DAVIDSON COUNTY TENNESSEE

WILLS & INVENTORIES

VOLUME TWO

1816 - 1830

Compiled by

HELEN C. & TIMOTHY R. MARSH

1989

SOUTHERN HISTORICAL PRESS, INC.
c/o The Rev. Silas Emmett Lucas, Jr.
275 West Broad Street
Greenville, South Carolina 29601

ISBN 0-89308-665-7

FOREWORD

Davidson County, North Carolina, now Tennessee, was created in 1783 as the most westward county in North Carolina and was named in honor of Brigadier General William Lee Davidson, a distinguished soldier of the American Revolution. The old original boundries roughly followed those of the old Mero District that encompassed most of the waters of the Cumberland River in north central Tennessee. This area was still a vast wilderness, virtually uninhabited except for the families that occupied the numerous block-house forts or stations that were scattered up and down the Cumberland River and northward to the Virginia, now Kentucky State line.

The majority of the early stations were occupied by pioneer families of the James Robertson, John Donelson, John Rains and Buchanan-Mulherrin parties that arrived at the French Lick in the winter of 1779-80. It was here at the French Salt Lick and Springs, on the Cumberland River and its tributaries, that modern civilization in middle Tennessee was born.

The old county boundries as constituted in 1783 remained unchanged until 1788 when the short lived Tennessee County was created on the north out of old Davidson. When statehood was achieved in 1796, it became Robertson and Montgomery Counties. In 1787, Sumner County on the north and east was formed out of Davidson. The parent county was again reduced in 1799 and 1803 with the creation of Williamson and Rutherford Counties on the south. Finally in 1856 a small portion was lost with the formation of Cheatham County. The county seat of Davidson County is Nashville, the capital of the state. Early names of Nashville were French Lick and Nashbourough.

The old original county records were often read with great difficulty, the writings having faded with age. Margins were often torn or missing. Great liberties were sometimes taken with the spelling of names. One can only imagine the variations in the spelling of unfamiliar names and places. The original court records in this publication are available on microfilm at the Tennessee State Library and Archives, Nashville, Tennessee.

Helen C. and Timothy R. Marsh

EARLY MIDDLE TENNESSEE

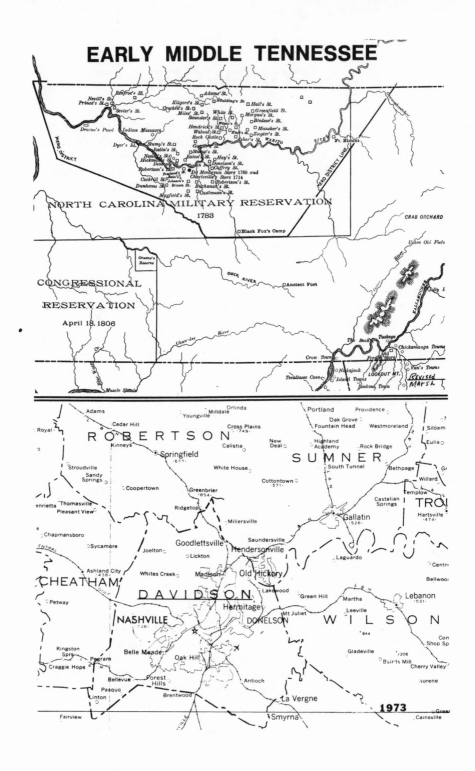

DAVIDSON COUNTY, TENNESSEE WILLS
WILL BOOK NO. 7
1816 - 1821

PAGE 1   Inventory of estate of thomas K. Harris, deceased.
June 10, 1816   Several items listed. Signed by Mary Harris, admrx and Richard
Moore, admr. Notes of said estate: Note given by Richard Moore, one by Hugh Caperton, one
by Thomas Robertson, one by William Priest, one by Thomas Vaughn, William Owen, William
Alexander, John Read, Elija Drake, William Price, Edmond Price, Henry Kirby, Benjamin
Weaver, Jeremiah Jones, William West, John Yorkland, George Stinnett, Isaac Koaby, James
Allison and James Townshead, John Shropshire, Alexander Lowry, Jeremiah Linton, Henderson
Cate, John Knowls, Jacob A. Lane, Stephen and Mark Renfro, H.G. Harris, John Cate a
corporal in the service of the United States to draw pay for a tour of duty of six months,
Solomon Harp a private in General Carroll's Division six months service, Thomas Lambert's
Power Attorney for a tour of six months duty in General Carroll's Division, William Ellis a
private in Militia in the service of the United States a tour of seven months under Captain
Asahel Rains' 2nd Regiment of West Tennessee Militia, Howel G. Harris transfer judgement
and also Murdock and Brown.   Memo of papers put in the hands of Dr. David Moore,
Huntsville, for collection and turned over to Harris in his lifetime, Lewis Winston kept for
two notes to collect one on William H. McBroom, one on Henry W. McBroom and William H.
McBroom, James McBroom & Co., Eliza Swift, William Rogers, a note on Alexander
Henderson and A. Stubblefield executed to Herron King & Co., Isham Bradley, James Witt,
Joseph Copeland, David Tittle, E.B. Brady, John Slogdon, Thomas Herbert and John W.
Gleeson. Memo of claims on Col. Meigs agent for Cherokee Indians this claim in of purchase
of the Hon. Mr. Strong of Vermont a member of Congress. One note on John C. Williamson,
John Taylor, Frederick Sexton, Peter Yorkham to Jas. Mitchell, Moses M. and Daniel Posy,
William Clark, Jesse Fondrom, Elijah Drossett, Clemon Gleman and Richard Shaddock, William
B. Nevills, William Lewis, Richard Lambertson, George White, William Webb, Robert Wolf,
William Webb, Joseph Cook and Jno. Gilliam, George Mattlock, William English, Willowby
Pugh, John Hall, Murry Webb, A.A. Wyche, M. Brookshire, Jacob Kennedy, Nathaniel Hunts,
William Bridges, William Dale, George Forbes and Nath. Haggard, John M. Carrick, William B.
Smith, William Huddleston, Samuel Huddleston, Michael McDonals, Woolsey W. Pierce, Smith
Jackson, John Johnson, Mrs. Merrits, Moses and Jesse Kennedy, William Barry, John Sublet,
Jesse Blakely, John F. Street, Aquilla Sugg, John H. Anderson, John Talley, Joseph Donals,
Margaret Barker, William Kennedy, John Daugherty, William Street, Spencer Pierce, Thomas
McLean, John Nothart, Benjamin Blackburn, George W. Donel, Thomas Simpson, William Were,
James Anderson, Anthony Hays, Reuben A. Higginbotham, Willie Barrow, Robert E. Lowry,
John Baker, Isaac Taylor, and Samuel Thomas. Signed by Mary Harris and Richard Moore.
Apr Term 1816.

Page 5   Inventory of estate of John Edmiston, deceased.
June 11, 1816   April 16, 1816. Several items listed. Note on William Neely and
one on Hugh Leeper. Signed by John Edmiston and Robert Edmiston. Apr Term 1816.

Page 5   Inventory of estate of Thomas Williams, deceased.
June 11, 1816   Several items listed. This 16 Apr 1816. Signed by Joshua P.
Vaughn, admr.

Page 5   Inventory of estate of Edmond Collinsworth, deceased.
June 11, 1816   Returned by Alsey Collinsworth, admrx. This Apr 23, 1816.

Page 6   Inventory of sale of estate of Prince Martin, deceased.
June 11, 1816   Feb 1, 1816. Persons listed, to wit, Charles Hart, Williamson
Jordan, John Bell, John Moore, William Pilliam, William L. Yarborough, Lewis Speice, John
Cobler, Henry Cromer, Joseph Youngblood, John Lucas, Noah Perry, Charles Hartly, and
James Gray. Signed by John Moore, admr. Apr Term 1816.

Page 6   Inventory of estate of Charles Burrow, deceased.
June 11, 1816   One superfine coat, vest and pantaloons, one pair boots and one
silver watch. Signed by Joseph Ward. Apr Term 1816.

Page 7   Inventory of estate of Enoch Oliver, deceased.
June 11, 1816   Several items listed. Apr 24, 1816. Signed by Josiah Phelps,
admr.

Page 7   Inventory of estate of Andrew Davis, deceased.
June 12, 1816   Taken by William Donelson, executor, this 16 Nov 1815. Several
items listed including one note on Jacob Dickinson and Ezekiel Young, one on Thomas G.
Bradford, one on Sally Blakemore and William Norris, and one on John W. Crunk and John
Brown. Part of the stock was sold by consent of Mrs. Nancy Davis, the widow. Persons
listed, to wit, Thomas Scruggs, Paul Dismukes, G. Payne, Reuben Payne, Greenwood Payne,
William Blakemore, John Dismukes, Lewis Basey, and Isaac Walton. Signed by William
Donelson, exr.

Page 7   Inventory of sale of estate of Stephen Roach, deceased.
June 12, 1816   Taken by Lydia Roach and John McCain, admrx and admr. Feb
16, 1816. Persons listed, to wit, Lydia Roach, Mordicai Kelly, Stephen Roach, Nelson White,
Zachariah Bell, Jesse Sulivan, Thomas Hill, Samuel Sulivan, John Berton, Jno. Stockard, Caleb
Cotton, Zadock Phelps, Charles Hays, James Whitsett, Daniel Mitchell, Enoch Ensly, William
Evans, John Right (Wright), Thompson Tomas (Thomas), Whiteside Thomas, Adam Carper,
Henry Seat, Joseph Moore, Demey Owen, William Erwin, J. Burnet, W. Turbeville, Benjamin
Barnes, Elijah Phelps, Wily Berton, Isaac Johnson, and Isaac Battle. The following possible
sale of negroes, Peter to Isaac H. Howlet, Hanah to William Bennet, Sam to Stephen Roach,
and Arthur to Lydia Roach. Other persons listed, to wit, L. Roach, William Gibson, John
McCain, John Dickson, Jno. Phelps, William P. Seat, Thomas Hill, Edmond Read, John M.
Right (Wright), James Whitsett, Enoch Ensley, Thomas Whitsett, John Canada, Jr., (blank)
Morton, Jacob Morton, Robert (blank), Edmond Collinsworth, Demey Barns, Demey Owen,
John Goodrich, Joshua Phelps, Thomas Johns, M.W. Gibbs, Godfrey Shelton, Nancy Farmer,
John Vanduzer, John Roach, Jr., Johnathan Procter, Jacob Cufman, Jno. M. Wright, Willis
Turbeville, Joseph Hopper, Willis Laurence, and William Marvum(?), and Benjamin Gray.
Signed by John McCain, admr and Lydia Roach, admrx. Apr Term 1816.

Page 10,   Fountain H. Gains, deceased.
June 13, 1816   F.H. Gains survivor of Horace and F.H. Gains returned by the
executors. Five negroes. Signed by James Trimble and Thomas Shackleford, executors. Apr
term 1816.

Page 10   Inventory of estate of Daniel Bell, deceased.
June 13, 1816   Apr 15, 1816. One (illegible) and 500 shingles. Signed by Samuel
Bell and John Bell, admrs. Apr Term 1816.

Page 10   Inventory of estate of Jonathan Walker, deceased.
June 13, 1816   Returned unto April Term 1816 by Lewis Dunn, admr. One sorrel
mare. Signed by Lewis Dunn, admr.

Page 11   Inventory of estate of Alexander Donelson, deceased.
June 13, 1816   By cash $266.88, a negro woman and two children, one negro boy,
horse, saddle and bridle. Signed by John Donelson, admr. Apr Term 1816.

Page 11   Inventory of estate of John Neely, deceased.
June 13, 1816   Taken at the house of John Edmondson, deceased, by Isaac Butler
and John Roberts the 23 Feb 1816, to wit, one large trunk and cloths, one large broad axe,
one tomahawk, one large butcher knife, one shoe hamer, a bag of small trumpery(?), one
saddle and bridle, one horse, one mare and colt, one hat, and two books. Signed by Samuel
Neely, admr. Apr Term 1816.

Page 11   Inventory of estate of William Hurst, deceased.
June 13, 1816   Several items listed, including a note on Thomas Gilbert and one
on John Pierce. Signed by Elizabeth Hurst, admrx. Apr Term 1816.

Page 11   Inventory of estate of Joseph Drake, deceased.
June 13, 1816   Returned unto April Term 1816. Two negroes, a boy named
Nelson and a girl named Cate. Signed by Christopher Stump, admr.

Page 12   Inventory of estate of James Camp, deceased.
June 13, 1816   Several items listed. Signed by William Peacock, admr. Apr
Term 1816.

Page 12   Inventory of estate of David Edmiston, deceased. April 15, 1816.
Several items listed including an account on Benjamin Capps, one on Thomas Thornburgh, one
on John Roberts, one of Thomas Golden, and a note on Evans Wilson, one on William Neely, an
account on William Allen, a note on Thomas Williamson, one on Samuel McSpadin, one on
Samuel A. Allen, one on Robert Hays, and one account on William Harris. Signed by Mary
Edmondson, admrx and John Edmondson, admr. Apr Term 1816.

Page 13   Inventory of estate of Rev. Elijah Hurst, deceased.
June 13, 1816   Several items listed including a note on Thomas Gilbert, and an
account due by Nathan Bennet. Signed by Elizabeth Hurst, admrx. Apr Term 1816.

Page 13   Inventory of estate of Edward Simmons, deceased.
June 13, 1816   Several items listed including one pocket Bible. Signed by John
Carter, admr. Apr Term 1816.
Page 13   Inventory of sale of estate of Joseph Engleman, deceased.
June 13, 1816   Taken in Nashville on Feb 16, 1816 atAuction. Several items
listed. Signed by Joseph Ward, admr. D. Robertson, auctioneer.

Page 14   Inventory of sale of estate of Exum Johnston, deceased.
June 14, 1816   Sold by Thomas Rivers, admr on Feb 14, 1814. Persons listed, to
wit, Joseph Brown, David Cole, Robert Taylor, John H. Camp, Kinchen T. Wilkerson, Benjamin
Branch, John C. Parker, David B. Love, Christopher Stump, James Everett, Jesse Everett,
Edmund Gamble, Jabias White, Samuel Wharton, Daniel Johnston, Joseph Hooper, Johnathan
Clay, Larken Clay, Thomas Faulks, Zachariah Stull, Joseph Chumbly, Rebecca Johnston,
Michael Gleaves, William Canon, Daniel Young, Jesse Johnston, John Brooks, Laban
Abernathy, Isaac David, Henry Lady, Nathaniel Wray, John Camp, Richard Merewithers, John
Irwin, William Parker, and Alexander Wray. Apr Term 1816.

Page 16   Settlement of estate of Exum Johnston, deceased.
June 14, 1816   Account current with Thomas Rivers, admr. Persons listed, to
wit, Hyde, Scott, Porter, Jno. L. Ewing, Ward, Johnston, Doctor May, Nathan Ewing, Lusk, E.
Gamble, Dehart's note, and John Stump. Balance in hands of admr $59.46. Signed by E.S.
Hall and W. Tannehill. Apr Term 1816.

Page 16   Settlement of estate of Richard Winn, deceased.
June 15, 1816   Thomas Crutcher, admr. Amount due the estate $111.48.

Page 17   We, Stephen Cantrell, Jr. and Wilkins Tannehill, Commissioners
Apr Term 1816   appointed to examine the account of Thomas Crutcher, admr. and
find a balance of $111.48 due the estate. This 27 Apr 1816.

Page 17   Inventory of estate of John Blair, deceased.
June 15, 1816   Several named negroes and several other items. One obligation
on Alexander Blair of Virginia and a balance due on F. Campbell's note. Signed by T.B. Rice,
admr. Apr Term 1816.

Page 17   Inventory of estate of Charles Beasley, deceased.
June 15, 1816   Several items listed. Signed by James Owen, admr. Apr Term
1816.

Page 18   Inventory of sale of estate of Thomas Hardy, deceased.
June 15, 1816   17 Apr 1816. Persons listed, to wit, Henry Cromer, Sally Hardy,
William Kent, Collin S. Hobbs, John Moore, John Stobough, R.B. Owen, Samuel Haney, A.
Conley, Levina Hardy, Joseph Page, Jno. Gordon, Joseph Vick, Whitlow's order to Ar. Lord,

Greenberry Fin's note, and Hardy Hobb's account at sale. Signed by Levina Hardy, admrx. Apr Term 1816.

Page 18,   Inventory of estate of Lemuel T. Turner, deceased.
June 15, 1816   Several items listed including a silver watch. Signed by E.S. Hall and Stephen Cantrell, admrs. A negro woman and child in Virginia. Apr Term 1816.

Page 19   Inventory of estate of John Dillahunty, Sr., deceased.
June 17, 1816   Taken Feb 1816. Several items listed. Signed by Thomas Dillahunty, executor. Apr Term 1816.

Page 19   Inventory of sale of estate of John Irwin, deceased.
June 17, 1816   Sold by David Irwin, admr. Several negroes and other items listed. Apr Term 1816.

Page 19   Inventory of sale of estate of Elizabeth Jones, deceased.
June 17, 1816   Feb 15, 1816. Several items listed. Signed by Robert Johnston, executor. Apr Term 1816.

Page 20   Inventory of sale of estate of John Strother, deceased.
June 17, 1816   Sold this 3 Feb 1816. Several items listed. Signed by James Lockhart, surveying exr of John Strother, deceased. Apr Term 1816.

Page 20   Inventory of estate of Elizabeth Jones, deceased.
June 17, 1816   As of Apr 17, 1816. One stone jug, one froe, two weavers stays, one grinfstone, and one set of iron wedges. Signed by Robert Johnston, executor. Apr Term 1816.

Page 20   Sale of estate of Edmond Blackman, deceased.
June 17, 1816   Feb 10, 1816. As sold by B. Blackman. Signed by Bennet Blackman, admr. Apr Term 1816.

Pahe 21   Inventory of estate of Asa Morton, deceased.
June 17, 1816   Balance of Jacob Morton. Asa Morton's claim for his services in general Coffee's Brigade of Mounted Infantry. Signed by Kingsley and Parrish. Apr Term 1816.

Page 21   Inventory of accounts of estate of John Pugh, deceased.
June 17, 1816   Accounts standing unsettled on John Pugh's book at his death. 1815. Persons listed, to wit, Richard Joslin, John Davis, Ivy Walk(er), Robert Clark, John Donley, William B. Robertson, Robert Thompson, Jesse Woodard, John D. Simonton, Richard Boyd, Zachariah Waters, Alexander Patton, Jacob Holt, Jacob Fudge, Jacob Watkins, George Elmore, Felix Robertson, Willie Joslin, Mrs. Ross, David Singletary, Archibald Walker, Martin Greer, James McNeely, Peyton Robertson, Solomon Clark, John Taylor, Isaac Watkins, John Whitfield, William Chuler, Samuel Inman, Thomas Grainger, Robert Young, David Martin, Neal Hopkins, John Singletary, Frederick Horne, William Blackard, Mathew Wamack, Peter New, Hugh Bell, Benjamin Joslin, Kiddy Robertson, Robert Mason, Mrs. Downey, David & Allen, Benjamin Greer, Jr., John Bosley, Robert Hewitt, Baalam Bannister, Aron Franklin, William R. Bell, Henry Liles, Mathew P. Long, Mason Fowler, Benjamin Wilks, Susannah Robertson, Laban Miller, George Pierce, Thomas Hobbs, David W(illegible), William Night (Knight), Thomas Porch, David Coen, Josiah Sugg, William Lucas, John Ledgert, Francis Newsom, John Richardson, David Jones, William Wren, Thomas Loftin, William Hobbs, Josiah Horton, William Grubbs, Benjamin Sturdivant, William Russell, Daniel Liles, William Gower, Peter Stewart, Stephen Nobbs, John Thornton, McCajah McQuerry, Thomas Thornton, John Hooper, Robert Brown, Samuel Hutton, Abraham Demoss, Canada Richardson, Robert Porch, John Johns, Sr., Robert McGaugh, Edward Woodard, Meshack Pinkston, Elijah Robertson, Johnston Vaughn, James Donley, Joel Jones, Daniel Dunham, Timothy Reeves, David Morrow, John Jones, Jr., Thomas Charter, Andrew Work, Wilkins Whitfield, William Miller, received of the hand of David Pugh balance of an estate from Virginia, Eldridge Newsom. This Apr 26, 1816. Signed by Solomon Clark, admr. Apr Term 1816.

Page 23   Sale of estate of Henson Hardy, deceased.
June 18, 1816   Mar 2, 1816.   Persons listed, to wit, William Kent, Robert Morton, James Gray, John Moore, Elizabeth Hardy, Archibald Vaughn, William L. Yarborough, and E. Brinson. Signed by John Moore, admr. Apr Term 1816.

Page 24   Will of George Strothers, deceased.
June 18, 1816   To my niece Mary Griffin wife of John C. Griffin and her children 4000 acres of land in West Tennessee lately devised to me by my late brother John Strother, deceased. To my niece Julia H. Clark wife of Gov. William Clark 1000 acres of land and to her children. To my mother Mary Lockhart and my step-brother James Lockhart all the residue of my real and personal estate of everkind. To my uncle Reuben Kinnerly 640 acres of land in West Tennessee. To Jeremiah Strother 1000 acres of land. I appoint my step-brother James Lockhart and Alpha Kingsley, executors. This 17 Feb 1816. Wit: Jno. Deatherage and Thomas Talbot. Apr Term 1816.

Page 25   Sale of estate of George Strother, deceased.
June 18, 1816   Sold 24 Apr 1816 by James Lockhart and Alpha Kingsley, executors. Several items listed. Apr Term 1816.

Page 25   Catharine Vaulx, her dower and dividend.
June 18, 1816   Jan term 1816, directed to the Sheriff of Davidson County to summond so many free holders to lay off to Catharine Vaulx, widow and relict of Daniel Vaulx, deceased, her dower of the land. They laid off 114 acres of land on the head waters of McCrorys Creek including the mansion house &c. Land bordered William Gowen's preemption, and John Gowen. This 2 Feb 1816. Signed by Richard Drury, William Murphy, James Carter, William Matlock, Richard Moore, Henry White, Jr., William M. Harwood, William H. McLaughlin, JOhn Gowen, Thomas Rutherford, Edmond Owen, and Peter Wright. Apr Term 1816.

Page 26   Division of estate of Daniel Vaulx, deceased.
June 18, 1816   Commissioners met to lay off and set apart Harrison Fussell and Susan his wife's portion of the personal estate of Daniel Vaulx, deceased, negroes sold. Persons listed, to wit, Mary Peebles, Littleberry Williams and Margaret his wife, Joseph Vaulx, to the heirs of Hannah Drake, deceased, John B. Seat and Pollyan his wife, James Drake, Martha Drake, and Mmary Drake. This 2 Feb 1816. Signed by W. Murphy, John Gowen, Edmund Owen, W.H. McLaughlin, and Peter Wright. Apr Term 1816.

Page 27   Inventory of estate of Robert Cartwright, deceased.
June 18, 1816   Apr 23, 1816. Several items listed. Signed by David Cartwright, executor. Property left to his grandson Edney Armstrong McCoy to be sold for said child. Apr Term 1816.

Page 27   John and James Patton, guardian return.
June 19, 1816   Joseph Ward, guardian for the estate of John and James Patton makes the return. Cash and notes amt of $693.77. Apr 25, 1816.

Page 28   Gray Washington, orphan guardian return.
June 19, 1816   Gray Washington orphan of Gray Washington, deceased.   To Elizabeth Washington, guardian. Dr. balance due guardian $67.50. Apr Term 1816.

Page 28   Nancy H. Washington, orphan guardian return.
June 19, 1816   Orphan of Gray Washington, deceased. To Elizabeth Washington, guardian. Due N.H. Washington up to Dec 25, 1815 $142.50. Apr Term 1816.

Page 28   Eliza and margery Childress, orphans guardian return.
June 19, 1816   Nashville, 24 Apr 1816. Eliza and Margery Childress daughters of Henry Childress, deceased. Cash $100.00 in hand 17 Jan 1816. Signed by Philip Shute, guardian. Apr term 1816.

Page 28   Inventory of estate of George Strother, deceased.
June 19, 1816   Sundry apparels, one sorrel mare, one portmanteau, one pair saddlebags, and one watch. Signed by Jas. Lockhart and Alpha Kingsley, exrs.

Page 29   Robert and Lemiza Lenier, orphans guardian return.
June 19, 1816   The estate of William Lenier, deceased, 1815. Persons listed, to wit, William Wilkerson, John Stump and John Cox. By note on John Lenier and David Parker for hire of a negro girl. The estate of William Lenier, deceased, 1815. Lemiza Lenier, and a note on John Brooks and William Ray. This Apr 26, 1816. Signed by Nathan Ewing. William Wilkerson, guardian.

Page 29   Supplementary to inventory of estate of Thomas Hardy, deceased.
June 19, 1816   Furniture in the shop formerly occupied by James G. Hicks now furnished 24 April 1816, to wit, one dish, one bureau, one small table also one half of a shop leased by Moore and Hardy formerly occupied by Prince the barber, deceased. Signed by Levina Hardy, admrx. Apr Term 1816.

Page 29   Lydia Roach, widow of Stephen Roach, deceased.
June 19, 1816   Privisions laid out for Lydia Roach this 16 Feb 1816. Several items listed. Signed by Charles Hays and bennet Blackman. Apr Term 1816.

Page 29   Rebecca Johnston, widow of Exum Johnston, deceased.
June 19, 1816   Provisions laid out to the widow of Exum Johnston, deceased, this 14 July 1814. Five barrels corn, 300 lbs bacon. Signed by Alexander Ewing and Joseph Hooper. Apr Term 1816.

Page 30   Additional inventory of estate of Isaac Rigney, deceased.
June 19, 1816   Made by Bignal Crook, admr. Feb 12, 1814. Several persons listed, to wit, Eldridge Newsom, William Herrin, John Hannah, Thomas Scott, William Miller, Philip Words, Allen Thompson, William Thompson, John Cooper, and Leonard P. Piles. Apr Term 1816.

Page 30   Settlement of estate of Meshack Hail, deceased.
June 19, 1816   Made Apr 27, 1816 by Nathan G. Hail, executor. Find on 8 Sept 1815 a mistake in the addition, instead of $2811.68½, should have been $2911.68½ and we proceed to divide between the legatees. Signed by C. Stump, J.P., and Jno. Stump, J.P. Apr Term 1816.

Page 30   Will of Stewart Farmbrough, deceased, of Davidson County.
June 25, 1816   To my beloved wife Susannah shall keep possession of my lands, stock, household furniture and farming utensils for the benefit of herself and raising my children during her widowhood but should she marry then she shall have only an equal child's part. To my son William Farmbrough at the age of twenty one all my landed estate and I have somewhere about $150.00 now let out on interest, which is to be collected, my debts to be paid and the balance be kept lent on interest until my daughter Jenny W. Farmbrough becomes of age and then she is to receive an equal child's part and the balance to remain on interest and to be divided to each of my children as they come of age. I also appoint my beloved wife Susannah and Robert Heaton and Samuel Weakley, executrix and executors. This 6 Apr 1816. Wit: Robert Farmbrough and Hannah Farmbrough. Apr term 1816.

Page 31   Inventory of estate of William Wharton, deceased, of Davidson
July 16, 1816   County. Several negroes listed also several items listed. Signed by Jesse Wharton, admr. July Term 1816.

Page 32   C. Stump of Ensley and Joyce of Davidson County.
July 18, 1816   I, Enoch Ensly and Thomas Joyce are bound unto Christopher Stump for $1200.00 to be paid. The said note os lost or misplaced that it cannot be had for the purpose intended and oath made to that amount by Parker Alexander. Damages to be void &c. This 17 July 1816. Signed by Enoch Ensley and Thomas Joyce. July Term 1816.

Page 33   Settlement of estate of Nicholas Raymond, deceased.
Aug 5, 1816   Persons listed, to wit, Arthur Dew, John L. Ewing, Nelson Tally, John W. Cocke, Reuben Rucker, William Byrn, Edward Bondurant, William Tarver, Andrew Hynes, H. Saunders, Henry Wells, Jacob and Asa Martin, Thomas Hudson, William Hill, Thomas Deadrick, Lewis White, John Dew, Alexander Walker, Ephraim H. Foster, John Dennis, John Greaves, John Goodrich, William Donelson, Stephen Cantrell, Thomas G. Bradford, Edward H.

East, John A. Walker, Jno. Smith, ? Norvill, Edward Harrison, Benjamin Capps, Nathan Barnes, Amos Walker, Ilai Metcalf, William Wray, and William Jones, and Samuel Chapman. Others listed, William Boke, George Burnett, and George Bell. Balance due estate $190.81¼. This 23 July 1816. Signed by John Goodrich and Alexander Walker. July Term 1816.

Page 34 Settlement of estate of Bird Evans, deceased.
Aug 5, 1816 Persons listed, to wit, Peter Wright, Nathan Ewing, Hickman & Searcy, Thomas Patton, Littleberry Williams, W.H. McLaughlin, and A.J. Edmondson. His pay for service against the hostile Creek Indians $37.74. Balance in hand of admr $33.44. Signed by Peter Wright, admr. Apr Term 1816.

Page 35 Settlement of estate of John D. Fly, deceased.
Aug 5, 1816 A total of $812.35 3/4 in vouchers and papers of the deceased. Signed by the Commissioners. This 16 July 1816. Cary Felts and B. Gray. July Term 1816.

Page 35 Settlement of estate of Micajah Woodard, deceased.
Aug 5, 1816 Made by Robert C. Foster and James Whitsett, executors. Persons listed, to wit, King Carson, William Lytle, Deadrick & Sommerville, James Manus, Jas. Riddle, Jos. Engleman, Thomas Rutherford, Henson Hardy, Felix Robertson, Jno. D. Fly, M.C. Dunn, William Beckum, Andrew Ewing, Everett, Mrs. Edwards, and Jeremiah Grizzard. This 22 July 1816. Signed by W. Tannehill and J.T. Elliston. July Term 1816.

Page 36 Settlement of estate of William McCollum, deceased.
Aug 5, 1816 Made by Levi McCollum, admr. Persons listed, to wit, John Demoss, William McMillen, Samuel Brooks, Hardy Mitchel, Samuel Crockett, and Levi McCollum. Zachariah Allen and Eldridge Newsom, Commissioners. This 15 July 1816. July Term 1816.

Page 36 James and Polly Dean, orphans of James Dean, deceased.
Aug 5, 1816 Paid Craighead for teaching James, paid Smiley Taylor, and furnished James with money. Balance due James and Polly Dean $2778.87¼. This 17 July 1816.

Page 37 Settlement of estate of Nimrod Weakley, deceased, of Davidson
Aug 5, 1816 County, with John Hannah, executor to the Last Will and Testament of James Hamilton, deceased, relative to the administration of James Hamilton, deceased, on the estate of Nimrod Weakley, deceased. Hannah reports that he drew said Weakley's wages from the paymaster which is $39.73. Settlement made with James Hamilton, admr to said estate in Oct Term 1815. We find said estate to owe the admr $23.28½. Allowance made the executor $2.00. Balance $14.34½. This July 20, 1816. Signed by William Hall and Cary Felts.

Page 37 Supplementary invention of James H. Koonce, deceased.
Aug 6, 1816 Of money received of Thomas Shackleford, viz, $136.86, likewise one note on Robert Cannada for $10.00, likewise one note on Betsey Jackson for $7.00. Signed by William Roach, Robert McMillon and George Koonce, executors. July Term 1816.

Page 37 Inventory of estate of William Hobson, deceased.
Aug 6, 1816 Several negroes (42) listed. Ten (named) set apart for Mrs. Hobson the widow and relict of William Hobson, deceased. Charles and Hall willed to John Hobson. Richard and Suckey willed to Nicholas Hobson. Dennis and Abby willed to Mary Hobson. Lewis and Maria willed to Elizabeth Hobson. Dave and Emily willed to Susan Hobson. Bob and Martha willed to William Hobson. Dave and Juggy and Caroline willed to Mr. N. McNairy. Violet and Peter willed to Mr. G. Hewitt. Seller and Alick willed to Mr. W. Lytle. Old Bob and old Beck, Billy, Miney, Jordinia, Perlina, Matilda, Gabriel, Sampson, Fanny, Jim, Critta and Pheby, thirteen undivided negroes and other items listed are set apart for Mrs. Hobson, the widow and relict. Signed by James Jackson, R. Weakley and John Hobson, executors. Also a list of persons, to wit, Abram Wright, R. Searcy and R. Foster, Robert Weakley, Leston Temple, Harris Gains, Fountain H. Gains, John and Daniel Chapman, Aaron Day, James Shavers, Joseph Coleman, Robert Stewart, Winfrey and Thomas Patterson, Thomas Williamson, Robert Farmbrough, John Stump, John P. Smith, W. and N. Carrolls, Thomas Shackleford, James Irwin, Stephen Farmer, James H. Gamble, Drury Hatcher, Samuel

7

Stegar's note of Virginia, William Allen, Isaac Clemmons, George Smith, Thomas Casey, Pain's bond, Richard Brown, James McGavock, Hugh Evans note, plank sawed and sold since the death of W. Hobson, Henry Cromer, and James Clemmons. Signed by James Jackson, R. Weakley and John Hobson, executors. July Term 1816.

Page 39   Sale of estate of William Hobson, deceased.
Aug 6, 1816   Several items listed. Signed by Johua P. Vaughan, admr.   July
Term 1816.

Page 41   Inventory of estate of Jonathan Johnson, deceased.
Aug 7, 1816   Several items listed. Signed by Barbary Johnston, admrx and
Gustavius Rope, admr. July Term 1816.

Page 42   Inventory of estate of John McKains, deceased.
Aug 7, 1816   Several items listed. Returned unto court by John Buchanan,
admr. July Term 1816.

Page 42   Inventory of estate of William Tait, deceased.
Aug 7, 1816   Taken 18 Apr 1816. A list of notes due the estate, to wit,
Joseph Scales, Thomas Shackleford, George and M.R. Newel, George and Robert Bell, to Hugh McClure, E. Nelson, James Gray, John Erwin, Edley Ewing, Nathan Williams, H.F. Bell, Joseph Hays, William Hays, Howel Tatum, David Clarke, John Price, M. Armstrong, James Moreland, William McGaugh, Robert Stothart, John Carr, James Young, Joseph Creech, William Turner, William Christmas, and Michael Sweetman. A list of conditional notes, to wit, Ilai Metcalf, David Allen, Moses Winters, and Edward Barker. A list of balance due the estate, persons listed, to wit, James Gowin, Joseph Sullivan, Samuel Hutchison (run away), James Stuart, Nathaniel Moody, Thomas Bearden, Kelly Williams, William H. Ramsey, Richard Hanks, Nelly (mulatto), Isaac D. Wilson, William Neely, Abner Vaughn, George Hall, Francis Scott (mulatto), Thomas Wadsworth, John Stewart, John Ward, Isaac Mayfield, John Brownlee, Jesse Pierce, William Daughlen, Reubin Westmoreland, Thomas Hobbs, John Pillow, William Dickinson, Frederick Ivey, John Barnes, Thomas Cates, Isaac Milberger, John McKleswain, Abraham Pinkley, Fancis McCawl, Rosannah Hoggins, Sarah Donelson, Samuel Jackson, William Gemain, Thomas Brewer, William Overton, Reuben Bedwell, Balam Thompson, William Beaty, John Prewer, Joel Mullin, James McCrory, Polly Pyles, Evan Bannister, Betsey Hopkins, Thomas Mustgrove, John Williams, James Gilham, Letty (negro wench), Thomas Thompson, Lady Butler, William Brady, Patrick Lyons, Kelly Singletary, John Black, John Drake, William Hurst, George Benn, Sr., Thomas Gorham, Jr., Joseph Park, John Dickinson, deceased, Robert Stothart, David Afflick, Ilai Metcalf, William P. Anderson, Hugh F.Bell, George Bell, Jr., Richard C. Cross, Shadrack Bell, Charles Davis, John L. Young, William Cole, John Newman, Thomas Shackleford, estate of Jno. Sommerville, estate of Thomas Masterson, Benjamin Morgan, David Robertson, Robert W. Hart, Doctor Holland, (blank) Trotter, estate of Mrs. Ann Hays, deceased, Mrs. Price, Burrell Temple, and R.T. Walker. Signed by R.T. Walker, one of the executors. An inventory of household furniture &c belonging to the estate taken 16 May 1816. Several items listed. Also at auction by Duncan Robertson on June 1, 1816. July Term 1816.

Page 46   Inventory of sale of estate of James Hamilton, deceased.
Aug 8, 1816   Sold on 8th and 9th May 1816. Persons listed, to wit, Ephraim
Phelps, John Huggins, Silas Phelps, John Phelps, George W. Charlton, John McNeel, Dennis McLendon, James Clemons, William Freeman, Edward H. East, Richard Hays, Burel Perry, William Huggins, John Johnston, Henry Hays, William Hannah, William Burnett, George Hannah, Thomas Gordon, William Green, Joseph Brown, William Rutherford, Newel Drew, Joseph D. Tait, Jas. B. Howe, Henry Wolf, Henry Seat, James Carter, Robert Hamilton, John Carter, Henry Castleman, James Allen, David Hughs, Jesse Griffin, William Hall, Levi McLaughlin, John L. Allen, David Hutchinson, Jos. Hamilton, Joab H. Barton, Joseph (illegible), Thomas Drenan, William Sharp, Charles McCombs, Claiborne Goodman, John Adams, Christopher C. Carter, Charles Hays, David Hughs, Joseph Burnett, Hezekiah G. Cook, Samuel Scott, Stephen Heard, James Lee, John Serrat, Godfrey Shelton, Zachariah Nowell, Allen Edmonds, James Baker, Isaac Sanders, George H. Hannah, John Hannah, William B. Dotson, Sewallen Campbell, William Eakins, William Wilson, Lewis Allen, William Warnack, John C. Hall, Thomas Sawyers, William Finney, G. Bradford, a note on Willis S. Shumate, and one on David Allen. Received of William Huggins and others already named above. Signed by

John Hannah, executor. July Term 1816. (long inventory)

Page 49   Sale of estate of James Camp, deceased.
Aug 9, 1816   Sale on 7 May 1816. Persons listed, to wit, Jno. Drury, Thomas
Williamson, Christopher Stump, McKernan & Stout, George Boyd, William T. Northern, Jas.
Erwin, E. Raworth, D. Robertson, A. Richardson, Jno. C. Hicks, Stainback, William Lintz,
Solomon Clark, James Jackson, N. Pryor, S. Tilford, Ra. Boyd, William Peacock, R. Dickinson,
Ellis Maddox, G.W. Boyd, R. Smiley, William Priestly, J.T. Elliston, Jas. Hanna(h), T.R.
Fletcher, and Jno. Garner. Signed by William Peacock, admr. July Term 1816.

Page 50   Will of John B. Jackson, deceased, of Davidson County.
Aug 9, 1816   To my beloved wife Lovy have first choice of my stock of horses
also a saddle and bridle that she is now in possession of also other items, during her natural
life and at her death the remaining is to be sold and the money be equally divided among my
male children. To my daughter Nancy one featherbed and furniture and $100.00 in cash. To
my daughter Salley one featherbed and furniture and $100.00 in cash. To all my male
children one featherbed and furniture. All the rest of my perishable property goes to my
beloved wife Lovy, also a tract of land whereon I now live containing 142½ acres. I appoint
John Davis, William Roach and Sterling Gunter my executors, and my wife Lovy my
executrix. This 13 Apr 1816. Wit: Guy Smith, Zachariah Allen and Willis Chambers. July
Term 1816.

Page 51   Additional inventory of estate of Robert Edmiston, deceased.
Aug 10, 1816   A note on John Haywood, Sr., one on David Cummins, one on
Sterling Davis, and one on William Demumbreum. Received of Nathan Ewing $30.00, received
of Col. Philip Pipkin one small heifer. July 15, 1816. Signed by Peter Wright, admr. July
Term 1816.

Page 51   Sale of estate of Thomas Hardy, deceased.
Aug 10, 1816   June 15, 1816. Sale of furniture sold, one desk $20.00, one table
$2.31, and one bureau $18.00. Whole amount $40.31¼. Signed by William L. Yarbrough.
Levina Yarbrough, admrx. July Term 1816.

Page 51   Inventory of estate of Squire Payne, deceased.
Aug 10, 1816   Several items listed. Signed by Sally Payne, admrx. July Term
1816.

Page 52   Additional sale of estate of Daniel Vaulx, deceased.
Aug 10, 1816   Sold on 22 June 1810 at the house of Mrs. Catharine Vaulx.
Items purchased, viz, one cow and calf to Moses Christenberry, one cow and calf to Catharine
Vaulx. Signed by Jas. Vaulx, admr. July Term 1816.

Page 52   Inventory of estate of Zachariah Hayes, deceased.
Aug 10, 1816   Wearing apparel, cash $150.00, one horse, bridle and saddle, and
one rifle gun. Signed by Henry Hays, admr. This July 20, 1816.

Page 52   Sale of estate of Isaac Drake, deceased.
Aug 10, 1816   The sale of negro Luce by C. Stump, admr. Sold to Abram
Wright. This July 25, 1816.

Page 52   Inventory of sale of estate of Joseph Drake, deceased.
Aug 10, 1816   The sale of negro Kate and Nelson by C. Stump, admr. Sold
negro Kate to Abram Wright and negro Nelson to C. Stump. This July 25, 1816.

Page 52   Inventory of estate of James Brannen, deceased.
Aug 10, 1816   Two hogs, one saddle and saddle bags, one mans hat, one pair of
boots, one pocket book, and one rifle gun. This July 23, 1816. E. Newsom, admr.

Page 53   Property of William Mathis, deceased.
Aug 10, 1816   Property valued. Several items listed. Whole amount $176.50.
July Term 1816. Eady Mathews, executrix.

Page 53   Additional sale of estate of Fountain H. Gains, deceased.
Aug 10, 1816   F.H. Gains survivor of the firm Horace & F.H.Gains made July Term 1816. Negro Ben to C. Stump, Charles to C. Stump, Billy to Josiah Mullin, Charles to Thomas Shackleford, and Joe to John Criddle. Signed by James Trimble and Thomas Shackleford, executors. July Term 1816.

Page 53   Will of Isaac Battle, deceased, of Davidson County.
Aug 11, 1816   This 12 May 1816. To my beloved wife Lucinda Atkinson Battle the tract of land whereon I now live and 150 acres of land out of my thousand acre tract adjoining the tract whereon I now live to be laid off to include the plantation whereon Joseph Mays now lives, to her during her natural life. Also to my wife I leave six negroes, a man Ridden, boy Dick, boy Nelson, one woman Lucy and her two children Trucy and Julia, also money of my estate to finish the house now on hand in a decent manner with brick or stone, chimneys, cellar and shed, and a kitchen with brick or stone chimney, also one years provision for my wife and children and family out of my stock and grain and then a child's part of all my stock and other items. Ay my death all my negroes (31) to be hired out until my daughter Charity Horn Battle or any of the rest, except Elizabeth Atkinson, comes of age or marries at which time I desire the said negroes be equally divided between my children. Elizabeth Atkinson's part to be given unto a suitable guardian for her having a sure support during her natural life and at her death, of the income and property that remains to be equally divided among my brothers and sisters. Charity H. Battle to have 150 acres. Susan Levina Battle 150 acres. Elizabeth A. Battle 100 acres. To my two sons William M. Battle and Joe A. Battle have the balance of my land including my cedar tract to be equally divided between them and at the death of my wife that part I left to her also be equally divided between my two sons. To Joel Allen that part whereon I now live. I appoint my friends Nathan Stansill and William Anthony my executors. Wit: Nelson White, B. Gray and Ellsey Roach. July Term 1816.

Page 55   Inventory of estate of Isaac Battle, deceased.
Aug 11, 1816   Several acres of land and other items listed. July Term 1816.

Page 56   Sale of estate of John Strong, deceased.
Aug 13, 1816   7 Feb 1816. Purchasers, to wit, Martha Strong, Thomas Peay, Samuel Morton, and Jacob Morton. Martha Strong, admrx. July Term 1816.

Page 56   Sale of estate of Charles Beasley, deceased.
Aug 14, 1816   Purchasers, to wit, Thomas Waller, Edmond Austin, James Owen, Robert Owen, Joseph Nants, Sarah Hill, Everet Owen, Moses Wooten, Joel Gray, John Hogan, Samuel Owen, James Cockrill, Jabez Owen, John Edmondson, Harbert Owen, Thomas Bradley, Turner Williams, William Maxwell, Delilah Beasley, and Sarah Hill. James Owen, admr. July Term 1816.

Page 57   Inventory of estate of Elizabeth Harding, deceased.
Aug 14, 1816   Several items listed. Signed by Silas Maddox, admr. July Term 1816.

Page 58   Amount of sale of estate of John Neely, deceased.
Aug 14, 1816   This 20 June 1816. Persons listed, to wit, William Hill, Isaac Butler, Enos Walker, Martin Gill, S.C. McDaniel, Jordan Sanders, William Wray, Godfrey Hicks, Samuel Neely, Baker Ayres, and William Ayres. Samuel Neely, admr. July Term 1816.

Page 58   Will of Jacob Dickinson, Sr., deceased, of Davidson County.
Aug 15, 1816   A provision for my wife whereas on the day of our marriage and before the marriage, a contract was made between me and her then Elizabeth Baker which was left in the possession of Captain James Burns. It was to secure to my children such property as I should retain at my death and to secure to her children such property then heirs by devise of her deceased husband Charles Baker as should remain at her death in case of my survivorship subject to our joint use during our joint lives. Being able to live without the use of such property and willing to aid the children of my wife, I have permitted them to enjoy the tract of land and plantation devised to her by her husband Charles Baker and also several of the negroes. I leave to my wife, negroes and other items and the dwelling house and outhouses whereon I now live. To my son Jacob Dickinson the tract of land I purchased of

James Dean containing 100 acres also the remaining part of the tract of land I now live on and that I do not in this will devise to my son William Thomas Dickinson a part of land supposing to contain about 80 acres to said Jacob. Also unto him several negroes all of which he has in his possession. To my son William Thomas Dickinson the plantation and part of the tract of land whereon I now live on, said land borders lands of Joseph Philips, Jacob Dickinson, Jr., Philip Walker, and William Moore. To my daughter Polly McKay a negro girl named Violet whom she has in her possession. To my daughter Charity Donelson all the negroes I have delivered to her. To my daughter Milberry McCrery all the negroes I have delivered to her. I appoint my friend William Williams my executor. Wit: William Denson, Nathan Williams and Josiah Williams. July Term 1816.

Page 60   Sale of estate of Thomas K. Harris, deceased.
Aug 16, 1816   Sold on 2 June 1816. Persons listed, to wit, Joseph Clark, James Franks, Christopher Swindle, James Allison, William Martin, Johnston Wilson, Jacob Franks, Ezekiel Waldrup, Richard Mitchel, Lemuel Franks, John Curtis, Thomas Walling, William Balch, Mary Harris, Henry Gill, Henry Hutson, George Harris, Andrew Irwin, Archibald Hutson, Richard Moore, John Chissom, Joseph Crabb, Henry Neal, Abraham Conner, Elijah Franks, Henry Franks, William Fisher, H.G. Harris, John Tonnsina, William Hawkins, H(illegible) B. Wright, Thomas Robinson, John Cotton, John Townsend, James Maise, Thomas Pate, George Pettillo, Joseph Hankins, Nath. Irvins, and Auson Gibbs. Signed by Mary Harris, admrx and Richard Moore, admr. July Term 1816.

Page 61   Inventory of estate of Thomas Mannifee, deceased.
Aug 16, 1816   One lot in the town of Shelbyville No. 128, one horse, saddle and bridle, and $130.00 cash. This July 17, 1816. James Mannifee, Jr., admr. July Term 1816.

Page 62   Sale of estate of William S. Gains, deceased.
Aug 16, 1816   By D. Robertson for account of Thomas Childress, executor of William S. Gains, deceased. Persons purchasing items, to wit, E.H. Foster, R. Goodlet one Bible, Jas. Trimble, John E. Beck, D. Robertson, and Doctor Smith. July Term 1816.

Page 62   Sale of estate of Elijah Hurst, deceased.
Aug 16, 1816   24 May 1816. Persons purchasing items, to wit, Thomas Heaton, John Lennoir, Asa Hurst, and Elizabeth Hurst. Signed by Elizabeth Hurst, admrx. July Term 1816.

Page 63   Sale of estate of William Hurst, deceased.
Aug 16, 1816   24 May 1816. Persons purchasing items, to wit, John Lenoir, Elizabeth Hurst, Asa Hurst, Jeremiah Pierce, James Fox, Thomas Dowling, James Martin, Harris Dowling, John Pierce, George Waters, and James Everett. Signed by Elizabeth Hurst, admrx. July Term 1816.

Page 63   Sale of estate of Jonathan T. Walker, deceased.
Aug 16, 1816   Persons purchasing items, to wit, William Stringfellow, Gustavious Rape, Jeremiah Baxter, Lewis Dunn, Benjamin Woodward, Peter Rape, and John Sanders. Returned by Lewis Dunn. July Term 1816.

Page 63   Inventory of estate of Daniel Morris, deceased.
Aug 17, 1816   The estate of Mathew Morris, Dr. to Daniel Morris, deceased $137.00. Dr. the wagons of Daniel Morris services $22.37. James Morris, admr. July Term 1816.

Page 64   Sale of estate of Robert Edmondson, deceased.
Aug 17, 1816   Sold on 3 & 4 May 1816. Persons listed, to wit, Andrew J. Edmondson, Aaron Everette, Peter Wright, Adam Stobaugh, Samuel W. Hope, Samuel Morton, Joseph Caldwell, Edward H. McNoel, William Edmondson, William Knight, Thomas Edmondson, Peyton Smith, Samuel Scott, William Cherry, Rebecca Edmondson, James Butt, James McCutchen, Adam Hope, Everate Owen, Hew Linch, Benjamin Bibb, Sterling Davis, John Blackman, Bennet Blackman, Samuel Fitzhugh, Joseph Nance, James Clinton, Henry Bibb, Thomas Bibb, Jenkin Whiteside, William Newton, Robert C. Reaves, William Howlet, Drewry Clanton, John Rains, William Ramsey, George Titus, Mathew Moore, James Pearson, Jacob W. Ramsey, and Isabella Edmondson. This 26 May 1816. Peter Wright, admr. July Term 1816.

Page 65   Sale of estate of Enoch Oliver, deceased.
Aug 21, 1816   Returned by Josiah Phelps, admr. Sale on May 15, 1816. Persons listed, to wit, Anny Oliver, Mordicai Kelley, Abner Morton, Guy McFaddin, Jacob Morton, and Josiah Phelps.

Page 66   Support laid off to Mary Edmiston.
Aug 21, 1816   To lay off for support of Mary Edmiston and family, late wife of David Edmiston. This 16 May 1816. Signed by L. Keeling and R. Edmiston. July Term 1816.

Page 66   Inventory of estate of John Lowe, deceased.
Aug 22, 1816   Cash $23.41½. Receipt of John Dobbs for the collection of a note on Francis M(illegible) for $1400.74. A note on Thomas Brown, two drafts on C. Stump, three negroes and other cattle &c, also household furniture willed to the widow her life time who has them now in possession. This July 26, 1816. Signed by C. Hewitt and Philip Shute, executors. July Term 1816.

Page 66   Inventory of estate of Laughlin McLean, deceased.
Aug 22, 1816   Negroes and other items listed. Notes on H. and F. Gains, A.H. Harris, Thomas Cartwright, William Harris, John Iredal, Sr., (blank) Menifee, J. Butler, Thomas Hudson, Cornelius Thomas, William Cornelius, Crutcher & McLean, A. Hope, Andrew Davis, William Donelson, R. Payne, and Peebles. July 16, 1816. Paul Dismukes, executor.

Page 67   Inventory of sale of estate of James Bibb, deceased.
Aug 22, 1816   Balance due on settlement with Robert C. Foster and S. Turley, Esquires. Amount of sale on 13 Aug 1814. James Bibb, admr. July Term 1816.

Page 67   Additional inventory of estate of Edmund Collinsworth, deceased.
Aug 22, 1816   Returned by Alsey Collinsworth, admr at Apr Term 1816. A discharge for a seven months tour in general Coffee's Brigade of Mounted Gunmen. July Term 1816.

Page 67   Inventory of estate of Robert Cato, deceased, of Davidson
Aug 22, 1816   County. Taken 15 July 1816. Several negroes and items listed. Mary Cato, admrx. July Term 1816.

Page 68   Inventory of sale of estate of Jesse Cox, deceased.
Aug 22, 1816   May 5, 1816. Persons listed, to wit, Wiseman Champ, Richard Champ, William Champ, Francis Mothershed, Polly Champ, Asahel Champ, Joseph Neely, and Arnel Russell. July Term 1816.

Page 68   Inventory of estate of David W. Edmonds, deceased, of Davidson
Aug 22, 1816   County. One note on Jesse Kirkland $40.00 being the only property or worth that I can find. This 10 July 1816. George Lile, admr.

Page 68   Support laid off for Anna Oliver of Davidson County.
Aug 22, 1816   John Johnston, Guy McFaddin and Candowr(?) McFaddin appointed to lay off one years provisions for Anna Oliver the relict of Enoch Oliver, deceased. Several items listed. This 10 May 1816. John Johnston and Cand. McFaddin.

Page 69   Support laid off for Alsey Collinsworth, the late wife of Edmund
Aug 22, 1816   Collinsworth, deceased, by John Johnston and Guy McFaddin and Cand. McFaddin. Several items listed. 10 May 1816.

Page 69   Inventory of estate of Oliver Johnston, deceased.
Aug 23, 1816   Several negroes listed also other items. David C. Snow, executor. July Term 1816.

Page 70   Sale of estate of Edmond Simmons, deceased.
Aug 23, 1816   Persons listed, to wit, James Lee, Christopher C. Carter, James Carter, David House, John Cannady, John Phelps, John Carter, William Harwood, Sherod Briant, Charles Macomes, and Joshua Fuqua. July Term 1816.

Page 71   Sale of estate of Edmond Collinsworth, deceased.
Aug 23, 1816   Returned by Alsey Collinsworth, admr. Persons listed, to wit,
Alsey Collinsworth, John Sullivant, William Ervan, Joseph Hopper, William P. Seat, Robert
Thompson, Adam Carper, Johnathan Williams, Susan Collinsworth, Thomas Warmouth, Charles
Hays, Reuben Smith, John Johnston, Sampson Edwards, John Kennedy, Sr., Caleb Goodrich,
William Vaulx, Joseph McKinney, Wyles Turberville, John Crutchfield, Robert Thompson,
James Clinton, John Collins, John Kennedy, William Tubiville, Allen (illegible), John Linch,
John Baley, Enoch Ensley, Silas Phelps, James Campbell, and Mordicai Kelly. Alsey
Collinsworth, admr. July Term 1816.

Page 72   Sale of estate of James H. Koonce, deceased.
Aug 23, 1816   Persons listed, to wit, Robert Shannon, Benjamin Pritchet, George
Koonce, William Nixon, Adam Weavers, Samuel Westbrook, James Conner, Thomas Cary, John
Jones, Joseph Tucker, Isaac Jones, William Jones, Newell Gray, Levi McCollum, Andrew Boyd,
John T(illegible), William McMillen, Josiah Glass, Daniel Glass, Dempsey Jones, Thomas
Cragg, James Pritchet, Samuel Orton, James Campbell, Thomas Atkins, Costin Sawyers, John
Harberson, James Allison, Mathew Lee, James Roades, James Acuff, William Jones, Lewis
Loyd, James Robertson, John Taylor, George Koonce, Bartholomew Steven (Stephen), Richard
Hart, Allen Forehand, Booker Richardson, John Linch, Samuel Jones, William Roach, Hardy
Mitchel, William Greer, Robert Cannady, Isaac Jones, Garman Stephens, Daniel Grey, Samuel
Maize, Wilkins Whitfield, James Gilliam, Robert Kennedy, Dempsy Sawyers, James Gilliam,
and John Aque, William Boyd, William Roach, and William Nixon. Sold by William Roach,
Robert McMillen and George Koonce, executors. July Term 1816.

Page 73   Indenture.
Aug 22, 1816   Made 15 July 1816 between James Leech of Wilson County of one
part and Peter Martin of Nashville other part. James Leech as guardian of Henry R.
Cartmell, infant son of Solomon Cartmell, deceased, hath with the free will and consent of
the said H.R. Cartmell hath bound the said Henry to Peter Martin as an apprentice to the
saddling business for and during the term of four years and eight months. He is to learn
reading, writing and arithmetic. He is to furnish sufficient diet, drink, washing and lodging
and good comfortable clothing. Signed by Peter Martin and James Leech. July Term 1816.

Page 74   James Austin, guardian and return, of Davidson County.
Aug 24, 1816   To sell the five tracts of land belonging to the heirs of Thomas
Dillon, deceased. Signed by James Austin, guardian of the heirs, by George Burnard his
agent. July 16, 1816.

Page 74   Will of Lucy White, deceased, of Davidson County.
Aug 24, 1816   To my son John White I give $15.00 and to my son Benjamin
White $15.00 and to my daughter Kesiah White $15.00, and to my grandson Willis White at my
death my boy Lewis and cows and calves, horse and other items. I appoint Allen Cotton and
Philip Campbell my executors. Wit: Henry Compton, James Campbell and James Crow. This
29 Jan 1816. July Term 1816.

Page 75   Sale of estate of John Edmiston, deceased.
Aug 24, 1816   Made by John Edmiston and Robert Edmondson, admrs. Persons
listed, to wit, Jane Edmiston, Robert Edmiston, Henry Graves, Elizabeth Edmiston, Daniel
Dennis, David Allen, Zach. Newel, Samuel Scott, John B. Hall, old Simon, John Drury,
Christopher C. Carter, James Carter, Jr., John Davis, and Lenrd. Keeling. July Term 1816.

Page 76   Sale of estate of David Edmiston, deceased.
Aug 24, 1816   Made by Mary Edmiston, admrx and John Edmiston, admr.
Persons listed, to wit, Robert Edmiston, Jeremiah Baxter, William Philips, Richard Drury,
Stephen Cason, William Knight, Edmond Owen, Craddock Fowlks, Mary Edmiston, Elizabeth
Edmiston, Peggy Bells, Baker Ayres, Christopher Brooks, Josiah Williams, Jeremiah Roberts,
David Allen, Meridith Wilkinson, James Carter, John Graves, Joshua Taylor, John Drury, and
John C. Hall. July Term 1816.

Page 77   Sale of estate of Robert Bell, deceased.
Aug 26, 1816   Persons listed, to wit, A.W. Morton, Nathaniel Bell, Thomas Bell,
Samuel Scott, Samuel Bell, James Baldridge, John Bell, Bennet Blackman, Jacob Morton,

David Bell, William Ogilvie, Thomas Williamson, Hugh Woods, Westley G. Nemo, John Allen, Daniel Mitchel, John Wattson, Robert Wood, James Turbiville, Bennet Blackman, Erel Fitzhugh, William Bell, Thomas Joyce, Samuel Philips, Jeptha Mosley, John Haywood, Joseph Williamson, Mr. Gooden, Jones Manifee, Morris Garret, William Marshal, Francis Bell, Thomas Bibb, Jane Bell, Neil Bell, W.G. Nemo, Abraham Bell, and James Baldridge. A note on John Gordon, one on Elijah Linkhorn, one on Shaw, and one due on James Stuart. Signed by Samuel Bell and John Bell, admrs. July Term 1816.

Page 79   Sale of estate of Rebecca Bell, deceased.
Aug 26, 1816   Purchases made by James Turbeville, Silvester Baker, and Jane Bell. Signed by Samuel Bell and John Bell, admrs. July Term 1816.

Page 79   William Harris, his freedom pass.
Aug 31, 1816   William Morris became my indented servant so that the said William Morris shall be considered by all concerned as fully dismissed my service, and as entirely free to act on his own behalf as he may think proper from the date of this instrument, done at the Seven Stars Aston Township, Delaware County, Pennsylvania. This 6 Sept 1815. Test: Joseph Piper and William Pennell. Signed by Joseph Nief.

Page 80   Alexander Nelson, his covenant from James Bradley.
Sept 18, 1816   I, James Bradley of Fayette County, Virginia, am indebted to Alexander Nelson for 200£ of Virginia currency. But to be void on condition that James Bradley made a good deed to all the lands he is entitled to as his military claim in Davidson County, North Carolina within six months after such deed is obtained. This 28 Mar 1814. Test: George Martin and Edward Bradley.

Page 80   Sumner of Sumner, receipt.
Sept 30, 1816   Davidson County, May 16, 1816. Received as the agent of Isaac Watts (or Walls) Sumner of Exum P. Sumner, executor of the Last Will and Testament of Jacob Battle Sumner, deceased, $300.00 which was a legacy left in this will of the testator to said Isaac Watts (Walls) Sumner, minor and son of the undersign. Duke W. Sumner. July Term 1816.

Page 80   Thomas James, his freedom pass.
Oct 24, 1816   Buckingham County Clerk's office Aug 14, 1809. Thomas James, a free mulatto, is duly registered and numbered 22. Aged 17 years, about five feet five and a half inches high, has no apparent mark or scar on face, head or hands and was born free. George Christon, J.P. Buckingham County Aug Court 1809.

Page 81   Settlement of estate of Thomas Ingram, deceased.
Nov 10, 1816   Made with Charles Cabiness, admr. Several items listed. William Hall, J.P. and Jos. Coleman, J.P. Nov 1, 1816. In 1809, paid Robert Goodloe. In 1811, paid T.G. Bradford, Andrew Ewing for a copy of the record Fanny Ingram VS Cabiness, admr. 1808, paid John E. Beck. 1816, paid Nathan Ewing for transcripts of record No. 9. 1816, paid Ephraim H. Foster. Balance due the admr $127.61. Also paid Jno. Dickinson No. 11, $75.00. Oct Term 1816.

Page 81   Settlement of estate of William Woodfin, deceased.
Nov 10, 1816   Made by Edmond Gamble, admr. Persons listed, to wit, Dr. McNairy, Dr. A. Newnan, Mr. Porter's note, Moody Harris, Washington Perkins, James Axum, William Basey, Dr. F. Robertson, James H. Gamble, Stephen Cantrell, Shadrack Casey, Hugh Birdwell, Oliver Johnston, M.C. Dunn, William Purnell, W.W. Hunt, Joshua Pilcher, William Perkins, T. Hall, Johnathan Clay, Thomas Mathis, and also sundries furnished, widow Sanders for her family in general support. James Read and Alexander Walker, Esquires. This 30 Oct 1816. Oct Term 1816.

Page 82   Settlement of estate of Isaac Shute, deceased.
Nov 11, 1816   Made with John Shute, admr. Money paid to the following person's vouchers: John Gowen, William Shute, Philip Shute, Robert Hewitt, Thomas Shute, Beal Bosley, Jno. Witherspoon, Jno. Harding, Asa Shute, and Peter Perkins. Notes on: James Jackson, Ilai Metcalf, William Mullen, John Martin, L. Norman, Pierce Maloy, Marques Divain, Mr. Mollhollen, and Nathan Eurn. Balance due John Shute, admr $182.82. E.S. Hall and M.B.

Lewis. Oct Term 1816.

Page 83   Settlement of estate of Roland Cato, deceased, of Davidson
Nov 11, 1816   County, made with Roland Cato, admr. Sold by John Stump and
James Read at the house of said Stump. Several vouchers, one bond on William Murrell.
Dividends paid were Roland Cato, Willis Alley, William Murrell, Thomas Runnals, Drewry
Jordan, Green Cato, and Mary Cato, each $202.95. Robert Cato, admr. is in debt to Robert
Cato on settlement $52.95. Also Roland Cato, admr is indebted to Lucy Cato on settlement
$167.60. This 15 Aug 1816. Oct Tern 1816.

Page 84   Settlement of estate of Samuel Buchanan, deceased, of Davidson
Nov 11, 1816   County, made with Peggy Buchanan, admrx. Eleven vouchers
amounting to $245.02½ and the body of the estate amount to $1250.69¼. Total $1005.66 3/4.
This 24 Oct 1816. Signed by Cary Felts and Thomas Williamson, J.P. and Samuel Bell. Oct
Term 1816.

Page 84   Settlement of estate of Thomas Dillon, deceased.
Nov 11, 1816   Made with James Austin, admr. Balance due by William Hall and
Robert Edmiston, Esquires, my agent George Bernard by examining Francis Saunders and
Jones Read, Esquires, for interest and principal of a judgement on Peter Bennett, also
retained by the Sheriff for McClung's claim under Stephen Haine's execution VS Thomas
Dillon. Received of the Clerk of Davidson County for John Ferguson. Balance due on Oct
30, 1816 $920.35½. Oct Term 1816.

Page 85   Settlement with Enoch Ensley, guardian to Henry Alexander's
Nov 12, 1816   heirs, At July Term 1816, the court ordered that Cary Felts and
Benajah Gray settle with Enoch Ensley as guardian to the orphans of Henry Alexander,
deceased.
and
Hire of negroes. Leave to Jerusha Parker and Patsey each share $346.46, to Milton Shurt and
Jerusha his wife $346.46, Parker Alexander yet due him $346.46, Patsey Alexander's share
$346.46. Yet due Patsey $327.09. This 26 Oct 1816. Oct Term 1816.

Page 86   Inventory of estate of Dr. William Dickson, deceased,
Nov 13, 1816   Several items listed including a Holy Bible, also several negroes.
Signed by Edward Ward and William C. Ward, executors. Oct Term 1816.

Page 87   Sale of estate of Dr. William Dickson, deceased.
Nov 16, 1816   Persons making purchases, to wit, James Carter, John Carter,
Robert Norman, Henry Hyde, Richard Oldham, J. & D. Maxwell, J. & J. Manifee, Richard
Williamson, Richard B. Owen, George M. Deadrich, S. Casey, W.T. Broadnax, Edward Ward,
Will Hart, J. Wharton, J. Whiteside, Turner Williams, W.W. Goodwin, L. Sturdevant, William
Knight, John Barnhart, John Frost, and R. Herbert purchased the Holy Bible, R. Turbeville,
William C. Ward, and benjamin B. Jones. Edward Ward and William C. Ward, executors. Oct
Term 1816.

Page 89   Sale of estate of Thomas K. Harris, deceased.
Nov 15, 1816   Nashville, Oct 27, 1816. Several items listed. Richard Moore,
admr. Oct Term 1816.

Page 90   Will of William W. Cook, deceased, of Nashville.
Nov 15, 1816   My library to be sold and amount to be laid out to my son Wilds
when he arrives at full age. The remainder of my estate to be left with my wife during her
life or widowhood and at her death or marriage to be divided among all my children except
my son Wilds. This 5 July 1816. Wit: Alexander Ewing and Eliza Grundy. Oct term 1816.

Page 90   Inventory of estate of John B. Jackson, deceased.
Nov 18, 1816   Taken on 29 Aug 1816. Several items listed. Signed by William
Roach, executor. Oct Term 1816.

Page 91   Mary Cato, relict of Robert Cato, support.
Nov 18, 1816   Part of the stock, also other items. This 16 Aug 1816. Signed by

Cary Felts and Jeremiah Ezell, Commissioners. Oct Term 1816.

Page 91   Inventory of estate of Lucy White, deceased.
Nov 18, 1816   Several items listed including a little wheel in possession of John
White. Allen Cotton and Philip Campbell, executors. Oct Term 1816.

Page 91   Mary Harris, relict of Thomas K. Harris, deceased, support.
Nov 18, 1816   Several items listed. Signed by T. Ezell, William H. McLaughlin
and John Gowen, Commissioners. Oct Term 1816.

Page 91   Inventory of estate of John Hope, deceased.
Nov 18, 1816   Now in possession of Ann Hope to be divided between the heirs of
John Hope, deceased. Seven head of horses, twenty head of cattle, forty head of hogs, and
twenty head of sheep. Oct 26, 1816. Signed by Ann Hope, executrix. Oct Term 1816.

Page 92   Inventory of sale of estate of Squire Payne, deceased.
Nov 18, 1816   Sold by Mrs. Payne. Persons making purchases, to wit, Sally
Payne, Greenwood Payne, George Pierce, and Robert Boothe. Signed by Sally Payne, admrx.
Oct Term 1816.

Page 92   John Hope, deceased, negroes.
Nov 18, 1816   Negroes to be divided between the heirs of John Hope, deceased.
Oct 26, 1816. Signed by Ann Hope, admrx. Caser and Phebe in possession of Adam Hope one
of the legatees. Stephen of Mathew P. Walker and Winney of James Buford who are also
legatees. Oct Term 1816.

Page 92   Inventory of sale of estate of Asa Shute, deceased.
Nov 18, 1816   Sold Aug 19, 1816. Purchasers, to wit, Ben Joslin, Thomas Shute,
William Griffin, John Harding, and Philip Shute. Total $1078.00. Jno. Harding, admr. Oct
Term 1816.

Page 92   Inventory of estate of Wright Gregory, deceased.
Nov 19, 1816   Oct 22, 1816. One bed, eight head of cattle, one axe, and one
chisel. Signed by Edward Gregory, admr. Oct Term 1816.

Page 93   Sale of estate of James D. Fish, deceased.
Nov 19, 1816   This 12 Aug 1815. Amount $36.62½. Joseph Smith, admr. Oct
Term 1816.

Page 93   Additional inventory of estate of James Brannen, deceased, of
Nov 19, 1816   Davidson County. Oct 27, 1816. Several items listed including a
note on Thomas Roach. Eldridge Newsom, admr. Oct Term 1816.

Page 93   Inventory of estate of Elizabeth Harding, deceased.
Nov 19, 1816   Several items listed. This 16 Aug 1816. Ellis Maddox, admr.
Oct term 1816.

Page 93   Joel Lewis of Daniel Adams, receipt.
Nov 19, 1816   Received of Joel Lewis former guardian to David Adams $167.55,
being in full, all includes his dividend of the estate of his brother George Adams, deceased.
This 20 Oct 1816. Daniel Adams, guardian. Oct Term 1816.

Page 93   Inventory of estate of David M. Edmonds, deceased.
Nov 19, 1816   Made by George Lile to the County Court of Davidson County
$40.48. Oct 21, 1816. Oct Term 1816.

Page 94   Mary B. Dickson, deceased, negroes.
Nov 19, 1816   Six negroes, viz, Dick, Gilpen, Betty, Polly, Sally An and Henry.
Betty Pleasant being dead. Edward Ward and William C. Ward, admrs. Oct Term 1816.

Page 94   Inventory of sale of estate of Isaac Battle, deceased.
Nov 19, 1816   Sold 22 & 23 Aug 1816. Persons listed, to wit, Lucinda A. Battle,

Charles Johnson, Humphrey Pope, Nathan Stancell, George A. Irion, Bennett Blackman, Rebecca Newsom, John P. Irion, Jacob Morton, John Kimbrough, Andrew Rodgers, William Kimbrough, Nelson White, William Hamilton, Henry Clanton, Johnathan Proctor, James Fitzhugh, William Nance, John Mayfield, David Barnwell, John McCutchen, David Haddock, Isreal McCarrell, Walter Kibble, John McCane, John Morton, James Morton, James Bosdell, John Lovett, Jr., Caleb Goodrich, Hancel Hervey, James Clinton, Bird Link, Robert Brown, Lewis Stephen, Britain Adams, William H. Nance, John Adams, William King, William Newsom, Ryleigh D. Murry, Green Seat, Francis Mays, Joseph Mays, P(illegible) Rodgers, James Gray, Abner Morton, Samuel McMurry, William Anthony, Robert House, Thomas Simmons, Andrew Rodgers, Andrew M. Johnston, and Henry Guthrie. Signed by Nathan Stancell and William Anthony, executors. Oct Term 1816.

Page 96   Settlement with Robert Thomas, guardian to Thomas Wilkes'
Nov 20, 1816   heirs. Robert Thomas as guardian to William A. Wilkes, Julia G.
Wilkes and Polly B. Wilkes, infant orphans of Thomas Wilkes, deceased. We, Giles Harding
and Robert Thompson have examined the accounts of the infants for year 1815 against said
Robert Thomas, guardian. This 18 Oct 1816. Signed by Giles Harding and Robert Thompson.
Oct Term 1816.

Page 97   Inventory of sale of estate of John Thomas, deceased.
Nov 20, 1816   Sold 3 Aug 1816. Persons listed, to wit, Archibald Pullen,
Christopher Carter, James Carter, Joshua Fuqua, William C. Carter, C.C. Carter, Hezekiah
Oden, John Drury, Edward East, Meredith Wilkerson, William L. Carter, Seth Cason, John C.
Hall, William McFerrin, James Drew, R.C. Drewry, and William Hall. Archibald Pullin, admr.
Oct Term 1816.

Page 97   Inventory of Isaac Edwards, deceased.
Nov 21, 1816   One sorrel horse, one bond for $123.00 and order for about
$40.00, one silver watch, one pair saddle bags half worn, one saddle and martingale and
bridle, and some wearing apparel. This 28 Oct 1816. Signed by Godfrey Shelton, admr. Oct
Term 1816.

Page 98   Sale of estate of John Blair, deceased.
Nov 21, 1816   Sold at the place where he died in Davidson County on 19 Mar
1816. Persons making purchases, to wit, Henry Compton, George Hodge, James Lester, Henry
Barnes, Capt. Coldwell, Jesse Cox, Theo. B. Rice, Allen Cotton, Mrs. McCutchen, and John
Overton, Thomas Herbert, Seth Norton, and James McPeck. Theo. B. Rice, admr. Oct Term
1816.

Page 98   Sale of estate of James Brannen, deceased.
Nov 21, 1816   Oct 28, 1816. Several items listed. Eldridge Newsom, admr.
Oct Term 1816.

Page 99   Will of Henry Bell, deceased.
Nov 21, 1816   To my beloved wife Betty Garrett Bell all the property that I
now have both real and personal including all claims that I have that is for the use of her and
all the children that I have or may have by her. Should my wife marry I give an equal share
of all the property during her life and at her death to be equally divided between my children
an equal share when they become of age or married. To my son John William Bell my gray
colt the reason whip. I have excluded him from having an equal share with my other children
is because he is well provided for in South Carolina. I appoint my wife as executrix. 26 Mar
1803. Wit: Sarah Hail, Thomas Jones and Jesse Webb. Oct Term 1816.

Page 99   Inventory of estate of Thomas Garrett, deceased.
Nov 21, 1816   Returned unto Oct Term 1816 by Samuel J. Ridley, admr.
Several items listed.

Page 100   Inventory of estate of Matthew Brooks, deceased.
Nov 21, 1816   Received by John Brooks, admr. Notes on Asa Green and a note
on Daniel Ramsey. One account received by Richard Crunk. Oct Term 1816.

Page 100   Will of Peter Perkins, deceased.
Nov 22, 1816   To my wife Rachael Jackson Perkins to have all my property real and personal during her natural life, except my negro woman Judy and her children which I wish to be free from my death. After the death of my wife I wish the whole of the property equally divided among my newphew, to wit, Peter Perkins Scales son of my sister Betsy, Nicholas Edmiston son of my sister Aggatha, Peter Perkins son of my sister Nancy, Constant Perkins son of my brother Nicholas. I appoint my brother Nicholas Perkins and my brother-in-law Thomas Edmiston, and my wife Rachael J. Perkins, my executors. This 1 Apr 1816. Wit: Nicholas Scales and Sally Perkins. Oct Term 1816.

Page 100   Will of Celia Atkison, deceased, of Davidson County.
Nov 22, 1816   To my brother Amos Atkinson one mare and colt now in his possession. To my sister-in-law Molly Atkinson one featherbed and furniture. To my friend Gabriel Smith one dutch oven, one earthen dish, two trunks and all my wearing apparel, also $80.00 in cash. I appoint my friend Gabriel Smith my executor. This 1 Oct 1816. Wit: Thos. Dillahunty, James Cooper and David Cartwright. Oct Term 1816.

Page 101   Will of James Wright, deceased, of Davidson County.
Nov 22, 1816   To my beloved wife Patty my three negroes, Hannah, Lucy and Bob as long as she remains single and afterwards to be equally divided among my daughters, Jenny, Betsey, Salley and Polly. Also to my wife the use of my land together with my stock of all sorts and my household furniture and farming utensils, afterwards the raising and schooling my small children to be equally divided among my sons, George Wright, Joseph Wright, Beverly Wright, John Wright, James Wright, and Jackson Wright and heirs, surviving heirs excepting and reserving to my wife the power to give my grand children, Weatherly Wright and Shaharazed (?) Wright any proportion she may choose so. I appoint my wife Patty and my son George Wright my only executors. Wit: John Buchanan and Jesse Fly. Oct Term 1816.

Page 102   John Kirkpatrick, deceased, negroes.
Nov 23, 1816   Nashville, August 5, 1816. Sale at auction. John Edmiston, admr. Robertson and Curry, auctioneers. Oct Term 1816.

Page 102   Inventory of estate of Jacob Dickinson, Sr., deceased.
Nov 23, 1816   Exclusion of legatees given the widow. Several negroes, a note of Francis Hailey, one on Joel Dun, one on Mathew Patterson, and negroes to be divided between Polly McCoy, Charity Donelson and Milly McCrory. This Aug 1, 1816. Will Williams, executor. Oct Term 1816.

Page 103   Inventory of estate of John Thomas, deceased.
Nov 25, 1816   One bay horse in the possession of William Hall. Several items listed. Signed by Archibald Pullin, admr. Oct Term 1816.

Page 103   James Austin, guardian return &c.
Nov 25, 1816   The orphans of Thomas Dillon, deceased, to James Austin, their guardian. To amount due and amount rendered unto 19 Oct 1815 $336.02½ to board and clothing for Thomas Davis Dillon and Edward Dillon from 19 Oct 1815 to 19 Oct 1816 at $30.00 each per year. Paid James H. Daugherty for schooling Thomas Davis Dillon and Edward Dillon. This 30 Oct 1816. James Austin appeared before Francis Saunders. Oct Term 1816.

Page 104   Sale of estate of Johnathan Johnston, deceased.
Nov 25, 1816   Made by Gustavus Rape, admr. Aug 9, 1816 sold at auction. Several items listed. Oct Term 1816.

Page 105   Sale of estate of Robert Cato, deceased.
Nov 25, 1816   Aug 16, 1816. Names of purchasers, to wit, Mary Cato, Rowling Cato, Henry Seat, Caleb Goodrich, John Wallpool, Charles McComb, Joseph Burnett, Henry Clanton, Joab Banton, Levi McGlothlen, Joseph Smith, and John Hill. Mary Cato, admrx. Oct Term 1816.

Page 106   Sale of estate of Elizabeth Harding, deceased.
Nov 26, 1816   Sold on 16 Aug 1816, property belonging to the estate of "Betsey" Harding, deceased. Purchasers, to wit, Giles L. Harding, H. Sturdevant, Edward Reves, Samuel Bell, William Jones, Ellis Maddox, A. Demoss, Polly Demoss, Jas. Hardgrave, B. Boon, Joel Yarborough, Skelton Hardgraves, Thomas Demoss, John Johns, Sr., Charles Walker, Robert Hodges, Henry Demoss, James Demoss, W. Whitfield, Samuel Kirkpatrick, John Thompson, Charles Saunders, David Jones, Robert Simpson, Jervis Jones, Josiah Maddox, William Bryant, and Johnathan Bell. Signed by Ellis Maddox, admr. Oct Term 1816.

Page 107   Sale of estate of Jesse W. Thomas, deceased.
Nov 27, 1816   Sold at the late residence of the deceased on Saturday May 18, 1816 by T.G. Bradford, executor. Purchasers, to wit, Sherwood Bryant, John Anglin, John B. Halls, John Drewry, Archibald Pullin, James Drew, Absolom Gleaves, Joseph Cook, Joshua Fuqua, Edmond Owen, John Thomas, William McMurry, John C. Hall, William Stewart, Zachariah Norvill, M. Thomas, Battersley Ballew, Alexander Buchanan, John Carter, Anthony C(illegible), Lemuel Keeling, David Castleman, and David Hays. This 25 Dec next. $53.28 brought in by Mrs. Thomas for herself and the family. Signed by T.G. Bradford. Oct Term 1816.

Page 108   Will of George Birdwell, deceased, of Davidson County.
Nov 21, 1816   I order that 160 acres of the land on which I now live lying along the south line of the tract to be seperated from the remainder of the tract by a line parallel to said south line to be sold to pay my debts &c. To my beloved wife Jane Birdwell possess and occupy and dispose of at her pleasure exclusively of all others. Whole estate to remain with my wife and my children except what shall hereafter be previously devised. I have given to my son Hugh Birdwell and to my son Isaac and my son Andrew each in property of different description to the amount of $60.00. My wife shall pay to my remaining children such property as she may think proper. To my beloved daughter Patsey $75.00 to be paid as above said. To my daughter Jinny $60.00 payable by her mother. To my son Samuel my mare commonly called the roan filly which he has full possession. To my son Milton also $60.00. To my daughter Polly $60.00. I appoint my beloved Jane executrix. This 30 July 1816. Wit: Francis McKay, Samuel Stull and William Neely. Oct Term 1816.

Page 110   William B. Wood of James Camp, guardian &c.
Nov 29, 1816   Receipt this 7 Aug 1815 of William B. Woods $491.09 in full to which Joseph W. Camp, Margarett B. Camp, Sarah P. Camp, and Mary M.B. Camp, infant children of Mary M.B. Camp, deceased are entitled or their mother and myself are entitled in consequence of any monies received of Margarett Woods which was considered as dower money. Children of Mary B. Camp. deceased and James Camp. Signed by James Camp, guardian. Test: James Trimble. Oct Term 1816.

Page 111   William B. Wood of James Camp, guardian &c.
Nov 29, 1816   Receipt. Aug 7, 1815 of negroes purchased by William B. Wood pursuant to a Deed of Trust executed by James Camp and Mary B. Camp his wife of one part and William B. Wood of other part, dated 25 Sept 1810, purchased a tract of land sold to William Shepherd it being a part of the one third part of the proceeds of sale to which Mary B. was entitled as one of the heirs of Joseph Wood, deceased. Land in the hands of Reynold Chapman. Signed by James Camp, guardian for his children. Test: James Trimble. Oct Term 1816.

Page 111   William B. Wood, executor &c of James Camp, guardian &c.
Nov 29, 1816   Aug 3, 1815 received of William B. Wood, executor of Margarett Wood, deceased, negroes, which were part of the dower negroes of Margarett Wood, deceased, which were allotted and set apart for Joseph W. Camp, Margaret B. Camp, Sarah P. Camp, Mary Miller, B. Camp, infant children of Mary Miller B. Camp, deceased. Signed by James Camp, guardian. Wit: William Quarles and James Trimble. Oct Term 1816.

Page 112   Michael C. Dunn, Sheriff bond of office.
Dec 14, 1816   We, Michael C. Dunn, David McGavock, Willie Barrow, George M. Deadrick, Elihu S. Hall, John Childress, and Felix Grundy, all of Davidson County, are bound unto his Excellency the Governor for $12,000.00 to be paid. Condition of the obligation is such that Michael C. Dunn is appointed Sheriff of Davidson County and he shall pay all fees.

July Term 1814.

Page 113   Michael C. Dunn, Sheriff's bond for collection of taxes.
Dec 14, 1816   The above named bind themselves to his Excellency the Governor
for $10,000.00 to be paid.   The condition is such that Michael C. Dunn will collect from the
inhabitants of Davidson County all public and county taxes. July Term 1816.

Page 113   Caleb Hewitt, Sheriff, bond of office.
Dec 16, 1816   We, Caleb Hewitt, Thomas Shute, Robert Hewitt, Elihu S. Hall,
Willie Barrow, Christopher Stump, John Stump, and William B. Lewis, all of Davidson County,
are bound unto his Excellency Joseph McMinn, Esq., Governor, for $12,500.00 to be paid. This
16 July 1816. Condition of the obligation is such that Caleb Hewitt is appointed Sheriff at
July Term instant, he is to pay all fees &c. July Term 1816.

Page 114   Caleb Hewitt, Sheriff's bond for collecting taxes.
Dec 16, 1816   The above mentioned men, all of Davidson County, are bound
unto his Excellency Joseph McMinn, Esq., Governor for $10,000.00. This 16 July 1816. Caleb
Hewitt is to collect taxes. July Term 1816.

Page 115   Joseph Philips, Sheriff's bond of office.
Dec 16, 1816   We, Joseph Philips, David McGavock, Jesse Wharton, William
Williams, and Stephen Cantrell, Jr., all of Davidson County are bound unto his Excellency the
Governor for $12,500.00 to be paid. This 22 Oct 1816. The condition is such that Joseph
Philips is appointed Sheriff of Davidson County. Oct Term 1816.
Page 115   Joseph Philips, Sheriff's bond for collecting of taxes.
Dec 16, 1816   The above named, all of Davidson County are bound for
$10,000.00 to be paid. This 22 Oct 1816. Joseph Philips is to collect all taxes. Oct Term
1816.

Page 116   Settlement of estate of Benjamin Liddon, deceased, of Davidson
Feb 17, 1817   County. We, Elihu S. Hall and Eli Talbot, Commissioners
appointed to settle with Sarah Liddon, admrx of estate of Benjamin Liddon, deceased. A bond
on Stephen Boonn for $80.00, a receipt on Henry Maxwell for $33.41, and a receipt on James
Evans for $24.58. Amounting to $137.96. Also she is allowed $100.00 for keeping Benjamin
F. Liddon, one of the children from Apr 1812 to Mar 1816. Jan Term 1817.

Page 116   Inventory of estate of Col. Peter Perkins, deceased.
Feb 18, 1817   Several items listed including a Bible. Signed by Nicholas Perkins
and Thomas Edmiston, executors. Jan Term 1817.

Page 118   Settlement of estate of Mathew Brooks, deceased.
Feb 18, 1817   Made with John Brooks, admr. persons listed, to wit, Nathan
Ewing, M.C. Dunn, A. Cheatham, R. McGavock, A. Green, Henry Fry, J.E. Beck, J.C.
McLemore, W. Shultz, David McGavock, Matthew Brooks, and Thomas Hickman. 16 Dec 1816.
Signed by E. Gamble and James Read. Jan Term 1817.

Page 119   Settlement of estate of John Waglee, deceased.
Feb 18, 1817   Made with Lazarus Inman, admr. Paid to Waightstill Avery, John
McGemsey, Eldridge Newsom, Sarah Wagley, Hardy Mitchell, Nathan Ewing, Ambros Hillburn,
John Harden, James Murphy, Jonathan Hargiss, Christian Inman, Lazarus Inman, and Felix
Grundy. Zachariah Allen and Levi McCollum appointed to settle with the admr. This 25 Jan
1817. Jan Term 1817.

Page 119   Settlement of estate of William Walker, deceased, of Davidson
Feb 18, 1817   County, as directed from Oct Term 1816. We have examined the
vouchers from the list of sales and money drawn from the United States for his service at
Orleans amounts to $483.68 3/4 and debt paid amounts to $49.25½, leaving a balance of
$434.43⅛. This 21 Jan 1817. Signed by Thomas Hickman and Jonathan Drake. Jan Term
1816.

Page 120   Settlement of estate of Philip Philips, deceased.
Feb 18, 1817   Made with Michael Campbell, executor. Persons listed, to wit,

Joseph Allen, Jos. Kirkpatrick, John P. Oldham, W.W. Cook, Isom Talbot, P. Philips, John Dickinson, Randol McGavock, John Thomas, Jos. Philips, James Campbell, G. Johnston, Isaac Herrel, William P. Duvall, Isom Inlow, P. Brown, E. McLean, Ben Thomas, N. Ewing, B. Helm, J. Morrison, B. Harden, John Rowen, John Philips, Andrew Ewing, James Chambers, James Neely, Miss Philips, M. & C. Campbell. Settlement made Oct 14, 1803 Davidson County Court. This 1 Feb 1817. W.B. Lewis, William Hall and R.C. Foster. Jan Term 1817.

Page 121   Inventory of estate of Elizabeth (Betsey) Harding, deceased.
Feb 19, 1817   Taken Dec 6, 1816. Cash received of Guy Smith $7.00. Signed by Ellis Maddox, admr. Jan Term 1817.

Page 122   James and Polly Dean, guardian return.
Feb 19, 1817   James and Polly Dean heirs of James Dean, deceased, account with Michael Gleaves, guardian. Paid Thomas H. Fletcher when F. McKay was guardian for year 1815. Paid William Neely for boarding James. Paid Josiah Williams for boarding James. Others paid, to wit, John Criddle, John Folwell, Thomas Dickinson for one bed for Polly, Thomas B. Craighead for teaching James, William James, William Lentz, Nathan Ewing, David Hunter, and D. Roberts. Michael Gleaves, guardian. Jan Term 1817.

Page 123   Will of Ephraim Drake, deceased, of Davidson County.
Feb 19, 1817   This 2 Dec 1816. All my perishable property to be sold, except my three beds and furniture and a spinning machine I wish to be divided equally between my three girls and when my son James Ford Drake becomes of age or marries I wish him to have a bed and furniture purchased out of the money coming from the sale of the property equal to the others. All my real estate or lands to be equally divided between my three girls and my son James F. Drake whenever they become of age or marry. I appoint my loving father Benjamin Drake and my loving brother William J. Drake my executors. Wit: Andrew Stewart and William Craddock. Jan Term 1817.

Page 124   William Feeland, deceased. Dec 1, 1815.
Feb 19, 1817   Received notes from William Martin and David T. Ethridge, one from Benjamin Moss and Wilson Gower, one from Joseph Morris, and one from Christopher Durham. All given Feb 13, 1815. Signed by Thomas W. Feeland. Jan Term 1817.

Page 124   James Drake, guardian return.
Feb 19, 1817   Account with James Vaulx, his guardian 1817. Balance $2.13.
Jan term 1817.

Page 124   Margarett Drake, guardian return.
Feb 19, 1817   Account with James Vaulx, guardian 1817. Balance $2.13. Jan
Term 1817.

Page 124   Martha Drake, guardian return.
Feb 19, 1817   Account with James Vaulx, guardian 1817. Balance $2.13. Jan
Term 1817.

Page 124   Sale of estate of Isaac Edwards, deceased.
Feb 19, 1817   Nov 7, 1816. Persons making purchases, to wit, Godfrey Shelton, William P. Seal, Ralph Neal, John Crow, and Ben. McCullock. Godfrey Shelton, admr. Jan Term 1817.

Page 125   Will of Charles Oldham, deceased, of Davidson County.
Feb 19, 1817   To my beloved wife Martha Oldham a negro man named Sam, a gray mare and side saddle and household furniture except one bed. To my son Peter Oldham a sorrel horse. To my daughter Sally Oldham one bed and furniture. I appoint my brother Richard Oldham my executor. This 10 Nov 1816. Wit: Samuel Matthew and William McCann. Jan term 1817.

Page 125   Inventory of estate of Selah Atkerson, deceased.
Feb 19, 1817   Jan 26, 1817. $80.00 cash, one dutch oven, one earthern dish, two trunks, one featherbed and furniture, one mare and colt which were in Amos Atkerson's possession now. Signed by Gabriel Smith, exr. Jan Term 1817.

Page 125   Inventory of estate of John Chiles, deceased.
Feb 19, 1817   Several items listed. Signed by Lois Chiles, admrx. Jan Term
1817.

Page 126   Sale of estate of Oliver Johnston, deceased.
Feb 20, 1817   Many items listed. Signed by David C. Snow, executor. Jan
Term 1817.

Page 128   Will of Rutha Turbiville, deceased, of Davidson County.
Feb 20, 1817   To my two grandsons Wiley Turbiville and Benjamin G. Turbiville
sons of Benjamin Turbiville a negro man named Gove, and my two sons Willis Turbiville and
Benjamin Turbiville shall keep said boy Gove and not to be hired out. To my son Willis
$40.00 which is in his hands. To my granddaughter Mary C. Turbiville one featherbed. To my
granddaughter Rutha Turbiville one featherbed. To my granddaughter Margaret Turbiville one
featherbed, daughter of Benjamin Turbiville. To my granddaughter Rutha Clinton daughter of
David Clinton one featherbed. All the rest of my property both real and personal I give to
my grandson Wiley Turbiville son of Benjamin Turbiville. This 5 July 1807. I appoint my two
sons Benjamin Turbiville and Willis Turbiville my executors. Wit: Richard W. Scruggs and
David Clanton. Jan term 1817.

Page 129   Inventory of estate of Ephraim Drake, deceased.
Feb 20, 1817   Taken Jan 23, 1817. Several items listed including one large
Bible, and a note on Benjamin Drake. Signed by William J. Drake, executor. Jan term 1817.

Page 130   Division of estate of William Walker, deceased, of Davidson
Feb 20, 1817   County. We find $60.84 to be their distributive share there being
Susannah Walker relict of the deceased and six children, namely, Polly, Elizabeth, Levi,
Henry, Patsey and William Walker. This 21 Jan 1817. Signed by Thomas Hickman and
Johnathan Drake. Jan term 1817.

Page 130   Settlement of estate of Joshua White, Jr., deceased, of Davidson
Feb 20, 1817   County. Made with Joshua White, Sr. A judgement on Bennett
Searcy. Received of W.C. Jamison. Received from the paymaster for Militia Services
$20.00. Paid William L. Brown's note. This 11 Jan 1817. Signed by George Wharton and
John Read. Jan Term 1817.

Page 130   Additional inventory of Thomas Garrett, deceased.
Feb 20, 1817   Returned unto Jan Term 1817 by Samuel J. Ridley, admr.
$142.00 in note of hand, all the corn and oats, wheat and hogs. Jan Term 1817.

Page 131   Dr. the executors of John Dickinson, deceased.
(No date)   Notes on William Tannehill, A. Caldwell, William Tait, W.L.
Hannum, J. Whiteside, Stephen Cantrell, and J. Trimble. Note on J. Hanna, Edmiston &
Blakely, Elliot's note, W. Miller, Constable, Deadrick & Sitler, Thomas Washington, Jane
Tucker, J. Stump, W. Eastin, C. Stump, J. Mulherrin, T.G. Bradford, E. Elliston, Jos. Erwin,
McClure & Elder, T.B. Craighead, Clifton Allen, Mrs. Caswell, B. McCullock, Deborah Elliot,
Jas. Lovell, Jno. Shelby, J. & C. Stump, Peter Bass, Jno. Nichols, W. Barrow, N.M. Williams,
T. Napier, and Ch. Cabiness. Cash from William Edmiston, S. King, T.H. Perkins, Thomas
Edmiston, ?. Williams, R. Smiley, A. Caldwell, Whiteside's note. Payment to guardian for
children's legacy: United States Stock, Nashville Bank Stock, Wilkins Tannehill, A. Caldwell's
note, also note on W.L. Hannum, J. Whiteside, S. Cantrell, and J. Trimble. Paid Mrs.
Dickinson, John White, William G. Dickinson, Chester & S. Gaylords, J.P. Batchelor, Jos.
Ward, T. Condon, D. McBean, Thomas Ramsey, Kirkman, Jackson & Erwin, Francis May,
Robert Farquharson, Thomas Childress, John Nichols, Tilford & Clopper, N.T. Perkins, Gideon
Blackburn, Thomas B. Wagoner, Roger B. Sappington, A. Foster, John Baird, Joseph T.
Elliston, R.B. Curry, M. & J. Norvel, E. Thursby, J. Metcalf, Ilai Metcalf, Felix Grundy, and
Stephen Cantrell. Signed by Josiah Nichols and James Trimble, executors. Jan Term 1816.

Page 133   Susan Woodfin's dower, of Davidson County.
Feb 21, 1817   Issued 2 Nov 1816. We have this day 2 Jan 1817 allotted to
Susan Woodfin of the personal estate of William Woodfin, deceased, Mr. Isaac Smith appearing
as her attorney and Major William Philip as guardian to the three children of said deceased,

22

several negroes. This 2 Jan 1817. Signed by D. Vaughn, William Maxey, Paul Vaughn, and Will Williams. Jan Term 1817.

Page 133   Division of estate of Samuel Buchanan, deceased, of Davidson
Feb 21, 1817   County.   Margaret Buchanan widow and relict of Samuel
Buchanan, deceased, gets one negro girl named Rose. Thomas Buchanan a negro fellow named Peter. Edward H. East a negro woman named Lucy. John Buchanan a negro girl named Phebe. Robert Buchanan a negro girl named Betsey. Also other items listed. This 5 Nov 1816. Signed by William Hall, James Carter, Henry White, Jr., Edmund Owen, and Peter Wright. Cary Felts, J.P. Jan Term 1817.

Page 134   Settlement made with Samuel Weakley, guardian to the heirs of
Feb 21, 1817   Benjamin Liddon, deceased. Samuel Weakley guardian of William
A. Liddon, Sarah Jane Liddon and Benjamin F. Liddon, heirs and minors of Samuel Liddon, deceased. Several items listed. Jan Term 1817.

Page 135   Joseph Vaulx, minor orphan, guardian's return.
Feb 21, 1817   Made with James Vaulx, his guardian.   Cash received of John
Goodrich, John C. Hall, Jno. and Richard Moores, and Thomas J. Reads. 31 Jan 1817. Jan Term 1817.

Page 135   John Hudson Sumner, minor orphan's return.
Feb 22, 1817   John Hudson orphan of Joseph John Sumner, deceased, made with
Duke W. Sumner, guardian. Several notes due also ten negroes. Jan Term 1817.

Page 136   Sale of estate of William Wharton, deceased.
Feb 24, 1817   Sale taken place at the plantation of the deceased on 26 & 27
July 1816. Purchasers, to wit, George M. Deadrick, Jenkins Whiteside, Charles Oldham, Samuel L. Wharton, George Wharton, Bernard McKernan, William Black, William Thompson, John Hamilton, Matthew Porter, Samuel Ridley, William Compton, Robert Hughs, L. Sturdevant, Samuel Hamm, John Topp, E. Ewing, Joseph Hopper, Johnathan Raines, John Nichols, John Alford, Jacob W. Ramsey, John Baccus, James N. Mannifee, Major Campbell, James Carter, Jonas Mannifee, (blank) Frazier, John Corbit, Beverly Ridley, Samuel C. McNees, Nicholas P. Walker, Zach. Nowell, and Jesse Wharton. Signed by J. Wharton, admr. Jan Term 1817.

Page 137   Isaac Battle, deceased.
Feb 24, 1817   Hire of negroes belonging to the estate of Isaac Battle, deceased,
Dec 30, 1816. Persons listed, to wit, Joseph Mays, John Mayfield, Jacob W. Ramsey, Charles Johnston, Alexander Buchanan, as taken off his hands by William King, Benjamin Bibb, Jacob Halfacre, William Ramsey, Jr., William H. Nance, Nathan Stancell, Isaac H. Howlet, John McCain, Thomas B(illegible), Lucinda A. Battle, C. Johnston, Nicholas Tomlin, and Thomas Hatchet, John P. Irion, William Anthony, John Blackman, James Gray, George A. Irion. Signed by Ariel Fitzhugh and William Anthony. Jan Term 1817.

Page 137   Amount of sale of property of Isaac Battle, deceased.
Feb 24, 1817   Sold Nov 15, 1816. Purchasers, to wit, Joseph Kimbrough,
Thomas Simmons, Nathan Stancell, Zachariah Bell, William Anthony, Isaac Nance, Thomas Joyce, Andrew Rodgers, Lucinda A. Battle, Thomas Claiborne, Robert Thompson, John L. Fielder, John Murry, Ralph Blair, Nelson Fields, Burnet Narren, Charles Johnson, Orren D. Battle, James S. Williams, William Nance, William Hamilton, Robert Thompson, Gideon Crutchfield, William Sorrel, Jesse House, John Gibson, John Morton, John Mayfield, David Haddock, Joseph Mays, David J. Robinson, Ephraim Thompson, David Barnwell, William K(illegible), James Moore, and Thomas Roberts. Signed by Nathan Stancell and William Anthony, executors. Jan Term 1817.

Page 138   Sale of estate of Wright Gregory, deceased.
Feb 24, 1817   Return by Edward Gregory, admr. One red steer, one blacn and
white cow and calf, a black cow, one white yearling, one white and black steer, a black steer, one bed, one axe and chisel. Nov 2, 1816. Jan Term 1817.

Page 139   Will of Joel Lewis, deceased, of Davidson County.
Feb 25, 1817   To my wife Marion all my estate both real and personal during her life or widowhood. She is to give to each of my children beginning at my son John when she chooses and thinks proper, not exceeding the sum of $3000.00 and from John decending to the next youngest child and so downwards to the youngest and whenever she shall die or marry all the property hereby disposed and divided among all my children. Wit: J. Haywood, Thomas Haywood and Jophah Moseley. Jan Term 1817.

Page 139   Lucinda A. Battle, widow of Isaac Battle, deceased, support.
Feb 25, 1817   At Oct Term 1816, court appointed B. Gray, William H. Nance, and Isaac Johnston to lay off and set apart one years provision for Lucinda A. Battle, relict. Several items listed. This 14 Nov 1816. Signed by B. Gray and William H. Nance and Isaac Johnston. Jan term 1817.

Page 140   Sale of negroes and other property of William Wharton, deceased.
Feb 25, 1817   Negroes sold at auction in Nashville on 21 Nov 1816. Other articles sold at the plantation of the deceased on 2 Dec 1816. Purchasers, to wit, Thomas Claiborne, John C. Hicks, N.T. Walker, J.T. Sims, William B. Lewis, Dr. John H. Marable, Joseph Park, Robert Searcy, Thomas Preston, Edmund Hyde, Richard Owens, Samuel J. Ridley, Thomas Rutherford, Willis Barker, (blank) Corbit, William W. Key, Mr. Harlin, Turner Sullivan, Samuel McChesney, Henry Questenberry, George W. Boyd, Jesse Wharton, and William Thompson. Signed by Thomas Claiborne and J. Wharton, admrs. Jan Term 1817.

Page 140   Additional inventory of estate of John Price, deceased.
Feb 25, 1817   Jan 1, 1817, then hired one negro man property of the deceased, let out one negro woman and five children. Signed by William Gilbert, executor. Jan Term 1817.

Page 141   Inventory of estate of Caleb Hewitt, deceased.
Feb 25, 1817   Purchasers, to wit, A. Balch, C. Stump, P.M. Humphries, John Pillow, John Davis, Jos. Dupree and assignee of the deceased a discharge for a tour of seven months service in General Coffee's Brigade of Mounted Gunmen, Henry Richards, Thomas Hickman, Kingsley & Parish, James Benning, Thomas Patterson, Thomas G. Bradford, Ilai Metcalf, John P. Broadnax, William Merryman, L. Earthman, Elisha Nicholson, W. Tannehill, Roger B. Sappington, William B. Robertson, Thomas Shute, John Haywood, John White, Thomas Gilbert, William Philips, Joseph and John Farrars, and Robert Macks. Jan 21, 1817. R. Hewitt, admr. Jan Term 1817.

Page 142   Sale of estate of John McCain, deceased.
Feb 25, 1817   Purchasers, to wit, Caleb Goodrich, Nelson Fields, William King, David Coldwell, Joseph Morton, Jeremiah Barnes, Joshua Briley, Riley D. Murry, Epps White, Alex. Morton, Alex. Buchanan, William Ogilvie, Abram Mason, James McCain, Isreal McCarroll, James Owen, Thomas Williamson, and John Bell. Signed by John Buchanan, admr. Jan term 1817.

Page 142   Sale of estate of David Beaty, deceased.
Feb 25, 1817   Aug 2, 1816. Purchasers, to wit, William Beaty, Philip Pipkin, Fred. Broadnax, Robert Newton, Robert Reaves, Shad. Bell, Lewis Sturdevant, Gabriel Smith, William Broadnax, Thomas Mitchel, David Pinkerton, John Corbit, Jesse Wharton, Robert Johnston, William R(illegible), George M. Deadrich, William Neely, Cad. Broadnax, William Compton, Jenkins Whiteside, Richard Oldham, James Cooper, Robert Scales, Henry Rutherford, Isom Fitzhugh, D.A. Durham, Thomas Hopper, Thomas McCrory, Philip Campbell, Martin Smith, John Broadnax, David Hughs, William Alford, and Henry Bateman. Lewis Sturdevant, admr. Jan Term 1817.

Page 143   Additional inventory of estate of John Dillahunty, deceased.
Feb 25, 1817   Taken May 7, 1816. Several items listed. Thomas Dillahunty, executor. Jan Term 1817.

Page 144   Sale of estate of John Dillahunty, deceased.
Feb 26, 1817   Purchasers, to wit, Benjamin Joslin, James Hodge, Rachael Dillahunty, Thomas Dillahunty, John Bosley, Joshua Dycas, Silas Dillahunty, David Pinkerton,

William Griffin, J.C. Bradshaw, Asa Becton, and William Compton. Thomas Dillahunty, executor. Jan Term 1817.

Page 144   Deed of Gift, Rachael Dillahunty of John Dillahunty.
Feb 27, 1817   For love and affection I, John Dillahunty, Sr., have for my grand daughter Rachael Dillahunty for her care and tenderness to me and my dear wife in our sickness, I do give unto her $50.00 in cash or good property out of my perishable estate. This 7 Feb 1816. Wit: Solomon L. Holder and Elizabeth Hopkins. Jan Term 1817.

Page 145   Sale of estate of Elizabeth Harding, deceased.
Feb 27, 1817   Sold 6 Dec 1816. Purchasers, to wit, John Whitfield, Harrison Whitfield, Charles Saunders, John Webb, Joel Yarborough, William Whitfield, Robert Hodge, James Shaw, John Hartgraves, William Parker, Ellis Maddox, John (blank), James Demoss, Polly Maddox, Timothy Reaves, Ellis Maddox, John Shaw, Canady Richardson, Henry Richardson, and Abraham Demoss. Signed by Ellis Maddox, admr. Jan Term 1817.

Page 145   Sale of estate of James Wright, deceased.
Feb 27, 1817   Several items listed. Patsey Wright, exrx. Jan Term 1817.

Page 145   Arthur Bland, a minor, guardian return.
Feb 27, 1817   Hires of negroes. Cash paid to Matthew Barrow, Josiah Nichol, T. Yeatman, W. Shumate, B. Hill, and E. Thompson. This Jan 30, 1817. Cary Felts, Esq., guardian. Jan Term 1817.

Page 146   Arthur Bland, a minor, guardian return.
Feb 27, 1817   The amount of hire of Arthur Bland's negroes, $215.25. Cary Felts, guardian. Jan Term 1817.

Page 146   Grey Washington, minor.
Feb 27, 1817   To Elizabeth Washington now Sims, guardian, to boarding, clothing and schooling up to 19 May 1817 $40.00. Hire out of negroes $25.00. Due Elizabeth Sims $15.00.
Nancy H. Washington, minor. To Elizabeth Washington now Sims (same as above). Due Nancy H. Washington $55.00. This 21 Jan 1817. Signed by William Hall, J.P. and Joseph T. Elliston, Commissioners. Jan Term 1817.

Page 147   Account &c of estate of John Dillahunty, Sr., deceased.
Feb 27, 1817   To Thomas Dillahunty. Paid to E. Hammon, Jno. Anderson, Deaderick & Somerville, William Black, Thomas W. Stockett, E.S. Hall, Harding & Stockett, to wine castor oil &c for mother, paid for coffin for father $11.00, paid Bradshaw for coffin for mother $6.00, F. Campbell, and paid your legacy to Rachel Dillahunty your grand daughter $50.00. Thomas Dillahunty, executor. Jan Term 1817.

Page 147   Henry C. Ewin, County Trustee &c, settlement.
Feb 28, 1817   July Term 1816. Elihu S. Hall and Willie Barrow, Esquires, Commissioners appointed to settle with Henry C. Ewin, County Trustee, make, report that they found in his hands $173.23½ which said Ewin then paid to the court.

Page 148   Josiah Nichol and John White, guardians of infant son of John
(No date)   Dickinson and Belinda Eleanor Dickinson, since deceased. Several items listed including a lot in Nashville, also by G.W. Campbell note. In account with henry Dickinson and sister. The amount of legacy left by John Dickinson, deceased, to his children $30,000.00. Jan Term 1817.

Page 149   Henry C. Ewin, County Trustee &c, settlement.
Feb 28, 1817   Duncan Robertson and Thomas Crutcher, Esquires, Commissioners appointed to settle with Henry C. Ewin, County Trustee now make report that they settled with Trustee indebted to the county the sum of $143.09½, paid 12 July 1816 and paid the clerk on 16 July 1816. Recorded in the minutes of July Term 1816, page 628.

Page 149   Inventory of estate of William Osborne, deceased.
Mar 11, 1817   Jan 6, 1817. Five negroes in the widow's possession. Several

other items listed. Signed by Shelton Hardgraves and John Vaughn. Jan Term 1817.

Page 149   Will of George M. Deadrich, deceased, of Davidson County.
Mar 22, 1817   All my estate both real and personal to rent out and apply the
proceeds to support and education of my son John George M. Deadrich now living at Ezekiel
Fitzhugh's and who I have adopted and wish to raise and educate. My executor sell all my
real estate to the best advantage at public auction reserving one fourth of an acre including
the graveyard and my plantation on Browns Creek in the center. Also to my son John George
M. Deadrich $15,000.00 and whatever to support and educate him until he arrives of age. To
Fielding Deadrich $10,000.00 and support to educate him until he arrives of age. To my
nephew Samuel M. Perry $6,000.00. To Elvira J. Searcy and Susan D. Searcy $2,000.00 each.
To Marcis M. Murrell and George M. Perry $3000.00 each. To each of my brother David
Deadrich's children $1000.00 excluding his son William. To each of my sister Murrell's
children excluding the before names George M. Murrell $1000.00. To each of my sister
Perry's children the before named Samuel M. Perry and George M. Perry $500.00. To my
nephew William Windle $2000.00. To my nephew William P. May $1000.00. To George M.D.
Cantrell son of Stephen Cantrell, Jr. $3000.00. To my nephew David S. Deadrich son of
Thomas Deadrick $1000.00. I give in trust to my executors $5000.00. The balance of my
estate and $500.00 to each of my executors for their trouble and attention. It is my will and
desire shall be equally divided between all the children of my brother David Deadrick, the
children of my sister Murrell, and the four sons of my deceased niece Elizabeth Searcy. I
appoint my friends Stephen Cantrell, Jr., Jesse Wharton and Robert Searcy, all of Davidson
County, my executors. This __ day of Nov 1816. Wit: John G.M. Deadrick, contested the
will of george M. Deadrick, deceased. A jury of men, to wit, William Whitsell, Philip Hurt,
Jacob Dickinson, Eli Cherry, William M. Harwood, William White, John McGaugh, James
Benning, William Lentz, John Philips, William Murphy, and William Atwood, being elected and
sworn and said that the paper to be the Last Will and Testament of George M. Deadrick,
deceased.

Page 152   Settlement of estate of William Payne, deceased.
May 20, 1817   Returned unto Jan Term 1817 by Joseph Payne, admr. They
found the amount of sales $45.37½, also the amount of services in the army $38.00. Total
$83.37½, found also vouchers amounting to $71.97. Leaving a balance $11.40½. This 19 Apr
1817. Signed by Edmund Goodrick, J.P. and William Donelson, J.P. Apr Term 1817.

Page 152   Settlement of estate of Daniel Vaulx, deceased.
May 20, 1817   Apr 18, 1817, with James Vaulx, admr. Several items listed.
Total $3930.22. Signed by Jeremiah Ezell and Cary Felts. Apr Term 1817.

Page 152   Settlement of estate of Samuel Buchanan, deceased.
May 20, 1817   Apr 18, 1817. Several vouchers listed. A balance of $656.09½ in
the hands of the administrators.   Signed by Jeremiah Ezell, Cary Felts and Thomas
Williamson. Samuel Buchanan, admr and Peggy Buchanan, admrx. Apr Term 1817.

Page 153   Settlement of estate of Amos Heaton, deceased.
May 21, 1817   Made with Enoch Heaton, admr. Amount of sale $55.00. Drew
for his pay for services in Creek Nation $37.50. Several vouchers, one on John Criddle and
John Stum(p). Paid Samuel Lenox and other items, leaving a balance in the hands of the
admr of $92.50. This 28 Apr 1817. Robert C. Foster and Braxton Lee, Esquires.

Page 153   Settlement of estate of Daniel Morris, deceased.
Apr (May) 21, 1817   Made with James Moses, admr. Several vouchers listed. Amount
of $147.24 now remains in the hands of the admr. This May 2, 1817. Signed by Joseph Love
and R. Weakley, Commissioners. Apr Term 1817.

Page 154   Settlement and division of estate of Lewis H. Lee, deceased.
May 21, 1817   Made with Braxton Lee, admr. Accounts paid to Braxton Lee,
Wilson Crocket, Gabriel Fuqua, Nicholas Hales, Samuel Miles, Richard Hydes, Elijah Spillers,
and James Stewart. Divide this sum amongst eight legatees makes a dividend of $23.60½.
This 25 Apr 1817. Robert C. Foster and Thomas Hickman. Apr Term 1817.

Page 155   Settlement of estate of John Simmons, deceased.
May 21, 1817   Nov 1, 1815. William Thompson, admr. Several items listed.
This 25 Apr 1817. Signed by Eldridge Newsom and William A. Anderson. Apr Term 1817.

Page 155   Settlement of estate of John Beck, deceased.
May 21, 1817   Paid John Henderson, Reubin Rucker, Dr. John H. Camp, William
Hayne, Robert Stainback, Arthur Dew, Philip Hart, William Wisenor, G(illegible) Scruggs,
William Hill, John S. Williamson, John E. Beck, James T. Love, John Newman, John Hoggatt,
Henry Graves, Hynes & Fletcher, and Thomas Hudson. Amount of sales $869.43 3/4, also sale
of Jan $250.00, and by Colonel E. Harris $49.00, and by (blank) Smith $28.00, and by Gideon
Eason, $15.00. A balance $96.29. John Goodrich, admr. Other paid, to wit, Thomas Talbot,
William Lytle, E.S. Hall, Joseph Fletcher, Jacob Morton, William Thompson, Doctor Richmond,
M. & J. Nowell, Ilai Metcalf, William P. Byrns, Nathan Ewing, Doctor Robertson, E. Cooper,
Peter Bass, William Wray, H.G. Harris, James T. Love, Jno. Camp, Samuel Neely, John Neely,
and Isaac Butler. This 21 Apr 1817. W. Tannehill and S. Cantrell, Jr. Apr Term 1817.

Page 156   Settlement of estate of Asa Shute, deceased.
May 21, 1817   To cash paid John Shute his note, Doctor Newman, Jno. Nichols,
Caleb Hewitt, Contantine Perkins for taxes, John Childress for note, Jno. Cockrell, J.
Whiteside for W. Anderson, Thomas G. Bradford, Philip Shute, N. Ewing, and Jno. Harding.
Amount of sales of personal property $1078.75. Also collected from Samuel Hale, A.
Kingsley, Howell Tatum, L.T. Turner, Asa Becton, and Daniel A. Dunham. Balance $1694.10.
Signed by Jno. Harding one of the admrs.

Page 157   The estate of Asa Shute, deceased.
(No date)   Account with Thomas Shute. Persons listed, to wit, Major Joseph
Lynn, Col. William Philips, Col. B.G. Stewart, Christopher Robertson, Samuel Parker, Lewis
Powers, David McGavock, William Stone, D(illegible) & Hudson, James H. Russell, William H.
Burton, Peter R. Booker, William Wilson, John C. Malone, Nathaniel Collins, Doctor Samuel
Sebastian, and Philip Shute his note. Collected from Samuel Sampson, Crofford Gooden, Joel
Maxey, George Hays, James McCann, Benjamin Hassell, and Peter Pinkston. Balance of
$433.28. Signed by Stephen Cantrell, Jr. and W.B. Lewis. Apr Term 1817.

Page 157   Settlement of estate of William Wright, deceased.
May 22, 1817   Made with Peggy Wright, admrx of James Wright, deceased, who
was admr of William Wright, deceased. Several vouchers listed. $280.78¼ remains in the
hands of the admrx. This 22 Feb 1817. Signed by J. Ezell and Cary Felts. Apr Term 1817.

Page 158   James Childs, his freedom, State of Virginia.
May 21, 1817   I, William Moss, Clerk of Fairfax County, Virginia, certify that
James a black man about 28 years of age, five feet nine inches high, very dark complexion,
this visage, pleasant countenance, was late the property of Gabriel D. Childs, who by his Last
Will and testament recorded in Fairfax County Court did among others forever emancipate
and set free the said negro James. I desired him to be registered in my office this 22 Sept
1813. Signed by William Moss, C.C.

Page 158   Sale of property of Ephraim Drake, deceased.
May 22, 1817   Sold Feb 12, 1817. Several items listed including a Bible $10.00.
William J. Drake, admr. Apr Term 1817.

Page 159   Additional inventory of estate of Ephraim Drake, deceased.
May 22, 1817   Taken Feb 12, 1817. Several items listed. William J. Drake,
admr. Apr Term 1817.

Page 159   Additional inventory of estate of William Cooper, deceased.
May 22, 1817   Received of the pay master $70.00, of William Monroe $12.00, of
William Edmondson $1.00. Total $83.00. May 3, 1817. Ephraim Brown, admr. Apr Term
1817.

Page 160   Sale of negroes of Stephen Roach, deceased.
May 22, 1817   Feb 18, 1817. Several negroes, total $2013.00. Signed by John
McCain, admr and Lydia Roach, admrx. Apr Term 1817.

Page 160   Sale of property of Thomas Liverton, deceased.
May 22, 1817   Purchasers, to wit, Samuel Eakin and Polly Liverton.   Total
$36.50. James David, admr. Apr Term 1817.

Page 160   Accounts of Thomas Williams, deceased.
May 22, 1817   Accounts against E.S. Hall, John Topp and J. & Joseph Woods.
Received from the book accounts $12.50. James Irwin note $301.88. Total $1210.44. Joshua
P. Caughan, admr. Apr Term 1817.

Page 160   Sale &c of estate of William Dickson, deceased.
May 22, 1817   Sales of sundries on __ Dec 1816. To Benjamin B. Jones, Edward
Ward, Edward Childs, John L. Williamson, T. Randolph, Henry Owens, Willis Barker, William
L. Yarborough, Thomas Claiborne, Richard B. Owen, Thomas Shackleford, Jas. Benning, John
G. Sims, and Jonas Mannifee. This 3 May 1817. Ben. B. Jones, one of the executors. Apr
Term 1817.

Page 161   Garritson Lanier, minor orphan, guardian return.
May 23, 1817   Three negroes, a note on John Lanier, and William Parker, one of
David Parker and John Lanier, one on John Henderson and John C. Parker, one judgement on
William Perkins and Kinchen T. Wilkinson, and a note on Thomas Wilkinson and W. Barnes.
Total $126.28½. This Apr 30, 1817. John Criddle, guardian. Apr Term 1817.

Page 162   Will of John Nichols, deceased, of Davidson County.
May 23, 1817   To my wife Sarah the land and plantation whereon I now live,
during her natural life with all my personal estate during her widowhood and for maintenance
and educating my children. To my youngest son now an infant an entry of land of 5000 acres
lying on the Mississippi River entered in the office of John Armstrong, lying on the west side
of the river Mississippi above the mouth of Hatchey River at the upper Hatchey Bluff. To
my son John the land whereon I now live, at the death of my wife. All the rest of my
residue to be equally divided among all my children, to wit, Nancy, John, Kezekiah, Susanna,
Harison, and my youngest son now an infant. I appoint General James Robertson, Thomas
Taylor and Bennet Searcy my executors. This 2 Nov 1796. Wit: James T. N(illegible),
William Lytle, Jr., and John Boyd, Jr. Apr Term 1817.

Page 163   Will of Kinchen T. Wilkinson, deceased.
May 23, 1817   To my beloved wife Martha Wilkinson, negroes. To my daughter
Amelia Wilkinson 136 acres of land adjoining Haysborough, also negroes. I wish no sale of my
property should take place. I wish my wife and child to live on my property during my wife's
widowhood, but if my wife should marry, I wish all property disposed of, for the benefit of
my child Amelia Wilkinson which to be educated. I wish my Haysborough property to be sold.
I appoint my beloved wife Martha Wilkinson, exrx and my brother Jesse Wilkinson, exr. This
__ Mar 1817. Wit: Thomas Hudson and Benjamin Hudson. Apr Term 1817.

Page 163   Sale of estate of William Osborne, deceased.
May 23, 1817   Apr 21, 1817. Several items listed. Amounts collected from
Daniel A. Dunham, Samuel Inman, Ezekiel Inman, and Robert Lazenberry. Skelton Hartgraves
and Johnson Vaughn, admrs. Apr Term 1817.

Page 164   Polly Feeland, her dower, laid off.
May 24, 1817   Jan Term 1817. A jury of twelve free holders are to lay off and
set apart to Polly Feeland, relict of William Feeland, deceased, her dower out of real estate.
James Lovell, Deputy Sheriff made return that he had summoned, to wit, Enoch Douge,
Thomas Hooper, William Levi, Jesse Garland, Richard Champ, Nicholas Hail, Meshack Hail,
William Douglass, Peter Dozier, Abram Tipps, George Hail, and John M. Lovell. They have
laid off to Polly Feeland the one third part of a tract of land which said Feeland died
possessed of containing 105 acres being a part of Shanklin's preemption. This Apr 11, 1817.

Page 164   Thomas Dillon, deceased, heirs guardian return.
May 24, 1817   The orphans of Thomas Dillon to James Austin, your guardian.
To Anthony Warwicks for clothing for Mary Ann and Elizabeth S. Dillon, also for George K.
Dillon, and Thomas D. and Edward Dillon. Paid James H. Daugherty for schooling Thomas
Davis Dillon and Edward Dillon. Paid John Hunter for tuition of Thomas D. and Edward

Dillon. Signed by James Austin, guardian. Apr Term 1817.

Page 165   Will of Mathew Karns of Town of Kittanning, Pennsylvania.
Aug 21, 1817   This 1 Mar 1817. To my father James Karns of Allegany County,
Pennsylvania $750.00 in bank notes which are deposited in the hands of Jos. and Rob. Woods
of Nashville, Tennessee to be paid to the order of my father only. To my brother Charles
Wilson Karns my horse, saddle, bridle and Saddle blanket now at Nashville, Tennessee. To all
my brothers and sisters the balance of my estate to be equally divided among them after my
debts are paid. I appoint my friend Robert Robertson, Post Master of Kittanning,
Pennsylvania my executor. Wit: Loderwick George, Richard Garrett and Jos. Woods. July
Term 1817.

Page 166   Will of Larkin Clay, deceased, of Davidson County.
Aug 22, 1817   All my estate should be sold except my land and negroes and
three figured counterpins which is to be divided among my three children. Negroes to be
hired out and the land rented until the children become of age at which time the negroes are
to be divided among the children. My land may be divided or sold and the money divided
among the children to be supported and schooled. I appoint my brother Johnathan Clay and
William H. Hamblen, my executors. This 28 July 1816. Supplement to the above. The land
to be rented and the negroes hired out. Wit: John Maxey, William A. Utley and Henry Seal.
July Term 1817.

Page 167   Will of Mary McWhirter, deceased, of Davidson County.
Aug 22, 1817   To my sold heir William Dorris I give all my personal estate, my
household furniture and stock also the land on which I now live, it being on Manskers Creek it
being part of a tract formerly belonging to William McWhirter, deceased, my former husband
containing 58 acres. To William Dorris and his heirs forever making null and void all other
wills &c. I appoint him William Dorris and Allen Mathis, executors. This 7 July 1817. Wit:
Allen Mathis, Isaac Walton and Beysey Tinnin. July Term 1817.

Page 167   Will of James Hanna, deceased, of Nashville, Tennessee.
Aug 22, 1817   Being about to commence a journey to Baltimore and Philadelphia
do make this my Last Will and Testament. To my wife Sarah Hanna one third part of the
value of whatever property I may be worth also the remaining two thirds of the same to my
seven children to be equally divided among them. I appoint my wife my executrix and James
Jackson her brother my executor. The house that I live in with, the store attached to it
which I lately purchased from Washington Jackson may constitute a part of the property
belonging to the children. This July 20, 1813. Test: Josiah Nichols, Peter A. Young and
William Allen. July Term 1817.

Page 168   Inventory of estate of David Earhart, deceased.
Aug 22, 1817   This July 21, 1817. 102 acres of land, 8 negroes and several
other items. Signed by Rodney Earhart, admr. July Term 1817.

Page 168   Inventory of estate of Ezekiel Brown, deceased.
Aug 22, 1817   Amount due him for services rendered the United States as a
Private in Captain Newman's Company of Tennessee Militia at New Orleans $27.14. Nashville
Aug 2, 1817. William Carroll, admr. July Term 1817.

Page 169   Nelson Lowry, guardian &c to Elizabeth Lowry.
Aug 22, 1817   Nashville, Apr 24, 1817. This day received of Elizabeth Lowry,
deceased, late guardian of Turner Lowry $364.00 in favor of said Turner Lowry part of the
estate of Absolom Lowry, deceased, the said Turner Lowry having choosen me as his guardian
from this time forward. Signed by Nelson Lowry. Test: Christopher Stump. July Term 1817.

Page 169   Inventory of estate of Benjamin Moss, deceased.
Aug 22, 1817   Inventory of money to the estate of Ben Moss. One note for
$55.00 John Robertson, one for $5.50 on Robert Gower, one for $1.25 on S. Wiley from the
United States $103.00. July 10, 1817. W.L. Gower, admr. July Term 1817.

Page 169   Additional sale of estate of Sarah Payne, deceased.
Aug 22, 1817   Sold by Flower McGregor, admr. One negro woman and two

children $650.00. July Term 1817.

Page 169   Settlement of estate of Jane Talbot, deceased.
Aug 22, 1817   Made with Thomas Talbot, admr. Several vouchers paid to: A.
Porter, Stump & Rapier, C. Stump, E.S. Hall & Co., Doct. W. Purnell, R.B. Sappington, J.
Talbot, and Thomas Talbot. Amount due the estate $695.78. This 30 June 1817. July Term
1817.

Page 170   Settlement of estate of William S. Gaines, deceased.
Aug 22, 1817   Made with Thomas Childress, admr. To amount of sales by D.
Robertson $140.81. To cash received of Peter Higgins for one gray horse $143.00. Cash paid
Duncan Robertson judgement also cash paid Henry Crabb. Balance left in hands of admr
$50.02 3/4. This Aug 1, 1817. Signed by William Hall, J.P. and John Stump, J.P. July Term
1817.

Page 170   Settlement of estate of Charles Bullock, deceased.
Aug 22, 1817   Made with E.W. Brookshire, admr. Vouchers amounting to
$886.83. This 24 July 1817. W. Barrow and Thomas Williamson. July Term 1817.

Page 171   Settlement of estate of William Feeland, deceased.
Aug 22, 1817   Persons listed, to wit, Thomas W. Feeland, Pharaby Feeland,
William Black and J. Williams, Nathan Ewing, Peter Dozier, E. Spiller, Hance Shaw,
Obedience Lucas, George S. Allen, J. Watkins, Feby Allen, William Douglass, J. Whiteside, and
Felix Grundy. William Russell and George S. Allen appointed to settle said estate. This 29
July 1817. Balance due $47.25. Thomas W. Feeland, admr.

Page 171   Settlement of estate of Robert Edmondson, deceased.
Aug 23, 1817   April Term 1817, made with Peter Wright, admr. Several
vouchers listed. July 28, 1817, we find still in the hands of admr a balance of $795.81 3/4.
J. Ezell and J. Felts. July Term 1817.

Page 172   Settlement of estate of Fountain H. Gaines, deceased.
Aug 23, 1817   Persons listed, to wit, John Nichols, Stephen Cantrell, Thomas
Ramsey, Doct. Robertson, Col. Butler, Charles Niles, P. Dodson, G.W. Campbell, John
Buchanan, R.B. Sappington, Robert Redding, W. Lytle, A. Hughey, M.B. Mumford, John C.
Hicks, J.P. Downs, John Rains, J. Downey, John Bosley, tax United States gold watch $2.00,
J. Sanford, J. Carter, Read & Washington, R. Clinton, John Harding, Camp & Peacock, D.
Robertson, Doc. Robertson, and J.B. Houston. Assets received due 25 Dec 1816. A lot sold
by J. Woods. Bu cash to be paid by S. Nothington. Others named, viz, T. Demumbreum, J.H.
Cobbs, W. Tannehill, Robert Simpson, L. McLeans, M. Helms, Jno. W. Cook, D. Robertson, F.
Helms, J. Whiteside, W. Wilkerson, L. Temple, Jacob W. Ramsey, and Boyd McNairy. C.
Stump, J.P. and E. Talbot, J.P. Thomas Shackleford and James Trimble, executors. July
Term 1817.

Page 173   Settlement of estate of John Price, deceased.
Aug 25, 1817   Made by William Gilbert, executor. Persons that has notes due
the estate, to wit, Taswell Hyde, James Everett, John Kennedy, Henry Lady, Richard Hyde,
Patsey Moody, Charley Cagle, Jordan Hyde, Jesse J. Everett, John Stump, John Criddle,
Thomas Hickman, and Thomas Watts. Contra credits agreeable to the vouchers, to wit,
Daniel Dunevant, William Martin, B. Hufman, R. Hyde, Joseph Washington, William Gillage,
James Martin, Nathan Ewing, Abraham Tippy, Thomas Pierce, Elizabeth Hurst, John L.
McCormack, John B. Durall, Thomas Heaton, Nathan Bennett, George Walters, William
Roland, John Stump, James Martin, James Fox, Benjamin O'Donaly, Isaac Mayfield, Daniel
Dunevant, John Tinnon, Thomas Hickman, and William Wallace. Johnathan Drake and Thomas
Hickman, Esq. July Term 1817.

Page 174   Settlement of estate of Isaac Basye, deceased.
Aug 25, 1817   Made by Samuel L. Wharton, admr. Paid to persons, to wit, John
Walker, L.C. Farrar, L. McLean, Thomas G. Bradford, John A. Walker, O. Johnson, Joshua
White, A. Balch, Jno. McCrunk, Jacob Morton, Nathan Ewing, and James T. Bayse. Balance
due by the admr $117.99 3/4. This 22 July 1817. John Goodrich and Alex. Walker. July
Term 1817.

Page 175   Second settlement of estate of Nicholas Raymond, deceased.
Aug 25, 1817   William Wisenor, admr. Persons listed, to wit, Nathan Ewing,
William Wray and Landon C. Farrar. Due the admr $18.75 3/4. This 28 July 1817. July
Term 1817.

Page 175   Settlement of estate of William Osborn, deceased.
Aug 23, 1817   Made by Skelton Hartgraves and Johnson Vaughn, admrs., July 25,
1817. Persons listed, to wit, John Gullet, Stephen Cantrell, J. Vaughn, A. Connelly, T.
Osborn, T. Hartgraves, William Armstrong, John Drury, and William Allen. Accounts on D.A.
Dunham, Ezekiel Inman, Samuel Inman, Peter Connelly, Robert Lazenberry, and S. Cantrell.
This 25 July 1817. Robert Thompson, J.P. and Zachariah Allen, J.P. July Term 1817.

Page 176   Account current of estate of John Ruger, deceased.
Aug 25, 1817   Made by John Hogan, admr. Received of the United States for
his services $128.25, also of Thomas Hutchings, Jno. Donnelson and Thomas Bedford, Jos.
Williams, Mr. Nutt, and Jos. M. Walker. Paid to William Clark, Samuel Smith, Richard D.
Holiday and William Howlet, Nelson Alford, Floyd Hurt, John Hogan, Thomas Bibb, Robert
Boothe, John Rains, Frederic Owen, Adam Stobough, and James Bibb. July Term 1817.

Page 176   Inventory of estate of James Hanna, deceased.
Aug 26, 1817   Taken on 7 June 1817. Several items listed. Merchandise listed.
(a very long inventory)
Sarah Hanna, exrx and James Jackson, admr.
A list of debts due the estate on 7 June 1817. Recorded 30 Aug 1817: Persons listed, to wit,
Horner & Wilson of Philadelphia, Duncan Robertson of Nashville, George M. Deadrich, Alfred
Balch, Pritchet and Shall, Mrs. Mary Lewis, Rev. J.B. Craighead, Thomas Easton, Moses
Hicken, Joel B. Harper, John Somerville, Ellis Maddox, Mrs. Holmes, Jacob Aaron, John
Graves of Giles County, Thomas Claiborne, Perry Cohu, Willie Barrow, James Irwin, Thomas
H. Fletcher, Doctor Butler, James Glasgow, John Chapman, Thomas Shackleford, William
French of Baltimore, Mrs. McCrory, John Davis of McMinnville, Briton Tully, Benjamin Joslin,
John Ashey, John Anderson, Doct. Saunders, James Earthman, John Harding, Christopher
Stump, John Donnelly, John Donaldson, O.B. Hayes, James Morton, Mrs. Dodds, William
Bosworth, Joseph Engleman, George W. Campbell, Mrs. Cannon, D.E. Biddle, Richard
Ba(illegible) of Baltimore, Margret Duffy, M.H. Quin, Thomas G. Bradford, Stokely Hayes,
Ralph Crabb, Samuel C. Hawkins of Palmyra, Daniel Horton of Springfield, James Camp,
Major Sevier, John Drury, John Fisher, Felix Grundy, W.W. Cooke, Edmond Cooper, John
Garner, David Tilford & Co. of Shelbyville, Thomas Moore of Shelbyville, Hugh T. Newell,
John Childress, John Tilford of Pulaski, Henry Jackson, Thomas Ramsey, James Lockhart,
(illegible) Willis a carpenter, Mrs. Sneed, James Tilford, John McNairy, John Tolville, Joseph
Coleman, Joseph Morton, William Leentz, Samuel McChesney, J. Duker, Robert Butler, Doct.
McNairy, James Priestly, Anthony Foster, Robert Bell, Conlon Rice, William Allen & Co.,
Hood and Walker, James Campbell, James Jackson, Jason Thompson, James Drury, Hugh
Young, Charles McLean, Charles Temple a carpenter, Jenkins Whiteside, Mont. Bell, Thomas
Shannon, Mrs. Fly, Micajah Fly, James D. Miller, Isaac Dortch, Peter Moseley, Howell
Tatum, Female Academy, Mr. Patterson, James Jackson & Co., Richard Garrett, William B.
Lewis, Robert Holmes, John L. Allen, Isaac Pierce, Samuel Bell, Archibald & G. McNeill,
Solomon Clarke, Elisha Fly, Philip Thomas, Terance Shaw, Jacob Curfman, Charles Cassidy,
Felix Robinson, Alexander Jones, Hugh Evans, Steam Mill Company, Margret Marlow, Doct.
Newman, John Lyons, Robertson & Kelton, John P. Erwin, Edmond Hewlett, Erwin & Baker,
Col. R. Hayes, JOhn C. Hicks, John Donaldson, Jr., Miss Green, Samuel Elam, Nicholas
Perkins, Doct. Hickman, Robert Smiley, Mr. Chester of Carthage, Levin Cator, McKernan &
Stout, Doct. Maxey, Washington Perkins, Peggy - James Jackson's girl, John W. Clay, Doct.
Shelby, Roger B. Sappington, General Jackson, Major Young, James Baxter, Miss Biddle,
Craddock & Read, John Erwin, Richard K. Adams, Robert Stothart, Zachariah (blank), Sally
Sneed, John W. Ewing, Big Pat - a negro woman, Judge Overton, Horace Gaines, Mr. Prior,
Bartley - James Jackson's boy, Richard Boyd, Thomas Waters, Robert Bell, Thomas Tunstall,
John H. Ligon of Wilson County, Mrs. Stone, Jesse Fly, Thomas C. Winthrow of Shelbyville,
William Shelton, S. Cowan, free Jeffry - a negro man, Mrs. Womac, Captain Abraham Wright,
Mr. B(illegible) Shumate, the widow Robinson, Buck - Doct. McNairy's negro man, Mrs.
Ramsey, Mrs. Morell, Allen Ward, William Rice of near Gallatin, old Joyce - a negro woman,
Mrs. White, David Williams, Catherine Rankin of Jefferson Road, Thomas Moss, Abe Cantrell,
George Barnett a yellow man, Patt Bigley, John Roy, and Boyd (blank). Creditors   of   the

estate: Jas. Baxter and R.T. Meriwether, J. Wharton, John C. Hicks, William B. Robinson, Robert Murray, Perry Cokes, Kennedy & Isom, Thomas Shute, Thomas Johnston, William Allen, Adam D. Hamilton, Joseph Ward, Solomon Clarke, William Winegardner, William Shields, Alpha Kingsley, H. Terass(?), John Baird of Shelbyville, William Chandler, Valentine D. Bary, Major Charles Sevier's transportation, Lieut. John Awalt, Ensign Abraham McMahan, and Doct. Saunders' transportation, Thomas Williamson, Thomas Deadrich, Cadman & Broadhurst of Sheffield, Arthur Redmonds, Talbot Jones of Baltimore, T. & P. Kelly of Philadelphia, Washington Jackson, Christopher Stump, Mrs. Clements, Kirkman & Jackson of Philadelphia, and the following are of Philadelphia: Richard Ashurst, James Potter, J. and G.M. Justice, George Slesman, Adam Everly, Adam Dural & Co., Benjamin Sharpneck, L(illegible) and C(illegible), Richard C. Potter, L. & S. Brown, John Gill, Jr. & Co., Thorp Sheddall & Co., and Thorp Hurley. Also N. Ewing for costs of Hooper's suit, F.E. Fisher, Alexander Scott, and Haislop and Vanleer. Bills payable to, viz, John Jackson of Philadelphia, James O'Neill, estate of William Tait, deceased, Young & Green, and Margret Marlow. Signed by Sarah Hanna and James Jackson, executors. (a very long inventory)

Page 198   Inventory of Hanna's personal estate. Many items listed. Signed
                            by Sarah Hanna, executrix and James Jackson, executor. July
Term 1817.

Page 199   Land divided, estate of Walter Fairfax, deceased.
Sept 1, 1817   (Plat on page 199) Walter Fairfax died intestate. Land adjacent
to town of Nashville containing four acres. We allott and give and divide their equal share of said land to Nathaniel Peck and his wife Elizabeth D. Peck which said Elizabeth D. is an heir of said Walter. His land bordering George W. Campbell, John McRainey, and Baird's line. We allott to Henry Fairfax, another heir of said Walter, the land bordering Nathaniel Peck and Elizabeth his wife, John McNairy, and John Baird. We allott to Matilda F. Fairfax, another heir of said Walter, as her equal share of land and bordering Henry Fairfax, John McNairy and John Baird. Lastly, we allott to John B. Fairfax, one other heir of said Walter, the land bordering Matilda F. Fairfax, John McNairy, Andrew Hynes, and John Baird. This 3 May 1817. Signed by Duncan Robertson, John Young, Mathew H. Quin, Felix Robertson, and David Moore. July Term 1817.

Page 201   John Davis, his freedom.
Sept 8, 1817   Nov Term 1816. Smith County, Tennessee. John Davis a man of
color, about 22 years of age, by two witnesses of Smith County Court, that he was born free and entitled to his freedom and a certificate. I, Robert Allen, Clerk of Smith County do certify to the foregoing as a true copy. This 29 Apr 1817. William Moore, Chairman pro tem of Smith County.

Page 201   Levina Melton, her freedom. Beaufort County, North Carolina.
Nov 2, 1817   Vina or Levina Melton is the daughter of a white woman named
Sally Melton and that Vina or Levina is and of right to be free and is about to remove out of said county and application having been made for a certificate of that fact. Wit: Thomas Snow, Clerk of Court, this 29 July 1817 at Washington.

Page 201   Settlement of estate of Sarah Payne, deceased.
Nov 11, 1817   Made with Flower McGregor, admr. Several vouchers listed.
Balance in the hands of the admr $874.06¼. Also a bond on William Walton. This Sept 6, 1817. William Hall and James Mulherrin. Oct Term 1817.

Page 202   Settlement of estate of William E. Gower, deceased.
Nov 11, 1817   Persons listed, to wit, J. Williams, McLeroy, L. Pierce, and T.
Simpkins, R. Williams, Nathan Ewing, and S. Jones. Oct 1, 1817. Jonathan Drake and Thomas Hickman. Oct Term 1817.

Page 202   Settlement of estate of Benjamin Moss, deceased.
Nov 11, 1817   Persons listed, to wit, Absolom Page, Henry Ewins(Ewing), T.
Hickman, and E. Gower. Oct 1, 1817. Jonathan Drake and Thomas Hickman. Oct Term 1817.

Page 202   Settlement of estate of Ruth Phipps, deceased.
Nov 11, 1817   Made with Zachariah Nowell, exr., with will annexed. Several

vouchers listed. Sept 6, 1817. William Hall and James Mulherrin. Oct Term 1817.

Page 203   Settlement of estate of Evan Green, deceased.
Nov 11, 1817   Persons listed, to wit, James Green's note, Justice's account,
Nathan Ewing, George Murphy, Louis Brent, S. Bellamy, Smith's cost, Young's account,
Murphy's note, S. Williams' receipt, Hogan's note, Nathan Ewing's account, Mr. Birdwell's
note, and Davis' note. 20 Oct 1817. John Stump, J.P. and Iredale Redding. Oct Term 1817.

Page 203   Settlement of estate of John Thomas, deceased.
Nov 11, 1817   Made with Archibald Pullen, admr. Several vouchers listed. Sept
19, 1817. William Hall, J.P. and James Mulherrin. Oct Term 1817.

Page 203   Settlement of estate of John Riger, deceased.
Nov 12, 1817   Made by Joseph Love and Thomas Edmiston, with John Hogan,
admr. Vouchers of William Howlett, William Clark, Samuel Smith, and Richard D. Hobdy.
Received of Thomas Hutchings, John Donelson and Thomas Bedford, Joseph Williams, and
others, Nelson Alford, Floyd Hurt, John Hogan, Thomas Bibb, Robert Boothe, John Rains,
Frederick Owen, Adam Stobaugh, and James Bibb. This 27 Oct 1817. Joseph Love, J.P. and
Thomas Edmiston, J.P. Oct Term 1817.

Page 204   Settlement of estate of Vincent Cartwright, deceased.
Nov 12, 1817   Ordered at July Term 1817 for Josiah Horton, Eldridge Newsom
and Zachariah Allen to settle with Leven Edney, admr of said estate, find $544.00 in the
hands of said Edney belonging to the estate of the orphans of said Vincent Cartwright,
deceased. This 13 Oct 1817. Eldridge Newsom and Zach. Allen. Oct Term 1817.

Page 204   Settlement of estate of Thomas Dillon, deceased.
Nov 12, 1817   Made with James Austin, admr. Persons listed, to wit, Francis
Sanders and James Read, Esqrs. Charges by agent George Bernard received account of
William Alexander, Clerk of the Circuit Court in Hawkins (County) 2 Dec 1816 for M. Lyons
execution on Jos. M. Anderson and Gabriel McCraw being the debt mentioned in the inventory
as due from William Cocke in the hands of John Kennedy $402.33 amount received of R.G.
Waterhouse. Signed by James Austin, admr by George Bernard his agent 21 Oct 1817.
William Hall and Eldridge Newsom, Justices of the Peace.

Page 205   Settlement of estate of John Longhorn, deceased.
Nov 12, 1817   Persons listed, to wit, Allen & Finch Scruggs, C. Stump, Jno.
Childress, John Dickerson, Thomas Rutherford, Thomas Kirkman, J. & W. Jackson, M.C. Dunn,
D. Moore, John Rankin, John Cox, William Tait, R.B. Sappington, Robert Hewitt, Ephraim
Parham, J.P. Downing, John Baird, Stump & Rapier, John Dickinson, L. Earthman, Thomas G.
Bradford, James P. Downs, Isom Hopkins, L. Chapman, Nathan Ewing, John C. Parker, and
George Boyd. This 25 Oct 1817. Oct Term 1817.

Page 206   Additional inventory of estate of Isaac Bayse, deceased.
Nov 12, 1817   Returned by Samuel L. Wharton, admr. One negro boy named
Dilliard, one bed, one trunk, and one woman's saddle. Oct 28, 1817. Oct Term 1817.

Page 206   Additional inventory of estate of Edmund Collinsworth, deceased.
Nov 12, 1817   Oct 20, 1817, made by Alcie Collinsworth, admrx. A note of
$7.00 and certificate of his copies at Instochopca Creek in the service of the United States
amounting to $45.00. Oct Term 1817.

Page 206   Negroes hired of the estate of Joseph McBride, deceased.
Nov 14, 1817   1 Jan 1817. One negro man, one negro woman with five small
children, one woman with one small child. Taken by P. McBride for maintenance, clothing
and taxes for one year. P. McBride, adnr and James Hodge, admr. Oct Term 1817.

Pahe 206   Inventory of estate of David Spence, deceased.
Nov 14, 1817   John Jones, Sr., admr. Due the estate by William Marrs and John
Jones. Note on Thomas Williams also one on Lodwick Williams. Oct Term 1817.

Page 206   Inventory of estate of Hiram Hurt, deceased.
Nov 14, 1817   Made by Robert Woods, admr. Oct 18, 1817. Several items
listed including Floyd Hart's account and Peter Owen's account. Oct 20, 1817. Oct Term
1817.

Page 207   Inventory of estate of John Hancock, deceased.
Nov 14, 1817   Several items listed. John New, admr. Oct Term 1817.

Page 207   Supplementary inventory of estate of William E. Gower, deceased.
Nov 14, 1817   Cash received from Cannon, execution of William E. Gower
$200.00, and one note on Samuel Gower for $46.00. Samuel M. Gower, admr and Patsey
Gower, admrx. Oct Term 1817.

Page 207   Inventory of estate of William C. Ewell, deceased.
Nov 14, 1817   Note against Absolom Gleaves, one against Sally Hayes and John
D. Campbell, one against John Harpath, one against William Stewart, Miles Jackson, Henry
Jones, and book accounts against Christopher Seabourne. One bed, one pot and one oven, and
one cow. Absolom Gleaves, admr. Oct Term 1817.

Page 207   Inventory of estate of Alexander Cowan, deceased.
Nov 14, 1817   Roger B. Sappington has been appointed admr of Alexander
Cowan, deceased, makes report that he knows of no goods and chattels at the time of his
death. He found one judgement against the heirs of John Rice, deceased. Oct 30, 1817.
Signed by Roger B. Sappington, admr. Oct Term 1817.

Page 207   Inventory of estate of Catherine Singletary, deceased.
Nov 14, 1817   Sept 10, 1817. Several items listed. Signed by Robert Williams,
admr. Oct Term 1817.

Page 208   Sarah and Lucy Clay, guardian.
Nov 14, 1817   Johnathan Clay reports on 5 May 1816 he received of David
McGavock $475.00 in lieu of a negro man Stephen given by William Parham to said Sarah and
Lucy which negro was killed by said McGavock and the above sum awarded by Samuel
Weakley and William Maxey persons chosen by said McGavock and said Clay. 22 Oct 1817.
Test: N. Ewing and Johnathan Clay, guardian. Oct Term 1817.

Page 208   Inventory of estate of Larkin Clay, deceased.
Nov 14, 1817   Several items listed including a note on Henry Seat, M.P. Walker,
Sam. Allen, and one due bill on M. Norvill, and a note on M. Pearce. Johnathan Clay by ?.
Williams. Oct Term 1817.

Page 209   Division of negro estate of Isaac Bayse, deceased.
Nov 14, 1817   To Frances Bayse, widow drew Fillie. To Lewis Bayse drew Suna.
To Lucinda Kimbro formerly Bayse drew Stephen. To James T. Bayse drew Cintha and
Delilah. To Sally Hill formerly Bayse drew Dilliard. To Frances Bayse daughter of the
deceased drew Daniel. To Nancy Bayse drew Harry. To Isaac Bayse drew Charles. This 13
Aug 1817. Signed by William Donelson and William Neely. Oct Term 1817.

Page 209   Negroes divided of estate of James Turner, deceased.
Nov 14, 1817   The said negroes are now in the possession of Martha Turner,
executrix, and to set off to Joseph Turner one of the heirs of said deceased one sixth part
thereof, being 21 in number. The whole value $9450.00. Signed by D. McGavock, Charles
Hayes and Willis L. Shumate. Oct Term 1817.

Page 210   Inventory of estate of James Porter, deceased.
Nov 16, 1817   Several items listed. Notes and accounts, viz, John C. Dunn,
James Lewis, Ephraim H. Foster, Roger B. Sappington, J. & W. Eubanks, Stephen Neal, Henry
Cromer, William McDonald, William Rutherford, William Dennison, Benjamin Turbiville,
Samuel Taylor, Thomas B. Hall, H. Petty, Charles Good, Allen & Billingsley, Campbell's note,
W.W. Cookes, Sheldon Thompson, Joshua Conger, Thomas Johnston, E.S. Baily, H. Johnston,
Edmond Harrison, Armstrong & Saunders, John McCutchen, K.T. Wilkinson, Christianna Irby,
Thomas Johnston, E.H. Foster for J. Patrick, William W. Cooke, Samuel Elam, William L.

34

Yarborough, Andrew Hayes, Robert Rentfro, William Burras, James Harris, and Jabus White for A. Patterson. Sundry accounts transferred from Hynes & Fletcher's books, viz, Thomas G. Bradford, Nimrod Fielder, Joseph D. Smith, D. Moore & Co., E. Bradley, Thomas B. Tunstall, Joel Lewis, James Priestley, Abner Hynes, James Radcliff, negro Ceasar, and Mrs. Clemins. Sundry accounts in James Porter's books, viz, Nathan Adams, Edmond Cooper, Robert McFarland, Wilkins Tannehill, Richard Garrett, negro Rose, Anthony Foster, McKeenan & Stout, E.A. Foster, William Woolfork, Willie Blount, and Stephen Cantrell. Due in A.P. & F. books, viz, Ephraim Hubbard, James Priestley, Catherine Rankin, Paul French, John Scoby, John Allen, James C. Clem, George Martin a cooper, Mrs. Hall, Hannah McCutchen, William Allen & Co., and John Wisehart for land in Kentucky. Notes belonging to James Porter, deceased, and Andrew Haynes jointly, viz, Robert Buckner, Jacob Enlow, Anthony Ragsdale, Charles Ramsey, Amos Williams, Jacob Pennebaker, Jabez White for A. Patterson, Christianna Irby, William Boyd, Terrence Shaw, Robert Rentfro, and Roger Gibson. Invoices of goods purchased by James Porter, deceased, in the spring of 1817, viz, Charles Faulks, Taylor & Howland, Samuel Carswell, Kirkman & Jackson, L. & S. Brown, John Gill, Jr., Large & Waln, William Schlatter, John Dubarry, Chapman Trinage & Co., C. Comegeys & Co., John Huffnagle, Adam Everly, Conrad & Kelly, Benjamin Warner, Henry Kirt & Sons, Philip L(illegible), James Cresson, McDonald & Ridgsley, Richard Ashurst, Mann & Couples, Craig Hutson & Co., Hockagey & Stout, Toland & Rockhill, Samuel Kilbourn, Bar Keys & Welch, Alexander Henry, L. Englebert, C.T. Hallowell, C.P. Tile, Hugh Ellis, James Kerr, Thomas Shevel, Joseph Gilbert, James Firtle & Co., Wright & Cook, Hoboury & Thompson, J.T. Elliston, McFarland & Scudder, J.P. Runier, Ann Hancock, J. & T. Woods, Fasset & White, Charles Cany, L. & H.C. Garentson, Brad(illegible) & Tiesure, J. Breban, Philip Piper, Bell & Son, Norvill & Jennings, Charles Jones, Rogers & Kinsman, James Potter, Ann Couton, Caoorley & Boyce, J. McAllister, Morland & Gray, J. Carlisle, H.R. Watson, J. Huffman, I(illegible) Bell, McGuire & Son, J. (illegible), Frederick Hammer, Nightingale & Ruth, L. Scudder, G. Gilmore, Conrad & Kelly, Bakewell Page & Bakewell, George Millinberger, John Little, Peebles & Tweedy & Co., Nathaniel Holmer, Robert Haslet, Isaac Wickersham, J. Roberts, Henry Showatter, McClurghs & McNight, James Brown, William Robinson, Jr., William Montgomery, Sutton & McNickle, and McDonald & Ridgeley. Amount of carriages to Pittsburgh also freight from Pittsburgh to Nashville. Signed by Joseph Porter, admr. Oct Term 1817. (a very long instrument)

Page 213   Will of Henry Burnett, deceased, of Davidson County.
Nov 18, 1817   To my son William Burnett 50 acres of land including his house and farm whereon he now lives. All my property both real and personal be kept together for the benefit of raising my family until my youngest son Richard Burnett arrives to 12(21) years of age unless my executors find it necessary to sell part of my perishable estate together with 200 acres of land lying in said county and joining the late James Hamilton then after my youngest son R.B. arrives at the age of 12 years. The residue of the tract of land whereon I live be equally divided between my three sons, Henry Burnett, Joseph Burnett and Richard Burnett. To each of my daughters, that is, Nancy McCombs, Elizabeth Burnett, Polly Burnett, Sarah Burnett, and Milly Burnett provided they continue on my family and aid and assist or raising my children be allowed $200.00 after my youngest son R. Burnett arrives to 12 years of age or in proportion for the time they stay in my family. It is my will that my children from Henry Burnett down be educated. All the residue of my estate be sold and divided among my children. I appoint Joseph Burnett and Elizabeth Burnett be executors. This 7 May 1817. Wit: Cary Felts, William Burnett and William Freeman. Oct Term 1817.

Page 214   Will of John Goodrich, deceased, of Davidson County.
Nov 19, 1817   To my daughter Mary Maria Courtney Goodrich when she arrives to the age of eighteen years or marries, four negroes. In the event of my wife having another daughter by me, I give to her three negroes. I lend unto my wife during her natural life the land and plantation whereon I now live also 8 or 9 negroes. All my sons may be educated to the bar as lawyers out of the profits of my estate lent to my wife either hiring out a part of the negroes. I lend to my wife horses &c and other items. I appoint my said wife Rhoda Goodrich and Edmund Goodrich, executrix and executor. This 11 Feb 1816. Wit: Willie Barrow and Edmond Lanier. Oct Term 1817.

Page 216   Thomas Napier, of James Robertson, covenant.
Nov 26, 1817   I, James Robertson of Davidson County am bound unto Thomas Napier of Davidson County for $300.00. This 1 Oct 1804. The condition is such that James

Napier a deed to a certain lot in the town of Nashville No. 149 being the lot which said Robertson purchased of the Trustees of Nashville. Test: William Black and Thomas Dillon. June Term 1817.

Page 216   John Drake, of George M. Deaderick, Covenant.
Nov 26, 1817   I, George M. Deaderick of Davidson County, am bound unto John Drake of same place for $5000.00. This July 17, 1800. Condition of the obligation is such that George M. Deaderick shall make a deed to that part of the tract of land which was laid out by order of the public including Heaton's Lick on the waters of Whites Creek which is not included within the lines of Amos Heaton's preemption originally granted to David Allison. Wit: R. Weakley and Isaac Roberts. Oct Term 1817.

Page 217   Milley Preston and Thomas, their freedom.
Dec 6, 1817   I, Charles L. Bird now of Natchez in the Mississippi Territory and for $1000.00 paid to me, do emancipate and forever discharge all my title or claim to the services of a certain mulatto woman named Milley and also to her two children, Preston and Thomas. This 10 Feb 1803. Wit: Will Turner and William Shipp. Registered in Adams County, Mississippi 16 June 1803.

Page 218   Kinchen Bouser, his freedom.
Jan 17, 1818   This 1 Jan 1818 appeared before me, Stephen Cantrell, Jr., one of the Justices of the Peace for Davidson County, make oath that a certain negro man named Kinchen Bouser, aged about 22 years old has, has lived with him several years, and that said boy was born free in the State of Virginia and that he has his freedom papers in his possession. Wit: Wythe Lyons.

Page 218   Will of Henry Jackson, deceased, of Nashville.
Feb 16, 1818   I bequeath all my estate after my debts are paid to my brother William Jackson now supposed to be living in the town of Ballybay, County of Monaghan, in one of the United Kingdoms of Great Britain called Ireland. I appoint James Jackson of Nashville my executor. This 8 Nov 1817. Wit: James Jackson, Jr., Alexander Jackson and Sarah Hannah. Jan Term 1818.

Page 218   Will of Philip Earhart, deceased, of Davidson County.
Feb 16, 1818   This 2 Feb 1815. To my beloved wife Catherine Earhart my land, stock and house, furniture &c during her natural life or widowhood and smith tools and still to be here also. To my beloved son John Earhart all the property and every part thereof that is above named to his mother at her death or marriage. My daughter Mary and my son Moses, and my daughter Naomi, and my son Abraham, and my son Jacob, and my daughter Nancy who has received their part already. Wit: Anderson Tait and JOhn Williamson. Jan Term 1818.

Page 219   Will of Williamson Harper, deceased, of Davidson County.
Feb 16, 1818   This 9 Oct 1817. To my beloved wife Sarah four negroes also all the perishable property with the household and kitchen furniture during her natural life or widowhood after my just debts are paid. To my son William Harper 50 acres of land on leatherwood Creek. The other property to my two daughters Sally and Winna equally divided between them. To my daughter Susannah Moleloy (Molloy) a negro boy named Bob now in her possession. To Daniel Joslin and Nancy Joslin his wife $1.00. To Sterling Williamson Mobly $40.00 to be raised out of the perishable property. I appoint my friend George Lile and Sarah Harper my executors. Wit: Jesse Newlin, John McIllwain and Thomas Scott. Jan Term 1818.

Page 220   Will of Francis May, deceased, of Nashville.
Feb 17, 1818.   To my beloved wife Mary M. May all my estate both real and personal during her widowhood and she is to divide it among my children as they marry or arrives to the age of 21 years. My said wife may dispose of any of the property as she sees fit. I appoint my beloved wife Mary M. May, executrix and my friends Hugh L. White and John Williams of Knox County, and John P. Erwin and Robert Searcy of Nashville, executors. This 11 Nov 1817. Wit: Felix Robertson and William Lytle. Jan Term 1818.

Page 220   Settlement of estate of Isaac Bayse, deceased, of Davidson
Feb 17, 1818   County, with Samuel L. Wharton, admr. A mortgage bond of

$150.00 No. 1, also a receipt for different bonds signed James Fishback No. 2, also a bond on Edmund James for $5.58 No. 3, also a receipt for money, no name, No. 4, also a bond on William Duling and Martin Corbin for one pound twelve shillings and seven pence half penny No. 5, and also an account for 18 shillings and six pence No. 6. Jan 30, 1818. William Hall and Alexander Walker. Jan Term 1818.

Page 221   Settlement of estate of Robert Stringfellow, deceased, of
Feb 17, 1818   Davidson County, made with James Carter, admr.   Several
vouchers listed.   Balance in hands of admr $906.90.   This Jan 30, 1818.   Test: James
Mulherrin and William Hall.   Jan Term 1818.

Page 221   Settlement of estate of John Evans, deceased.
Feb 17, 1818   Made by Sherwood Bryant, admr.   Paid to persons, to wit, Charles
M. Hall, David Castleman, Alexander Stuart, Frederick Pinkley, T.G. Bradford, William
Newcom, John Blair, Clerk, Henry Blackwell, Philip Pierce, Frank Scott, Andrew Hays, John
Hoggatt, Jacob Waggoner, and William Hall.   Credit by account of sale in the army $59.00.
Credit by account by services done in the army $93.25.   Test: James Mulherrin and William
Hall.   Jan Term 1818.

Page 222   Settlement of estate of Isaac Edwards, deceased.
Feb 17, 1818   Nov 28, 1817, made with Godfrey Shelton, admr.   Several
vouchers listed.   Balance in hands of admr $82.38 3/4.   This 28 Nov 1817.   J. Ezell and Cary
Felts, Commissioners.   Jan Term 1818.

Page 222   Settlement of estate of David W. Edmonds, deceased.
Feb 17, 1818   William Anderson and Eldridge Newsom to settle with George
Lile, admr.   This Jan 5, 1818.   Several vouchers listed.   Jan Term 1818.

Page 223   James Drake, a minor orphan, guardian return.
Feb 18, 1818   Made with James Vaulx, admr. $229.15.   Margaret Drake, minor
orphan guardian return, with James Vaulx, admr $229.15.   Martha Drake, minor orphan
guardian return with James Vaulx, admr $229.15.

Page 223   Inventory of estate of Joseph Dickson, deceased, of Nashville.
Feb 18, 1818   July 18, 1816.   One mare, bridle and saddle, one pair of saddle
bags, one pair of shoe boots, one big coat, one close bodied coat, one hat, five vests, nine
neck cloths, two pair of flannel drawers, and two pair of pantaloons.   Enoch Dickson, admr.
Jan Term 1818.

Page 223   Inventory of sale of estate of Joseph Dickson, deceased.
Feb 18, 1818   Persons making purchases, to wit, Enoch Dickson, James Dickson,
and William Malone.   Amount $87.50.   Enoch Dickson, admr.   Jan Term 1818.

Page 224   James and Polly Dean, minor orphans guardian return.
Feb 18, 1818   James and Polly Dean, heirs of James Dean, deceased, with
Michael Gleaves, guardian.   Persons paid, viz, Nathan Ewing, Hood & Walker, John Baird,
Thomas Ramsey, John Folwell a tailor, Exum P. Sumner for shoe making, Henry Douglas for
ferriage, and Thomas Gleaves for his wife Polly.   Balance due James and Polly Dean, minors,
$1575.10½.   Jan Term 1818.

Page 224   Division of the personal estate of James Dean, deceased.
Feb 18, 1818   Four small slaves valued at $2400.00 and Lot No. 1 which
includes two negroes valued $120.00 was drawn by James Dean the minor son of the deceased.
And Lot No. 2 which includes Alexander and Jim valued $1200.00 was drawn by Thomas
Gleaves and Polly his wife who is the daughter of the deceased.   Dec 13, 1817.   Test: James
Read, Alexander Ewing and Duke W. Sumner.   Jan Term 1818.

Page 224   Inventory of estate of Henry Burnett, deceased.
Feb 18, 1818   Several negroes and other items listed.   Signed by Elizabeth
Burnett, exrx.   Jan Term 1818.

Page 225   Inventory of estate of Sterling Northington, deceased.
Feb 18, 1818   Made with Thomas Hill, admr. An equal interest in articles
which were purchased at New Orleans in the spring of 1817 for account and risk of
Northington and Hill. Several items listed including the barge "Priscilla Covington", also
interest on money on goods brought on board said barge to the following persons, viz, James
Charlton, G. Thurman, and E. Edwards. Northington & Hill for services of two negroes, Jack
and Darr from New Orleans to Nashville on said barge. Jan Term 1818.

Page 225   Sale of estate of Sterling Northington, deceased.
Feb 18, 1818   Account of sales of the cargo of the barge "Priscille Covington"
sold by Thomas Hill. Sold Nov 25, 1817. Long list of items. Jan Term 1818.

Page 228   Will of Littleberry Williams, deceased, of Davidson County.
Feb 19, 1818   Wife Margaret Williams shall have the use of the whole of my
property of every description until my daughter Catherine Williams comes of age or marries,
unless my wife should marry then said property is to be divided between my wife Margaret
and my daughter Catherine Williams. My said wife should dispose of the whole or part of my
property, land and negroes excepted, as she thinks to raise money to pay my debts and for
use for her and daughter. I appoint my wife Margaret Williams and her brother James Vaulx
my executors. This 5 June 1816. Wit: William Murphy, Jeremiah Ezell and William Vaulx.
Jan term 1818.

Page 229   Inventory of estate of Littleberry Williams, deceased.
Feb 20, 1818   Made on Jan 15, 1818. Nine negroes and several other items
listed. James Vaulx, executor. Jan Term 1818.

Page 229   Inventory of sale of estate of Littleberry Williams, deceased.
Feb 20, 1818   Sold on 15 & 16 Jan 1818. Purchasers, to wit, James Pearson,
James Howell, James Vaulx, Andrew J. Edmondson, Benjamin Bibb, Samuel Scott, James
Carter, George Goodwin, James Baker, Alexander Martin, Charles Hays, Samuel Ridley,
Joseph B. Turner, John Knight, Wilson Lerrat, Arthur A. Redmond, Edmund Chism, Robert
Goodlett, Samuel W. Hope, Thomas Haywood, Nicholas Tomlin, Thomas Shackleford, Jenkin
Whiteside, Walter Kibble, Henry Wade, William L. Wilson, Peter Wright, Richard B. Owens,
Lemuel Kennedy, William A. McLaughlin, Sampson Wright, William Hollingsworth, William
Hays, Zachariah Noell, Brazier Lewis, Ebenezer Titus, Thomas Walter, William Vaulx,
Washington Pullion, Jeremiah Burge, William Ramsey, John Blackman, Andrew Clark, Peter
Owen, Hezekiah Cook, Harrison Fussell, Joseph Buchanan, Mary Peebles, J.W. Ramsey, Robert
Reaves, William Matlock, Edmond Owen, Thomas Buchanan, Edward A. East, George C.
Boothe, Moses Christenberry, John Skelly, and William Hollingsworth. Jan 30, 1818. James
Vaulx, executor. Jan Term 1818. (a very long inventory)

Page 232   Settlement of estate of John Pugh, deceased.
Feb 20, 1818   Made with Solomon Clark, admr. Said Clark is indebted to the
estate $1597.09¼, $174.00 interest arising from the sum of $850.00 which the negroes sold for.
This 29 Jan 1818. R. Hewitt, J.P. and D.A. Dunham and J. Harding. Jan Term 1818.

Page 232   Inventory of estate of Elizabeth Roland, deceased.
Feb 21, 1818   Made by William Roland, admr. Several items listed. Jan Term
1818.

Page 232   Additional inventory of estate of Henry Hyde, deceased.
Feb 21, 1818   A land warrant of two hundred acres sold John C. McLemore,
cash in hand paid $40.00 and his note five months after date for $60.00. Given 3 Nov 1817.
Richard Hyde, admr. 30 Jan 1818. Jan Term 1818.

Page 232   Inventory of estate of William McChesney, deceased.
Feb 21, 1818   Made by Samuel McChesney, admr. Returned into court $180.00
in the hands of E. Hewitt for which suit is brought in court. 31 Jan 1818. Jan Term 1818.

Page 232   William P. Campbell, a minor's guardian return.
Feb 21, 1818   Nov 22, 1817 then received as guardian for William P. Campbell
$1500.00 in cash. Cr. by expense for clothing $30.19. To cash paid $4.00. Expense total

$34.29. William P. Seat, guardian. Jan Term 1818.

Page 233   Inventory of estate of Larkin Clay, deceased.
Feb 21, 1818   Sept 4, 1817, property sold.   The plantation rented and three negroes hired to Thomas Patterson, one to John Thomas and a woman to Greenwood Payne. Instected at A. Page warehouse two hogshead of tobacco, weight net 2198. Johnathan Clay, executor. Jan Term 1818.

Page 233   Division of negro estate of William Hobson, deceased.
Feb 21, 1818   Negroes to be divided between the heirs of said estate on 1 Jan 1817. Nathaniel A. McNairy had in his possession at the death of said Hobson, Dave worth $250.00 and Aggy worth $250.00. Negroes allotted to N.A. McNairy, Bob worth $300.00 and Beck worth $200.00. Negroes in possession of William Lytle, Jr. at the death of said Hobson, Silla worth $300.00 and Aleck worth $250.00. Negro allotted to said Lytle, Miney worth $800.00. Negroes in possession of George Hewlett at death of said Hobson, Violet worth $300.00 and Peter worth $200.00. Negro allotted to said Hewlett, Billy worth $550.00. Negroes in possession of John Hobson at death of said Hobson, Charley worth $400.00, Hal worth $300.00, this amount out of the price of Delpha sold under the will of the deceased and directed thereby to be applied to the redemption of Charles that was pledged by John Hobson with James Jackson for $400.00. Negroes allotted to Nicholas Hobson, Richard worth $450.00 and Suckey worth $450.00. Negroes willed to Mary Hobson, Denny worth $475.00 and Abby worth $450.00. Negroes willed to Elizabeth Hobson, Lewis worth $275.00 and Maria worth $275.00, also negroes allotted to Elizabeth Hobson, Jurdiana worth $150.00 and Polina worth $125.00 and Critty worth $100.00. Negroes willed to Susan Hobson which she already has in her possession, Emily worth $250.00 and Davey worth $250.00, also negroes allotted to her, Fanny worth $225.00 and Matilda worth $125.00 and Jim worth $150.00. Negroes willed to William Hobson which he has in his possession, Bob worth $400.00 and Martha worth $200.00, also negro allotted to him, Sampson worth $375.00. Pheby in possession of Marshal B. Mumford which is unsound. Making $1050.00 each. Signed by James Jackson and R. Weakley, executors. Jan Term 1818.

Page 233   Inventory of estate of James Hodge, deceased.
Feb 23, 1818   Several items listed including negroes and a note on Robert Hodge, a bond or note on Roger B. Sappington and Thomas Hickman and Thomas Dillahunty security, a judgement on Joseph Dawson. Signed by Nancy Hodge and Samuel D. Bells, admrx and admr. Jan Term 1818.

Page 235   Will of Thomas Faulks, deceased, of Davidson County.
Feb 23, 1818   To my beloved wife Mary Faulkes my negro man James during her natural life or widowhood also 10 negroes, also the tract of land whereon I now live together with all the household and kitchen furniture, stocks &c.   To my grandson John Joseph Anthony Faulks my negro fellow named Dick, Charlotte and Mary Ann and Littleton. To my daughter Lucy Trotter negroes, Mary, Washington, Williby, Abram, and Isabel now in her possession and a negro fellow now in my possession named Gilbert. To my grandson John M. Hamblin negroes, Juda, Edmund, Austin, Hubbard, and Harriet. To my grandson William Henry Hamblin negroes, Lewis, young Anthony, Julia, Milley, Edwin and Nathan also a bed and furniture and other items including my watch. At the death of my wife or marriage all the property I have lent to her I give unto my two sons William Parham Faulks and Thomas Henry Faulks, the land and plantation whereon I live together with all my household and kitchen furniture &c. To my grandson William Henry Hamblin negroes, Big Anthony, Nanny, Nancy, Anderson, Cato, Booker, Betsey, Vina, Isaac and Mariah. I appoint my wife Mary Faulks, William Hope and William H. Hamblin, executors. This 5 Dec 1815. Wit: Samuel L. Wharton, Lucinda Wharton, Rebecca Frazier, D. Frazier, and Ebenezer Frazier. Jan Term 1818. (a very long will)

Page 237   Inventory of estate of Ira Stout, deceased.
Feb 24, 1818   One note on Thomas Hodges and Joseph M. Millen, H. Ragsdale, Brice M. Garner, and J.V.D. Stout. One receipt on W. Henderson, account on McKernan & Stout, also other items. Samuel V.S. Stout, admr. Jan Term 1818.

Page 237   Inventory of sale of estate of Frederick Thompson, deceased.
Feb 24, 1818   Made by James Gray, executor. Sold unto Edward Ward about

300 acres of land in North Carolina, Onslow County. Sold to William Waldron 90 acres of land. To Cyrene Gray one Testament and other items. Jan Term 1818.

Page 237   Inventory of estate of David McCullock, deceased.
Feb 24, 1818   Several items listed. James Bradford, admr. Jan Term 1818.

Page 238   Martha Lanier, a minor, orphans guardian return.
Feb 24, 1818   Jan 27, 1818.   John Criddle guardian for Martha Lanier.   One negro woman and three children, and other items. Nathan Ewing. Jan Term 1818.

Page 238   Joseph Vaulx, a minor, guardians return.
Feb 24, 1818   Made with James Vaulx, guardian. Cash paid Littleberry Williams and Margaret Williams for their interest of the tract of land whereon Mrs. C. Vaulx now lives for you. By your part of the rent of the Mill Creek plantation for 1816 and also by your part of the rent for the home plantation for 1817. Total $955.06¼. Jan 30, 1818. Jan Term 1818.

Page 238   Elizabeth, Polly and Martha Jackson's guardian return.
Feb 24, 1818   I, Obediah Jackson, guardian of the minor orphans of Jesse Jackson, deceased. The money belonging to the estate is loaned out on interest. Also other items. Jan 19, 1818. Jan Term 1818.

Page 239   Frances Basye, widow dower laid off.
Feb 24, 1818   Land laid off below the south west corner on Dry Creek, containing 42 2/3 acres. This 22 Sept 1817. Signed by William Donelson, D. Frazier, Thomas Faulks, John Frazier, Samuel L. Wharton, Thomas Cartwright, Jacob Cartwright, William Hope, Reuben Payne, Greenwood Payne, Spencer Payne, and Peter Bashaw. Jan Term 1818.

Page 239   Nancy Hodge, widow of James Hodge, deceased, support.
Feb 25, 1818   Her support laid off. Several items listed. This 23 Jan 1818. Signed by Giles Harding, Johnston Vaughn and Joseph Coldwell. Jan Term 1818.

Page 239   Inventory of estate of Josiah Hurt, deceased.
Feb 25, 1818   Jan 15, 1818. Several items listed. This 19 Jan 1818. Elizabeth Hurt, admrx.

Page 240   John H. Sumner, a minor, orphan's guardian return.
Feb 25, 1818   John Hudson Sumner, orphan of Jos. Jno. Sumner, deceased, account with Duke W. Sumner, guardian. Several items listed. $6195.65½. Jan 24, 1818. Jan Term 1818.

Page 240   Inventory of estate of William H. Utley, deceased.
Feb 25, 1818   Estate now in the hands of the admr Jan 29, 1818. Several items listed. Persons listed, to wit, Matthew P. Walker, Isaac Hudson, William Hope, Larkin Clay, Peter Bashaw, George Wharton, Thomas Faulks, Philip Walker, Isham A. Parker, Joseph Pierce, Elizabeth Cartwright, Ebenezer Micance, Thomas Craighead, Mrs. Basey, Simon Williams, Mrs. Stratten, William White, Samuel Allen, Henry Wray, Josiah Porter, and William Williams. Signed by Isaac Hudson, admr. Jan Term 1818.

Page 241   Inventory of sale of estate of Catherine Singletary, deceased.
Feb 26, 1818   Purchasers, viz, John E. Bradshaw, Elizabeth Smith, William Hardy, Robert Williams, Solomon Holder, Stephen Barefoot, Daniel A. Dunham, Henry Wade, William Thomas, and Robert McGaugh. Signed by Robert Williams, admr. Jan Term 1818.

Page 242   Arthur Bland, a minor, orphan's guardian return.
Feb 26, 1818   The hire of negroes for the year 1818, total $267.25.   Other items listed.   Paid $4.00 to William Sharp for tuition. Signed by Cary Felts, guardian. Jan Term 1818.

Page 242   John Pugh, deceased, estate to Betsey Pugh. Nov 9, 1816.
Feb 26, 1818   To boarding and washing for John Pugh, Jr., aged 15 years from Nov 9, 1815. To boarding and washing for Polly Pugh, aged 17 years from Nov 9, 1815. To boarding and washing for Sally Pugh, aged 16 years from Nov 9, 1815.   To boarding and

To boarding and washing for Hannah Pugh, aged 12 years from Nov 9, 1815. To boarding and washing for Samuel Pugh, aged 9 years from Nov 9, 1815. To boarding and washing for Hampton Pugh, aged 6 years from Nov 9, 1815. To boarding and washing for Isaac Green Pugh, aged 4 years from Nov 9, 1815. Signed by Solomon Clark, admr. Test: Isaac Watkins and Betsey Pugh, widow. Jan Term 1818.

Page 244   John and John S. Singletary, deceased, land divided.
Feb 27, 1818   No. 1 to Mahala Singletary for 12 acres and 115 poles.
No. 2 to William Hardy for 12 acres and 115 poles.
No. 3 to Elizabeth Smith for 12 acres and 115 poles.
No. 4 to Ruth Owen for 13 acres.
No. 5 to Sterling Kendrick for 12 acres and 126 poles.
No. 6 to Elsey Williams for 12 acres.
No. 7 to John S. Singletary for 12 acres and 79 poles.
The said lands being the contents of a Deed of Gift from James Thompson to his grandson the said John Singletary containing about 50 acres and dated the 15th Aug 1791 also the west end of Deed of Conveyance from Robert Thompson to John Singletary father of the said John Singletary and which he claimed as heir said last mentioned deed containing 130 acres and bears date 14 Apr 1792. This 20 Jan 1818. Jno. Davis, surveyor. Test: Martin Greer, D.A. Dunham, John Johns, and Jas. Donnelly, Commissioners. Jan Term 1818.

Page 246   Molly Goff, her freedom papers. Powhatan County.
Apr 22, 1818   I, James Poindexter, Clerk of County Court of Powhatan, certify that Molly Goff was this day registered in my office and is of the following description, to wit, about the age of 34 years, of a yellow complexion, about five feet one and a quarter inches high, has a scar on her right arm and was emancipated by a Court of Appeals by virtue of the will of John and Johnathan Pleasant. This 21 Apr 1813. Wit: Letty Mosley and John McNunnally.

Page 246   Richard Allen, his freedom papers. City of Richmond, Virginia.
Apr 28, 1818   Registered in the office of the Court of Hastings for the city 20th Aug 1816, No. 571, Richard Allen, a mulatto man, about five feet nine inches high, twenty eight or nine years of age and was born free as appears by the oath of William H. Taylor. Test: Thomas C. Howard, Clerk.

Page 246   John A. Cowley, his freedom papers. City of Richmond, Virginia.
Apr 28, 1818   Registered in the office of the Court of Hastings for said city this 11th June 1811, No. 467. John Cowley a dark mulatto man about five feet seven inches high, seventeen years old and born free as appears by the certificate. This 20 Aug 1816. Test: Thomas C. Howard, Clerk.
I, William White, certify that John A. Cowley, a free man of color, born in Richmond, Virginia, has been in my employ for seven months last past and is now about leaving this place for Nashville on board Sterling Northington's barge as Cabin Stewart, is an honest, sober and upright man and a man of trust. New Orleans, June 24, 1817.

Page 247   Will of John Walker, deceased, of Davidson COunty.
May 19, 1818   To my son-in-law Charles Miller $150.00 in cash. To my son Matthew Patton Walker the tract of land I possess on the head of Gibsons Creek containing 320 acres, a negro girl named Lizzy and two boys Henry and Bill and the half of my stock of cattle. To my sons Alexander Walker, Abraham Walker, Joseph Walker's heirs John Walker, James Walker and Aney Enochs and Rebecca Andrews my daughters an equal division of all my other property, viz, a negro man named Stepon, a woman named Patience, girls Caroline, Jincy, Mary and Comfort, also household furniture and the balance of my stock of horses and sheep. I also give unto my daughter Rebecca Andrews a negro girl named Vina. I appoint my sons Alexander Walker, Abraham Walker and James Walker my executors. This 17 Mar 1816. Wit: James H. Cobbs and Langhorn Scruggs. Apr Term 1818.   ·

Page 248   Inventory of estate of John Walker, deceased.
May 18, 1818   Taken 18 Apr 1818. 320 acres of land on the head of Gibsons Creek, a negro girl named Lizza, one boy named Henry, one boy Bill, 17 head or the half of the stock of cattle which was devised unto Matthew Patton Walker. Also a negro girl Vine devised unto Rebeccah Andrews. Also a negro man Stepon, woman Patience, a girl Comfort,

one girl Jinney, one Maxey, one Caroline also seven head of cattle and other items devised to Alexander, Abram. Joseph's heirs John and James Walker and to Ann Enocks and Rebeccah Andrews. Also several household items and negroes devised to (same as above named). Also one negro boy child Michael, a negro child a girl and one old 80 gallon still $96.00 in cash, not devised. Apr Term 1818.

Page 248   Personal estate divided of Ennis Hooper, deceased.
May 19, 1818   Lot No. 1 which includes Milly and child Sealey and child and Minerva valued $1700.00 was drawn by Anthony Durdin and Hulda his wife a daughter of the deceased. No. 2 which includes Lucy, Tom, Sophia and Matilda valued $1800.00 was drawn by Hooper son of the deceased. This 5 Mar 1818. Signed by Alexander Ewing, William Caldwell and Jones Read, Commissioners. Apr Term 1818.

Page 249   Supplementary inventory of estate of William Hobson, deceased.
May 18, 1818   Purchasers, viz, Terrence Shaw, Ilai Metcalf, A.B. Hays, John H. Smith, Woody Holts, McDowell & Riley, J. & J.W. Little, Thomas Patterson, David Vaughn, Hugh Evans, John Nichols, Sr., Robert W. Stewart, Mr. Crow the butcher, Temple Gaines, W.B. & U.L. Lewis, Willis Barrow for two lots in Nashville, Samuel Weakley, Stephen Farmer, Doctor Priestley, Doctor John Newnan, John Hobson, and William Griffin. This May 2, 1818. Signed by James Jackson, R. Weakley and Jno. Hobson. Apr Term 1818.

Page 249   Inventory of estate of Williamson Harper, deceased.
May 19, 1818   Several negroes, and other items, also one Bible. Signed by Sally Harper and George Lile,executors. Apr Tern 1818.

Page 250   Additional inventory of estate of Ann Hays, deceased.
May 19, 1818   For July Term 1816. Part of Lot No. 6 allotted to said A. Hays, estate also other items, also a second sale of Lot No. 167. Signed by Thomas Crutcher, surviving executor. Apr Term 1818.

Page 250   Sale of estate of James Hodge, deceased.
May 19, 1818   Persons purchasing items, to wit, Nancy Hodge, Samuel D. Bell, Polly Hodge, James Hodge, A(illegible) Hodge, Henry Compton, Francis Slaughter, George Hodge, Jas. Caldwell, Robert McCutchen, William Parker, Benjamin Butler, Thomas Loftin, William Sneed, Lewis Hartgraves, John Butler, Benjamin Evans, James Moore, Joel Yarberry, Robert Goodlet, John Brooks, John Scruggs, Peter Conly, Thomas McRory, William Edmiston, and M. Jackson. Samuel D. Bells, admr. Apr Term 1818.

Page 252   Inventory of sale of estate of John Hancock, deceased.
May 20, 1818   Nov 20, 1817. Persons listed, to wit, Sarah Hancock, John New, Spencer New, and Jno. Swain bought one silver watch, and Dennis Miller. Signed by John New. Apr Term 1818.

Page 252   Settlement of estate of Oliver Johnston, deceased.
May 20, 1818   Made by David C. Snow, executor, with the heirs of O. Johnston. Several vouchers listed to people, viz, N. Ewing, William Perkins, William Neely, C. Perkins, T.L. Shannon, Doctor Hadley, Jno. Chapman, William Arthur, D.C. Snow, W. Butterfield, Winslow Johnston, William Y. Probast, A.W. Johnson, O.C. Johnson, Jno. Caulfield, Parnelle Johnson. Legatees: David C. Snow, Isaac Fisk and Calvin Statton. A.W. Johnson, guardian for Mary T. and Clarissa Johnson. David C. Snow, executor. Signed by J.T. Elliston and Stephen Cantrell of the Commissioners. Apr Term 1818.

Page 253   Additional inventory of estate of Oliver Johnston, deceased.
May 20, 1818   Nov 21, 1816. Several items listed. Signed by David C. Snow, executor. Apr Term 1818.

Page 253   Inventory of sale of estate of John Irwin, deceased.
May 21, 1818   Made by D. Irwin, admr. Purchasers, viz, Montgomery Bell, D. Irwin, Robert Jamison, and Robert C. Clow. D. Robertson, auctioneer. Apr Term 1818.

Page 253   Settlement of estate of Alexander K. Gower, deceased.
May 21, 1818   Made by Mrs. Edith Gower, admrx. Notes on William Anderson,

Elisha Gower, W.L. Gower, and John B. Demumbro. One debt on Russell Gower due 28 Oct 1816. Sales returned by N. Ewing paid by Thomas Hickman. This Apr 20, 1818. Signed by Jonathan Drake, J.P. and Thomas Hickman, Esqrs., two of the Commissioners.

Page 254   Additional inventory of estate of Jesse Cox, deceased.
May 21, 1818   One mare and two hogs. Wiseman Champ, admr.   Apr Term
1818.

Page 254   Settlement of estate of Jesse Cox, deceased.
May 21, 1818   Court appointed Eldridge Newsom and William Anderson to settle
with Wiseman Champ, admr. Paid to Ephraim A. Foster for his services. This Apr 14, 1818.
Apr Term 1818.

Page 254   Additional inventory of estate of Francis B. Sappington, deceased.
May 21, 1818   Made by Roger B. Sappington, executor. 161 acres of land on the
headwaters of Mill Creek in Davidson County as part of said deceased proportion of the firm
of A.Foster & Co. Apr Term 1818.

Page 254   Settlement of estate of Abraham Nolin, deceased.
May 21, 1818   Apr 24, 1818. Vouchers paid and taken up by the admrx, to wit,
John L. Young, John B. Goldsberry, John E. Beck, N. Ewing, Stump & Cox, Lewis Earthman,
and Joseph Chumbley. Signed by Jonathan Drake and Thomas Hickman.   Elizabeth Nolin,
admrx. Apr Term 1818.

Page 255   Settlement of estate of Sterling Northington, deceased.
May 21, 1818   Made with Thomas Hill, admr. Paid Joseph Smith, William Y.
Probart, and Nathan Ewing. William Carroll for hire of negro girl Creesy for two and one
half years. Balance due estate $2855.14. Signed by E. Talbot and S. Cantrell, two of the
Commissioners. Apr Term 1818.

Page 255   Settlement of estate of Joseph Dickson, deceased.
May 21, 1818   Made with Enoch Dickson, admr. Found $82.00 credit by three
accounts $83.00. This 21 Apr 1818. Signed by William H. Nance and Cary Felts, two of the
Commissioners. Apr Term 1818.

Page 256   Will of John B. Gwathney, deceased.
May 21, 1818   To my friend William Saunders my whole estate both real and
personal after my just debts are paid. This 1 May 1816. Signed by Peter Houson and
Woodson Jackson, Commissioners. Apr Term 1818.

Page 256   Inventory of estate of John Nichols, deceased.
May 22, 1818   Returned by John Nichols, admr., with will annexed, viz, personal
property in the possession of widow Sarah Nichols which she is entitled to hold during her
widowhood. Twenty three negroes and other items listed.
Bonds and notes on, viz, James Taylor, J. Martin, Thomas M.D. Reed, William Young and
Thomas Blair, W. Loggins, Poindexter Tullock, Archibald Lytle, Burwell Boils, Bazzella Taylor,
Bagley Butler, Joseph J(illegible), James Butler, William Price, William Maclin, James
Bedford, and Reubin Carter. This May 1, 1818. John Nichols, admr. The last twelve notes
some of which were given by prople in England. Apr Term 1818.

Page 257   Inventory of estate of Moses Eakin, deceased.
June 9, 1818   Several items listed including a large Bible. Signed by Isabella
Eakin, admrx. Apr Term 1818.

Page 257   Account of sale of estate of David McCullough, deceased.
June 9, 1818   10 Feb 1818, made by James Bradford, admr. Purchasers, to wit,
Jesse Fly, William P. Seat, William Hamilton, William Marcum, James Bradford, Thomas
Thompson, Mordicai Kelly, Adam Carper, R.S. McFaddin, Benajah Gray, Jordan Jones, Bennet
Sullivan, William Johnston, Guy McFaddin, William Orr, John M. Knight, and James Bradford.
James Bradford, admr. Apr Term 1818.

Page 258   Settlement of estate of Robert Cartwright, deceased.
June 9, 1818   Received of Gordon & Brooks of Jonathan Ramsey, Henry Jackson, Elizabeth Cartwright, Jesse Cartwright, a total of $676.50. Paid out, viz, Randol McGavock, O.B. Hayes, Nathan Ewing, Jas. Rutherford, Thomas Cartwright, Jacob Cartwright, Stephen D(illegible), &c. Total balance $221.17. This 8 Apr 1818. William Donelson and James Byrn, Esquires, Commissioners. Thomas, David and Jacob Cartwright, executors. Apr Term 1818.

Page 259   Inventory of estate of Thomas Faulkes, deceased.
June 12, 1818   1 Dec 1817. Several negroes listed. Notes and accounts on John Goodridge, William Trotter for heirs of Gilbert, William Rutherford, George R. Dismukes, Jonathan Clay, (blank) McGavock, Edmond Goodrich, William Philips, Solomon Russel, Moses Russel, and John McGavock. William H. Hamblin, executor. Apr Term 1818.

Page 259   Division of estate of Isiah Mathias, deceased.
June 12, 1818   Several items listed and divided unto the heirs being legal and no debts, to wit, Mary Mathias, Samuel Stull for Elizabeth Mathias, Rachael Stull, Stephen Mathias, and Thomas Mathias. The residue given to the widow to dispose as she may think proper. This 28 Feb 1818. Test: Isaac Clemons.
I, Thomas Mathias, on my own right &c agree to the within division of the estate of my deceased father. This 28 Feb 1818. Apr Term 1818.

Page 260   James H. Gamble, County Trustee, a settlement.
June 15, 1818   Amount received from N. Ewing and others, total $5169.20. Signed by Eli Talbot and Stephen Cantrell, Jr. This 17 Apr 1818. Apr Term 1818.

Page 261   C. & William O. Evans and G.L. Gayden, their agreement.
June 20, 1818   All of Adams County, Mississippi Territory, certify that they all agree to the division of property, viz, Charlotte Evans is to have several negroes and a sorrel and a gray horse. Gayden is to have several negroes. W.O. Evans is to have several negroes. This 10 Feb 1817. Signed by Charlotte Evans, G.L. Gayden and W.O. Evans. Test: William Evans and Nicholas Hail. Apr Term 1818.

Page 262   Samuel Ogg, freedom papers, No. 219.
Aug 6, 1818   I, Beverly Chew, Collector of the District of Mississippi, do hereby certify that Samuel Ogg, an American Seaman, aged 38 years, of 6¼ inches high, wooly hair, black complexion and black eyes, a native of the State of Delaware, has a scar in the corner of the left eye and two nails on the left foot, has this day produced to me proof directed by the act entitled "An Act for the relief and protection of American Seaman". Also that Samuel Ogg is a citizen of the United States. At New Orleans, this 21 Oct 1817. Signed by Bev. Chew, Collector.

Page 262   Eli Welch, his freedom papers.
Aug 6, 1818   Made this 9 May 1803, made between Judy Welch and Eli Welch of the County of Nelson, Kentucky of one part and James Bard of said county of other part, said that Eli Welch with approbation of Judy Welch, his mother, put and placed and bound himself and to serve with him the said James Bard to dwell and as servant with him the said James Bard to dwell till Eli Welch shall attain the age of 21 years during which time Judy Welch doth covenant and agree to and with said James Bard shall well and faithfully serve in all such lawful business as Eli Welch shall be put into by his moster. Test: James Brown, Daniel James and Abenezer Baird. 30 July 1818.

Page 263   Settlement of estate of Daniel McBean, deceased.
Aug 18, 1818   Made by Angus McPhail, admr. Nov 15, 1815. Several items listed. Cash paid Thomas G. Bradford, also Duncan Robertson, J.R. Ruble, and Thomas Yeatman, M.C. Dunn, James Irwin, Gideon Blackburn, Elizabeth Jones, William Compton, Nathan Ewing, William Smith, R. Farquharson, Alexander Hutchinson, John Bosley, Samuel Cox agent for James H. Williams, A. Balch, R. Hewlett, Henry Crabb, Norvell & McLean, John Boyd, Henry Harding, James Roans, William Bosworth, Thomas Bradford, Henry Evans, William Lynch, J. Trimble, Robert McFarland, E. Hewlett, J.E. Beck, Jno. Falwell, Nancy McBain, and William Bosley. Angus McPhail, admr. Several other items listed. 28 July 1818. July Term 1818.

Page 265   Settlement of estate of Ann Hay, deceased.
Aug 18, 1818   Paid cash to James B. Houston, Moses Eakin, Samuel Weakley, M.C. Dunn, David Moore, Andrew Hynes, John Buchanan, S.P. Willet, Henry Douglas, James Hanna, Benjamin Kidd, Henry Hunter, Nathaniel S. Anderson, Kirkman & Irwin, Thomas Yeatman, William Wilkerson, John Conger, Francis May, Martha Dunnevant, Stephen Cantrell & Co., Peter Bass, Richard Garrett, Stephen Cantrell, Jr., Thomas Moseley, Thomas G. Bradford, Christopher Stump, George Poyzer, James Condon, Archibald Scott, Alexander McDowell, Moses & Jos. Norvell, William Seat, W.T. Lewis' executors, Felix Robertson, Nathan Ewing, Thomas Crutcher, and William Tait. This 20 July 1818. July Term 1818.

Page 265   Settlement of estate of Daniel Jones, deceased.
Aug 18, 1818   Made with John Jones, Jr., admr. Several vouchers listed. This 18 July 1818. Signed by Eldridge Newsom and William H. Shelton, Commissioners. July Term 1818.

Page 266   Settlement of estate of James Brannon, deceased.
Aug 19, 1818   Made with Eldridge Newsom, Esq., admr. A note on Thomas Poarch and several vouchers listed. This 18 June 1818. William Anderson and William H. Shelton, J.P.'s. July Term 1818.

Page 266   Settlement of estate of Joseph McBride, deceased.
Aug 19, 1818   Amount of debts against Joseph McBride, deceased 308.77\frac{1}{2}$. Balance due estate to be collected $579.89. This 10 July 1818. R. Hewitt, Jos. Coldwell and Jno. Harding, Commissioners. July Term 1818.

Page 267   Settlement of estate of Stephen Roach, deceased.
Aug 19, 1818   Made with John McCain, admr and Lydia Roach, admrx. Several vouchers listed. Apr 24, 1818 balance remaining in the hands of admrs 3007.38\frac{1}{2}$. J. Ezell and Cary Felts. July Term 1818.

Page 267   Settlement of estate of Edmond Collinsworth, deceased.
Aug 19, 1818   made with Alsie Collinsworth, admrx. Several items listed. This 20 June 1818. J. Ezell and Cary Felts, Esqrs.

Page 267   Settlement of estate of Jonathan Walker, deceased.
Aug 19, 1818   Made with Lewis Dunn, admr. Several vouchers listed. This 26 June 1818. E. Newsom, J.P. and William Anderson, J.P. July Term 1818.

Page 268   Settlement of estate of David Spence, deceased, of Davidson
Aug 19, 1818   County, made with John Jones, Sr., admr. Notes on, to wit, Thomas Williams, Lodwick Williams, William Marrs, and John Jones. Several vouchers. This 26 June 1818. Eldridge Newsom, J.P. and William Anderson, J.P. July Term 1818.

Page 268   Settlement of estate of Wright Gregory, deceased.
Aug 19, 1818   Held at the house of Mr. Godfrey Shelton, with Edward Gregory, admr. They found three vouchers. This 7 Mar 1818. J. Ezell and Cary Felts. July Term 1818.

Page 268   Settlement of estate of John McCain, deceased.
Aug 21, 1818   July 20, 1818, made with John Buchanan, admr. Three vouchers. This 20 July 1818. J. Ezell and Thomas Williamson. July Term 1818.

Page 269   Settlement of estate of James Koonce, deceased, of Davidson
Aug 21, 1818   County, made with William Roach, Robert McMillon and George Koonce, executors of the Last Will and Testament of James Koonce, deceased. Persons listed, to wit, Thomas Shackleford, Robert Kennedy, Betsey Jackson, Elisha and Frederick Davis, Richard Hart, Thomas Edington, Lazarus Inman, John Harbinson, Daniel Jones, Jose Ervis, Daniel Gray, Henry Forehands, Alson Linton, William Nichson, John Taylor, Constan Sawyer, John Demoss and William Barrow. Several vouchers listed. This 20 July 1818. Eldridge Newsom and William Anderson.

Page 169   Estate of Robert Cato, deceased.
Aug 21, 1818   Hire of negroes belonging to said estate for year 1817. Rollen Cato a boy, Mary Cato a woman and two children, Mary Cato one woman and one child, and Mary Cato one girl. Mary Cato, admr. Also hire of negro woman and two children by Jos. Whitsett, and Mary Cato one woman and child also one girl. July Term 1818.

Page 270   Additional inventory of Caleb Hewitt, deceased.
Aug 21, 1818   Received of Nathan Ewing, Clerk, also of Jacob McGavock, Clerk of Circuit Court. Received by R. Hewitt, admr. July 20, 1818. July Term 1818.

Page 270   Additional inventory of estate of Stephen Roach, deceased.
Aug 21, 1818   Returned by Lydia Roach and John McCain, admrs. John Dickson and Polly his wife received of S. Roach in his lifetime in money $25.00 also one sorrel mare, one negro girl, and collected from Adam Cooper, from John Canady, Jr., also from William Blakely, and Benjah Pipkin. July Term 1818.

Page 270   Debts collected for the estate of Daniel McBean, deceased.
Aug 21, 1818   Several items listed including from E. Foster. Angus McPhail, admr. July Term 1818.

Page 270   Gray and Nancy H. Washington, minor orphans.
Aug 21, 1818   Estate now in the hands of their guardian, one note on E. Hallums, three on Leonard H. Sims, one on John B. West, and for the hire of a negro, and on James Buck. T.H. Everett. July Term 1818.

Page 271   Will of John E. Beck, deceased.
Aug 21, 1818   The executors to have entire use and control of all the profits arising from my estate after my debts are paid for the purpose of educating my children supporting my family until the legatees become entitled to it by marriage or by becoming of age. To sell of part of my Lot No. 35 sold to Moses Norvell and Eli Talbot. At the marriage of my wife it is my desire all the balance of my personal estate property to be sold and profits arising from my estate be so divided that my wife have a child's part forever. It is my desire that a division of my real estate be made at the marriage of my wife or the coming of age of either of my children so that my wife may get one third thereof forever. Two equal parts to be divided between my half brother William C. Beck if then living and the children of my sister Ann E. Barrow if then living. Whereas Miss Ann James holds a note of mine for $250.00. I appoint my wife Levinia Beck and Felix Robertson, executors. This 15 June 1818. Wit: A. Foster, R.C. Foster and Thomas Crutcher. July Term 1818.

Page 272   Will of Philip Bley, deceased.
Aug 22, 1818   To my nephew Philip Noland all my estate real and personal. I appoint my sister Elizabeth Noland sole executrix. This 25 Aug 1798. Wit: Thomas Malloy and Daniel Ross. July Term 1818.

Page 272   Joshua White and Thomas Murrey, Covenant.
Aug 22, 1818   I, Thomas Murrey of Davidson County, am bound unto Joshua White of Halifax County, North Carolina, for $500.00 to be paid to said White. This 15 Nov 1796. Condition of obligation is such that Thomas Murrey make over unto said Joshua White a lawful deed to 75 acres of land lying between Birdeville preemption and Varner's tract &c. Test: James Dean, Robert Hulm and William Shaw. July Term 1818.

Page 273   Additional inventory of sale of estate of John Pugh, deceased.
Aug 25, 1818   Sold on 12 May 1818. Purchasers, to wit, Betsey Pugh, John Johns, Jr., John Pugh, Sr., Solomon Clark, Frederic Harwell, Henry Wate, Polly Pugh, Hannah Pugh, Sally Pugh, Richard Oldham, Thomas Mitchell, William Miller, David Pugh, and John Covy and William Johns. Solomon Clark, admr. May 12, 1818. July Term 1818.

Page 274   Will of Reuben Westmoreland, deceased, of Davidson County.
Aug 24, 1818   I lend unto my beloved wife Elizabeth Westmoreland all my personal property for the support of the children until my oldest son comes of age. Then to be valued, my wife to have one third her lifetime, then to be equally divided between the children and my eldest son to have an equal part of the balance and the rest of the children

in the same way as they become of age. To my children, William G. Westmoreland, Jesse Westmoreland, Labourn Westmoreland, and Martha L. Westmoreland one tract of land containing 62½ acres in Giles County to be leased or rented until my eldest son comes of age, then to be divided equally between the children. I appoint Elizabeth Westmoreland my sold executrix. This 10 May 1818. Wit: Joseph Scales, John William Robertson, Benjamin Moore, and Elizabeth Drake. July Term 1818.

Page 275   Will of James Everitt, deceased, of Davidson County.
Aug 24, 1818   July 4, 1818. To my son Simon Everett my horse named Dearick. To my daughter Patsy one cow and calf. To my daughter Polly one bay mare, saddle, cow and calf, featherbed and furniture. To my two little boys Amariah and Charles, the rest of my property equally divided after all debts are paid, for the purpose of raising and schooling them. All my negroes to be kept together for the use of the family until the year 1821 and then to be equally divided among all my children. I appoint my son Jesse Everitt, executor. Wit: James Martin and William Gilbert. July Term 1818.

Page 276   Inventory of estate of John Philips, deceased.
Aug 24, 1818   A bond on William Jackson, an account against Robert B. Curry. One large Bible and several items listed. Returned by Elisha William S(illegible), admr. July Term 1818.

Page 276   Inventory of estate of Joshua White, deceased, of Davidson
Aug 24, 1818   County. Several items listed, including a bond against Kinchen T. Wilkinson, a judgement against Claybourn G. Gentry, one bond on Thomas Murrey, one on J.R. Ruble given to Alexander McDowell without assignment to Joshua White. Signed by Jabez White and Wilson White, admrs. July Term 1818.

Page 277   Sale of estate of Moses Eakin, deceased.
Aug 24, 1818   Purchasers, to wit, George S. Hampton, Lewis Spiece, Richard Mannard, David L. Thompson and James, John Boyd, Michael Brown, John Webber, Charles Wilson, and Isabella Eakin who bought several items. Sale on 1 July 1818. Isabella Eakin, admrx. July Term 1818.

Page 278   Sale of estate of John Walker, deceased.
Aug 24, 1818   John B. Walker, several items listed. A.B. Walker several items listed. M.P. Walker several items listed. Dickerson Williams several items listed. Other named, viz, Thomas Gleaves, William Wray, Sr., James H. Hope, Gray Anders, Jesse Fulcher, John Frazier, Moses B. Frazier, Nelson Lowry, John Butterworth, William H. Hamblin. Total amount $3901.37½. Signed by Alex. Walker, Abm. Walker and James Walker, executors. July Term 1818.

Page 279   Inventory of sale of estate of John Fielder, deceased.
Aug 26, 1818   Persons named who bought property, to wit, Daniel Hamer, Nimrod Fielder, Benjamin Morgan, John L. Fielder, John McBean, David Cummins, William Black, Ann Overton, Thomas Williamson, Joel Riggs, Samuel Haggard, Robert Olive, Bart Stovall, Moses Wooten, John Wood, Joseph Honeel, William Simpson, John Champ, Samuel Bell, William Erwin, James Dickson, Samuel G. Bell, Ann Leah, John Turner, and James Sneed. July 21, 1818. Returned by John L. Fielder, executor. July Term 1818.

Page 280   Settlement of estate of Ruth Phipps, deceased, of Davidson
Dec 24, 1818   County. Made with Zachariah Noell, admr. Amount in the hands of the admr $18.88. Came into the hands of admr from State of Virginia $107.25. Total $126.13. Paid to Mary Atkinson a legatee $18.88, vouchers &c. Remains in the hands of admr $100.40. This Oct 19, 1818. James Mulherrin and William Hall, Commissioners. Oct Term 1818.

Page 280   Inventory of estate of Robert Edmondson, deceased.
Dec 24, 1818 $187.00 received from different persons. This 23 Oct 1818. Peter Wright, admr. Oct Term 1818.

Page 281   Settlement of estate of Thomas Wilcox, deceased, of Davidson
Dec 24, 1818   County, made with Zachariah Noell, executor. $203.66 in hands

of the executor. James Mulherrin and William Hall, Commissioners. This Oct 19, 1818. Oct Term 1818.

Page 281   Inventory of sale of estate of Thomas Faulkes, deceased, of
Dec 24, 1818   Davidson County.   10 Oct 1818.   Sale of negroes.   Persons
purchasing negroes, viz, W.H. Hamblin and Mary Faulkes. Signed by William H. Hamblin, one of the executors. This 19 Oct 1818. Oct Term 1818.

Page 281   Inventory of estate of Gregory T. Meany, deceased.
Dec 24, 1818   22 Oct 1818.   Several items listed.   John Bosley, admr.   Oct
Term 1818.

Page 282   Settlement of estate of Thomas S. Brown, deceased.
Dec 24, 1818   Made with Moses Brown, admr. In the hands of the admr $21.00
also collected for the services as a soldier in the United States service $62.05, also vouchers.
Oct 17, 1818. William Hall and James Mulherrin, Commissioners. Oct Term 1818.

Page 282   Settlement of estate of Stephen Roach, deceased, of Davidson
Dec 24, 1818   County, made with John McCain, admr and Lydia Roach, admrx.
Amounting remaining the hands of the admrx $3329.98½. This 11 Sept 1818. J. Ezell and Cary Felts, Commissioners. Oct Term 1818.

Page 282   Inventory of estate of James Everitt, deceased, of Davidson
Dec 24, 1818   County, on Oct 17, 1818. Several items listed. Jesse J. Everitt,
executor. Oct Term 1818.

Page 283   Inventory of estate of George Poyzer, deceased, late of Nashville.
Dec 25, 1818   Has exclusive right to a patent machine for washing, patent right
making sod oil, patent machine for shelling corn, also several other items listed. Benjamin Poyzer, admr. Oct Term 1818.

Page 283   Will of Thomas Smith, deceased, of Davidson County.
Dec 28, 1818   To my wife Sarah Smith during her life all my lands &c including
negroes and at the death of my wife, to be equally divided between my children. I appoint my wife Sarah Smith and my son William Smith, executors. This 12 Sept 1815. Wit: James Whitsett, Edwin Smith, John F. Smith and George F. Critz. Oct Term 1818.

Page 284   Inventory of estate of Nathan Peebles, deceased.
Dec 25, 1818   Several items listed. This 30 Oct 1818. William Vaulx, admr.
Oct Term 1818.

Page 284   Will of Benjamin Pack, deceased, of Davidson County.
Dec 26, 1818   To my beloved wife Mary Pack during her natural life all my
household and kitchen furniture that I now possess also other items. To my grand daughter Emmily Jervis Lovell one bed and furniture. To my wife one note on my son Benjamin D. Pack for $40.00 due 25 Dec 1819, also one note for $7.00, also the note I have on John M. Lovell for $50.00 due 25 Dec 1818 or payable by 1819 and all other notes on Lovell. At the death of my wife Mary Pack, all the money and property to be equally divided between my five children and heirs &c, Nancy Rape, Susannah Lovell, Benjamin D. Pack, Melissa Levin(?), and Mary Garland. The money that comes to my daughter Mary to remain in the hands of my executors to be paid when they think proper as it is not my wish that Elisha Garland should have the disposal of the same. I appoint John M. Levell and Benjamin D. Pack my executors. This 1 Sept 1818. Wit: Wiseman Champ and Keziah Champ. Oct Term 1818.

Page 285   Settlement of estate of Enoch Oliver, deceased, of Davidson
Dec 26, 1818   County, made with Josiah Phelps, admr. Amount of sale $129.27.
An account due the estate against said Phelps $33.00. Total of charges $162.27. Vouchers and widow's part deducted left a balance $94.64. This Oct 17, 1818. Signed by B. Gray, Enoch Ensley and Cary Felts. Oct Term 1818.

Page 286   Land division of estate of William Hobson, deceased. (plat on
Dec 26, 1818   page 286) Davidson County.   John Hobson drew 203 acres,

Nicholas Hobson drew 203 acres and William Hobson drew 203 acres on both sides of the Cumberland River. John Hobson's land begins at a road leading from Nashville by the upper ferry to Haysborough and borders James Jackson's line and David McGavock. Nicholas Hobson's land begins in the center of the above road as the beginning of John Hobson's tract, borders James Jackson's line, Robert Weakley and David Shelby's line. William Hobson's land begins on the bank of the Cumberland River, David Shelby's corner and borders Nicholas Hobson and Robert Weakley. Surveyed and divided 20 Apr 1818. Signed by Samuel Weakley, Surveyor and Commissioner, D, Vaughn and R. Weakley. Oct Term 1818.

Page 288   Inventory of estate of John Anderson, deceased.
Dec 27, 1818   On Oct 23, 1818. Several items listed. Elizabeth Anderson, admrx. Oct Term 1818.

Page 189   Inventory of estate of Richard K. Adams, deceased.
Dec 27, 1818   Taken 16 Sept 1818. Eliza Adams, admrx and Robert J. Clow, admr. Several items listed. Oct Term 1818.

Page 290   Enos Walker of John Anderson, Covenant.
Dec 28, 1818   I, John Anderson of Nashville formerly purchased at Sheriff's Sale all the rights of Charles Cabiness to a certain tract of land lying in Neely's Bend of Cumberland River in Davidson County, conveyed by deed from William Neely to said Cabiness, that I have agreed with Enos Walker that if the sum of $1600.00 shall be paid to me within the present year and also is a written memo given by me to Charles Cabiness shall be given to me or cancelled. I will convey the said tract of land to the wife and children of said Neely or to some person intrust for them &c. This 22 Jan 1816. Test: M. Barrow. Oct Term 1818.

Page 291   Inventory of estate of Reuben Westmoreland, deceased.
Dec 28, 1818   Taken 15 Oct 1818. Several negroes and several other items including notes of Joel Childress, and one on John Anderson. A receipt on William Howlett, an obligation on Jos. Porter, a note on Elisha Tidle, accounts on Tilman R. Daniel, John Erwin, Mr. Brown, Jesse Wharton, John Hall, Nathaniel Curtis, and Christopher Metcalf. Tilman R. Daniel, admr. Oct Term 1818.

Page 292   Will of Susannah Ewing, deceased, relict of Andrew Ewing,   late
Jan 22, 1819   Clerk of Davidson County. I desire that all my estate and property after my death (except what may be coming to me from the estate of Thomas Malloy) shall be first valued by two honest men pointed out by my executors herein after named, bank stock to be considered as cash and after all the property to be divided among all my children, sons and daughter. My son William Ewing should own my watch. My son Nathan Ewing hold as his share 30 shares of Nashville Bank Stock and he paying to the rest of his brothers and sisters all ever his part within 12 months with interest. My son William Ewing shall transfer the said Bank Stock after my decease to my son Nathan. The estate of Thomas Malloy has been attended with great trouble and many expenses and vastly troublesome lawsuits and knowing that my late husband got his son Nathan to do all that was done on his part as one of the executors and having heard him say that if any benefit was reserved from it to him he wishes his son Nathan to have it knowing it could not be much after claims were settled, considering all this I desire that my son Nathan have all such part of said Malloy's estate. I appoint my sons William and Nathan my executors. This 4 Sept 1813. Wit: Thomas Claiborne, Henry C. Erwin and John Overton. Jan Term 1819.

Page 293   Settlement of estate of Thomas Williams, deceased.
Mar 31, 1819   The estate of Thomas Williams, deceased, debtor to Joshua P. Vaughn, admr. Several items listed. This 2 Jan 1819.

Page 294   Inventory of estate of Ephraim Drake, deceased.
Apr 1, 1819   20 Jan 1819. Amount $271.00. William J. Drake, admr.   Jan Term 1819.

Page 294   Inventory of estate of John Fielder, deceased.
Apr 1, 1819   Sold on 19 Dec 1818 by John L. Fielder, executor. Sold Negro for $551.00. Jan Term 1819.

Page 294   Inventory of estate of Thomas Williams, deceased.
Apr 1, 1819   Sale of two negroes $1449.23. 23 Jan 1819. J.P. Vaughn, admr.
Jan Term 1819.

Page 294   John Price, deceased, orphans account.
Apr 1, 1819   Jan 1, 1818. Hire of negroes of the orphans of John Price,
deceased, $127.50. William Gilbert, guardian. Jan Term 1819.

Page 294   Inventory of estate of Charles Mathews, deceased.
Apr 1, 1819   Returned by Jan 20, 1819. Several items listed. John B. West,
admr. Jan Term 1819.

Page 294   Inventory of estate of Craddock Faulks, deceased.
Apr 1, 1819   William Hill, Samuel Faulks, Enos Walker, (illegible) Lock, Charles
Biveans, and Thomas Gleaves. This Jan 18, 1819. Samuel Faulks, admr.

Page 295   Inventory of estate of Francis May, deceased.
Apr 2, 1819   Notes, viz, Washington L. Hammons, Aaron Days, John C. Hicks,
Jos. D. Smith, Simpson Cox, Thomas G. Bradford, James Estill, Brice M. Garner, Robert
Searcy, W.B. & W.Y. Higgins, Thomas Shackleford, Stump & Cox, Richard Rapier, and
Christopher Metcalf. Other notes on Dickinson, Jacob Dickinson, ?. Moyer, Thomas B. Smith.
Other persons listed, to wit, Captain William Bell, Moses Norvell, Robert Bell, William Lytle,
Joseph Park, Doctor Shelby, and J. Davis. John P. Ervin, executor. Several items listed.
Jan Term 1819.

Page 296   Inventory of estate of David Cartwright, deceased.
Apr 2, 1819   A bond on William White, and one on Enoch Cunningham it being
for the price of David Cartwright's part of his father's land, directed to be sold by his
father's Last Will and Testament for the beneficiaries. George Wharton, executor. Jan Term
1819.

Page 296   Inventory of estate of Nancy Davis, deceased.
Apr 2, 1819   Taken 16 Jan 1819. A note on Dunn & Philips, and several other
items listed. William Donelson, admr. Jan Term 1819.

Page 296   Inventory of estate of Joshua White, deceased.
Apr 2, 1819   Several items listed. Jabez White, admr. Jan Term 1819.

Page 296   Jesse Jackson's orphans guardian return.
Apr 2, 1819   Davidson County. I, Obediah Jackson guardian to Elizabeth, Polly
and Martha Jackson, minor orphans of Jesse Jackson, deceased. Return to Jan Court 1819,
60¢. Paying for Elizabeth, Polly Jackson's schooling $5.00. This 26 Jan 1819. Jan Term
1819.

Page 297   Inventory of estate of William Merryman, deceased, of Davidson
Apr 2, 1819   County. Several items listed. Judith Merryman, admrx.   Jan
Term 1819.

Page 297   Settlement of estate of John Dickinson, deceased.
Apr 2, 1819   Persons listed, to wit, Mrs. Dickinson, G.M. Campbell, W. Lytle,
F. Grundy, E.H. Foster, Williamson, McKeennan & Stout, O.B. Hays, J. Trimble, J. Whiteside,
John B. Hogg, James M. Lewis, Thomas H. Benton, Edward B. Littlefield, James Davis, James
& George Mayfield, Greenwood Payne, Absolom Payne, William Thomas, White & Chumbly,
Isaac Boyce, W.L. Wilson, C. Duval, A. Lowry, William Eastin, J. Frazier, and B. Turman.
James Trimble, executor. Jan term 1819.

Page 298   Account of estate of Henry Jackson, deceased.
Apr 3, 1819   Made with Jas. Jackson. Persons listed, to wit, Doctors McNairy
and Shelby, J.B. Houston for coffin, T.G. Bradford's note also a note on W.L. Hillegible).
Amount due estate $1550.50.

Page 298   Inventory of estate of Thomas Williams, deceased.
Apr 3, 1819   Persons listed, to wit, Elihu S. Halls, and J. & R. (illegible). J.P.
Vaughn, admr. Jan Term 1819.

Page 299   Settlement of estate of Andrew Ewing, deceased, of Davidson
Apr 3, 1819   County. Made with Anthony Ewing, executor. Cash paid to
James Condon, M.C. Dunn, Constant Perkins, Duncan Robertson, J.F. Williams, Susanna
Ewing, Patrick Darby for A. Nelson heir &c, E. Cooper, Richard Garrett. Will Williams and
R.C. Foster, Commissioners. Nathan Ewing, one of the executors. Jan Term 1819.

Page 299   Sale of estate of Nathan Peebles, deceased.
Apr 3, 1819   Sold on 22 Dec 1818. Purchasers, viz, Mary Peebles, John Davis,
James Carter, Daniel Peebles, Francis Saunders, Edward East, Watkin Brown, Caleb Goodrich,
William Vaulx, George Driskell, Charles Hays, Lewis Hollinsworth, and William H. McLaughlin.
William Vaulx, admr. Jan Term 1819.

Page 300   John Hudson Sumner, a minor, orphan's guardian return.
Apr 3, 1819   John Hudson Sumner orphan of Jos. Jno. Sumner, deceased,
account with Duke W. Sumner, guardian. Several accounts and items listed. Jan Term 1819.

Page 300   Inventory of estate of Thomas Faulks, deceased.
Apr 3, 1819   Several items listed. William H. Hamblin, executor. Jan Term
1819.

Page 301   Inventory of estate of Susannah Ewing, deceased, of Davidson
Apr 5, 1819   County. Notes on the following, to wit, Andrew Ewing and R.B.
Sappington, Andrew Casselman & Moses Speers, William Ewing, Thomas Shannon, and Nathan
Ewing. Nathan Ewing, executor. Jan Term 1819.

Page 302   Sale of estate of Richard K. Adams, deceased.
Apr 6, 1819   Sale on Jan 7, 1819. Several items listed including one silver
watch. Robert J. Clow, admr. Jan Term 1819.

Page 304   Sale of estate of John Anderson, deceased.
Apr 6, 1819   Sale on Nov 23, 1818. Several items listed. This 26 Jan 1819.
Jan Term 1819.

Page 305   Samuel Stull of Isaac Clemons, receipt.
Apr 7, 1819   Received 18 Jan 1819 of Samuel Stull late guardian of Elizabeth
Mathias who was lately intermarried with me, the sum of $200.00 in full of all demands and
the personal estate has been given up to me, and I do hereby release him from all claims
whatever touching said guardianship. Wit: Henry Ewing. Jan Term 1819.

Page 305   Arthur Bland, a minor orphan's giardian.
Apr 7, 1819   Jan 1, 1819. Arthur Bland for expenses to C. Felts. Other
names, to wit, Nathan Ewing, S. Cantrell, and W.P. Seat. Jan Term 1819.

Page 305   Joseph McBride's heirs, guardian return.
Apr 7, 1819   Several items listed. Test: Nathan Ewing. Signed by George
Hodge, guardian for the heirs. Jan Term 1819.

Page 306   William Parker. Martha Lanier and Churchwell Lanier, legatees
Apr 7, 1819   of William Lanier, deceased, or lawful guardians. To William
Parker, to boarding and clothing of said Martha and Churchwell Lanier for eight years
$400.00. Jan Term 1819.

Page 306   Nathan Peebles, deceased.
Apr 7, 1819   I, William Vaulx, have through mistake inventories of the property
of Nathan Peebles, deceased, which belongs to Mary Peebles. Several items listed. William
Vaulx, admr. Jan term 1819.

Page 306   John Simmons' orphans guardian return. 1818.
Apr 7, 1819   Several items listed.   William Arant, guardian of the orphans.
Jan Term 1819.

Page 307   Sale of estate of John Philips, deceased.
Apr 2(7 or 8) 1819   Sold by Elisha Williams, admr.   Purchasers, to wit, Isaac
Clemmons, William Jackson, Will Williams, Paul Vaughn, Josiah F. Williams, Henry Graves,
David Pully, Charles Bivens, Elisha Williams, James B. Moore, Rodney Thomas, William
Jackson, Jeremiah Sadler, Doctor Maxey, Lemuel F. Greene, Bible bought by Will Williams for
$3.12½, Family Bible by Elisha Williams $2.00, and Samuel Faulkes. Jan Term 1819.

Page 307   Sale of estate of William C. Ewell, deceased.
Apr 8, 1819   Made by Absolom Gleaves, admr, on 8 Nov 1817. Several items
listed. Jan Term 1819.

Page 308   Sale of estate of Benjamin Pack, deceased.
Apr 8, 1819   On Jan 18, 1819. Purchasers, to wit, B.D. Pack, Thomas Lofton,
John Cooper, Henry Eleson, Richard Champ, Isaac Harris, Peter Rape, Jesse Reynolds,
Mayberry Gilland, William Anderson, and William Covel. Benjamin D. Pack, executor. One
note on John Jovill also one on B.D. Pack and one on Noah Kelly. Jan Term 1819.

Page 308   Sale of estate of Gregory F. Meaney, deceased.
Apr 8, 1819   Sale on 28 Nov 1818. Purchasers, to wit, Maria H.F. Meaney,
Charles Bivens, John Bosley, George Harris, Edward D. Hobbs, William Bryant, Henry Eakin,
and John Harris. John Bosley, admr. Jan Term 1819.

Page 308   Jesse, Ely, Sally and Aaron Roach, minor orphans guardian return.
Apr 8, 1819   J.B. Gray, guardian for said orphans of Stephen Roach, deceased,
received 23 Jan 1818 of John McCain, admr of said estate of Stephen Roach, deceased,
$327.92 for Jesse Roach. For Ely Roach $321.84. For Sally Roach $321.84. For Aaron
Roach $321.84, paid to the widow Lydia Roach for boarding and clothing the said Sally Roach
for the year 1818 up to the 23 Jan 1819 also for boarding and clothing Aaron Roach. This
Jan 29, 1819. Benjah Gray, guardian. Jan Term 1819.

Page 309   Inventory of estate of John Anderson, deceased.
Apr 8, 1819   Several items listed. This Jan 20, 1819. Elizabeth Anderson,
admrx. Jan Term 1819.

Page 309   Sale of estate of James Everett, deceased.
Apr 8, 1819   Persons listed, to wit, Jesse J. Everett purchased one Bible,
James Martin, Henry Lady, Jeremiah Pierce, Leban Abernathy, Isaac Mayfield, Jeremiah
Saddler, Williamson Jordan, Amariah B. Everett, Charles E. Everett, and Jesse J. Everett.
Sale on 12 Nov 1818. Jesse J. Everett, executor. Jan Term 1819.

Page 310   Division of negroes of Joshua White, deceased.
Apr 8, 1819   Sarah White relict of Joshua White, deceased, drew Will, Dempsey
White drew Nancy, Jacob White drew Sue, Samuel Copeland and Polly his wife drew Jenney,
Thomas Harmon and Elizabeth his wife drew Jim, Wilson White drew Bason, Sally White drew
Bill, and Jabez White drew Melinda and child. This 23 Jan 1819. Signed by Alexander Ewing,
Samuel L. Wharton and William Neely, Commissioners. Jan Term 1819.

Page 310   Sale of estate of Henson Hardy, deceased.
Apr 9, 1819   Purchasers, to wit, William Kent, Jacob Brasher, E. Hardy, John
Moore, James W. Holly, William L. Yarbro, and William Ray. Signed by Elizabeth Hardy,
admrx. Jan term 1819.

Page 311   Inventory of estate of Nathan Patterson, deceased.
Apr 9, 1819   Jan 29, 1819. A note on William Wilson, a receipt given by
Mathew Patterson, a note on Thomas Harney given by J.P. Downs to Jos. Shaw, one other
made to John Patterson on David Earhart, also one bank note on the Merchants Bank of
Alexandria. Signed by Matthew Patterson, admr. Jan Term 1819.

Page 311   Inventory of estate of Asahel Champ, deceased.
Apr 9, 1819   Jan 25, 1819. Several items listed including a note on Clement McDaniel. Nancy Champ, admrx. Jan Term 1819.

Page 312   Inventory of estate of Robert Evans, deceased.
Apr 9, 1819   Jan 21, 1819. Several items listed including two receipts on B.W. & W.H. Bedford for his claim for property lost in the Military Service of the United States which they promise to pay before the next Session of Congress. Eldridge Newsom, admr. Jan Term 1819.

Page 312   Inventory of estate of Joseph Coleman, deceased, of Davidson
Apr 20, 1819   County. Several items listed including a large family Bible. This 20 Apr 1819. Anna M. Coleman, admrx and Blackman Coleman, admr. Apr Term 1819.

Page 314   Will of Jesse B. Wilkinson, deceased, of Davidson County.
June 7, 1819   To Mrs. Martha Wilkinson a negro woman named Siller during her lifetime and afterwards to her daughter Amelia Wilkinson. To my sister Lucy Gibson a negro girl named Kitty. To Eliza Putney a negro girl named Matilda. I appoint Jesse Taylor, executor. This 5 Sept 1818. Wit: Benjamin Y. Hudson and James B. Craighead. Apr Term 1819.

Page 314   Will of Zachariah Stull, deceased, of Davidson County.
June 8, 1819   My wife Nancy Stull shall have her lifetime on the plantation that I now live on with all the land that lies east of the Dry Branch leading through blew grass lot by the dog hole to the Big Rode and at her death said land is to belong to my son George Stull. My son George Stull to have all the land that lies west of the said Branch that leads by the dog hole. My son Samuel Stull shall have all the land that lies east of the big rode his lifetime and at his death it shall belong to my wife unless he should have an heir then the place must be rented out til the boys becomes of age and then to the heir. My son George shall have the management of the plantation as it is to return to him if there be no heir. My wife Nancy Stull shall have half the money that I have and my son George shall have the other half. No witnesses. Able Elmore and Francis McKay swore that the will was of Zachariah Stull's hand writing. And Edmond Gamble, Samuel Weakley, John Maxey, and James H. Gamble swore that that are acquainted with the hand writing of Zachariah Stull, deceased, and believes it to be his writing &c.

Page 315   Inventory of sale of estate of Joseph B. Turner, deceased.
June 8, 1819   Jan 5, 1819. Several items listed. Ingram Blanks, admr. Apr Term 1819.

Page 315   Inventory of sale of estate of Robert Evans, deceased.
June 8, 1819   Feb 3, 1819. Taken by Eldridge Newsom, admr. Persons listed, to wit, Benjamin Joslin, Elizabeth Robertson, Richard Hobbs, Arthur Exum, William Parker, Lewis Demoss, Eldridge Newsom, William Penn, John C. House, William Grubbs, Susanna Robertson, Henry Robertson, John Taylor, Lucy Evans, James Anderson, Lewis Hardgraves, James Taylor, Isaac Tillit, William Hobbs, George Pierce, John Webb, Thomas Loftin, John Exum, Mabry Walton, John Hardgraves, William R. Evans, John Evans, David Penn, Isaac Watkins, and Charles Scot. Apr Term 1819.

Page 316   Inventory of estate of Robert Evans, deceased.
June 9, 1819   Feb 3, 1819. Several items listed including one account dated May 25, 1813 against the estate of Daniel Cowen, deceased, and a receipt on Eldridge Newsom given to Lewis Loyd. Eldridge Newsom, admr. Apr Term 1819.

Page 317   Inventory of sale of estate of Nancy Davis, deceased.
June 9, 1819   Sold on 2 Feb 1819 by William Donelson, admr. Purchasers, to wit, Robert Stewart, William Donelson, Coleman McDaniel, Reuben Payne, William Lefever, Jesse Fulcher, Clement McDaniel, Nicholas Pryor, and Samuel Fowlkes. Apr Term 1819.

Page 317   Additional inventory of sale of estate of Andrew Davis, deceased.
June 9, 1819   Sold on Feb 2, 1819. Purchasers, to wit, Hendly Russel, Benjamin Butterworth, William Donelson, John Crunk, Caleb Willis, Reuben Payne, Ralph Hall, George

Hall, Robert Bates, Axum Sumner, Zachariah Payne, Ezekiel Young, Robert (illegible), Clement McDaniel, Greenwood Payne, William Dorris, Sarah Cain, Morris Cain, John Leak, Elizabeth Blakemore, William Philips, Thomas Blakemore, Frederick Laciter, Thomas Glaves, Theophilus Scruggs, James Boothe, John Wadkins, Lewis Basey, Thomas Cartwright, William McLawrence, Robert Goodlet, and James Clement being all the (illegible) that I could find after the death of Mrs. Davis on the plantation, George Hall and Rice Cobb. Andrew Davis in his will gave one featherbed and furniture to Joseph Payne a nephew of Mrs. Davis. He gave to each of his grand daughters one featherbed and furniture, one bed Mrs. Davis sold. Sold negro man Jacob to Thomas Glaves, Ezekiel Young, Zachariah Payne, Stephen Cantrell, Alexander Donelson, Thomas Overton for $650.00, sold negro woman Judy to Zachariah Payne for $200.00. William Donelson, executor. Additional sale of the old horse mill sold on 20 July 1816 and purchased by William Donelson. Apr Term 1819.

Page 319   Inventory of estate of George Fredrick Jerow, deceased.
June 10, 1819   Several items listed including one silver watch.   W. Wallace,
admr. Apr Term 1819.

Page 319   James Dean, minor orphan, guardian's return.
June 10, 1819   Made with Michael Gleaves, guardian. Paid Nathan Ewing, Peter
H. Martin, B.W. & W.H. Bedford, Thomas Ramsey. Balance due James Dean, minor, $1359.70.
Apr Term 1819.

Page 319   William A., Julia G. and Polly B. Wilkes, guardian's return.
June 11, 1819   Jan 1, 1818. Robert Thomas to William Albert Wilkes, Julia G.
Wilkes and Polly B. Wilkes. Robert Thomas, guardian. Apr Term 1819.

Page 320   Inventory of sale of estate of Asahel Champ, deceased.
June 11, 1819   Sold Feb 20, 1819. persons listed, to wit, George Rasberry,
Nancy Champ, Richard Champ, Wiseman Champ, Samuel Eakin, Arnold Russell, John Jordon,
Andrew Job, Jr., Thmas Lofton, Reuben Brown, Jeptha Hooper, Jeremiah Pierce, Thomas
Hooper, and Jesse Woodard. Nancy Champ, admr. Apr Term 1819.

Page 320   Inventory of sale of estate of Benjamin Pack, deceased.
June 12, 1819   Mar 12, 1819. One note on Thomas Levy, one on John Lovell,
one on Jesse Garland, one on John Dimon, one on Henry Rape, one on William Gordon, and
one on James Lovell. B.D. Pack, executor. Apr Term 1819.

Page 320   Sale of negroes of estate of Nathan Peebles, deceased.
June 12, 1819   Sold at Nashville 13 Feb 1819. Purchasers, to wit, Mary Peebles,
William Murphy, William H. McLaughlin, and Jno. Stobough. Whole amount $2013.50. William
Vaulx, admr. Apr Term 1819.

Page 321   Inventory of sale of estate of William Moring, deceased.
June 12, 1819   Made by Benjamin Cox, admr. 100 lbs bacon, to cash received
for said Moring serving in the United States $157.00, one certificate $14.00 for lost property
in the United States $22.50. Amount $206.00. One note on William P. Smith and Samuel
Brown. Apr 3, 1819. Apr Term 1819.

Page 321   Additional inventory of estate of Reuben Westmoreland, deceased.
June 12, 1819   One account on Thomas Shackleford and one on Jeremiah Allen
who lives in Virginia. An obligation on Joseph Porter when in fact it was only the receipt on
James Porter for an obligation given by William Welch and Henry Adams who lives in the
State of Kentucky. Signed by Tilman R. Daniel, executor, with Will annexed.   Apr Term
1819.

Page 321   Churchhill Lanier, guardian's return.
June 12, 1819   Apr 20, 1819. Note in the hands of John Lanier, guardian.
Several items listed. Apr term 1819.

Page 322   William P. Campbell, guardian's return.
June 12, 1819   Received July 25, 1818. Several items listed. This 30 Apr 1819.
William P. Seat, guardian. Apr Term 1819.

Page 322   Sale of estate of William Merriman, deceased.
June 15, 1819   Feb 1, 1819, sold to the following persons, to wit, Judy Merriman,
B. Lanier, C. Elmore, Henry Douglas, Jno. Morgan, Allen Knight, James Boon, Isaac
Earthman, Ruben Michel, Alfred Justice, David Wills, William Coltharp, Thomas Eddington,
and Robert Merriman. Judith Merriman, admrx. Apr Term 1819.

Page 323   Lucy Evins, widow, support laid off.
June 15, 1819   One years support laid off to widow of Robert Evins, deceased,
her late husband. Several items listed. Feb 1, 1819. Thomas Lofton, Francis Newsom, and
John Harwood appointed to lay off support. Apr Term 1819.

Page 323   Will of Nimrod Williams, deceased, of Davidson County.
June 15, 1819   To my son Turner Williams 204 acres of land whereon he now
lives also a negro man named Harry with all the stock, household furniture &c in his
possession by his paying to his five sisters, viz, Mary Hamton, Nancy Reiley, Elizabeth
Garner, Eunice Estes and Sally Watson, sum of $1200.00 equally divided when collected from
the sale of land which he sold to Joseph Garner. Appointed my son Turner Williams,
executor. This 27 May 1818. Wit: John Ensley, Martin Gray and Richard Davidson. Apr
Term 1819.

Page 324   Sale of estate of Nathan Patterson, deceased.
June 16, 1819   Feb 27, 1819. Several items listed. Mathew Patterson, admr.
Apr Term 1819.

Page 324   Will of Peyton Parham, deceased.
June 16, 1819   My will is that my estate be equally divided between my two
nephews Josiah Pennington son of Robert Pennington, and William Rains Pennington son of
Graves Pennington, all of Davidson County. I appoint Robert Pennington and Graves
Pennington, both of Davidson County, my executors. This 25 Feb 1819. Wit: Leonard Keeling
and William Rose. Apr Term 1819.

Page 324   Nancy Champ, widow support laid off.
June 16, 1819   Nancy Champ widow and relict of Asahel Champ, deceased, with
five children, one years support. Several itens listed. This 20 Feb 1819. Thomas Hooper
and James Lovell, Commissioners. Apr Term 1819.

Page 325   Sale of estate of Joshua Curtis, deceased.
June 16, 1819   Made by George W. Curtis, executor, of sale on Mar 4, 1819.
Purchasers viz, George W. Curtis, Nathaniel Curtis, Constant Curtis, and Mr. Farmer.
Amount $163.98 3/4. Apr Term 1819.

Page 325   Settlement of estate of Thomas K. Harris, deceased.
June 16, 1819   Several accounts including amount of R. Moore account for
expenses in attending to the business for the estate, also by amounts of Mrs. Harris' account
for money made use of for the support of children and negroes, Col. Meigs' claim for $238.15.
Mary Harris, admrx and Richard Moore, admr. William S. Fulton and Jas. Lockhard. Apr
Term 1819.

Page 326   Settlement of estate of William Moring, deceased.
June 17, 1819   Made with Benjamin Cox, admr. One note due 15 Oct 1815 on
William P. Smith and Samuel Brown, cash received for bacon, and to cash received of the
United States for William Moring, deceased, service $157.00, advance for certificate for lost
property while in the service of the United States $14.00. Several vouchers listed. This 13
Apr 1817. Test: Eldridge Newsom and William H. Shelton. Apr Term 1819.

Page 326   Inventory of George Keeling, deceased.
June 21, 1819   Several personal items listed. Edward A. Keeling, admr. Apr
Term 1819.

Page 327   Additional inventory of estate of Craddock Faulks, deceased.
June 21, 1819   Crop of Tobacco $87.72. This Apr 19, 1819. Samuel Fawlkes,
admr. Apr Term 1819.

Page 327   Inventory of estate of William Baird, deceased. $500.00 stock in
June 21, 1819   the Nashville Bank. Apr 19, 1819. John Baird, admr. Apr Term
1819.

Page 327   Settlement of estate of Amos Heaton, deceased.
June 21, 1819   Made with Enoch Heaton, admr. Found receipts in full of the
estate of said Heaton. This Apr 20, 1819. Jonathan Drake and Braxton Lee, Commissioners.
Apr Term 1819.

Page 327   Settlement of estate of Ephraim Drake, deceased.
June 21, 1819   Made with William J. Drake, admr. To the amount of the sale
$1243.00. To the hire of the negroes $171.00. To the rent of the plantation $100.00. His
service $100.00. Several receipts and credits listed. Balance due from the admr to the
estate $1332.77. This 20 Apr 1819. James Read, J.P. and Braxton Lee, J.P. Apr Term 1819.

Page 328   Anna, Selah and Jane Roach, guardian's return.
June 21, 1819   I, John McCain, guardian for Aney Roach, Selah Roach and Jane
Roach, orphans of Stephen Roach, deceased, have in my hand 23 Jan 1818, to wit, for Anna
Roach $337.92. For Selah Roach $337.92, and for Jane Roach $337.92. Several items
purchased for said orphans. This 30 Jan 1819. John McCain, guardian. Apr Term 1819.

Page 328   Thomas Dillon, deceased, heir's guardian return.
June 29, 1819   The orphans of Thomas Dillon - To James Austin their guardian:
Board and clothing for Thomas Davis Dillon, and Edward Dillon. Paid Benjamin Newman for
schooling said orphans. This 27 Apr 1819. James Austin, guardian. Apr Term 1819.

Page 329   Settlement of estate of Thomas Dillon, deceased.
June 29, 1819   Made with James Austin, admr. Balance due me by William Hall
and Eldridge Newsom, Esquires. Charges by my agent George Bernard. This Apr 27, 1819.
Apr Term 1819.

Page 329   Settlement of estate of Susannah Ewing, deceased.
June 29, 1819   Made with Nathan Ewing, her executor. Paid Lewis White for
tombstone, William Garner for coffin, and other persons named, to wit, Elizabeth Berry,
William Ewing, legatee, Thomas Shannon, Andrew Castleman, Moses Speer, Andrew Ewing and
paid Henry C. Ewing for his time and trouble coming from Kentucky to prove descendants to
the will. Also Nathan Ewing's own part of descendants estate. Balance due by the executor
$15.00. This Apr 23, 1819. Jesse Wharton and Elihu S. Hall, Esquires, Commissioners. Apr
Term 1819.

Page 330   Inventory of estate of Edmond Hewlett, deceased.
Aug 18, 1819   This 28 Apr 1819. Several items listed, to wit, stock in trade of
Edmond and William Hewlett. Several other items listed including a Family Bible. Signed by
William Hewlett and Nicholas Hewlett, admrs. July Term 1819.

Page 330   Inventory of estate of Severn Donelson, deceased.
Aug 19, 1819   Twenty six negroes and several other items listed. Signed by
Elizabeth Donelson, admrx. July Term 1819.

Page 331   Inventory of estate of Jonathan Williams, deceased.
Aug 19, 1819   July 17, 1819 Davidson County. Several items listed. Signed by
Charity Williams, admrx. July Term 1819.

Page 331   Will of Samuel L. Philips, deceased.
Aug 20, 1819   This 2 Feb 1818. To my brother Edward Philips all my estate
both real and personal also I appoint him my executor. Wit: John Pirtle, William Walton and
Isaac Walton. July Term 1819.

Page 332   Inventory of estate of Arthur Exum, deceased.
Aug 20, 1819   Twelve negroes and other items listed. Benjamin Phillips
$300.00, Eldridge Newsom due bill for ginned cotton. Hartley's note $17.00. Jesse Reynolds
note. John Exum, admr. July Term 1819.

Page 332   Inventory of estate of Zachariah Stull, deceased.
Aug 20, 1819   July 15, 1819. A note on Benjamin Phillips, one on John Walker
agent for Nashville Steammill Co., one on Robert Murdock, one on Daniel & Merriman
McGuire, and one on William Jackson. Cash received of Peter Martin and James Jackson.
Other persons named, to wit, Richard Hicks and Rosanna Murray. Several items listed along
with nine negroes. Samuel Stull, admr. July Term 1819.

Page 333   Inventory of estate of Daniel Frazer, deceased.
Aug 21, 1819   After his death, July 22, 1819. 420 acres and 13 negroes, cattle,
hogs and several other items listed. Bonds and notes on Sampson Sawyer, Jeremiah Harlan,
Benjamin Wright, John Are (Orr), George Wharton, Stephen C. McDaniel, Clement McDaniel,
Jacob Dickinson, Ebenezer Titus, one town lot in Haysborough, and two town lots in
Waynesborough. Rebecca Frazer and Moses B. Frazer, admrs. July Term 1819.

Page 334   Inventory of estate of James Hamilton, deceased.
Aug 23, 1819   Delivered by John Hannah, late executor. This July 28, 1819.
Notes on George W. Charlton and Young Green and Robert Armstrong, John L. Allen, and
David Allen. Two grants of 1258 acres of land lying in Middle District, north side of
Tennessee River on the waters of Coldwater Creek, one duplicate grant for 274 acres of land
in Davidson County, one quit claim deed to 50 acres of land in Davidson County, one grant
for 20 acres of land in Davidson County entered by said Hannah as executor, one obligation
on John Rosson for lease of land in Giles County, one execution on Ephraim and Zadoc
Phelps, a negro man named Peter now in possession of James Mulherrin, Esquire, one negro
man named Reuben now supposed to be in the possession of John L. Allen, a negro man
named Sterling in possession of Z. Noell, one named Harry, Milly and her four children hires
by Joseph Hamilton, one boy named Littleton hired by Young Green. Also a note on Reuben
Witten and one on James Blackburn. Willis L. Shumate, admr, with will annexed. July Term
1819.

Page 335   Land divided of John Williams, deceased.
Aug 23, 1819   Division among the heirs of said deceased giving to Benjamin F.
Williams and William Murphey their parts and the heirs of Littleberry Williams the balance.
To Benjamin F. Williams one lot of land conveyed by James Titus to said J. Williams and
bordering lands of William H. McLaughlin, William Murphy and William Wright and containing
56 acres and 52 poles. To William Murphey land bordering Benjamin F. Williams and William
Wright and containing 56 acres and 52 poles. The balance of the tract allotted and set apart
to the heirs of L. Williams and containing 232 acres and 56 poles. This 31 Oct 1818. Signed
by Jeremiah Ezell, William Hall, Jno. Gowen, Edmund Owen, and Peter Wright. July Term
1819.

Page 336   John Topp, perpetuating testimony.
Aug 23, 1819   On the application of John Topp for the purpose of perpetuating
testimony of the corners and boundaries of a tract of land in Davidson County and on the
waters of Mill Creek granted to Peter Caltron by Grant No. 111 for 640 acres, dated 17 Apr
1786 of which said tract 320 acres are held by said Topp by deed dated 7 Sept 1803. Land
borders John Buchanan, Mill Creek, William Simpson, and Jesse Maxwell. A deposition of
John Buchanan was taken by the Commissioners at Jan Term 1819. July Term 1819.

Page 337   Sale of estate of George F. Jerrow, deceased.
Aug 24, 1819   Persons listed, to wit, A. Page, J. Parker, Thomas Walston, J.
Page, Patsey Brooks, Zach. Tate, John Page, Thomas Taylor, W. Wallace, and W. Moses. W.
Wallace, admr. July Term 1819.

Page 337   Settlement of estate of James Hamilton, deceased, of Davidson
Aug 24, 1819   County and made with John Hannah, executor. Several items
listed including the funeral expenses for Jas. Hamilton, deceased, and wife $10.00, Charles
Hayes, John Huggins, Joseph Brown, Benajah Gray, Elijah Hamilton, Thomas Greer, Cary
Felts, John McNeal, William P. Hannah, George Hamilton, John E. Beck, John C. Hannah,
Joseph Hamilton, Samuel Weakley, John Carter, George H. Hannah, Charles Heard, Benjamin
Hooker, Edward H. East, Charles M. Hall, James Erwin Whyte, Esq., Henry Crab, Ephraim H.
Foster, John C. McLemore, Joseph Smith, Joseph Burnett, Mathew Barrow, Nathan Ewing,
Micaja Peacock, Thomas G. Bradford, Balaam Edmons, John Buchanan, Ransom Gwyn, William

Allen for schooling for George F. Hamilton an heir, Stump & Cox, R.C. Foster & Son, J.G. Martin, Josiah Nichol, Thomas Yeatman, J. Parker, Duncan Robertson, Hannah Porter, Samuel Donnell, Elijah Hamilton, James Jackson, George W. and Jane Charlton, Milberry Hamilton, James Hamilton for Hanah and Polly Hamilton's use. Signed by James Mulherrin and William Hall. July Term 1819.

Page 339
Aug 25, 1819
July Term 1819.

Thomas Cox, a minor son of Greenberry Cox, deceased.
Made with Thomas Cox, his guardian. Paid to Charles Mead.

Page 340
Aug 25, 1819

Settlement of estate of William C. Ewell, deceased.
Made with Absalom Gleaves, admr. Several items listed. This
July 5, 1819. William Hall and James Mulherrin. July Term 1819.

Page 340
Aug 25, 1819

Settlement of estate of _____ Faulkes, deceased.
Persons listed, to wit, William Rutherford, E. Goodrich, Mary
Faulkes, William H. Hamblin, Mrs. Faulkes, Jonathan Clay, William Cayton, Robert Adams, William Donelson, Nathan Ewing, and William Hope as guardian for William B. Faulkes. Signed by E. Goodrich and George Wharton, Commissioners. July Term 1819.

Page 341
Aug 25, 1819

Ann M. Coleman, widow's support laid off.
June 1, 1819. Ann M. Coleman relict of Joseph Coleman,
deceased, one years support for herself and family. Robert C. Foster, Acting J.P. Several articles listed. William B. Lewis and E. Pritchett.

Page 341
Aug 26, 1819

Inventory of estate of Samuel L. Philips, deceased.
Several items listed including one watch. This July 19, 1819.
Edward Philips, executor. July Term 1819.

Page 341
Aug 26, 1819

James Hodge, deceased, negroes hired.
Persons listed, to wit, Nancy Hodge, Thomas M. Burlin, Samuel
D. Betts, and William Armstrong. Signed by Nancy Hodge, admrx and Samuel D. Betts, admr. July Term 1819.

Page 342
Aug 26, 1819

William P. Campbell's, guardian return.
May 15, 1819. Paid the tailor for making a close coat and
finding trimming, and paid for boarding and schooling. This 29 July 1819. William P. Seat, guardian. July Term 1819.

Page 342
Aug 26, 1819

Robert Cato, deceased. Negroes hired.
Mary Cato one woman and child, Dennis McClendon one woman
and child, Mary Cato one girl, and Rowland Cato one boy. Mary Cato, admrx. July Term 1819.

Page 342
Aug 26, 1819

John and Isaac G. Pugh, minor orphans, guardian return.
John Davis, guardian to John Pugh, minor, Dr. to $180.00
received the 29th April 1818 as his dividend of John Pugh, deceased, personal estate as far as divided $180.00 30 July 1819. This July 30, 1819. Jno. Davis. John Davis guardian to Isaac G. Pugh, minor, Dr. to $180.00 received 29 April 1818 as his dividend of John Pugh, deceased, personal estate as far as divided 30 July 1819. This July 30, 1819. July Term 1819.

Page 343
Aug 26, 1819

Robert Stringfellow's heirs, guardian return.
Aug 30, 1818. Received of James Carter, admrx $412.22½. Paid
Nathan Ewing $2.95. Signed by Jeremiah Baxter. July Term 1819.

Page 343
Aug 26, 1819

Jas. and Jason Wilson.
I, William H. Nance, hold a bond on James and Jason Wilson for a
title of land to me and others Thomas Shackleford and John Bradford and the said Wilson having made a deed therefore I will deliver unto them the said bond when called on at my house. Test: James H. Wilson. Signed by William H. Nance, March 5, 1818. July Term 1819.

Page 343   Settlement of estate of Robert Edmondson, deceased.
Aug 28, 1819   The following list of vouchers, produced by Peter Wright, admr.
This July 27, 1819, viz, paid Alexander Alicke as a witness for Robert Edmondson lessee
against John Greer and others, paid Amos Balch as a witness for Robert Edmondson lessee,
against John Greer and others, paid William McClelan as witness for Robert Edmondson
lessee,against A. Ferguson, paid Richard Martin as a witness for Robert Edmondson lessee,
against John Greer and others, paid Anthony Ragor as a witness for Robert Edmondson lessee,
against John Green and others, also paid James Bright for surveying land, also James Bright,
Jr. for chain carrying, and Jenkin Whiteside as attorney. Signed by William Hall and R.
Weakley, J.P. July Term 1819.

Page 344   Settlement of estate of Robert Cato, deceased.
Aug 28, 1819   Made with Mary Cato, admrx. Several items listed. J. Ezell and
Cary Felts, Commissioners. July Term 1819.

Page 345   Settlement of estate of Robert Edmondson, deceased.
Aug 30, 1819   Made with Peter Wright, admr. Twenty seven vouchers listed.
Jan 20, 1819. J. Ezell and Cary Felts, Commissioners. July Term 1819.

Page 346   John Pugh's heirs guardian return.
Aug 30, 1819   Returned by Solomon Clark, guardian for part of the heirs of
John Pugh, deceased, Apr 29, 1819. Polly Pugh, minor, to Solomon Clark, Sally Pugh, minot,
to Solomon Clark, Hannah Pugh, minor, to Solomon Clark, and Hampton Pugh, minor, to
Solomon Clark. July Term 1819.

Page 347   Judith Merryman, her support laid off.
Oct 9, 1819   This 6 May 1819. We believe that $225.00 is as little as Mrs.
Merryman and her family can be supported for one year. Signed by Lewis Earthman, Jno.
Criddle and Henry Douglass. July Term 1819.

Page 347   Sale of estate of Daniel Frazor, deceased.
Nov 15, 1819   Oct 7, 1819. Persons listed, to wit, Rebecca Frazor, John M.
Dickson, Jesse Butterworth, Ebenezer Frazor, Daniel Frazor, Samuel Lotter, Moses B. Frazor,
Reuben Payne, John Jourdon, Edward Vaun (Vaughn), John Criddle, Thomas Rimmer, Jacob
Dickinson, John Scruggs, George Harris, James Frazor, and Landon C. Farrar. Moses B.
Frazor, admr. Oct 18, 1819. Oct Term 1819.

Page 349   Sale of estate of Severn Donelson, deceased.
Nov 16, 1819   Friday 15 Oct 1819. Purchasers, viz, Elizabeth Donelson, E.
Donelson, and William Bryant. Elizabeth Donelson, admrx. Oct Term 1819.

Page 350   Sale of estate of Arthur Exum, deceased.
Nov 16, 1819   27 Aug 1819 by John Exum, admr. Persons listed, to wit, John
C. House, Widow Exum, George Reaves, Joseph Exum, William Exum, Robert Exum, Sarah
Reynolds, Peggy Exum, Richard Boyd, Mabry Walton, Widow Hannah, Thomas Loftin, Howel
Harris, James Joslin, William S. Gordon, Widow Evins, E. Edwards, Hiram Anderson,
Theophilus Fulgum, Francis Newsom, William S. Miller, Robert Simpson, James Hartgraves,
Balaam Newsom, William Walden, Thomas Stroud, James Lovell, Eli Methers (Wethers), Jesse
Shelton, James Anderson, John T. Scott, Robert Hughs, Lewis Demoss, Jesse Garland, Elisha
Garland, Huston Cooper, Jeptha Hooper, Jesse Reynolds, Jahua Cloid, Mathew P. Long, John
Hughs, E. Cloid, Mrs. Hughs, William R. Evins, William Downey, Abner Driver, Thomas Scott,
Jacob Sanders, Henry Elliston, William Shelton, and John Exum. Items sold on 27 and 28 Aug
1819. John Exum, admr. Oct Term 1819.

Page 352   Will of Benjamin Branch, deceased.
Nov 17, 1819   To my son Robert Branch one negro man named Daniel, bed and
furniture, a horse, saddle and bridle which property he has in possession on loan. To my son
John Branch a negro man named Sam, a bed and furniture, also the tract of land whereon he
now lives which property he has in possession on a loan. To my son Wallace Branch a negro
boy named Moses, a bed and furniture, a horse, bridle and saddle, also a tract of land in
Montgomery County which property he has in possession on a loan. To my daughter Lizzy
Taylor two negroes named Sophia and Alford, one bed and furniture which she has in

possession, also a negro girl named Artemissa at my death. To my daughter Milley Allen two negroes named Airry and Aggy, one bed and furniture which property she has in possession, also a negro giel named Tilda at my death. To my grand daughter Permelia Taylor one negro girl named Charlotte, a bed and furniture which is in the possession of Thomas Taylor, also a negro girl named Julia at my death. To my grand daughter Sally Murry a negro girl named China, one bed and furniture. To my grand son James Murry a negro boy named Brit, also a tract of land whereon Rosanna Murry now lives provided the land should be recovered in my favor which land is to be divided equally between my grand daughter Sally Murry and James Murry. To my grand son William Cocke Young one negro girl named Harriet now in the possession of Daniel Young. To my son James Augustus Branch the tract of land whereon I now live also two negroes named Ennis and Jerry, together with all my household and kitchen furniture, plantation utensils and my stock of every description, subject to my wife's lifetime or widowhood. To my beloved wife Nancy Branch one negro man named Isaac also Betty and child together with my household and kitchen furniture, plantation utensils and stock of every description during her lifetime or widowhood, also a negro boy named Caleb, and at her death the whole of the property left to be given to my son James Augustus Branch. To my daughter Julia Ware two negroes named Linda and Jane, one bed and furniture which she now has in possession. I appoint Josiah Williams and my son Wallace Branch my executors. This 28 May 1819. Wit: Samuel L. Wharton and Jabez White.

Codicil: To my daughter Juliet Ware one negro woman named Dilly at the death of my wife, and the balance of my estate not otherwise willed, my will and wish to be equally divided between Robert Branch, John Branch, Wallace Branch, Lizzy Taylor, Juliet Ware, and Milley Allen at the death of my wife. This 9 June 1819. Wit: Samuel L. Wharton and John C. Parker. Oct Term 1819.

Page 353   Inventory of estate of Benjamin Branch, deceased.
Nov 18, 1819   Several items listed including notes on the following, to wit, William Perkins, Washington Perkins, A.B. and J.A. Taylor, J.H. Gamble, Jesse H. Cartwright, Christiana Irby, Valentine Branch, John Clinard, Jabez White, C.Y. Hooper, Henry Clinard, Joseph Page, Henry and Zach. Duncan, John C. Parker, William Shaw, George Foster, Henry Wilson, John Stump and George Zachariah, McDowell & Lyons, and D. and W. Perkins. Also bank notes listed. Oct 19, 1819. J.F. Williams, executor. Oct Term 1819.

Page 354   Will of Liston Temple, deceased, of Nashville.
Nov 18, 1819   After all my debts are paid, all remaining to be equally divided between my dear wife Harriett and two dear children, Agness and Charles. To my brother William Tample and my father-in-law Duncan Robertson to act as my executors. This 2 May 1819. Wit: J. Roane and Hugh Roland. Oct Term 1819.

Page 355   Inventory of estate of John Patterson, deceased.
Nov 19, 1819   Several items listed including two Bibles and two Testaments. Signed by Elender Patterson and Robert Patterson. Oct Term 1819.

Page 356   Inventory of estate of Aquilla Carmack, deceased.
Nov 19, 1819   Items that came into the hands as executor of the deceased Aquilla at the death of his wife which took place on the 7th April 1819. Several items listed including one large Family Bible. Oliver Williams, acting executor. Oct Term 1819.

Page 356   Inventory of estate of Stephen Lock, deceased.
Nov 20, 1819   Oct 18, 1819. Several items listed including one note on Nelson P. Jones. Signed by Rebecca Lock, admrx. Oct Term 1819.

Page 357   Additional inventory of estate of Littleberry Williams, deceased.
Dec 16, 1819   Made by James Vaulx, executor. One note on William L. Willis, items sold to William Hollinsworth, also items sold unto Thomas Buchanan, Jno. Topp, I. and J. Seller. Oct Term 1819.

Page 357   Sally Exum, widow's support.
Dec 16, 1819   Widow of Arthur Exum, deceased, one years support for her and her family. Several items listed. This 27 Aug 1819. Test: William Anderson. Oct term 1819.

Page 357   Inventory of estate of Moody Harris, deceased.
Dec 16, 1819   Made by Sally Harris, admrx. Several items listed. Oct Term
1819.

Page 358   Inventory of estate of Robert Evans, deceased.
Dec 16, 1819   Made by Eldridge Newsom, admr. June 30, 1819 received of
Thomas Hickman, Sheriff of Davidson County, $215.40 in full of a judgement that was
recovered against James Robertson and Susannah Robertson. One account against the estate
of James Brannon, deceased, for $10.00, $2.50 for one pair of saddle bags that was sold at
Evan's sale and was not delivered in the account of sale. Oct Term 1819.

Page 358   Settlement of estate of Larkin Clay, deceased.
Dec 16, 1819   Made by Jonathan Clay, executor. Rent of plantation, hire of
negroes to Thomas Patterson and John Thomas and G. Payne, tobacco sold to Reuben Payne.
Cash to Clanton, Jos. Philips, Mary Faulks, S. Allen, S.C. McDaniel, John Perry, Martin
Pierce, Thomas Cufman, Thomas Patterson, Dennis Mann, Jos. Nichol & Co., Darby
I(illegible), John W. Allen, John Jennings, Patsey Rice, M. Allen, Doctor Massey, E. Porter,
Peter Bashaw, and to board of three children from 1 Aug 1817. William Donelson and George
Wharton, Commissioners. Oct Term 1819.

Page 359   Settlement of estate of John Walker, deceased.
Dec 16, 1819   Did on 9 Oct 1819 examine the account of Alexander Walker,
Esq., and as executor of estate. Each legatees portion, Alexander Walker, Abraham Walker,
Samuel Dickson, Gray Andrews, John P. Walker, admr of Joseph Walker, deceased, John B.
Walker, and James Walker. Paid to Doctor John Newnan's fee, Doctor John Massey's fee,
Matthew P. Walker, McLean & Tunstall, Nathan Ewing, and N.G. Childress. Signed by E.
Goodrich and George Wharton. Oct Term 1819.

Page 359   Inventory of estate of David Pulley, deceased.
Dec 17, 1819   Several items listed including a note on William H. Alley. D.
Vaughn, admr. Oct Term 1819.

Page 359   Inventory of estate of Peter Randolph, deceased.
Dec 17, 1819   One negro man sold, one horse sold, two bonds given by Henry
Williams to said Randolph and Williams is believed to be insolvent. he has got possession of
said bonds and has torn his name off them says also that he has paid them. It is believed
that he was not of full age when said bonds were given. Peyton Randolph, admr. Oct Term
1819.

Page 360   Will of Lewis Harrison, deceased, of Davidson County.
Dec 17, 1819   To my beloved sister Franky Parham I give the services of a
negro woman called Winney and her posterity during her lifetime and at her death to be given
to her children. Mary and her daughter Rushiana, Maria, Samond, Isaac all of whom being
sisters and brothers do I give solely to my much beloved brother Richard B. Owen. This 13
Sept 1819. I appoint Richard B. Owen my sole executor. Lewis Harrison. Test: John
Stobough and R.B. Owen, Jr. Oct Term 1819.

Page 360   Will of James P. Downs, deceased.
Dec 17, 1819   To my adopted son William Downs that he shall have my estate.
I also wish Mrs. Polly Moreman formerly the wife of William Roper to have a competency for
the support of her yearly while she remains single and at her death or marriage to be taken
and applied to the benefit of William Downs. I also wish my negroes sold and applied to
boarding and schooling of William Downs to be conducted by William L. Willis and Nathan
Ewing, executors. July 31, 1819. Wit: Susannah H. Snead and Sarah H. Snead. Oct Term
1819.

Page 361   Inventory of estate of Severn Donelson, deceased.
Dec 17, 1819   One whip saw and one cross cut saw. Elizabeth Donelson, admr.
Oct Term 1819.

Page 361   Settlement of estate of William Tait, deceased.
Dec 17, 1819   Made with R.T. Walker, executor. Persons listed, to wit, Stump,

Thomas Edmiston, C. Perkins, William P. Anderson, C. Hewitt, Doctor Smith's bill, Henry Lyle, Kingsley & Parish, Jno. Murdock, Jno. L. Allen, R. Ruble, Thomas G. Bradford, Hood & Walker, Jas. Gordon, Jno. McNairy, T. Washington, Henry West, Thomas Johnston, Jno. Dickinson, William Ray, N. Perkins, Lyons, Jno. Erwin, George Neville, W. & R. Butler, George & M.R. Newell, Sampson Williams, Thomas Hill, Nathaniel McCreasy, G. Patton, Jas. Johnson, Mr. Moore, Nathan Williams, Duncan Robertson, E. Cooper, William B. Bell, Jno. Johnson, Jeremiah Pierce, Jno. Pierce, C. Metcalf, Jno. Summerville, Jos. Ward, Jos. McGavock, R. Stothart & R. Hughes, M.C. Dunn, Samuel Weakley, Doctor Irwin, Thomas Ramsey, Joseph Scales, Mary Watson, A. Kingsley, Stephen Cantrell, Josiah Nichol & Co., D. Robertson, Doctor Hadley, M. & J. Norvell, William Carroll, Thomas Childress, L. Stull, Elisha Williams, C. Perkins, Lewis Sturdevant, Laban Abernathy, William Davis, Jesse Everett, Isaac Mayfield, David Williams, Harris Dowlens, H. Tatum, Jas. Martin, Robertson & Currey, Nathan Williams, George W. Deadrich, Jno. H. Patton, Edmond Cooper, R.C. Cross, Jos. T. Elliston, J. Brahan, N.T. Perkins, Henry McIllwain, Doctor May, William Leintz, Robert Tait, Daniel McBean, Eliza Weston, Ilai Metcalf, Ann Fay, deceased, Jno. Armstrong, E. Williams, William M. Bell, McNeill & Greer, William Barker, William Montgomery, Jno. Murdock, R. McGavock, T. Thompson, Thomas Crutcher, John Mays & William Chandler, William Haynies, Shadrack Bell, Thomas Talbot, Thomas Watts, Thomas B. Craighead, Jno. Bosley, William Barker, Daniel Smith, Jno. H. Smith, Richard Sutton, James Gordon, A. Foster, William Arthur, R. Bowers, Jane Stothart, C. White, T. Masterson, Jno. Elder, J. & J.W. Sitler, William Griffin, and Jno. Carrs. Balance due the estate $8556.73. Joseph T. Elliston and Wilkins Tannehill, Commissioners. 19 Feb 1819. Robert Bell, James Gordon and Robert T. Walker, executors.

Page 365   George F. Hamilton, a minor, guardian return.
Mar 17, 1820   Report by Willis L. Shumate, guardian. Several items listed. Paid to Nichol Vaulx, M.H. Quinn, Thomas Yeatman, James E. Willis, and N. Ewing. This 28 Jan 1820. Jan term 1820. Test: Nathan Ewing.

Page 366   Settlement of estate of Lemuel T. Turner, deceased.
Mar 17, 1820   Made with Stephen Cantrell, Jr. and Elihu S. Hall, executors. Found a balance in the hands of Stephen Cantrell of $2389.04 of which a credit of $600.00 money laid out in the purchase of a negro woman and child for the benefit of the widow and children of said deceased. This 29 Jan 1820. W.B. Lewis, D.A. Dunham and W. Tannehill, Commissioners. Jan Term 1820.

Page 366   Ephraim H. Foster of Adam Caldwell, Covenant.
Mar 17, 1820   Sept 2, 1818 Adam Caldwell agrees to sell Ephraim H. Foster twenty five feet of his lot on Cedar Street, bordering Foster's new improvements and running up towards the Public Square, to the lot of James Porter, deceased. Foster is to pay Caldwell $1500.00 in cash and $1250.00 in 12 months from this date secured by a note in bank with endorsers. Foster agrees to put up a good post and rail fence between him and said Caldwell running back the full length of the lot equal to a post and rail fence around the lot at present occupied by Robert W. Armstrong in the front thereof. Signed by Ephraim H. Foster and Adam Caldwell. Jan term 1820.

Page 366   Inventory of estate of Johnathan Williams, deceased.
Mar 18, 1820   Several items listed. Charity Williams, admrx. Jan Term 1820.

Page 367   Sale of estate of Johnathan Williams, deceased.
Mar 18, 1820   Sold Aug 22. Charity Williams purchased several items, also Lamb Lawrence, R(illegible) Jourdon, and Aaron Lewallen. Charity Williams, admrx. Jan Term 1820.

Page 367   Settlement of estate of Jacob Dickinson, deceased.
Mar 20, 1820   Made with Will Williams, executor. Persons listed, viz, Will T. Dickinson, Mathew Patterson, Francis Hale, and William Thomas Wilkinson. Signed by Thomas Claiborne and W.B. Lewis. Jan Term 1820.

Page 368   Henry Dickinson, a minor, guardian return.
Mar 20, 1820   A note on George W. Campbell also interest on bank stock &c, also on John Childress and Jno. White, O.B. Hays, Jas. Trimble, and Thomas Shackleford

notes. Paid to, viz, Doctor Dickinson expenses of B.E. Dickinson's funeral, H. Petway, W. Banks, and A. Lytle. Cash advanced by J. Nichol for shoes. Paid Rogers for schooling, R.C. Foster & Sons, William Nichol, Vaulx & Co., John Carson, Shelby & McNairy, and J. Whiteside's note. Josiah Nichol, guardian. 29 Jan 1820. Jan Term 1820.

Page 369   Settlement of estate of Catherine Singletary, deceased, of
Mar 20, 1820   Davidson County. Made with Robert Williams, admr. and find the
amount of sales to be $182.75. Found he had paid out $138.56½, leaving a balance of $44.18½. This 25 Jan 1820. R. Hewitt and J. Horton. Jan Term 1820.

Page 369   Settlement of estate of Thomas Moseley, deceased.
Mar 20, 1820   Made to E. Moseley. Paid Josiah Morris for medicine &c, also
Dr. S. Easten for medicine. Richard Terrell for board and lodging also for attendence while sick, coffin and funeral expenses. Paid cost of two suits (illegible) Thomas Williamson, admr of Thomas, deceased and Williamson said Thomas Moseley, deceased, also paid judgement against E. Moseley as admr of T. Moseley, deceased. This 18 Jan 1820. J. Horton and Jno. P. Erwin. Jan Term 1820.

Page 370   Inventory of estate of John Lester, deceased.
Mar 20, 1820   Several items listed. Alexander Lester, admr. Jan Term 1820.

Page 370   Inventory of estate of John Lowe, deceased.
Mar 20, 1820   Received of Richard Lowe $194.00 admr of Mary Lowe, deceased,
received for the heirs of John Lowe. Philip Shute, executor of John Lowe's Last Will and Testament. Jan Term 1820.

Page 370   Inventory of estate of James Russell, deceased.
Mar 20, 1820   Several items listed. Wilson Crocket, admr. Jan Term 1820.

Page 370   Will of John Sanders, deceased, of Davidson County.
Apr 10, 1820   To my loving son Robert L. Sanders the following property, to
wit, Isaac, Nancy his wife, Abraham, Sarah and her two children, Redman, one girl Mahala, one boy Jesse, also all the money due me in the State, to wit, Tennessee and in North Carolina, now in the possession of Absolom Sanders being in Pitt County supposed to be $2500.00 or $3000.00, also $1000.00 due me in the hands of Col. John Criddle whose note I have in my possession. To my loving daughter Eliza Ann Sanders the following property, to wit, Primus, Betty his wife now in Chathan County, North Carolina and her child Nancy in the possession of William Hobson, Briant, Satra, Simon, Philis, and Patty, all the residue of my property not named I wish to be sold and the money equally divided between my children Robert L. Sanders and Eliza Ann Sanders. It is my desire that my children and the property should be removed to the County of Pitt and State of North Carolina. I appoint Absolom Rogers of Rutherford County, Tennessee my executor to manage said estate of the children until they can be conveyed to Pitt County, North Carolina, to the care of Absolom Saunders who I also nominate as my executor. This 28 Sept 1819. Wit: Richard Sutton and William Sutton. Jan Term 1820.

Page 371   Inventory of estate of William Y. Probarts, deceased.
May 18, 1820   Several items listed. Sally Probart, admrx. Jan Term 1820.

Page 372   Inventory of estate of John Sanders, deceased.
May 18, 1820   Jan 27, 1820, made by Absolom Rogers, executor. Several items
listed including a note on Colonel John Criddle and Lemuel Kennedy. This 28 Jan 1820. N. Ewing. Jan term 1820.

Page 372   Sale of estate of John Patterson, deceased.
May 18, 1820   Persons listed, to wit, Ellen Patterson, Robert Patterson, Jabez
White, William Patterson, John Shields, James Barns, Isaac Coffman, William Wilson, John Cleaves, David Parker, William Wilkinson, Robert Hood, James M. Eddington, William Kirkwood, Robert Wilson, John Nowlan, and John Patterson. Ellender Patterson, admrx and Robert Patterson, admr. Jan Term 1820.

Page 373　　　　　　　　　　Will of William S. Smith, deceased, of Davidson County.

May 19, 1820　　　　　　　　A negro woman named Abby and her son named Washington and several other negroes, all which slaves are now in the town of St. Martinsville, Louisiana, also other negroes five of which are in the care of Mr. Alexander Black Smith of Baton Rouge, Louisiana, $400.00 due me as my part of an obligation executed by John and Esther Wood of Adams County, Mississippi, in favor of Watkins and Smith, which obligation bears interest, $600.00 supposed to be my part of property sold in Nashville by John Rains of Davidson County, a negro boy named Leven who was decoyed or taken out of my possession by the Quakers near Winchester, Virginia, which said negro the John Rains has an equal property with myself, a negro woman that ran away from me at N(illegible) River in Virginia, the joint property of John Rains and myself. George Dugan of Virginia owes John Rains and myself $150.00 my part being $75.00, John Smith of Bayou, Sarah Louisiana owes my $45.00, in the hands of my present landlady $50.00 in money also my riding horse, saddle and bridle, a silver watch, all may be sold and converted into cash for the benefit of my heirs hereinafter named. To my beloved niece Nancy Smith a daughter of my deceased brother Edward Smith the sum of $1200.00 and devested in a bank in Nashville, Tennessee for her until Nancy comes of age or marries. To my beloved nephew David Hogan Smith a son of my deceased brother Edward the sum of $1200.00 of which $200.00 to go to educate him and the $1000.00 to be vested in the bank in Nashville until he shall be of age to manage the same. To my beloved nephew Samuel Smith a son of my deceased brother $1200.00. To my beloved sister Elizabeth Adams wife of Hodge Adams of Tennessee all the rest and residue of my estate. I appoint my friends Hodge Adams and John Hardin of Tennessee, executors. I also will and desire that my friend Ransom Eastin will attend to my funeral &c. This 6 Sept 1819 at St. Martinsville, Louisiana. Wit: John S. Sewart and Ransom Eastin.John Muggah, Gary, Richard Fennesy, A. Rulong, and James Davis, witnesses at St. Martinsville, Louisiana, Parish of St. Martin. Davidson County, Jan Term 1820.

Page 375　　　　　　　　　　Sale of estate of Aquilla Carmack, deceased.

May 20, 1820　　　　　　　　Sold by Oliver Williams, acting executor, on 12 and 13 Nov 1819. Persons listed, to wit, R.B. Sappington, G.G. Washington, John Corbitt, Daniel Carmack, John Linch, Mathew Porter, Henry Critchelow, Susanna Mandley, Turner Williams, Richard Mandley purchased one large Bible, Caleb McGraw, Charles Hollandsworth, Syrus Roberts, John Chadwell, Mordica Pillar, Slith M. Patterson, Henry Quishenberry, Silas Mourton, Thomas Walter, Martin Smith, Robert Goodlet, James Howel, Arthur Redman, Isaac L. Crow, Jno. Hathway, (illegible) Dunaway, Buckley Walker, John Hall, Samuel J. Ridley, Jemima White, Samuel Scott, and Meredith Corbit. This 28 Jan 1820. O.W. Williams, acting executor. Also named Gilbert G. Washington. Jan Term 1820.

Page 377　　　　　　　　　　Will of James B. Owen, deceased, of Davidson County.

May 22, 1820　　　　　　　　To my beloved wife Polly Owens all my stock of every kind and all my household and kitchen furniture and all my farming tools and all and everything that belongs to me at this time and all my corn and fodder. I apppoint my son John W. Owens my executor. This 28 Nov 1819. Wit: D.J. Hunphreys, Marthey Strong and Elijah Humphreys. Jan term 1820.

Page 377　　　　　　　　　　Elizabeth Childress, widow's support.

May 23, 1820　　　　　　　　Woodland, Nov 15, 1819. We have laid off and set apart to Elizabeth Childress relict of John Childress, deceased, one years support for the use of herself and family. Several items listed. Thomas Crutcher, Edmond Cooper and Duncan Robertson, Commissioners. Jan term 1820.

Page 378　　　　　　　　　　Inventory of estate of John Childress, deceased.

May 23, 1820　　　　　　　　Several items listed including a note on hand, James Baldriges, John Parks, Philip Anthony, James Kennedy, William Davis, Jacob McKees, Sterling C. Robertson, Alfred Nichols, H.F. Prells, John Dockeys, Thomas B. Bowins, James Jackson, John H. Smith, Taswell Hide, Sterling and C.B. Robertson, E. Benoit, Benjamin B. Jones, Elizabeth Childress, Abraham Barren, and Jesse Larance. A certificate of the managers of the Cany Creek Camp. Signed by Samuel B. Marshall, admr and Elizabeth Childress, admrx. Jan Term 1820.

Page 379　　　　　　　　　　John Hudson Sumner's guardian return.

May 24, 1820　　　　　　　　John Hudson Sumner orphan of Jos. John Sumner, deceased, with

Duke William Sumner, guardian. Several items purchased for said orphan. This 28 Jan 1820.
Jan Term 1820.

Page 380   Rebecca Lock, widow's support laid off.
May 24, 1820   Commissioners laid off and set apart one years support for
Rebecca Lock widow and relict of Stephen Lock, deceased. Several items listed. This 5 Nov
1819. Test: Z. Noell, Nathan Williams and William Matlock. Jan Term 1820.

Page 380   Arthur Bland, a minor orphan's guardian return.
May 25, 1820   May 19. Several items listed. Paid cash to W. Seat for crying
negroes. Also the hire of Arthur Bland's negroes for year 1820. This 28 Jan 1820. Cary
Felts and N. Ewing. Jan Term 1820.

Page 380   Ellender Patterson, support laid off.
May 25, 1820   Ellender Patterson widow and family of John Patterson, deceased.
300 bushels corn, pork, family expenses. Alex. Ewing, Michael Gleaves, William Caldwell, Jr.
appointed to lay off said support.

Page 381   Settlement of estate of William H. Utley, deceased.
May 25, 1820   15 Jan 1820. To settle with Isaac Hudson, admr. Several items
listed. To paid William Hope, Doctor J. Roane, Doctor Jno. Maxey, Doctor J.B. Wilkinson,
John Perry, and Mathew P. Walker. E. Goodrich, J.P. and George Wharton, Commissioners.

Page 381   Will of Walter Sims, deceased.
May 26, 1820   Now living on my farm called Woodland in Davidson County. To
my beloved wife Rebecca Sims all my household furniture and other items listed. Also to my
wife Rebecca during her lifetime that part of my farm which I now live, that lies south of
the branch which divides and runs through the said farm with all the improvements thereon or
that maybe made thereon. To my wife during her natural life the interest on the (illegible)
to Walter B. Sims and John S. Green for which I hold their bond for $20,000.00, the bond is in
the hands of John G. Sims, it may be loanes to my son Walter the one half and the other half
to my executors.   I desire that my property in Philadelphia County, Pennsylvania,
Penntownship be sold by my executors, to be invested and interest shall be paid to my wife
until my son William Poston Sims arrives at age of 21 years and that he be educated. To my
son William one half of my land on Richland Creek, Giles County, Tennessee when he arrives
to the age of 23 years. My son Walter B. Sims to have one half of my land on Richland
Creek in Giles County, Tennessee, also to him all my right and interest in the tract of land
that I hold jointly with my son John G. Sims also in the contract entered into with my son
John for building mills and a distillery &c. It is my will that $10,000.00 of the sum loaned to
Walter B. Sims and John S. Green may be loaned to my son Walter. It is understood that
John G. Sims is to convey for the use of the mills and distillery a piece of land on which the
mills are built on south side of Duck River. It is my will that the land certificates to the
amount of 5,000 acres now in the hands of Captain John A. Rogers of Hawkins County,
Tennessee when they shall be received from him and when my account with the heirs of G.
Denison is settled the proportion of the said warrants which cannot be less than 2500 acres
shall be divided between my son Walter B. Sims and my daughter Elizabeth. To my son David
Sims the part of my farm where I now live that lays to the north of the branch that runs
through and divides the farm. To my son David Sims the one half of my interest in the land
in Bedford County known by the name of Scullcamp tract near Shelbyville. Also to my son
David Sims the tract of land in Bedford County that I purchased from Jonathan Graves
consisting of 391 acres. To my daughter Elizabeth Scudder the one half of my tract of land
in Bedford County known by the name of Scullcamp tract the other half having been
bequeathed to my son David. To my daughter Elizabeth Scudder all my interest in my tract
of land in Bedford County known by the name of the Fishing Ford tract excepting 400 acres
which 400 acres I hereafter bequeathed. To my nephew John Sims Green 400 acres of my
land in Bedford County in the tract known by the Fishing Ford tract, other places be settled
or selected between my said nephew John S. Green and my son-in-law Philip J. Scudder. My
land in Hawkins County may be sold by my executors soon after my death as can be done and
the debt due me from the estate of Gideon Denison Maybe collected and when the lands shall
be sold and the debts shall be collected that the proceeds thereof shall be divided amongst
my children, John G. Sims, Walter B. Sims, David Sims, and Elizabeth Scudder. The debt due
me from the estate of Nicktin & Griffith shall be attended, tax divided amongst my children.

To my grandsons Walter Sims and John E. Sims $1000.00 each. To my namesake and connection, Walter Sims McNairy, $1000.00 to be paid to his father for his use. To my son William my gold watch. I appoint my sons John G. Sims and Walter B. Sims and my son-in-law Philip J. Scudder, guardian of my son William P. Sims. I appoint my dearly beloved wife Rebecca Sims as executrix and my son John G. Sims and my son William B. Sims, and my son-in-law Philip J. Scudder and my nephew John S. Green, executors. This 20 Feb 1819. Wit: John Sigler and Boyd McNairy.
Codicil: If my son William Poston Sims should die before he arrives to age of 21 years, unmarried, the foregoing is to be divided amongst his brothers and sister. This 19 Mar 1819. Signed by Boyd McNairy, Robert Wood and Anne E. Hewson. (a very long will)

Page 388   Jesse, Eli, Sally and Aaron Roach, minors &c guardian return.
May 29, 1820   Beneja Gray to each of the orphans: To Jesse Roach $364.40, to Eli Roach $353.71½, to Sally Roach $332.04, and to Aaron Roach $329.79. Also credit by a receipt of Lidia Roach. This 25 Jan 1820. R.C. Foster and Jno. P. Erwin. Jan Term 1820.

Page 389   Churchill Lanier, minor orphan, guardian return.
May 29, 1820   Jan 27, 1820. The hire of two negroes for $139.93 3/4. Jno. Lanier, guardian. Nathan Ewing for C. Lanier. Jan Term 1820.

Page 389   John Jos. A. Fowlkes, minor orphan, guardian return.
May 30, 1820   The amount of hire of John Jos. A. Foulkes' negroes willed to him by his grand father Thomas Foulkes for year 1820. This 17 Jan 1820. Nathan Ewing and William H. Hamblen, guardian. Jan Term 1820.

Page 389   Joseph McBride's orphans, guardian return.
May 30, 1820   George Hodge return guardian of the heirs of Joseph McBride, deceased, Jan 1, 1820 rented out their part of the land for $43.00 for one year, also hire of a negro woman and child for $35.00 and a girl for $25.00 and a boy for $15.00 due in 12 months. This 22 Jan 1820. Nathan Ewing. Jan Term 1820.

Page 389   John Price heirs, guardian return.
May 30, 1820   Hire of negroes of the heirs of John Price, deceased, for the year 1819-1820. In notes a/c $200.00. William Gilbert, guardian. Jan Term 1820.

Page 390   William A. and Polly B. Wilkes, orphans, guardian return.
May 30, 1820   Jan 1, 1820. Robert Thomas to Polly B. Wilkes interest on #155.00, rent on two acres, and for her board $13.30. Also Robert Thomas to William A. Wilkes hire of a negro boy $10.00, rent of 6¼ acres $12.50. This Jan 29, 1820. Nathan Ewing. Robert Thomas, guardian. Jan Term 1820.

Page 390   Priscilla McBride, her dower, of Davidson County.
May 30, 1820   We being summoned by R.B. Sappington, Deputy Sheriff, to lay off and allot to Priscilla McBride, widow of Joseph McBride, deceased, have laid off 37½ acres of land as her dower of two tracts, one containing 100, the other 40 acres and 90 poles lying on the waters of Little Harpeth, bordering lands of William Sneed. Priscilla McBride paying to George Hodge guardian of Sally McBride, Joseph McBride, Polly McBride, and Priscillla McBride $90.00. This 30 Dec 1819. Signed by John Harding, John Johns, Martin Greer, Henry Barnes, William Bumpass, Thomas Cox, John F. Owen, Philip Campbell, Joseph Caldwell, Johnson Vaughn, Samuel Stull, and F. Campbell.

Page 391   Sale of estate of George M. Deadrick, deceased.
May 31, 1820   Several items listed. This Jan 28, 1820. Signed by Stephen Cantrell, Jr., and J. Wharton. Jan Term 1820. (a very long list)

Page 396   Settlement of estate of George M. Deadrick, deceased.
June 3, 1820   Made with Wilkins Tannehill, William B. Sims and Daniel A. Dunham. This 28 Jan 1820. Jan term 1820.

Page 397   Will of Benjamin Philips, deceased, of Davidson County.
June 5, 1820   To my son Jesse Hinton Philips all the land beginning at the mouth of the Stone Lick Branch, intersects the line of the land I purchased of William

66

Watkins where it crosses the branch, to southeast corner of the land I purchased of James Hocket. Also to my son John Hinton Philips all the balance of my land whereon I now live. To my eldest daughter Anne and John T. Williamson, her husband, two negroes, to wit, Patience and Clary, which they have received. To my other two daughters Rebecca and Eliza four likely young negroes each als two boys and two girls. To my grand daughter Martha Anne Williamson two negroes. The balance of my negroes not otherwise appropriated I give unto my sons and two daughters Rebecca and Eliza, to be equally divided among them. My distillery be equally divided together with my mills, between my two sons. Each son and daughter is to have a bed and furniture. This 26 Dec 1818. Wit: Simon Johnson, Robert Gillespie and James Tatum. Jan Term 1820.

Page 398   Land divided of the estate of Jonathan F. Robertson, deceased,
June 5, 1820   of Davidson County. Commissioners are to divide the lands of
Jonathan F. Robertson, deceased, among the several heirs and claiments of said Robertson, the said land whereon the said Jonathan F. Robertson formerly lived and adjoining hereto being held by three Deed of Conveyance from James Robertson to said Jonathan F. Robertson, the first being recorded in Davidson County Register's Office in Book F, page 27, Aug 26, 1810, and also a deed from Peyton Robertson to Jonathan F. Robertson for 95 acres dated 23 Mar 1811 and registered first of April 1812, and also one other tract of 640 acres lying on both sides of Big Harpeth River held by deed as above from James Robertson, registered June 7, 1804, and also one other tract of 250 acres lying in the County of Maury on the south side of Duck River at the waters of Lytles Creek held by deed from Joseph Brown to the heirs of said Jonathan F. Robertson and being part of a grant issued by State of North Carolina to James Brown for 3980 acres. Also Lot No. 14 and part of Lot No. 15 in town of Nashville held by deed from John Gordon to Jonathan F. Robertson. Another tract of land of 640 acres lying on south west side of Big Harpeth River and on the Sulphus Fork of Jones Creek which was granted by the State of North Carolina to Jonathan F. Robertson by No. 2802 and dated 6 June 1796 in what was Davidson County now in Dickson County. Another 301 acres in County of Dickson on the Sulphur Fork of Jones Creek granted by North Carolina to Jonathan F. Robertson No. 2801 and dated 6 June 1796. And also one undivided half of a 640 acre tract of land in Dickson County on both sides of the upper Main Fork of Bartons Creek held by grant issued by the State of Tennessee to John Davis and Jonathan F. Robertson for 640 acres No. 8607 and dated 1 Feb 1816. Several other tracts listed. No. 1 of James R. Robertson, No.2 of Jonathan F. Robertson, No. 3 of Henry U(V). Robertson, No. 4 of Fanny G. Robertson, No. 5 of Felix Robertson, No. 6 of Elizabeth Cheatham, No. 7 of Frederick D. Robertson, and No. 8 of Benjamin F. Robertson. To Benjamin F. Robertson two quarters of Lot No. 14 and part of No. 15. This 18 Jan 1820. Jno. Davis, Surveyor. Signed by O.R. Hewitt, Solomon Clark, Peyton Robertson, D.A. Dunham, Jno. Harding, and Lewis Joslin. Jan Term 1820. (long description of lands)

Page 403   Sale of estate of James Russell, deceased.
June 10, 1820   Purchasers, to wit, Elizabeth Russell, Stephen Russell, Martin
Patterson, Samuel Work, Richard Champ, and Nancy Hooper. Sold on 19 Feb 1820. Signed by Wilson Crocket. Apr Term 1820.

Page 404   Jesse Wharton of George M. Deadrick, Covenant.
June 9, 1820   I, George M. Deadrick, will made a Deed or Deeds of Conveyance
to Jesse Wharton his heirs to the following parts of lots in the town of Nashville, to wit, No. (blank) the lot whereon John Sommerville now lives to be laid off by a divisional line north and south the half does not include the dwelling house of Sommerville to be conveyed when requested. One lot No. (blank) being the lot adjoining Mrs. Hay below held in common by David Deadrick of Jonesboro and the heirs of Edwin Hickman to be conveyed whenever a division is made by Commissioners to be appointed for that purpose. This Oct 17, 1804. April Term 1820.

Page 404   Will of William Donelson, Sr., of Davidson County.
June 10, 1820   All my children under 21 years of age live with their mother my
beloved wife Charity Donelson until they marry or arrive at the age of 21 and that my wife keep and raise with them my dear little grand daughter Mary Eliza Overton Hamblen, the only child of my daughter Mary Hamblen, deceased, and all my children who are not educated to be supported and educated from the proceeds of the farm whereon I now live, namely the tract I bought of George Blackamore of 149 acres, one other tract of land adjoining the above

tract on the west which I bought of (blank) Collings and containing about 100 acres, also the tract of land I bought of (blank) Marney and conveyed by Thomas Kilgore containing 320 acres, also one small tract of land containing 20 acres bought of George M. Deadrick, deceased, also one tract of land bought of Adam Clements containing 320 acres, and another tract of land known by the name of Bunker Hill tract containing 616 acres, all of which I bequeath to my beloved wife Charity Donelson during her natural life. All my negroes are to remain together on my farm and under the direction of my wife until my eldest son or sons marry or settle on their land hereafter willed to them. My wife is to have her choice of seven negroes until she marries or my youngest daughter comes of age. All stock to remain with my wife until my eldest child settle to themselves or marry and until the youngest comes of age or marry. All my young stock to be sold to support my wife and children and the education of my five younger children including my little grand daughter Mary Eliza Overton Hamblen who is to be educated. To my eldest son Severn Donelson all my tract of land situate in the fork of Cumberland and Stones Rivers in Davidson County containing 640 acres. To my second son Jacob Donelson all my two tracts of land that adjoin each other lying in Williamson County and near Big Harpeth River patented to me by the State of North Carolina and which contains about 800 acres or more. To my eldest daughter, now living, Milberry Donelson, my tract of land in Wilson County and which lies on Big Cedar Creek the same being conveyed to me by Hugh Henry and Isaac Henry and containing about 640 acres. To my second living daughter Patsey Donelson my tract of land lying on Spencers Creek in Wilson County and conveyed to me by my brother Severn Donelson, deceased, containing about 640 acres. To my third son William Donelson my tract of land lying on both sides of Big Harpeth River in Williamson County which was conveyed to me by James Scurlock and containing 430 acres and also a tract of land in Rutherford County containing 432 acres, it being the tract whereon Mr. Alexander formerly lived and being part of a tract conveyed by John G. and Thomas Blount to my brother John Donelson and myself. To my grand daughter Mary Eliza Overton Hamblen, only child of my beloved daughter Mary Hamblen, deceased, my tract of land in Wilson County on Cumberland River and containing 200 acres, it being the tract conveyed to me by George Green, also one other tract of land in Rutherford County containing 303 acres, it being the tract whereon Thomas Coffee formerly lived and being part of a tract conveyed by John G. and Thomas Blount to my brother John Donelson, but should she die without issue then said tracts of land be equally divided among all my children, also she is to have negro girls named Harriet and Raina. To my fourth son Andrew Jackson Donelson and to my youngest daughter Eliza Donelson to be divided equally and at the death of my wife, tracts of land heretofore named and composing the farm whereon I now live and containing 100 acres of land. I appoint my loving brother John Donelson, my beloved wife Charity Donelson, my beloved sons Severn and Jacob Donelson and my friend Andrew Jackson, my executors. This 10 Apr 1820. Wit: Samuel S. Cogg, W.P. Anderson and James D. Booth. Apr Term 1820. (long will)

Page 407   Will of James Glasgow, Sr., deceased, of Davidson County.
June 12, 1820   To my daughter Nancy McMinn five shillings with what she has had which is in full of the part she is to receive of my estate. To my daughter Elizabeth Anderson five shillings with what she has had, which is in full of the part she is to receive of my estate. To my daughter Phereby White five shillings with what she has had which is in full of the part she is to receive. To my son James Glasgow all and singular my lands, tenements &c that I have in this State or elsewhere. To my daughter Susan Haywood the six negroes, viz, Isaac, Jenny, Rachel, Elijah, Shadrick, and Perry. To my daughter Mary Glasgow five slaves, to wit, Lucy, Jim, Mary, India, and Minerva with one featherbed and furniture. To my daughter Clarinda J. Glasgow six negro slaves, to wit, Mary, Joe, Nancy, Henry, Harriet, and Tennessee with a featherbed. To my daughter Maria Anderson Glasgow five negro slaves, to wit, Rachel, Henry, Emeline, Morris, and Charles with a featherbed and furniture. I revoke all Deeds of Gift except the one made to my son James for negroes, Sarah, Dick, Dempsey, Lucy, Wilfred, and Willie. I also give to my said son, Lucinda and Charles. My son James is to pay all my debts. My grandson James G. Martin and my son James Glasgow to be my executors. This 11 Nov 1819. Wit: E. Anderson, P. Whyte (White), C.J. Glasgow, and M. Whyte (White). Apr Term 1820.

Page 409   Will of Benjamin Wilkinson, deceased, of Davidson County.
June 13, 1820   To my wife Polly Wilkinson all my real and personal property during her natural life and if anything is left should be equally divided among my five children, Delilah Wilkinson, Lucinda C. Wilkinson, Nancy P. Wilkinson, Benjamin J. Wilkinson,

and Peter Wilkinson. To my son Benjamin J. Wilkinson my Family Bible and other books. To my son Peter Wilkinson books. To Joseph Locket a mulatto apprentice boy of mine $50.00 when he arrives at lawful age. I appoint my wife Polly Wilkinson my executrix. This 7 Jan 1820. Wit: Samuel Scott and Philip Anthony. Apr Term 1820.

Page 409   Will of Daniel Woodard, deceased.
June 14, 1820   To my dear wife Sarah Woodard, if she should live longer than myself, my two negro women Sarah and Silvey to wait on her and maintain her, her ligetime and she shall have the use of the house and furniture that I now live in, and any other property that is hereafter willed to my son Edward Woodard that may be necessary to support her during her life. To my son Pitt Woodard 120 acres of land of the east end of the tract of land that we both live on at this time to be laid off of the east end of said tract by a north and south line to extend across said survey, also to Pitt the following negroes, viz, Jacob, Aggey, Jinney, Sall, Clary, Henry, Alexander, Minerva, Ennos, and Jacob, all of which are now given to Pitt as his own. To my son Edward Woodard all the balance of the tract of land that I now live on including the plantation whereon I now live and containing 200 acres, also the following negroes, viz, Pegg, Isaac, Sarah, Silvey, John, Anderson, Charlotte, Siney, Eliza, and Anzeda, and also other stock of all kind and all the household and kitchen furniture and farming utensils, also he is to have my still and tubs subject in the meantime to the use of his brother Pitt Woodard to still his fruit whenever he may have any to still, also to Edward all my bonds, notes and accounts and all the property that I am owner of that is not yet willed. I appoint my friend Samuel Shannon my executor. This __ of ___ 1820. Apr Term 1820.

Page 411   Will of Andrew McCormac, deceased, of Davidson County.
June 14, 1820   To my daughter Elizabeth Martin $1.00. To my son Moses McCormac $1.00. To my son Andrew McCormac $1.00. To my son Magness McCormac $1.00. To my son George McCormac, and to Richard N. McCormac and my daughter Mary Ann McCormac to them three last named all the land I possess of in the County and State above written including the farm I now live on to be divided in the manner following, to wit, that after my death them three shall each of them choose a man and them three men so choose shall divide said land equally between George McCormac, Richard B. McCormac and Mary Ann McCormac, also give to my daughter Mary Ann now living with me one red cow and calf, two featherbeds and furniture and other items listed. This 20 Jan 1820. Wit: E. Walker, John Tomlin, Sr., and Clement T. Walker. Apr Term 1820.

Page 412   Inventory of estate of Tully Williams, deceased.
June 14, 1820   Several items listed. William S. Gordon, admr. Apr Term 1820.

Page 412   Sale of estate of Joshua Owen, deceased.
June 15, 1820   Sale on Feb 4, 1820. Purchasers, to wit, Mary Owen, Benjamin Bibb, John (illegible), Jabez Owen, Jeptha Moseley, Ira H. Owen, Jacob W. Ramsey, Nathan Owen, Nelson Alford, William Ogilvie, James Butt, James C. Owen, Jacob Bolinger, and Robert Bell. Jabez Owen, admr. Apr Term 1820.

Page 413   Inventory of estate of Mathew Williams, deceased.
June 16, 1820   Taken 26 Apr 18(illegible). Several items listed. Patience Williams, admrx. Apr Term 1820.

Page 413   Inventory of estate of Thomas B. Pipkin, deceased.
June 16, 1820   One bay mare and colt, one sorrel horse, and one bay filly. Philip Pipkin, admr. This Apr 25, 1820. Apr Term 1820.

Page 414   John Simmons, orphans guardian return.
June 16, 1820   Paid for their schooling to William Thompson. Paid to William Thompson for certificate. For the year 1812 William Arant Dr. Apr 6 to the orphans of John Simmons, to pension money barrowed of them. William Arant, guardian. This 24 Apr 1820. Apr Term 1820.

Page 414   Mary Owen, widow's support.
June 16, 1820   We have set apart of Mary Owen, widow and relict of Joshua Owen, deceased, for one years support for herself and family. 800 lbs pork, 25 bushels of

corn and one stock of corn fodder. This 4 Feb 1820. Signed by Henry Cruchlow, John Alford and Jno. Watson, Commissioners. Apr Term 1820.

Page 414   Sale of estate of John Sanders, deceased, of Davidson County.
June 17, 1820   Purchasers, to wit, Lemuel Cannady, Jason Thompson, John McEwin, Willis White, John Corbett, Allen Cotton, Josiah Mullen, Anderson Tucker, William Ray, John Canady, Samuel Fitzhugh, Earl Fitzhugh, John Hathway, Washington Curtis, John Hall, Richard Sutton, Absalom Rodgers, Jeremiah Hunt, Thomas C. Smith, Davis Cobler, George W. Boyd, Thomas Hopper, William Night, William Whitsett, James M. Whitsett, Henry Bateman, and John M(illegible). Absalom Rogers, admr. Apr Term 1820.

Page 415   Inventory of estate of Joshua Owen, deceased.
June 19, 1820   Several items listed including an account of John P. Hill and one against Samuel Bell, one order from Robert C. Reives to Samuel Bell dated Sept 14, 1818, and two notes on James Owen. Jabez Owen, admr. Apr Term 1820.

Page 416   Will of Sarah White, deceased, of Davidson County.
June 19, 1820   The negro man Will which fell to me in the division of my deceased husband Joshua White's estate I give to my son Wilson White. I give the balance of my estate to my surviving children, viz, Dempsey White, Jacob White, Polly Copeland, Elizabeth Harman, Sally White, Wilson White, and Jabez White each one. I appoint my son Wilson White my executor. This 3 July 1819. Wit: Duke W. Sumner and Jacob Dickinson. Jan term 1820.

Page 416   Sale of estate of Benjamin Philips, deceased.
June 20, 1820   Sale taken 1 Feb 1820 also hiring of the negroes of Benjamin Philips, deceased, commenced on 11 Feb 1820 by Joseph Philips, admr., with will annexed. Several items listed including a collection of R.W. Green, a bill on Pleasant Tally, on Thomas Porter, on Jacob Robertson, on E.M. Symms, on Eli Mills, on Stump & Cox, on Simon Johnson, Lewis Joslin, on Michael Waggoner, William Philips (Sheriff of Hickman), an execution in favor Benjamin Philips against Robert and Thomas Green, on N.H. Robertson, a due bill on Exum P. Sumner, on William Gower, Francis Owen, Samuel Johnson, Mrs. King, and Davis Cobler. Purchasers of items listed, viz, Presley Sheppard, Duncan Robertson, J.R. Bosley, Jesse Wharton, D. Robertson, T.C. Bradshaw, T.S. Williamson, Henry Wade, James Ridley, E. Smith, Jno. S. Williamson, William Bosworth, Joseph Sewell, C. Stump, Ch. D. McLain, David Hunter, Samuel Stull, Olive Weeks, H.F. Newel, Solomon Clark, Robert Goodlet, Thomas Shannon, Beal Bosley, Terry Sadler, Robert Smiley, Robert Williams, Robert Lazenberry, Isaac Watkins, Joseph Philips, Peyton Robertson, Richard Garrett, Fred Taylor, Benjamin Hyde, David McGavock, Richard Johnson, Richard Hyde, John Shute, James Ridley, Robert Gillespie, Isaac Watkins, Thomas Hickman, Thomas Claiborne, William Temple, C. McCarahan, D.W. Sumner, Josiah Mullens, Andrew Hynes, Lavinia Beck, J.N. Manifee, L. Warfield, B. McKernan, F. Harwell, Thomas Martin, J.H. Smith, R. Goodlett, J. Fowlks, W. Hamilton, M. Barrow, D. Hunter, T. Maxwell, A. Tucker, J. Jewell, (illegible) Shepard, T.L. Lockhart, E.P. Sumner, J. Hooper, N. Williams, W. Munty, J. Tilman, Dr. Shelby, J. Irwin, T. Edington, R. Briggs, J. Leak, W. Knight, T. Ramsey, J. McN. Robertson, A. Porter, Spencer Loving, A. Page, Oakley Jones, T. Huggins, Craven Jackson, Martin Smith, M. Porter, Boyd McNairy, J. Shelby, J. Corfman, W.L. Willis, R. Oldham, Z. Waters, J. Dean, and D.H. Dunham. This 23 Apr Term 1820. Joseph Philips, admr. Apr Term 1820. (a very long list)

Page 421   Noncupative Will of Benjamin Philips, deceased.
June 23, 1820   On motion of John S. Williamson in favor of Benjamin F. Williamson his infant son, to have the Last Will of Benjamin Philips altered by a noncupative will in favor of said Benjamin F. giving of him two negroes to be selected by the executor of the same description that is given to John S. Williamson's other child by the said Will of Benjamin Philip who died the (blank) day of January 1820 and it being proven by Martha A. Williams and Olive Weeks all parties being present that the deceased at his own residence and where he had resided many years in Davidson County a few days before his death and in his last sickness made his noncupative will in their presence giving slaves as above stated to said Benjamin F. Williamson of the same description as given to his sister by his testators written will and all other legal request being proven to the satisfaction of the Court that said will was duly made, the Court orderd that said will stand of record in favor of said B.F. Williamson that he have of the state of Benjamin P(Philips), deceased, his grandfather two

slaves given to said Ben. F.'s sister in Ben. F.'s will and that Jos. Philips execute this will he being executor to the written will of Benjamin Philips. Apr Term 1820.

Page 421   Inventory of estate of Daniel Young, deceased.
June 23, 1820   Several items listed including notes on Jeremiah Williams, William Coltharp, John L. Young, Joseph Porter, Oliver E. Porter, Whitmill Harrington, William Caldwell, Henry Boner, Cornelius (illegible), Benjamin Hyde, Vincent Carney, John Lanier, Michael Waggoner, More & Son, James Sims, Joseph T. Elliston, Doctor Newman, and Doctor Roanes. Hardy L. Bryan, admr. Other named listed, viz, Alexander Luster, John Peoples, John McElroy, and John Blair. An execution against Stephen Stuberfield, William Shaw, Joseph Love, Zinis Tate, Nicholas Tulls, George Cagle, Sr., and David Wells. Apr Term 1820.

Page 422   Personal estate divided of Zachariah Stull, deceased.
June 23, 1820   The division of the personal property of Zachariah Stull, deceased, between the widow and heirs of said deceased. We have proceeded to divide said property, to wit, To Nancy Stull, widow, negroes, viz, Piety, Easther and Memory. To Samuel Stull negroes, viz, Jack, Sally and Matilda. To George Stull negroes, viz, Anthony and Mary. Other items divided between Nancy Stull, Samuel and George Stull. This 25 Apr 1820. Signed by Samuel Weakley, D. Vaughn and James H. Gamble, Commissioners.

Page 422   Sale of estate of Arthur White, deceased.
June 24, 1820   Sale on 24 July 1819. Several items listed. Will Temple, admr.
Apr Term 1820.

Page 423   Division of negroes of William T. Lewis, deceased.
June 24, 1820   Negro Lot No. 1 to W.B. Lewis, by Jos. Coleman and R.C. Foster 6 Dec 1816. Negro Lot No. 2 to T.H. Eaton by Jos. Coleman and R.C. Foster 7 Dec 1816. Negro Lot No. 3 to C. Lewis by Jos. Coleman and R.C. Foster 6 Dec 1816. Negro Lot No. 4 to Alfred Balch by Jos. Coleman and R.C. Foster 6 Dec 1816. April Term 1820.

Page 424   Division of estate of William T. Lewis, deceased.
June 26, 1820   Whereas William B. Lewis for himself and as natural guardian for Mary Ann Lewis his infant daughter, and Charlotte Lewis did petition the Court of Pleas and Quarter Sessions for Davidson County to appoint Commissioners to divide the estate of William T. Lewis, deceased, between them. Andrew Jackson, Anthony Foster, JOhn C. McLemore, Thomas Crutcher, and Jenkin Whiteside, appointed Commissioners for that purpose. To William B. Lewis and Mary Ann Lewis his daughter all that part of the tract of land lying near Nashville which lies on the south east side principally of Browns Creek, bordering lands of the heirs of Joel Lewis, deceased, when the road leading from Nashville to Buchanans Mill crosses the same, and where the waters breaks out of the creek at high waters and known as Sandy Hollow to Cumberland River, survey of Thomas Crutcher. Also to William B. Lewis half of lot known in the plan of town of Nashville by Lot No. 8 being that half lying on the Public Aquare and Market Street and bounded by Lot No. 7 including the Nashville Inn, also one fourth of Lot No. 7 of Nashville being that fourth part which belonged to William T. Lewis, deceased, which adjoins Market Street and Lot No. 8 that William B. Lewis and his daughter Mary Ann Lewis to have and to hold, also left to them negroes, viz, Hercules, Lew, Litia, Francis, Emily, Annaca, Lucy, Sally, and Paris and to said Charlotte Lewis which is not set apart to William Bond and Mary Ann his daughter the following, to wit, land bordering Richard Cross, lands belonging to the heirs of Joel Lewis, deceased, middle of Browns Creek, Cumberland River, Willie Barrow, and academy lands, also one fourth part of Lot No. 8 in plan of Nashville which lies between William B. and Mary Ann Lewis' part of said lot and also Lot No. 31 in Nashville. We also allott to Charlotte Lewis, viz, Sam, Filly, Margaret, George, Kitty, Roy, (illegible), Dealy, Nann, Lee, and Hannah. This 26 Apr 1820. Signed by Andrew Jackson, A. Foster and Thomas Crutcher, Commissioners. Apr Term 1820.

Page 426   Division of real estate of Henson Hardy, deceased, of Davidson
June 28, 1820   County. To divide part of the one half of Lot No. 69 in town of Nashville which said Hardy owned at his death into six lots or parcels of ground. Nancy now Mrs. Fly drew Lot No. 1 which begins on the north east corner of Craven Jackson's lot and Jno. Moore's line to Broadway, which includes a stable and another small house. Mary Ann

drew Lot No. 2 which begins at north east corner of Lot No. 1, to Broadway, and to Moore's line. Elizabeth drew Lot No. 3 which begins at north east corner of Lot No. 2 and borders Moore's line, including a small cedar log stable. William drew Lot No. 4 which begins at the south east corner of Jno. Moore's lot on Cherry Street, and borders Lot No. 3, including a stone shop. George Washington drew Lot No. 5 which begins on the south east corner of Lot No. 4 on Cherry Street, to Lot No. 3 and Lot No. 4, including the greater part of a red frame house. Rebecca drew Lot No. 6 which begins on the south east corner of Lot No. 5 on Cherry Street, joins Lot No. 3 and Lot No. 5, including a stone and brick smokehouse and one of the back kitchens. The rest of the lot owned by said deceased at his death having been laid off by a jury as dower to the widow. This 18 April 1820. Signed by W.B. Lewis, Duncan Robertson, J.T. Elliston, and Will Lytle. Apr Term 1820.

Page 427   Elizabeth Hardy, of Davidson County, widow's dower.
June 29, 1820   We, the jury, met to lay off and set apart to Elizabeth Hardy, widow of Henson Hardy, deceased, her dower out of Lot No. 69 in the town of Nashville, beginning at said lot at the intersection of Cherry and Broad Streets, thence with Cherry Street 40 feet, thence at right angles with Cherry Street and parallel with Broad Street 80 feet, thence 40 feet to Broad Street, thence 80 feet to beginning. Including the Mansion house and kitchen on said Lot No. 69, and put into her possession of the same her dower in the lot in Columbia yet to be ascertained. This 11 Feb 1820. Signed by Thomas Deadrick, J.D. Miller, George Crockett, J.H. Smith, S. Tilford, Will Lytle, A.W. Johnson, J.G. Martin, John Baird, Thomas Hill, R. Buchanan, and John Price, Commissioners. Apr Term 1820.

Page 427   Settlement of estate of Isaac Battle, deceased, of Davidson
June 30, 1820   County, with the executors. Allowed the widow $347.44 and also $48.03¼, leaving a balance infavor of the orphans $2892.67½. Executors are chargeable with the hire of the negroes belonging to said orphans $587.31½ also for rent of lands belonging to the said orphans, also other items. This 28 Apr 1820. William H. Nance and Thomas Williamson, Esquires, to settle with William Anthony and Nathan Stancil, executors.

Page 428   Division of personal property of estate of Aquilla Carmack,
June 30, 1820   deceased. We have proceeded to divide the personal estate of Aquilla Carmack, deceased, among his several heirs, viz, To Daniel Carmack negroes, Dol, Tim, Sarah, and Nelly, and he paying to his brother Samuel $220.00. To William Carmack negroes, Linson, Fanny and Amy, and he, William, paying to his brother Samuel Cormack $15.00. To Samuel Carmack allotted negro woman Hannah and her two children Mary and Tom. This 31 Jan 1820. Signed by M.C. Dunn, William Black, Jesse Maxwell, and Thomas Edmmiston. Apr Term 1820.

Page 428   Sale of estate of leston Temple, deceased.
June 30, 1820   Sept 30, 1819, sales by auction of Robertson & Curry. Signed by Will Temple, executor. Apr term 1820.

Page 429   Settlement of estate of John Pugh, deceased.
June 30, 1820   Made with Solomon Clark, admr. Found in the hands of said Clark money collected $88.00 and for the hire of a negro girl $20.00, total $108.00 and which he is to pay over to the guardian of the following heirs, to wit, to the guardian of John Pugh $12.25, to Sally Pugh's guardian $28.25, to Polly Pugh's guardian $36.46, to Hannah Pugh's guardian $30.87. We also find that Betsey Pugh widow of John Pugh, deceased, is indebted to the estate for goods &c purchased at the sale and for hire of a negro girl up to 1 Jan 1820 $300.00, which is divided among the following heirs or their guardians, to wit, To Jnoathan Pugh $75.00, to Samuel Pugh $75.00, Hampton Pugh $75.00, and Isaac G. Pugh $75.00. This 27 April 1820. Signed by E. Hewitt and Jno. Harding. Apr Term 1820.

Page 429   Wilmouth Bishop, minor orphan.
July 3, 1820   Settlement with Edward D. Hobbs, guardian. In account with Miss Wilmouth Bishop, received her portion of the personal estate of Edward Hobbs, deceased, $141.00 and interest of $64.00, received a negro boy named Jeffrey and hire of said negro after he was 10 years old until 1819, total $345.00. Several expenses paid in Virginia her portion of boarding and going to school for 8 months. We, Alpha Kingsley and John P. Erwin, two of the persons appointed to settle with Edward D. Hobbs, guardian. This 19 Feb 1820. Apr Term 1820.

Page 430   Sale of estate of David Pulley, deceased.
July 3, 1820   Oct 6, 1819. List of the property of David Pulley, deceased, by
D. Vaughn, admr. Persons named as purchasers, to wit, George W. Boyd, William M. Hinton, John Kennell, John McGavock, R.A. Higginbotham, David Vaughn, Abraham Smith, Tabitha Ray, Samuel Weakley, Hezekiah Manifee, Silas M. Morris, Edmond Lanier, Andrew Smith, James Clemens, William Pulley, Samuel F. Green, Jabez White, and Robert Stuart. Apr Term 1820.

Page 430   William H. and Jesse H. Philips, minor orphans guardian return.
July 3, 1820   Made with Mathew Barrow, guardian, reports that he has rented the plantation and distillery whereon said Benjamin Philips formerly lived to James Ridley. This Apr 28, 1820. Apr Term 1820.

Page 431   Jane Fletcher, her dower &c.
July 4, 1820   Met to allot and set apart to Nelson Gillespie and Jane Gillespie in right of said Jane his wife, her dower in Lot No. 153 in the town of Nashville, together with the house thereon. Jane Gillespie who was widow of James H. Fletcher. The said lot borders Whyte's line, Spruce Street, and parallel with Broad Street. This 18 Mar 1820. Signed by Josiah Nichol, Isaac Sitler, Richard B. Owen, R. Farquharson, Jno. Nichol, E. Pritchett, David Irwin, R. Buchanan, Thomas Ramsey, Will Lytle, Thomas Deadrick, and S.V.D. Stout, Jurors. Apr Term 1820.

Page 431   Isaac Basye, minor orphan guardian return.
July 4, 1820   To Francis Basye, guardian, Aug 25, 1817. For schooling, boarding and clothing $169.68 3/4. Cr. by Charles hire $30.50, also Doctor for Charles.
Nancy Basye, minor orphan, guardian return to Francis Basye, guardian, Aug 25, 1817. For clothing Harry also boarding and clothing, total $158.00. Francis (her X mark) Basye. Apr Term 1820.

Page 432   Settlement of estate of John Nichols, deceased.
July 4, 1820   Made with John Nichols, admr. persons listed, to wit, R. Fainbrough, James Trimble, Young (Sheriff), Cooper receipt, McChesney account, Doctor Newman's account, J. Hinton's account, R. Weakley, David Parker, Thomas Washington, Cocks (Sheriff) receipt, Goodall receipt, Nathan Ewing, Lewis White's account tombstone, Peter Bass, Baiker taxes, Garrett's receipt, Everton's note, William Lytle, Napier note transferred to Lytle, Basilla Toller, Goodall & Young's receipt, James Trimble, John Nichols, and Robert Foster. Contra. received of Baley Butler, Joseph Enxplett, Bazilla Talors, and James Martin. This 29 Apr 1820. Signed by J.P. Erwin and Stephen Cantrell. Apr Term 1820.

Page 433   Sale of estate of Joshua White, deceased.
July 5, 1820   Aug 21, 1818. Purchasers, to wit, William White, Wilson White, Samuel Copeland, Jabez White, George Wharton, William H. Hamblin, Jacob Dickinson, Dempsey White, Jeremiah Saddler, Sally Sumner, James McGavock, Isaac Clemons, Matthew P. Walker, Exum P. Sumner, Ebenezer McCance, John Dickson, Joseph Philips, James Deen, Rodney Earhart, Langhorn Scruggs, Benjamin Branch, David Hunter, and Wilson White purchased the cloths of Joshua White, deceased, $1.00. Jabez White and Wilson White, admrs. Apr Term 1820.

Page 434   Robert and Elizabeth Evans, deceased.
July 6, 1820   Land divided. Plat on page 434. Heirs of Elizabeth Evans, 61 acres; Lucy Evans, dower for $19\frac{1}{2}$ acres; No. 1 for Lucinda Evans $15\frac{1}{2}$ acres; No. 2 Nancy Evans $5\frac{1}{2}$ acres; No. 3 Patsey Evans $5\frac{1}{4}$ acres; No. 4 Betsey Evans $5\frac{1}{4}$ acres; and No. 5 Salley Evans $5\frac{1}{4}$ acres. Land on south side of Harpeth River. This 14 Jan 1820. Signed by Jno. Davis, D.S., Thomas Lofton, Eldridge Newsom, David Wrenn, William Wrenn, and Jno. Harwood. Before William H. Shelton, J.P. Apr Term 1820.

Page 436   James Camp's orphans, settlement.
July 6, 1820   Made with their guardian. Several items listed including paid D. Robertson for books, Mrs. Camp for the children, sundries purchased at Thomas Hills, paid Doctor A.G. Goodlett, paid Mr. Martin's bill, sundries at J. Porter, paid Shannon & McClellan's account, also D. McIntoshe's account. In account with Thomas H. Fletcher, R.C. Foster, Jr., N. Peck, H. Cromer, Thomas Childress, Jas. Tilford, J. McNairy, R.B. Sappington,

R.B. Sappington, Benning & Hills, R. McFarland, E. Brookshire, J. Garner, J.L. Allen, and L. Temple. Note on W.L. Hannums. This 20 Apr 1820. Signed by J.P. Erwin, W.B. Lewis and Thomas H. Fletcher. Apr Term 1820.

Page 439   Andrew Jackson of William Donelson, Covenant.
July 19, 1820   I, William Donelson, bind myself &c to convey unto Andrew Jackson when called on for undivided half of the 640 acres of land originally granted by the State of North Carolina to Hugh Hays, lying on the south side of Cumberland adjoining the land on the north whereon said Andrew now lives and known by the name of Hugh Hays Preemption which said tract of 640 acres was bought by me and Samuel Donelson in his lifetime from said Hugh Hays. This 11 Dec 1806. Test: Jno. Coffee. July Term 1820.

Page 440-441   Missing.

Page 442   After a settlement with each heir, we find and allot to each of
July 28, 1820   the following, viz, No. 1 to James Hamilton negro Harry, and also in the notes we pay him his dividend, Lot No. 2 to John B. Hamilton his dividend, Lot No. 3 to George W. and Jane G. Charlton negro Sterling, Lot No. 4 to George F. Hamilton negro Peter, No. 5 to Milberry Hamilton negroes Littleton and Maria, Lot No. 6 to Hannah P. Hamilton receives Reuben and Alfred, and No. 7 to Mary B. Hamilton receives Milly, Harriett and Milly the younger. This July 28, 1820. Signed by William Hall, James Carter, John Gowen and Z. Noell. July Term 1820.

Page 442   Settlement of estate of Henson Hardy, deceased.
Aug 24, 1820   Nashville, Apr 29, 1820. To Elizabeth Hardy paid to Thomas S. King, A.M. Wade, Thomas Sewel, Thomas Norton, Thomas Rutherford, Jno. Newman, and (illegible) Hunt. Received cash of James Goodlett, Richard Owen, John Rains, Thomas Everett, Thomas Claiborne, Bignal Crook, W. Barrow, William Hayes, and Mrs. Windell. Paid to Pritchet, R. Dotson, David Cobler, B. Stanley, J.B. Houston for coffin, James Halley, Jacob Shafer, Caleb McGraw for stone wall, John Blurton, Jas. D. Mills, F. Robertson, and A. Rodgers for schooling children. Estate Dr. to boarding and clothing five children four years and six months each $60.00 per year. To Dr. one child before her marriage two years and six months. Amount due the administrator $1128.00. Signed by R.C. Foster and W. Barrow. July Term 1820.

Page 443   Sale of estate of Littleton Green, deceased.
Aug 24, 1820   Purchasers, to wit, Balser Huffman, Freeman Abernathy, Thomas Edington, James Green, Freeman Fry, Truman Fry, Felix Demumbry, D.P. Davis, Rebecca Green, Charles Cagle, Thomas Morris, Richard Lester, and Jacob Cagle. Nancy Green, exrx. July Term 1820.

Page 444   Settlement of estate of John Philips, deceased.
Aug 25, 1820   Made with Elisha Williams, admr. Persons listed, to wit, William Jackson's note, R.B. Curry's account, vouchers on J.B. Houston, John Elliston, Doctor Roanes, Doctor Maxey, Lawyer Crabb, Berryhill & McKees, Attorney Foster, and Thomas H. Fletcher. Signed by D.A. Dunham, George Shall, and Stephen Cantrell. July Term 1820.

Page 445   Settlement of estate of Reuben Westmoreland, deceased.
Aug 25, 1820   Made with Tilmon R. Daniel, admr. Paid to Jesse Wharton, McLean, Joseph T. Elliston, McNairy & Shelby, William Howlett, Thomas Shackleford, David Abernathy, James Perry, taxes on land in Giles County, Richard Hyde, Enoch Kennedy, Nathan Ewing, John Dismukes, Dixon & Shelton, John Abernathy, Josiah F. Williams' taxes Davidson County, Elias F. Rape for tuition of three children for six months, Jos. Scales, E.H. Foster, E.J. Porter for coffin, and H. Crabb. To note on Joel Childress, John Anderson, William Welch, Henry Adams, Elisha Riddle, Tilmon R. Daniel, John Erwin, Mr. Porter, Mr. Brown, Nathaniel Curtis, Christopher Metcalf, Jesse Wharton, Thomas Shackleford, Jeremiah Allen, Mrs. William L. Yarborough, and John Hall. This July 20, 1820. Signed by Alpha Kingsley, J.P. and D.A. Dunham. July Term 1820.

Page 446   Settlement of estate of Stephen Lock, deceased.
Aug 26, 1820   Made with Rebecca Lock, executrix. Several vouchers listed. Paid Richard Smith's voucher, William Faulkner, Saunders & Chandler, Jesse W. Grizzard,

Jesse Clement, James Carter, Francis Hamilton, and John Bruce. Balance in the hands of the executrix $103.66 3/4. This July 24, 1820. Signed by William Hall and James Mulherrin. July Term 1820.

Page 447   Nancy H. Washington's guardian settlement.
Aug 28, 1820   Thomas Everett, guardian. In account with Nancy H. Washington.
Received William Goodwin, A. Redmond, and Bass & Spence. Contra paid E. Marshall, T. Edwards, J. Litton, C. Stone, W. Stoddard, Boone & Hayes, L.H. Simms, Mrs. McWhirter, L.H. Sims for board and schooling, and N. Ewing. Balance due by T.H. Everett $519.98. This 31 May 1820. Signed by J.P. Erwin and G. Wilson. July Term 1820.

Page 447   Grey Washington, guardian settlement.
Aug 28, 1820   Made with Thomas H. Everett, guardian. Paid L.H. Simms pr voucher. This 31 May 1820. Signed by J.P. Erwin and G. Wilson. July Term 1820.

Page 448   Settlement of estate of Isaac Edwards, deceased, of Davidson
Aug 28, 1820   July 28, 1820, made with Godfrey Shelton, admr. Found that a former settlement returned Jan term 1818 the estate of said Isaac Edwards, deceased, to be $82.08 3/4 plus interest of $7.12. Vouchers on Richard Moore, N. Ewing, Thomas Mitchel, and said Shelton. Signed by Benajah Gray, J.P. and Cary Felts, J.P. July Term 1820.

Page 448   Settlement of estate of John Hancock, deceased.
Aug 28, 1820   Made with John New, executor. Received from E.H. Foster, from judgement VS Metcalf, Jos. Nichols & Co., R.C. Foster, and J. & R. Woods. Amount paid Doctor Roberts and C(illegible). Balance due $500.68. Signed by J.P. Erwin and Alpha Kingsley. July Term 1820.

Page 449   Inventory of estate of William Donelson, Sr., deceased.
Aug 29, 1820   A list of 48 negroes and description on each, also other items listed. Bonds, debts and notes on the following, to wit, Beverly Williams, John Ore, William and George Boyd, Zachariah Payne, Purtle & More & Purtle, John Deaderick, Azariah Bruice, Thomas Overton, Michael Gleaves, Col. George Smith, William Bonds & Mathew Rice, Reuben Payne, William P. Anderson, John Dismukes, Elizabeth Donelson, Benjamin Butterworth, Stokeley D. Hayes, Ezekiel Young, Francis McCoy, Shadrick Jones, Francis Rice, John Jennings, John McNice, Edward Ward, Greenwood Payne, Robert Bates, David Dunn, Jeremiah Hampton, Thomas G. Bradford, Isaac Hudson, Robert Booth, William Arrant, William Campbell, John Bosley, Stephen C. McDaniel, Marshall B. Mumford, Walter Kible, Nancy Davis, Abimelech Herrin, Joseph Wise, James M. Lewis, Timothy Demumbra, Jesse Cartwright, and John Lyons. Notes on the deceased one third John Donelson, one third John Peyton, one third the notes in the hands of John Donelson. Also notes &c on Rawley & Samuel Morgan to John and William Donelson, John Fletcher, Cary Morgan, Travis C. Nash, and John P. Wiggins. Debts desperate, viz, David Nandrew, Robert Hays, John P. Wiggins, Peter Edwards, Pines Ingrum, William Black, Hans Trusty, Peyton Martow, Jacob McDermit, William Welch, Hugh and William Gibbs, and Thomas H. Fletcher. Several other items listed. July 21, 1820. Severn Donelson, executor. July Term 1820.

Page 452   Supplementary inventory of estate of John Childress, deceased.
Aug 30, 1820   Three notes given by Sterling & Eldridge Roberts, total $7665.00.
July 27, 1820. Samuel B. Marshall, admr. July Term 1820.

Page 452   Settlement of estate of John Fielder, deceased, of Davidson
Aug 31, 1820   County, made with John L. Fielder, executor. Found the whole amount of the estate to be $933.25¼. Legal vouchers amount of $97.03 3/4. Balance in favor of the legatees $836.21⅛. July 17, 1820. Signed by Thomas Williamson, J.P. and William H. Nance, J.P. July Term 1820.

Page 452   Will of John Bowyer, deceased, of Davidson County.
Aug 31, 1820   Jan 14, 1820. To my beloved wife Hannah Bowyer all my real estate, the tract of land whereon she now lives containing 125 acres, also my stock of horses, cattle, hogs &c also the household and kitchen furniture. I give unto my beloved wife not forgetting my children as I thing I have done as much for them as I am able to do and I do appoint my beloved wife Hannah Bowyer my executrix. Wit: William Arrant, William

Anderson and David G. Thompson. July Term 1820.

Page 453   Inventory of estate of Foster Sayre, deceased, who died on 4 July
Aug 31, 1820   1820. Persons listed, to wit, Ilai Metcalf, J. Fisher, Patton
Anderson, Leston Temple, Jos. Coleman, Francis McKoy, Thomas Hickman, B. Randolph, John
Young, R.B. Sappington, Williamson Adams, C.D. McClain, Benjamin Patterson, H. Langford,
Brown & Foster, E.S. Hall, J. McLean, and J.L. Allen. Balance in favor of the estate in the
hands of Alexander Richardson $231.37. Several negroes listed and also other items. Signed
by Samuel Seay, admr. July Term 1820.

Page 454   Sale of estate of Stephen Spain, deceased.
Aug 31, 1820   Auction July 25, 1820, Stephen Cantrell, admr. Several items
listed including one silver cased watch. Signed by Robertson & Curry, auctioneers. July
Term 1820.

Page 454   Inventory of estate of Stephen Spain, deceased.
Sept 1, 1820   Stephen Cantrell, admr. Aug 11, 1818, by cash received on
Gray's note, and other items listed. July Term 1820.

Page 454   Will of William Davis, deceased, of Davidson County.
Sept 1, 1820   To my wife Mrs. Sarah Davis all the estate and property I own or
have right to, real, personal or mixed subject to the following legacy, to wit, the sum of
$2000.00 which I bequeath to my daughter Mrs. Anne Bass to be paid as soon as Mrs. Davis
can raise the money from my estate allowing to Mrs. Bass legal interest from my death until
the legacy is paid. In case Mrs. Davis should marry after my death, it is my desire that my
estate be divided equally between herself and my children, Mrs. Bass, Mrs. Abram Wright,
Mrs. Giles Harding and Mrs. John Goodman. Should my wife Mrs. Davis never marry, the
first clause in my will shall not be restricted, except so far as respects Mrs. Bass, all the
estate she received from me shall dispose of as she thinks fit by will or otherwise. I appoint
my wife Mrs. Davis sole executrix. This 24 Mar 1820. Wit: Ephraim H. Foster, John S. Topp
and William L. Willis. July Term 1820.

Page 455   Inventory of estate of Andrew McCormack, Sr., deceased.
Sept 2, 1820   Taken Feb 1, 1820. Several items listed including the property
given to his daughter Mary Anne as designated in the will is not named in his inventory. C.L.
Byrd, executor. July Term 1820.

Page 456   Sale of estate of Thomas B. Pipkin, deceased.
Sept 4, 1820   Made June 30, 1820. Lot No. 1 Bay mare and colt - Philip
Pipkin $100.00. No. 2 a sorrel filly - Philip Pipkin $100.00. No. 3 a two year old filly -
Philip Pipkin $110.00. Total $310.00. Philip Pipkin, admr. July Term 1820.

Page 456   Sale of estate of John Lester, deceased.
Sept 4, 1820   Made by Alexander Lester, admr. Several items sold to the
following persons, to wit, Susan Lester, John Lanier, William Parker, Kitury Lester, Richard
Lester, Alexander Lester, D.P. Davis, and R.B. Sappington.

Page 456   Settlement of estate of Nathan Patterson, deceased, of Davidson
Sept 4, 1820   County, made with Matthew Patterson, admr. Found the estate
to be $488.39, also vouchers. Signed by Thomas Williamson, J.P. and A. Walker, J.P. July
Term 1820.

Page 457   Will of Emila Drake, deceased. (Female)
Sept 4, 1820   To my brother Logan Drake my bed and all Mary's increase, Mary
being my slave for life. To my brother-in-law Freeman Abernathy of Davidson County my
slave named Mary for life. I also appoint Freeman Abernathy, sole executrix. This 2 June
1820. Signed by Jonathan Drake and Elizabeth Drake. July Term 1820.

Page 458   Inventory of estate of Benjamin Wilkinson, deceased.
Sept 4, 1820   Several negroes named. Lot No. 113 in said town $125.00.
Robert W. Green's bond, J.B. Houston's note, Philip Anthony's note, and notes on Thomas and
William Hamilton, Stamp & Cox's bond, Washington Perkins a Notary Public of Davidson

County, account on Archar Duel. Books willed to Benjamin J. Wilkinson and one large Bible, books willed to Peter Wilkinson. Signed by Polly Wilkinson, executrix. 24 July 1820. July Term 1820.

Page 459   Inventory of estate of William Priestley, deceased.
Sept 5, 1820   Several items listed including a horse that was long called his, he left for the use of his youngest brother. The bill for some of his cloths I have paid since his departure. He consigned to Thomas Hill of this place goods to the amount of $(blank). The remainder of which was $5423.36 as Mr. Hill's account sets forth put into the hands of General William Carroll as William's friend, who is was supposed might be accountable for the prices of those goods at Orleans. Thomas Fletcher claims a balance about $120.00, I think and Mr. Drury for fourteen. James Priestley, admr. July Term 1820.

Page 460   Sale of estate of Daniel Young, deceased.
Sept 5, 1820   Made 14 July 1820. Purchasers, viz, Hardy S. Bryan, John L. Young, Freeman Fry, John Criddle, the widow, William McLaurence, Norvel H. Robertson, Lucy Young, Henry Boner, Alexander Ray, Samuel Campbell, Maxmillian Redding, Charles Cale, William Homes, Sally Strawthers, C.Y. Cooper, Lewis Bryan, Joseph Jewel, one Bible to Hardy S. Bryan for $3.18 3/4, Drury Scruggs, John Lucas, Mrs. Patterson, Joseph Hooper, Mrs. Ray, and George Waggoner. Hardy S. Bryan, admr. July Term 1820.

Page 461   Sale of estate of Tully Williams, deceased.
Sept 6, 1820   Sold on 3 June 1820. Purchasers, viz, John Gibbs, Cyntha Williams, William S. Gordon, Samuel Miles, Jr., William Simmons, Charles Cagle, Emanuel Hunter, James Lewis, James Sanders, Charles Campbell, James Durin, and Hardy Miles. William Gordon, admr. July Term 1820.

Page 462   Ephraim Drake, heirs guardian return for year 1819.
Sept 6, 1820   The hire of negro boy Frank, hire of Frank is doubled the collection. Hire of Eve and Peter. William J. Drake, guardian to the heirs. July 24, 1820. July Term 1820.

Page 462   Polly, Sally, Hannah and Hampton Pugh, orphans guardian return.
Sept 6, 1820   Made with Solomon Clark, guardian to Polly Pugh, minor 1819. Solomon Clark, guardian to Sally Pugh, minor, 1819. Solomon Clark guardian to Hannah Pugh, minor, 1819. Solomon Clark guardian to Hampton Pugh, minor, 1819. July Term 1820.

Page 463   John and Isaac G. Pugh, orphans guardian return.
Sept 7, 1820   John Davis guardian to John Pugh, minor, 1819. Also John Davis guardian to isaac G. Pugh, minor, 1819. Interest now in the hands of Betsey Pugh, mother of said minors, $75.00 and $250.00. Paid Betsey Pugh for boarding and clothing $25.00. July Term 1820.

Page 463   Settlement of estate of Thomas Dillon, deceased.
Sept 4, 1820   Account with James Austin, admr. Persons listed, to wit, R. McGavock, J.M. Lewis, Thomas Dillon, David Shannon, Nathan Ewing, John Mayes, William Kelly attorney in Giles County, George Keeling, A.V. Brown, Thomas Cain, George Bernard, Gideon Pillers, P.M. Miller of Knox County, Hawood Bennet, William Tyrells, John Crabbs, John Coleman, Charles R. Dillon, John Bouldins, Lewis Spiece, Willie(s) Featherstone, Joseph Watkins, in 1815 put into the hands of William A. Allen of Prince Edward County, Virginia to be delivered unto James Austin, admr of Thomas Dillon. James Austin, admr. July 22, 1820. Alpha Kingsley, J.P. and Jno. P. Erwin, J.P. July Term 1820.

Page 465   Settlement of estate of Stephen Spain, deceased.
Sept 7, 1820   Stephen Cantrell, admr. Cash paid to Houston, Lintz, Dr. McNairy & Co. Cash paid to H. Petway. This 28 July 1820. J.P. Erwin and D.A. Dunham, Commissioners. July Term 1820.

Page 465   Will of Lewis Demoss, deceased, of Davidson County.
Nov 10, 1820   To my beloved wife Hannah my plantation or tract of land whereon I now live together with the grist mills attached thereto also all the plantation or farming tools and all the household and kitchen furniture not to be removed nor disturbed also

77

my wagon and cart and other items including negroes, to my two youngest sons Shelton T. Demoss and William L. Demoss benefits of the work hands , land and mills as far as they may agree in taking care of the same for her support all she makes on the farm to dispose of as she thinks proper, also to my wife land I bought of Bryant Boon lying on west side of the river together with all the property given to her, negroes excepted to be divided between my two youngest sons Shelton T. Demoss and William L. Demoss, and I bequeath unto my two sons Abraham Demoss and JOhn Demoss the benefit of the labor of my two negroes, Jack and Hardy. During the life of my wife Hannah excepted one month in each year they and one of the negroes fellows given to my wife is to work for my son James Demoss. All stock of horses, cattle, hogs and sheep not already given to my wife to my four children, Delila Taylor, Abraham Demoss, John Demoss and Sally Driver excepting two young steers my son James Demoss is to have four oxen also James to have his bread corn from the mill during his mother's life. I give what money is due me, after paying Bryant Boon for the land I bought of him, to my seven children and my beloved wife Hannah to be equally divided. My brother James Demoss' land borders my land also said Taylor. To my grand daughter Lucinda Taylor $100.00 and a horse or mare and cloths. To my grand daughter Kitty Taylor a good horse or mare worth $60.00 with saddle and bridle, and also cloths. To John William Demoss my grandson, my riding saddle and sword and no more. To my grandson James L. Demoss one pistol and a heifer. All the negroes, after the death of my wife to be equally divided. This 8 Sept 1820. Wit: Silas Dillahunty, Bryant Boon and William B. Rutland. Oct Term 1820.

Page 467   John Watson of Stephen Spain's heirs, a Power of Attorney.
Nov 13, 1820   We, William Spain, Henry Spain, John Spain, Cad L. Spain, and Francis E. Spain, brothers and heirs to a whole share each of the estate of Stephen Spain, deceased, and Spencer Spain son of Richard Spain, deceased, who was a brother of the said Stephen Spain, deceased, and is heir to a half share of the estate and Thomas W. Eckles who intermarried with Piety Spain a daughter of the said Richard Spain, deceased, and is entitled to the other half share and John B. Spain the admr of Daniel Spain, who was a brother of Stephen Spain, deceased, of the County of Dinwiddie, Virginia. I appoint John Watson of Williamson County, Tennessee my attorney to recover and receive all the estate of every kind which did belong to Stephen Spain, deceased, who departed this life sometime in the year 1817 in Nashville without having made a disposition of his estate by a will. This 10 Jan 1820. Wit: John F. Smith and Herbert Reise. Dinwiddie County, Virginia, 21 Feb 1820. Davidson County, Tennessee Oct Term 1820.

Page 469   Sale of estate of Daniel Frazor, deceased.
Nov 14, 1820   Purchasers, to wit, Rebecca Frazor, M. Pierce, M.B. Frazor, John Pierce, John M. Dickson, Carter Allen, and Daniel M. Frazor. M.B. Frazor, admr. Oct Term 1820.

Page 469   Inventory of estate of Elijah Earhart, deceased.
Nov 15, 1820   A balance of #1224.49½. Due the estate from Rodney Earhart as he was purchaser of 248 acres of land that was sold by the Sheriff of Davidson County to satisfy a judgement of $217.00 cost $8.40½ at the instance of Matthew Patterson and purchased for $1450.00. This Oct 24, 1820. Oct Term 1820.

Page 469   Will of John Lee, deceased, of Davidson County.
Nov 15, 1820   To my beloved wife Jane Lee all my property during her natural life or widowhood. I also give to my son Tarlton Lee a gray horse called Davy, a sorrel horse colt, also it is my will that there shall be a horse raised for my son Lewis Lee equal to one of them and it is my will that my wife shall give to my daughters that are yet single beds as she shall think proper, viz, Patsey, Betsey, Polly, Nancy, and Thirza. It is my will that at my wife's death or marriage that everything be sold and equally divided among all my children and if either of my children die without an heir that their part be equally divided among the rest of my children. I appoint my beloved wife Jane Lee, my son Henry T. Lee and my son-in-law James R. Stewart as executors. This 21 Aug 1820. Wit: W. Wallace and Braxton Lee. Oct Term 1820.

Page 470   Will of Robert Searcy, deceased, of Nashville.
Nov 15, 1820   To my brother Thomas Searcy my watch if he should survive me, if not I give it to my son Orville. To my daughter Elvira J. my negroes, Lewis and his wife Winney and their increase. To my daughter Susan D. my two negroes Clem and his sister

Grace and her increase. To Elizabeth S. Cantrell daughter of Stephen Cantrell my time piece now in the possession of her mother. To my children, Robert E., Orville H., Elvira J., Susan D., Granville D., William, and James all the balance of my estate to be equally divided among them, except $1000.00 to each of my three youngest sons, Granville D., William and James which I leave them inconsideration of my having educated my other children set of my joint property. They are to each a bed and furniture a piece owned by each of my daughters and such articles as table furniture as I have now in the possession of Mrs. Cantrell and which I hereby give to my said daughters to be equally divided between them. I give to my son Orville my large Bible and which he is not to be charged with that he will let my other children have it occasionally and it is my earnest wish that it may never be sold or transferred out of the family. I appoint Stephen Cantrell, Jr., James W. Sitler, Thomas Crutcher and Jesse Black---, my executors. This 23 Aug 1820. Wit: Edmond Cooper and Ephraim H. Foster and J. Overton. Oct Term 1820.

Page 471   Sale of estate of Foster Sayre, deceased.
Nov 16, 1820   Auction on 2 Sept 1820. Several items listed. Samuel Seay, admr. Oct Term 1820.

Page 472   Sale of estate of John Childress, deceased.
Nov 15, 1820   Auction near Florence, May 18, 1820. Purchasers, to wit, Thomas Childress, Jesse Evans, James Hood, James Hanna, David Brown, James Benham, John Floyd, William Griffin, Patrick Andrew, and J. Coulter. Samuel B. Marshall, admr. Oct Term 1820.

Page 473   Settlement of estate of Robert Cato, deceased, of Davidson County, Oct 27, 1820, to settle with Mary Cato, admrx of Robert Cato, deceased. Several vouchers listed, also negroes. Benajah Gray, J.P. and William H. Nance, Commissioners. Oct Term 1820.
Nov 17, 1820

Page 473   Inventory of estate of Moody Harris, deceased.
Nov 17, 1820   Purchasers, to wit, Moody Harris and Sarah Harris. Signed by James McGavock, admr. Oct Term 1820.

Page 474   Inventory of estate of Foster Sayre, deceased, who died on the 4th June 1820. Persons listed, to wit, Ilai Metclaf, J. Fisher, Patton Anderson, Liston Temple, Joseph Coleman, Francis McCoy, Thomas Hickman, B. Randolph, John Young, Roger B. Sappington, Williamson Adams, C.D. McLean, Benjamin Patterson, H. Langford, Brown & Foster, E.S. Hall, and J.L. Allen. Balance in the hands of Alexander Richardson $231.37, also five negroes. Samuel Seay, admr. Oct Term 1820.
Nov 17, 1820

Page 474   Will of Thomas H. Perkins, Jr., deceased, of Davidson County.
Nov 20, 1820   To my beloved wife Mary N. Perkins all my negroes during her natural life and at her death they are to be equally divided between my niece Leah America Cannon and my nephews William Perkins Cannon and Giles Harden Scales and if either of them dies before they arrive at the years of maturity and after the decease of my beloved wife, my negroes be equally divided between the survivors and my last mentioned nephew Giles Harden Scales, should they both die in their minority my will is that my nephew Giles Harden Scales shall have one half of my negroes, the other half to be equally divided between the balance of my sister Sarah P. Scales' children. To my wife Mary N. Perkins all the residue of my estate both real and personal. I appoint my brother Nicholas Perkins and my brother-in-law Newton Cannon, Robert Scales and Thomas Hardeman, Jr., my executors. This 1 Aug 1820. Wit: Thomas Edmiston and Henry Cruchlow. Oct Term 1820.

Page 475   Inventory of estate of Thomas H. Perkins, Jr., deceased.
Nov 21, 1820   Returned by Robert Scales, acting executor. Several items listed including one Bible and one silver watch. Notes on William Lynch, James Walker, Nicholas Perkins, Dickinson & Cooper, S.H. Laughlin, and R.A Higginbotham. Received on Constant Scales for a note on Thomas L. Trotter, William Wilson, C. Wilson, John D. Edney, C. Pryor, G. Goodlett, and Mr. G. Bradford. Signed by Robert Scales, executor. This 27 Oct 1820. Oct Term 1820.

Page 476   Inventory of estate of Moody Harris, deceased.
Nov 21, 1820   James McGavock returns a negro boy now in the hands of John
Nichols both belonging to the estate of Moody Harris, deceased, also a note on John Nichols.
James McGavock, admr. Oct Term 1820.

Page 476   Settlement of estate of Stephen Lock, deceased.
Nov 22, 1820   Made with Rebecca Lock, admrx. We find on July 24, 1820,
there remained in the hands of the admrix $103.66 3/4, paid by the admrx as pr voucher a
total of $41.75. There remaining in the hands of the admrx $61.91 3/4. Signed by William
Hall and Thomas Williamson, Commissioners. Oct Term 1820.

Page 477   Division of estate of Henson Hardy, deceased, of Davidson
Nov 22, 1820   We, David Moore, William Lytle and Joseph T. Elliston being
appointed to divide the personal estate of Henson Hardy, deceased, among his heirs, finding
seven heirs and five negroes have allotted Lovey to Mrs. Hardy, and Moses to Mich. Fly,
Charles, Sandy and Paul we have allotted to Rebecca Hardy, William Hardy, G.W. Hardy,
Mary Ann Hardy, and Elizabeth Hardy. Mrs. Hardy shall pay to the five children $173.22 and
that said Mich. Fly shall pay the said five heirs $135.72. Oct Term 1820.

Page 477   Inventory of estate of Daniel Woodard, deceased.
Nov 22, 1820   Taken by Samuel Shannon, executor. There are 21 negroes and
several other items listed. This 28 Oct 1820. Oct Term 1820.

Page 478   Thomas Hickman, Sheriff's bond.
Nov 22, 1820   We, Thomas Hickman, Roger B. Sappington, James Mulherrin,
Josiah Horton, John Stump, Daniel Ross, Begnal Crook, and Felix Robertson, all of Davidson
County, are bound unto his Excellency Joseph McMinn, Esquire, Governor, for sum of
$12,500.00 to be paid. This 20 Oct 1818. Condition of this obligation is that Thomas
Hickman is appointed Sheriff of Davidson County. Oct Term 1820.

Page 479   Thomas Hickman, his bond for collection of taxes as Sheriff.
Nov 22, 1820   We, Thomas Hickman, Roger B. Sappington, James Mulherrin,
Josiah Horton, Jno. Stump, Daniel Ross, Bignal Crook, and Felix Robertson, all of Davidson
County, are bound unto his Excellency Joseph McMinn, Esquire, Governor, for $10,000.00 to
be paid. This 20 Oct 1818. Thomas Hickman shall collect taxes.

Page 479   Josiah Horton, Sheriff's bond.
Nov 22, 1820   We, Josiah Horton, William B. Robertson, Joseph W. Horton, Felix
Grundy, Eldridge Newsom, William E. Watkins, Francis Newsom, Thomas Williamson, George
Wharton, William Hall, Silas Dillahunty, and Richard Boyd, all of Davidson County, are bound
unto his Excellency Joseph McMinn, Esquire, Governor, for $12,500.00 to be paid. This 17
Oct 1820. Oct Term 1820.

Page 480   Josiah Horton, his bond for collection of taxes as Sheriff.
Nov 23, 1820   We, Josiah Horton, William B. Robertson, Joseph W. Horton,
William E. Watkins, Francis Newsom, Thomas Williamson, Felix Grundy, Eldridge Newsom,
George Wharton, William Hall, Silas Dillahunt, and Richard Boyd, all of Davidson County, are
bound unto his Excellency Joseph McMinn, Esquire, Governor, for $10,000.00 to be paid. He
is to collect the tazes. Oct Term 1820.

Page 481   Will of William McKey, deceased.
Nov 23, 1820   18 Jan 1820. I appoint John Alford, Sr., and Henry Crutchlow,
my executors. To my beloved wife Elizabeth and for her to have a comfortable support.
Whereas my daughter Nancy are married to Nicholas T. Walker, and my daughter Elizabeth to
Lee Alford, did receive certain property and household furniture from me, it is my desire that
my daughter Sally when she marries or becomes of age for her to receive from my estate like
property and household furniture. To my son Tandy has received from me one horse and
saddle, two cows, one bed and furniture. To my sons John and Martin when they marry or
become of age should receive from my estate the same or the value thereof in some other
property except a horse and saddle my son John has received from me. After my wife's
death it is my desire that all my estate be sold and the money equally divided among my
children. This 18 Jan 1820. If my son Tandy should die before his wife Delila that all his

property that came from my estate to go to his heirs when they become of age. Wit: George W. Alford, Thomas Alford and Nancy N. Alford. Oct Term 1820.

Page 481   Sale of estate of Matthew Williams, deceased.
Nov 24, 1820   July 3, 1820. Purchasers, to wit, Reuben Holt, Jacob Binkley, Adam Binkley, James Darrow, James Lenox, Patience Williams, Gideon Harris, Daniel Darr, William Houston, Hardy Walker, Thomas Harris, James Coon, and Peter Binkley. Patience Williams, admrx. Oct term 1820.

Page 482   Settlement of estate of John Hancock, deceased.
Nov 24, 1820   Made with John New, admr. Balance due by J. New $346.58. Cash for rent of plantation $20.00. Total $386.58. Several vouchers listed. Signed by J.P. Erwin and Alpha Kingsley, J.P. Oct Term 1820.

Page 483   Sale of estate of John Childress, deceased, of Davidson County.
Nov 24, 1820   Purchasers, to wit, Elizabeth Childress, Sterling Robertson, Benjamin Jones, C. Hyde, E. Benoit, James Jackson, and John H. Smith. Robertson & Curry, auctioneers. Samuel B. Marshall, admr and Elizabeth Childress, admrx.

Page 486   James Dean's guardian return.
Nov 27, 1820   Made with Mich. Gleaves, guardian. Paid Nathan Ewing also State and County on 1 Jan 1820 settlement made in full with J. Dean. Total $1731.88. Oct Term 1820. James Dean, a minor orphan.

Page 486   Account of estate of Larkin Clay, deceased.
Nov 27, 1820   Made with Jonathan Clay, executor. Paid cash to Willis for shoes $1.25, also other items listed. This 3 Oct 1820. Oct Term 1820.

Page 487   Settlement of estate of William Merriman, deceased.
Nov 27, 1820   Made with Judith Merriman, admrx. A note on Riley Fletcher. Balance due J. Merriman, admrx $1220.51 3/4. Paid vouchers, viz, Stump & Cox, Stump & King, Allen Knight, Jno. Huffman, Vincent Carney, Thomas Washington, Lewis Earthman, Macey Francis, Isaac Earthman, James Hay's note, John Boyles, Herbert Alley, and Henry Douglas. Other names, viz, Christopher Elmore, John Waggoner for money collected for him in Robertson County by intestate, Lewis Earthman, Ritchey's voucher, Jno. Stump, and William L. Brown. Signed by Joseph Love, J.P. and Thomas Claiborne, J.P. Oct Term 1820.

Page 488   Settlement of estate of James Hodge, deceased, of Davidson
Nov 27, 1820   County, made with Samuel D. Betts, admr. Eleven negroes valued at $4600.00 and debts to $2582.00 which distribute as follows, to Mrs. Nancy Hodge a negro man named Doze valued $798.00; to Betsey Hodge or Mrs. Betts negro man Jacob valued $300.00 and $498.00 money; Polly Hodge, Jacob and Thorton valued $500.00 and $298.00 money; and Alvy Hodge, Will and Ellis valued $450.00 and $348.00 money. This 13 Sept 1820. Signed by R. Hewitt and Jno. Harding. Oct Term 1820.

Page 488   Settlement of estate of James Hanna, deceased, Nashville.
Nov 29, 1820   Oct 18, 1820. We have examined the accounts by Mrs. Hanna, executrix and find that $32,510.36 has been paid to the creditors by her and that $65265.68½ has been received, leaving a balance in her hands in favor of the estate of $32,755.32½, also a schedule of bad debts amounting to $430.43½. Also a schedule of the real estate not heretofore returned. Signed by Alpha Kingsley, J.P. and W. Barrow, J.P. Oct Term 1820.

Page 489   Thomas Thompson, his perpetuated testimony.
Nov 29, 1820   We have proceeded to take the testimony of John Buchanan and James Mulherrin relative to the lines and corners of a 640 acre tract lying on Browns Creek in Davidson County granted to Thomas Thompson by Grant No. (blank), the same being the tract on which said Thomas Thompson now lives after being duly sworn in presence of Jonas Manifee and William Windle, saith that John Buchanan saith he went in company with James Mulherrin, surveyor, and William Ellis and Jason Thompson, chain carriers, to survey Thomas Thompson's Preemption on Browns Creek. Survey borders Jonathan Drake, William Simpson, north of the head of a spring and passing Nicholas Gentry, to the west side of the ridge on which the old trace passed from Nashville to a pond within said survey. Signed by John

Buchanan. This 4 Sept 1820. Thomas Edmiston, J.P. and Thomas Williamson, J.P. Oct Term 1820.

Page 490   Land divided of estate of Thomas Finney, Jr., deceased, of
Nov 30, 1820   Davidson County. Among the several heirs and claimants of the deceased, the tract of land which Thomas Finney, Jr. held as heir of his father Thomas Finney, Sr., and is designated in the division as Lot No. 4 and is part of a 2560 acre tract granted by the State of North Carolina to said Thomas Finney, Sr. We, the Commissioners, divided the land into three divisions of equal quantities yet of equal value and numbered the said divisions as appears in the written plan and report as follows. First, No. 1 to Augustus Moore, it being on Richland Creek of 96 3/4 acres. No. 2 to Thomas J. Finney, borders Lot No. 1, John Johns' line, west bank of a fork of Richland Creek of about 150 acres. No. 3 to William H. Finney, borders No. 2 and containing 70 3/4 acres. This __ day of Oct 1820. Signed by Jno. Harding, Giles Harding and John Johns. Oct Term 1820.

Page 491   Land divided of estate of James Hodge, deceased.
Nov 30, 1820   Divided among his heirs. Nancy Hodge No. 1 - 16 containing $19\frac{1}{4}$ acres. Alva Hodge No. 2 - 9 containing 13 3/4 acres. William Hodge No. 3 - 15 containing $19\frac{1}{4}$ acres. Asa Hodge No. 4 - 12 containing $19\frac{1}{4}$ acres. James Hodge No. 5 - 13 containing $19\frac{1}{4}$ acres. Mary Northern No. 6 - 10 containing 13 3/4 acres. Elizabeth Betts No. 7 - 11 containing $20\frac{1}{4}$ acres. Ann Hodge No. 8 - 14 containing 13 3/4 acres. Signed by D.A. Dunham, Robert Hill, Jno. Harding, Giles Harding, and Johnson Vaughn, Commissioners. Oct Term 1820.

Page 492   Will of Samuel Bell, Sr., deceased, of Davidson County.
Feb 28, 1821   Sept 18, 1819. To my beloved wife Jane Bell possession of my now dwelling house and kitchen and so much of the kitchen furniture and other household items during her natural life, also a negro girl named Betsey during her lifetime then to be disposed of. To my son John Bell the land I have deeded to him on the waters of the Harpeth, his share. To my son-in-law Samuel Scott whose wife is dead the sum of $5.00 besides what I have already given him. To my beloved daughter Jane Orr $40.00 besides what I have already given her. To my beloved daughter Issabella Williamson $5.00 besides what I have already given her. To my beloved daughter Sarah Bell one third of a negro girl Patsey after the decease of my wife Jane Bell besides what I have already given her. To my beloved daughter Martha Bell now single, two thirds of the negro girl Patsey after the decease of my wife, also one horse, saddle and bridle also other items. To my son Samuel Green Bell $20.00 besides what I have already given him. To my beloved son James Bell $35.00 besides what I have already given him. To my son Robert Bell $60.00 besides what I have already given him. To my beloved son Thomas Bell the plantation whereon I now live also other items and he is to provide every necessary for the support of his aged mother during her natural life. I appoint my two sons John and Thomas Bell and Charles Hays as executors. This 18 Sept 1819. Wit: Thomas Williamson, John Bell and Thomas Bell. Jan Term 1821.

Page 494   Inventory of estate of Samuel Bell, Sr., deceased.
Feb 28, 1821   This 10 Jan 1821. Several items listed. Signed by Thomas Bell and John Bell, executors. Jan Term 1821.

Page 494   Will of John Wilson, deceased.
Feb 28, 1821   To my beloved wife Agnes Ann Wilson all my household and kitchen furniture. To my son Robert Wilson my tract of land I live on. After my death all my stock be sold and money equally divided among all my children. To my son William Wilson have all my cloths. I appoint my beloved son Robert Wilson and Samuel Shannon my executors. This 13 Nov 1820. Wit: David B. Love, Jas. Love and John Patterson. Jan term 1821.

Page 495   Inventory of estate of John Wilson, deceased.
Feb 28, 1821   Several items listed including one note on John Lanier. This 23 Jan 1821. Signed by Robert Wilson, executor. Jan Term 1821.

Page 495   Additional inventory of estate of Thomas H. Perkins, Jr.,
Feb 28, 1821   deceased, of Davidson County, returned by Robert Scales, acting executor. Negroes named Bob and Jerry, Anderson, Julia and other items. This Jan 19, 1821.

Jan Term 1821.

Page 496   Sale of estate of Thomas H. Perkins, deceased, of Davidson
Mar 1, 1821   County, returned by William Perkins on 23 Nov 1820. Purchasers,
to wit, Thomas Hardeman, William Perkins, Joel Waller, Jacob W. Ramsey, Robert Scales,
Frederick Owen, Constant P. Sneed, Everett Owen, William Perkins purchased one silver
watch, Richard Herbert, William N. Holt, Thomas Edmiston, and Samuel Bell. Robert Scales,
executor. Jan 19, 1821. Jan term 1821.

Page 497   John H. Sumner, minor orphan guardian return.
Mar 1, 1821   John H. Sumner orphan of Jos. Jno. Sumner, deceased, with Duke
W. Sumner, guardian. Items paid for the orphan, and paid Doctor Hogg. This 27 Jan 1821.
Jan term 1821.

Page 497   Sale of estate of Lewis Demoss, deceased.
Mar 1, 1821   Purchasers, to wit, F. Fulgham, James Rhodes, Abram Demoss,
David Bridgeforth, Thomas Jefferson, Eldridge Phipps, Abner Driver, E.B. Cl(illegible), Thomas
Osborne, Jas. Demoss, William Demoss, A. Demoss, B. Richardson, Jno. Demoss, Edwin
Barham, Jno. Jones, E. Gibson, Howland & Allen, and Jas. Trailor. John Demoss, executor.
Jan Term 1821.

Page 498   Sale of estate of Daniel Young, deceased.
Mar 1, 1821   Made Dec 21, 1820. Persons listed, to wit, Jeremiah Sadler, the
widow, N.H. Robertson, Hardy S. Bryan, C.Y. Hooper, R. McGavock, David Love, Lucy Young,
Sally Strowther, Robert Wilson, Alexander Ray, and John L. Young. Hardy S. Bryan, admr.
Jan term 1821.

Page 499   Inventory of estate of Robert Thompson, deceased, of Davidson
Mar 1, 1821   County. Jan 15, 1821. One half of a tract of land lying on
Browns Creek containing 252 acres, 64 acres of said tract being now contended for by suit at
law leaves 188 acres of clear of dispute. A bond on his brother John Thompson for a Deed of
Conveyance to the one half of a tract of land on Browns Creek adjoining the above tract
containing 52 acres held by conveyance from Joseph Irwin to John Thompson being (illegible)
acres which is contended for by suit at law. One note on James Chambers for $5250.00
payable at the bank of the State of Mississippi. This 1 Mar 1821. John Thompson and Philip
Campbell, admrs. Jan Term 1821.

Page 499   Sale of estate of Foster Sayre, deceased.
Mar 1, 1821   Dec 5, 1820. Four negroes and also other items listed. Samuel
Seay, admr. Jan Term 1821.

Page 499   Settlement of estate of George Keeling, deceased.
Mar 1, 1821   We, George Wharton and Samuel Shannon, appointed to settle
with E.A. Keeling, admr. Vouchers and accounts amounted to $90.18 3/4. E.A. Keeling,
executor, account against said estate to travelling to Elkton and back twice $40.00, T.G.
Bradford receipt for $1.50. Doctor Newman's receipt $10.00. John C. Hicks' receipt $20.00.
To riding three times to Nashville $3.00. Paid fees to Nathan Ewing $1.50. Attorney's fees
of James Austin not known 7 Dec 1820. Jan Term 1821.

Page 500   Inventory of estate of Lewis Demoss, deceased.
Mar 1, 1821   Notes on the following, to wit, Charles Hartley, Shelton T.
Demoss, Charles Walker, John Demoss, Lazarus Inman, John Hardgraves, Andrew Russell,
Bryant Boon, Barnet Varden, John Taylor, Jr., John Jones, James Roach, George Wade, Daniel
Dansby, Robert Hill, Thomas Norman, and Eldridge Newsom. Other items listed. John
Demoss, executor. Jan Term 1821.

Page 500   Inventory of estate of Benjamin Philips, deceased.
Mar 1, 1821   Returned to Jan Term 1821. Persons listed, to wit, J. Ridley,
Robert W. Briggs, J.S. Williamson, John Drury, Anthony W. Vanleer, S. Cantrell, W.D.
Whitsell, Roger B. Sappington, William H. Robertson, William Hinton, Boyd McNairy, Jno. S.
Green, Bignal Crook, William P. Cobles, J. Nichols, Richard Garrett, Luke A. Vanleer, John
Woodcock, Simon Bradford, Robert Woods, James Ridley, Braddock Richmond, M. Barrow, and

83

D.H. Dunham. This 17 Jan 1821. Joseph Philips, executor. Jan Term 1821.

Page 501   John Criddle, Philip Shute and Thomas Shute VS Phinehas Cox
Jan __, 1821   Barbara Cox. July Term 1820 of Court of Pleas and Quarter
Sessions. On 28 July 1820 appeared John Criddle, Philip Shute and Thomas Shute offered for
probate a paper writing of the Last Will and Testament of Frederick Stump, deceased, to wit,
I, Frederick Stump of Davidson County, make this my Last Will and Testament and is not to
effect any Deed of Gift made, nor a will made the 25 Nov 1819 in favor my wife Catherine
in the hands of John Catron. I appoint John Criddle, Philip Shute and Thomas Shute my
executors of this my will. I vest unto my executors for 20 years from my death a tract of
land called Old Tavern Place whereon Mr. Tait now resides lying on Whites Creek in Davidson
County whichthey are to hold for the said term should my son John Stump so long live or his
wife so long live. I appoint my son John for and in behalf of his family (illegible) agent and
receiver of the rents, profits &c, and to support my son Christopher Stump's family of self,
wife and four children, two by his former and two by his present wife. To my grand children
John F. and Jacob Stump, and Sarah Whitworth $250.00 each. To my daughter Barbara Cox
two negroes. This 19 Mar 1820. Wit: Jno. H. Smith, Jno. Lanier, James Marshall, and
Richard H. Barry.

Page 504   Christopher Stump VS Phineas Cox and Barbara Cox.
July Term 1820   28 July 1820, Christopher Stump offered for probate the
following paper purporting to be the Last Will and Testament of Frederick Stump, deceased.
Another copy of his Last Will and Testament. To my wife Catherine Stump 300 acres of land
where I now live including the house, bordering Jacob Stump, Whites Creek, Mill Pond,
including the 300 acres, also negro girl Caroline and girl Aggy, a man Sam. This 25 Nov
1819. I appoint Christopher Stump, my son, my executor. Wit: John Catron and Zenas Tait.
Jan term 1821. A jury of men, viz, Austin Hainey, Thomas E. Smith, John Falwell, William
Lytle, Thomas Loving, Robert W. Green, Richard Hanks, John Hall, Robert J. Clow, William
W. Goodwin, James Harris, and Eli Cherry said the paper to be the Last Will and Testament
and to be entered of record.

Page 505   Will of Sarah Davis, deceased, widow, of Davidson County.
May 21, 1821   I, Sarah Davis, about to set out for the Mississippi from hence by
the will of providence I may never live to return, do make this my Last Will and Testament.
I give to my two grand daughters Sarah Jane Bass and Mary Ann Bass, children of my
daughter Ann Bass, all my estate real, personal or mixed of every description. Mrs. Bass
shall for the support of herself and support and education, my said grand children have the
use and occupation of all my estate. I appoint my daughter Mrs. Bass, my executrix. This
Feb 20, 1821. Wit: E.H. Foster and Robert Smiley. Apr Term 1821.

Page 506   Will of Rosanna Murray, deceased, of Davidson County.
May 22, 1821   The rent, corn, bacon, hogs or household and kitchen furniture,
farming utensils &c be spared from the support of my son Henry Murry also my funeral
expenses to be paid. To my son Henry Murry my share of all the rents and profits of the
plantation of 150 whereon I now live also other household items &c and at his death to be
equally divided between Thomas Murry, Jane Holland and John Murry. I appoint Thomas
Murry, my son, and Hemp Holland, my son-in-law, and John Murry, my son, my executors.
This 28 Mar 1821. Wit: Francis McKay and Jane Birdwell. Apr Term 1821.

Page 507   Will of Mary Clow, deceased, of Davidson County.
May 22, 1821   To my beloved husband Robert J. Clow the following lots of land
in the town of Nashville, situated in the south field distinguished by the survey and partition
made between James Trimble, Willie Barrow, Montgomery Bell, R. McGavock, Robert J. Clow
and his wife Mary Clow by the following numbers, to wit, 31, 36, 38, 43, 47, 48, and 51, also
an undivided third in each of the lots known and designated in the above plan of said South
Field sivision by numbers 16 and 45, all of which several parcels or lots of land, together with
hereditaments &c thereto belonging, I do give to my beloved husband Robert J. Clow forever.
To Nancy B. Clow my kind and affectionate daughter the lot of land designated in the
aforesaid South Field plan by No. 28 to have and to hold forever. To my beloved husband
Robert J. Clow all the landed or freehold estate, which descended to me from my brother
John Irwin's estate which is my portion of about 20,000 acres of land lying principally in the
Counties of Robertson, Sumner and Wilson. I appoint my husband Robert J. Clow, sole

executor. This 19 Sept 1820. Wit: Leonard P. Cheatham and Frederick D. Robertson. Apr Term 1821.

Page 507   Additional inventory of estate of James Russel, deceased.
May 22, 1821   Pension money $48.00. Wilson Crockett, admr. Apr Term 1821.

Page 508   Will of Sarah Nichols, deceased, of Davidson County.
May 23, 1821   To my grand daughter Sarah Elizabeth Dupree one bed and furniture and $118.50, furniture to be delivered to her by my executor amd money to be delivered when she arrives at full age or marries and should she die before she marries or arrives at full age then it goes to my grandson John Nichols son of Alfred Nichols. To my grandson John Nichols son of Alfred $118.50 with interest to be paid to him at the time he arrives at age of 21 years. To my son Alfred Nichols' children all the rest and residue of my estate to support his family and educate his children during their minority. This 19 June 1820. Wit: Nathan Ewing and Henry Ewing. Apr Term 1821.

Page 509   Inventory of estate of James Hennon, deceased.
May 23, 1821   Returned by James Trimble, admr. Bonds taken by deceased, viz, Reuben A. Higginbotham $1146.86, money left in the hands of the admr to be loaned by directions of the deceased $2664.12½, Higginbotham's note was in suit before his death, William Eastin note $2533.23, a suit in chancery James Hennon VS Allen & Large & Co. of $500.00. Apr Term 1821.

Page 509   Sale of estate of Daniel Young, deceased.
May 23, 1821   Sold 3 Apr 1821 also on 19 Apr 1821. Persons listed, to wit, John H. Smith, Roger B. Sappington, Daniel P. Davis, Hardy S. Bryan, Norvel H. Robertson, Lucy Young, Sally Strowther, Eleanor Young, and Richard Berry. Returned by Hardy S. Bryan, admr. Apr term 1821.

Page 510   Will of Francis Saunders, deceased, of Davidson County.
May 23, 1821   To my living wife Elizabeth Saunders two negroes, viz, Joseph and Cilva, two featherbeds and furniture. To my daughter Maria Buchanan and my son-in-law John K. Buchanan two negroes. Sally and Kitty also two featherbeds and furniture and all other gifts now in their possession. To my daughter Elizabeth Saunders two negroes, Thursday and Simon also two featherbeds and furniture. All my estate both real and personal after the above legatees are taken out be equally divided, and be either allotted or drawn for among my wife Elizabeth, my daughters Maria and Elizabeth. I appoint William Saunders and John Gowen, Sr., executors. This 18 Jan 1821. Wit: Willis L. Shumate, George Hartman, John Scally, and Betsey Hartman. Apr Term 1821.

Page 511   Cary Felts of Arthur Bland guardian receipt.
May 24, 1821   Jan 27, 1821. Received of Cary Felts, Esquire, in full of all dues and demands which I have against him respecting his guardianship for me on account of the estate of Arthur Bland, deceased. Test: Jerem. Ezell and William P. Seat. Signed by A. Bland. Apr Term 1821.

Page 511   Patsey McBride's support laid off, Davidson County.
May 24, 1821   Allotted to Patsey McBride widow and relict of James McBride, deceased, hath laid off and set apart for her support and family as follows, bacon, corn, flower (flour), salt, sugar, coffee, and clothing for children. This Feb 10, 1821. Signed by Robert Wood and William C. Rodgers and Abraham Hite. Apr Term 1821.

Page 511   Sale of estate of John Wilson, deceased.
May 24, 1821   Made by Robert Wilson, executor. Purchasers, to wit, Robert Wilson, Jabez Wilson, James Wilson, William Wilson, James Love, John M. Murray, Norvel H. Robertson, Robert Patterson, and Agnes Ann Wilson. Also one note on John Lanier. This Apr 14, 1821. Apr Term 1821.

Page 512   Settlement of estate of Asahel Champ, deceased.
May 25, 1821   Made by Nancy Champ, admrx &c. As Calculated on the return is $243.93 3/4. A note on Daniel McDonald $100.00. Vouchers $176.42½. Total $167.51¼. This 15 Apr 1821. Eldridge Newsom and W. Russell. Apr Term 1821.

85

Page 512   Eleanor Young, dower laid off. Davidson County.
May 26, 1821   Allotted and set off to Eleanor Young widow and relict of Daniel
Young, deceased, the one third part of the lands &c which Daniel Young died possessed of
having met this 21 Feb 1821 at the late residence of said Young and after being duly sworn
report that they have laid off to the widow one third of the tract of land on which said
Young lived at the time of his death, lying on Whites Creek and containing 349 acres. Signed
by Alexander Ewing, Absalom Page, William Wilkinson, John Criddle, Jr., William Nelson,
Joseph Love, and Clem Stubblefield. Apr Term 1821.

Page 513   Settlement of estate of Thomas Hail, deceased, of Davidson
May 28, 1821   County, with Stephen Hail and Jane Hail, admrs. Found amount
of sales to be $64.47. Also several vouchers total $412.01. Test: B.H. Lanier, J.P. and
Braxton Lee, J.P. 3 June 1820. Apr Term 1821.

Page 513   Sale of estate of Thomas Harrison, deceased.
May 28, 1821   Persons listed, to wit, Elizabeth Harrison, Emily Harrison,
Richard Harrison 640 acres lying on the Springfield road the mansion dwelling of Mrs.
Harrison, deceased, David Smiley, Joseph Standley, Lowe Harrison, Pason Woodard, Zachariah
Betts, Thomas Dorris, George Holt one tract of land lying on the Kentucky road, Spencer
Moss, Ferdinand Ryneman, Robert T. Richey, John Bolson, and Lowe Harrison 320 acres of
land lying in Smith County. Richard Harrison, executor. Apr Term 1821.

Page 514   Sale of estate of Samuel Bell, deceased.
May 29, 1821   Made 1 Feb 1821. Persons listed, to wit, Jane Bell, Robert Bell,
John Bell, Sr., Thomas Bell, Jr., Washington Campbell, Robert Orr, William Whittemore,
Hartwell Seet (Seat), William B. Erwin, Joseph Burnett, Thomas Hope, John Watson, Jeremiah
Ezell, Robert Woods, Edward Woods, John Bell, Jr., William N. Hamilton, Andrew Baldridge,
Franklin Collins, Silas Morton, Adam Carper, Thomas Johnson, John N(illegible), Mordicai
Pillow, William Bruer, Benjamin Farrow, Robert Turner, Martha Brown, Nicholas Tomberlin,
George R. Claiborne, William Seat, William Trimble, Arthur Bland, Franklin Collinsworth, and
John Hays. Apr 16, 1821. Signed by John Bell and Thomas Bell, executors. Apr Term 1821.

Page 516   Inventory of estate of James McBride, deceased.
May 30, 1821   26 Jan 1821. Several items listed. Edward H. East, admr.   Apr
Term 1821.

Page 516   Sale of estate of James McBride, deceased.
May 31, 1821   Several items listed including one watch. Edward H. East, admr.
Apr Term 1821.

DAVIDSON COUNTY, TENNESSEE WILL BOOK NO. 8
1821 - 1826

Page 1   Inventory of estate of Doctor James Priestley, deceased.
June 5, 1821   The library consisting of 3110 volumes, a telescope, two
microscopes, and several other items listed. Sarah Priestley, admrx. Apr Term 1821.

Page 2   Settlement and division of estate of Daniel Young, deceased, of
June 5, 1821   Davidson County. We, Samuel Shannon, Samuel Weakley, Peter
Woodson, and Robert Weakley have proceeded to divide the personal estate, to wit, negroes
and real estate of the deceased late of Davidson County among his heirs and legal
representatives. First, we set apart to the widow and relict of Daniel Young the following
negroes, to wit, a woman Vina, a boy Harry, a nd a woman Chloe. Secondly, to his daughter
Anne Hooper the mother of Claiborne Y. Hooper who appears to be one of the legal
representatives, a negro woman. Also we do charge said Claiborne Y. Hooper, as heir to his
mother, property as stated in the desposition of John L. Young herewith annexed and marked
A and set the same apart as so much of his Claiborne Hooper's part of said estate. Thirdly,
to his daughter Catherine Bryan, to wit, one mare, two beds and furniture, and two cows and
calves and one negro boy George. Also one negro man Joe. Fourthly, to his daughter Susan

86

Herring, to wit, one negro woman, one featherbed and furniture, three cows and calves, also one negro man Boswell. Fifthly, to his daughter Sarah Strother, to wit, one negro woman, one horse, one featherbed and furniture, three cows and calves, also one negro man Simon. Sixthly, to Mary Young one negro man Dave, also one negro woman Charlotte. Seventhly, to Lucy Young one negro man Jack, also one negro woman Charity. Eightly, to Sina Young one negro woman Dilcy also a negro woman's child Nelson and also a negro man Simon. Ninethly, to William Young one negro woman Harriett, and a negro boy Alfred. Tenthly, we are of the opinion that the real and personal property given to his son John L. Young amounts to an equal proportion of the estate of Daniel Young, deceased, and we called on John L. Young to render to us an account of said estate given by his father Daniel Young, but he refused. Mar 24, 1821, this day John L. Young personally appeared before me, Robert Weakley, a Justice of the Peace of Davidson County, and made oath that his father Daniel Young, deceased, in his lifetime, to wit, sometime after the intermarriage of Enis Hooper with his sister Anne Young, that his father gave to said Hooper and his wife a featherbed and furniture, also a bay mare, also gave said Hooper two sows and some pigs, also one sow and five shoats indifferent, also Enis Hooper having received of his father the plantation whereon he lived previous to his death. One half of which I understood to be a gift from his father for the other half of the tract said Enis Hooper agreed to pay his father $500.00 and in making the payment paid $120.00 by way of a mare to Major Coffield as his father Absalom Hooper was indebted to said Coffield for $500.00 with balance of $380.00 remaining, which sum of said father gave to Enis Hooper in corn, also to Enis Hooper money I think upwards to $200.00 to pay a fine for a breach of the peace on Arthur K. Turner. Signed by John L. Young. Wit: R. Weakley, J.P. Mr. Norvell H. Robertson, agent for Mr. C.Y. Hooper.
Division of two tracts of land, one lying on the east fork of Whites Creek and one on Sycamore Creek. No. 1, 64 acres to Sarah Strother, on Whites Creek, bordering the widow Eleanor Young's dower in the north boundary line of a preemption of 640 acres granted to David Rounsville, and by Alexander Ewing. Lot No. 2, 48 acres to Susan Harring, adjoining No. 1 in the dower line, and Alexander Ewing. Lot No. 3, 45 acres to Lucy Young adjoining Lot No. 2, Ewing's line and dower's line. Lot No. 4, 50½ acres to Mary Young adjoining Lot No. 3 in the dower line and Ewing's line. Lot No. 5, to Sins Young, 340¼ acres on west side of Sycamore Creek adjoins John Crockett's lands. Lot No. 6, 374½ acres to Claiborne Y. Hooper lying on Sycamore Creek adjoining Lot No. 5, Henry Rutherford and Spring Branch. Lot No. 7, 708¼ acres to William Young lying on Sycamore Creek and adjoining Lot No. 6 and Crockett's corner. We have allotted to Hardy S. Bryan 25 acres out of the Whites Creek tract which is represented by the plot together with a tract whereon he lives which said Daniel Young conveyed him. The 25 acres is bounded by William Homes line. This Apr 23, 1821. Signed by Sam Weakley, Surveyor, Peter Woodson with T. Shannon and R. Weakley, Commissioners. Apr Term 1821.

Page 7   Settlement of estate of Nathan Peebles, deceased.
June 6, 1821   Made with William Vaulx, admr. Found the whole estate to amount $2580.60¼. Vouchers amount to $40.00. Found in the hands of the admr $2540.60¼. Several vouchers listed. This 11 Apr 1821. Signed by William H. Nance and Cary Felts, Commissioners. Apr Term 1821.

Page 8   Archellus Cox children account with Richard Garrett, agent.
June 6, 1821   Archellus Cox (in his absence) with R. Garrett, agent. Cash paid to, viz, Joseph Litton, John Cootes, and R. Garrett. Cash received of James Irwin for hire of negroes. Total $163.13. Signed by Duncan Robertson and M.H. Quinn. Apr Term 1821.

Page 9   Andrew McCormack, deceased, heirs receipt.
June 6, 1821   Feb 2, 1820, Davidson County. The legatees of the Last Will and testament of Andrew McCormack, deceased, met and divided the personal property and received each their share. Test: E. Walker. Signed by George McCormack, Richard B. McCormack and Mary Ann McCormack. Apr Term 1821.

Page 9   William H. and Jesse H. Philips, orphans settlement.
June 6, 1821   William H. Philips to Matthew Barrow. Paid Edmund Lanier for board, Robert Smiley, John S. Williamson for boarding, Moses Stephens for tuition, Duncan Robertson for books, Robert C. Foster, Treasurer to Cumberland College, tuition, Gordon & Walker, Keys & Webb, George Wilson & Tunstall & Norvell for printing for the rent of plantation, and John S. Williams for boarding. Received of Joseph Philips, admr with will

annexed, and received of James Ridley in favor of E. Lanier. Matthew Barrow, guardian of William H. Philips and Jesse H. Philips, minor sons of Benjamin Philips, deceased. Signed by Duncan Robertson and M.H. Quinn. Apr Term 1821.

Page 10   Land division of estate of Andrew McCormack, deceased, of
June 7, 1821   Davidson County. We having been appointed by the legatees, to wit, George McCormack, Richard B. McCormack and Mary Ann McCormack, to divide the land of the said deceased, to wit, George McCormack No. 1, and 4, No. 1 containing 16¼ acres and also No. 4 bordering George Campbell, Elinor Walker's line and containing 28 3/4 acres. Richard B. McCormack No. 3, 5, 6, & 7, No. 3 containing 16 acres, also No. 5 containing 6 acres, being the land whereon said R.B. McCormack now lives, also No. 6 & 7 being two small entried made by said Andrew McCormack, deceased, containing 8 acres and adjoining No. 5, in all 30 acres. Mary Ann McCormack No. 2, bordering George Campbell, Lot No. 3 & Lot No. 4 and containing 48½ acres. This 29 July 1820. Signed by John N. Crossway, Thomas Dill and Richard Harrison. Test: E.C. Walker and William Davis. Apr Term 1821.

Page 12   Inventory of estate of John Wilson, deceased.
June 23, 1821   Returned by Robert Wilson, executor. One pair of steelyards, one auger, ten head of geece and sundry clothing. This Apr 14, 1821. Apr Term 1821.

Page 12   Will of Elisha Davis, deceased, of Davidson County.
Aug 11, 1821   To my beloved Polley Davis one plantation and tract of land containing 75 acres whereon I now live, also one other tract of land containing 640 acres which I bought of Robert Cartwright lying on the waters of Obeys River also one other tract of land containing 274 acres which I bought from Thomas Adkins adjoining the 640 acre tract on Obeys River, also other household items and negroes. To my son David Pritchard one tract of land of 640 acres which I bought from Simon Baker's heirs and lying on the Caney Fork in Sumner County, No. 2249. To my niece Sallah Davis and the heirs of my niece Mary Pearce five 640 acre tracts of land on Caney Fork River in Sumner County. I appoint my loving wife Polley Davis and John Davis and Arthur Pearce, executors. This 16 May 1802. Wit: Dd. Davis, R. McDaniel and A. Pearce. July Term 1821.

Page 13   Will of Sarah T. McConnell, deceased, of Davidson County.
Aug 13, 1821   To my mother, should she survive me, during her natural life, all my estate of every kind, also all the money. Out of the money due me from David Allen and my portion of the debt due me from James Martin Lewis a sum sufficient to purchase a good gold repeater watch to be given as a token of my affection to John Claiborne the son of Thomas Claiborne of the town of Nashville. I give John Campbell Marshall son of Doctor Lewis Marshall of Buck Pond the sum of $50.00 as a token of my regard of said child and attachment to its parents, which sum I wish appropriated to the purchase of a good pony for said child. I give to Eliza A, Lewis, Louisa Lewis, Anna Lewis and Darthula Lewis, Thomas Claiborne Lewis and (blank) Lewis, the two sons of James M. Lewis, Jr. and John Claiborne the sons of Thomas Claiborne, my negro girl Dorcas and her increase to be equally divided among them when John Claiborne shall come of the age of twenty one or dies, and in the meantime the annual profits of said slave and her increase after the death of my mother shall be equally divided among the last mentioned devisees. To my little relation Mary Clayton Claiborne daughter of Thomas Claiborne my negro girl Cleste after the death of my mother. If I should survive my mother, my brother John P. McConnell and my sister Nancy Allen shall have my share of the negro boy Sam. I appoint my brother John P. McConnell and my friend John H. Eaton, executors. This __ day Dec 1820. Wit: John H. Lewis. The above was put down through mistake not being proven.

Page 14   Will of Morris Shain, deceased.
Aug 13, 1821   This 18 May 1821. To my beloved wife Pheba Shain the use of the house and cleared land and all other property for the support of the family so long as she remains a widow and at her marriage or death a division to be then made of every thing. To my youngest son Cornelius Shain 100 acres of the land I now live on including the apple orchard. To my sons James Shain and Jacob Shain the balance of the land I now live I now live on supposed to be 100 acres to be equally divided between them. To my daughter Sarah Stephens the use of three acres of cleared land that is most convenient to her and one acre round her house to have while she remained a widow. My daughter Elendar Shain has to be

supported off of the land while she remains a single woman with the use and privilege of the house. To my two daughters Rebecca Shain and Margarett when they leave this place an equal share of my property with them thats married and as to all the rest remainder and residue of my perishable property to be equally divided among my daughters. I appoint Absalom Gleaves and William Stewart, executors. This 18 May 1821. Wit: William Stewart and Jesse Waldron. July Term 1821.

Page 15   Will of John Castleman, deceased, of Davidson County.
Aug 13, 1821   To my beloved wife Martha Castleman one featherbed and furniture and a sufficient of cooking utensils and cupboard ware for her use also three cows and calves, two ewes and lambs and also her maintainance off the land as long as she lives also ten young hogs. To my son Benjamin Castleman the one half of all the land that I own and also one featherbed and furniture. To my daughter Margaret Green's heirs that is the lawful heir or heirs of her body the other half of all the land that I own. My son Benjamin and my daughter is to take good care and maintain my son Andrew Castleman, an idiot, so long as he lives and lastly as to all the rest residue and remainder of my personal estate should never be sold and to be divided among all my children. My son Benjamin Castleman and Isaiah Green, executors. This 25 Apr 1821. Wit: Sam Steele, Thomas Spurg and Campbell Hays. July Term 1821.

Page 15   Will of John Coots, deceased, of Davidson County.
Aug 14, 1821   To my wife Mary Coots the plantation whereon I now dwell, containing about 150 acres, for her natural life and then the decend to my two daughters, namely, Letitia Coots and Elizabeth Coots. To my nephew John Cunningham his choice of 200 acres our of the land I now possess and hold in Maury County on Duck River and waters of Flat Creek conveyed to me by John McCrory. The residue of my lands to be sold and the amount thereof be equally divided among my joint heirs. Rest of the residue of my estate to be disposed of as follows, to wit, my household and kitchen furniture to be and remain for the use of my wife Mary Coots. My two negro men, to wit, Ben and Frank, to be sold also my stock of horses, cows, sheep, hogs, farming utensils &c, and the proceeds to be equally divided among my joint heirs. The residue of my negroes to remain on the plantation for the use of my wife Mary Coots during her natural life and at her death to be sold and proceeds to be divided among his heirs. I appoint my dear wife Mary Coots, Letitia Coots and Elizabeth Coots, as sole exrxs. This 28 Apr 1821. Wit: Andrew Wilson, Jason Thompson and John McEwin. July Term 1821.

Page 16   Sale of estate of Mark Philips, deceased.
Aug 14, 1821   Sold by Elizabeth Philips, admrx. Persons listed, to wit, William Homes, Elizabeth Philips, Robert Huggins, Joel Philips, Joseph Chumbley, Freeman Abernathy, George Guy, N.H. Robertson, James Green, Henry Boner, John Jackson, and Clem Stubblefield. July Term 1821.

Page 17   Division of the estate of Jesse Mullen, deceased.
Aug 14, 1821   Division among his heirs. We have allotted to Polly Mullen widow of Jesse Mullen, deceased, one negro girl Celia also the sum of $184.79 which sum Polley received together with the sum of $148.90, $102.06 of the last mentioned sum is in the hands of administrators and $46.84 in the hands of Josiah Mullen who is guardian of her children. To Isaac Mullen a negro woman Lucy also sum of $533.69 now in the hands of Josiah Mullen, guardian. To Sally Mullen a negro woman Cherry also sum of $383.69 now in the hands of said guardian. To Nancy Mullen a negro lad Andy also $650.00 and also sum of $183.69 in the hands of said guardian. To Jesse Mullen a negro man Bobb also $183.69 also in the hands of said guardian. This 15 May 1821. Signed by William H. Nance and Thomas Edmiston, Commissioners. July Term 1821.

Page 17   Inventory of sale of estate of Thomas B. Pipkin, deceased.
Aug 14, 1821   June 31, 1820. Philip Pipkin purchased amount of $310.00. Philip Pipkin, admr. July Term 1821.

Page 18   Will of Naomi Rains, deceased, of Davidson County.
Aug 14, 1821   My landed interests more or less to my mother Ursula Rains during her natural life and at her death to be equally divided between all my brothers and sisters. My undivided interest also in the negro slave estate I give to my mother forever. I

appoint my mother Ursula Rains my executrix. This 26 Apr 1821. Signed by Naomi J. Rains. Wit: R.C. Foster and Wilford H. Rains. July Term 1821.

Page 18   Polly, Sally, Hannah and Hampton G. Pugh, orphans guardian
Aug 14, 1821   return. Polly Pugh debtor to S. Clark, guardian. Cash paid due
from estate of John Pugh, deceased. Sally Pugh Dr. Solomon Clark, guardian, also Hannah
Pugh Dr. to S. Clark, guardian, and Hampton G. Pugh Dr. to S. Clark, guardian. This 27 July
1821. July Term 1821.

Page 19   Sarah Priestley, widow support laid off, of Davidson County.
Aug 15, 1821   Support set apart for the use of Sarah Priestley relict of James
Priestley, deceased. Bacon, corn, fodder, oats and salt. This June 2, 1821. James Mulherrin,
John Buchanan and L. Keeling. July Term 1821.

Page 19   Settlement of estate of Jesse Mullin, deceased, of Davidson
Aug 15, 1821   County. Made with David Cummings and Josiah Mullins, admrs.
Several vouchers listed. William H. Nance and Thomas Edmiston. July Term 1821.

Page 19   Settlement of estate of James Everett, deceased.
Aug 15, 1821   Several vouchers listed, ?. Hickman's receipt, William Quarles,
Newman's receipt, Enoch Kennedy, Balsor Huffman, Jesse J. Everett, Nathan Ewing, William
W. Brown, William Martin, Benjamin Smith, Goldsberry's receipt, Simon Everett, John Criddle,
Sr., and also find in the hands of the executor $346.28½. This July 17, 1821. Jonathan Drake,
J.P. and Braxton Lee, J.P. July Term 1821.

Page 20   Jesse Jackson, deceased, orphans guardian settlement, of
Aug 15, 1821   Davidson County, with Obediah Jackson, guardian. Furnished
Elizabeth Jackson for school and boarding. Paid Saunders & Chandler for goods furnished.
Furnished Polly Jackson to schooling and boarding. Paid Ramsey for schooling. Furnished
Martha Jackson for merchandise by Saunders & Chandler and to Ramsey for schooling.
Furnished Jerima(?) Jackson for merchandise &c. This 14 June 1821. Signed by William
Saunders and William Chandler. Jul Term 1821.

Page 20   Settlement of estate of george F. Jerow, deceased, of Davidson
Aug 15, 1821   County, with William Wallace, admr. Found $99.87¼. Also found
vouchers to the amount of $93.30, $6.57¼ is the amount of estate left. Signed by G.S. Allen,
J.P. and B. Lee, J.P. July Term 1821.

Page 21   Divided estate of Francis Saunders, deceased, of Davidson
Aug 15, 1821   County. Return by William Saunders, executor of the Last Will
and Testament of Francis Saunders, deceased, to divide and set apart to the heirs in the will
mentioned their portion, to wit, one tract of land Lot No. 1 including the place where said
deceased last resided in his lifetime. To Elizabeth Saunders, Sr., land of 368 acres. 2nd Lot
to Elizabeth Saunders, Jr., one tract of land including the tract known by the name of the
Singletary tract including other land adjoining it, bordering lands of Hartman's tract, Gowen's
tract, and containing 471 acres. Lot No. 3 to Maria Buchanan wife of John K. Buchanan one
tract of land known by the flood tract containing 347 acres. To the heirs of the estate of
Thomas Saunders eight negroes, and that Elizabeth Saunders, Sr. has allotted to her three
negroes. Elizabeth Saunders, Jr. has allotted to her one negro, three negroes. Maria
Buchanan and John K. Buchanan has allotted to them two negroes, and that the guardian of
Elizabeth Saunders, Jr. pay to Elizabeth Saunders, Sr. and John K. Buchanan to each of them
$16.66 2/3. Paid J. Burnett, surveyor, to John Gowen for eight days attendance, to E. Owen
for three days, to C. Felts, Esquire, to Jeremiah Ezell for writing report. This 17 July 1821.
Jeremiah Ezell, John Gowen, Edmund Owen, and Cary Felts. July Term 1821.

Page 22   Inventory of sale of estate of Francis Saunders, deceased.
Aug 15, 1821   Sold 7 May 1821. Several items listed. William Saunders,
executor. July Term 1821.

Page 23   William Howlett's land perpetuated testimony, of Davidson
Aug 15, 1821   County. July 6, 1821. Thomas Williamson, Benajah Gray and
John Currin to take the deposition of James McCutchin as respect to the perpetuating the

north west corner of James Foster's original preemption in John Tucker's original boundary line is also the beginning corner of a 38 acre tract granted to Peter Wright No. 10508 and dated 11 Aug 1817 agreeable to a notice given to John Rains, Jr. We have taken the despsition of said McCutchen, to wit, in winter of 1816 that myself and Robert Edmonston was going from my house and on the way somewhat took place about our land he asked me if ever I saw his south west corner and I said I had not. This 6 July 1821. Test: Benajah Gray, J.P. and Thomas Williamson, J.P. and John Currin. July Term 1821. All the desposition of Major John Buchanan taken.

Page 24   Inventory of estate of Morris Shain, deceased.
Aug 18, 1821   200 acres of land, one deed found on Julius Saunders for 366 acres of land. Notes on Samuel Steel, and several other items listed. This 4 July 1820. Test: Absalom Gleaves and William Stewart, executors. July Term 1821.

Page 24   Inventory of sale of estate of Edward Coglin, deceased.
Aug 18, 1821   Purchasers, to wit, William Brooks one gold watch, Jones, Lockhart, and J. Wilson. William Brooks, admr. July Term 1821.

Page 25   Division of estate of Robert Cato, deceased, of Davidson County.
Aug 20, 1821   Negroes, Peggy, Judah, Jesse, Lucy, Ivey, Jacob, and Monroe. Number of legatees are six, each share $470.83. Legatees names and their lots. Benjamin Barnes, Judah and pays $29.17. Evelina Cato, Lucy and receives $20.83. Mary A. Cato, Ivy and receives $120.83. Louisa Cato, Jacob and Monroe and pays $4.17. Robert Cato, Peggy and receives $20.83. Melissa Cato, Jesse and pays $129.17. Some notes remaining not settled said to be about $106.00 remaining in the hands of the admr and some debts to pay. This 30 Jan 1821. Jerm. Ezell, Edmund Owen, John Gowen, Cary Felts, and William Hall. July Term 1821.

Page 25   Inventory of estate of Nathaniel Herbert, deceased.
Aug 20, 1821   May 26, 1821. 174¼ acres of land, five negroes, two large Bibles, and several other items listed. Richard Herbert, admr. July Term 1821.

Page 26   Settlement of estate of Robert Evans, deceased.
Aug 20, 1821   Made with Eldridge Newsom, admr. Cash received of Thomas Hickman and of Jas. Brannon. Cash paid to J. Richeson, M. Tennison, Felix Robertson, Charles Hartley, Mary Evans, John Evans, Nathan Ewing, Charles R. Saunders, Robert Simpson, Moses Greer, Guy Smith, John C. Hicks, William Hobbs, Francis Slaughter, Benjamin Joslin, Thomas Washington, James Jackson, William Brannon, B.W. and W.H. Bedford, Ep. H. Foster, Isaac Tillet, Benjamin Cox, and the widow. This 24 July 1821. E. Hall and W. Barrow. July Term 1821.

Page 27   Additional inventory of estate of Robert Evans, deceased.
Aug 20, 1821   This June 1, 1821. Received of B.W. and W.H. Bedford $45.47 which money they collected from the United States on a claim that said Evans had on the United States in 1819 for the use of his horse at 40¢ per day. July 16, 1821. Eldridge Newsom, admr. July Term 1821.

Page 27   Jesse Mullin, deceased, orphans guardian settlement.
Aug 20, 1821   Josiah Mullen guardian of the minor orphan children of Jesse Mullin, deceased, viz, Isaac, Sally, Nancy and Jesse Mullins. Paid Polly Mullin for raising, clothing and schooling of the minor orphans. Paid E.H. Foster, Esq., paid Physician for doctoring negroes, and paid Ilai Metcalf for taking and selling negro Tom in the Natchez Country. Signed by Josiah Mullin, guardian. 15 May 1821. Thomas Edmiston, J.P. and William H. Nance, J.P. July Term 1821.

Page 28   John and Isaac G. Pugh, minor orphans guardians return.
Aug 21, 1821   Made with John Davis guardian to John Pugh, minor. Part returned by Solomon Clark, admr. Total $213.85. John Davis guardian to Isaac Green Pugh, minor. Part returned by Solomon Clark, admr. July Term 1821.

Page 28   Will of James Tatum, deceased, of Davidson County.
Nov 10, 1821   After my debts are paid the residue of my property after such

such payments shall be made, I will in the second place should go to and be enjoyed by my friend and only brother Howell Tatum. This 8 Sept 1821. Wit: William Williams, Josiah F. Williams and John P. Hunter. Oct Term 1821.

Page 29   Will of Elizabeth Richardson, deceased.
Nov 10, 1821   June 6, 1821. For services rendered by my daughter Lany Molly I give $100.00 and several other items, which is now in her possession. To my daughter Milly Franklin one white sheet and one calico bedquilt. To my grand daughter Lucinda Robertson one cow that stays at Robertsons. To my daughter Charlotte Hull's children four head of sheep. To my son Henry Richardson two steers, six head of sheep, one pot, and all the hogs and my crop that is growing. To my grand daughter Elizabeth Smith one big pot, skillet and oven, cow and calf and one heifer, one rose blanket, one cotton sheet, all the cotton and wool, one wheel, and one pail. To my daughter Charlotte Hill two wheels, two chairs, the meat must be equally divided between my daughter Charlotte Hill and Elizabeth Smith. To sister Letty Greer one folding table. I have no claim against John Richardson horse and he must be given up to Aron Franklin. Wit: Lucinda Demoss and Tabitha Charter. Oct Term 1821.

Page 29   Will of Edward Bondurant, deceased, of Davidson County.
Nov 12, 1821   To my beloved wife Magdaline Bondurant my plantation whereon I now live during her natural life or widowhood also all my plantation tools and utensils also all stock of every kind. I also give the use of my negroes, to wit, David, Philip, Eady and Cootney, but at her death to be divided among my children or lawful heirs. My estate to be kept together for the use of my wife to raise and school my younger children as long as she lives a widow and afterwards for the use of my young children until the youngest child becomes of age or marries. I wish after my son Edward Bondurant has completed his education that he be furnished with money to attend the lectures to complete him for a Physician and that money be charged to his account. The same for the rest of my sons and daughters. I appoint my beloved wife Magdaline Bonurant, Jacob M. Bondurant and Robert M. Bondurant, my executors. This 10 July 1820. Wit: John Maxey, Zach. B. Pryor and Jane Pryor. Oct Term 1821.

Page 31   Will of John Bowle, deceased, of Davidson COunty.
Nov 12, 1821   To my sister Margaret Chambers $500.00 which is now in my possession. To David Chambers the balance of my estate both real and personal, son of Margaret Chambers and her daughter Nancy Chambers alias Nancy Woodward except $5.00 I will to her son John Chambers a citizen of Alabama, also John Chambers my real property in an interest in a lot of ground in the town of Nashville held in partnership by myself, Thomas Edmiston, Esq., Michael C. Dunn, David Vaughn and Samuel Crockett, my own interest being $1836.62, which is in agreement between the partners lodged in the hands of Josiah Nichol in Nashville, Balance of notes on, viz, Joseph Hopkins', deceased with Daniel A. Dunham and John Johns, security for $350.00, one on Joseph Scales for $400.00 and Joel Waller, security, also one other note on said Scales for $131.00 his son Henry, security. Also $336.00 on Thomas G. Bradford taken in four notes. Notes all in my possession. I appoint Thomas Edmiston, Esquire and Robert Hill, executors. This 31 Aug 1821. Wit: John Motheral, Francis Hodge, John Ralston, and Thomas G. Pritchett. Oct Term 1821.

Page 32   Will of Sarah P. McConnell, deceased, of Davidson County.
Nov 12, 1821   To my mother all my estate of every kind, should she survive me, during her natural life, the money to be used by her for her own benefit should she need it. The money due me from David Allen and my proportion of the debt due from James Martin Lewis a sum sufficient to purchase a good gold repeater watch as a token of my affection to John Claiborne the son of Thomas Claiborne of the town of Nashville. I give to John Campbell Marshall son of Doctor Levi Marshall of Buck Pond the sum of $50.00 as a token of my regard for said child, to purchase of a good pony for said child. To Eliza A. Lewis, Louisa Lewis, Anna Lewis and Darthula Lewis - Thomas Claiborne Lewis and (blank) Lewis the two sons of James M. Lewis, Jr. and John Claiborne the son of Thomas Claiborne my negro girl Dorcas and her increase, when John Claiborne shall come of age of twenty one or dies. To my little relation Mary Clayton Claiborne daughter of Thomas Claiborne my negro girl Celeste after the death of my mother. If I should survive my mother, my brother John P. McConnell and (illegible) Nancy Allen shall have my negro boy Sam. I appoint my brother John P. McConnell and my friend John H. Eaton, executors. This __ day of Dec 1820. Wit:

92

John H. Lewis. Oct Term 1821.

Page 33   Inventory of estate of Craven Jackson, deceased.
Nov 13, 1821   Notes on James N. Manifee, Michael Campbell, J.B. Houston,
A.R. Freeman, John C. Hicks, Thomas Patterson, and William Adams, John Stump and Richard
Hanks. Other persons listed, to wit, Henry Terace, John Moore, Thomas Washington, Doctor
Roane, Hugh Roland, the Mason's hall, Washington Pullian, account with the building
committee of the Mason's hall balance due $74.00, and J.D. Miller an assignee to Jackson.
There is an unsttled account with the Presbyterian Church. Note on David Irwin. Several
items listed. This Oct 25, 1821. Signed by Elizabeth Jackson and Nathaniel A. McNairy,
admrs. Oct Term 1821.

Page 34   Settlement of estate of James Russell, deceased, of Davidson
Nov 13, 1821   County, July 18, 1821. Found amount of sales $128.56½ and
vouchers on Wilson Crockett, Enoch Douge, W.L. Gower, and money paid out by
administrators. Signed by William Wallace and Braxton Lee, Esquires, Commissioners. Oct
Term 1821.

Page 34   Ephraim Drake's orphans guardian return.
Nov 13, 1821   The profits of the estate of Ephraim Drake is as follows, to wit,
rent of the upper plantation and the rent of the lower plantation, hire of negroes, Frank, Eve
and Peter. William J. Drake, guardian. Oct Term 1821.

Page 35   Inventory of sale of estate of Robert Searcy, deceased.
Nov 11, 1821   Sale by auction. Several items listed. Notes due, viz, Stephen
Cantrell has paid, Samuel Elam and William ?. Williams, Alfred Balch, Sam G. Murray & Co.,
Jno. P. Erwin, Moses Stephens, Daniel (illegible), John C. McLemore, Thomas H. Fletcher, H.
T(illegible), E.D. Jones, Duke W. Davis, Orville H. Searcy, Andrew Erwin, Jr., Andrew Hays,
Charles Cooper, Whiteside & Balch, George Bell, John M. Wilford, and Samuel Tilford. Signed
by Stephen Cantrell, one of the executors. This 26 Oct 1821. Oct Term 1821.

Page 36   Inventory of estate of John Castleman, deceased.
Nov 15, 1821   Taken 12 Oct 1821 by Absalom Gleaves, admr with the will
annexed. Several items listed. Oct Term 1821.

Page 36   Elizabeth Saunders, minor orphan, guardian return.
Nov 15, 1821   Edward H. East to Elizabeth Saunders, minor orphan. Hire of
negroes for food and cloths, two beds and furniture left by the will, the land owned by said
minor was not rented. This 25 Oct 1821. Oct Term 1821.

Page 37   Inventory of estate of William Hobson, deceased.
Nov 15, 1821   That part directed to be sold by his Last Will and testament
together with the monies due said estate and disbursed as directed by said will between the
heirs and legatees by James Jackson, Robert Weakley and John Hobson, executors. Persons
paid, to wit, R.C. Foster the treasurer of Cumberland College, John Hobson to return negro
Charles from James Jackson, Thomas Eastland, Thomas Deaderick, Eastland & McNairy, J.B.
Houston, N.A. McNairy, Benjamin Eddins for Dr. Smith, David Irwin, Jos. Scales, John T.
Dismukes for Thomas H. Watson, Stephen Farmer, Nicholas Hobson, Robertson & Curry, and
Doctor Maxey. Cash received from, to wit, R.C. Foster and Robert Searcy, Abram Wright,
Thomas Williamson, Thomas Shackleford, Robert Farmbrough, Duke Sumner, Michael Gleaves,
Hugh Evans, Robert Stewart, Stephen Farmer, Joseph Coleman, N. Hobson, Doctor Priestley,
Carroll & Smith, Robert Weakley, K. Green & Thomas Ramsey, Dr. Hadley, Nicholas B. Pryor,
William Hobson, Nathan Ewing, John Newman, David Vaughn, John Hobson, James G. Hicks,
Thomas G. Bradford, Dr. McNairy for medicine, George Hewlett, William Lytle, Nicholas
Hobson, Mary Hobson, Susan Hobson, Elizabeth Hobson, and William Hobson. Notes, viz, John
Stump, Chapman's note, William Allen, Thomas Claiborne, John Newman, David Vaughn, Isaac
Clemmons, George Smith, Thomas Cary, Pain's bond, Richard Brown, Robert Stewart, John H.
Smith's note, Willie Barrow, William Griffin, James McGavock, Thomas Patterson, V. Winfrey,
James Irwin, Liston Temple, J. & Jos. Sitler, Hugh Evans, James Clemmon, Jos. Coleman,
Jas. Jackson, Elizabeth Hobson by her guardian N.A. McNairy, Susan Hobson by her guardian
N.A. McNairy, William Hobson by his guardian William Lytle, James H. Gamble, William B. &
V.L. Lewis, A.H. Harris, Thomas Patterson, and Willie Barrow. Total $5675.60 3/4. This 7

Oct 1821. W.B. Lewis and J.P. Elliston. Oct Term 1821. (long list)

Page 39   Inventory of estate of Arthur Exum, deceased.
Nov 15, 1821   Oct 23, 1821 a return of money by John Exum, admr. Collected
from John Bosley $6.25, from Elisha Sullivant $12.00, from Robert Hughs $4.00, and from
Abner Driver $1.50. Oct Term 1821.

Page 40   Inventory of estate of Isham A. Parker, deceased.
Nov 15, 1821   Fourteen negroes and several items listed including one house and
two lots. Margaret Parker and John Maxey, admrs. Oct Term 1821.

Page 40   Settlement of estate of Stephen Lock, deceased.
Nov 15, 1821   The accounts of Rebecca Lock, admrx found in the clerk's office
$61.91 3/4. Several vouchers listed. This 23 Oct 1821. E. Goodrich, J.P. and Thomas
Williamson, J.P. Oct Term 1821.

Page 41   Inventory of sale of estate of Nathaniel Herbert, deceased.
Nov 15, 1821   Sept 5, 1821. Persons listed, to wit, Richard Herbert, Henry
Woten, John Frost, Richard Herbert, Harrison Ogilvie, Frederick Owens, Jr., James Butt,
William Ogilvie, Gurshern Hunt, Samuel Hope, John Rains, Stephen Briant, John Watson,
Thomas Ray, Thomas Boles, Silas Mourton, John Currin, William McCanles, David Cummins,
Roland Stone, Miles Bass, James Sneed, John Gibson, John Edmiston, William Cherry, Luther
Champ, Constant Sneed, Jabez Owen, David Philips, William M. Calas, Thomas Pu (Pugh),
Thomas Waller, Levi Gardner, Thomas Worler, and Everett Owen. Signed by Richard Herbert,
admr. Oct Term 1821.

Page 43   Settlement of estate of William Y. Probart, deceased.
Nov 16, 1821   Made with Sarah Probart, admrx. Paid vouchers, to wit, Isaac
Sitler, Tunstall & Norvell, Alexander Porter & Son, Jacob McGavock, James Roane, John R.
W(illegible), John L. Hadley, Thomas Talbot, Robertson & Waters, Felix Robertson, John H.
Eaton, paid for burial and tombstone $21.17, and T.G. Bradford. Cash received from Matthew
Walker, Wilkins Tannehill, Thomas Talbot, and John Newman. Balance on hand $738.96.
Duncan Robertson and Samuel V.D. Stout, Commissioners. Oct 26, 1821. Oct Term 1821.

Page 43   Sale of estate of James Everett, deceased.
Nov 17, 1821   Feb 13, 1821. J.J. Everett, executor. Several negroes.   Oct
Term 1821.

Page 44   Inventory of estate of John Coots, deceased.
Nov 19, 1821   Returned by Letitia Coots, executrix. Persons listed, to wit,
John B. Craighead, Joseph Scales, Richard Garrett, Samuel Bell, and John Cobler. Several
items listed. 150 acres of land in Davidson County, 400 acres in Maury County, one silver
watch, and judgements against Christopher Stump. Oct Term 1821.

Page 44   Inventory of sale of estate of John Coots, deceased.
Nov 19, 1821   Returned by Letitia Coots, acting executrix, on 5 Sept 1821.
Purchasers, to wit, Letitia Coots, John Thompson, James Dillon, Benton Harris, William
Hinton, Thomas Chilcutt, Josiah Mullin, J.W. Ramsey, Jno. C. Chadwell, Robert Scales, Philip
Campbell, Jno. Hathaway, James Campbell, William Whitemore, James Harris, Esther
Dickinson, Richard Sutton, William Hooser, William Windle, Jno. Harrison, Henry Bateman,
Jeremiah Hunt, William Brent, William Ramsey, Edmund Reaves, Benjamin Malone, Leaven
Marshall, Eliza Coots, and Austin M. Wade. This 23 Oct 1821. Oct Term 1821.

Page 46   Division of estate of Isaac Basey, deceased.
Nov 19, 1821   Division of the negroes between the legal heirs. Each heir's
share $233.75. Total valuation $1870.00. No. 1 Lewis Basey draws negro George. No. 2
Francis Basey, Sr. draws cash $233.75. No. 3 Nancy Basey draws negro Malinda. No. 4
James Basey draws a negro Winney. No. 5 Francis Basey, Jr. draws negro Elizabeth. No. 6
William Kimbrow and wife draws cash $233.75. No. 7 Isaac Basey draws negro Nelson. No. 8
Thomas Hill and wife draws negro Aggey. This 3 Oct 1821. Signed by Enoch Ensley, John
Johnston and William P. Seat. Oct Term 1821.

Page 46   Inventory of estate of Daniel Clark, deceased.
Nov 20, 1821   Several items listed including notes on Jesse Olen, JamesLesher,
Williamson Adams, James and Snodgrass. One silver watch, one anchor, and unexpired term
of a negro man. Sept 3, 1821. William S. Clark, admr. Oct Term 1821.

Page 47   John Rains land perpetuating testimont, Davidson County.
Nov 20, 1821   We are directed to take the desposition of John L. Fielder on the
25 Aug 1821 relative to what he may know with regard to the south east corner of a 640 acre
tract of land granted by the State of North Carolina to Philip Catron. John L. Fielder said
that to the best of his knowledge he was at an oak corner in year 1796 in company with
Jonathan Philips and Benjamin Herendon and Jonathan Philips stated that was the south east
corner Philip Catrons survey and the said oak was then standing and marked as a corner
which was at the spot where we now are taking his deposition being about 24 feet east of a
sugar tree marked a day with the letter W. Borders James Foster's preemption. Signed by
John L. Fielder. William H. Nance, Thomas Williamson, and Jno. Watson. John Rains and
John Buchanan present at this deposition.
A deposition was taken of Jacob W. Ramsey to what he may know about the south east
corner of a 640 acre tract of land. Deposition was taken 25 Aug 1821, saying he was along
two or three times the date of 1799 when the surveyors began at a hickory, Philip Catron's
south west corner and run east to this place. Signed by J.W. Ramsey. Oct Term 1821.

Page 48   Benjamin Philips, deceased, minor orphans, of Davidson County.
Nov 21, 1821   In Feb 1820 James Ridley leased the plantation whereon Benjamin
Philips lived and died, from Matthew Barrow guardian of William H. Philips and Jesse H.
Philips sons of Benjamin Philips. Ridley failed to comply to enter into bond with security.
Barrow resigned his guardianship and the subscriber was appointed in his stead. Signed by
Joseph Philips. Oct Term 1821.

Page 49   Estate of Larkin Clay, deceased, to Jonathan Clay, executor.
Nov 21, 1821   Amount paid to William Nichol Vaulx & Co. for articles, to
James Stewart and Co. for shoes, tuition, to Armstrong for sundries, homespun clothing,
board of three children for 12 months. Oct Term 1821.

Page 50   Settlement of estate of Robert Searcy, deceased.
Nov 21, 1821   Made with Stephen Cantrell. Cash discount at Nashville Bank, F.
& M. Bank, and Branch Bank. Cash received balance on O.B. Hayes, paid to A.A. & W.R.
Woods, Thomas Henderson, Ewing for recording will, paid Boon for taking up and keeping
horse, cash inclosed in a book found in the vault of N. Bank, and cash paid T.B. Tunstall.
Others named, viz, Charles Hays, Gordon & Walker, Mitchell's note, Harrison's account, Drs.
Hogg and Bronaugh's account, R. Farquharson, George A. Bedford, James B. Houston, Franky
Harrison, tuition at female academy, Dr. Overton's bill, Ewing for copy of will, Tilford's note,
William Lytle's note, suit VS Willis Wray & Walker, John S. Topps fee in said suit, Walker,
Rhea & Whiteside, Whiteside & Bell's note, Norvell & Tunstall, McLemore's note, William
Bosworth, Robert Smiley, Moses Stevens, Robertson & Curry, Edmond Cooper, Henderson &
Marshall, R. Doak's note, John H. Eaton, Esquire, R.P. Dunlop, Whitfield's debt, P. Mosely's
note, Charles Hays, William L. Williams, Benjamin Sewell's note, George W. Hockey, John P.
Erwin, George Shall's account, J. Shalls, S. Cantrell, Jr. & Co., Yeatman's bill, Rhodes for
surveying land, and Dr. Robertson. This 27 Oct 1821. George Wilson and Daniel A. Dunham,
Esquires, Commissioners. Oct Term 1821.

Page 54   Settlement of estate of John Childress, deceased.
Nov 22, 1821   Made with S.B. Marshall, admr. Persons listed, to wit, Moses
Stephens, George Wilson, Robert B. Curry, John Newnan, Stephen Cantrell & Co., John P.
Erwin & Co., Kendall Webb, Jesse Evans, James N. Smith, Robert Smiley, A.W. Bell, James
Odel, Thomas Deaderick, Jno. B. McCauliss, Will Griffin, Jno. Parks, W.C. Bruce, James
Jackson & Co., Will. Thompson, Matthew Porter, Thomas Hickman, Henry Ewing, Thomas Gill,
Nathan Ewing, Thomas Claiborne, James Copeland, Andrew Caradine, Raworth & Gordon,
Peyton Randolph, David & James Irwin, Whiteford & Williams, C. McKerahan, Robert J. Clow,
Matthew Barrow, Robert W. Green, Edmund Hewitt, Jos. & Robert Woods, James B.
McCanliss, Will Hunt, and James B. Houston. Cash paid to John H. Smith, Josiah Nichols &
Co., Will Griffin, Will McCaffrey, James McMannus, Will Lintz, cashier Columbia Bank, and
Samuel Wilson. Other names, to wit, Robert Hewitt, Alpha Kingsley, J.B. Leroy, Will Hume,

95

J. Simonton, Edward Daniel, John Shute, Nathan Ewing, D. Frazor, B.S. Harrison, J. Horton, Doctor Alexander in Alabama, Will Dubarry, B.W. & W.H. Bedford, George Hewitt, C.G. White, Kirkman & Erwin, P. Nelson, Jno. Andrews for salt and bacon (Alabama) and for land warrants, B. Vick, Pritchett & Shall, Hayes & Roane, Thomas Yeatman, Will Nichol, Vaulx & Co., W. Tannehill, Mr. Polk, Will Eastin, Will Fanning, James Trimble, Jno. McNairy, Marshall & Watkins, Eldridge B. Robertson, Berryhill & McKee, James Stewart, taxes in Alabama, Jno. Harding, Robert Farquharson, George W. Gibbs, Beal Bosley, W.L. Hannum, James Mulherrin, Alexander Porter, paid auditor's account at Huntsville, Thomas Deaderick, Philip Thomas, Tunstall & Norvell, Davis & S.C. Robertson, B. Vick for the use of the farm in Alabama, Robert & Will Armstrong, and Mrs. E. Childress and Doctor Solomon. Paid Mrs. Childress for her and sons expenses travelling and taxes on land, travelling to Alabama and back. By cash received of James Jackson on account of Packolet, received in Natchez, cash received of Caney Creek Land Company, cash on note from John Parks, received of John H. Smith, also received of T. Hyde, S.C. Robertson, cash received for land rent in Giles County, cash paid of Peter R. Booker, cash paid for ground rent in Nashville. Cash for property sold in Alabama. Mrs. Childress, admrx. Signed by J.T. Elliston, J.P. and D.A. Dunham. Oct Term 1821. (long article)

Page 57   Settlement of estate of John Irwin, deceased, of Davidson
Nov 24, 1821   County. Made with D. Irwin, admr. Sixty eight vouchers listed.
Signed by William Wallace, J.P. and Braxton Lee, J.P. Oct Term 1821.

Page 58   Settlement of estate of Charles Beasley, deceased, of Davidson
Mar 18, 1822   County. Made with James Owen, admr. Twenty vouchers listed.
This 16 Jan 1822. William H. Nance and Thomas Edmiston, Commissioners. Jan Term 1822.

Page 59   Division of estate of William Donelson, deceased, of Davidson
Mar 18, 1822   County. Commissioners appointed to lay off and set apart to
Severn and Jacob Donelson, heirs of William Donelson, their portion of the personal estate
agreeable to the direction of William Donelson's will and we report, viz, 48 negroes and each
of the legatees, Severn and Jacob, being entitled to $1968.25 each, it being one eighth part of
the same. Negroes being divided. This 17 Jan 1822. Signed by David Dunn, A. Matthis and
E. Goodrich, Commissioners. Jan Term 1822.

Page 60   Settlement of estate of Joseph Coleman, deceased.
Mar 18, 1822   To Ann M. Coleman. Persons listed, to wit, James Stewart, J.
Litton, T. Yeatman, R. Foster & Son, W. & S. Creys, M. Adams, Gordon & Walker, Aron Day,
William Hume, D. McIntosh, William Hewlett, Moses Stevens, Jno. Falwell, A. & J. McNull,
Edmond Reaves, G.C. Boggs, Jno. W. Walker, F.G. Pearcy, Doctor Irskin & Irby, Robert
Reaves, Crockett & Adams, B. Bibb, A. Porter, William Gardner, Burrel Perry, Jno. Stobough,
G. Bedford, J. Johnston, R.W. Green, Doctor G. Bedford, D. James Priestley, Sarah Bigloe,
J.B. Houston, Richard Garrett, D. Robertson, R. Smiley, E.J. Porter, Andrew Denton, E.
Owens, Roan & Hays, J.C. Hicks, B.W. Bedford, Berryhill & McKee, Ingram & Loyd,
Powhatton Coleman, William H. Coleman, and Joseph G. Coleman. Notes on Hill, Scott, R.
Garrett, William Temple, B. Bibbs, B. Coleman, J. Johnson, K. Green, and Mrs. Stringfellow.
Mrs. Ann M. Coleman now Mrs. Legrand, admrx. 8 Jan 1822. Signed by R.C. Foster and
W.B. Lewis, Blackman Coleman, admr. Several vouchers listed. Jan Term 1822.

Page 63   Settlement of estate of Benjamin Branch, deceased.
Mar 18, 1822   Josiah T. Williams, executor. Notes on the following, to wit,
Washington Perkins, John Clinard, Jabez White, Henry Clinard, John C. Parker, William Shaw,
George Foster, and D. & Wash Perkins, Jesse H. Cartwright, William Perkins, A.B. & J.A.
Taylor, C.Y. Hooper, Christiana Irby, Valentine Branch, Jos. Page, H. & Z. Duncan, Wilson
Stump & Zachariah H. Wilson, A.W. Dawell & J. Lyons, and James H. Gamble. Received, to
wit, Robert Taylor, Thomas Taylor &c. Allen. To Clerks receipt from, to wit, Nancy Branch
and others. This 19 Jan 1822. John Love and George Wharton, Esquires. Jan Term 1822.

Page 64   Settlement of estate with the heirs of James Camps, deceased.
Mar 19, 1822   I was appointed guardian of the heirs of James Camp, deceased,
viz, Joseph, Margaret, Sarah and Mary Camp. Twenty one negroes named. R.C. Foster their
guardian. Cash paid to the following, viz, E.H. Foster an attorney, Benjamin S. Harrison for
boarding, Edward Daniel a jailor, Matthew Barrow for tuition, Samuel Lyons for coffin, Mary

Wharton for mid-wife, Pleasant Craddock for boarding, Braddock Richmond a merchant, Robert Smiley a tailor, Duncan Robertson for books, Willis Barker for shoes, Matthew Quinn for books, Samuel J. Ridley for boarding and tuition, Josiah Nichol a merchant, Doctor Roane a Physician, William Osmore for making cloths, Thomas B. Craighead for boarding and tuition, G. & J. Shall merchants, Richmond & Flint jewelers, R.C. Foster, Jr. for boarding, J. McComb for coffin, the boarding of Margaret Camp, Sarah Camp and Mary Camp, also Joseph Linton a merchant, and others. This 1 Feb 1822. W. Tannehill and W.B. Lewis, Commissioners. Jan Term 1822.

Page 66   Henry Dickinson's guardian return.
Mar 19, 1822   Josiah Nichol and John White guardian of Henry Dickinson. Notes due on John Childress, John White, A.B. Hays, James Trimble, Thomas Shackleford, T. Martin, R.C. Foster & Sons, Dickinson & Cooper, B. McNairy, G.W. Campbell, G. Bell, and E.H. Foster. 28 Jan 1822. Jan Term 1822.

Page 68   William Wright's orphans settlement.
Mar 19, 1822   Made with John Johnston, guardian of two of the minor orphans. Several vouchers listed. This 28 Jan 1822. William H. Nance and B. Gray, J.P. Jan Term 1822.

Page 68   John Jas. A. Fowlke's guardian settlement.
Mar 19, 1822   Made with William Henry Hamblin, guardian. Notes on, viz, M.P. Walker and Sam Allen. Persons named, viz, William Hope and Sam Hope. Cash paid J. Pierce and Nathan Ewing. E. Goodrich, J.P. and George Wharton, J.P. Jan Term 1822.

Page 69   John Simmons' orphans settlement.
Mar 19, 1822   Made with William Arrant, guardian. Cash received of Stephen Cantrell for pension from the United States to the orphans. Cash paid to the following, to wit, William Thompson, Washington Perkins, Nathan Ewing, William Williams, Hickman, Horton, and Sappington. 7 Jan 1822. Eldridge Newsom and Silas Dillahunt. Jan Term 1822.

Page 70   Settlement of estate of John Patterson, deceased.
Mar 19, 1822   We, James Read and Samuel Shannon, being appointed to settle the estate of John Patterson, deceased, with the admr and admrx and proceeded on this 28 Jan 1822 to settle with Robert Patterson, admr and find as follows, vouchers on, to wit, R.A. Higginbotham, George Gill, James Barnes, S. Shannon, Jos. Marshall, Robert Wilson, A. Page, Robert Patterson, and Nathan Ewing. Jan Term 1822. Robert Patterson, admr and Ellender Patterson, admrx.

Page 70   Inventory of estate of James Tatum, deceased.
Mar 20, 1822   Several items listed. Ho. Tatum, admr. test: R. Sanderson. Jan Term 1822.

Page 71   Inventory of estate of John Peabody, deceased.
Mar 20, 1822   Taken Nov 2, 1821. Several items listed. Braddock Richmond, admr. Jan Term 1822.

Page 71   Inventory of estate of Jacob Dickinson, deceased.
Mar 20, 1822   Several items listed. Patsey Dickinson got negroes. Signed by Patsey Dickinson, admrx. Jan Term 1822.

Page 72   Inventory of estate of George Hewitt, deceased, intestate.
Mar 20, 1822   Several items listed including one gold watch and one silver watch. Ann M. Hewitt, admrx. Jan Term 1822.

Page 72   Inventory of estate of Elizabeth Hardy, deceased.
Mar 20, 1822   Taken Jan 29, 1822. Several items listed. Micajah Fly, admr. Jan Term 1822.

Page 73   Inventory of estate of Terrence A. McGuiggin, deceased, on the
Mar 20, 1822   evening he was shot by Col. John Smith. Notes on C. Robertson, Sterling Brewer, John H. Hydes, John Read, and Field Farrar. Also one small gold watch,

gold seal and key and other items listed including a note on William T. Crouse. James Irwin, admr. Jan Term 1822.

Page 73   Inventory of estate of Edith Gower, deceased.
Mar 20, 1822   Several items listed. Thomas Hickman, admr. Jan Term 1822.

Page 74   Inventory of estate of Edward Bondurant, deceased.
Mar 20, 1822   Made by the executor of the Last Will and Testament. Several items listed including a judgement against Alpha Kingsley. Robert M. Bondurant, executor. Jan Term 1822.

Page 74   Elizabeth Jackson, support laid off.
Mar 21, 1822   Nashville, Nov 2, 1821. Support for Elizabeth Jackson widow of Craven Jackson, deceased, $400.00 and two cows with the corn as on hand and the use of the house and lot where said widow now lives. Duncan Robertson and David Irwin, Commissioners. Jan Term 1822.

Page 75   Will of William Harper, deceased, of Davidson County.
Mar 21, 1822   To my affectionate wife Elizabeth Harper for her natural love to my children and her capacity to manage my affairs, all my estate both real and personal. This 20 Dec 1821. Wit: Duncan Robertson, W. Hewlett, George Hewlett, and Daniel Cameron. Jan Term 1822.

Page 75   Will of Jesse Smith, deceased, of Nashville.
Mar 21, 1822   All my personal property after payment of my just debts to my beloved (torn away) ---ther Anson Smith. This Sept 21, 1821. Also that Anson Smith my executor. Wit: Ira Ingram and J. Roane. Jan Term 1822.

Page 76   Will of John Carter, deceased.
Mar 21, 1822   July 20, 1820. To my beloved wife Elizabeth all the stock, the household and kitchen furniture along with 196 acres of land including the plantation where we now live. Two negroes, Suck and Essix and their three children, Eve, Ann and Lucy and Tom and three children except such as is hereafter mentioned, I give to my wife during her life, then to be given to my three youngest children, Polly Simmons, Partheney and John to be equally divided at her death, the above negroes. I wish two apiece to go to each of the three youngest children when they are of lawful age and leave the above property in the hands of my brothers James and William L. Carter for the use above mentioned. To my grand children Pelina, Minerva, Sophia, Madison and a boy six months old and not named, 50 acres of land in the south end of my land, and negroes namely, Hardy and Deley for Christopher and his wife's use while they live but left entirely in the hands of James Carter for their use and at no time at all to be at Christopher's disposal. I will to my son Walter O. Carter 50 acres of land in the east end of my tract of land including the mill and two negroes, Wilson and Bill, a negro girl named Mary I give to my wife forever. I appoint James and William L. Carter my executors. Wit: James Carter, Jr. and William L. Carter. Jan Term 1822.

Page 79   Will of Anna Randall, deceased, of Davidson County.
Mar 21, 1822   To Aquilla Randall the land whereon I now live containing 133½ acres with one bed and furniture also I leave to Micha and Sarah Randall my negro boy named Charles, negro woman named Patsey with all my household furniture, also I leave Isaac Randall Harrison one bed and furniture, also Norman Randall $5.00, also Isaac Randall $5.00, also Jehu Harrison and heirs $5.00, also John Randall $5.00, also Hannah Martin and heirs $5.00. also Peggy Logue and heirs $5.00, also Greenberry Randall's heirs $5.00. Note Micha and Sarah Randall their part to include their father's estate. If Micha and Sarah Randall should die without heirs the property to belong to Aquilla Randall. I appoint Aquilla Randall executor. This 10 Feb 1817. Wit: John S. Galbreath and Pitt Bowers. Jan term 1822.

Page 78   Will of Grizle McCutchen, deceased, (female) of Davidson
Mar 21, 1822   County. To my beloved brother John McCutchen one note of $300.00 given to me by Anthony and McClellan and dated 19 Nov 1821, also to him all my part of legacy that I am entitled to by the death of Patrick McCutchen, deceased, also to John one bed and furniture and bedstead, side saddle, and one chest. Also to John all my

personal estate, goods and chattels. I also appoint my beloved brother John McCutchen sole executor. This 28 Nov 1821. Test: James McCutchen and John Hogan. Jan Term 1822.

Page 79   Will of Edmund Owen, deceased, of Davidson County.
Mar 21, 1822   To my beloved wife Sarah owen during her natural life the tract of farm house and improvements whereon I now live, also one negro girl named Lucinda or her choice of negroes, one featherbed and furniture, table and furniture, one horse, saddle and bridle, and riding chair. The rest of mu residue of my estate be equally divided among my children, to wit, Henry, Elizabeth, Edmund, James, Silas, Sarah, Nancy, Mary and David. This 1 May 1816. James Beasley, James Owen and Robert owen. Jan 1822.

Page 81   Inventory of estate of Edmond Owen, deceased.
Mar 22, 1822   Several items listed including two Bibles and one new Testament. This 2 Feb 1822. Henry Owen, executor. Jan term 1822.

Page 82   Sale of estate of John Criddle, deceased.
Mar 22, 1822   Nov 22, 1821. Several items listed including John C. Colour's receipt for a note on Thomas Whitmill and E.W. David, Robert Batson receipt Sheriff of Dickson County for collection of two notes, one on Ann and Thomas Whitmill and one on Thomas Whitmill, Isaac Earthman's receipt for a note on Kindred Jackson and James Marshall, also one note on Solomon Clark. Sarah Criddle, Jonathan Drake and Sevier Drake, admrs. Jan Term 1822.

Page 83   Inventory of estate of James Mannifee, deceased.
Mar 22, 1822   Several negroes and several other items listed including notes, viz, Samuel Anderson of Murfreesborough, William Hansborough, W. Barfield, H. Trott, W.B. Bart(illegible), Allen Goodrum, and B. Biggs, in the hands of Jerred Mennifee for collection. J.N. Mannifee and James Mannifee, admrs. Jan Term 1822.

Page 84   Inventory and sale of estate of Craven Jackson, deceased.
Mar 22, 1822   Several items done by C. Jackson hands after his death at D. Irwins. Nathaniel A. McNairy, admr of Craven Jackson, deceased. Persons making purchases, to wit, George Jackson, William Kent, Moses Stevens, Joseph Mounts, Elizabeth Jackson, N.A. McNairy, William Goodwin, John Webber, Hugh Roland, and John Moore. Jan Term 1822.

Page 85   Hire of negroes of John Saunders, deceased.
Mar 22, 1822   Twenty negroes. This 29 Dec 1822. Absalom Rogers, executor. Jan Term 1822.

Page 86   John H. Sumner, minor orphans guardian return.
Mar 22, 1822   John H. Sumner, orphan of Jos. Jno. Sumner, deceased, made with Duke W. Sumner, guardian. Several items purchased for said orphan. Jan Term 1822.

Page 87   Nancy H. Washington, minor orphan's guardian return.
Mar 22, 1822   Thomas H. Everett, guardian. This Jan 21, 1822. Jan term 1822.

Page 87   William C. Beck, minor orphan guardian return.
Mar 22, 1822   William C. Beck to Mary beck. Boarding, clothing and tuition. 29 Jan 1822. Mary Beck. Jan Term 1822.

Page 87   John Price's orphans guardian return.
Mar 22, 1822   William Gilbert, guardian for orphans. 22 Jan 1822. Jan Term 1822.

Page 88   Elizabeth Saunders, minor orphan's guardian return.
Mar 22, 1822   Edward H. East to Elizabeth Saunders, a minor orphan. Hire of her negroes and rent of her land. 30 Jan 1822. Edward H. East. Jan Term 1822.

Page 88   Settlement of estate of Andrew Davis, deceased.
Mar 22, 1822   July 10, 1821. A note on John W. Crunk and John Brownlee, Blakemore Davis, George and Drury Scruggs, and William Donelson. Also note on Morris Shain, executor of William Donelson, deceased. Vouchers in the hands of the executor

relative to the estate of Andrew Davis, deceased, by Stephen C. McDaniel and L. Scruggs, Reuben Payne and Thomas Walton, John Leaks, and Greenwood Payne, Zachariah Payne, Spencer Payne, Thomas Gleaves, James Dean, William Philips, James Clemmons, Frederick Lasiter, William McLaurine, John Hobson, George Holland, Ezekiel Young, Benjamin Butterworth, Lewis Basye, Samuel Fowlkes, John Crunk, George Hall, Caleb Willis, Thomas Blackemore, John Brownlee, Blackemore Davis, George K. and Drury Scruggs, Robert Stewart, John Hobson, Robert Bates & William Davis, Nicholas B. Pryor and Daniel Frazor. By Robert Goodlett and N.B. Pryor, Zachariah Payne, Ezekiel Payne. By receipt for C. Willis and Thomas Blackemore's note, Thomas Gleaves, John T. Dismukes and Paul Dismukes. Estate of Andrew Davis, deceased, with the executor of William Donelson, deceased. Signed by D. Dunn and George Wharton. Jan Term 1822.

Page 89   Divided estate of James Hanna, deceased, of Davidson County.
Mar 25, 1822   Estate to be divided among the heirs of James Hanna, deceased, part of Lot No. 24 in Nashville including the improvements formerly occupied by James Hanna, and two lots of land adjacent to the town of Nashville containing 9 acres and 141¼ poles having first set apart one third in value of said two lots of land to Sarah Hanna widow of said James Hanna, deceased, as follows, to wit, To Sarah Hanna one third of said two lots lying next to the road running through said land past A. Foster's. Anf to Robert H. Hanna one fourth part of the residue of said land adjoining above tract of land. And to Ellen H. Hanna is set apart one other fourth of said residue adjoining the last said tract. And to Sarah J. Hanna one other fourth of said residue of the aforesaid two lots adjoining the last tract. And to Letitia H. Hanna is set apart the remaining fourth of said residue of the two said lots. And to James Hanna is set apart the part of Lot No. 24 in town of Nashville heretofore owned by James Hanna, deceased, that was conveyed by Washington Jackson of his deed 22 Aug 1814. To Robert H. Hanna $1980.00. To Ellen H. Hanna $1980.00. To Sarah Hanna, Jr. $1980.00. To Letitia H. Hanna $1980.00. 31 Jan 1822. Andrew Morrison, executor. James Erwin, Thomas Crutcher, A. Foster, and J.P. Erwin, Commissioners. Jan Term 1822.

Page 91   Settlement of estate of John Saunders, deceased.
June 5, 1822   Made with Absalom Rogers, executor. Found negroes and whole estate $3024.42¼. Several vouchers listed. This 3 Apr 1822. Signed by William H. Nance and Thomas Williamson, Commissioners. Apr Term 1822.

Page 92   Settlement of estate of John Lester, deceased.
June 5, 1822   Made with Alexander Lester, admr. Persons listed, to wit, Susanna Lester, M.H. Quinn, Richard Lester, Richard P. Hayes, E. Smith, Benjamin Drake, E. Daniel, Jno. Lanier, S. Drake, Robertson & Curry, Daniel P. Davis for Jno. Young, Th. G. Bradford, William Wilkinson, David Abernathy, Th. Washington, George Wilson, Lewis Earthman, Nathan Ewing, Absalom Page, Alexander Lester's own account $75.00. This 9 Feb 1822. W.B. Lewis and William Lytle, Esquires, Commissioners.

Page 93   Settlement of estate of Joshua Owen, deceased.
June 5, 1822   Made with Jabez Owen, admr. This 12 Apr 1822. Several vouchers. Vouchers paid by Cary Bibb, Samuel Bell, B.W. & W.H. Bedford, Drury Clanton, Nelson Fields, Nathan Owen, Robertson & Waters, and Nathan Ewing. Signed by William H. Nance and Thomas Edmiston, Esquires, Commissioners. Apr Term 1822.

Page 94   Sale of estate of George M. Deadrick, deceased.
June 5, 1822   On 11 & 12 May 1820 in Nashville. To whom sold, viz, Joseph Woods 242 3/4 acres of the home plantation, Francis Linch 205½ acres of the home plantation, William Windle 99 3/4 acres of the home plantation, Jesse Wharton 183¼ acres of the home plantation which since transferred to George W. Campbell, Robert B. Curry 162 3/4 acres of the home plantation, John McNairy 38 feet on the Public Square including two houses. Robertson and Curry's plan No. 1, George Shall 40 feet on Deaderick Street No. 2 as Robertson's plan, John Drury 40 feet transferred to George Wilson No. 3 as Robertson's plan, George Wilson 40 feet No. 4 as Robertson's plan, S. Cantrell & Co. 60 feet No. 5 Robertson's plan, S. Cantrell & Co. 40 feet, 4 inches on Cherry Street No. 6 Robertson's plan, Edmund Cooper 62 feet, 6 inches on Cherry Street extending back on Deadrick Street 94 feet No. 7 Robertson's plan, Edmund Cooper 40 feet on Deadrick Street No. 8 Robertson's plan, Thomas Yeatman 40 feet on Deadrick Street No. 9 Robertson's plan, George Shall 40 feet on Deadrick

Street No. 11 Robertson's plan, George Shall 20 feet on the Public Square west with Deadrick Street No. 12, Stephen Cantrell & Co. 20 feet on the Public Square running back westward with Shall's line 85 feet No. 13, Joseph Litton 25 feet near the Public Square ground rent running back westwardly with Thomas Yeatman's line to a 16 foot Public Alley No. 15 Robertson's plan, Thomas Yeatman 25 feet near the Public Square on College Street ground rent running back westwardly with Joseph Litton's line a 16 foot alley No. 16, John McNairy 23 feet, 3 inches near the Public Square College Street ground rent running back westwardly with Thomas Yeatman's line to a 16 foot alley No. 17, at the same time and place was sold a white frame house to John McNairy. This house stood upon the ground where Deadrick Street now is. Also an old log stable standing on the 16 foot alley sold to Thomas Yeatman. Total for above $79,392.57. Also sold on 16 June 1821 (illegible) feet ½ adjoining Price's warehouse on College Street to John Waters. Also (illegible) feet joining the above was sold to Samuel L. Wharton.

Memo: This 23 Apr 1822 Lots No. 10 on Deadrick Street and No. 14 on the Public Square according to Duncan Robertson's plan was struck off to James G. Martin but he failed to give his bond and on 12 of Nov 1821 totally refused to execute bonds at all. He refused to sign statement. They finally took his notes. The two lots therefore from this compromise or rather necessity remain yet unsold. J. Wharton, executor and Stephen Cantrell, executor. Apr Term 1822.

Page 96   Settlement of estate of Thomas B. Pipkin, deceased.
June 6, 1822   Madw with Philip Pipkin, admr. One bay mare and colt, one sorrel mare, also one bay filly, and feed for a bay mare &c. This 17 Apr 1822. Signed by S. Shannon, J.P. and Thomas Williamson, J.P. Apr Term 1822.

Page 96   Inventory of estate of Ulric M. Dancer, deceased.
June 6, 1822   Apr 15, 1822. One horse and one bridle and saddle bags. Manuel Hunter, admr. Apr Term 1822.

Page 97   Settlement of estate of Andrew McCarmack, deceased.
June 6, 1822   Made with Charles L. Byrns, executor. Several vouchers listed. Cash in hand $5.42 3/4. $4.00 directed by absent legatees not in the hands left by the testator's will. Two grants not collected. This 6 Apr 1822. Signed by George Wharton and Joseph Love. Apr term 1822.

Page 97   Settlement of estate of John Wilson, deceased.
June 6, 1822   Made with Robert Wilson, executor. This 15 Apr 1822. By Jos. and Martha Love received $75.00, A. Ralston $75.00, James Wilson $75.00, William Wilson $75.00, Jas. and Margaret Marshall $75.00, Ellenor Patterson $75.00, and Robert Wilson $75.00. Signed by E. Goodrich, J.P. and William Faulkner. Apr Term 1822.

Page 98   Will of Alexander Ewing, deceased, of Davidson County.
June 6, 1822   To my beloved wife Sally during her natural life one third of all the lands I own in Davidson County including the mansion house, out houses and all other buildings on the tract of land whereon I now reside to be laid off by my executors, also to her the use of one half of the stock upon my farm and farming utensils to be divided by my executors, also the whole of the household and kitchen furniture with the exception of beds and bed furniture which are to be equally divided by the executors between her and my three sons, Alexander, Randol McGavock and William Black, taking into such division the beds and bed furniture which have recently been given to Alexander and Randol or which may be given to them previous to my death. My wife should not be restricted in the disposition or sale of any the above personal property bequeathed to her but that she should sell or dispose of such part as she may think necessary or proper. Also she is to have one half of all the slaves. To my son James Ewing a tract of land on Smiths Fork of Caney Fork in Wilson County containing 640 acres, also a tract of land on Elk River in Franklin County containing 640 acres, also the seven slaves now in his possession, also 25 slaves of the Capital Stock of the Bank of State of Tennessee. To my son Alexander Ewing one half of the tract of land in Williamson County near Franklin containing 538 acres, also two lots or part of lots in the town of Nashville on Water Street which were conveyed by Hall and McNairy to C. Stump by him to Thomas Shute and by him to me, also several named slaves also 25 shares of Capitol Stock of the Bank Of State of Tennessee. To my son Randol McGavock Ewing the other half of said tract of land of 538 acres to be equally divided between him and Alexander, also a

part of Lot No. 6 in town of Nashville on Water Street including Stump's warehouse which was conveyed by James Trimble also by Thomas Shute to me. Also several named slaves and fifty shares of bank stock of Nashville Bank. To my son William Black Ewing the tract of land whereon I now live in Davidson County containing about 500 acres subject to the life estate of my beloved wife, also 60 acres of land on Stones River in Rutherford County, Tennessee, also the other half of the stock on my farm and farming utensils and also upon the death of my wife the stock, farming utensils, household and kitchen furniture which may remain also the other half of my slaves are to be equally divided between my sons Alexander, Randal McGavock and William Black, also to my son William B. 50 shares of the capitol stock of the Nashville Bank. To my grandson Alexander Ewing McGavock a tract of land containing 320 acres on Loosa Hatcher River in the 11th District in Range 2, Section 4. To my grandson Oscar Smith Ewing a tract of land containing 300 acres in the 11th District in Range 3, Section 7. To my grand daughter Nancy Kent McGavock my negro girl slave named Cynthia and her increase provided my grand daughter should live to attain the age of 18 years or should marry but should neither happen the said slave and her increase are to be divided with the residue of my estate hereinafter mentioned. I give to my son William B. my gold watch. All the rest and residue of my lands not herein before devised, I give to my sons James, Alexander, Randal McGavock and William Black and their heirs forever. All the rest and residue of my personal estate of every description not herein devised to be equally divided after payment of my just debts, to my beloved wife and my sons, Alexander, Randal McGavock and William Black and their heirs. All the aforesaid devises and bequeaths to my son Alexander Ewing are to depend on the contingency that he does not marry Sarah Jefferson and the event that he should not comply with my desire and should marry her, he is to take nothing and bequeathed to my sons Randal McGavock and William Black and their heirs. I appoint my friends Oliver B. Hayes and William L. Brown and my son Alexander Ewing executors. This 6 Feb 1822. Wit: Jacob McGavock, Robert W. Green and Jacob Perkins. Apr Term 1822.

Page 100   Inventory of estate of Alexander Ewing, deceased.
June 6, 1822   Several items listed including several negroes and other items also several bonds and notes, viz, Robert Jarman, Shadrack Jarman and A. Harris, Thomas Childress to A. Ewing by his attorney Robert W. Green, W.B. Ballentine of Kentucky, C. Gibs, George Elliot, and James Jackson in hands of William Hadley, Stump & Cox, T.H. Fletcher endorsed by G.G. Washington also by Young Green & Co. Signed by O.B. Hayes and W.L. Brown, executors. Apr Term 1822.

Page 102   Inventory of estate of Edmond Owen, deceased.
June 7, 1822   Made this 15 Apr 1822. Note on James Wright, George G. Brown, Michael Campbell given Christopher Seabourn. Henry Owen, one of the executors. Apr Term 1822.

Page 102   Sale of estate of Edmond Owen, deceased.
June 7, 1822   Persons listed, to wit, James Carter, Esq., Henry White, Russel Sulivant, Robert Sample, Nelson W. Pigg, George Hartman, M. Corbit, E.H. East, Sarah Owen, Edmond Owen, M. Wall, John Kenedy, John Charlton, N.B. Owen, Z. Nowel, Thomas Hambleton, Robert Goodlet, John Carnal, Henry Owen, J.K. Buchanan, J.C. Smith, M. Smith, A. Height, Jeremiah Roberts, A. Redmond, Silas L. Owen, Presley Jones, N.W. Pigg, W.M. Harwood, James Pigg, J. Roberts, James Wright, William Hays, A. Martin, Robert Ridley, J. Baker, Howel J. Carnel, Jr., William Hervey, James Howell, J. Whitsett, Henry Ferebee, Joseph Allison, Thomas Rutherford, William Richardson, Nancy R. Owens, John Carnel, Sr., P.S. Owen, R.C. Drury, Henry Owen bought one Bible for $1.00, James Owen, William Franks, William Murphey, Thomas Buchanan, H. Wilcox, M. Kettle, Richard Bradberry, and R. Pully. Henry Owen, executor. Apr Term 1822.

Page 104   Will of William Perkins, deceased.
June 8, 1822   To my beloved wife Susanna Perkins during her natural life that part of the tract of land on which I now live which was conveyed to me by Nicholas T. Perkins, also negro woman Winney and two of her children also other negroes, also household and kitchen furniture she is to give to my youngest daughter Eliza Fearn when she marries or comes of age, two beds and furniture, also one half of the farming tools and one half of my horses and mules and one third of my cattle &c and my carriage that I bought from Colo. Cannon. To my youngest daughter Eliza Fearn negroes, one horse, saddle and bridle. To my

son Nicholas my negro boy Meshack. To my daughter Sally Price Scales my negro boy Jacob and girl Maria. All the balance of my estate except my land after paying my just debts I wish to be divided equally between Sally Price Scales, Eliza Fearn Perkins each one third part, and my two grand children America Carmon and William Perkins Cannon one third part between them, all that part of my land which I have not given to my wife, I wish to be sold by my executors. I appoint my beloved wife Susanna Perkins, executrix and Daniel Perkins, Samuel Perkins and Thomas Edmiston, executors. This 8 Mar 1822. Wit: James Walker, J. Overton and Henry Crichlow.
Codicil: To my beloved wife my negro man Saul and at her death to be disposed. This 12 Mar 1822. Test: James Walker and Henry Crichlow. Apr Term 1822.

Page 106   Patsey McBride's dower.
June 10, 1822   Patsey McBride widow of James McBride, deceased, one third part of the tract of land on which the said deceased did live, bordering lands of Richard Drewry. Also she is to have the mansion house and all the other houses with all the waters. This 2 Mar 1822. J. Ezell, Richard Drury, David Hays, Henry White, Jr., Robert Wood, John Gowen, Richard Smith, J.K. Buchanan, John Buchanan, James Mulherrin, James Carter, and Thomas Rutherford, Jurors. Apr Term 1822.

Page 107   Sale of estate of Arthur Exum, deceased.
June 10, 1822   Sold by John Exum, admr. One small pair of Mill Stones and tobacco. Apr 20, 1822. Apr Term 1822.

Page 107   Sale of estate of Williamson Adams, deceased.
June 10, 1822   Purchasers, to wit, James Carter, Thomas Fuqua note, William Hinton note, John Corbit note, Richard Drury note, Solomon Clark note, William Trepperd note, and Samuel Morleys, and Rebecca Adams note. Apr 25, 1822. Aor Term 1822.

Page 107   Inventory of estate of Anne Harris, deceased.
June 10, 1822   Nashville, 23 Apr 1822. Negro woman Kate and three children, Hetta, Mary Ann and Jefferson which were sold by the guardian of the minor distributee of the wife of the adminstrator of value of $1000.00. One negro boy by the name of Belley sold by the guardian as above to Mrs. Beck of the value of $500.00. Benjamin S. Williamson, admr. Apr Term 1822.

Page 108   Ensley & Johnston's Land Testimony Perpetuated, Davidson
June 10, 1822   County. On 12 Apr 1822, appeared John Buchanan before me Benjah Gray an acting Justice of the Peace, one of the Commissioners, to take the deposition of said Buchanan relative to the north west corner of a tract of land originally granted to Jason Thompson for 274 acres lying on the waters of Mill Creek east of Carpers Branch of Collinsworth Creek the waters of the east fork of Mill Creek, Thomas Fletcher's land, John Thompson's survey, Jason Thompson's 274 acre survey. Signed by John Buchanan. Test: Sherwood Green, Joseph Brewer, Benjamin F. Collinsworth, Samuel Weakley, William Johnson, Elisha Phelps, Alexander Buchanan, and Simon Jenkins. Benajah Gray, J.P. Apr Term 1822.

Page 109   Sale of estate of Jacob Dickinson, deceased.
June 10, 1822   Persons listed, to wit, Patsey Dickinson, George Wharton, Robert Wilson, William H. Hinton, Jabez White, William Dorris, Silas McKay, Francis McKay, Patsey Dickinson, James Dean, Whidha White, David Love, Jos. Jewell, Nelson Talley, Martin Pearce, James Wilson, Ellis E. Dismukes, William Parker, Edward Butler, Thomas Hopson, John Jourdon, S.C. McDaniel, and Mrs. Dickinson. Patsey Dickinson, admrx. Apr Term 1822.

Page 110   Sarah Owen, widow's support, Davidson County.
June 10, 1822   Support to lay off and set apart unto Sarah Owen widow of Edmond Owen, deceased. Several items listed. This 22 Feb 1822. William Murphey and John Gowen, two of the Commissioners. Apr Term 1822.

Page 111   Winney McFarland, widow's support, Davidson County.
June 13, 1822   Support to lay off and set apart unto Winney McFarland, widow of R.P. McFarland, deceased. Several items listed. Duncan Robertson and Collin S. Hobbs, two of the Commissioners. Apr Term 1822.

Page 111   Catherine Powell, widow's support.
June 13, 1822   Allowed Catherine Powell $140.00 for support of herself and her six children. Apr 26, 1822. John Stump and Lewis Earthman. Catherine Powell is widow and relict of Willie Powell, deceased. Apr Term 1822.

Page 111   Additional inventory of Francis Saunders, deceased.
June 13, 1822   This 4 Mar 1822. Z. Noel collected as an officer $7.50. Leather sold $40.37½. Auction $689.68 3/4, and cash at sale $32.68 3/4, and Neal book $2.56¼. This 22 Apr 1822. William Saunders, executor.

Page 112   Sale of estate of Elizabeth Hardy, deceased.
June 13, 1822   Persons listed, to wit, Joseph Dougal, Harriet Temple, Joseph Mount, John Webber, John Moore, James Holt, Micajah Fly, Lewis Spiece, Samuel McMurria, one Bible sold to Lewis Spiece, Isaac Allen, Jesse Brown, C.S. Hobbs, Enoch Fly, (blank) Whitney, Jno. Woodcock, E. McDaniel, and William Kent. Apr Term 1822.

Page 112   Sale of estate of Lemuel Kennedy, deceased.
June 13, 1822   Notes, viz, Foster & Wells, Gillespie, Falwell, E.H. Foster, one silver watch sold for $8.33, and several other items listed. One note on William Brooks. John Criddle, admr. Apr Term 1822.

Page 113   Inventory of estate of Jesse Smith, deceased. (Mr. Jesse Smith)
June 13, 1822   One gold watch, note books and other items. Notes on Jacob Shall, Keys & Webb, James Roanes, E.W. Brookshire, George Dillons, John H. Lewis, Joel M. Smith, Daniel Clark, John Beattie, Robert H. Adams, Richard M(illegible), Nelson Tyler, Duke W. Davis, Jno. Witherow, Jno. Flemming, Amasa Jones, Edward Perlee, Benjamin Hamlin, Ridley Wynn, Wilson Lyon, James Reed, Flavius Harris, Williamson Adams & Benjamin Brookshire, Joseph Norvell, George Wilson, Duncan Robertson, Thomas Blount, Sterling H. Lester, Henry Lake, William Quarles, James Porter, Richard Jones, Chauncy Shipman, Henry Manus, widow Adams, James C. Lee, Thomas H. Flemming, William Alexander, Margaret Chism, Levi Farrell, E.B. Roach, Elezer Baker, Samuel Howard, Samuel K. Green, Marmion Lowe, Edmund Lanier, E. Eddy, Jno. M. Harnett, Jno. McNairy, Isaac Millikins, John W. Crunk, William Rutherford, Samuel Maclin, Gilbert Pew, J. Barry, Henry Rutherford, John Cox, T.W. Williams, Moses Matthew, Robert Sea, John Hill, Jeffrey B.M., Jno. D. Stovall, Robert Gilmore, Judah M.W., George West, Francis Jones, Anthony Butler, Thomas Beal, Hugh Young, and Daniel Turner. Several items listed. (a very long list) Other notes on viz, Harwell Dunham, J. Roan, Samuel Scott, R.P. Hays, Dyer Quarles, Robertson & Waters, Boyd McNairy, Jno. Shelby, and George A. Bedford. Accounts due on, viz, Ingram & Lloyd, Samuel Hoit & Co., James Roane, Keys & Webb, E.W. Brookshire, Jno. Harding, James B. Houston, Manus & Dillon, E. Benoit, Roman Watson, A. Kingsley, Jos. Norvell, William Hewlett, R.P. Hays, and Thomas Beal. Nashville Apr 15, 1822. Ira Ingram, admr. Apr Term 1822.

Page 119   Will of Joseph Philips, deceased, of Davidson County.
Sept 3, 1822   To my daughter Sally Williams six negroes. To my daughter Peggy Williams eight negroes. To both my daughters Sally and Peggy jointly all my land and mill situate lying and being in what is called McLean's Bend of Cumberland River. To Jesse Wharton to hold and dispose of interest for the three children of my daughter Polly Wharton, deceased, viz, John Overton Wharton, Joseph Philip Wharton and Sally Angeline Wharton six negroes and $3000.00 being sixty shares of my stock in the Nashville Bank, and also to said trustee to hold in trust for Sally Angeline Wharton, and my negro girl named Martha. To Francis McGavock to hold in trust for the children of my daughter Patsey Martin or in case of his death or refusal to act before the said trust is completed, to Jacob McGavock in trust for the same purpose $4000.00 of my stock in the Nashville Bank, being eight shares which is to remain in bank for the benefit of the children of said Patsey Martin and under the control of my said trustee and the dividends or interests arising from the whole sum, after deducting there from an adequate conpensation in equal shares to each as they may marry of come of lawful age. To my son William Duncan Philips the land on which I now live together with all that which I purchased of James Ross and James Mores except what I sold to Duke William Sumner, all my household and kitchen furniture, farming utensils and tools of every description, my wearing cloths, still and tubs, wagon and gears, a team of good horses, two brood mares and his colt, also other items including 12 negroes. I will and order such sum as may be necessary in the opinion of my executors, be by them expended in inclosing the family

graveyard. The rest of my residue, after all my just debts are paid, to be equally divided between my daughters Sally Williams and Peggy Williams, but if the fund created is insufficient, it is my desire that Josiah F. Williams whom I appoint guardian to my son William D. Philips, shall set apart so much of the personal property given to my son William as will be sufficient to pay the balance of my debts. The property left to my son William be kept together on the farm under the direction of his guardian and that the distillery on said farm be carried on or rented yearly and a person employed to attend to the business from year to year, and that his property maybe given up to him when he arrives at twenty one years of age or sooner if his guardian may think proper. I appoint my friends William Williams, Josiah F. Williams and David McGavock as executors. This 1 Jan 1820. Wit: Stephen Cantrell, Jr., Matthew Barrow and E. Pritchett. July Term 1822.

Page 121   Will of David Moore, deceased, of Davidson County.
Sept 3, 1822   To my brother Samuel Moore ten shares of my Nashville Bank stock and one half of my wearing apparel. To the children of my late sister, late wife of Robert Hill of Pittsburg, the remaining thirty shares of my Nashville Bank stock to be divided among them. To my niece Elizabeth Hagen wife of James Hagen, Rutherford County, during her natural life, my tract of land on Bradshaw Creek of 142 acres, being the tract granted to me by Grant No. 3272 from the State of North Carolina, also 100 acres of my tract of land on Kellys Creek being the remainder of said tract after taking off 400 acres given to John and Polly Moore, also my negro woman Patsey and after the death of my niece Elizabeth Hagen I give said two tracts of land and my negro Patsey to her heirs. To my nephew David Moore one undivided moiety of my house and lot on Water Street being the house and lot where I now live and being the ground purchased from William L. Boyd at two separate purchases, see his deed Book L, page 537 and book N, page 72. To Patrick Moore, brother of David Moore, the other moiety of the above named or described house and lot. To John Moore, son of my deceased brother James Moore, 200 acres of land on Kellys Creek having about 500 acres in one body granted by several grants to be laid off at the lower end next to the river, also one half of the net proceeds from the sale of my house and lot on Market Street being part of Lot No. 1 of the College Lots lying near the Stone Bridge being the lot purchased by me from Bernard McKeenan, 30 feet front running back the depth of the lot, the remaining half of my wearing apparel. To my niece Mary Moore, daughter of my brother James Moore, deceased, 200 acres of land on Kellys Creek, to be laid off next to above the tract devised to her brother John Moore, also all my household furniture. To my friend and relation Ann Ridley, wife of James Ridley, the remaining part of my lot of ground adjoining the town of Nashville, granted to me by the State of Tennessee by Grant No. 329, also by Quit Claim from John McNairy being the residue after satisfying the deeds of John Drewry and John Hamilton. To my friend and relation Nathaniel A. McNairy my patent lever silver watch with gold chain, seal and key with a request that the same may be kept in the family as a token of my regard. To my friend Kitty McNairy, wife of N.A. McNairy, my white pony. To my young friends John McNairy, son of N.A. McNairy, and John McNairy, son of Boyd McNairy, a note of hand executed to me by Thomas H. Fletcher for $431.00 with interest. To my friend Duncan Robertson of Nashville my lot on Sumner Street 43 feet front being part of Lot No. 41 of the College Lots being the same I purchased of James Grizzard, also my silver mounted spectacles and case. To Musador(?)(in margin of page) B. Campbell, daughter of my good friend William P. Anderson, the 200 acres of land given to me by William P. Anderson, dated 19 Jan 1813. To my niece Susan Hill in addition to the former devise one moiety of the net proceeds of the sale of my before described house and lot on Market Street. To the Female Charitable Society of Nashville $50.00 current money to be paid within 12 months after my decease by Duncan Robertson. To my kind friend Daniel Cameron as a token of my regard, I give my shot gun, razor and other shaving utensils also my pocket knife and walking cane. My executors are to sell my house and lot on Market Street near the Stone Bridge and when in funds discharge the legatees to John Moore and Susan Hill. I appoint Nathaniel A. McNairy and John Elliston as executors. This 11 June 1822. Test: Addison East, David Cameron and William Garner. July Term 1822.

Page 123   Will of Martin Greer, deceased, of Davidson County.
Sept 3, 1822   To my beloved daughter Nancy May one horse, saddle, featherbed and furniture, cow and calf, two ewes and lambs being the property already delivered her after marriage. To my beloved son Joseph Greer one horse, saddle, featherbed and furniture, cow and calf, two ewes and lambs being the property already delivered him after marriage. To my beloved son Benjamin Greer one horse, saddle, featherbed and furniture, cow and calf,

two ewes and lambs being the property already delivered him after marriage. To my beloved daughter Polly Vaughn one horse, saddle, featherbed and furniture, cow and calf, two ewes and lands being the property already delivered her after marriage and no more until after mine and her mother's death then she is to have ten pounds and no more. To my beloved son Green B. Greer one horse, saddle, which he has received, also one featherbed and furniture, cow and calf, two ewes and lambs. To my beloved daughter Elizabeth Greer one horse which she received also one featherbed and furniture, one cow and calf, and two ewes and lambs. To my beloved son James W. Greer one horse, saddle, featherbed and furniture, cow and calf, two ewes and lambs. To my beloved son William H. Greer, horse, saddle, featherbed and furniture, cow and calf, ten ewes and lambs. The residue of my property both real and personal remain in the hands and possession of my beloved wife Mary during her natural life or widowhood to support her and my children and school them and at the death or marriage of my beloved wife, all the property both real and personal that is left, to be sold at public sale and the monies collected and all debts due me to be equally divided among all my children except Polly Vaughn. I appoint my two beloved sons Joseph and Benjamin Greer with my beloved wife Mary, my executors. This 11 Mar 1822. Wit: Robert Thomas and Alex. Waites. July Term 1822.

Page 125   Will of Seth Davis, deceased, of Davidson County.
Sept 3, 1822   To my beloved wife Lucy amd my children, to wit, Joshua, Meddy, Stokeley, Wilson, James, Nancy, Laurecy, Julia and Seth Davis, all my real and personal estate to be equally divided amongst them. To my beloved wife Lucy all the household and kitchen furniture. The tract of land lying and being in Williamson County, Tennessee, on the waters of Harpeth River on which my sons Joshua and Stokeley now reside, shall be included among my other property. I appoint my worthy friends John Davis, Newton Edney and B. Russell Howland, my executors. This 16 May 1820. Wit: Newton Edney, Edmond Edney, Demsey Jones and B. Russell Howland. July Term 1822.

Page 126   Will of David Wills, deceased, of Robertson County, Tennessee.
Sept 4, 1822   To my beloved wife Polly Wills a certain piece or parcel of land lying in Davidson County on what is called the Blue Spring Branch on the waters of Sycamore Creek containing 80 acres which land I purchased of Joseph Binkley to her and her heirs forever. Also to my wife Polly all my stock together with all my household and kitchen furniture, all the farming and working tools and all my money, notes &c. I appoint my wife Polly to be my whole sole executrix. This 22 Feb 1822. Wit: Asa Bryan and John Cochran. July Term 1822.

Page 127   Will of George Bell, deceased, of Davidson County.
Sept 4, 1822   Being of extreme old age, make this will. To Adeline Nelson, daughter of Elizabeth Nelson, my daughter, my bureau as a token of my great regard and love for her. To my beloved son George Bell all my property of all kinds, negroes &c, he is the only child to whom I never gave anything. I desire that my negro boy Buck be free at the age of 21 and I do hereby enjoin on my son George Bell that he will obtain the freedom of said negro boy Buck so as to effect his freedom legally, and george Bell be the guardian and protector of said boy Buck. I appoint my son George Bell my sole executor. This 16 July 1819. Wit: George Bell, John McNairy and Samuel Gallaway. July Term 1822.

Page 128   Will of Mary Scott, deceased.
Sept 4, 1822   Court of Pleas and Quarter Sessions held in Nashville on 3rd Monday in July A.D. 1822 the following cause on to be heard, to wit, Mary Scott's executors, plaintiff VS William L. Carter and wife, defendants. Apr 15, 1822. This day appeared Thomas Scott and Sinkler Scott in person and offered a paper in writing for probate purporting to be the Last Will and testament of Mary Scott, to wit, I, Mary Scott of Davidson County, do this 11 day April 1816 make my Last Will and Testament. To my son William Scott $1.00 and the property and money he had in his possession at his father's death. To my son George Scott $1.00 and the property and money he had in his possession at his father's death. To my daughter Lucretia Patterson $1.00 and the property and money she had in her possession at her father's death. To my daughter Sarah Yeats $1.00 and the property and money she had in her possession at her father's death. To my son Thomas Scott and Sinkler Scott the tract of land I now live on containing 314 acres. To Thomas Scott the upper end of said land by a line being run across the land agreeable to the way the lane now runs. To Sinkler Scott the lower end of said tract of land also one mare, that one he now claims and

one of his choice of cows, and one bed. My will is that Thomas Scott and Sinkler Scott shall maintain my son John Scott his lifetime and whichever keeps him Thomas Scott or Sinkler Scott the other shall pay him whatever it is worth as they agree. To JOhn Scott the bed he now lies on during his natural life. To my son Moses Scott $200.00 to be raised out of the stock. To my daughter Polly Thompson the one half of the value of all the rest of the household and kitchen furniture together with a still that is now in possession of William L. Carter along with all the farming utensils, stock that remains over and above making Moses Scott's part. To my daughter Rhoda Carter the other half of the value of the property I gave to Polly Thompson to be sold or divided as they can agree. My desire that my negro woman Moll and the land warrant, that the land was lost by Woods claim, and the balance of the land that Woods claim did not take shall be sold to pay my just debts and if any remain to be divided between Polly Thompson and Rhoda Carter. I appoint my son Thomas Scott and Sinkler Scott my executors. Wit: Edward Woodward, Charles Scott and John Exum.

William L. Carter and Rhoda Carter, his wife, came into court and said that the said paper writing purported is not the Last Will and Testament of said Mary Scott, deceased, and the said Thomas Scott and St. Clair Scott, executors, likewise. A jury was called, to wit, Hugh F. Newell, William Matlock, Robert W. Greene, Philip Shute, Mordicai Pillow, Frederick E. Fisher, Richard H. Barry, Edmund Grizzard, John Searcy, Greenwood Payne, Daniel Whiting, and Charles Abernathy being sworn and said that the paper writing is the Last Will and Testament of Mary Scott, deceased.

Page 130   Isaac Battle's heirs guardian settlement.
Sept 4, 1822   Jesse Stancil, executor of Nathan Stancil, deceased, who was the former guardian of the minor heirs of Isaac Battle, deceased. Vouchers on the following, to wit, David Manns, Zilpha Collins, Doctor S. Morton, Nelson Fields, Dorcas McClain, Thomas Kings, William Scruggs, and Doctor Pryor's receipt. Notes of the following, to wit, Joshua Cutchin and D.J. Robinson, William Scruggs, Jas. Moore, and David Barnhill, Nehemiah Taylor and E. Lawrence, E. Hall and J.H. Hall, George Bennett and Edwin Austin, R.W. Robinson and Jos. Nevan, Thomas Lance and Thomas Johnson, Mrs. Betsey Sadler and D. Barnwell, Jas. Moore, Thomas Shelton, Mack Roberts and Thomas Roberts, Thomas Lane and Thomas Johnson, John S. Russworm, Sterling Davis and J.H. Howlett, Allen Goodrum and Jos. Brittain, Jas. Taylor and Jos. Scott, Edwin Austin and D.J. Humphrey, William Adams, Brittain Adams, and John H. Hall. This 4 July 1822. Signed by Jno. S. Russworm, Thomas S. King and William H. Nance. July Term 1822.

Page 131   Inventory of estate of Joseph Jewell, deceased.
Sept 5, 1822   Made by Mary E. Jewell, admrx. Several items listed. July
Term 1822.

Page 132   Settlement of estate of Lemuel T. Turner, deceased.
Sept 4, 1822   Made with Stephen Cantrell. Cash paid to the following, to wit, Thomas G. Bradford, and John S. Williamson. Cash received of Richard Rapier & Co. by Will H. Bedford. Cash paid to John S. Williamson, Mr. Ewing, and Ann W. Turner. This 19 July 1822. Signed by Will Lytle and W.B. Lewis. July Term 1822.

Page 133   Jesse Jackson, deceased, heirs.
Sept 6, 1822   Elizabeth bought of Mr. Saunders merchandise, also Mary bought merchandise, Martha bought as above, and Jessina bought as above. 8 July 1822. Court has examined the guardianship of Obediah Jackson of the orphans of Jesse Jackson, deceased, and he has laid out for them $57.00 as stated and do allow him $1.00 to each child per year since commencing. Signed by William Saunders and Fra. Saunders. July Term 1822.

Page 133   Settlement of estate of Elijah Earhart, deceased, of Davidson
Sept 6, 1822   County. We, Edmond Gamble and Samuel Shannon, appointed settle with Rodney Earhart, admr of estate of Elijah Earhart, deceased, and made return, viz, notes on Jonathan Clay, Nathan Ewing's receipt, William Douglass account, T. Hill assignee and Isaac Weakley, George Waggoner note, J.F. Williams receipt. Proven by Andrew Birdwell. Received of Matthew Patterson, Elijah Earhart by the hand of John Earhart, by William Stognes, and by David Earhart. This 23 July 1822. Signed by S. Shannon, J.P. and E. Gamble. July Term 1822.

Page 134   Settlement of estate of David Earhart, deceased, of Davidson
Sept 6, 1822   County. We, Edmond Gamble and Samuel Shannon appointed to settle with Rodney Earhart, administrator. J. Williams' receipt, also Thomas Taylor, Ephraim Foster, William Richey, John Bayres(?), Thomas Rutherford, William Parker, Joseph Love, John B. Goldberry, Robert Taylor, James T. Love, John C. Parker, Langhorn Scrugg, John Newman, Thomas Coles, Matthew Patterson, Thomas Deaderick, John H. Smith, Josiah Horton, Joseph Hooper, Exum P. Sumner, Peter Bass, James Everett, J.F. Williams, James Bryson, Jno. C. Hicks' account for coffin and trimmings, Zachariah Stulls, Archibald Scott, John Lanier, John H. Smith, James Harris, David Parker, William Wallace, Thomas Casey, Nathan Ewing, and David B. Love. This 23 July 1822. July Term 1822.

Page 135   Settlement of estate of Thomas Wilcox, deceased.
Sept 6, 1822   Made by Z. Noell, executor. Persons listed, to wit, James Askins, A. Whitehead, A. Porter, and John Kernal. Paid William Gibson, Robert Wood, Robert W. Green, and Littleton Perry. This 20 July 1822. Test: James Carter, J.P. and Will Lytle, J.P.

Page 136   Inventory of estate of Moody Harris, deceased.
Sept 6, 1822   Made by James McGavock, admr. Returned by agreement of the heirs and legatees of said Moody Harris, deceased, to wit, note on John W. Page and Absalom Page and John W. Page having returned to me negroes, Ben and Matilda the consideration of said note. July Term 1822.

Page 137   Inventory of estate of Lemuel Kennedy, deceased.
Sept 6, 1822   A judgement on Stump & Cox and one debt on John Kennedy, one debt on Charles Ballentine and one on William L. Carter. Signed by John Criddle, admr. July 26, 1822. July Term 1822.

Page 137   Sale of estate of John Castleman, deceased.
Sept 6, 1822   Amount of sale $184.62½. This 22 July 1822. Absalom Gleaves, admr. July Term 1822.

Page 137   Account of Larkin Clay, deceased.
Sept 6, 1822   Made with J. Clay, executor. Persons listed, to wit, N. Ewing, E.E. Dismukes, McCain for tuition, E.H. Foster, Nichol Vaulx & Co., Hendly Ballance, J.P. Clark, and R. & W. Armstrong. July Term 1822.

Page 138   Mary E. Jewell, widow support.
Sept 6, 1822   To Mary E. Jewell's support being three in family, we find the $80.81, we find for Mary E. Jewell for one year. This 25 July 1822. Signed by Joseph Love, William Neely, James Wilson, and Simon Williams. July Term 1822.

Page 138   Patsey Dickinson, widow support.
Sept 6, 1822   We have laid off and set apart to Mrs. Patsey Dickinson, widow and relict of Jacob Dickinson late of Davidson County, deceased, for the support of herself and family for the present year. Several items listed. This 6 Feb 1822. Signed by William Neely, Duke W. Sumner and Simon Williams. July Term 1822.

Page 138   Inventory of sale of estate of Ulric Dancer, deceased.
Sept 6, 1822   Sold one horse and bridle for $35.00, one pair saddle bags $1.81¼. Total $36.81¼. Manuel Hunter, admr. July Term 1822.

Page 139   Inventory of estate of John Childress, deceased.
Sept 6, 1822   Received of S.C. Robertson a note on Mordicai Pillow $150.80, this note was paid by said Robertson to me as admr as the full part of Jno. Childress, deceased, in a tract of land in Giles County, Tennessee to John McCanless. Balance of sale of cotton in 1820 $5.37. Total $155.37. Samuel B. Marshall, admr. July Term 1822.

Page 139   John Pugh and Isaac G. Pugh.
Sept 7, 1822   John Davis guardian to John Pugh, minor, returned by Solomon Clark, admr, dated Apr 1820. John Davis guardian to isaac Pugh, minor, returned by Solomon Clark, dated Apr 1820. July Term 1822.

Page 140   Elizabeth A. Carter's dower.
Sept 7, 1822   Commissioners met to lay off to Elizabeth A. Carter widow and
relict of John Carter, deceased, her dower on 27 April 1822, allotted a tract of land
bordering Grizzard's line and containing 98 2/3 acres, also personal property and the one sixth
part of all money or dues to said estate when collected. This 27 Apr 1822. Signed by Jerm.
Ezell, John Buchanan, Thomas Buchanan, James Buchanan, John K. Buchanan, Robert
Buchanan, William Matlock, Anthony Clopton, James Pigg, Richard Smith, Samuel Blair, and
William McMurray. July Term 1822.

Page 140   Inventory of estate of Arthur Redmond, deceased.
Sept 7, 1822   Inventory of the late firm of Redmond & Branche, viz, Several
items listed including one gold watch. Frances M. Redmond, admr. July Term 1822.

Page 140   Inventory of estate of David Moore, deceased.
Sept 7, 1822   Persons listed, to wit, Notes on John Elliston, William L. Boyd,
and Thomas H. Fletcher. Several items listed. Notes on Boyd McNairy, Duncan Robertson
and William W. Goodwin. N.A. McNairy and Jno. Elliston, executors. 500 acres on Kellys
Creek, 142 acres on Bradshaw Creek, one house and ___ on Water Street, William P. Anderson
bond for 200 acres of land, one lot near the Stone Bridge, 43 feet of lot on Cherry Street,
and remainder of lot joining Whiteside and Balch, purchased of McNairy. July Term 1822.

Page 142   Inventory of estate of Walter Sims, deceased.
Sept 7, 1822   Several items listed. The personal property was left to the
widow by his will except the negroes in which a life estate only is given and are in the
possession of said widow. This July 15, 1822. John G. Sims, admr. July Term 1822.

Page 143   Settlement of estate of Joseph Coleman, deceased.
Sept 7, 1822   To Peter Legrand in behalf of his wife Ann M. Legrand, admr.
Several items for William and Powhatton, and Joseph Coleman. Cash let Powhatton have to
go to Huntsville $8.00. Boarding Powhatton Coleman from April 1821 to April 1822 $100.00.
Boarding of William Coleman $90.00. Boarding Joseph Coleman $75.00. To cash paid for the
heirs of Joseph Coleman, deceased. Cash paid Edward Daniel, Moses Stevens, and G.
Blackburn, as per vouchers. Hire of negroes. One third off widow's dower. By cash for rent
of one house in town for eight months at $6.50 per month. R. Weakley, J.P. and Will Lytle.
July Term 1822.

Page 145   Will of Samuel Leonax (Lenox), deceased, of Davidson County.
Dec 16, 1822   To my beloved wife Minit Lenox the house and plantation
whereon I now live together with all the personal estate I possess during her natural life or
widowhood, except one dunn mare and saddle which I give to my nephew Levi Walker incase
my wife marries, I wish my property to be equally divided between her and all my beloved
children after all my just debts are paid. To my beloved wife keep together and raise my
little (blank) in the best way that she can, at her decease what remains to be equally divided
among my children, that is to say, Nancy, Polly, William and Martha. I appoint my wife
Minit Lenox and Cardy C. Peebles, as executors. This 7 Aug 1822. Wit: Jeremiah Ellis and
Thomas Pierce. Oct Term 1822.

Page 146   Inventory of estate of Samuel Lenox, deceased.
Dec 17, 1822   Davidson County Oct 24, 1822. Several items listed including
one dun mare that was given to Lucy Walker in by will and $70.00 in bank notes and notes on
Gideon Harris and George Huffman and book account on Thomas Pierce, also $6.00 in the
hands of Christopher Brooks for collection. Signed by Cardy C. Peebles and Minit Lenox,
executors. Oct Term 1822.

Page 146   Account of sale of estate of Mary Scott, deceased.
Dec 17, 1822   Sept 6, 1822. Purchasers, to wit, Thomas Scott, St. Clair Scott,
John Exum, William L. Carter, John McElwain, Joel Smith, Joshua Dillingham, Daniel Martin,
Preston V. Thompson, George Scott, William Hail, John T. Scott, William Brown, Jesse
Reynolds, Moses Patterson, Samuel Thompson, Elijah Lake, Granny Moll, Benjamin Smith,
William Davidson, and Benjamin D. Pack. Thomas and St. Clair Scott, executors. Oct Term
1822.

Page 147   Inventory of estate of William Perkins, deceased, of Davidson
Dec 17, 1822   County, taken by Samuel Perkins, executor, on 19 Oct 1822.
Household furniture, two bedsteads at Samuel perkins bought in lifetime of the deceased and
not taken away. Several items listed. A bond on Jonathan Hill. Received James W. Perkins
his bond, to Thomas H. Perkins' bond. Oct Term 1822.

Page 148   Inventory of estate of Allen Dodson, deceased.
Dec 18, 1822   Taken 31 Oct 1822. Several items listed. Timothy Dodson,
admr. Oct Term 1822.

Page 148   Inventory of estate of Seth Davis, deceased.
Dec 18, 1822   Items not included for disposal in his will, several items listed.
Jno. Davis and Newton Edney, executors. Oct Term 1822.

Page 149   Account of sale of inventory of Joseph Jewell, deceased.
Dec 18, 1822   July 27, 1822. Purchasers, to wit, Francis McKay, Maxmillion
Redding, William Neely, John Patterson, John Beasley, William McCaslin, Jabez White, John
Brown, Joseph T. Hope, P. Woodard, Samuel Neely, Andrew Birdwell, Landon Farrow, William
Hope, Moses B. Frazier, Duke W. Sumner, Jane Brown, Mary E. Jewell, Patsy Dickinson, S.W.
Hope, William Porter, Leonard Hunter, David Walker, Josiah Williams, Daniel M. Frazier,
Jemima Hall, George Wharton, Robert Wilson, Jane Wilson, William Williams, Robert Wilson,
Thomas Dill, Jeremiah (illegible), David Love, S. Williams, William Neely, Pitt Woodard,
Whitley White, and George W. Trimble. Mary E. Jewell, admrx. Oct Term 1822.

Page 150   Inventory of estate of Jarrot Nelson, deceased.
Dec 18, 1822   Several items listed including cash received of Stephen Cantrell
$21.50. This Oct 21, 1822. Jno. Nelson, admr. Oct Term 1822.

Page 150   Inventory of estate of William Coltard, deceased, of Davidson
Dec 18, 1822   County, taken 17 Oct 1822. Two beds and furniture, one table,
sundry chairs, sundry cooking utensils, crockery ware, tin ware, books, two trunks, mirrow,
and one cloak and one cow. Sarah Coltard, admrx. Oct Term 1822.

Page 150   Inventory of estate of Andrew Graham, deceased, of Davidson
Dec 18, 1822   County, taken 17 Oct 1822. Two beds and furniture, two tables,
sundry chairs, sundry cooking utensils, crockery ware, tin ware, books, two chests, and one
cow. Margaret Graham, admrx. Oct Term 1822.

Page 151   Inventory of estate of Martin Greer, deceased.
Dec 18, 1822   Inventory which has come into the hands of the admrx and admr
of the Last Will and testament. Negroes, cattle and several other items listed including a
note on John Erwin, one on John Demoss, one due bill on R.W. Hart, account against Joseph
Greer, one against John Jobe, one against James Fudge, one order from Jacob Fudge, a claim
on the United States for property lost and service of horse in the Seminole Campaign
amounting in the gross to $110.00 subject to a deduction of 40¢ per day for services for three
months, and one Bible and testament. Signed by Benjamin Greer and Joseph Greer. Oct
Term 1822.

Page 152   Account of sale of estate of Arthur Redman, deceased.
Dec 19, 1822   And Paul Branche, surviving (partner). Names of purchasers, to
wit, Paul Branche, John Beaty, Duncan Robertson, William Gibson, H. Wade, Hoover & Co.,
George Louther, D. Robinson (Duncan Robertson), Mrs. Redman, and John Byrne. Signed by
Frances M. Redman, admrx. Oct Term 1822.

Page 153   Ephraim Drake's heirs guardian return.
Dec 19, 1822   Rent of the plantation, hire of Frank & Eve and Peter. The
money was given for building of a house on the upper plantation. William J. Drake, guardian.
Oct Term 1822.

Page 153   William Creel receipt from E. Cooper, guardian.
Dec 20, 1822   Nashville, Nov 14, 1816, received of Captain William Creel,
executor of Benjamin Seabourne, deceased, money for the hire of said deceased, to wit, James

Seabourne, Howell Seaborne, Benjamin Seaborne, and Isaac R. Seaborne. Edmund Cooper, guardian. Proven by Robert Saunderson and Charles Cooper. Oct Term 1822.

Page 154   Jesse J. Everett, his receipt from Henry Lady.
Dec 20, 1822   Jesse J. Everett, executor of James Everett, deceased, $261.59 in full, it being the full amount of said legatees share of all the assets received this 13 Feb 1822. Signed by Henry J. Lady. Test: Will Lytle. Oct Term 1822.

Page 154   Jesse J. Everett, his receipt from David Abernathy.
Dec 20, 1822   Jesse J. Everett, executor of James Everett, deceased $261.59 in full, it being the full amount of said legatees share of all the assets this 13 Feb 1822. David Abernathy. Oct Term 1822.

Page 154   Jesse J. Everett, his receipt from Simon Everett.
Dec 20, 1822   Jesse J. Everett, his receipt of $261.59 in full, it being the full amount of legatees share of all the assets this 13 Feb 1822. Simon Everett. Oct Term 1822.

Page 154   William Brown, a minor, guardian return.
Dec 20, 1822   Eldridge Newsom and John Davis, Commissioners appointed to settle with John Exum, admr of Arthur Exum, deceased, who was guardian to William Brown, minor. They found the paper to be the Last Will and Testament of William Brown father of said orphan and from a settlement made by James Hart and Charles Donoho with Arthur Exum one of the executors, both of which appears to be copies from the record of Sumner County. 30 Aug 1822. Oct Term 1822.

Page 155   Settlement of estate of Arthur Exum, deceased.
Dec 20, 1822   Made with John Exum, admr. Cash received of Benjamin Philips, Charles Hartley, John Bosley and Elisha Sullivant. Cash paid Richard Brown, guardian, William Brown, Robert Hughs, William Walden, Elisha Mathis, James Black, Nathan Gatlin, Leonard Burnett, Samuel Joslin, Eldridge Newsom, Cary Bibb, John C. House, Robert Phipps, William P. Brown, Robert Black, Nathan Ewing, John Exum, John Stover, and for articles for widow. 26 Oct 1822. Oct Term 1822.

Page 155   Inventory of estate of Benjamin Philips, deceased.
Dec 21, 1822   Notes &c found among the papers of Joseph Philips, deceased, by William Williams, his executor, to wit, John Bosley and Frederick Harwell, J.S. Williamson and D. Robertson, McNairy & Shelby & Cantrell & Co., Boyd, McNairy & J. Shelby, James Ridley and Boyd McNairy, Simon Williams and E. Pritchett, Duke W. Sumner and David Hunter, W.B. Robertson and J. Bosley, John Leak and Thomas Patterson, William Howlett, J. Manifee and William Porter, N.H. Robertson for R.W. Briggs and J.S. Williamson, J. Drury and John S. Williamson, R.B. Sappington and Bignal Crook, Boyd McNairy and J.S. Green, James Ridley and B. Richmond, N.H. Robertson and William Hunter, William Cobler and John Nichols, J. Woodfork and B. Crook, and Edward Daniel and Richard Garrett. Hire of several negroes. Note to J. Philips, guardian of W.H. and J.H. Philips. Solomon Clark for rent, Jesse Ashley and Sol. Holder, and George Taylor. Signed by Will Williams, admr. Oct Term 1822.

Page 157   Milberry Philips, her dower.
Dec 21, 1822   Made this 22 Oct 1822, made by the executors of the Last Will and Testament of Joseph Philips, late of Davidson County, to allot and set apart for Milberry Philips, widow and relict of the deceased, and to her own proper use and for her support &c during her natural life. The following property real and personal, to wit, negroes and the western end of the dwelling house, the Pizza (a veranda) and free use of the passage, the room in the south end of the kitchen, the meat house, spring house, and diary and the double cabin next to the garden for her negroes, the east end of the grainery and stables attached thereto and the crib and free use of the thrashing floor, the half of the graden, the kitchen, and one section of the vineyard on the other side, the pasture lot between the house and Dickinson's line, and that around the chip and that part of the meadows west of the little branch and the small field adjoining the orchard fence and half of the orchard, half of the big field called the Still House Field, her half to be next to the creek and the field on the side next to Wilson's and grinding free from tole, also other items. Signed by Will Williams and J.F. Williams. Oct Term 1822.

Page 158   Wilford H. Rains.
(No date)   Commissioners met to divide and set apart to Wilford H. Rains, one of the heirs of William Rains, deceased, his portion as heir to 200 acres of land and ten negroes which William Rians held by deed from his father John Rains which deed is dated Oct 16, 1795, containing 221¼ acres. They have set apart 27¼ acres of land as his portion, bordering John Rains' preemption. Also set apart one negro boy named George on condition of his paying to the other heirs $22.33 1/3 on 29 Aug 1822. This 10 Sept 1822. S. Shannon. Signed by Samuel Weakley, J.N. Manifee and Samuel J. Ridley. Oct Term 1822.

Page 158   Settlement of estate of George M. Deaderick, deceased.
Dec 23, 1822   Made with the executor of the Last Will and Testament of George M. Deaderick, deceased, and found a balance $10,721.65 due to the estate. This 2 Nov 1822. W.B. Lewis and Will Lytle. Oct Term 1822.

Page 159   Will of Ephraim Pritchett, deceased.
Dec 23, 1822   James Trimble and George Yerger and George Shall, executors. His negro to be free when he buys himself, the boy to have time to do so. George Yerger to have $10,000.00 for five years then to be given to Ephraim Pritchett Shall bank stock and Ephraim Shall, executors to sell all his real property, the lot which he owns in partnership with John Baird to be sold to said Baird. Wit: Boyd McNairy and J. Roane. Ephraim Pritchett asked Doctor McNairy to sign his name. Oct Term 1822.
The noncupative part of the Last Will and Testament of Ephraim Pritchett, deceased. To John Ragan of Hagerstown, Maryland $2000.00. John Baird, James P. Irwin, John Wright which having, which having been reduced to writing. This __ day of Sept 1822 at George Shall's in Nashville where he had resided.

Page 160   Will of Ezekiel Smith, deceased.
Dec 23, 1822   Nashville, Davidson County, on 3rd Monday in Oct 1822. To wit, Thomas Smith and others, heirs of Ezekiel Smith, deceased VS Noell W. Watkins and others als heirs of E. Smith, deceased. Contested Will - To Susannah Lester 40 acres of land lying and being on Whites Creek, the place they now live on within the boundary that Stull run off, I do also give to my two elder sons Jesse Smith and Thomas Smith the balance of said tract of land on Whites Creek. Jesse the upper half and Thomas the lower half. Also unto Thomas Smith one set of blacksmith tools. To my two younger sons all my land lying on Sulphur Creek to be equally divided between the two. Also all the stock of all kinds and household and kitchen furniture to be equally divided between Abner Smith and Ezekiel Smith, also to stills to Abner Smith and negroes. To Nancy Watkins a negro girl named Matilday. To Sally Watkins and Elizabeth Gleaves all the cash I have by me. This 10 Jan 1822. Wit: Thomas Pierce, Thomas Watts and Sabret Choat. Oct Term 1822. A jury was elected and found that the will is the Last Will and Testament of said Ezekiel Smith, deceased.

Page 161   Inventory of estate of Ezekiel Smith, deceased.
Dec 23, 1822   Taken by Abner Smith. Oct 29, 1822. Several items listed. Oct Term 1822.

Page 162   Settlement of estate of Robert Searcy, deceased.
Dec 24, 1822   Made with Stephen Cantrell, executor. Persons listed, to wit, Nathan Ewing, John J. Erwin, Jesse Searcy, Charles Cooper, Jesse Wharton, John C. McLemore, A.B. Shelby, Thomas B. Tunstall, John S. Topp, James Campbell, Esq., Samuel Murry, Franky Harris, and James Trimble, Esq. This 24 Oct 1822. D.A. Dunham and Will Lytle. Oct Term 1822.

Page 164   Settlement of estate of Craven Jackson, deceased.
Mar 6, 1823   Made to Nathaniel A. McNairy. Cash paid to Alexander Richardson, Nashville Bank, Jo. & R. Woods, Doctor Roane, James B. Houston, J. Moore, James D. Miller, Nathan Ewing, Gibbs & Fogg, and Harwood (constable). Gave Mrs. Jackson a note on Freeman. Cash paid Robertson and Waters, Thomas Claiborne, David Irwin, David Cartwright, William Faulkner, Jas. Cooper, T. Deaderick, admr., James Grizzard, E.H. Foster, Att., James Gray, Elizabeth Jackson, and Branch Bank. This 10 Jan 1823. Signed by Duncan Robertson and J.P. Erwin. Also notes on John C. Hicks. This 20 jan 1823. Jan term 1823.

Page 165   Settlement of estate of Alexander Ewing, deceased.
Mar 6, 1823   Made with the legatees. To cash paid J.B. Houston, Mrs. Snow, Alexander C. Ewing, in part of his legacy, Randal M. Ewing in part of his and his mother's legacy, Jacob McGavock, guardian of W.B. Ewing, Nathan Ewing, William White, Newman & Ewing, Alexander C. Ewing & Sally Ewing in part of their legacy, cash collected of John Barber, and by William Hadley of George Elliot. Balance in the hands of O.B. Hays $1224.23. Jan 29, 1823. E. Talbot and Will Lytle, J.P. They have proceeded to divide the slaves among Sally Ewing and William B. Ewing. The executors have received the dividend on the Nashville Bank Stock and have paid the same to R.M. Ewing and W.B. Ewing to whom the same is bequeathed. Jan 1823. O.B. Hays, executor. Jan term 1823.

Page 166   Settlement of estate of John Carter, deceased.
Mar 6, 1823   Made with James Carter, executor. A note on J. Carnel, on William L. Carter, and on John C. Brown, William Hays, John Huggins, James Carter, G.W. Charlton, Jesse Fuqua, Elizabeth Carter the widow, William Harwood, C.C. Carter, Walter B. Carter. James Carter, executor. Note on James Carter, Sr., A. Pullen, E. East, and C.C. Carter. Money paid to the estate of R. Smith, William H. McLaughlin, Thomas Washington, John A. Bacchus, William Faulkner, Sh. Bryant, James Carter, E.H. East, and Erwin. Mrs. Ca(illegible) for tending the negroes, Noell's receipt for services and Houston for defending the will. Allowed James Carter for services, receipt E. Carter, William L. Carter's receipt and allowed Mrs. Carter one years support. This 16 Nov 1822. R.C. Foster and John Buchanan. Jan Term 1823.

Page 167   Settlement of estate of Peter G. Bowyer, deceased.
Mar 6, 1823   John T. Dismukes, admr. Pais cash to S. Seay, and Dwyer. Balance due the estate $100.69. Nov 16, 1822. E. Talbot and E.S. Hall. Jan term 1823.

Page 168   Settlement of estate of Thomas Harrison, deceased, of Davidson
Mar 6, 1823   County. Made with Richard Harrison, executor. Two notes to Mary Harrison. Other persons listed, to wit, Thomas Powell, Thomas Johnson, Edwin S. Moore, Daniel Kennedy, Doct. Allen Mathis, Connell & Walton, and John Cook. Jan 13, 1823. Signed by D. Dunn, George Perry and John Pirtle, Commissioners. Settled Jan 18, 1823. Jan Term 1823.

Page 169   Will of John Harwood, deceased, of Davidson County.
Mar 7, 1823   As much of my perishable part of my estate to be sold to pay my just debts. I lend to my beloved wife Rebecca Harwood, the land, household and kitchen furniture, farming tools and all my stock and four negroes, Davy, Moses, Priss, and Lucy, for her natural life or widowhood then to be expended of as hereafter mentioned. The land to be equally divided between my three youngest sons John Harwood, Benjamin Franklin Harwood and Charles Harvey Harwood and all the balance of my estate to be divided equally between my three sons, above mentioned, and my daughter Sarah Washington Downey provided that she has an heir of her body, and my daughter Eliza Harwood provided that she has an heir of her body. I appoint William Wrenn my executor. This 3 May 1822. Wit: Benjamin Cox, Sr., Benjamin Cox and Rebecca Jorden. Jan term 1823.

Page 170   Will of Francis P. Ford, deceased, of Davidson County.
Mar 7, 1823   To my sister Sally Boyd three negro slaves for life named David, Franky and Mary. To my brother Philip Ford my negro fellow Abraham. To my nephew James Drake and my three nieces Adeline Drake, Susan Drake and Polly Drake, negroes for life, to wit, Lydia, Charles and Catherine, first after the youngest of my nieces become of age and not before, but to be kept in and by my brother-in-law William L. Boyd until my youngest niece Polly Drake becomes of the age of 21 years, then William L. Boyd is to give up to them the said three negroes together with their increase. The money and notes of hand and book accounts together with the residue of my property goes to my brother-in-law William L. Boyd who I appoint my sole executor. This 6 Jan 1823. Wit: Jno. Boyd, M. Fly and John M. Cha(illegible). Jan term 1823.

Page 171   Will of John Elliston, deceased, of Nashville.
Mar 8, 1823   To my beloved wife Ann T. Elliston one undivided fourth part of my real and personal estate after my debts are paid. Also to her my furniture, horse, gig and cows. To my daughter Mary Ann Elizabeth Elliston one undivided fourth part of my real and

personal estate after my debts are paid. To my son William Heter Elliston one undivided fourth part of my real and personal estate after my debts are paid. To my son John Elliston one undivided fourth part of my real and personal estate after my debts are paid. I appoint Josiah Mullen guardian for my daughter Mary Ann Elizabeth Elliston. I appoint Joseph T. Elliston guardian for my two sons William Heter Elliston and John Elliston. I appoint Joseph Joseph T. Elliston my sold executor. He is to sell all my tools, materials and work that belongs to my shop. I wish my wife and executor to divide equally among the guardians of my children for them. This 12 Jan 1823. Wit: Addison East and Matthew H. Quinn. Jan Term 1823.

Page 172   Will of John N. Haynie, deceased, of Davidson County.
Mar 8, 1823   To my beloved brothers George M. Haynie, Austin R. Haynie and William R. Haynie all my worldly effects, viz, horse, wagon and gears, riding saddle, cattle, hogs, a cherry table, a bed, bedstead and furniture, ploughs and hoes. The whole of the above named property is to remain in the possession of my father John Haynie during his life and he to enjoy the benefit and after his death it is to be sold and proceeds be equally divided between my before mentioned brothers. My father John Haynie my sole executor. This 12 Jan 1822. Wit: William G. Evans, Cyrus Murray and John G. Chiles. Jan term 1823.

Page 172   Will of Robert E. Searcy, deceased.
Mar 10, 1823   A Lieutenant of the Navy of the United States being frequently in hazardous situations, and knowing that life is uncertain, do make this my Last Will and Testament. To my Issabella Ritchie Searcy one third of all my property both real and personal and as soon as my property can be disposed of, I give to my said wife Issabella R. Searcy her proportion without delay, the card tables and looking glasses I made her a present of before we were married, they are exclusively hers and at her own disposal. The other two thirds of my property to my child should I have one, should I not have one, it is my request that it be divided between my brothers and sisters, viz, Orville H., Elvira J., Susan D., Granville D., William, and James Searcy, their share. Remainder of proceeds to my wife. To my oldest child should it be a son my double cased gold patent lever watch, chain and seals with request that he never will part with it, as it was a present from my father to me, but let it decend from generation to generation of the family in the male line, should I not have a son I give it to my brother Granville D. Searcy with the same request. I appoint Stephen Cantrell and Robert Armstrong of Nashville and William M. McCauley of Washington City, executors. I here put down the value of property lying in Nashville as valued by my father in 1819, if I have any other property it is more than I know of, one half lot and a two story brick house fronting on Market Street $10,000.00, one half lot and one story brick house fronting on college street $8,000.00, and two unimproved lots at $4,500.00 - Total $22,500.00. This 16 July 1822. Wit: John B. Forrest and Thomas Howard. District of Columbia, Washington County, 16 Nov 1822. This 18 Nov 1822. Henry C. Neal, Register of Wills for Washington County, D.C. Jan Term 1823 (Davidson County, Tennessee)

Page 174   Real estate divided of John Carter, deceased.
Mar 10, 1823   Commissioners appointed and named the petition of Christopher C. Carter, James Carter guardian of Parthena Carter and Polly Simmons, William L. Carter guardian of John Carter heirs of John Carter, deceased, and Walter O. Carter praying to the court to divide certain lands to the heirs, to wit, Lot No. 1 beginning at Thomas Gillaspie's corner, to McCrorys Creek, containing 39 2/3 acres. Lot No. 2 beginning at corner of Lot No. 1, widows dower, McCrorys Creek, containing 43 acres and 45 poles. Lot No. 3 beginning at Thomas Everett's corner, McCrorys Creek, Lot No. 3 and Lot No. 2 containing 58 acres. Lot No. 4 beginning at Thomas Everett's corner, Lot No. 2, containing 34 acres. And Lot No. 5 beginning at corner of Lot No. 4, Jeremiah Grizzard, Lot No. 4 containing 34 acres. To Parthena Carter Lot or Parcel No. 1. To John Carter Lot or Parcel No. 2. To Polly Simmons Lot or Parcel No. 3. To Christopher C. Carter Lot or Parcel No. 4. To Walter O. Carter Lot No. 5. Paid to Jeremiah Ezell for surveying, to William McMurrey, James Buchanan, John K. Buchanan, Thomas Buchanan, and John Buchanan, Commissioners. Jan term 1823.

Page 175   Division of personal estate of John Carter, deceased.
Mar 10, 1823   To C.C. Carter negro girl Julia, boy Henderson, and boy Bluford. To Walter O. Carter negro woman Lucy, a boy Hardy, one boy Wilson and a boy Austin. To Polly Simmons a negro man E(illegible), one woman Susanna, and one child Doctor. Parthena

114

Carter negro woman Eve, boy Anthony and a girl Mary. To John Carter a negro woman Ann, boy Bill and a girl Dilcy. This 22 July 1822. Signed by William McMurphy, Edmund Owen, John K. Buchanan and Thomas Harding, Commissioners. Jan Term 1823.

Page 176   Inventory of estate of James McBride, deceased.
Mar 12, 1823   Notes on the following, to wit, Strother Keys, Calvin Strater, William Tinnin, Lucien Dollars, Elizabeth Stevison, William L. Barry, Elizabeth Simpson, Sarah S. Harrison, George Cooper, M.W. Wilson, and David Wilson. Received of John Buchanan, Moses Burton, John Newman, J. Brahan by the hands of Robert Weakley, Richardson C. Drewry, and Robert Wood and Rogers and others. Note on Solomon Blair and John Downy. To cash received of Benjamin F. Lewis. This 31 Jan 1823. Edward H. East, admr. Jan Term 1823.

Page 177   Settlement of estate of Moody Harris, deceased.
Mar 12, 1823   Made with James McGavock, admr. Cash collected of Matthew Harris, of Sarah Connelly, of William Rogers, of James Harris, of John Hobson, John Nichols, of Moody Harris, and of Sarah Harris. Total $159.75. Cash paid James Harris, Tabitha Wray, Norvell H. Robertson, McNairy & Shelby, Jacob McGavock, Robertson & Waters, Doctor Roane, the Sheriff, O.B. Hayes for defending suits VS John W. and Absalom Page, Nathan Ewing, and Duncan Robertson. Signed by Robert Weakley, J.P. and Will Williams. Jan Term 1823.

Page 178   Inventory of estate of David T. Ethridge, deceased.
Mar 12, 1823   Taken by Dennis Dozier and Penina Ethridge, admrs. This 29 Jan 1823. Several items listed. Jan Term 1823.

Page 178   Susannah Perkins, widow support.
Mar 12, 1823   Susannah Perkins widow and relict of William Perkins, deceased, allotted several items for years support. This 15 Nov 1822. G.G. Washington and M.C. Dunn. Jan Term 1823.

Page 179   Elizabeth Carter, widow support.
Mar 12, 1823   Elizabeth Carter widow and relict of John Carter, deceased, her years support. Several items listed. This 16 Nov 1822. R.C. Foster and John Buchanan. Jan Term 1823.

Page 179   Inventory of estate of Henry Cooper, deceased.
Mar 12, 1823   This 26 Jan 1823. Several items listed. One note given by Daniel McDaniel and Thomas Hart and Haston Cooper his executor. Allen Thompson, admr. Jan Term 1823.

Page 180   Inventory of estate of Arthur Exum, deceased.
Mar 12, 1823   Sold by John Exum, admr. One negro girl named Jane, one pair cart wheels, flat irons and dutch oven. This Jan 28, 1823. Jan Term 1823.

Page 180   Inventory of estate of Seth Davis, deceased.
Mar 12, 1823   A note on hand given by William Spence to said Davis. Signed by John Davis, executor. Jan Term 1823.

Page 180   Lucy Davis, widow support.
Mar 12, 1823   Several items listed. This 15 Nov 1822. Leven Edney and William Roach and William Dillahunty. Jan term 1823.

Page 180   Elizabeth Saunders, minor.
Mar 12, 1823   Edward H. East to Elizabeth Saunders, a minor orphan. Hire of negroes and rent of land, $109.37½ for year 1823. Edward H. East, guardian. Jan Term 1823.

Page 181   Sale of estate of William Perkins, deceased.
Mar 13, 1823   Sale on 23 Oct 1822 and Dec 30, 1822. Purchasers, to wit, Susan Perkins, Robert Scales, Jno. Chadwell, Edmond Edney, Frederick Owen, James Campbell, Nicholas Perkins, Jr., James Walker, Henry Crutcher, Silas Morton, Thomas Casey, Daniel Vaughn, Wright Ramsey, Newton Cannon, Robert Gray, John Fitzhugh, John Hughs, Martin

Smith, John Nichols, Daniel P. Perkins, James G. Jones, William Maxwell, Thomas H. Perkins, and Nicholas Perkins. Samuel Perkins, executor. Amount sales on Oct 23, 1822, to wit, Susanna Perkins, Robert Scales, James Walker, Henry Crutcher, Robert R. Bell, John Hogan, James Campbell, Mathew Johnson, George W. Alford, George W. Curtis, Stephen Sutton, Everett Owen, William Thompson, Thomas Edmiston, J. Bell, Bright Ramsey, and William Thompson. Samuel Perkins, executor. Jan Term 1823.

Page 183   Sale of estate of Henry Ferebee, deceased.
Mar 13, 1823   Sold on 9 Nov 1822. Persons listed, to wit, to Celia Ferebee, William McMurry, Edmond Owen, John Hartman, Thomas Ferebee, William Richardson, John Hall, William H. McLaughlin, and John K. Buchanan. Thomas Ferebee, admr. Jan Term 1823.

Page 184   Sale of estate of William Wells, deceased.
Mar 13, 1823   Notes on the following persons, to wit, David Abernathy, Charles Abernathy, George Waters and Richard (blank), Jontahan Drake, Freeman & David Abernathy, Richard Hydes, Rolan Cato and Isaac Earthman, John Lanier, John Vaughn and John McClure, Green Cato, John Kennedy and John Pierce, Jeremiah Pierce and Thomas Pierce, Reuben Biggs, John Pierce and John Kennedy and Jeremiah Pierce, Thomas James, Taswell Hyde, William Parker, William J. Drake, William Curtis, Willis Alley and Rolan Cato, Benjamin Smith, Laban Abernathy, Jr. and Laban Abernathy, Sr., John C. Parker, Benjamin Hyde, and Hiram Wells. Cash in Hiram Wells $88.00. Tabitha Wells account for $42.37½. Solomon Wells for $151.00. Total amount $606.27. Hiram Wells, admr. Jan Term 1823.

Page 184   Joseph McBride's heirs, guardian return.
Mar 13, 1823   Plantation rents, hire of negro girl Rachael, one boy Henry hires, one boy Jim and a woman and three children hires. George Hodge, guardian. Jan Term 1823.

Page 185   Joseph McBride's heirs, guardian return.
Mar 13, 1823   Guardian for the heirs of Joseph McBride, namely Sally McBride, Mary McBride, Joseph McBride, and Priscilla McBride for the year 1821. Land rented, hired of negro girl Rachael, one negro boy Henry, one named William, a negro woman and three children fired for the pay of the board of Sally, Mary, Joseph and Priscilla McBride. George Hodge, guardian. Jan term 1823.

Page 185   Sale of estate of Ezekiel Smith, deceased.
Mar 13, 1823   Returned by Abner Smith, admr. Items sold unto Ezekiel Smith, George Waters, Abner Smith, Jesse Smith, and John Pierce. This 27 Jan 1823. Abner Smith, admr. Jan Term 1823.

Page 186   Sale of estate of Richard R. Jones, deceased.
Mar 13, 1823   Several items listed. J. Jameson, admr. Jan Term 1823.

Page 186   Division of negroes of estate of Isaac Battle, deceased.
Mar 14, 1823   We have allotted to Martin Clark and Charity H. Clark, his wife formerly Charity H. Battle, the following negroes, viz, Jacob, Amey, Daphney, Charlotte, Harriet, Jacob, Aron, Shadrack, Hannah, Clarisia, Augustus, and Eliza. To William M. Battle, viz, Sharper, Leah, Maria, Parlee, Sharper, Nathan, Evelina, R(illegible), and James. To Joel A. Battle, viz, David, Jenny, Silvey, Milley, Pompey, Amos, Sarah, Violet, Jenny, and Joseph. To Susan L. Battle, viz, Cillar, Tempey, Phillis, Sabra, Piety, Sally, Anna, Alsa, Abram, Harry, and Henry. This 27 Dec 1822. William H. Nance, Enoch Ensley and William Scruggs, Commissioners. Jan Term 1823.

Page 187   Inventory of estate of Ezekiel Smith, deceased.
Mar 13, 1823   Several items listed. Thomas Watts, Sevier Drake and Jonathan Drake. Jan Term 1823.

Page 187   John H. Sumner, minor orphan.
Mar 15, 1823   John Hudson Sumner, orphan of Jos. Jno. Sumner, deceased, with Duke W. Sumner, guardian. Several items listed. Paid Josiah F. Williams for boarding the orphan. Duke W. Sumner, guardian. Jan Term 1823.

Page 188   Ephraim Pritchett, deceased.
Mar 17, 1823   Notes on the following, viz, F. Saunders and W. Chandler, Duke W. Sumner, Joseph Philips, James Trimble, David Dunn, Boyd McNairy, Joseph Philips, Stephen Cantrell & Co., Samuel Hogg, P.H. Darby, E.P. Sumner, Thomas P. Jones, Thomas Claiborne, George Bell, S.D. Hayes, William Rutherford, George Shall, and W. Barrows. Feb 1, 1823. George S. Yerger, James Trimble and George Shall. Jan term 1823.

Page 189   Settlement of estate of Benjamin Philips, deceased.
Mar 17, 1823   Made with Joseph Philips, admr. Persons listed, to wit, C. Dodd, D.W. Sumner, C. Johnson, Lewis Joslin, R. & T. Greer, E. Sumner, J. & J.W. Sitler, Allen for Armstrong, J.S. Williamson, Hogg & Bronaugh, R. Buchanan, R. Boyd, J. Blackmans, R.D. Barry, G. Wilson, J. Trimble, J.C. Bradshaw, J. Wharton, J.R. McMean, R. Hewitt, T. Hills, J.D. Miller, A. Demoss, E.P. Sumner, T. Hickman, Branch Bank, J. Hooper, A. Weeks, B. Bosley, B. and Spence, S. Stull, A. Porters, W. Howlett, G. Taylor, R.W. Green, T. Wilson, M. and Watkins, J.M. and R. Johnson, A. Richardson, J. Sumner, H. Ewing, G. Wilson, and J.B. Lockhart. Rendered by Will Williams, admr of B. Philips and executor of Joseph Philips. Jan Term 1823. Others named, to wit, N. Branch, William Kent, J. Horton, D. Robertson, J. Scales, T. Crutcher, A. Exum, (blank) Shall, C. Williams, W. Maxey, and G. McConnico. Jan Term 1823.

Page 191   Division of land of Isaac Battle, deceased.
Mar 17, 1823   Plat on page 191. Commissioners met to set apart to Martin Clark and Charity H. Clark formerly Charity H. Battle, 200 acres of land out of the east corner of 1000 acre tract which Isaac Battle died seized of. This 23 Dec 1822. Signed by William Scruggs, William H. Nance and Enoch Ensley and B. Bray. Jan Term 1823.

Page 192   Will of William Douglass, deceased.
Mar 17, 1823   The following cause came to be tried, to wit, the executrix of William Douglass, deceased, Plaintiff VS Thomas Douglass, Defendant - Contested Will. Oct Sessions 1823. This 28 Aug 1815 made and published the Last Will and Testament. To my beloved wife Elizabeth Douglass 100 acres of land including all the improvements, said land lying in the County of Davidson on the south side of Cumberland River, also negro woman Lettice, negro boy Harry, all stock, household and kitchen furniture during her natural life after just debts being paid. To my brother Thomas Douglass $1.00. To my sisters Elizabeth Hill and Nancy Douglass 50¢ each. At the death of Elizabeth Douglass, William Ethridge the eldest son of David T. Ethridge is to hire the property land and negroes, Lettice and Harry. David T. Ethridge and Elizabeth Douglass, executors. Wit: W. Wallace, E. Gower, G.S. Allen, and Enoch Douge. Thomas Douglass by George W. Gibbs and Francis B. Fogg, Esquires, his attorney prays to be admitted to contest the validity of said paper writing and leave is granted him so to do. Thomas Douglass who is admitted to defend and contest the validity of the paper presented for probate. And the plaintiffs likewise Foster. A jury was elected, to wit, William E. Watkins, William Kent, James R. Robertson, Floyd Hurt, John M. Robertson, Thomas Hamilton, Jason Thompson, Benjamin Turbeville, Philip Shute, Benjamin S. Williamson, Oakley Jones, and Mark R. Cockrill and agreed that the paper purporting to be the Last Will and Testament of William Douglass, deceased, said that the paper writing is the Last Will and Testament of William Douglass, deceased.

Page 194   Inventory of William Douglass, deceased.
Mar 17, 1823   Taken by David T. Ethridge Oct 16, 1822 and then taken by Dennis Dozier this 25 Jan 1823 to the records of Davidson COunty, 100 acres lying on Brush Creek and several items listed. Jan Term 1823.

Page 194   Inventory of estate of John Childress, deceased, of Davidson
Mar 17, 1823   County, taken by John Catron, admr and unadministered by Samuel B. Marshall and Mrs. Childress, former administrators. Several items listed. To a mortgage on Sterling C. Robertson in favor of Mrs. Childress. Notes on Sterling and Eldridge Robertson for land lying in Giles County. Note on James Kennedy on suit of Alexander McCall, note on Jno. B. Hogg, Samuel Nelson, James Dobbins, Alfred Nichol, Jas. Jackson and Jno. Childress, Zachariah Duncan, Patton Anderson, and William P. Anderson. The above property was purchased at a high price and with the best intention by Mrs. Childress and Captain S.B. Marshall, her co-administrator. This 1 Dec 1819. Wit: Elizabeth Childress and S.B. Marshall. Several items listed including one Holy Bible. This Jan 29, 1823. John

Catron. Jan Term 1823.

Page 198   Inventory of estate of Elizabeth Childress, deceased.
Mar 18, 1823   Taken by John Catron, admr. Mrs. Childress was entitled on the
death of her husband to the nineth part of the personal property of her husband, there were
nine children, but James Marshall between eight and nine before her father's death, married
and was advanced $10,000.00 in notes on Whiteside and Bell, and Whiteside and Balch, all
endorsed by Mr. Childress, negro girls and sum personal property amounting to her share and
more of the personal property after debts are paid.   The remaining personal property is
undivided except a couple of negro girls given by Mrs. Childress to her daughter Matilda on
her marriage.   The will void confusion &c injury as the distributees of John and Elizabeth
Childress' estate are the same except Mrs. Marshall who is entitled to a nineth of Mrs.
Childress, her mother's estate which if indebted with the personal property claimed by Mrs.
Childress and charged with the $2700.00 note mentioned in the inventory of John Childress'
estate. Personal property of Mrs. Childress, viz, a mare gotten from Sterling Robertson and
gotten by him for land sold in Montgomery County, also a mortgage for $259.40.   One third
of Alexander Hamilton's note for iron delivered in Nashville, note executed to Eldridge
Robertson and other items listed. This 29 Jan 1823. Jan Term 1823.

Page 199   Divided land of David Earhart, deceased.
Mar 18, 1823   Plat on page 199. No. 1 to Lucinda Earhart for 10½ acres. No. 2
to Franklin Earhart for 10½ acres.   No. 3 to David Earhart for 10½ acres.   No. 4 to Rodney
Earhart for 10½ acres.   No. 5 to John Earhart for 10½ acres.   No. 6 to Mahala Sadler for 10½
acres.   No. 7 to Elijah Earhart for 10½ acres.   Widow's dower for 36½ acres.   The division of
David Earhart and Elijah Earhart among their heirs.   No. 7 to the heirs of Elijah Earhart.
Also negroes allotted to David Earhart's heirs, Rodney Earhart, to the heirs of Elijah Earhart,
David Earhart, the widow, Lucinda Earhart, Franklin Earhart, Mahala Sadler, and John
Earhart. This 28 Jan 1823. Signed by Samuel Weakley, Edmond Gamble and Duke W. Sumner.
Jan Term 1823.

Page 201   Inventory of estate of Craven Jackson, deceased.
Mar 25, 1823   Notes of J.W. McCombs, and one on George W. Campbell.
Received for Toby sold James Gray and amount due by the Presbyterian Church $40.30.
Total $1599.14. N.A. McNairy, admr. Jan Term 1823.

Page 201   Will of Micha Randall, deceased, of Davidson County.
Mar 25, 1823   To my brother Aquilla Randall and my sister Sarah Randall all
the property and estate that may and will decend to me from my mother's estate by will, to
be equally divided among them. I appoint Aquilla Randall my sole executor. This 30 Sept
1822. Wit: John S. Galbreath and Isaac Harrison. Jan Term 1823.

Page 202   Jacob Wright of george M. Deaderick, bond.
Apr 12, 1823   George M. Deaderick sold unto Jacob Wright of Maury County a
certain tract of land lying on Duck River adjoining Tyra Rhodes and the place where
Adonejah Edwards lives, containing 440 acres owned by myself and Howel Tatum. This 7 Dec
1810. Signed by George M. Deaderick. Wit: Nathaniel A. McNairy. This 9 July 1822.

Page 202   Inventory of estate of Alexander Brinkley, deceased.
June 16, 1823   Two mares, one colt, one cow and calf, one mans saddle, one
ladies saddle, one featherbed and furniture, one pot and pot hooks, one skillet, one dish, ten
plates, one bridle and other items. Lewis Earthman, admr. Apr Term 1823.

Page 203   Inventory of estate of Frederick Stump, deceased.
June 16, 1823   Negroes, shares in the Nashville Bank. Persons named, to wit,
John Counselman, Lewis Greene, Clayborne Gentry, Zenas Tait, Lewis Earthman, James
Yerber, L. McCarmack, David Caldwell, Thomas White, George Pinkly, Peterson Vaden,
Alexander Staley, Daniel Waggoner, Willis Seat, Benjamin McIntosh, John Shelby, John B.
Darrow, John Wilson, William Atchardson, George Maxwell, W.W. Hud(illegible), Joel Olive,
David C. Irvine, John Barrow, Robert Sammons, Sherod Winningham, Lewis Williams, George
Pinkly, Caleb Bosmer, John Peoples, R.C. Phelin, William Graham, Claiborne Gentry, William
Gilliam, John Sto(illegible), John Tulley, and George Jefferson. Several items listed. Signed
by Philip Shute, one of the executors. Apr Term 1823.

Page 204   Inventory of estate of Gabriel Fuqua, deceased.
Apr 16, 1823   Taken Apr 28, 1823 by Judy (Judith) Fuqua and William Anderson,
admrs. Several items listed. Apr Term 1823.

Page 205   Will of Absolom Page, deceased, of Davidson County.
June 17, 1823   It is my will that my ferry be rented annually until my daughter
Betsy Page arrives at the age of 21 and the profits arising to be applied to defray the
expense of boarding and educating my children also to educate Cyprissa Brooks and Angeline
Brooks the two youngest daughters of my wife Patsy Page then the same with three acres of
land thereto adjoining to be sold and proceeds to be equally divided between my two youngest
sons Jesse and Jefferson Page. To my wife Patsy Page have the use and benefit of my
dwelling house and as much of the farm whereon I live to support or maintain her during her
widowhood and also a sufficient number of negroes to cultivate that part of the farm
allotted. All my property not otherwise devised except the tract of land whereon I live shall
be sold and the proceeds to be equally divided between all my children deducting the value of
the property that I have already given to my married children from their proportion. After
the death or intermarriage of my wife, the property devised to her and the farm whereon I
live be sold and proceeds to be equally divided between my children. I appoint John H. Smith
and Samuel Shannon, executors. This 8 Feb 1823. Wit: John Shelby and John Earhart.
Codicil: $100.00 to Cyprissa Brooks and the like sum of $100.00 to Angelina Brooks to be paid
to them by the executors. 8 Feb 1823. Apr Term 1823.
Martha Page, widow and relict of Absalom Page, deceased.

Page 206   Will of Nicholas Crossway, deceased, of Davidson County.
June 17, 1823   To my four sons James Cole, Pilmore Cole, John Henry and
Lenenton Lockart that tract of land formerly owned by William McAdams including 200 acres
to be so laid off as not to interfere with the tract of 250 acres that I now live on. I also
give to my son James Cole one sorrel horse that he has now in possession. To my son
Pilmore Cole one sorrel horse that he has now in possession. Each of my other sons shall
have a horse, apiece, worth $60.00 when they come of age. To my son Elions 50 acres of
land to be laid off in the lower end of the tract of land that I now live on so as to take any
of the land is now under fence. To my beloved wife Ann shall remain in possession of the
tract of land whereon I now live and all my negroes, household and kitchen furniture, also all
my stock, my farming utensils, my stills and apparatus &c, but should she marry again then
she shall have a child's part of all that has been named to her. The balance to be equally
divided among my five sons. I appoint my two eldest sons John Cole Crossway and Pilmore
Cole Crossway my sole executors. This 26 Apr 1823. Wit: Pitt Bower, Jesse Glasgow and
Isaac Walton. Apr Term 1823.

Page 207   Inventory of estate of Corbin Noles, deceased.
June 17, 1823   Several items listed including notes on the following, to wit,
Solomon Clark, Burwell Harton, James Pengleton, James Long, John Pierce, and John
McKenzie. Also several negroes. This 30 Jan 1823. Signed by James Boyd, admr. Apr Term
1823.

Page 208   Sale of estate of William Douglass, deceased.
June 17, 1823   This 3 Mar 1823, with Dennis Dozier, admr. Persons listed, to
wit, Elijah Nicholson, Elisha Nicholson, John Gibbs, Mathew Lee, Wilson Crockett, James
Schooley, Richard Brown, Dennis Dozier, Jane W. Shelton, Samuel Davidson, Penina Ethridge,
John C. Glasgow, Enoch Dozier, Nicholas Hail, Jr., Jno. B. Demumbrum, George Hail,
Meshack Hail, John Exum, Larkin Scott, Wilson L. Gower, Widow Douglass, William Shelton,
John W. Page, Timothy Durat, George S. Allen, William Brown, and Reuben Biggs. Dennis
Dozier, admr. Apr Term 1823.

Page 209   Inventory of estate of John Childress, deceased.
June 19, 1823   Taken by John Catron, admr. Inventory of slaves then in
Davidson County and including the slaves on the farm in Alabama. Several negroes named.
This May 6, 1823. John Catron, admr of John and Eliza. Childress. Apr term 1823.

Page 209   Inventory of estate of Charles Cagle, deceased.
June 19, 1823   100 acres of land and several items listed including a note on
George McCarmack, Jr., an account on Roger B. Sappington, one on Joseph ?. Woods, and one

on Robertson and Curry. William Wallace, admr. Apr Term 1823.

Page 210   Sale of estate of Henry Cooper, deceased.
June 19, 1823   Sale on Feb 14, 1823. Persons listed, to wit, Houston Cooper, Allen Thompson, William Thompson, George Reynolds, John Elliston, John Strawn, John Cooper, John Jones, John Travilson, Isaac Greer, Frederick Hunt, Royal Ferguson, William Canndy, William B. Evans, Josel Smith, John O. Bennett, Leroy Burnett, William Ellison, Hiram Anderson, Henry Stuart, William Jewell, David G. Thompson, and William R. Evans. Allen Thompson, admr. Apr Term 1823.

Page 211   Settlement of estate of Arthur Exum, deceased.
June 19, 1823   Made with John Exum, admr. Persons listed, to wit, Benjamin Philips, John Bosley, Charles Hartley, Elisha Sullivant, Richard Brown guardian of William Brown, Robert Huse, William Walden, Elisha Mathis, James Black, Nathan Gatlin, Leonard Burnett, Samuel Joslin, Eldridge Newsom, Cary Bibb, John C. House, Robert Philips, William P. Barrow, Nathan Ewing, John Exum, John Stovers, Alexander Y. Brown, and widow. This 18 Apr 1823. Signed by S. Prowell and Thomas Scott. Apr Term 1823.

Page 212   Sales of estate of David T. Ethridge, deceased.
June 20, 1823   Mar 10 & 11, 1823. Persons listed, to wit, William Fuqua, Penina Ethridge, Elisha Gower, Churchwell Hooper, Frederick Gullage, Reuben Wallace, Gabriel Fuqua, John D. Demumbrum, William Vick, Timothy Durat, Isaac Mayfield, Robert Work, William Champ, Theophilus Hart, Wilson L. Gower, Russell Gower, Dennis Dozier, Isaac Watkins, Wilson Crockett, Robert Hart, James Kerney, George S. Allen, John W. Page, Isaac Mayfield, James Russell, and Frederick Gullidge. Lewis Earthman's receipt, William Douglass, Thomas Williams, Thomas Spence, James Hollis, Thomas Colier, E. Gower, William Wallace, Isaac Earthman, Henry Crabb, L.P. Cheatham, Churchwell Hooper, Anthony Sota, Enoch Dozier, Aron Dean, Robert Vick, Timothy Duratt, Reuben Bigg, Josiah League, John Page, and William Willis. Dennis Dozier and Penina Ethridge, admrs. Apr Term 1823.

Page 214   Settlement of estate of William Thomas Dickinson, a lunatic.
June 20, 1823   On 22 Apr 1823 the Commissioners settled with Francis McKay, guardian of William Thomas Dickinson, a lunatic, reported bonds on sundry persons belonging to said Dickinson, also a balance of 26 3/4 acres of land not returned, hire of negroes, also received of Jabez White, Joseph Philips, and Joseph Jewell for corn and for rent. Persons listed, to wit, Francis McKay, Joseph Philips, William Donelson, Jacob Dickinson, Exum R. Sumner, Thomas Hickman, Josiah Wharton, N. Ewing, Henry Crabbs, Felix Grundy, E.H. Foster, James Trimble, G.W. Gibbs, Gordon and Walker, Dr. Goodlett, R.T. and J. Walker, Robert Smiley, Doctor Newman and Ewing, Patsy Dickinson, William G. Evans, Sugg Fort, William Thomas Dickinson's receipt, Greenwood Payne, Whitford and Williams, Jacob Dickinson, William Dickinson, Duke W. Sumner, S.L. Wharton, William Neely, Joseph Jewell, G.W. Trimble, Wilson White, Simon Williams, Severn Donelson, D. and G.W. Trimble, J. Nichols, William Gibson, George Wharton, David Hunter, S.W. and K. Hope, P. Walker, M.B. Frazier, W. Hope, William T. Dickinson, Jas. R. Hooper, Robertson and Curry, Sumner and Moore, William Bosworth, John Price, Crockett and Adams, James Dean, John Nichols, William and R. Gibson, Martha Lottan, John Cole, S.L. Wharton, John Porter, John Gordon, Milton Birdwell, Patsy Martin, Peter Ter(illegible), A. Porter and Sons, Whitley White, Joseph Lottan, Drury Scruggs, John Manus, R.W. Green, F. Links, Thomas P. Yates, A. McNabb, M.H. Sampson, William B. Cox, P. Moore, A. Walker, William D. Philips, and Robert Wilson. This 22 Apr 1823. Signed by Edmond Goodrich, J.P., Samuel Shannon, J.P. and R. Weakley. Apr Term 1823.

Page 215   Additional inventory of estate of Henry Ferebee, deceased.
June 21, 1823   The amount of cotton that was not picked in at the time that I made return of the property that was sold at the sale. 394 lbs in, the seed at $1.31¼ per hundred $5.15 3/4. Signed by Thomas Ferebee, admr. Apr Term 1823.

Page 216   Settlement of estate of Elizabeth Hardy, deceased.
June 21, 1823   To cash paid Joseph Mount, Robertson and Waters, Mr M(illegible), Micajah Fly, J. Howlett, and J. Scott. Signed by Eli Talbot and William Lytle, Esquires. 28 Apr 1823. Micajah Fly, admr.

120

Page 216   Guardian return settlement of Thomas Hail's heirs.
June 21, 1823   We have proceeded to settle with Gabriel Sanders, guardian to Thomas Hail's heirs and we find $51.00 in favor of the guardian which he is willing to give to the heirs. This 2 Dec 1822. Signed by William Wallace and Braxton Lee. Apr Term 1823.

Page 216   James Green and others, orphans.
June 21, 1823   Thomas Green, guardian for James Green, Rebecca Green, William Green, Sally Green, and Samuel Green, makes return that he came into his hands, there was 57¼ acres of land on waters of Heatons Creek in Davidson County which he sold agreeable to the provisions of the will of Littleton Green, father to the above named minors and on 23 Nov 1822 and William Huffman became the purchaser at $301.16¼. Also a note on Nicholas Eddington and James Cantrell. Thomas Morris, guardian. Apr Term 1823.

Page 217   Settlement of estate of Daniel Frazier, deceased, of Davidson
June 23, 1823   County. Made by admr. Persons listed, to wit, Mathew Walker, Alexander Hutchison, Doctor Mathews, James T. Basey, N.W. Moore, James Trimble, John Buchanan, William G. Kimbro, Stephen C. McDaniel, J. Bell (decedent), George Wharton, J. Watkins, B. Wright, J.L. Moland, Walker & Hope, N. Ewing, James Ollivant, Gordon & Walker, W. Whites, Lemuel Bevers, A. Kingsley, VS Frazier's admr., Samuel Stull, N. Ewin, Micklebury, and Tunsell & Norvill, allowance made the widow of Daniel Frazier, deceased, Moses B. Frazier, and Harris. Signed by David Dunn and Alexander Walker, Esqrs. Apr Term 1823.

Page 217   Henry Murry, lunatic, guardian return.
June 23, 1823   Paid to Kemp Holland for boarding and other items. Signed by Kemp Holland, guardian. Apr Term 1823.

Page 218   Inventory of estate of Zachariah Betts, deceased.
June 23, 1823   One tract of land in Davidson County , Manskers Creek, 561¼ acres, one on R.C.(Robertson County) 428 acres, negroes, notes on John Sigler. Several items listed. Signed by Enoch P. Connell and Seldon Betts, admrs. Apr Term 1823.

Page 218   Penina Eatheridge, support laid off.
June 24, 1823   Support to be laid off to the widow and family, widow of David T. Eatheridge, deceased. Several items listed. This 10 Mar 1823. Braxton Lee, Esquire and Elisha Gower, Commissioners.

Page 218   Additional inventory of estate of William Perkins, deceased.
June 24, 1823   Several items listed. 27 Apr 1823. Samuel Perkins, executor.
Apr Term 1823.

Page 219   Sale of estate of Howell Tatum, deceased.
June 24, 1823   Made at Robertson's and Sanderson's. Several items listed. Nashville, Apr 29, 1823. Stephen Cantrell, Jr., admr. Apr Term 1823.

Page 219   Settlement and division of estate of Severn Donelson, deceased.
June 24, 1823   Apr 28, 1823, settled with Elizabeth Donelson, admrx., to divide the estate among the heirs. Report - That they have not made petition of the land of said estate. Signed by Robert Butler, Francis Sanders and John Donelson, Sr., Commissioners.
Item B: Mar 28, 1823, paid to Mrs. Jane Hays, William Watson, Thomas Overton, William McNight, Joseph Litton, John Bernard, Timothy Dodson, Harris, Edward Bondurant, A. Porter, Shelton Pride & Hugh Hays, James R. Glaves, James Erwin, George Williamson, B.F. Saunders, James G. Martin, Francis Saunders, Leven Donelson, John McNice, Moses Brook, John Baker, Thomas Gleaves, Eli Cherry, and Stephen Cantrell. 9 Apr 1823.
Elizabeth Donelson, Item C: Purchasers of negroes, to wit, William Donelson, Rachel Donelson, James Donelson, John Donelson, Thomas Jefferson Donelson, Samuel Donelson, Lucinda Donelson, and Alexander Donelson. Jan 31, 1823. Apr Term 1823.

Page 221   Nancy B. Clow and others, division of lots.
June 25, 1823   Made on 28 Apr 1823. Nancy B. Clow Lot No. 28 and one third of No. 116. Jane H. Clow Lot No. 36 and one third of No. 45. Eleanor (Ellen) M. Clow Lot No. 38 and Lot No. 51. John J. Clow Lot No. 31. Robert J. Clow Lot No. 43 and 47. Each

child to have one fifth part of Lot No. 48 including the houses. This 29 Apr 1823. Signed by Thomas Claiborne, Alpha Kingsley, Thomas Crutcher, John McNairy, and N.A. McNairy and S.T. Tilford. Apr Term 1823.

Page 221   Inventory of estate of John Elliston, deceased.
June 25, 1823   A list of the accounts on the books of John Elliston, deceased, to wit, Thomas Talbot, Samuel McChesney, Isaac Erwin, John McNairy, (blank) Turley, Rodney Earhart, Richard Garrett, William McCade, William Stuart, M(illegible) R(illegible), William Linch, Thomas Hill, Bernard McKernan, Malachi Carlile, (blank) Lawrence, A. Nichols, S. Snell, William Joslin, Jno. B(illegible), William Handsberry, Charles D. McLain, Joel Smith, John Baukem, John Driver, Samuel Elam, (blank) Hamilton, (blank) Scruggs, Daniel McIntosh, James Harris, Cane Glasgow, William Garner, Henry Wade, Thomas D. Smith, (blank) Simpson, John Newman, Joseph Henrich, Jesse Ashworth, William B. Lewis, John Woodcock, John Lyons, George Simpson, George Peay, B.W. Monroe, Leonard Kennedy, James Ridley, Beverly Ridley, William Sneed, Moses Norvill, Samuel Ralston, P.H. Darby, E. Daniel, William Phills, Josiah Mullen, James Boon, Williamson Adams, William W. White, John T. Dismukes, Thomas Hitter, Daniel Sandefer, Sherrod Arnold, (blank) Baker, Alexander Porter, Christopher Metcalf, Thomas Norton, James L. Hutchens, John Page, (blank) Simmons, Conrad Mandal, (blank) Harper, Jeffrey a negro, Nathaniel Peck, Samuel Nothern, George Boyd, Daniel A. Dunham, John Pryor, (blank) Corbett, Edward Willis, Thomas Yeatman, Jonathan Rains, Raworth & Gordon, Thomas P. Henson, Gen. Thomas Johnson, James P. Irwin, Robert Goodlett, Lewis White, Doctor Burns, Gorden Williams, John Miller, Amsey Jones, Thomas Claiborne, Daniel Lyons, Moses Marshall, Doctor Shelby, Mrs. Priestly, Robert S. Greene, Robert H. Greene, John L. Young, John Scruggs, T.H. Fletcher, Brent a post rider, John Young, Gil Pew, Edward Blackman, Jos. T. Hun, Charles Davis, Thomas Morefield, John Nichols, George Ridley, (blank) Gibbs, William M. Berryhill, Whitfield Moore, Christopher Carter, Asa White, W.H. Barefoot, William Mothers, John Gardner, Little B. Horn, R.B. Owen, M. Lile, (blank) Payne, John W. Clay, James Davis, John Buchanan, James Trimble, Woods (Sam negro), Aron Day, (blank) Vaught, Michael Raney, John T. Pennington, John Leak, O. Harrow, (blank) Shopshire, John Estill, John Chapman, William Bosworth, Hide C(illegible), Samuel D. Read, Thomas Green, (blank) Lucky, William B. Robertson, E. Phipps, John Pickering, John B(illegible), William Brooks, Samuel Ridley, Mrs. Porter (now Ferguson), Joseph Gammell, James G. Martin, Collin S. Hobbs, N. McNairy, Jas. C. Lee, Benjamin Stump, John Thomas, Duncan Robertson, William Compton, Mrs. Harris, N. Gardner, Philip Thomas, William W. Watson, John Kersey, Thomas P. Henson, William Alexander, (blank) Benson, (blank) Laurence, Thomas N. Edington, John Stobuck, John M. Page, Benjamin Atkinson, Edward Ward, Jesse Smith, Priestly Sheppard, (blank) Watson, William B. Gardner, Wilson Sanderlin, Richard Lyon, William S. Turner, James H. Gamble, Joseph Payne, Lazarus Inman, Samuel Harwood, Isaac Howlett, John Gunning, Robert Smiley, M.H. Quinn, Morris Harding, Miss Elliot, Campbell Carlile, (blank) Shewman, Alexander Smiley, Jason Thompson, H. Smith, Samuel K. Green, John Sommerville, Frederick Harwell, James Lockhart, Zachariah Waters, John Bosley, William P. Campbell, Samuel Martin, James Craighead, Pleasant Craddock, Zadock Forbs, James Stuart, E.D. Hobbs, J.T. Elliston, Allen Goodrum, John Adams, Joseph Herrin, John Folwell, (blank) Grubbs, James Dean, James Manifee, James Grizzard, Willis Branch, Joseph Litton, William Park, Benjamin T. Lewis, Henry Crabb, (blank) Douglass, David Irwin, Boyd McNairy, Mrs. Boyd, W.M. Parks, William Campbell, Robert Weakley, William Lytle, Stout & Long, Micajah Fly, Bernard Vanleer, Jobe Gill, John Nichols, Doctor Overton, William Barrow, Ann James, Robert W. Green, (blank) Grant, Colonel William Philips, Arith Foster, Edward Scruggs, Daniel Davis, A. Hynes, Alpha Kingsley, Samuel M. Brice, Young Philips, Jacob Donelson, Doctor Higginbotham, Thomas Irwin, (blank) Norris, James M. Elliston, Robert Armstrong, Isaac Earthman, Robert Campbell, (blank) Warson, John Kibble, John Spence, Benjamin Bedford, James McGavock, Samuel Houston, Jesse Wharton, Samuel Seay, (blank) Goodman, George W. Campbell, Robert Woods, Josiah L. Shaffer, Soloman Clark, Josiah W. Harton, Andrew Morrison, Rhody Goodrich, Knox Merchant, William Gibson, George K. Dillon, Capt. Shaw, Michael Hoover, John B. Williams, Sarah King, Felix Grundy, and John Hays. Notes on, viz, H. Bateman, J. Wilkins, John L. Cobler, John Chanler, James M. Elliston, John Inman, Alfred Osborne, Winson Edney, Nichl. Garaway living in Kentucky, William Wood, Alex. McCullock, William Brooks, Exum P. Sumner, P. Mc. Priestley, Robert Ridley, William Wilson, John Chapman, William Whitfield, Conrad Mandle, William Hewlett, Sarah Abernathy, Henry Daugherty, Charles Hartly, William H. Morton, George Whitney, Joseph Gammill, Jesse B. Porter, Edmd. Lanier, John Hewlett, Thomas Dilworth, Moore P. Love, A.D. Hamilton, Richard Robins, Samuel Williams, Zadock Forbs, William Rutherford, H.O. Hare, George Smith

in Kentucky, John A. Gruber, and Benjamin Elliston living in Kentucky. Signed by J.T. Elliston, admr. Apr Term 1823.

Page 224   Amount of sale of estate of John Elliston, deceased.
June 26, 1823   Sold Mar 1, 1823. Purchasers, to wit, Solomon Clark, John Grundy, Miller & Murrell, G. Wharton, N.W. Robertson, Wilburn, Manchester, Brooks, Shall, Thomas Welch, McGavock, Crenshaw, J. Dicken, and Richmond. J.T. Elliston, executor. Apr Term 1823.

Page 225   Division of land of Seth Davis, deceased.
June 27, 1823   Plats on page 225. Lot No. 1 to Lucy Davis 56½ acres. Lot No. 2 to James Davis 58 acres. Lot No. 3 to Julia Davis 44½ acres. Lot No. 4 to Wilson Davis 55½ acres. Lot No. 5 to Joshua Davis 34 acres. Lot No. 6 to Minervia Davis 19 acres. Lot No. 7 to Stokley Davis 21 acres. Lot No. 8 to Merion Winstead 20 acres. Lot No. 9 Nancy Davis 20 acres. Lot No. 10 to Seth L. Davis. Land on east and west side of Harpeth River and on headwaters of Trace Creek and the place whereon he resided in his lifetime. This 29 Apr 1823. Newton Edney and John Davis. Apr Term 1823.

Page 228   Andrew McNairy - Deposition - Davidson County.
June 27, 1823   We, Willie Barrow and William Lytle, J.P.'s on 10 Apr 1823. We met on the land in question and at the trees represented in the deposition, proceeded to take and take the deposition of the witnesses, to wit, the depositions of John Rains, Sr., John Duffield and Jason Thompson, duly sworn &c said at a corner of a 640 acres on which Thomas Thompson now resides for the purpose of establishing where the west boundary of Thomas Thompson and the east boundary of David Mitchell. He, John Thompson, son of Thompson who says he owns the land now being present and acknowledges that he received notice to attend. They proceeded to take the deposition of John Rains, Sr. on the land, he being duly sworn and said that a forked cherry tree, one fork being out (now down), standing near said Thompson's fence and east of the road, the tree was originally marked by Roger Top and David Mitchell as a conditional line between them, that Top marked one fork of the tree and Mitchell the other, this was done in or about the last days of Jan 1780 which I have always understood to be the conditional line between them until Top's land was run out, and that Top's marks are still on the tree. This 10 Apr 1823. Will Lytle, J.P. and W. Barrow, J.P. Signed by John Duffield.

Page 232   William Ellis' deposition. Limestone County, Alabama.
June 30, 1823   Apr 3, 1823. A call was made for Mr. Thompson who had a subpoena for William Ellis of Giles County to attend at Nashville on 10 Apr 1823 to give evidence in a case of controversy wherein Andrew McNairy is Plaintiff and Thomas Thompson is Defendant. The said witness being a resident of this county and also being in a low state of health not likely to recover, the said Thompson thought fit to take the following measures. The Witness is about 83 years of age and being duly sworn on the Holy Evangelist and he said he did carry the chain for James Mulherrin to run out a tract of land for Thomas Thompson lying on the waters of Browns Creek near Nashville, along with Jason Thompson. Several other questions were asked and he answered. Apr Term 1823.

Page 233   Settlement of estate of Daniel Young, deceased.
July 1, 1823   Made with Hardy S. Bryan, admr. Persons listed, to wit, Cyrus Campbell, Doctors McNairy & Shelby, Cornelius Waggoner, Thomas M. Ross, Balser Huffman, Waggoner & Huffman, Michael Waggoner, Farquharson, Robert Wilson, Benjamin Moore, Samuel Williams, David Wills, George W. Gibbs, E.H. Foster, John Elliston, Samuel Shannon, Willis Seat, Doctor John Newman, Clement Stubblefield, Drury Scruggs, Samuel Stull, J.W. Horton, Robert Weakley, James Sims, Samuel Weakley, Buchanan Lanier, Henry Johnston, John C. McLemore, Shederick R(illegible), Peter Woodson, Elenor Young, Robert C. Foster, N.H. Robertson, William Coldwell, Lewis Earthman, Jeremiah Williams, T. & Joseph Porter, Whitmell Herrington, Henry Boner, Benjamin Hydes, Michael Waggoner, Alexander Lester, James Shires, George Cagle, Cyrus Campbell, John Lanier, H. Dooling, William & Coltharpe, Oliver C. Porter, James Cornelius, Vincon Carney, John McElroy, John Blair, William Shaw, Stephen Stubblefield, Joseph Love, Joseph T. Elliston, and J. Peebles. Apr Term 1823.

Page 234   Isaac Battle, deceased, orphans guardian return.
July 2, 1823   Sherwood Green to the minor heirs as their former guardian.

Persons named, to wit, Jesse Stancell, executor of N. Stancel, deceased, who was former guardian of said heirs. Also Brittain Adams' note, also Martin Clark, Miss Susan L. Battle, Joel A. Battle, William A. Battle, Robert C. Foster, John W. Hall, Joshua Cutchin, D.J. Roberson, Edward Adams, and Jonathan Proctor. 24 Feb 1823. Thomas S. King and William H. Nance. Also a list of 32 negroes. Apr Term 1823.

Page 235   Settlement of estate of James McBride, deceased.
July 2, 1823   Made with Edward H. East, admr. Several vouchers. A balance in the hands of admr $35.09. This 29 Apr 1823. Signed by Will Lytle and L. Keeling. Apr Term 1823.

Page 236   Settlement of estate of Jesse Smith, deceased.
July 2, 1823   Made with Ira Ingram, admr. Persons listed, to wit, Keys & Webb, James Roan, E.W. Brookshire, Jno. Harding, Jas. B. Houston, Manus & Dillon, E. Benoit, R. Stothart, R. Watson, D. Robertson, N. Ewing, J. Haskell, Jno. H. Wilkins, M. Watson, Will Hewlett, S. Hart, Ingram & Lloyd, Jos. Norvell, George Wilson, R.P. Graham, A. Kingsley, R.P. Hays, Thomas Beals, E.D. Edy, Ira Ingram, Thomas Blount, Sterling Lester, Henry Lake, Jacob Shall, Will Quarles, James Porter, James Grizzard, C. Shipman, Robertson & Curry, Henry Minus, George Dillon, J.M. Smith, Jno. Shelby, Boyd McNairy, Dyer Pearls, Samuel Scott, George Wilson, George A. Bedford, Thomas Beal, Amza Jones, F. Jones, and R.H. Adams. This 20 Jan 1823. Will Lytle and D.A. Dunham. Apr Term 1823.

Page 237   Settlement of estate of Francis Saunders, deceased.
Sept 29, 1823   Made with William Sanders, executor. Persons listed, to wit, John Neel, Z. Noel, Jno. Cox, A. Bland's note, and vouchers on James Carter, Zachariah Noel, B. Burnett, E. Brewer, G. Hartman, J. Purson, and Jos. Howel. Accounts of John Newman, Edmond Owen, and Samuel Blair. Signed by William H. Nance and Cary Felts, Commissioners. July Term 1823.

Page 237   Jesse and Eli Roach, orphans estate settled.
Sept 29, 1823   As ordered by the court at Apr Term 1823, we have proceeded to settle with Enoch Ensley, guardian to the heirs of Stephen Roach, deceased, and find him charged as follows, we find in favor of Isaac Roach, July 19, 1819 $364.40. Interest on that sum from July 19, 1819 $87.45. Rents of land for 1819 up and including 1823 with interest $38.00, total $489.85. Credit by Enoch Ensley account with Jesse Roach $26.65, leaving due him $461.20. We find in favor of Eli Roach July 19, 1819 $347.72, interest from 19 July 1819 to 19 July 1823 $83.45, rents on land for 1819 to 1823 $38.00, total $469.17. Credit by E. Endsley account with Eli Roach $28.53. Leaves due him $440.64. This 18 July 1823. July Term 1823.

Page 238   Settlement of estate of Henry Bailey, deceased.
Oct 1, 1823   Persons listed, to wit, Moses Norville, Brown & McAdams, N.B. Norton, John Kerr, F. Bailey, Jesse Brooks, J. & R. Woods, J. Brown, John Falwell, Simon Glens, A. Richardson, James Irwin, John Caldwell, Briggs, Doctor Overton, R. & Curry, and George Battle. David Irwin, admr. This 30 July 1823. Eli Talbot and William Lytle, executors. July Term 1823.

Page 239   Settlement of estate of Nathaniel Herbert, deceased.
Oct 2, 1823   Made with Richard herbert, admr. Several items listed. Also persons listed, to wit, John Lanier, John L. Fielder, John Currin, Doctor Stith, Ephraim H. Foster, James Brett, J.H. Hewlett, David Cummins, Mr. Ogilvie, and Mr. Cherry. Articles purchased for, viz, Judith Herbert, Richard N. Herbert, Thirza, Rosey and John Herbert. This 11 June 1823. Thomas Edmiston and William Ramsey. July Term 1823.

Page 240   Inventory of estate of Absalom Page, deceased.
Oct 2, 1823   Nineteen negroes, $70.35 in silver which was exchanged for Tennessee money, $114.75 in Tennessee and Alabama paper, $13.25 in Kentucky paper, and 30¢ in North Carolina paper, and several other items listed including two ferry boats and notes on E.D. Barnes, Joseph Page, Henry Clark, John T. Dismukes, James Camels (Campbell), Rodney Earhart, John G. Porter, J.L. Young, James Marshall, Mary Fowlkes, William Falkner, Frederick Barefield, R.C. Phealday, George Davidson, Gideon Gary & Co., John Drury, A. Nichols, R.C. Brown, D.S. Butler, William Black, Stump & Cox, and Skinner & Cox. Signed by

Samuel Shannon, executor. July Term 1823.

Page 242   Account of sales of estate of Absolom Page, deceased.
Oct 3, 1823   Made by Samuel Shannon, executor. Persons making purchases,
viz, Warren Page, Shadrack Fl?ellen, Thomas Porter, Martha Page, Stephen Johnston, Jesse
Birdwell, Harrison Whitfield, Exum P. Sumner, William Page, Reuben Wallace, William Roach,
John W. Page, David Parker, Samuel Shannon, Isaac Newland, Joseph Page, George Wharton,
Joel Philips, Duncan Robertson, James Scruggs, John Newland, Jesse Hobdy, Drury Scruggs,
David Love, Debbis Dozier, Henry Bonner, William Philips, William Wallace, Bass & Spence,
Thomas Sadler, Sarah Jones, Henry Wade, William Gill, Willis Ally, Jno. Hinton, John
Morehead, James Hooper, James Falkner, Jas. Yarbro, Cyrus Campbell, E. Gamble, William
Yarbrough, Wilson Gower, Berkley Thomas, Thomas Smith, G.W. Waters, George Waters,
Thomas Ivey, John C. Parker, Jesse J. Everett, John Lanier, Christopher Brooks, Frederick
Gulledge, Langhorn, Scrugs, Harriet Page, Roger B. Sappington, Robert Martin, Luiza Page,
Richard Minor, Gilbert Marshall, Thomas Talbot, William Brooks, William Moore, Vinson Page,
Edward Vaughn, John Criddle, J.R. Jefferson, Samuel F. Graves, Joel Beavers, James
Woodard, William Lytle, Joseph Love, Jno. B. Demembrum, William Fuqua, Braxton Lee,
William Anderson, Arnold Russell, Reuben Biggs, William Shelton, and Wilson Crockett.
Samuel Shannon, executor. July Term 1823.

Page 246   Account of sale of estate of Charles Cagle, deceased.
Oct 4, 1823   Sold by William Wallace, admr the 10th May 1823. Persons
purchasing, viz, Jacob Cagle, John Hufman, John Waggoner, George Cagle, and John L.
Young. July Term 1823.

Page 246   Inventory of estate of John Harwood, Sr., deceased.
Oct 6, 1823   Taken 14 Feb 1823 by William Wrenn, executor. Several items
listed. July Term 1823.

Page 247   Inventory of estate of William P. Bowers, deceased.
Nov 6, 1823   Several items listed including notes on Greenwood Payne, James
McDaniel, Sumner & Weakley, William Williams, Joshua Drake, Alexander Cunningham, John
Dicken, John Harrison, Ezekiel Philips, William Warmack, Richard Harrison, John Tomlinson,
Robert Boothe, Thomas Dorris, James Bowers, David Logue, George Campbell, Thomas Ragan,
R.T. Richey, John Kennedy, P.M. Randal, King Liston, John Bowers, James Priestley, Will
Crawford, John Jordon, E.S. Moore, John R. Byrn, Charles Stuart, Lot Warren, John S.
Galbreath, William Campbell, William Hill, Sally Winchester, William Watson, Richard B.
McCarmack, James B. Conger, Robert Bates, William Baker, John Sutton, Samuel P(illegible),
Robert Campbell, David Kennedy, Jesse Glasgow, Dismukes & Boothe, and Philip Hurt. John
M. Morton's receipt, and J.D. Huddleston's receipt. Executions on Josiah Warren, L.C.
Farraw, and John P. Hogan. Signed by E.P. Connell and George Campbell, admrs. July Term
1823.

Page 248   John Pugh, guardian return.
Oct 7, 1823   John Davis, guardian and Solomon Clark, admr. Isaac Green
Pugh, a minor. Betsy Pugh, mother of the minor. July Term 1823.

Page 249   Account of sale of estate of Zachariah Betts, deceased.
Oct 7, 1823   Sold 29 May 1823. Persons purchasing items, viz, Catherine
Betts, Eliza Betts, Seldon Betts, William Perry, Richard Harrison, Theophilus Scruggs, Isaac L.
Glasgow, John S. Galbreath, G.R. Elmore, Stephen Cantrell, Thomas Dorris, William Kennedy,
Isaac Walton, George Campbell, John Stuart, John G. Galbreath, P.M. Randal, Thomas Powell,
C(illegible) Freeman, Thomas Ragan, James McDaniel, Charles L. Byrn, John R. Byrn,
Frederick Lasiter, John Betts, John Harrison, S.W. Hope, B.W. Minus, David Logue, Anderson
Byrn, and E.S. Moore. E.P. Connell and Seldon Betts, admrs. July Term 1823.

Page 250   Inventory of estate of John Bowle, deceased.
Oct 7, 1823   Notes on Joseph Scales, Henry Scales and Joseph Hopkins,
deceased. Interest in a lot in Nashville, horse, saddle and bridle, and three notes on Thomas
G. Bradford. James Maxwell and Robert Hill, executors. July Term 1823.

Page 250   Martha Page, support laid off.
Oct 8, 1823   Several items listed. Signed by Joseph Love, Jno. Criddle,
William Neely, David Hunter, and James Marshall. July Term 1823.

Page 251   Will of Jain Bell, deceased.
Oct 8, 1823   Apr 26, 1823. Widow of Samuel Bell, deceased, of Davidson
County. To my daughter Martha Brown my two beds and furniture, one chest, cupboard
furniture and kitchen furniture, one big wheel, and one flax wheel. To my grand daughter
Jain Bell only and daughter of Sq. Bell. I appoint my friend Charles Hays and John Bell,
executors. Test: John Barnhart, William B. Erwin and Thomas Bell. July Term 1823.

Page 251   Will of George Porter, deceased, of Davidson County.
Oct 8, 1823   To my beloved wife Lydia Porter my real and personal estate. I
appointed my beloved wife Lydia Porter my executrix. This 18 May 1823. Wit: Thomas
Claiborne and Nathan Ewing. July Term 1823.

Page 252   Inventory of estate of Jeremiah Allen, deceased.
Oct 8, 1823   Taken 21 July 1823. Several items listed. Notes and accounts,
viz, Wilson Woodroff, David Cartwright, Benjamin Moores, William Thomas, Philip Campbell,
Thomas Roundtree, John Hall, Stephen Shelton, Robert Johnson, Edward H. Jones who lives in
Virginia, Edward Pignim(?) who lives in Virginia, Mr. Foster, Sidney Smith, Lewis Sturdevant,
Edwin Smith, Elizabeth Thacker who lives in Virginia, and Thomas Neely who lives in Virginia,
as I am informed by the widow of the intestate have been long since paid. Tilman R. Daniel,
admr. July Term 1823.

Page 253   Catherine Betts, her support laid off, of Davidson County.
Oct 8, 1823   Support laid off for Catherine Betts and family, widow of
Zachariah Betts, deceased, several items. This 29 May 1823. Signed by Allen Mathis, Charles
L. Byrn and Thomas Powell, Commissioners. July Term 1823.

Page 253   Elizabeth Saunders, a minor, guardian return.
Oct 9, 1823   Edward H. East, guardian. Several items. July Term 1823.

Page 253   Inventory of estate of Joseph Coldwell, deceased, late of
Oct 9, 1823   Davidson County. Returned unto court by Sidney Coldwell, admr.
and Stuart Pipkin, admr. Several negroes listed and several other items including one Bible.
Account of Mr. Richard, Albert G. Wilks and Robert Page and John Mosley. July Term 1823.

Page 254   Judith Fuqua, support laid off.
Oct 9, 1823   Several items listed. This 19 May 1823. Judith Fuqua, widow of
Gabriel Fuqua, deceased. Signed by B.(Braxton) Lee and Wilson Crockett, two of the
Commissioners.

Page 255   Account of sale of estate of Gabriel Fuqua, deceased.
Oct 9, 1823   Made on June 12, 1823. Persons listed, to wit, Judith Fuqua,
John B. Demumbry, William Fuqua, James Fuqua, William Anderson, Robert Vick, Elisha
Gower, Charles Cagle, Isaac Anderson, J.B. D(illegible), John Fobbs, William Evans, Felix
Demumbry, Lewis Earthman, John N. Blankenship, Timothy Durat, Wilson Crockett, Harris
Dastin, C. Peebles, Aron Dean, Joseph Page, Wilson L. Gower, and note on Samuel Taylor of
Virginia. This 19 July 1823. Judith Fuqua and William Anderson, admrx and admr. July
Term 1823.

Page 256   William Young, a minor orphan, guardian return.
Oct 10, 1823   Hardy S. Bryan, his guardian. Paid Mr. Riley for tuition, Malcom
Buie, Robert W. Biggs, McBride Taylor, McNeill, S. Young, Thomas Spence, Jos. Childress, Mr.
Perly, and Mr. Rynman for items for William. In estate of William's father, there was
divided $8779.11 which if divided among eight of the heirs will give to William $1097.39.
708⅛ acres of land on Sycamore Creek which are two small farms. Balance due the estate
$366.16¼. Hardy S. Bryan, guardian. July Term 1823.

Page 257   Land divided of Ezekiel Smith, deceased.
Oct 10, 1823   Plat on page 257. Land lying on Sulphur Creek, north side of the

Cumberland River. To his two sons, viz, Abner Smith and Ezekiel Smith, Jr., beginning at an oak tree in the western boundary of the survey of 237½ acres whereon said Smith lived last before his death, bordering lands bought of Edmond Hyde, leaving to each legatees an equal value and equal quantity of acres giving to Abner Smith the south side of the dottied lines of the surveys, we gave to Abner Smith 78¼ and to Ezekiel Smith 62¼ acres north of the dotted line and to include the mansion house and orchard and plantation or part thereof and of the 50 acre survey we gave to Abner Smith 16 2/3 acres on the south end of the survey running at right angles and to Ezekiel Smith the residue of the survey. Signed by Thomas Hickman, Jeremiah Ellis, Thomas Watts, Jonathan Drake, and Edmond Hyde, Commissioners. JJuly Term 1823.

Page 258   Anne, Celah, Jane, Sally and Aron Roach, minor orphans,
Oct 10, 1823   guardian return. To settle with John McCain, guardian to the
heirs of Stephen Roach, deceased. Several items for each of the orphans. Balance due (Anne (Anny) Roach $452.07. Balance due Celah Roach $452.58. Balance due Jane Roach $444.21. Balance due Sally Roach $388.06. Balance due Aron Roach $386.41. This 18 July 1823. Benajah Gray and Cary Felts, Esquires, Commissioners. July Term 1823.

Page 259   Oct 10, 1823   Account of sale of estate of Samuel
Leonox, deceased.
Oct 10, 1823   Sold by Cardy C. Peebles and Minet Lenox, executors, on 5 Nov 1823. Cardy C. Peebles purchased several items also George W. Waters and Joseph W. James and Levi Walker. July Term 1823.

Page 259   Churchill Linear, a minor orphan's return.
Oct 10, 1823   Hire of several negroes for year 1821. John Lanier, guardian.
July Term 1823.

Page 259   Divided estate of James Hanna, deceased.
Oct 10, 1823   Set apart to James J. Hanna one house and the ground attached thereto lying in Nashville and it being represented to the court that the ground allotted to James J. Hanna is not truly described and that there is a part of said ground constituting an alley from the stables to College Street which is not set out by metes and bounds though so intended by the Commissioners. The court do therefore adjudge and decree that the said James J. Hanna have and hold to himself and his heirs forever as well the house and ground described in the aforesaid partition as also the alley attached to said ground running to College Street. The bounds will appear in the deed from Jenkin Whiteside to James Hanna (now deceased) for part of Lot No. 24 in Nashville and by deed to Jesse Wharton and others, whereby a part of said ground purchased from Jenkin Whiteside was conveyed away and the alley reserved. July Term 1823.

Page 260   Will of Samuel Overton, deceased, of Davidson County.
Oct 11, 1823   Formerly a resident of Louisa County, Virginia. I desire that the money recovered and received for a tract of land of 1000 acres lying on Pleasant River in the State of Kentucky, bequeathed me by my father James Overton, deceased, of Louisa County, Virginia, the net proceeds or so much as be necessary be applied to discharge of a debt due Colonel Richard Marins of Louisa COunty, Virginia. Any contract that my brother John Overton may have made or any that he may hereafter make relative to the (illegible) of the aforesaid tract of land bequeathed me by my father in Kentucky, I do ratify and confirm. To my brother John Overton and his heirs a negro named Lew and also $250.00 on condition of his paying the legacies hereafter bequeathed, viz, those legacies that are to be paid in money. To my nephew Samuel Overton Nelson $250.00. To my nephew John Samuel O. Claybrook $100.00. To Samuel O. Murdock of Lincoln County, Tennessee, son of John Murdock $50.00 out of respect of his having been named after me. To my nephew Samuel Overton, son of Walter Overton, my shot gun that has my name engraved on the barrel and lock. To my sister Sarah Claybrook all my books, a feather bed and also any other estate now in the possession of her husband John Claybrook, writing desk &c and intended for her children. To my sister Ann Coleman $25.00 and a request that she may have a mourning ring made with the same to wear for my sake. I appoint my brother John Overton and my two nephews Samuel Overton and John H. Overton, sons of Walter Overton, executors. This 26 May 1819. Wit: (illegible) Overton. Codicil: I give and bequeath residue of my estate if any remain of every description at the time of my death after paying the legatees &c in said will to my two

nephews Samuel Overton and John W. Overton, equally. This 30 May 1819. July Term 1823.

Page 261   Settlement of estate of John and Elizabeth Childress, deceased.
Oct 13, 1823   To Mrs. Elizabeth Childress, cash received as admrx, and for the heirs of John Childress, on the cotton farm after 26 Oct 1821, date of her settlement with the Commissioners. Persons listed, to wit, Robert Walker, James Jackson, Doctor Robertson, Fitzpatrick, and Davis in Florence. Notes of James and Jesse Darden, John Parks, McKee's note paid, James Kennedy, Benjamin W. Jones, Mr. Fogg, Andrews & Harrison, White of Lincoln, Robert C. Foster, William Robertson of Lincoln, Mrs. Childress, Esquires Elliston & Dunham, Burwell Butler, A.W. Vanleer, Andrew Erwin, Robert Green, Nathan Ewing, Edwin Smith, McNairy & Shelby, G.W. Campbell, M.B. Winchester, B. Vick, Campbell Graves, Gordon & Walker, Samuel Weakley, William Ward, Thomas Hamilton, Kirkman & Erwin, Marshall & Watkins, Capt. Marshall, Jos. G. Martin, Samuel Seay, Norvell & Hill, Edwin Smith, John Wilson, Samuel B. Marshall, N.B. Pryor, and Rapier & Simpson. May 6, 1823. John Catron. Apr Session 1823. We, Wilkins Tannehill and Eli Talbot have this day 6 May 1823, John Catron, admr and exhibited to us the amount of Elizabeth Childress, which is signed by John Catron, dated 6 May 1823, says the account stands corrected charged and that Elizabeth Childress stands indebted to the estate of John Childress for $1802.96¼. July Term 1823.

Page 266   Inventory of estate of James Campbell, deceased.
Dec 18, 1823   Several items listed. Signed by Sally Campbell, admrx. Oct Term 1823.

Page 267   Will of William Maxey, deceased, of Davidson County.
Dec 18, 1823   To my beloved wife Margaret during her life my tract of land and plantation whereon I live, also nine negroes, with all my stock and the plantation utensils. To my son John Maxey one negro boy named Washington and other items. To my son Bennett Maxey a negro boy named Royal and other items. I have already given to my son William a horse, saddle, bridle and $500.00, also I have given him a negro boy named Stephen and a bed and furniture, cow and calf and other items. I have already given to my son Merit a horse, saddle and bridle which he has received, also a negro girl named Mandy, a bed and furniture and other items and $500.00. To my daughters Theodotia, Sally P. Mason, Margaret, Rebecca, Elizabeth and Henrietta at their marriage or death of their mother shall have one negro each out of those not already named, also a horse, saddle and bridle and bed and furniture and other items. To my two younger sons Elisha and Powhaton shall be put to school and receive a good english education. I appoint my son John Bennett and William and his wife, executors and executrix. This 9 Sept 1822. Wit: Samuel Weakley, Samuel Stull and George Stull. Oct Term 1823.

Page 268   Will of Robert Sample, deceased, of Williamson County,
Dec 18, 1823   Tennessee. I wish all my property to be sold at public sale and money to be divided among my children. To my daughter Sarah her horse, saddle and bridle, all my household goods and furniture and three shares of my Nashville Bank and other items, also my grand daughter Ann Carroll. I appoint my sons John and Thomas Sample and my friend William Montgomery, Esq. of Sumner County, Tennessee, executors. This 9 Apr 1817. Wit: Daniel Montgomery and Robert Montgomery. Oct Term 1823.

Page 269   Will of Martin Sisk, deceased, of Davidson County.
Dec 18, 1823   June 10, 1822. To my beloved wife during her life or widowhood to do as she thinks best with it and to make use of the profits arising therefore as she pleases. To my son Jordon one $50.00 horse, and then a equal share with the rest of the children. My daughter Betsy Roberts is not to have any share in Vina, Bill and others, equal share of all the property besides. My wife Mary Sisk, my executrix. Wit: Isom Wooten and Elizabeth Wooten. Oct Term 1823.

Page 270   Will of Martha Camp, deceased, of Davidson County.
Dec 18, 1823   To my daughter Martha Jones wife of Wood Jones, all of my wearing apparel and large trunk given me by my mother. To my daughter Martha Jones, wife of Wood Jones, one-half of all my bed cloths, and other items. To my son John W. Jones, in trust for the maintenance of his, my daughter Martha Jones, wife of Wood Jones, during her life, a negro woman named Abby and a negro boy named Jack to be disposed of by her at her death amongst the heirs of her body. To my son John W. Jones, in trust, for the support,

comfort and maintenance of my grand daughter Martha Ann Jones during her life, a negro woman named Nelly and a girl named Mahala to be disposed of by her at her death amongst the heirs of her body. To my son John W. Jones, in trust, for the support, comfort and maintenance of my grand daughter Marthy Virginia Jones during her life, a negro woman named Mariah and a girl named Sophia to be disposed of by her at her death amongst the heirs of her body. To my son John W. Jones, in trust, for the support, comfort and maintenance of my grand daughter Eliza Jones during her life a negro boy named Rowland and a girl named Polly to be disposed of by her death amongst the heirs of her body. To my son Thomas B. Jones a negro woman named Sukey and a boy named Pompey. To my son Richard H. Jones my gigg and harness, horse and colt, loom and furniture, spinning wheel and cards for the support of his children. To my son John W. Jones the side board I bought of Richard Smith. All the monies that I may have on hand and that may be due me should be equally divided between my three sons Richard H., Thomas B. and John W. Jones after paying all my just debts. My stock of cattle, hogs, and sheep should be equally divided between my two sons Richard H. and John W. Jones. To my grand daughter Eliza Jane Jones one small featherbed. To my son Richard H. Jones one half of my bed cloths, table cloths &c. I appoint my son John W. Jones executor. This 25 Sept 1823. Wit: William Saunders and Jane H. Thomas. Oct Term 1823.

Page 272   Will of Robert Smiley, deceased.
Dec 19, 1823   I appoint my friend John Nichol of Nashville my sole executor. To my dear wife Mrs. Smiley all my household and kitchen furniture and all my cattle and stock, my wearing apparel and also my books, also to her my negro boy Charles and at her death that belong to my children then living and that he is not to be sold to any person. The rest of my negroes to be kept for the use of my wife and children. All the rest of my estate to be sold and proceeds to be used for the benefit of my wife and children and at my wife's death to my children. Negroes to be sold for the support of my wife and my aged friend and mother-in-law, Mrs. Love, who I wish to remain with my wife during her life. All my children to remain with my wife until they obtain the age of 21 or marries or at a proper age. i wish that my wife and after consulting on the subject to my friend John Nichol do carry on my business. This 6 Sept 1823. Wit: James Roans and Roswell P. Hayes. Oct Term 1823. Robert Smiley signed his will in presence of E.H. Foster.

Page 273   Inventory of estate of Robert Sample, deceased.
Dec 19, 1823   477 acres of land and several other items listed. Thomas Sample, executor. Oct Term 1823.

Page 273   Inventory of estate of Samuel Philips, deceased.
Dec 19, 1823   Several items listed. Signed by David Philips, admr. Oct Term 1823.

Page 274   Larkin Clay's orphans, guardian return.
Dec 19, 1823   To Jonathan Clay, guardian. persons listed, to wit, R. & W. Armstrong, Daniel Berry for tuition &c of Martha. Also William Nichol Vaulx & Co., David Tally, L. Watson, paid Gibson for tuition of Maria and Permelia and Martha for three months. Oct term 1823.

Page 274   Inventory of estate of Williamson Baker, deceased.
Dec 22, 1823   Oct 21, 1823. Several items listed. Moses T. Brooks, admr. Oct Term 1823.

Page 274   Mary Allen, support, of Davidson County.
Dec 22, 1823   We, William Bumpass, Willis White and Robert Johnston were appointed to set apart for Mary Allen and family one years provisions out of the estate of Jeremiah Allen, deceased, several items listed. This 13 Sept 1823. Oct Term 1823.

Page 275   Settlement of estate of John Sanders, deceased.
Dec 22, 1823   Robert L. Sanders to Absalom Rogers, executor, several items listed and persons named, to wit, H. Crabb, Canady & Criddle, Hopper, Grimmer, Higginbotham, and Jno. M. Watson. Eliza Ann Sanders to Absalom Rogers, executor, several items listed and person named paid was Jno. W. Watson. This 20 Oct 1823. Signed by Benajah Gray, J.P. and William H. Nance, Commissioners. Oct Term 1823.

Page 275   Inventory of estate of John Farrer, deceased.
Dec 22, 1823   Several items listed. Signed by William Farrer, admr. Oct Term
1823.

Page 276   Account of sale of estate of Jeremiah Allen, deceased.
Dec 22, 1823   Made by T.R. Daniel, admr on 15 Sept 1823. Purchasers, to wit,
Mrs. Allen, William Westmoreland, Tilman R. Daniel, William White, Mr. Temple, Maj. William
Grubb, Simon Everett, Edwin Smith, Dick Manly, William Temple, Jno. Thompson, Henry
Compton, Jackson Foster, Thomas Roundtree, F. Abernathy, Jeremiah Hunt, Philip Pipkin,
Harvey D. Parish, Sidney R. Smith, James Bradley, William Bains, Benjamin Moore, and
Thomas Campbell. Oct Term 1823.

Page 277   Sidney Coldwell, support laid off.
Dec 23, 1823   Commissioners met to lay off one years provisions for Mrs.
Sidney Coldwell, widow of Joseph Coldwell, deceased, and her family. Several items listed.
This Sept 4, 1823. Signed by Jno. Harding, Giles Harding and James Cooper, Commissioners.
Oct Term 1823.

Page 277   Isaac Basye, orphan, guardian return.
Dec 23, 1823   Made by Francis Basye, guardian. Clothing for Charles, clothing
and boarding Isaac, Doctor's bill for Charles, to cash Elishman Basye's heirs, also paid to
Samuel Wharton $2.62, and other items. This Oct 7, 1823. Signed by William Williams and E.
Goodrich. Oct Term 1823.

Page 278   Nancy Basye, orphan, guardian report.
Dec 23, 1823   To Francis Basye, guardian. Schooling and boarding for Harvey
and Nancy, also Samuel Wharton $2.62½. Oct 7, 1823. Signed by Will Williams and E.
Goodrich. Oct Term 1823.

Page 278   Inventory of estate of James David, deceased.
Dec 23, 1823   Several items listed. Signed by George David and Jno. Davis,
admr. Oct Term 1823.

Page 279   Account of sale of estate of Allen Dodson, deceased.
Dec 23, 1823   Sold by Timothy Dodson, admr. Nov 15, 1823. Purchasers, to
wit, Mary Dodson, widow, and Ann Dodson, John P. Dix, Mary Dodson, Joseph Dodson, Jas.
Gleaves, Hugh Hays, Timothy Dodson, Thomas Creel, William Briant, Samuel Scott, Joseph
Hamilton, Abner Cowgill, Thomas Jones, Thomas Bradshaw, William Saunders, William
Sanders, William Hays, David Caselman, Jno. Wilson, Sr., Zadock Tally, Francis Sanders, Jas.
Cook, Obediah Jackson, Meridith Wilkinson, John Wilson, Thornton Dodson, and William Creel.
Oct Term 1823.

Page 280   Inventory of estate of Elisha Brewer, deceased.
Dec 24, 1823   Oct 6, 1823. Several items listed. Accounts on Joseph Kimbro
and Mason Philips. This 25 Oct 1823. Catherine Brewer, admrx. Oct Term 1823.

Page 281   Account of sale of estate of Joseph Coldwell, deceased.
Dec 25, 1823   Sold 5 & 6 Sept 1823. Purchasers, to wit, Sidney Coldwell, John
M. Allen, William Compton, Harriet Pipkin, Martha Coldwell, Burkley Thomas, Braddock
Richmond, William Thomas, Abraham Caselman, Joseph Ensley, Edwin Smith, Silas M. Morris,
Stuart Pipkin, Nancy Overman, Willis Davis, William Chatham, Robert Page, D. Cartwright,
Samuel McDowell, Robert Goodlett, Thomas McCrary, John Williams, Opie Dunnaway, William
Briant, John Hill, Richard Vaughn, Henry Wade, Evan Bateman, William Thomas, Jno. B.
Craighead, David Campbell, Benjamin Malone, Richard Joslin, James Campbell, Thomas
Bradley, William B. Hopkins, Henry Stuart, Allen Cotton, William McCrary, and Benjamin
Brown. Sidney Coldwell, admrx. and S. Pipkin, admr. Oct Term 1823.

Page 282   Settlement of estate of Morris Shane, deceased.
Dec 25, 1823   Absalom Gleaves and William Stuart, executors. Paid the
following, viz, William Tait, Phebe Shane, Doctor Butler, and Sheriff for taxes. Received of
Samuel Steel $60.00. This 15 Oct 1823. Signed by L. Keeling and Jas. Carter. Oct Term
1823.

Page 283   Settlement of estate of Robert Evans, deceased.
Dec 25, 1823   Made by Eldridge Newsom, admr. Received of B.W. and W.H.
Bedford for claim of deed against the United States, also received of B. and R. Joslin. Paid
cash to, viz, John Evans, Alexander Liston, E.H. Foster, Francis Newsom, the Sheriff, H.
Ewing, B. Joslin, and nathan Ewing. This 23 Oct 1823. Signed by Elisha S. Hall and Thomas
Claiborne, Esq., Commissioners. Oct Term 1823.

Page 284   Settlement of estate of Sarah Payne, deceased.
Dec 25, 1823   Made with Flower McGregor, admr. Sept 6, 1817. Paid to Paul
Dismukes guardian of George W. Payne, one of the distributees, also to Zachariah Payne,
Greenwood Payne, R. Booth, Gideon Pillow, Spencer Payne, and William Payne. Bond on
William Walton. Signed by Eli Talbot and Elisha S. Hall, Commissioners. This 2 Oct 1823.
Oct Term 1823.

Page 284   Settlement of estate of George Hughlett, deceased.
Dec 26, 1823   Made by Mrs. Ann M. Hewlitt, admrx to various persons as per
vouchers, to wit, John Hobson, Josiah Nichols, Newman & Ewing, James Gould, John Elliston,
Jeremiah Terry, John R. Grundy, R.A. Higginbotham, Micajah Fly, James Irwin, Joseph
Herrin, James Grizzard, Joseph W. Horton, James Lockhart, Robert W. Green, Nathan Ewing,
J. Mount, T.G. Bradford, W.W. Barber, B. Atkinson, Simon McClendon, M.H. Quinn, John
Thomas, Nathaniel A. McNairy, David Perkins, Isaac Allen, James B. Houston, John Nichols,
R. and W. Armstrong, Martin New, W.C. Coldwell, George Nelson, Francis Lock, Andrew
Graham, Branche   & Co., John L. Allen, Peter Bass, Bass & Spencer, William Compton,
Solomon Clark, Wood T(illegible), H. and R.W. Hill & Co., and Thomas A. Duncan. Persons
paid, to wit, Solomon Clark for brick work, for a frame house, John Boyd for rent, Will
Shields for stone work, and Joseph Herrin for schooling. This 31 Oct 1823. Oct Term 1823.

Page 285   Settlement of estate of Benjamin Philip, deceased.
Dec 26, 1823   Made with Jos. Philips. Persons listed, to wit, J.S. Williamson,
Nichols and Lytle. Others named were Will Williams, Rhody Boyd, Thomas Crutcher, Sam
Lowry, Duncan Robertson, D. Hughs, F. Moore, and Williams. Signed by Daniel A. Dunham
and Thomas Edmiston. Oct Term 1823.

Page 286   Additional inventory of estate of Robert Evans, deceased.
Mar 2, 1824 $149.11 received of the United States by the hands of B.W. and
W.H. Bedford, which money I made a return before the Commissioners that settled the estate
with me at Oct Term 1823 but had not made a return of the same to court. Eldridge
Newsom, admr. Jan term 1824.

Page 286   Sale and hire of negroes of Zachariah Betts, deceased.
Mar 2, 1824   Dec 20, 1823. Purchasers and persons hired negroes, to wit,
Catherine Betts, Lovel Betts, Daniel Ralston, Edward Butler, and John Betts. Enoch P.
Connell and Seldon Betts, admrs. Jan Term 1824.

Page 287   Sale of estate of James Campbell, deceased.
Mar 4, 1824   Several items listed. Sarah Campbell, admrx and Patrick W.
Campbell, admr. Jan Term 1824.

Page 288   Joseph McBride, deceased, orphan's guardian return.
Mar 4, 1824   A return for the heirs of Joseph McBride, deceased, for year
1823. Rent and hire of negroes. Jan term 1824. George Taylor, guardian.

Page 289   Inventory of estate of Harris Ogilvie, deceased.
Mar 4, 1824   Several items listed. William Ogilvie, admr. Jan term 1824.

Page 289   Inventory and account of sale of estate of John David, deceased.
Mar 4, 1824   Sold on 31 Oct 1823. Purchasers, to wit, Susan Davis, John
Canada, John Bell, Loyd Davis, William Harvey, George Goodwin, William B. Erwin, Charles
Hays, Willis L. Shumate, Thomas Shilcutt, William Thompson, Thomas Collins, Sterling Davis,
Edmond Owen, John Hays, Thomas Bell, Abraham Whittmore, James Wright, John Carper,
John Buchanan, Dempsey Corbet, James Goodrich, William Vaulx, John Wammoth, and
Isham Pearson. A note on Adam Casper and Charles H. Pickering. Charles Hays, admr. Jan

Term 1824.

Page 290   Nancy Phillips, widow support laid off.
Mar 4, 1824   We have allotted Nancy Phillips, widow of Samuel Phillips,
deceased, several items for her and her family. This 13 Nov 1823. John C(illegible), John
Watson and John Bell, Commissioners. Jan Term 1824.

Page 291   William C. Beck, minor orphan guardian return.
Mar 4, 1824   William O. Beck to Mary Beck to boarding, clothing and
schooling. Mary Beck to William C. Beck, hire of negro boy Henderson and hire of negro boy
Jackson. Rent of 12 acres of land. Mary Beck, guardian. Jan 27, 1824. Jan Term 1824.

Page 291   James Camp's, deceased, orphans guardian return and Settlement.
Mar 6, 1824   To R.C. Foster, their guardian. Pocket money furnished Joseph,
paid to S.J. Ridley for board and tuition, also paid to Samuel Crocket, Dyer Pearl, Sarah
Camp's expense to Alabama, Charlotte Hart for midwife, shop money gave Margaret in
Franklin, Mary Wheaton for midwife, Joseph Witcher for coffin, John Gregory for sexton,
G.W. Charlton for horse for Joseph, William B(illegible), McLung & Sons, Gregg & Johnson,
dress for Margaret, boarding Joseph Camp, saddle and bridle and shoes for Margaret, dress for
Mary Camp, McGavock, Joseph Litton, Willis Barker, McCombs for coffin, Norvell printer,
R.C. Foster, Jr. board Joseph and Margaret, Robert Smiley tailor, Doctor Roane a Physician,
Josiah Nichols a merchant, cash furnished Joseph Camp to go to Alabama for Sarah Camp,
Doctor Ewing, Moses Norvell, Joseph Litton a merchant, Edward Daniel a jailor, Whyte &
Lynn for Sarah, and Mary Wheaton a midwife. Cash of James B. Houston, John Thomas,
Moses Norvell, T.H. Fletcher, William Compton, Thomas Patterson, Robert Farquharson, Mrs.
Boyd, Robert P. Cunin, Robert Smiley, Whitney, McCombs, William Ozmore, Moses Norvell,
and Smith hire of negro. 27 Jan 1824. W.B. Lewis, Thomas Crutcher and Charles J. Love.
Jan term 1824.

Page 294   Inventory of estate of Fairley Brookshire, deceased, of Nashville,
Mar 6, 1824   Tennessee, Jan 15, 1823. Several items listed. E.W. Brookshire,
admr. Jan Term 1824.

Page 295   Inventory of sale of estate of Sabina Farrow, deceased.
Mar 8, 1824   Persons listed, to wit, Adam Casper, William Harris, Joseph
Senalt, John Bell, Guss M. McFaddin, Nicholas Tomberlin, Ralph S. McFaddin, Willis L.
Shumate, John Roberts, Edmund Owen, Hugh M(illegible), William Hamilton, Enoch Ensley,
Floyd Davis, John Hood, Isham Pierson, Thomas Bell, Hugh Mansone, William B. Erwin, H.P.
Seat, H. P(illegible), Elizabeth Farrow, Polly Farrow, Richard Harfort, William Whittemore,
William Thompson, Charles Hays, and Arthur Bland. William Farrow, admr. Jan Term 1824.

Page 296   Nancy H. and Gray Washington's guardian return.
Mar 9, 1824   Thomas H. Everett guardian for Nancy H. Washington and Gray
Washington, minor heirs of Gray Washington, deceased, for the hire of the negroes belonging
to Nancy H. Washington since the year 1819, money remained in the hands the sum of
$445.61⅛ plus interest, and deducted from the sum $291.80¼. Total $419.16 1/3. The amount
received for Gray Washington for the heirs of negroes $274.80 and deducted $274.80. Signed
by Thomas H. Everett, guardian. 19 Jan 1824.

Page 297   Account of sale of estate of Robert Sample, deceased.
Mar 11, 1824   Made by Thomas Sample, executor. Purchasers, viz, Sarah
Sample, Thomas Sample, William Brannon, Andrew Ewing, James McC(illegible), Laban Eastis,
R. Eastis, W. Pully, M. Maxwell, William Grubbs, C.C. Carter, John Broughton, William
Hollingsworth, Robert Woods, M. Francis, Ab. Eastis, John W. Jones, George
Boyd, Samuel Hite, and H. Graves. Jan 26, 1823 by auctioneer Duncan Robertson. This 26
Jan 1824. Nathan Ewing and Thomas Sample. Jan Term 1824. Persons listed in account with
Thomas Sample, to wit, Richard Smith, John Osborne, Robert Wood, Randal Kennedy, W.
Harding, and John Gordon. This 26 Jan 1824. Stephen Cantrell, J.P. Jan Term 1824.

Page 299   Settlement of estate of Benjamin Phillips, deceased.
Mar 11, 1824   Made with William Williams, admr. J.S. Williams, guardian.
Vouchers on the following persons, to wit, Garretts, Litton, R. Boyd, Daniel, Coltarts Williams,

Crabbs, Edmiston, Horns, S. Clark, Nichols, Lakes, Watson, Ewing, McNairy, Crutcher, J.L. Halls, and Williamson. Jan Term 1824.

Page 300   Division of negroes of Corban Noles of Davidson County.
Mar 11, 1824   Among the heirs, to wit, to the widow, James Boyd and Ann Tennessee Noles. Duncan Robertson, Jno. Nichols and John Shute, Commissioners. Jan Term 1824.

Page 300   Additional inventory of estate of Thomas H. Perkins, deceased, of
Mar 11, 1824   Davidson County. Note on Thomas H. Perkins by Jas. M. Perkins which was left in the hands of William Perkins and came to my hands on 21 Oct 1822 to the amount of $317.16. 25 Jan 1824. Robert Scales, executor. Jan Term 1824.

Page 301   John H. Sumner, minor orphan, guardian return.
Mar 11, 1824   John H. Sumner orphan of Joseph J. Sumner, deceased, with Duke W. Sumner, guardian. Several items purchased for John H. Sumner. Jan Term 1824.

Page 302   Tabitha Baker's widow support laid off, of Davidson County.
Mar 12, 1824   Shelton Pride, Edmond Melvin, Sr. and William Jackson, Commissioners, have laid off one years provisions for Tabitha Baker and children, widow of Williamson Baker, deceased. 550 lbs pork, 16 barrels corn, 2 bushels salt, 85 lbs sugar and coffee. This 8 Nov 1823. Jan term 1824.

Page 302   Divided estate of James Camp, deceased, of Davidson County.
Mar 12, 1824   The Commissioners met to divide and set apart to Benjamin S. Tappan and Margaret his wife, formerly Margaret Camp, one of the devisee of John S. Wood, deceased their part or portion of sundry negro slaves and their increase which was devised to her by said Wood, proceeded to divide and allott to Benjamin S. Tappan and Margaret his wife, six slaves and their increase. This 27 Jan 1824. W.B. Lewis, Thomas Crutcher and Charles J. Love, Commissioners. Jan term 1824.

Page 303   Account of negro hire &c of Jeremiah Allen, deceased.
Mar 13, 1824   Hired 20 Dec 1823. Persons listed, to wit, (negro hired by) Thomas Vaughn. Other estate purchased by the following, viz, Stewart Pipkin, Thomas Roundtree, Sidney Smith, Freeman Abernathy, and William Westin. Tilman R. Daniel, admr. Jan Term 1824.

Page 303   Account of estate of Thomas Hill, deceased.
Mar 13, 1824   To Jan 19, 1824. Note on Washington and Coldwell, and P.H. Darby. Received of Moses Norvell & Co. for account of Thomas Hill's furniture sold by him also other items sold. Notes held by J.P. Clark. Robert Hill, admr. Notes on the following persons, to wit, Alpha Kingsley, Benjamin Turberville, Stump & Cox, George Hicks, Thomas H. Fletcher, Charles Lewis, Lewis Dent, John H. Wilkins, Samuel Elam, Robert W. Hart, William Wilson, John C. Hicks, William McEwin, William Rutherford, Martin Beard, Hiram Dunnigan, A. Sledge, Uzziah Lockhart, John Read, Joseph Stone, Henry Cromer, William Saunders, Thomas J. Read, James Watson, Hiram Allen, Layton Yancey, and John C. Dew. Total $3175.08. Robert Hill, admr. Jan term 1824.

Page 305   William C. Wilson of Williamson Baker, bond.
Mar 15, 1824   I hereby bind myself to William C. Wilson for a tract of land lying on Stones Creek and joining the land of said Wilson on the west, containing 33 acres. This 10 Mar 1823. Test: Robert Butler. Signed by Williamson Baker. Jan Term 1824.

Page 305   Samuel Perkins with N. Cannon, Covenant.
Mar 15, 1824   Suit between Samuel Perkins, executor of William Perkins, deceased, Complainant and the widow and children of said William Perkins, which is to have the proper construction of said will declared the widow having decended (illegible) it and to obtain from the court instructions how the widow's share is to be ascertained and how the balance undivided which may not be included in the widow's share shall be distributed among the widow and children of the deceased and how the said Samuel Perkins as executor may pay over to an distribute amongst them the assets which may be remaining in his hands after the payment of debts, some of the children having been advanced in the testators lifetime. The

suit is to be dismissed by consent of the widow, as her share, seven negroes. Eliza Fearn Perkins, William P. Cannon, Leah America Cannon and Sally P. Scales are the only heirs of William Perkins, deceased. Newton Cannon binds himself to (illegible) said Samuel Perkins his heirs, admrs and assignees against the operation of such claim and the delivery over of said property to said widow and provided Eliza F. Perkins and her heirs should (illegible) any right to said property, the undersigned Susannah Perkins guardian of Eliza F. Perkins doth bind herself against such claim and delivering over said property and provided Sally Price Scales and her heirs to (illegible) any right to any portion of the said property the undersigned Robert Scales the husband of said Sally P. Scales, binds himself to Samuel Perkins. This 23 Jan 1824. Wit: Thomas Edmiston, Mary Bell and John Alford. Signed by Newton Cannon, Susannah Perkins and Robert Scales. Jan Term 1824.

Page 307   Inventory and account of sale of estate of William Williams,
Mar 16, 1824   deceased. Several items listed including James Stratton's receipt for Caleb B(illegible)'s note. In acknowledgement by the Commissioners of the town of Jackson that William Williams had bought Lot No. 97 which they acknowledge they will make a title to when paid for. Three notes on Isaac Williams. William Bedford's receipt for a certificate of a lost horse. S. Shannon, admr. Persons purchasing items, to wit, Joshua Rooks, Isaac Williams, Warren Page, Nelson Jackson, Spencer Lacey, William Porter, Thomas Morris, Jesse Hobdy, Samuel Shannon, and Franklin Looney. Samuel Shannon, admr. Jan Term 1824.

Page 308   Sale of property of Samuel Phillips, deceased.
Mar 16, 1824   13 Nov 1823. Purchasers, to wit, Nancy Phillips, Jonathan Phillips, Adam Hope, Samuel Owen, William Brown, David Phillips, Silas M. Morton, Elizabeth Phillips, Martin Clark, John Fitzhugh, George Goodwin, Amos Moore, Osborn Reaves, Thomas Wright, William Degraffenseed, Samuel Barton, Dempsey Corbit, Samuel Bell, Charner Degraffenceed, Samuel Fitzhugh, Ezekiel Fitzhugh, James Butt, Thomas Hope, Joseph Tait, William Black, Silas Morton, and one note of hand on Charles H. Pickering. David Phillips, admr. Jan term 1824.

Page 310   Account of sale of property of Elisha Brewer, deceased.
Mar 16, 1824   Nov 14, 1823, sold by Admrx. Purchasers, to wit, Catherine Brewer, Eli Brewer, Nancy Brewer, Patsey Brewer, Joseph White, Hugh Mars, William Goodman, William Kent, James Linton, Edwin Austin, Hiram Gambriel, William Weatherly, William Brewer, George Goodwin, Thomas Whiteside, Joseph Kimbro, John Hays, Amos Moore, Adam Casper, John Bell, John Roberts, Denny Lane, William N. Hamilton, James Thompson, Joshua Crutcher, Enoch Ensley, Naomi Bland, S. Greene, John Johnston, Samuel Cuney, Samuel McMurrey, Ephraim Thompson, Thomas Lane, and B.F. Collinsworth. Catherine Brewer, admrx. Jan term 1824.

Page 312   Henry Dickinson, minor orphan guardian return.
Mar 18, 1824   Josiah Nichol and John White, guardians. Two notes on T. Martin, note on R.C. Foster and Sons, James Trimble, J. Shackleford, Dickinson & Cooper, Boyd McNairy, G.W. Campbell, G. Bell & James Gordon, and E.H. Foster and others. Paid to, viz, Josiah Nichols and John Topps. Notes on, to wit, John C. McLemore, Shelby & Claiborne, J.G. Washington and Thomas Washington, J. Norvell and R. Woods, G. Bell and Jas. Gordon, Martin Smith and T.C. Smith, James Trimble and F. Grundy, William B. Lewis and T. Crutcher, also one lot in Nashville. This 20 Jan 1824. Jan Term 1824.

Page 314   Settlement of estate of William Perkins, deceased.
Mar 18, 1824   Made with Samuel Perkins, executor. Receipts on, to wit, H. Crutcher, N. Cannon, J. Dempsey, Chadwell, E. Reaves, George Beatty, Robert Scales, Newnan & Ewing, Darby & Vanpelt, G. Griffin, R.A. Higginbotham, and N. Ewing. Notes on W. Shute, P. Pinkston, S. Perkins, Robert Scales, J.H. Royal, H. Crutchlow, J. & R. Bell, Eliza T. Perkins, Smith & Almstead, S. Sutton, R.T. & J. Walker, A.W. Johnson, Robertson & Waters, J.B. Houston, M. Bostevick, McNairy & Overton, T. Washington, E. Scales, T. Williams, J.P. Perkins, R. McGavock, Matthew Johnson, Curtis & others, Campbell & others, Daniel Scales, R.B. Sappington & M. Smith, W. & J. Alford, Morton & Owen, Ray Alford, and Wright Ramsey. Jan 20, 1824. Elisha S. Hall and David Dunn, Commissioners. Jan term 1824.

Page 315   Valuation of estate of John Childress, deceased.
Mar 18, 1824   We, Joseph T. Elliston and Duncan Robertson, have this day 14
May 1823, examined and valued the property of John Childress which was left undisposed of
by Mrs. Elizabeth Childress at the time of her death. Several items listed including items
that Mrs. Childress gave to Marilda, and a note on John Catron. Jan Term 1824.

Page 318   Inventory of estate of Williamson Baker, deceased.
Mar 30, 1824   Several items listed. Moses T. Brooks, admr. Jan Term 1824.

Page 319   Will of Thomas Russell, deceased, of Davidson County.
Mar 30, 1824   To my beloved wife Angely Russell all my lands, stock and
household and kitchen furniture, during her lifetime ot remains my widow and to be kept in
peaceful possession to raise my three youngest children by my executor but not with power to
sell or dispose of any of my real estate. At the death of my wife Angely or marriage, my
land and property remaining shall be sold and equally divided between my then living children
or their lives, except my daughter Polly Daugherty and she is to have $5.00 of money. I
appoint my son Isaac Russell and John M. Lovell, executors. This 30 Dec 1823. Wit: Alston
Hooper and John Benningfield. Jan Term 1824.

Page 320   Isaac Battle's heirs, guardian settlement.
June 3, 1824   Martin Clark, guardian. Notes on the following persons, to wit,
J.H. Hall and Breathitt, N. Scales and R.W. Hyde, J. Cutchin and D.J. Robinson, E. Austin, J.
Proctor and G. Stevens, E. Stancel and W. Scruggs, E. Stancill and M. Clark, W. Scruggs and
S. Glass, N. Williams, and Jesse Stancill and N. Williams, received of viz, Jesse Stancill, W.
Weatherby, and B. Gray. Several vouchers listed. 8 Apr 1824. Enoch Ensley and William H.
Nance, Commissioners. Jan Term 1824.

Page 321   Settlement of estate of Robert P. McFarland, deceased.
June 3, 1824   Made with Winney McFarland, admrx. Persons paid, to wit, Jno.
B. Lyons, A.R. Haynie, James Mulherrin, Jos. Grizzard, Enoch Laws, Newman and Ewing,
James B. Houston, George A. Bedford, Robert Stothart, R. & W. Armstrong, Adam Woods,
SamuelHogg, Quinn Elliston & Sons, Isaac Davis, Charles Mosley, (blank) Wilson, Nathan
Ewing, Robertson and Waters, and (blank) Norvell. By cash received, to wit, Mrs. Witt, Mr.
McCutchen, Thomas Washington, James Read, Fred. E. Fisher, William McLaurin, Kirkman and
Erwin, B. Castleman, Thomas J. Read, Jno. Bell, Esq., Ed Hall (Hill), James Cannon, Adam A.
Woods, J.B. Houston, Isaac Davis, William Seat, Francis M. Allen, E.H. Foster, Thomas
Deaderick, J. and J.M. Sitler, Jno. H. Eaton, William Coldwell, John Thomas, D. Shelby,
Oakley Jones, John Dowry, J. Roane, William Bryant, Jno. Goodman, Mark Young, Nicholas
Gordon, and Samuel Chapman. Signed by Eli Talbot and Elihu S. Hall, Commissioners. 29
Apr 1824. Apr Term 1824.

Page 323   Settlement of estate of Lemuel Kennedy, deceased.
June 3, 1824   Made with John Criddle, admr. To cash paid and received, to
wit, Ewing, Horton, McGavock, William Homes, estate of Stakett, Edward Daniel, S. Manning,
William Gibson, Foster and Wells, Gillespie, Falwell, J. Tuckett, Brook's note, Stamp and Cox,
Jno. Kennedy, James Erwin, Robert Lanier, James Bonner, Nathan Ewing, Bradford, C.
Ballentine, and William L. Carter. Apr 8, 1824. Signed by Jonathan Drake and William
Faulkner, J.P.'s. Apr Term 1824.

Page 324   Settlement of estate of David Moore, deceased.
June 3, 1824   Made with Nathaniel A. McNairy, executor. Persons listed, to
wit, Daniel Cameron, W.L. Boyd, Boyd McNairy, Duncan Robertson, and William Goodwin.
Vouchers, to wit, James Higgins, S. Clark, (blank) (illegible), J. Ridley, M. New, J. Bright, J.
Grizzard, S. Thomas, M.C. Hays, M.B. Campbell, J. Moore, and John Elliston. Signed by Elihu
S. Hall and Eli Talbot, Commissioners. Apr Term 1824.

Page 325   Settlement of estate of Frederick Stump, deceased.
June 3, 1824   Made with Philip Shute, executor. Persons listed, to wit, Philmer
Whitworth in part of legacy lefy his wife, Mrs. Powell, E.S. Hall for taking a deposition, John
Stump for despositions, Mrs. Huffman for weaving, Jacob Stump for his legacy left by the
will, N. Ewing for recording will, Eli Talbot for taking depositions, a note given by Lewis
Earthman paid to R.H. Barry as part of the legacy left John Stump, Jacob Stump's brother,

by will, D.P. Davis for liquor drank while selling perishable property, Nathan Ewing forcasts of two suits Jno. McNairy VS Stamps, executors and Stump, executors against Jones Read or Moseley, money spent going to Florence to take deposition of Jas. Jackson and Thomas Childress, Mrs. Lester as midwife, Jacob McGavock cost of suit, Sevier Drake for serving notices, Josiah Childress for serving notices, Isaac Howlett for serving notices, D.P. Davis for serving notices, Samuel Shannon's account, Waggoner and Huffman's account, Nathan Ewing for copy of will and survey of land, Jacob McGavock for cost of suit, Lewis Earthman's account against F. Stump also on Earthman's note, paid Steamboat Leopard to pursue Jno. S. Cox who ran off negroes of estate, paid William Hinton for his services on trip after negroes, paid Logan Drake and Mr. Perkins as chain carriers when surveying the Tavern Tract to sell to the Ewings, paid N. Ewing for copy of grant of old Tavern Tract, Randal McGavock for cost of suit, paid Samuel Stull for surveying Old Tavern Tract, paid M. Gleaves, D. Sheriff, for executions in favor of Jno. Hood and also paid Joel M. Smith, D. Marshall, for same, paid Edmond Daniel, Jailor, his fee of negro put in by M. Gleaves, D. Sheriff, to $5607, amount of claim due Alexander Ewing's executor, paid Jefferson Stump's expenses to Western District after Thomas Shute to get his name to deed of land sold to the Ewings, paid Fogg for drawing deed to land, paid Ewing for taxes of John Stump's children of property in will, paid Darby and Vanpelt for advertising Tavern Tract for sale and also Norvell and Wilson same, paid E.H. Foster for services in suit James Hood, the executor, paid McNairy and Shelby and Doctor Higginbotham's account, paid John P. Erwin for services, paid Richard H. Barry balance of Jno. Stump's legacy, paid Newman and Ewing for attending on negro George, paid Criddle for cloths, paid R. McGavock for copy of B. Lanier's deposition, paid Robert Lanier for his service in trip after negroes taken off by Cox, paid John Stump his expenses to Fort Massacre to cross examine George McCormack, paid C. Brooks for trip down river after negroes, paid N.S. McNairy for copy of Hoods judgement, paid Francis Linch for Doctor Robertson's bill, paid Doctor Overton's bill, paid Robertson and Sanderson for hiring negroes, paid Jno. Criddle's expense in going to Carthage to see to business of the estate left in the hands of Hogg, paid Bradford to settle up business, paid Duncan Robertson for selling three negroes and hiring out negroes, paid Josiah Nichols for all spice &c, paid to let Col. Stump have for the use of his family, and paid Hall's note at Steam Mill. Signed by Ephraim H. Foster and Matthew Barrow. Apr Term 1824.

Page 330   Settlement of estate of John Castleman, deceased.
June 6, 1824   Made with Absalom Gleaves, admr. Balance in hands of admr
$152.86½.   Credit of legal vouchers to Moses T. Brooks, Daniel and Thomas Richmonds, Thomas Gleaves, and Nathan Ewing. 10 Apr 1824. William H. Nance, J.P. and Leonard Keeling, J.P. Apr Term 1824.

Page 330   Inventory of estate of George W. Sommerville, deceased, late of
June 6, 1824   the United States Navy. One silver watch and balance due him
at time of his death from the government of the United States for his service and proceeds of the sale of his effects he had with him at the time of his deceased as per account rendered to the undersigned by the pension of the Comr. Porters Squadron on the West India Station, of the effects such as his clothing and sold, with the exception of the above and a few articles of wearing apparel and an old trunk containing the same lately received by the undersigned from Philadelphia, he does not know of any other property either real and personal belonging to the deceased nor does he know of any debts due to him except the above. At the time of the death of George W. Sommerville it appears from the claims made that he owed to John W. Saunders of Philadelphia for loans of money. Robb and Winelenner, Merchant, Tailors and Charles C. Watson and Son, tailors. Apr 20, 1824. John Sommerville, admr. Apr Term 1824.

Page 331   Inventory of estate of John Davis, deceased.
June 6, 1824   Additional inventory of the open accounts on the blacksmith's
bookd of John Davis, deceased, which are unsettled. $155.11. Charles Hays, admr. Apr Term 1824.

Page 331   Sally Campbell, widow's support, of Davidson County.
June 6, 1824   Support laid off for one year for Sally Campbell widow of James
Campbell, deceased. Several items listed. This 22 Nov 1823. Jeremiah Ezell, Cary Felts and Jos. Burnett, Sr., Commissioners. Apr Term 1824.

Page 332   Sale of estate of Corbin Noles, deceased.
June 6, 1824   Nashville, June 15, 1823 by Jas. Boyd, admr. Persons listed, to wit, Mrs. Noles, James Boyd, S(illegible) Beaty, S. Johnson, D. Robertson, R.B. Sappington, John Jobe, John Chatham, R. Garret, H. Martin, Mich. Stean, W. Woodwin, John Cockrill, and Mrs. Noles. Apr Term 1824.

Page 333   Inventory of estate of Willis L. Shumate, deceased.
June 6, 1824   Notes on, viz, Jno. Dungey, Willis Menifee, account against Battersby Ballow, obligations on Jere. Roberts, William Goodrich, Benjamin Wright, William Harrison, Thomas G. Bradford, Hubbard P. Scott, Thomas Rutherford and McNeal, Enoch Ensley, William Bibby, Arthur Bland, Lawson Jones, Caleb Goodrich, James Howell, and several items listed. Signed by Cary Felts and Jerem. Ezell, admr. Apr Term 1824.

Page 334   Division of estate of Harris Ogilvie, deceased.
June 6, 1824   Commissioners has allotted to Elizabeth Ogilvie three negroes, and allotted to John Rains and Frances Rains his wife daughter of said Harris Ogilvie, deceased, two negroes, and allotted to George H. Allen and Mary Allen his wife daughter of said Harris Ogilvie, deceased, two negroes, and also to Henry Bailey and Nancy Bailey, his wife daughter of said Harris Ogilvie, deceased, two negroes, and also to William Ogilvie two negroes. This 20 Apr 1824. Signed by William H. Nance, Alexander Buchanan and Charles Hays, Commissioners. Apr Term 1824.

Page 335   William Young, a minor, by Hardy S. Bryan his guardian.
June 6, 1824   Persons listed, to wit, N. Ewing for several items, paid Washington Ryburn for tuition. On note on Doctor Jno. Newman for hire of negro girl Harriet and boy Alfred. This 30 Apr 1824. Apr Term 1824.

Page 335   Will of William Levy, deceased, of Davidson County.
June 6, 1824   Mar 18, 1824. I want as much of my property sold to pay my lawful debts and after that I lend to my wife my plantation and land where I now live and all my stock of horses, cattle, hogs, and sheep and also my household furniture during her lifetime or widowhood and after her death or marriage to be equally divided between my lawful heirs. I appoint William Russell and Parker Levy, my executors. Wit: Jesse Hooper, Isaac M. Hooper and Elizabeth Hooper. Apr Term 1824.

Page 336   Sale of estate of Harris Ogilvie, deceased.
June 6, 1824   This 10 Feb 1824. Purchasers, to wit, Elizabeth Ogilvie, George H. Allen, John Rains, Jr., William Ogilvie, Jno. Watson, Jr., Adam Carper, Benjamin Bibb, Joseph Taylor, David Bibb, William Pumroy, Lemuel Laurence, James N. Menifee, James Condon, James Leah, Peter Owen, John Fitzhugh, Frederick Owen, Benjamin Cobler, James C. Owen, Henry Bailey, James Baldridge, Daniel Carmack, David Bell, Ezekiel Fitzhugh, Amos Moore, William Menifee, Alexander Robison, Edmond Hyde, Alexander Buchanan, and David Cummins. William Ogilvie, admr. Apr Term 1824.

Page 337   Sale of estate of Jonas Menifee, deceased.
June 6, 1824   On 13 of ___ 1821. Purchasers, to wit, Nancy Menifee, Barnet Sisk, Jeptha Moseley, Thomas Hopper, M.C. Dunn, Isaac Erwin, J.N. Menifee, Major Wall, Philip Wolf, Matthew Porter, Charles J. Love, William Alford, John Waitman, Thomas Edmiston, John Corbet, Gilbert G. Washington, Fairley Brookshire, John R. Buchanan, Jonas Menifee, John Harrison, Thomas Wray, James Dillon, Joseph Burnett, W.L. Shumate, John Watson, Silas Morton, Samuel Edmiston, Bondurant, Pulliam, Armstrong, and Jno. Chadwell. James N. Menifee, admr. Apr Term 1824.

Page 339   Ephraim Drake's heirs guardian return.
June 7, 1824   Apr 27, 1824. The hire of negroes and rent of lands. William J. Drake, guardian. Apr Term 1824.

Page 339   Inventory of estate of Peter Oldham, deceased.
June 7, 1824   Apr 27, 1824. Several items listed. Richard Johnson, admr. Apr Term 1824.

Page 340   Will of Ermin Johnston, deceased, of Davidson County.
June 7, 1824   To my eldest son Isaac Johnson and daughter Parmelia Johnson, each one bed and furniture, saddle and two thirds of the money coming to me from the Farmers and Smithing and all the rest, residue and remainder of my personal estate goods and chattels, after my debts are paid. To my youngest son Edward Christopher Johnson one bed and furniture, one third of the money coming from the Farmers and Smithing and all that is coming from Johnson and Bain, also that my property lying and being in the County of Madison, Tennessee in 10th District, 1st Range and 8th Section. To my beloved mother Susannah Lester, cow and calf and the use of lands &c during her natural life whom I appointed executrix. This 18 Oct 1823. Wit: Daniel P. Davis, Richard Lester and George Waggoner. Apr Term 1824.

Page 340   Winney McFarland, widow support.
June 7, 1824   Widow of Robert McFarland, deceased, allowed to her bacon, lard and $200.00 in cash, this large allowance of money is to defray the expense of the birth and death of an infant and expense of illness. Signed by Duncan Robertson and Colin S. Hobbs. Apr Term 1824.

Page 341   William H. and Jesse H. Philips, minor orphans.
June 7, 1824   Orphans of Benjamin Philips, deceased, to John S. Williamson, guardian. Several items bought for Jesse H. and tuition. Paid Thomas Adams for tuition, Taylor Stanbach, John Parker for shoemaking. Several items for William H. Philips also paid Doctor George B. Hopson for negro. Paid Robert and M. Armstrong's account against both minors. Paid Jesse Shanklin and John E. Finns. Miss Eliza Philips, minor of Ben Philips account with John S. Williamson for shoes, silk &c, Miss Rebecca Philips, minor of Ben, Philips, deceased, for goods &c and horse bought of Richard C. Woolfork. Notes on James Ridley and Boyd McNairy, received of Jas. Philips former guardian of said minors, William Hinton, J.J. Hinton, John Bosley, Crockett and Adams, R. Drewry, John Baird, C. McCarrahan, William M. Berryhill, James Irwin, and J. Decker. This 28 Apr 1824. Apr Term 1824.

Page 342   Inventory of estate of Martha Camp, deceased.
June 7, 1824   Two negroes devised to John W. Jones in trust for Martha Jones wife of Wood Jones. Negroes devised to John W. Jones in trust for Martha Ann Jones. Negroes devised to John W. Jones in trust for Mary Virginia Jones. Negroes to John W. Jones in trust for Eliza Jones. Negroes devised to Thomas B. Jones. Large trunk, wearing apparel and table furniture devised to Martha Jones wife of Wood Jones. Bed cloths, table cloths, towels and toilet devised to Richard H. Jones and Martha Jones wife of Wood Jones. Small featherbed devised to Eliza Jones. Sideboard devised to John W. Jones. Bay horse and yearling colt, gig and harness, loom and furniture, spinning wheels and cards devised to Richard H. Jones. Hogs, sheep and cattle devised to Richard H. and John W. Jones. John W. Jones, executor. Apr term 1824.

Page 343   Sale of estate of Martha Camp, deceased.
June 7, 1824   Purchasers, to wit, John W. Jones, Robert Wood, Samuel Hite, William Dickinson, Jno. Wray, Charles Ballentine, Zachariah Noell, Sherwood Bryant, Thomas H. Everett, Edward Matthews, Jno. Esters, Laban Esters, William L. Carter, William Bryant, Abraham Manuel, Wood Jones, William Harding, Richard H. Jones, Robert Buchanan, and William Walker. Jno. W. Jones, executor. Apr Term 1824.

Page 343   Additional inventory of estate of Frederick Stump. deceased.
June 7, 1824   Several items listed. persons listed, to wit, Stump & Cox, John Counselman, Lewis Green, Claiborne Gentry, Zenas Tait, James Yarbers, L. McCormack, David Coldwell, Thomas White, George Pinkley, Peterson Vaden, Alexander Staley, Daniel Waggoner, Benjamin McIntosh, Jno. Shelby, John B. Darrow, John Wilson, William Atchardson, Jno. George Maxwell, W.W. Hudnall, Joel Olive, Daniel C. Irvine, John Darrow, Robert Samons, Sherrod Winningham, George Pickly, Lewis Williams, Caleb B(illegible), Jahu Peoples, R.C. Phelan, William Grayham, William Gilliam, John Stopes, and John Tuley, and George Jefferson. This 22 Par 1824. Signed by Philip Shute, executor. Apr Term 1824.

Page 345   Sale of estate of William P. Bowers, deceased.
June 8, 1824   Sale on 20 and 21 Aug 1823. Purchasers, to wit, William P.

Bowers, William Watson, Frederick Lasiter, William Williams, Sally Bowers, Enoch P. Connell, Theophilus Scruggs, Carney Freeman, George Hall, John Bowers, Charles B. Perry, Samuel Saveley, William Porter, Matthew Rice, David Logue, James Black, Thomas Powell, Charles Pierce, Thomas Watkins, Reuben Payne, Thomas Dorris, Josiah Warren, Hugh McBride, John McCasland, Isaac L. Glasgow, Elijah Warren, Joseph Dorris, James Sprouse, William Grizzard, Isaac Perry, George Campbell, John Kirkpatrick, B.W. Menice, Jas. McDaniel, Thomas Powell, John C. Glasgow, William Joyner, Joshua Harrison, Stephen Bowers, Richard B. McCormack, Ezekiel Philips, E.P. Connell, J.M. Glasgow, Lemuel Bowers, Burnell Robinson, Aquilla Randal, Rolla Harrison, Isaac Clemmons, James B. Conger, and Edmund Richards. E.B. Connell and G. Campbell, admrs. Apr Term 1824.

Page 347   Division of negroes of William Perkins, deceased.
June 8, 1824   To William P. Cannon and America Cannon allotted four negroes.
To Sarah P. Scales allotted four negroes. To Eliza F. Perkins three negroes, and Sophia allowing Sarah P. Scales to pay $48.33 1/3 to William P. and America Cannon and $3.33 1/3 to Eliza F. Perkins. This Jan 23, 1824. Signed by Thomas Edmiston, John Alford and Henry Crichlow, Commissioners. Apr term 1824.

Page 347   Mrs. Ogilvie, widow support.
June 8, 1824.   Feb 10, 1824. Several items listed out of the estate of Harris Ogilvie, deceased. Signed 10 Feb 1824 by legatees, G.H. Allen, Jno. Rains, Jr., H. Bailey and William Ogilvie. Apr term 1824.

Page 348   Rebecca and Eliza Philips, minor orphans.
June 8, 1824   Made with Josiah F. Williams, guardian. Persons listed, to wit, Mr. Beal Bosley, note on James, one note on Sitler, D. Robertson and son for books, G. Wilson, Cartmell and Munsey, R.P. Garrett, J. Wright, R.T. and J. Walker, N. Ewing, M.T. Williams, Mr. Crutcher, and R. Philips. This Apr 27, 1824. Apr Term 1824.

Page 349   Codicil to the will of Samuel Overton, deceased.
June 8, 1824   Traveller's Rest, 3 July 1822. I am putting this will in the power of my brother John Overton to own Lew, a negro slave bequeathed by my deceased father, in trust to the said Jno. Overton upon his paying $450.00 and his being one of the executors of my will now in possession of Jesse Wharton, Esquire. The said negro Lew is to remain a servant to both or either of my nephews Samuel R. Overton and John W. Overton, not to be sold out of the Overton family. To Col. Richard Morris, now deceased, whatever may be recovered from grants of land bequeathed to me by my deceased father James Overton. Apr Term 1824.

Page 349   Confirmatory inventory of John Childress, deceased.
June 16, 1824   John Catron was appointed administrator of estate of John Childress, deceased, in Oct 1822 instead of Samuel B. Marshall who was released, but was declared invalid. A suit of Samuel B. Marshall, Perry Cohea at Columbia and at Session of 1823 of Tennessee Legislature an act was passed authorizing the Davidson County Court to confirm said administration &c. It confirmed that John Catron was appointed admr of said estate and Samuel B. Marshall was released from said administration. This Feb 13, 1824. Apr Term 1824.

Page 350   Settlement of estate of John Criddle, Jr., deceased.
Sept 2, 1824   Notes on the following persons, to wit, William Drake, Benjamin Hyde, John McNairy, Smith Criddle, Elijah Carney, Simon Everett, William B. Cox, John Huffman, Jacob McGavock, James P. Clark, Jesse J. Everett, J.B. Houston, William Courts, William McCasland, R.A. Higginbotham, William Nichols and Vaulx & Co., Robert W. Green, Joseph W. McCombs, Cornelius Waggoner, N.H. Robertson, J.M. Horton, Henry Ewing, Criddle order to Whitmell, Hardy S. Bryan, Christopher Waggoner, William Roach, Ephraim Robertson, Thomas B. Matthews, J. Roach, and N. Ewing. Signed by Will Lytle and S. Shannon, Commissioners. July Term 1824.

Page 351   Settlement of estate of Richard R. Jones, deceased.
Sept 2, 1824   Made with James Jamison, admr. Several items listed. Robert Butler, William Saunders and Frs. Saunders, Commissioners. July Term 1824.

Page 351   Settlement of estate of John Lester, deceased.
Sept 2, 1824   Made with Alexander Lester, admr. Several items listed. This
31 July 1824. E. Talbot, E.S. Hall and G. Wilson, Commissioners. July Term 1824.

Page 352   Settlement of estate of Walter Simms, deceased.
Sept 2, 1824   Made with J.G. Simms, admr. Persons listed, to wit, Isaac
Wharton, Thomas S. Murray, Samuel Seay, Richard Smith, Minos Cannon, Jo. Norvell, George
Hewlett, Gordon & Walker, Gilchrist an attorney, Nathan Ewing, James P. Clark, Foster an
attorney, Robert Woods, William Kent, William Perkins, Mr. Minn & Colbert, Samuel & D.
Stuart, Sheriff Horton, James Gordon, William White, James Trimble, William Bacotes of
Philadelphia, Hickman & Erwin, S. & M. Allen of Philadelphia, and Sims & Green. This 15
July 1824. Eli Talbot and William Lytle, Commissioners. July Term 1824.

Page 353   Settlement of estate of Corban Noles, deceased.
Sept 3, 1824   Made with James Boyd, admr. Persons listed, to wit, H. Ewing,
Nathan Ewing, Higginbotham, James W. Sitler, James Boyd in right of his wife Patsey Noles,
Lucy Noles a distributive share, E.H. Foster, James Long, and D. Robertson. This 22 July
1824. Eli Talbot and William Lytle, Commissioners. July Term 1824.

Page 354   Settlement of estate of Thomas Hill, deceased.
Sept 3, 1824   Persons listed, to wit, Thomas Everett as guardian, Scott & Rule
of St. Louis, Washington & Coldwell, M. Norvell on N. & Hills account, and Mason Pelcher.
July 23, 1824. July Term 1824.

Page 354   Jesse Jackson's orphans settlement.
Sept 3, 1824   Elizabeth Jackson to Obediah Jackson her guardian, Alexander
and Martin, Thomas Yeatman, Mary Jackson to Obediah her guardian, W.B. Goodman, Martha
Jackson to Obediah Jackson her guardian, Joana (Josina) Jackson to Obediah Jackson her
guardian, heirs of Jesse Jackson, deceased, Elizabeth, Mary, Martha and Josina Jackson.
Signed by William Saunders and Francis Saunders, Commissioners. July Term 1824.

Page 355   Hire of negroes of John Saunders, deceased.
Sept 3, 1824   Made with Absalom Rogers, executor, on 29 Dec 1823. Persons
who hired negroes, to wit, David Adams, Ewin Smith, Thomas Hopper, John McEwin, Jeremiah
Terry, Mathew Porter, and Jeptha Moseley. Also John Corbit. July Term 1824.

Page 355   Henry Murrey, a lunatic.
Sept 3, 1824   Kemp Holland guardian for Henry Murrey made report on his
ward. Paid for boarding, clothing, &c. July 19, 1824. Robert Weakley and William Lytle,
Commissioners. July Term 1824.

Page 356   Will of (Gen) Thomas Overton, deceased, of Davidson County.
Sept 3, 1824   To my son Walter H. Overton $1000.00. To my daughter Jane
Moore $1000.00. To my two grandsons Thomas Butler and John Butler $500.00 each. To my
daughter Harriet B. Overton and her heirs the tract of land which I purchased of John H.
Camp, also to her five negroes. The remainder of my real and personal estate to be left to
my wife Penelope Overton to be kept by her for the space of seven years from the date of
this my Last Will until the executors believe it may become necessary to distribute it among
my children by her begotten. I appoint my brother John Overton, my friend General Andrew
Jackson and my nephew Archibald M. Overton, executors. This 24 Feb 1822. Wit: N.B. Pryor
and Samuel R. Overton. July Term 1824.

Page 357   Inventory of estate of Skelton T. Demoss, deceased.
Sept 4, 1824   Made by John Demoss, admr. A negro boy named Lee levied
upon by attachments of James Demoss as being assets in the hands of Charles Kelly in
Arkansas who qualified there as admr of said Skelton T. Demoss, $130.00 in S(illegible), and
one half of a stud horse named Royal Exchange. July Term 1824.

Page 357   Inventory of estate of John Criddle, Jr., deceased.
Sept 4, 1824   A return of monies belonging to the heirs of said John Criddle,
Jr., also rent of plantation, jury tickets, Garrett's account, also for keeping Mrs. Roland and
children. Jonathan Drake, admr. July Term 1824.

Page 357   Inventory of estate of Richard R. Jones, deceased.
Sept 4, 1824   2250 lbs of cotton which was to have gone to William E. Butler,
note given by said Jones in his lifetime for cotton but was not done through mistake $45.00.
Money due in Virginia $112.78. Total $157.78. James Jamison, admr. July Term 1824.

Page 358   Will of James Richardson, deceased, of Davidson County.
Sept 4, 1824   To my dear beloved wife Nancy Richardson all my estate both
real and personal during her widowhood or lifetime and after her death to my son Daniel
Richardson $100.00 to be paid to him out of the sale of the land also to my son Jubal
Richardson $100.00 to be paid out of the sale after his mother's death. The remaining money
from the sale to be equally divided between Mason, Jenny, Peggy, Milley, Sally, Nancy, and
Matilda and Booker. I appoint my beloved wife Nancy Richardson my sole executrix. This 3
Feb 1823. Wit: William Greer and Nathaniel Gilliam. July Term 1824.

Page 358   Sally Shumate, widow's support.
Sept 4, 1824   Widow of Willis L. Shumate, deceased. Several items listed.
May 15, 1824. William Vaulx and John Gowen, Commissioners. July Term 1824.

Page 358   Susan Davis, widow's support.
Sept 4, 1824   Widow of John Davis, deceased. Support to Widow and family.
Several items listed. William Vaulx , John Bell and Thomas Bell. July Term 1824.

Page 359   Inventory of estate of Ezekiel Fitzhugh, deceased.
Sept 4, 1824   July 15, 1824. Several items listed. Polly Fitzhugh, admrx and
John Fitzhugh, admr. July Term 1824.

Page 359   Will of James B. Houston, deceased, of Nashville.
Sept 4, 1824   I have not yet paid for the real estate on which my cabinet shop
is situated and which I purchased of John Deatherage. To the legal representatives of Craven
Jackson the residue purchase money due on the lot of ground on which I live and which I
purchased of said Jackson. To my wife Mrs. Houston my gray horse and other items including
my large Bible and Methodist Hymn Book. To my daughter Martha Ann Elizabeth one bureau
to be selected by her mother or grandfather Herndon. To my brother William my double
barrel gun. I desire my executors to purchase out of the finds of my estate two mourning
dresses of black crepe to be presented one to my mother and one to Mrs. Martha Herndon.
The remainder to my wife Mrs. Houston and my children Martha Ann Elizabeth and Samuel.
I appoint my friends Randal McGavock, Sr., Joseph T. Elliston, Thomas Crutcher, and Joseph
Herndon, executors. 21 May 1824. Wit: William Hume and Ephraim H. Foster. July Term
1824.

Page 359   Settlement of estate of John Saunders, deceased, of Davidson
Sept 6, 1824   County. July 26, 1824. Made with Absalom Rogers, executor.
Persons listed, to wit, to tuition and paper to Hugh S. to Ferguson, also paid for cloths &c,
also to R.C. Foster, Franklin, N. Ewing, and Criddle & Kennedy. We find said R.L. Sanders
charged on the oath of said A. Rogers for $129.45. This 24 July 1824. Benajah Gray, J.P.
and William H. Nance, J.P., Commissioners. July Term 1824.

Page 362   William C. Young, a minor, guardian return.
Sept 6, 1824   Made with Hardy S. Bryan, guardian. Persons listed, to wit,
Nathan Ewing, Alfred Justice, Washington Reborne, and Doctor Newnan. July Term 1824.

Page 363   Benajah Gray of Wheaton and others, a Bond.
Nov 20, 1824   We, John Wheaton, William Wilkinson and James Wilson, all of
Williamson County, Tennessee, are held and firmly bound unto Benajah Gray of Davidson
County for sum of $5000.00, this 18 May 1820. The condition of the above obligation is such
that the above bound John Wheaton, William Wilkinson and James Wilson has this day
bargained and sold unto Benajah Gray and his heirs, one thousand acres of land in the Western
District of the State of Tennessee and John Wheaton is heir to west of the Tennessee River.
This 8 May 1824. Wit: Enoch Ensley and John Barfield. Oct Term 1824.

Page 364   John Jordon of James Trimble, Covenant.
Nov 24, 1824   Whereas I am entitled to an equal undivided one eighth part in

fourteen tracts of land of five thousand acres each, on the waters of the Hatchee River in Tennessee which tract are all granted to John Rice, one half of each tract was purchased by John McCampbell from Patience Westead of Philadelphia and is now owned by said McCampbell, Robert Searcy, John C. McLemore and myself making my share in each tract 640 acres. I do hereby convenant and bind myself &c to convey to John Jordon his heirs &c 640 acres of land being my interest or share in one of the said tracts. This 1 Feb 1820. Signed by James Trimble. Oct Term 1824.

Page 365   Will of Thomas Edmondson, deceased, of Davidson County.
Nov 27, 1824   The tract of land on which I now live, I will to my two sons Samuel and John Black to be divided as follows, viz, Beginning on the great road where my line and John Topp's meet, then with the road until it crosses the creek, thence up the ridge to the top to an oak tree marked as a line between James McCutchen land and my land, my son Samuel to have all the land east of the line mentioned and my son John Black to have all the land on the west thereof. To my dear beloved wife Martha all that part of the land which I have bequeathed to my son John Black, during her life or widowhood, also to my wife Martha five negroes and at her death or marriage to those of my children who are now single with this exception, viz, that negro Peter is to descend to my son Samuel and to my son John Black negroes, viz, Alfred, Green and Micajah. To my daughter Elizabeth my negro woman named Rose and her child Horace. To my daughter Martha a negro girl Tildy. To my daughter Esther a negro giel Silvy. To my daughter Rachel a negro girl Paulina. To my daughter Louisa two negroes named Harriet and Mariah. The balance of my property to my beloved wife Martha and my son John Black allowing to each of my single daughters when they marry one horse and as many cattle as my wife thinks can be spared, also one bed and furniture. I have a lawsuit in the Circuit Court of Bedford County for a certain tract of land situate in Lincoln County, now in case I should be successful in the termination of said suit. I give one hundred acres of said tract to each of my grandchildren, Hugh McClung and Obediah, sons of William Edmondson. I appoint my son Samuel and my friend William Black, my executors. This 17 Sept 1821. Wit: Michael C. Dunn and John R. Dunn.
Schedule: Whereas Rose has a second child named David, I give to my daughter Elizabeth. Oct Term 1824.

Page 366   Will of William Newell Menifee, deceased, of Davidson County.
Dec 4, 1824   To my brother John B. Menifee 20 acres of land and negro fellow Lillard, blacksmith, and slave for life, my tools and 3 head of horses and other negroes and named which are to remain in the hands of my brother John B. Menifee until first day of Jan 1828, also all the money due me on my shop book account, also my saddle and share of crop this season, and should he die of the present sickness that he now labors under, to be divided equally between my brother Jonas Menifee and my sister Mary D. Menifee. To my brother Jonas Menifee all the balance of the land I die seized of in the county aforesaid, also all my interest to a claim against my father's estate of $496.62½ and I require him to pay to my sister Mary D. Menifee $200.00. To my beloved sister Mary D. Menifee three negroes for life, viz, Alfred, Lucy and Jenny. I give all my undivided interest I may have in several lots of ground in different places in this State and Alabama. I enjoin my brothers Jonas and John to pay each one half of the money that I am legally bound for as security for my brother Jonas N. Menifee and I also release him (Jonas) from the payment of $100.00 which he owes me, loaned money. I enjoin my brothers Jonas and John tp pay to my niece (each one equal part) to Nancy Menifee, daughter of Garrett Menifee, a negro girl. I appoint my brothers Jonas and John B. Menifee my executors. This 16 Aug 1824. Wit: John R. Dunn, William Nichols and Matthew Porter. Oct term 1824.

Page 368   Will of James Trimble, deceased.
Dec 3, 1824   To James P. Clark my law library and my interest being the one equal fourth part in two tracts of land in the western part of this State of 1000 acres each one of which is granted to Edward Cox and the other to Joseph Ross which I hold jointly with John C. McLemore, John McCampbell and Robert Searcy. To my dear wife Letitia B. Trimble all my personal estate except the debts due me, to hold for herself and support of my children for their education as they come of age. To my daughter Susan P. Trimble, negroes Alley and Louis. To my son John negro boys Jack and Tom. To my son Thomas negro boys Maddison and Alexander. To my daughter Mary Ann negro girl Caroline and Margaret. I desire my wife Letitia B. Trimble to make provision for my dear children Eliza Malvina and Margaret Louisa which shall be equal to my other children. I appoint James P.

142

Clark, John Nichols, Josiah Nichols, and Randal McGavock, executors. This 18 Apr 1823. Feb 10, 1824: I hereby ratify the above will. It is my desire in the event of the death of my wife before all my children are grown or settled, that they take equal portions of my estate and it is also my wish that each of my children to be educated out of the general fund of my estate. Oct Term 1824.

Page 370   Polly Fitzhugh, her support laid off.
Dec 6, 1824   We have laid out for Polly Fitzhugh the relict of Ezekiel Fitzhugh, deceased, several items for the use of the family. This 5 Aug 1824. Signed by Alexander Buchanan, Jno. Watson and Jno. Currin. Oct Term 1824.

Page 371   Account of sale of estate of Ezekiel Fitzhugh, deceased.
Dec 6, 1824   5 Aug 1824. Purchasers, to wit, Polly Fitzhugh, John Fitzhugh, Frederick Owen, William Maxfield, Benjamin Fitzhugh, John Rains, Absalom Rogers, William Ogilvie, William Grubbs, Jas. Cooper, William N. Menifee, Adam Cooper, Jno. Carper, Pierce P. Pigg, David Whiteside, Benjamin Bibb, Thomas Ray, David Ray, Opie Dunnaway, James Howell, Charles Hays, James Butler, _____ Smith, and Benjamin Turberville. Oct Term 1824. Several notes, to wit, notes on Thomas Dillworth and John and Henry Stobaugh. Signed by Polly Fitzhugh, admrx and John Fitzhugh, admr.

Page 372   Division of negroes of Joseph Coldwell, deceased.
Dec 7, 1824   Made by Sidney Coldwell, admr and Stuart Pipkin, admr. Also to divide the personal property in Davidson County. Owing to the short time since the death of Mr. Coldwell, the admrs were not prepared to account and produce their vouchers and therefore no settlements were made. All the personal property being sold and division of negroes: Persons drawing negroes, Andrew Coldwell, Joseph Coldwell, Samuel Coldwell, James Coldwell, Mrs. Sidney Coldwell, Stuart Pipkin and wife Harriet, Martha Coldwell, and Polly Coldwell. Signed by Daniel A. Dunham, John Shute and William Compton, Commissioners. Oct term 1824.

Page 373   Will of Woodson Clay, deceased.
Dec 14, 1824   Past a citizen of Nashville and in a very bad state of health. To my friend Warren C. Richmond of Nashville my silver watch a testimony of respect and attachment to him. To my friend Richard Dobbs all my wearing apparel. All the rest of my residue of my estate to my father Levi Clay of Lunenburg County, Virginia. I appoint my friend Richard Dobbs my sold executor. This 12 Aug 1824. Wit: Henry Ewing and Nathan Ewing and Woodson Clay. Oct Term 1824.

Page 374   Will of Abigail Clemmons, deceased, of Davidson County.
Dec 14, 1824   To my son James Clemmons during his natural life my negro woman named Rose and my little negro girl named Lucy, they and their increase shall be equally divided among the children of my son James and his present wife Lydia. Also all my bed and household and kitchen furniture shall be given to my son James and it is my wish that whenever his son Henry and his daughter Nancy Clemmons shall come of the age of 21 years or shall marry that my son James shall give to each of them a bed and furniture. Also to James all my stock of cattle and poultry. I have purposely omitted to give anything to my son Isaac because he is already well provided for and because I have already done more for him than I am able to do for James and his children. This is the only way I have of disposing of my property in the manner I have done because I was governed by and considerations of affection. I appointed my two sons James Clemmons and Isaac Clemmons my executors. This 14 Aug 1824. Wit: Nathan Ewing and Henry Ewing. Oct Term 1824.

Page 375   Will of Daniel Reaves, deceased, of Davidson County.
Dec 14, 1824   To my beloved wife Ellender Reaves all my estate both real and personal during her natural life and at her death or at her discretion. I give unto my grandson James Chessor one good cow and calf. At the death of my wife I give unto my daughter Anne two-thirds of the residue of my estate. After the death of my wife I give unto my daughter Nancy Simpkins the remaining one third of the estate. I appoint my well beloved wife Ellender Reaves my sole executrix. This 18 Aug 1824. Wit: Thomas Hickman and Aquilla Price.

Page 376   Will of Henry J. Love, deceased.
Dec 15, 1824   To my dearly beloved wife Jane N. Love and her heirs the
following property, to wit, proceeds of my land lately sold lying in the District of Columbia,
my negroes (10), also the proceeds of my land in Bledsoe County in Lot No. 2 which I desire
to sell at public sale. To my beloved niece Frances M. Love and her heirs a negro woman
called Eliza and her three children and their future increase. These negroes are bought from
Samuel Worthington. To my beloved little nephew Richard M. Scott Love youngest son of
Charles J. Love a 500 acre tract of land lying in the Western District which said 500 acres of
land I bought of my brother Charles J. Love and desire him to make the deed to my said
nephew Richard M. Scott love. I appoint my brother Charles J. Love my executor. This 4
Oct 1824. Wit: John Dixon, Just. A. Brown and Thomas Dixon. Oct Term 1824.

Page 377   Inventory of estate of Christopher C. Carter, deceased.
Dec 15, 1824   Taken 19 Oct 1824. Several items listed. Signed by Walter O.
Carter, admr. Oct Term 1824.

Page 378   Larkin Clay's orphans guardian return.
Dec 15, 1824   Made by Jonathan Clay, executor. Persons listed, to wit, D.C.
Landen, R. & W. Armstrong, Thomas Patterson, Blackamore, Nichol and Vaulx. Paid for
board of children. This 20 Oct 1824. Oct Term 1824.

Page 378   Settlement of estate of Lemuel T. Turner, deceased.
Dec 15, 1824   Made with Stephen Cantrell, executor. Persons listed, to wit,
Mrs. Turner, Thomas Talbot, Joseph Greer, Mr. Welch, Mr. Clark, E.H. Foster, and T. Rapier.
This 28 Oct 1824. Signed by Eli Talbot and Daniel A. Dunham, Esquires, Commissioners. Oct
Term 1824.

Page 379   Settlement of estate of John Harwood, deceased.
Dec 16, 1824   Made by William Wrenn, executor. Persons listed, to wit, paid
Robert Simpson for making John Harwood's coffin $8.00, others paid for various items, Edwin
Harris, Benjamin Cox, Sr., John D. Stover, William M. Harwood, Henry and Jos. Brown, E.H.
Foster, Jos. Norvell, Peter Booth, Doctor McCalls, John Nichol, John Davis, Rebeccah
Harwood, and Nathan Ewing. This 26 Oct 1824. Signed by John Davis and Silas Dillahunt,
Commissioners. Oct Term 1824.

Page 380   Will of James Moncrieff, deceased, of Davidson County.
Dec 16, 1824   To my friend Daniel Cammeron all my wearing apparel, my silver
watch, chain and seal also my riding mare. To my beloved father Alexander Moncrieff of
Perthshire in Scotland I give one third of my estate. To my affectionate sister Elizabeth
Thomson of Perthshire in Scotland one other third of my estate. To my worthy maternal aunt
Elizabeth Robertson of perthshire in Scotland the remaining one third of my estate. I appoint
Daniel Cammeron my sole executor. 29 Sept 1824. Wit: Duncan Robertson, Frederick
Sehemiras, James Gray and Hugh Elliot. Oct Term 1824.

Page 381   Will of John Hoggatt, deceased, of Davidson County.
Dec 16, 1824   To my beloved wife Dianna Hoggatt my large gray mare and colt
and my bay horse, also all my household and kitchen furniture of all kind. To my daughter
Rhoda Clopton in addition to what I have previously given her, 37 acres of land lying in
Franklin County, Tennessee at the mouth of Cove Spring Creek, also 10 acres of land lying in
Lincoln County, Tennessee near the tract known by the name of Cantrell Tract, said 10 acres
was bought of Josiah Riley, also a small part of my 1000 acre tract in Lincoln County,
Tennessee on Elk River, the number of acres not known, the part given and attended to is the
north east corner separated from the main tract by Elk River and lies near Mr. Reaves. Also
to my daughter Rhoda Clopton two bonds on William P. Anderson, one binding him to make a
warrant deed to 165 acres near my 1000 acre tract dated 22 Nov 1820. The other for
$758.04 to be paid in land in Lincoln County dated 20 Feb 1821. To my daughter Rhoda
Clopton two negroes John and George. To my eldest son Abraham S. Hoggatt, in addition to
what I have already given him, seven negroes. To my second son James W. Hoggatt, in
addition to what I have already given him, a negro boy Ben. To my youngest son John H.
Hoggatt, in addition to what I have already given him, six negroes. I give unto my wife's
three nephews George Sandifer, John B. Sandifer and Abraham Sandifer 200 acres of land
lying in Franklin County, Tennessee on waters of Rock Creek which land, may at the request

of George Sandifer at the time he becomes of age, be sold and one third of the money given to said George and the remaining part to be equally divided between John B. and Abraham. To my wife's two nieces Ann Jane Sandifer and Mary Ann Sandifer each a small negro girl. The remaining part of my 1000 acre tract in Lincoln County supposed to be about 700 acres after laying off what is sold to James Forsythe and the part given to my daughter Rhoda Clopton I give to my two sons Abraham S. Hoggatt and James W. Hoggatt equally divided. At the death or marriage of my wife, the estate to be equally divided among my children. I appoint Abraham S. Hoggatt, James W. Hoggatt and John H. Hoggatt, executors. This 22 July 1824. Wit: Thomas Harding, William McMurry and John C. Hall. Oct Term 1824.

Page 383   Will of George Wharton, deceased, of Davidson County.
Dec 17, 1824   To my son William Henry Wharton and to my daughter Elizabeth Caroline Wharton all the property which I received of my intermarriage with the deceased mother, several negroes. One of which I sold and the sum of which I have expended in the education of my said son William H. I direct that a negro boy or girl of the same value be given to my daughter Elizabeth out of the negroes before mentioned. The remainder of the estate to be equally divided between my son William H. and Elizabeth C. I appoint my friends William Donelson, Esq., David McGavock and Joseph Philips, Esq., as executors. This 26 Oct 1815. Wit: J. Wharton, John Nelson and Eliza A. Wharton.
Codicil: I appoint Samuel L. Wharton and Samuel Seay, executors and whereas Samuel Seay has had the misfortune to loose a negro boy named Jack which I gave him upon his intermarriage with my daughter Jane. This 21 Aug 1824. Wit: William Hume, J.O. Wharton and Enoch Cunningham. Oct Term 1824.

Page 385   Will of Thomas J. Parmer, deceased.
Dec 17, 1824   We, being present when he was in his last sickness and until his death, doth certify that he the said Parmer made the following statement respecting his children and property, viz, he wished Stephen Micher to sell all his property that he had in this State and after the money for said property was collected and some money that were due and Parmer at Louisville he then wished said Micher to school his children and after they were educated divided among his children. This 2 Sept 1824. Signed by Thomas Gilbert and Samuel Coldwell. Oct Term 1824.

Page 385   Inventory of estate of Francis Wright, deceased.
Dec 17, 1824   Several items listed. 23 Oct 1824. J.H. Howlett, admr. Oct Term 1824.

Page 386   Will of John Strawn, deceased, of Davidson County.
Dec 18, 1824   To my beloved wife Polly Strawn the whole lands during her lifetime and at her death to be equally divided between my relations and her relations. This 20 Sept 1823. Wit: William Greer and Zachariah Jones. Oct Term 1824.

Page 386   Inventory of estate of Thomas J. Parmer, deceased.
Dec 18, 1824   Taken Aug 25, 1824. In United States paper money $40.00, Mississippi $10.00, In Louisiana $10.00, in Tennessee $35.00, one receipt given by S.A. Cook for two notes $170.00. One note on David Thomas, 24 in Commonwealth paper Kentucky, and several items listed. Signed by Stephen Micher, admr with will annexed. Oct Term 1824.

Page 387   Will of Clemment (Clem) Hall, deceased.
Dec 18, 1824   To my friend Edward Ward all my estate both real and personal within the State of Tennessee except one gold watch which I bequeath to his wife Ann Ward and her heirs. I appoint my friend William C. Ward, executor. This 5 July 1824. Wit: Martin W.B. Armstrong and William Hume. Oct Term 1824.

Page 388   Inventory of the estate of George W. Sommerville, deceased.
Dec 18, 1824   Inventory of the personal estate of the late George W. Sommerville of the United States Navy, deceased, came into the hands of John Sommerville, admr. Balance of account due to him from the United States as settled and allowed at the Navy Department $176.50, one silver patent lever watch purchased in Nashville $80.00, and several other items. This 28 Oct 1824. Oct Term 1824.

Page 388   Account and inventory of estate of George W. Sommerville,
Dec 20, 1824   deceased. A late Midshipman. Persons listed, to wit, John W.
Sanders of Philadelphia, S.P. Todd of United States Nacy by J.W. Downing of Philadelphia,
E.R. Call of United States Navy by J.W. Downing of Philadelphia, Robb and Winbrume, a
merchant tailors of Philadelphia by J.H. Eaton, and Charles C. Watson and Son, merchant
tailor of Philadelphia by J.H. Eaton. Received from United States Navy Department balance
due to the deceased for his pay of the sale of his clothing agreeable to the rules of the Naval
Service, one silver patent lever watch given to the deceased by his father purchased in
Nashville, and one new marshall great coat. This 10 Oct 1824. Signed by Eli Talbot and
William Lytle, Esquires, Commissioners. Oct Term 1824.

Page 389   Inventory of estate of Henry Bennett, deceased, late of Nashville.
Dec 20, 1824   Several items listed. James Christian, admr. Oct Term 1824.

Page 389   Debts due Corbin Noles, deceased.
Dec 20, 1824   Persons listed, to wit, Willis Joslin, B.W. Sneed, Lewis
D(illegible), Mr. Burnett, Daniel Joslin, John Garrett, John Loyons, John Barry, Mr. Stephens,
Mr. Lovin, Charles B(illegible), Joseph Wilson, Jas. Lovell, William Carpenter, George Griffin,
Thomas Connell, John Freser (Frazer), John Flatts, Robert Clark, Mr. Hodge, Moses Bonner,
Frederick Ivey, Asa Harris, Charles McCombs, Mr. Cherry, Peter Smith, John Stinnett, Mr.
McChesney, Edney Smith, John Walker, Arthur Hanks, Mr. Taylor, Charles Guire, John
Hamilton, Claiborne Robertson, Col. Hart, Mr. Montgomery, Collin Hobbs, Solomon Holder,
Jesse Reynolds, William Harris, Mr. McGavock, Mr. Malone, Mr. Norwood, Jas. Bonds, C.
Barnes, Isaac Saunders, Jno. McKinsey, Burwell Hartham, Thomas Wright, Capt. William
Evans, Mr. Wade, William Eddie, William Noland, Buck Anderson, James David, William Joslin,
Mr. Hartley, Mr. Hobbs, Thomas Long, George D. Clark, Casey Harris, Jas. R. Robertson,
John Platts, Robert Loure, and Samuel Hutton, Nathan Gatlin, Elijah Jones, William Ramsey's
due bill to John Dillon, and Asa Harris. James Boyd, admr. Oct Term 1824.

Page 390   Division of real property of John E. Beck, deceased, of Davidson
Dec 20, 1824   County. We have divided and laid off and set apart to them
equal parts, all the real estate of John E. Beck, deceased, between John B. Craighead and
Levina Craighead his wife formerly Levina Beck, Susannah Beck and Georgiana Beck, children
and legatees of John E. Beck, deceased. Lot No. 1 of one house and Lot No. 35 in Nashville
allotted to John B. Craighead and wife. Lot No. 2 of 350 acres being a part of the Dentons
Lick tract and adjoining the tract of land belonging to Beal Bosley and extending from David
McGavock's line to the river. Lot No. 3 houses and lots in the suburbs of Nashville joining
the south field and the two little tracts of land joining the Stone Lick one of 86 acres and
the other 25 acres and also 155 acres being part of the Denton Tract to be taken off the
upper end of said tract adjoining the land lines of David McGavock's tract &c. This 15 Sept
1824. Signed by Robert Weakley, David Vaughn, Robert C. Foster, William B. Lewis, and
Thomas Crutcher, Commissioners. Oct Term 1824.

Page 392   Land divided of Edward Collinsworth, deceased.
Dec 20, 1824   Lor No. 1 to George Collinsworth of 28 acres and 74 poles. Lot
No. 2 to Jno. Collinsworth of 28 acres and 32 poles. Lot No. 3 to James Collinsworth of 28
acres and 53 poles. Lot No. 4 to Permelia Davis of 28 acres and 53 poles. Lot No. 5 to
Susanna Cockrell of 28 acres and 53 poles. Lot No. 6 to Elizabeth Collins(worth) of 28 acres
and 53 poles. And Lot No. 7 to B.F. Collinsworth 30 acres and 5 poles. Surveyed 16 Aug
1824 land being on Hurricane Creek bordering lands of John Buchanan and Roach's line. Jos.
Burnett, D.S. Jno. McCain, Jos. Watkins and E. Ensley, C.C. This 26 Oct 1824. Signed by
Joseph Burnett, Enoch Ensley, Benajah Gray and Joseph Watkins. W. Barrow, J.P. Oct Term
1824.

Page 395   Joseph W. Horton's bond as Sheriff.
Dec 22, 1824   We, Joseph W. Horton, Josiah Horton, John Davis, Andrew Hays,
William E. Watkins, Ephraim H. Foster, and Michael Gleaves, all of Davidson County, are held
and firmly bound to his Execllency William Carroll, Esquire, Governor for $12,500.00 to be
paid. This 22 Oct 1824. The condition of this obligation is such that Joseph W. Horton is
this day appointed Sheriff of Davidson County, to pay all fees &c unto the proper office. Oct
Term 1824.

Page 396   Joseph W. Horton, Sheriff's bond for collections of taxes.
Dec 22, 1824   We, Joseph W. Horton, Josiah Horton, John Davis, Andrew Hays, William E. Watkins, Ephraim H. Foster, and Michael Gleaves, all of Davidson County, are bound unto his Excellency William Carroll, Esquire, Governor of Tennessee, for sum of $10,000.00 to be paid. The obligation of the above is such that Joseph W. Horton does well and truly collect from the several inhabitants of Davidson County, all public and county taxes. Oct Term 1824.

Page 396   Joseph W. Horton, Bond as Sheriff.
Dec 22, 1824   We, Joseph W. Horton, Josiah Horton, Ephraim H. Foster, William E. Watkins, John Davis, John Bell, Daniel A. Dunham, David B. Love, William Faulkner, and Absalom Gleaves, all of Davidson County are all firmly bound unto his Excellency William Carroll, Esquire, Governor of Tennessee for sum of $12,500.00 to be paid. This 19 Oct 1824. The condition of the obligation is such that Joseph W. Horton is this day appointed Sheriff of Davidson County. Now if Joseph W. Horton shall well and truly execute and due return make of all such (illegible) and (illegible) as directed and pay and satisfy all fees and sums that he may receive to such office as agents &c. Oct Term 1824.

Page 398   Joseph W. Horton, Sheriff's Bond for collection of taxes.
Dec 22, 1824   We, Joseph W. Horton, Josiah Horton, Ephraim H. Foster, William E. Watkins, John Davis, John Bell, Daniel A. Dunham, David B. Love, William Faulkner, Michael Gleaves, and Absalom Gleaves, all of Davidson County, are bound unto his Excellency William Carroll, Esquire, Governor of Tennessee, for sum of $10,000.00 to be paid. The condition of the obligation is such that Joseph W. Horton does well and truly collect from the several inhabitants of Davidson County all public and county taxes and account for and pay over all monies. Oct Term 1824.

Page 399   Settlement of estate of Joseph Coldwell, deceased.
Mar 21, 1825   Made with Stuart Pipkins and Sidney Coldwell, admr and admrx. To cash paid Stockill's executors, E.H. Foster, M.H. Quinn, Sheriff for taxes, Norvill for advertising, F. Campbell, John Hodge for J. Philips, Jesse Philips, Robertson & Waters, Executors of J.B. Houston, deceased, A. Foster for tuition, William Compton, B.W. & W.H. Bradford, and N. Ewing. Credit by cash received of E. Smith, Thomas McCrory, S. McDowell, Henry Wade, H. Stuart, William Compton, Berkley Thomas, William Thomas, A. Casselman, Ensley, Nancy Overman, Willis Davis, W.P. Hopkins, A. Cotton, B. Malone, J. Campbell, Thomas Bradley, Jesse Philips, W. Chapman, David Cartwright, Goodlett, P. Pipkin, Opie Dunnaway, William Rains, E. Bateman, Jno. B. Craighead, Jno. Hill, and John Moseley. This Jan 28, 1825. Signed by Philip Campbell and William Compton. Jan term 1825.

Page 400   Jonas Menifee, deceased. Settlement and Division of estate.
Apr 7, 1825   Made with Jonas Menifee, admr. Vouchers on the following, viz, Fairly Brookshire, John Eaton, J.W. Horton, Jno. Coltart, Joseph Hopper, Henry La(illegible), Will Lytle, Joseph Litton, Samuel Weakley, Matthew Porter, James Overton, Jeptha Mosley, William Nichol & Co., Thomas Washington, James B. Houston, Newman & Ewing, Isaac H. Howlett, William Howlett, Joseph Wright, Robert Smiley, Jos. W. Horton, Christopher Brooks, Zachariah Noell, James Ridley, John Boyd, and Josiah Nichol & Co., Nathan Ewing, Doctor Higginbotham, William W. Goodman, Mathew Quinn, David Adams, James N. Menifee, J.W. Horton, W.W. Brown, Samuel Seay, and R. Farquharson. Also sold negro boy David to Bondurant, and negro girl Elizabeth to W. Pulliam, a negro woman Charlotte to Robert Armstrong, a negro boy Joe to Mark R. Cockrill, also negro Jeffrey, a horse to William Ramsey. Also Mrs. Menifee's account for articles purchased at public sale. Several negroes sold to Mrs. Menifee, to Mary, Jonas, John, William, and Jarrat Menifee. This 2 July 1824. Signed by Thomas Edmiston, R.C. Foster and William B. Lewis. Jan term 1825.

Page 401   Inventory of sale of estate of Christopher C. Carter, deceased.
Apr 8, 1825   Several items listed including a Bible for $1.00.   Walter O. Carter, admr. Jan Term 1825.

Page 403   James Camp, deceased, orphans guardian return to R.C. Foster, Apr 8, 1825   guardian. Trimming for Sarah's bonnet, cash to Mary for sundry articles of clothing, cash by Capt. Tappan for Joseph Camp, cash paid Gregory a gravedigger for Ensley's child, cash paid Mr. Garner for coffin for Ensley's child, cash paid Smiley's executor for Joseph Camp, cash to Doctor Roane and McNairy attending negroes, cash paid Joseph when getting married, cash to Jane Foster for Sarah Camp, cash to James H. Foster for dresses &c, cash paid Nathan Ewing Clerk of Court, cash paid Robertson & Sanderson hiring negroes, cash paid Josiah Nichol for Sarah, cash paid Doctor Ewing for attending negroes, and cash paid Capt. Tappan's account. Negroes hired out. A judgement made 15 Aug 1823 for $781.02 case of chairman of Davidson County was plaintiff and Thomas Fletcher, Moses Norvell and William Compton as defendants, which was for the benefit of James Camp's children which was relinquished except as to mary M.B. Camp. negores have been delivered to them. Jan Term 1825.

Page 404   Additional sale of estate of Ezekiel Fitzhugh, deceased.
Apr 8, 1825   Made on 13 Nov 1824. Adam Carper one still and twelve tubs, Polly Fitzhugh to two tubs, Charles Hays to five barrels, Samuel Fitzhugh, Jr. to fourteen barrels of corn. Signed by Polly Fitzhugh, admrx and John Fitzhugh, admr. Jan term 1825.

Page 405   Settlement of estate of Alexander Ewing, deceased.
Apr 8, 1825   Made with the executors. Persons listed, to wit, Mrs. Sally Ewing, Jacob McGavock guardian of William B. Ewing, Randal M. Ewing, Alexander C. Ewing, and R.M. Ewing. This Jan 15, 1825. O.B. Hays, executor. E. Talbot and E.S. Hall, Commissioners. Jan Term 1825.

Page 406   Robert Weakley and others receipt from William Hobson,
Apr 9, 1825   legatees. Received Nashville Jan 3, 1824 of Robert Weakley, James Jackson and John Hobson, executors of William Hobson, deceased, the following notes, viz, John Chapman, Thomas Martin and John C. McLemore for $241.87½ with a credit of $80.00. A note on Nicholas Hobson, note on J.W. Brooks, on William Brooks, Isaac W. Brooks, Tally and Clement, Nicholas and Edmund Hewlett, and John Hobson. Test: W.M. Berryhill and Jos. Lockhart. N.A. McNairy guardian for S.E. Hobson, James Knox by N.A. McNairy, A.M. Hewlett by N.A. McNairy, N. Hobson, Jno. Hobson, and A.W. Johnston. Jan term 1825.

Page 406   Solomon Clark's receipt from William W. Brown.
Apr 9, 1825   Received Nov 22, 1824 of Solomon Clark, guardian to Polly L. Pugh, now Polly L. Brown $13.80 her full share of money that said Clark received of guardian of John Pugh, deceased, estate. Jan Term 1825.

Page 406   John Criddle, Jr., deceased, additional inventory.
Apr 9, 1825   A return of the rent of the plantation for 1824 and 50 barrels of corn. This Jan 27, 1825. Signed by Jonathan Drake, one of the admrs. Jan Term 1825.

Page 407   Will of John Baird, deceased, of Davidson County.
Apr 9, 1825   To my dear and loving wife Frances H. Baird one fourth of all my real and personal estate. The other three fourths to my dear children, Mary Jane, Eliza Ann, and John Baird to be equally divided between them. I appoint my dear wife Frances H. Baird my executrix. This 8 Sept 1822. Apr Term 1825.

Page 408   Will of John L. Goodwin, deceased, of Davidson County.
Apr 9, 1825   To my beloved wife Nancy Goodwin all my real and perishable property for her support &c and for schooling my six children during her widowhood. If she should marry I will that an equal division take place between my wife and my six children, namely, Greenberry, Polly, Nancy E., George W.H., Jesse G., and Jeremiah S.J. Goodwin. Should my wife not remarry, when Greenberry comes of age or marries, he is to have his share of the estate and as each child becomes of age or marries then they shall have their share. I appoint my wife Nancy Goodwin and William W. Goodwin my sole executors. This 19 Oct 1824. Wit: Hugh Allison and George Goodwin. June Term 1825.

Page 409   Will of Andrew Boyd, deceased, of Davidson County.
Apr 11, 1825   To my dear beloved wife Isabella Boyd shall have full possession of all my property both real and personal during her natural life or widowhood. To my son Patterson Boyd shall have all my landed estate at his mother's death. To my son James Henry Boyd my negro man Sampson at the death of his mother. As touching my other children, Anna, Peggy, Polly, Martha, Zaney and Elizabeth Jane to have the balance of my estate to be equally divided between them. My wife has full power to give them respectively

when each comes of age, their share. I appoint my wife Isabella Boyd and my eldest son Patterson Boyd my executors. This 25 Sept 1824. Wit: William H. Shelton and John Herbison. Jan term 1825.

Page 410   Will of John Spence, deceased, of Davidson County.
Apr 11, 1825   It is my will that my estate shall be disposed of as follows, to wit, according to the laws of this State, and I appoint Benjamin W. Bedford, Joseph Spence and William G. Campbell my executors. They are to dispose of such property as is vested in me by conveyance from John M. Telford and should the proceeds amount to more than the sum to be paid by that agreement. It is my will that the surplus should be paid over to said John M. Telford, his heirs or assignees. It is also my will that my said executors shall appropriate for the use of my son John Spence of Murfreesboro as soon as advisable or when he arrives at the age of 21 years the sum of $2000.00. This 15 Dec 1824. Wit: M. Spence and A.D. Campbell. Jan Term 1825.

Page 410   Account of sale of estate of Alexander Brinkley, deceased.
Apr 11, 1825   Made on 19 May 1823. Several items listed including notes on George Guy and Peter Marr, Isaac Earthman, Sr., and Henry Brinkley. Lewis Earthman, admr. Jan term 1825.

Page 411   Additional inventory of estate of David T. Eatheridge, deceased.
Mar 11, 1825   Notes David T. Eatheridge took up for William Douglas. One receipt for money paid to Lewis Earthman in favor of John H. Smith. A note payable to Enoch Douge, one receipt of Nathan Gatlin which Floyd Hurt assignee of W.S. Gordon obtained against said Douglas on 10 June 1822, also an order from James Read, Esq., to pay balance due. One account due to John Stump and was paid by Etheridge. This 25 Jan 1825. Dennis Dozier, admr and Penina Etheridge, admrx.

Page 411   Settlement of estate of Seth Davis, deceased.
Apr 11, 1825   Made with Newton Edney and John Davis, executors. Persons named, to wit, Joshua Davis and as guardian for Laverna(?) Davis, Lucy Davis as guardian for Seth Lewis Davis, Stockely A. Davis as guardian for Nancy Davis, William C. Winstead, Wilson Davis as guardian for Julia Davis and James Davis. John Davis dr. to James Gilliam's note belonging to the estate. Signed by William H. Shelton and Abraham Demoss. Jan term 1825.

Page 412   Inventory of estate of John Stron, deceased.
Apr 11, 1825   Several items listed including notes on the following, viz, A.W. Evans, William Taylor, Theoderick Hunt, and Abner Driver. The above notes in the hands of David G. Thompson, Constable, for collection, also a note on John T. Walker and on B.H. Anderson given to John T. Walker, also one note on John Allison. Polly Stron, admrx. Jan Term 1825.

Page 413   Divided land of Frederick Stump, deceased.
Apr 12, 1825   We have met to lay off and set apart to Catherine Stump, widow and relict of Frederick Stump, deceased, 300 acres of land. Plat on page 413. Beginning at south west corner of Jacob Stump's preemption on the south bank of the Dry Fork of Whites Creek. The land which Frederick Stump willed to Charistopher Stump's wife and children by numbers one, two, three, four, and five. Lot No. 1 of 297 acres given to Rachel Stump, widow of Christopher Stump. Lot No. 2 to Thomas J. Stump of 209 acres. Lot No. 3 to John F. Stump of 214 3/4 acres. Lot No. 4 of 232 3/4 acres to Philip S. Stump. Lot No. 5 to Tenny (Tennessee) M. Stump of 155 acres. Catherine Stump 300 acres. This 19 Jan 1825. Wit: Will Lytle, J.P. Signed by Samuel Weakley, Surveyor and Commissioner, Joseph Love, William J. Drake, James Marshall and David Cloyd. Jan term 1825.

Page 417   Settlement of estate of Robert E. Searcy, deceased.
Apr 13, 1825   Made with Stephen Cantrell, executor. Persons listed, to wit, Samuel McManus, Mrs. Searcy, S. Cantrell, and Mr. Pilcher, and L. Sperry. Amount due the estate $499.23. This 26 Jan 1825. Signed by Eli Talbot and Daniel A. Dunham, Commissioners.

Page 417   Elizabeth Carter, her dower, of Davidson County.
Apr 13, 1825   We met to lay off and set apart to Elizabeth Carter, widow of

C.C. Carter, deceased, her dower, beginning at Robert Marrs west corner running down McCrary Creek to marrs line thence with the garden and yard fence to the hen house, 3 1/3 acres and to include the dwelling house and all other buildings. This 5 Nov 1824. Signed by James B. Williams, Thomas Harding, Edmond Owen, A. Clopton, Thomas Buchanan, Robert Marr, James Buchanan, Benjamin W. Williams, John K. Buchanan, William Matlock, John McMurry, and William McMurry, Commissioners. Jan Term 1825.

Page 418   Settlement of estate of Benjamin Philips, deceased.
Apr 14, 1825   Made with William Williams, admr. Persons listed, to wit, Clark Ewing, J.F. Williams, D. McGavock, Hales, (Eliza) R. Garrett, (Eliza) P.H. Overton, M. Williams, Robertson & Waters, J. Nichols (Eliza), J. Catron, S. Williams, J. Herndon, and Cartmell & McKinney (Eliza). Other names, viz, William and Rebeccah. Signed by John Davis and William Lytle, Esquires, Commissioners.

Page 419   Settlement of estate of Jeremiah Allen, deceased.
May 23, 1825   Made with Tilman R. Daniel, admr. To cash paid Nathan Ewing to lay off widow's support, W.S. Grass, Thomas Roundtree, W.G. Westmoreland, Henry Ewing, Francis Campbell, Willis White, Lewis Sturdevant, A. Foster for tuition of two scholars, Benjamin Moore, Sidney R. Smith, Edwin Smith, Freeman Abernathy, Thomas Vaughn, J.B. Houston for coffin, and Ephraim H. Foster. Notes on the following, to wit, Wilson Wood & David Cartwright, Benjamin Moore, William Thomas, Philip Campbell, Thomas Roundtree, John Hall, Stephen Sutton, Robert Johnston, Edward H. Jones, Edward Pegram, Mr. Foster given by Sidney Smith, Lewis Sturdevant, Elizabeth Thacker who lives in Virginia, Thomas Nolly, Stewart Pipkin and Thomas Roundtree, Mary Ann Allen, and Thomas Vaughn. Philip Campbell, William Compton and Allen Cotton, Commissioners. Jan term 1825.

Page 421   Jeremiah Allen, deceased, widow's part laid off.
May 25, 1825   Five negroes, notes on hand, to wit, Stuart Pipkin, Martha Allen, and Thomas Vaughn. Thomas Vaughn has rendered the following accounts against the heirs of said Allen, deceased: Martha Allen for boarding, clothing and schooling, Eary Allen for boarding, clothing and schooling, Margery Allen for clothing and boarding, and Susan Jane Allen for clothing and boarding. Jan 20, 1825. Signed by Philip Campbell, William Compton and Allen Cotton, Commissioners. Jan term 1825.

Page 422   Account of sale of estate of Henry Hyde, deceased.
May 25, 1825   Made on Oct 28, 1824. Purchasers, to wit, Mary Hyde, William Philips, Thomas Ray, Menaah Bostick, Allen Duffell, Thomas Bowles, Charlotte G. Hyde, Philip Campbell, Edmond Hyde, Jeremiah Hunt, James Campbell, William Vaulx, William Brent, J.H. Howlett, Stephen Bradley, John Cooper, William Ogilsby, Robert Rives, John Frost, Willoughby Williams, William Philips, William H. Simmons, and A.D. Carden. Notes on, viz, James Fitzhugh, John Hogan, A.D. Carden, Thomas James, F. Binkley, Thomas Smithwith, Nathan Reaves, Thomas Farmer, Stump & Cox, J. Hall, Samuel Madra, S. Green, M. Boyd, and R. Woodson. Mary Hyde, admrx. Jan Term 1825.

Page 423   Negroes hired of estate of John Saunders, deceased.
May 25, 1825   Made on Dec 29, 1824 by Absalom Rogers, executor. Thomas Hopper, Jeremiah Terry, William Temple, Richard Sutton, Sr., Henry Rogers, David Adams, James M. Ewing, and Joseph Wright. Jan Term 1825.

Page 423   Elizabeth Carter's one years support laid off.
May 25, 1825   We, Thomas H. Everett, Thomas Harding and William McMurry met at the residence of Elizabeth Carter to lay off and set apart one years support for Elizabeth Carter, widow and relict of Christopher C. Carter, deceased, and her family, to wit, 12 barrels of corn, 1600 lbs pork, 25 lbs sugar, 12 lbs coffee and 5 bushels of salt. This 5 Nov 1824. Signed by Thomas Harding, Thomas H. Everett and William McMurry. Jan term 1825.

Page 424   Benjamin Philips, deceased, part of his estate allotted for.
May 26, 1825   We assigns and set off to Patrick Henry Overton in right of his wife Rebeccah Overton, four negroes. Signed by Jesse Wharton, Beal Bosley and Solomon Clark, Commissioners. Jan term 1825.

Page 424   Inventory of estate of John L. Goodwin, deceased.
May 26, 1825   Several items listed. A note on William Henry, one on John
Travelar, and Nathan Greer. Also one negro Zack. Nancy Goodwin, admrx. Jan Term 1825.

Page 425   Account of sale of estate of Francis Wright, deceased.
May 26, 1825   Purchasers, to wit, William Bryant, Hardy Conly, William Burras,
William Parkman, Alexander McDonel, Wyatt Parkman, James N. Williamson, Patrick Hughs,
and James Shane. J.H. Hewlett, admr. 4 Nov 1824. Jan Term 1825.

Page 425   Division of estate of Ephraim Drake, deceased.
May 27, 1825   We proceeded to divide the personal property of Ephraim Drake,
deceased, between his heirs, to wit, six negroes divided as such, to wit, Frank No. 1 to James
F. Drake, Peter No. 2 to Polly N. Drake, Eve and Fanny No. 3 to Judith A. Marshall, George
and Isam No. 4 to Susan S. Drake. This 21 Jan 1825. Wit: James Marshall, J.P. Signed by
David Cloyd, Benjamin Hyde and John T. Hunter. Jan Term 1825.

Page 426   Inventory of notes and accounts of estate of John Hoggatt,
May 27, 1825   deceased. $94.12½ left with James Forsythe obligation to pay
$400.00 for a certain tract of land. Peter Mosely and Edward Ward's note, one on John Ellis,
William and James Drake, Frederick Binkley's note and William Cummins, Robert Sample,
Nicholas S(illegible), Mrs. R. Goodrich, Mrs. Priestly, John Brown, Abraham Manuel, Francis
Sanders, Leonard Keeling, Robert Man, James Lee, Thomas Creel, Nathan Williams, James
Buchanan, Alexander Fosset, Caleb Cherry, De(illegible), Richard Jones, John Edmunds,
Thornton Dodson, John Jones, Jesse Thompson, Thomas Harden, John Broughton, Balaam
Edmunds, William Hays, and Charles Ballentine. Also several other items listed. James W.
Hoggatt, executor. Jan Term 1825.

Page 427   Inventory of estate of Abraham S. Hoggatt, deceased.
May 27, 1825   One 39 acre tract of land in Rutherford County, Tennessee, a 350
acre tract in Lincoln County, Tennessee, according to the will of John Hoggatt, deceased.
Fourteen negroes. Notes, viz, William Hall, James Robertson, Abraham Johns, Isham
Childress, Trott J. Newman, Andrew Jackson, William Chandler, Thomas Creel, Richard Jones,
John Graves, Anthony Clopton, Ballentine Sims, Charles Ballentine, Robert Pully, William
Perkins, Jesse Fuqua, and Walden. Jan term 1825.

Page 428   Account of sale of estate of Abraham S. Hoggatt, deceased.
May 27, 1825   Purchasers, to wit, James W(M). Walker, Sherwood Bryant, Nelson
C(illegible), Zach Noell, Abrahan Hyht, Robert Turner, Miles Myre, Samuel Hyht, and Jno.
Broughton. This Nov 30, 1824. James W(M). Hoggatt, admr. Jan Term 1825.

Page 429   Division of part of the estate of James Turner, deceased.
May 28, 1825   This 22 Jan 1825 had divided and set apart to Robert B. Turner
as his distributive share as portion of the negroes and other personal estate of which James
Turner, deceased, died seized, to wit, a negro man Austin, boy Abner, woman Viney and her
child Granville and other items listed. David McGavock, Charles Hays and Cary Felts,
Esquires, Commissioners. Jan term 1825.

Page 429   George W. Campbell and Jno. Childress, deceased, heirs division
May 30, 1825   of Lot No. 43 in Nashville, Davidson County. We, the
Commissioners have laid off and set apart to George W. Campbell 3/4 parts in value out of
10 pole square of Lot No. 43 in Nashville owned by said Campbell jointly with the heirs of
Elizabeth Childress, deceased, the part of Lot on College Street including the houses wherein
Mrs. Elizabeth Robertson now lives, near Public Square, assigned to the heirs of said
Elizabeth Childress, Samuel B. Marshall and Jane his wife, John Catron and Matilda his wife,
Louisa M., George C., Elijah R., Ann, Maria, John, Elizabeth, and James R. Childress. This
24 Jan 1825. Josiah Nichol, Jno. C. McLemore and Duncan Robertson. Jan term 1825.

Page 430   Divided in part of estate of Hugh Brent, deceased.
May 30, 1825   Negroes, money and property due to said William B. Brent out of
the estate. 23 Oct 1824. John Thompson, Jason Thompson, John Bradford, Jeremiah Terry,
and Samuel J. Ridley, Commissioners. Jan term 1825.

Page 431   Account of sale of estate of John Hoggatt, deceased.
May 31, 1825   Made on 23 Dec 1824. Purchasers, to wit, James W. Hoggatt,
Dianna Hoggatt, Thomas J. Winston, JOhn C. Brown, Philip L. Linsley, Sherwood Bryant, Miles
Myres, O.B. Gordon, John Hoggatt, Jno. McMurry, James Lee, and John C. Hall. James W.
Hoggatt, executor. Jan Term 1825.

Page 431   Account of sale of estate of Thomas J. Parmer, deceased.
May 31, 1825   Made Sept 28, 1824. Purchasers, to wit, Zachariah Owen, John
Gibbs, John Sharp, James Campbell, Joseph Mitchell, Jas. Connell, Henry Aronsden, Jacob
Mohe, Jacob Hunter, Isaac Sanders, Joseph Morris, William Birdwell, Joseph Witcher, James
Campbell, William Miles, James Simmons, William Brown, Esom Brading, Isaac Sanders, Jr.,
Hardy D. Miles, Gabriel Sanders, Samuel Coldwell, Zadock Owen, Abner Gupton, Stephen
Martin, Thomas Gilbert, Stephen McCall, Robert Squares, Jno. Jones, Christopher Williams,
John W. Gibbs, Jeremiah Morris, Isaac Morris, John Sharp, Patrick Kenney, Joseph Smith,
Arseneth Stuart, Jane Conner, and Robert Duke. Jan term 1825.

Page 433   Division of estate of Edmond Owen, deceased, of Davidson
May 31, 1825   County. We have allotted to Mrs. Sarah Owen, the widow, the
mansion house with 63 acres of land the south west corner of which Edmond Owen, deceased,
died, also allotted her a child's part of the personal estate, to wit, Dinah and Martha,
servants, along with $284.22½. We have allotted to Henry Owen, a legatee, $995.00 &C. To
Edmond Owen, a legatee, $995.00 and other property advanced to him by his father in his
lifetime. To James Owen, a legatee, $995.00. To Silas Owen, a legatee, $995.00. To Nancy
Owen, a legatee, $995.00 which she has received land No. 4 containing 31½ acres. To Polly
Owen, a minor legatee, $995.00. To David Owen, a minor legatee, $995.00. Each legatee
received land, and negroes, $143.00 to be paid to Mrs. Hamilton and $42.00 to each of the
other legatees for education of two minors. This 20 Dec 1824. William B. Lewis, William
Murphy, Henry White, Jr., Robert C. Foster, and John Gowen, Commissioners. Jan Term
1825.

Page 435   Inventory of estate of Thomas Edmondson, deceased.
June 2, 1825   Taken 18 Oct 1824. Several items listed including one Bible.
Signed by Samuel Edmondson and William Black, executors. Jan Term 1825.

Page 435   Inventory and accounts of sales of inventory of John B. Houston,
June 2, 1825   deceased. Taken by Joseph Herndon, executor, sale on 12 Aug
1824. Several items listed. Persons listed, to wit, Mrs. Houston, the widow. Note on Phebe
Coldwell, Davis Cobler, Edward Hall, Thomas Claiborne, Timothy D. Lawrence, Jno. R. Burke,
J. Love, Thomas Cayse, John G. Wilson, Benjamin Gholson, G.W. Campbell, James Grizzard,
Joseph Norvelle, and Gen. Sam Houston. Judgement against Andrew Hays, one against Jno.
Caufield in Rutherford County. Bad notes on, viz, John Jobe, James Hays, Thomas Shute,
Enos H. Dickson, George Wharton, John Woodcock, Christopher Brooks, William E. Kennedy,
and Jno. Newman in Davidson County. Other debts: Anderson & Knox, Mrs. Isabella Eakin,
Mrs. Martha Adams, Samuel Bell, Sr., Charles Bosley, Misses Bradford and West and Simon,
Bradford & B.B. West, William L. Brown, Esq., Mrs. Levina Beck, Mr. John R. Burk, Joseph
Coldwell, James P. Clark, Esq., Lemuel P. Cheatham, Esq., Mrs. Phebe Coldwell, Henry
Crabb, Esq., the Corporation of Nashville, Col. Michael Campbell, Rev. A.D. Campbell of
Nashville, Thomas Duncan, Esq., Thomas Deaderick, Capt. John Donelson, Capt. Andrew J.
Donelson, Davidson County, Col. Jeremiah J. Everett, Ephraim H. Foster, Esq., George W.
Gibbs, Esq., Felix Grundy, Esq., Thomas Hill, Hoover & Thomas & Philip Hoover, William
Horn, Joseph K. Kain, Col. John McIver, Nathaniel G. McKee, Maj. John Nichols, Joseph
Norvell, Susannah Perkins, Duncan Robertson, Samuel Seay, Emily Stuart, Robert Samples'
estate, _____ Stephens, Doctor John Shelby, Robert Sanderson, B. Sherwood, Joseph & Robert
Woods, W. Williams, Josiah Williams John G. Wilson, Robert T. Walker, W.W. Goodwin, James
Walker, James Wood, and Hazzard & Arrill and Robert A(illegible). Four Lots in Nashville,
540 acres in Sumner County, Tennessee, a claim to a large portion of the estate of Samuel
Houston, deceased, the father of said James B. Houston which is still in the possession of the
widow and executor of Samuel in East Tennessee. Jos. Herndon, executor. Jan term 1825.

Page 441   Inventory of estate of Thomas Lane, deceased.
]June 3, 1825   Several items listed. A note on Guy McFaddin and one on
William Peay. 23 Jan 1825. Ralph S. McFaddin, admr. Apr Term 1825.

Page 442   Settlement for Isaac Battle's orphans.
June 3, 1825   The hire of negroes and rent of land for support of heirs.
Several vouchers, viz, M.M. Battle, Joel A. Battle, and J.L. Battle. This 8 Apr 1825. William
H. Nance and Enoch Ensley, Commissioners. Apr term 1825. Settled with Martin Clark,
guardian of orphans.

Page 443   Will of John Graves, deceased, of Davidson County.
June 6, 1825   To my beloved wife Sally Graves the use of one half of the tract
of land I now live on and one half of the cleared land that I now live on also six negroes, also
two horses, cattle &c for her support during her widowhood or death. To my son Henry
Graves the land and plantation whereon he now lives also the land and plantation known by
the name of the Old Place and containing the long pond also four negroes. To my son David
Graves the tract of land whereon I now live adjoining Graves Pennington and Henry Crabbs.
To my daughter Frances Pennington two negroes now in the possession of Graves Pennington.
To my daughter Jane Gibbins a negro boy which she has in her possession also a negro woman.
To my daughter Betsy Pennington two negroes which are now in her possession. To my
daughter Nancy Seat two negroes and other household items. To my three grandchildren,
Mary M. Allen, Jane Allen and Betsy Ann Allen, children of my daughter Susannah Allen two
negroes being the negroes I give to my daughter Susannah Allen. The residue of my estate to
be sold and after my just debts are paid, to be equally divided among all my children, to wit,
Henry Graves, David Graves, Jane Gibbins, Betsy Pennington, Nancy Seat, and my daughter
Susannah Allen's part to her three daughters, Mary M. Allen, Jane Allen and Betsy Ann Allen.
At the death of my wife, the property loaned to her is to be equally divided among my
children and my three grandchildren. I appoint my son David Graves and my two sons-in-law
Robert Pennington and William Seat, my executors. This 8 Feb 1822. Wit: John Maxey. Apr
Term 1825.

Page 444   Account of sales of estate of Henry Bennett, deceased.
June 6, 1825   Made on Nov 6, 1824. Purchasers, to wit, John Landsdown, Mr.
Peacock, Noel Cox, Mr. Hunt, Paul Branchey, William Chapell, Noel Perkins, Patrick Collins,
and William Doherty. James Christian, admr. Apr Term 1825.

Page 445   Inventory of estate of William Wallace, deceased.
June 6, 1825   Several items listed including a watch and a Bible and one order
drawn on Lewis Earthman by Frederick Carpenter, Isaac Earthman's receipt for R.B.
Sappington's note, a note on Ambrose Downs, Cave Johnston's receipt for a note on D.H.
Outlaw and C(illegible), Arnold Russell's receipt for a receipt on James Bland for two notes,
one on John Lucas, one on William Hall, Isaac Earthman's receipt for five certificates on
Thomas Rutherford, a note on Samuel Shannon, a receipt on Cheatham & Hays for Willis H.
Cunningham's note, and a note on Lewis Earthman. David Read, admr. Apr Term 1825.

Page 445   Account of sale of estate of Thomas Lane, deceased.
June 6, 1825   Made Feb 17, 1825. Purchasers, to wit, Rebeccah Lane, John
Lane, James Hamilton, James Campbell, John Hood, B.W. Campbell, John M. Wright, Elisha
Crutchfield, Godfrey Shelton, John Bell, Silas Morton, Henry Lundy, Dennis Lane, William
Weatherby, Benjamin Weaver, Thomas Hill, Aristarcus Collins, Henry Walden, Greenberry
Ozment, Wallace Cosby, William Hamilton, and Ralph S. McFaddin. Ralph S. McFaddin, admr.
Apr Term 1825.

Page 447   Inventory of estate of John Baird, deceased.
June 8, 1825   Made on Feb 1, 1825. Cash received of Eli Talbot, J.W. Horton,
Joel Parish, Achillis Sneed for Thomas Watson, notes on Dyer Pearl, cash of E. Grizzard, A.
Whitney, and Debt of Doctor R.P. Hays for rent. Also several items listed. Also notes on
Samuel H. Laughlin and Thomas A. Duncan. This Apr 18, 1825. M.C. Dunn, acting executor.
Apr Term 1825.

Page 447   Absalom Gleaves receipt from Benjamin Seaborne.
June 8, 1825   Apr 8, 1825. Received of A. Gleaves my guardian the sum of
$571.95 being in full of all the estate which has come into the hands of said Gleaves as my
guardian and now being of full age, made final settlement with him. Benjamin Seaborne.
Wit: Henry Ewing. Apr term 1825.

Page 448   Inventory of estate of Robert Sanderson, deceased.
June 8, 1825   Made Feb 25, 1825. Several items listed. Zebulon P. Cantrell,
admr. Apr Term 1825.

Page 448   Account of sale of estate of Robert Sanderson, deceased.
June 9, 1825   Notes on the following, to wit, J. & J.W. Sittler, B. Poyzer,
James Knox & Jno. L. Brown, R.C. Campbell & D. Crockett, C. & W. Brooks, John Wright, J. Wharton, David Craighead, John Harris & Z.P. Cantrell, M. Porter, M. Sanderson & John Franklin, Isaac Sittler, John Beaty & P. Clifford, E. Burke, John C. McLemore, David Hughs & Robert Martin, Johnston & Smith, Duncan Robertson, P. Craddock, Doctor M(illegible), E.H. Foster, George W. Campbell, Jones & Lysander McGavock, William Brooks, S.V.D. Stout, James Erwin, D(illegible) & Dyer, James Cutler & E. Wilborn, JOhn M. Hill, Jno. Franklin, and John S(illegible), John & James R. Franklin, W.P. Smith, Free Jeffrey, E. Long, John B. Long, Robert Martin, Anderson & Knox, Thomas Wells, F. Fisher, J.F. Williams, and R. Barber, an account on Jesse Wharton, Joseph Dugan, J. & J.W. Sittler and R. Elliott. Zebulon P. Cantrell, admr. Apr Term 1825.

Page 449   Will of Anthony Foster, deceased, of Davidson County.
June 8, 1825   After all just debts are paid the residue to be divided into two
equal parts, one half of which I bequeath to my step-son Richard Winn the only son of my late departed wife Mrs. Elinor Foster, and the other half of my estate, money or bonds I bequeath in equal shares and portions to the daughters of my sister Mrs. Patsy Gray and my brother Edmond Foster who at the time of my death shall be living and or married. Wit: Will Lytle and Henry Crabb. Apr Term 1825.

Page 450   Will of James Byrn, deceased, of Davidson County.
June 9, 1825   To Mary Byrn consort of James Byrn, deceased, that tract of
land on which she now lives during her natural life and after her death to be sold and proceeds to be equally divided among her surviving heirs. The land being on north side of Manskers Creek. To my son William Byrn and my son Charles L. Byrn, jointly, a tract of land of 50 acres lying and being on the waters of Sulphur Fork, Robertson County. To my son Charles L. Byrn all my household and kitchen furniture, all farming and carpenter tools. Also to my sons William and Charles Byrn my blacksmith tools and my wagon jointly. To my grandson Stephen Byrn a featherbed, having given Preston and James Byrn his brothers each a bed which they have received. My son Charles Byrn is to pay my three grandsons as a balance of $365.00 he having their receipts for what is paid &c. I appoint William Byrn and Charles L. Byrn as executors. This 2 June 1823. Wit: A. Mathis and E.P. Connell. Apr Term 1825.

Page 451   Account of sale of estate of Willis L. Shumate, deceased.
June 9, 1825   Made on 17 May 1824. Purchasers, to wit, Sally Shumate, John
Wright, J. Casper, James Howse, William Whitemore, J.G. Campbell, William Huggins, Caleb Goodrich, George F. Hamilton, John Neal, John Bell, William Campbell, William B. Erwin, Andrew Hartman, Elisha Crutchfield, Thomas Bell, John C. Brown, Herbert Towns, G.W. Charlton, William M. Neal, Capt. R. Turner, James Carter, Esq., Jeremiah Ezell, William Bibby, Matthew Corrither, William Thompson, Edward H. East, Bernard Seat, Henry Hurt, A. Mason, and John Hartman. Jeremiah Ezell, admr. Apr term 1825.

Page 452   Inventory of estate of Abigail Clemmons, deceased.
June 9, 1825   One negro woman Rose, one negro girl Sucky, two beds and
furniture, household and kitchen furniture, stock of cattle, poultry of all kinds which said property was willed to James Clemmons the son of said Abigail Clemmons by her Last Will and Testament and dated 14 Aug 1822 and which said will has been acknowledged in the County Court of Davidson County. James Clemmons, executor. Apr term 1825.

Page 452   Inventory of estate of William Gulledge, deceased.
June 9, 1825   Several items listed. Wilson Crockett, admr. Apr Term 1825.

Page 453   Settlement of estate of Jacob Dickinson, deceased.
June 9, 1825   The Commissioners met at Mrs. Patsy Dickinson's on 12 Apr 1825
made report. Persons listed, to wit, James Dean, S. Bond, R. Taylor, F. McKay, _____ Coltharp, William Neely, Sr., _____ Byrns, Jno. Maxey, Jno. Newman, R. Smiley, Joseph

Philips, Sumner & Moore, Robert Wilson, R. McGavock, Joseph Litton, S.C. McDaniel, R.W. Green, William Philips, Joseph Norvell, L.C. Farrar, Joseph Jewell, _____ McCalle, D. & G. Trimble, T.T. Shaw, J. Newland, W. White, N. Ewing, and _____ Shannon. Edmond Goodrich and William Neely, Commissioners. Apr Term 1825.

Page 454   Division of negroes of Joseph Hooper, deceased.
June 9, 1825   Commissioners met at the residence of the late Joseph Hooper, deceased, on 26 Jan 1825 and divided the negroes between the heirs, viz, Mrs. Elizabeth Hooper, wife and late consort of said deceased, Lot No. 1 of 11 negroes, also other items for her support for the present year. To James H. Hooper Lot No. 2 of 12 negroes which 5 of them were given to him by his father. To Richard Hyde Lot No. 3 of 12 negroes which 10 of them were given to the said Richard by the said Joseph Hooper, deceased, during his lifetime. To Claiborne Y. Hooper Lot No. 4 of 12 negroes which 6 were given to him by said deceased in his lifetime. Signed by Duke W. Sumner and J.F. Williams and William Neely. Apr Term 1825.

Page 455   Mary Hyde, her dower.
June 10, 1825   The jury of men met to lay off and set apart to Mary Hyde relict of Henry Hyde, deceased, her dower in the lands of which said Hyde died seized and possessed of in Davidson County, on 7 Feb 1825. She received her dower of 760 acres adjoining John Alford corner, Owen's corner, Ben. Bibb's corner, in one tract and another tract containing the mansion house on which the said Hyde lived before his death and all the out houses and improvements &c. This 7 Feb 1825. Signed by Samuel Weakley, Thomas Waller, Turner Williams, John Alford, Samuel Fitzhugh, Benjamin Bibb, Jesse Maxwell, Henry Crutchlow, James Walker, Joel Walker, Peter Owen, and Robert Scales, Commissioners. Apr Term 1825.

Page 456   Division of the estate of Henry Hyde, deceased, of Davidson
June 10, 1825   County. To the widow Mrs. Mary Hyde two negroes and $129.94 in notes. To Allen D. Carden two negroes and $179.94 in notes. To Miss Charlotte Hyde a negro and $279.94 in notes. To Edmond Hyde two negroes and $254.94 in notes. To John J. Hyde one negro and $279.94 in notes. To Jordon Hyde one negro and $279.94 in notes. To Mary Hyde two negroes and $154.94 in notes. To Elizabeth H. Hyde three notes and $154.94 in notes. To Westley W. Hyde two negroes and $129.94. Signed by J.H. Hewlett, Turner Williams, Thomas Edmiston, Benjamin Bibb, William Ramsey, and Samuel Fitzhugh, Commissioners. Apr term 1825.

Page 456   Account of sale of estate of John Baker, deceased.
June 10, 1825   Sale on 13 Apr 1825. One bed, one cow and yearling and one pair shears. Martin W.B. Armstrong, admr. Apr Term 1825.

Page 457   Inventory of estate of John Baker, deceased.
June 10, 1825   Made on 1 Apr 1825. One bed, one cow and yearling, one pair of shears, also a Revolutionary Claim against the United States as a pension amounting to $38.00. Martin W.B. Armstrong, admr. Apr Term 1825.

Page 457   Account of sale of estate of John L. Goodwin, deceased.
June 10, 1825   Purchasers, to wit, John Beech, James Clawed, Francis Newsom, John Travelan, Isaac Greer, John Jones, Walter Greer, John Arthur, Moses Greer, John Elliston, Shelton Hardgraves, William Pritchard, Thomas H. Stewart, John Edgar, Thomas Glass, Theoderick and Edward Mobley. Nancy Goodwin, executrix. Apr Term 1825.

Page 457   Inventory of estate of Isham Felts, deceased.
June 10, 1825   One wagon, two horses and grar, thirteen head of cattle, thirty head of hogs, eight head of sheep, five featherbeds, and one rifle gun. This Apr 15, 1825. Hardy D. Felts, admr. Apr Term 1825.

Page 458   Settlement of estate of Howell Tatum, deceased.
June 10, 1825   Made with Stephen Cantrell, admr. Persons listed, to wit, J.B. Houston, John Gregory, N. Ewing, James Elders, T. Talbot, Jos. Greer, N. Gordon, J.P. Clark, R. McGavock, Doctor Roan, George Wilson, C. Talbot, W.L. Brown, Esq., William Rawls, Esq. in Philadelphia, and John B. Evans, admr. This 23 Apr 1825. E. Talbot and D.A. Dunham, Commissioners. Apr Term 1825.

Page 458   Additional inventory of estate of Craven Jackson, deceased.
June 10, 1825   Made by N.A. McNairy, admr. Persons listed, to wit, G.W. Campbell for negro and Mr. McCombs for rent of the dwelling houses. Apr Term 1825.

Page 459   Settlement of estate of Alexander Brinkley, deceased.
June 11, 1825   Made on Apr 25, 1825. Persons listed, to wit, Theo. Stogner, Andrew Patterson, Nathan Ewing, George Guy, William Evans, Isaac Earthman, Peter Binkley, Henry Binkley, John Cagle, and Lewis Earthman. Lewis Earthman, admr. Also Nelson P. Jackson and Jas. Marshall. Apr Term 1825.

Page 459   Inventory of estate of George Wharton, deceased.
June 11, 1825   Eighteen negroes and several other items listed. This 1 Jan 1825. Samuel Seay, executor. Apr Term 1825.

Page 460   Sale of estate of Daniel Binkley, deceased.
June 11, 1825   Sold on Feb 5, 1825. Purchasers, to wit, Catherine Binkley, John Binkley, John Aheart, B. Eastis, G.W. Charlton, William Binkley, John Huggins, Thomas Strong, Hollis Wright, David Casselman, Isaac Binkley, E.H. East, William Strong, John Brown, Anthony Binkley, and Moses Brown. Notes on Jacob Shares, Micajah Fly and Josian Shaffer. George W. Charlton, admr. Apr Term 1825.

Page 461   Settlement of estate of William P. Robinson, deceased.
June 11, 1825   We met at Mrs. Jane Robinson on 5 Apr 1825 and found several vouchers. Also paid, to wit, John Camp, H. Crabb, _____ Benoit, _____ McNairy, _____ Shelby, _____ Goodlett, John Exum, B. Patterson, M. & J. Norvell, Kynes & Fletcher, and N. Ewing. Edmond Goodrich,and William Neely, Commissioners. Apr Term 1825.

Page 461   Elizabeth Pugh, her dower.
June 11, 1825   Apr 7, 1825. We have met and laid off and set apart to Elizabeth Pugh, widow, her dower her land out of 314 acres, her share being 102½ acres. This Apr 7, 1825. Signed by Jno. Davis, Peter Booth, Benjamin Greer, Henry Wade, John Harding, Giles Harding, Benjamin Joslin, Thomas Demoss, Henry Lile, E. Raworth, Lewis Joslin, and Moses Knight, Commissioners. Apr Term 1825.

Page 462   Amanda F. Hoggatt, support laid off, of Davidson County.
June 13, 1825   Several items laid off to Amanda F. Hoggatt, widow of A.S. Hoggatt, deceased. This 10 Feb 1825. Signed by Leonard Keeling, William Harding and Thomas Harding, Commissioners. Apr term 1825.

Page 462   Inventory of Martha Hooper, deceased.
June 13, 1825   Six negroes and notes and accounts due next February. 24 Apr 1825. Claiborne Y. Hooper, admr. Apr term 1825.

Page 462   Catherine Binkley, support for one year.
June 13, 1825   Two cows, 110 bushels of corn, 1400 lbs pork, 25 lbs coffee, and 5 bushels salt. Signed by John Hall and Eeazer Hamilton. Apr Term 1825.

Page 463   Divided estate of Jesse and John Wallace, deceased.
June 13, 1825   We have met to divide the estate of Jesse Wallace, deceased, between the widow and other distributees, viz, Hartwell H. Wallace, William P. Wallace, and Thomas Wallace, each received negroes, notes &c from the estate of John Wallace, deceased. This 23 Apr 1825. Signed by Benjamin Bibb, William Ramsey, S.H. Howlett, Humphrey Grayson, and Samuel Edmondson, Commissioners. Apr Term 1825.

Page 464   Account of sale of estate of Corbin Noles, deceased.
June 13, 1825   Made by James Boyd, admr, at Nashville June 18, 1823. Purchasers, to wit, Mrs. Noles, James Boyd, _____ Sneary, _____ Beatty, S. Johnson, D. Robertson, R.B. Sappington, John Jobe, John Chatham, J. Grose, R. Garrett, Henry Martin, Michael Steen, William Woodruff, John Cockrell, and _____ Quinton. Apr Term 1825.

Page 465   Hire of negroes of Zachariah Betts, deceased.
June 14, 1825   Made on 1 Jan 1825. Henry to John Betts, Daniel to David Ralston,

Spurlett to John Betts, Allen to John Sigler, and Jesse two years old, lowest bidder, to C.L. Byrn. Enoch P. Connell and Seldon Betts, admrs. Apr Term 1825.

Page 465   Account of sale of estate of Gabriel Fuqua, deceased.
June 14, 1825   Made on 15 Mar 1825. One 85 gal still to Judy Fuqua, one set of mill irons to Judy Fuqua, and the half of a wheat (illegible) to William Fuqua. William Anderson and Judith Fuqua, admrs. Apr Term 1825.

Page 466   Catherine Brewer, her dower.
June 14, 1825   Davidson County, Mar 10, 1825. A jury met to lay off and designate to Catherine Brewer, widow and relict of Elisha Brewer, deceased, her dower in land out of 85 acres. And marked off the said Catherine Brewer assigns Mordicai Kelly, 28 acres and 55 poles out of the 85 acres. Signed by Benajah Gray, Thomas Collins, Joseph Burnett, Adam Casper, George Stephens, Patrick W. Campbell, Ralph S. McFaddin, William W. Hamilton, James A. Procter, William Weatherby, and Samuel V. Endsley, Commissioners. Apr term 1825.

Page 467   Divided land of William P. Bowers, deceased.
June 14, 1825   Plat of division on page 467 and 470. Sarah Bowers, widow's dower of 95 acres, Lot No. 1 to Stephen C. Bowers of 52 acres, Lot No. 2 to Lavina Bowers for 57½ acres, and Lot no. 3 to Thomas Powel for 44 acres. Second plot: Lot No. 4 to John Bowers of 48 acres, Lot No. 5 to Lemuel Bowers for 30 acres, Lot No. 6 to William P. Bowers for 45 acres, No. 3 to W.P. Bowers for 45 acres, No. 2 to Lemuel Bowers for 16 acres, and No. 1 to John Bowers for 44 acres. Signed by Charles L. Byrn, Aquila Randal, John Pyrtle, Benjamin Williamson, and James Williamson, Commissioners. Apr Term 1825.

Page 471   Hire of negroes of William P. Bowers, deceased.
June 20, 1825   Willis to James B. Conger, Isaac to Lemuel Bowers, Lewis to William P. Bowers, Readen to Lemuel Bowers, Minerva and Levi to Hugh Tilford, Judy and three children for food and cloths to William P. Bowers, and Edmond to William P. Bowers. Jack, lowest bidder to keep, William P. Bowers. Enoch P. Connell and George Campbell, admrs. Apr term 1825.

Page 471   Support laid off to Rebecca Lane.
June 20, 1825   We, John M. Wright, John Johnson, and Edwin Austin, have laid off to Rebecca lane, widow and family of Thomas Lane, deceased. Several items listed. This 26 June 1825. Apr term 1825.

Page 472   Settlement of estate of Craven Jackson, deceased.
Sept 30, 1825   Made by N.A. McNairy, admr. Persons listed, to wit, J.N. Menifee, Michael Campbell, J.B. Houston, A.R. F(illegible), J.C. Hicks, T. Patterson, Jno. Stamp, R. Hanks, H. Turner, _____ Moses, T. Washington, Doctor Roane, Hu. Roland, M. Hall, W. Pulliam, Mrs. Hall and J.D. Miller, _____ McCombs, A.R. Freeman, and Foster & Fogg. Signed by J.P. Erwin, Duncan Robertson and Ephraim H. Foster. July Term 1825.

Page 472   Settlement of estate of Charles Cagle, deceased.
Sept 30, 1825   Made with David Read, admr of William Wallace, admr of Charles Cagle, deceased. Persons listed, to wit, Michael Gleaves, Edward Vaughn, _____ Drake, Lewis Earthman, Nathan Ewing, R.B. Sappington, Matthew Harris, and Isaac Earthman. Signed by Robert Weakley, Jonathan Drake and William Faulkner, Commissioners. July Term 1825.

Page 473   Settlement of estate of Gabriel Fuqua, deceased.
Sept 30, 1825   Made with William Anderson, admr and Judith Fuqua, admrx. Persons listed, to wit, Arnold Russell, Crabb & Bell, J. Earthman, Henry Ewing, William (illegible), Silas Equals, William Fuqua, Lewis Earthman, Nathan Ewing, Dennis Dozier, J. Fuqua, B. Lee, William Anderson, William H(illegible), William Rogers, J.B. Demumbrum, Aron Dean, B.H. Lanier, and R. Hyde. Robert Weakley and Jonathan Drake, Commissioners. July Term 1825.

Page 474   Settlement of estate of John Sanders, deceased, of Davidson
Sept 30, 1825   County. Made with Absalom Rogers, admr. We find that Robert L.

157

Sanders, one of the legatees, entitled to one note on John Criddle for $1000.00. Also find that Robert L. Sanders is entitled to one half the amount of the sale of said deceased estate. This 18 July 1825. Benajah Gray, Commissioner and William H. Nance. Also find that Eliza Ann Sanders, one of the legatees, entitled to one half of amount of sales of said deceased estate. This 18 July 1825. Benajah Gray, Commissioner and William H. Nance. July Term 1825.

Page 475   Inventory of estate of Absalom Page, deceased.
Oct 1, 1825   Made by Samuel Shannon, executor. Persons listed, to wit, Henry Faulkes, William Wilkinson, D.B. Love, and Vinson Page 1033 acres of land on Marrabone. The following are yeorsman at the ferry in 1823: Jeffrey Johnson, James Scruggs, George Guy, Elijah Carney, George Cagle, Duke W. Sumner, David Parker, Franklin Earhart, John Cato, Thomas Parker, John Thomas, John Galledge, Langhorn Scruggs, (blank) Mathis, Benjamin Smith's negro, (blank) Canady, Charles Abernathy, John Blare, Andrew Smith, Exum P. Sumner, Jones Read, Jesse Parker, Robert Hood, Roland Cato, Benjamin Drake, David Craddock, Vinson Carney, John Parker, William Ewing, Thomas Alley, Randal Ewing, Gabriel Huggins, Henry Boner, John Hollis, Alexander Lester, John Hinton, Balser Huffman, (blank) Butler, John Clinard, Pleasant P. Smith, L(illegible) Man, William Holmes, William Parker, William Wingo, William Rolan, James Powell, Joseph Hooper, W. Daniel, (blank) Chriton, Reuben Biggs, Isaac Smith, William G. Evans, (blank) Farrow, Thomas Fairley, John Lanier, Thomas Morris, John Cloyd, William Fuqua, William White, William Huffman, James Marshall, Samuel Shannon, widow Kirkwood, John Stump, John Earhart, William Nicholson, Thomas Dill, William James, Michael Gleaves, Isaac Coffman, David Cloyd, Henry Fowlkes, Joseph Wasson, Lewis Williams, William Ray, widow Stump, Pitt Woodward, Thomas Taylor, Nelson Talley, David House, Cornelius Waggoner, Richard Lester, Laban Abernathy, Jr., Matthew Patterson, Smith Criddle, Ned Walkins, Jacob Harden, Charles Cagle, Mr. Howe, Thomas T. Shaw, Charles Abernathy, David B. Love, Jacob Cagle, D.P. Davis, Edward Butler, and Lewis Williams. All of the above ferrying accounts for the year 1823 was toˈ be divided with Martha Page by contract for keeping the ferry the balance of that year 1823. Robert Martin $32.00. Signed by Samuel Shannon, executor. July Term 1825.

Page 476   Sale of estate of Absalom Page, deceased.
Oct 1, 1825   Credit: James B. Houston, James Marshall, Stephen Childress, Newman & Ewing, Darby & Van(illegible), Langhorn & Scruggs, Moses B. Frazer, John Forbes, Dennis Dozier, Warren Page, William Page, Jacob McGavock, Thomas Deaderick, Alexander Ray, A. Porter, Jno. C. McLemore, John W. Page, Porter & Wright, James Boyd, J.H. Lenier, William Shields, James Scruggs, James Hooper, Jno. B. Demumbrum, Wilson Crockett, H. Ewing, E.H. Foster, Matthew Patterson, Jno. Blare, Robert Martin, Jacob Vick, B.W. & W.H. Bedford, William Wood(illegible), E. Fairley, E. Vaughn, William Brooks, J. Curry, M. Gleaves, John Criddle, Joseph Love, Theophilus Horne, Thomas Washington, John Harrison, J.W. Horton, Boyd McNairy, C. McKeenan, H. Crabb, James Grizzard, John Shelby, Nathan Ewing, Samuel Weakley & B. Hyde, Gabriel Saunders, Lewis Williams, Thomas Watts, D. Robertson, R. Minor & E. Davidson, William Bosworth, Daniel Brim, N. Young, A. Porter & Son, S. Shannon, D. Vaughn, John Hobson, M. Stean, George Wilson, John Catron, Robert Lanier, William Faulkner, D.B. Love, Jos. Norvell, C. Brooks, V. Page, William Anderson, S. Weakley, G.W. Gibbs, S. Johnson, E. Richards, John Earhart, Martha Page, John H. Smith, R. Wallace, J.W. Horton, H.W. Ryburns, and Joseph Love. Joseph Love and William Faulkner, Commissioners. July Term 1825.

Page 478   Division of negroes of James Campbell, deceased, of Davidson
Oct 3, 1825   County. Enoch Ensley and Jeremiah Bell and Benajah Gray, Commissioners appointed to divide the negroes belonging to the estate of James Campbell, deceased, between the heirs and legatees, to wit, widow, Sally Campbell four negroes, P.W. Campbell five negroes, Sophronia McDonald five negroes, William P. Campbell five negroes, James C. Campbell five negroes, A.G. Campbell four negroes, and L.D. Campbell four negroes. 5 Jan 1825. July Term 1825.

Page 478   Land divided of estate of James Campbell, deceased of Davidson
Oct 3, 1825   County. Plat on page 478. Lot No. 1 of 69 acres and 80 sq. poles to Albert G. Campbell. Lot No. 2 of 60 acres to William P. Campbell. Lot No. 3 of 97 acres and 80 sq. poles to Ludilphus D. Campbell. Lot No. 4 of 97 acres and 80 sq. poles to Sophronia W. McDonald. Lot No. 5 of 84 acres and 80 sq. poles to James G. Campbell.

Joseph Burnett, Deputy Surveyor. This 19 July 1825. Signed by Enoch Ensley, Benajah Gray and Jeremiah Ezell, Commissioners. July Term 1825.

Page 480   Division of negroes of William Donelson, deceased.
Oct 4, 1825   We met at Mrs. C. Donelson's on 13 May for the purpose of dividing the negroes. The one fifth part of $9275.00 value of seven negroes was set apart for John McGregor and his wife $1855.00. This 13 May 1825. Edmond Goodrich, Enoch P. Connell, Esquires and Allen Mathis, Commissioners. July Term 1825.

Page 480   Sally Shumate's dower.
Oct 4, 1825   Widow of Willie L. Shumate. They laid off 373 acres. This 16 June 1825. Joseph Burnett, John Johnson, Henry Owen, William Burnett, John McCain, Godfrey Shelton, Robert McCain, George Peay, William A. Seat, James Pigg, Ralph S. McFaddin, and Thomas Johnson. July Term 1825.

Page 481   Elizabeth Philips, widow's dower.
Oct 4, 1825   Widow and relict of Merrell Philips, deceased. Land bordering William Mitchell's Spring Branch, William Homes' land, Jones Read's land, Norvell H. Robertson's land, heirs of Christopher Stump's land, containing 26¼ acres. This 17 June 1825. Signed by David Parker, Matthew Patterson, Samuel Weakley, Sr. and Jr., and Jno. Criddle, Jones Read, Thomas Taylor, N.H. Robertson, John J. Hinton, John T. Hunter, Isaac Coffman, William Nelson, and William Yarborough, Commissioners. July Term 1825.

Page 481   Inventory of estate of John Spence, deceased.
Oct 4, 1825   Several items listed. Jos. Spence, executor. July Term 1825.

Page 482   Inventory of estate of James L. Byrn, Sr., deceased.
Oct 4, 1825   Several items listed including one Bible. This 25 July 1825. July Term 1825.

Page 483   Will of Willie Barrow, deceased.
Oct 5, 1825   I, Willie Barrow of Nashville, appoint my wife Anne Barrow sole executrix. She is to pay my just debts and the rest of my estate to support my wife and my four youngest children. This June 5, 1825. Wit: Felix Robertson and James Roane. July Term 1825.

Page 483   Will of Richard Dobbs, deceased, of Davidson County.
Oct 5, 1825   My executors shall sell 100 acres of the tract of land on which I now reside, purchased by me of Richard Drewry and to include the place where Michael Gill now resides, to raise funds to pay my debts. To my daughter Julia Hawkins during her natural life and no longer, a negro girl Belinda and at her death I give to the heirs of her body. To my wife Mrs. Elizabeth Dobbs all the rest and residue of my estate both real and personal for her use and such of my children as are under age and at death or widowhood to be equally divided among my children. I have already given to my married daughters $600.00 each and what my son John Dobbs has received from me at $100.00 with these sums I do hereby charge my said three named daughters and my son John and that they shall not have anything until the note of my children shall receive the like amount. I appoint my friend Robert C. Foster of Davidson County and Henry Ewing of Nashville, my executors. This Apr 26, 1824. Wit: Ephraim H. Foster, Samuel J. Ridley and James Dobbs.
Codicil: To my daughter Elizabeth Gill residue of my estate. This May 20, 1825. Wit: Jno. ?. Ewing. July Term 1825.

Page 485   Inventory of estate of Gabriel Fuqua, deceased.
Oct 6, 1825   One execution on William Henson returned by Isaac Earthman. Signed by William Anderson, admr. July Term 1825.

Page 485   Additional inventory of William P. Bowers, deceased.
Oct 6, 1825   Persons listed, to wit, John Kirkpatrick, David Smiley, William Warmack, David Logue, Jehu Harrison, Rolla Harrison, Edmond Gamble, Lou Harrison, Jemima Hackney, Charles L. Byrn, George Perry, James Williamson, John Bowers, E.S. Moore, B.W. Minus, D. Powell, Harden Campbell, Robert Stothart, F. Lasiter, Isaac Pearce, Eleanor Logue, Anderson Byrn, and Cana Freeman. Enoch P. Connell and George Campbell,

admrs. July Term 1825.

Page 485   Settlement of estate of Robert Evans, deceased.
Oct 6, 1825   Made with Eldridge Newsom, admr. A settlement with E.S. Hall,
Thomas Claiborne and B. & W.H. Bedford. 28 Apr 1825. Jno. Davis and Silas Dillahunt,
Commissioners. July Term 1825.

Page 486   Account of estate of Larkin Clay, deceased.
Oct 6, 1825   Made by Jonathan Clay, executor. To cash paid Nichol Vaulx &
Co., Butterworth, Turner, Baker, C. Beasley, R. & W. Armstrong, Ingram & Loyd, and John
C. Rea. June 30, 1825. July Term 1825.

Page 486   Inventory of estate of Reuben P. Biggs, deceased.
Oct 6, 1825   One gray horse, one cow and calf, seven head of hogs, one bed and
furniture, one pot and one skillet, one weeding hoe, one plough, two axes, one chair, five
plates, four cups and six knives and forks. Wilson Crockett, admr. July Term 1825.

Page 486   Inventory of estate of James David, deceased.
Oct 6, 1825   Several items listed. Jno. Davis and George David, admrs. July
Term 1825.

Page 486   Inventory of estate of Martha Hooper, deceased.
Oct 6, 1825   One note on James H. Hooper and one note on Richard Hyde. July
13, 1825. Claiborne Y. Hooper, admr. July Term 1825.

Page 487   Additional inventory of estate of Robert Sample, deceased.
Oct 6, 1825   Returned by Thomas Sample, executor. One note on John Buchanan.
July Term 1825.

Page 487   Inventory of estate of Thomas Logan, deceased.
Oct 6, 1825   Several items listed. Margaret Logan, admrx. July Term 1825.

Page 487   Sale of estate of John Baird, deceased.
Oct 6, 1825   Made by Michael C. Dunn, executor. Purchasers, to wit, Doctor B.
McNairy, W. Williams, Thomas Rutherford, Mrs. Frances H. Baird, and John H. Smith. This
21 July 1825. July Term 1825.

Page 488   Division of negroes of John Graves, deceased, of Davidson County.
Oct 7, 1825   Stephen drawn by Henry Graves, Sam and Kittie drawn by David
Graves, Viney and her child Maria drawn by Susanna Allen's heirs, Harry drawn by Elizabeth
Pennington, Bob drawn by Nancy Seat, and Charles drawn by Jane Gibbins. This 20 Apr
1825. Signed by L. Keeling, Thomas Sample and Graves Pennington, Commissioners. July
Term 1825.

Page 488   Sale of estate of William Gulledge, deceased.
Oct 7, 1825   Sold on 28 May 1825. Purchasers, to wit, Frederick Gulledge, John
Gulledge, Jo. Philips, Norvell H. Robertson, J.B. Demumbre, H.S. Bryant, Joel Beavers,
Wilson L. Gower, Edward Scruggs, William Homes, William Gulledge, William Yarbrough,
Alexander Meryman, Jonh(John) Gulledge, Jacob Cagle, Alexander Cliner, Cyrus Campbell,
Edward Vaughn, and A. Smith. Wilson Crockett, admr. July Term 1825.

Page 489   Division of land of Henry Hyde, deceased.
Oct 7, 1825   Plat on page 489. Lot No. 1 of 122½ acres to Elizabeth Hyde, Lot
No. 2 of 100 acres to Westley W. Hyde, Lot No. 3 of 100 acres to Mary D. Hyde, Lot No. 4
of 100 acres to Maria W. Carden, Lot No. 5 of 100¼ acres to John J. Hyde, Lot No. 6 of 76½
acres to Jordan M. Hyde, Lot No. 7 of 76½ acres to Edmond Hyde, and Lot No. 8 of 76½
acres to Charlotte G. Hyde. This 14 May 1825. Signed by Sam Weakley, Surveyor, Robert
Scales, Turner Williams, Benjamin Bibb, John Alford, and William Ewing. July Term 1825.

Page 491   Inventory of estate of John Graves, deceased.
Oct 8, 1825   Sold 6th and 7th May 1825. Purchasers, to wit, William Seat, David
Graves, Sally Graves, Harris Wilbourn, Robert Pennington, Henry Graves, Robert Woods, John

160

Puckett, Isaac D. Sullivan, John Faulks, John Carmell, John Brice, Thomas Ivy, Levin Watson, Isaac B. Sullivan, Abraham Hite, Benjamin Williamson, Moses Drue, Graves Pennington, Anderson Puckett, Samuel Hite, Hiram Hite, Edmund Finch, William M. Harwood, David T. Hatch, Leonard Keeling, John Broughton, James M. Goodrich, and Baker Ayres. Notes on the following, viz, John and Douglas Puckett, Mr. Abercrombie, James Priestly, Alexander Stewart, William and Samuel Neely, John Barnhart, Stump & Cox, James Woodroff, Elizabeth Braten, Thomas Harney, Bernard Verden, Moses Drew, Samuel Mays, Elizabeth C. Cole, Kinchen T. Wilkinson, Edmund Finch, David Hays, Jo. W. Kean, Russel Sullivan, James Brown, Isaac David, John Brown, and Lemuel Ballentine. William Seat, executor. 27 July 1825. July Term 1825.

Page 494   Settlement of estate of John Davis, deceased.
Dec 5, 1825   Made with Charles Hays, admr. Several vouchers listed. One proven account Robert and William Armstrong, receipt from Nathan Ewing, Receipt from George Peay, and receipt from Enoch Ensley. 19 Oct 1825. William H. Nance and William Ramsey, Commissioners. Oct Term 1825.

Page 494   Inventory of personal estate of Richard Boyd, deceased.
Dec 5, 1825   Several negroes and several items listed. Rachel Boyd, admrx. Oct Term 1825.

Page 495   Inventory of estate of Robert Perry, deceased.
Dec 5, 1825   This legacy from estate of George M. Deaderick, deceased, $500.00. William Windell, admr. Oct Term 1825.

Page 496   Account of sale of estate of Caleb Cherry, deceased.
Dec 5, 1825   Purchasers, to wit, John Meraw, Thomas Ivey, Thomas Cherry one large Bible, John Williamson, Severn Donelson, Robert Wood, David Graves, John Morgan, Hiram Hill, Henry Mullen, John Broughton, Moses Drew, Leonard Keeling, Edmond Finch, Laban Estes, Eli Ballow, J.M. Goodrich, and Jane Cherry. Jane Cherry and Thomas Cherry, admrs. Oct Term 1825.

Page 496   Account of sale of estate of Reuben Biggs, deceased.
Dec 5, 1825   Purchasers, to wit, Elizabeth Biggs, and several others listed. Wilson Crockett, admr. Oct Term 1825.

Page 497   Settlement of estate of Allen Dodson, deceased.
Dec 6, 1825   made with Timothy Dodson, admr on 25 Oct 1825. Total account $736.37½. Several vouchers &c. William Sanders and Absalom Gleaves, Esquires, Commissioners. Oct term 1825.

Page 497   Account of sale of estate of Thomas Logan, deceased.
Dec 6, 1825   Sold on Aug 13, 1825. Purchasers, to wit, Joseph Pinkerton, John Shute, Hugh Logan, Margaret Logan, Martha Logan, Robert Clark, Hiram Blackwood, William Brown, Abrm. Casselman, Thomas Logan, George Clark, William H. Philips, Joel (illegible), Joel Swinney, and Hugh F. Newell. Margaret Logan, admrx. Oct Term 1825.

Page 498   Settlement of estate of Samuel Philips, deceased.
Dec 6, 1825   Made Oct 24, 1825. Account Doctor N. Newman & Ewing, James Gilven for coffin, J.H. Howlett, Nathan Ewing, and Nathaniel Bells. William H. Nance, John Curren and Alexander Buchanan, Commissioners. Oct Term 1825.

Page 498   Account of sale of estate of James David, deceased.
Dec 6, 1825   Sold on 1 Dec 1823. Private sale $466.12½. John Davis and George David, admrs. Oct Term 1825.

Page 499   Settlement of estate of William Baker, deceased.
Dec 7, 1825   Made with Moses T. Brooks, admr on 22 Oct 1825. Several vouchers and leaving a balance $32,51¼. William Saunders and Absalom Gleaves, Esquires, Commissioners. Oct 25, 1825. Oct Term 1825.

Page 499   Settlement of estate of Sebina Farrow, deceased, of Davidson
Dec 7, 1825   County. Guy McFaddin & Ralph S. McFaddin to settle with William
Farrow, admr. Remaining due the estate $96.19. Six heirs each received $16.03. Nothing
remains. This Oct 18, 1825. Oct Term 1825.

Page 500   Will of Thomas James, deceased, of Davidson County.
Dec 7, 1825   To my beloved wife Elizabeth James my farm whereon we now live,
13 negroes, all my household and furniture, stock, horses, cattle &c during her life or
widowhood, as many of the children are young and small. She is to support and give them
education and as the elder children come of age. She is to give them $500.00 in good
property or money if they stand in need of it and my desire is that my tract of land in
Kentucky containing 270 acres on Highland Creek, may be sold. 200 acre tract of land on
the Mississippi below the Walnut Hills opposite the upper end of the Three Island I am
informed the place is called Palmira. 200 acres of land on the north side of a large creek
called (illegible) lying on the first bluff about three or four miles from its mouth, the grant
is in the name of Anna Sturns my first wife. One other tract of 950 acres lying about two
miles from the mouth of Bopeer, this grant was landed by the British when Pensacola was
taken by the Spaniards, 200 acres including a high mound and several other smaller ones,
about 2 miles east from the mouth by Byopeer, the grant is in the name of Susannah Jacobs
and is filed in the office at Natchez. One other tract containing 500 acres beginning on
Susannah Jacobs first line nearly opposite the high mound running towards the head of
James' Creek. The grant is in my name and is in the office at Natchez. To my grandson
Thomas James Fennie(?) $500.00 it being the desire of his mother to be paid him when he is
21 years of age. To my grand daughter Julia Greenfield Davis $500.00 to be paid her at 18
years of age. I desire that my land in the Natchez Country be sold and proceeds to be
equally divided among the following children, viz, Polly Turner James, Joseph W. James,
Thomas G. James, Patsy Field Wells, John D. James, George Washington James, Henry F.
James, Julia Anna James, and Daniel David James. The land whereon I now live may be sold
after the death of my wife Elizabeth James, whom I appointed my executrix with my two
sons Joseph W. James and Thomas G. James. This 12 Aug 1823. Oct Term 1825.

Page 501   Will of Josiah Mullen, deceased, of Davidson County.
Dec 8, 1825   To my wife Elizabeth Mullen all the tract of land on which I now
live. To my son John Mullen the house and lot in Nashville on Market Street where I
formerly lived. All the rest of my estate to be divided between my wife Elizabeth and my
son John. If my son should die without a wife or issue then the residue to be equally divided
among the children of my brother Henry Mullen. I appoint Ephraim H. Foster guardian for
my son John who is authorized to sell all that part of the estate that may fall to my son
John except the house and lot and negroes. I appoint Ephraim H. Foster my executor. This
27 July 1825. Wit: John Thompson and M.H. Quinn. Oct Term 1825.

Page 502   James B. Conger of W.P. Bower, Covenant.
Dec 8, 1825   I, W.P. Bower of Davidson County, am bound to James B. Conger of
Davidson County for sum of $600.00 but to be void on condition that I make a deed to said
Conger for a small tract of land including the mills where said Conger now lives and being in
Davidson County on waters of Manskers Creek and bounded by lands of William Warnack,
John S. Galbreath, the Mill Dam and head race. This 14 Mar 1823. Signed by Pitt Bowers.
Oct Term 1825.

Page 503   Division of land of Arthur Exum, deceased.
Dec 8, 1825   Lot No. 1 of 9 acres and 34 poles to Margaret Champion. Lot No.
2 of 8 acres and 60 poles to Elizabeth Edwards. Lot No. 3 of 6 acres and 112 poles to
Martha Walton. Lot No. 4 of 5 acres and 198 poles to Arthur Exum. Lot No. 5 of 5 acres
and 138 poles to William Exum. Lot No. 6 of 5 acres and 138 poles to Elijah Exum. Lot No.
7 of 5 acres and 138 poles to Polly Reynolds. Lot No. 8 of 5 acres and 138 poles to John
Exum. Lot No. 9 of 5 acres and 138 poles to Sally Reynolds. Lot No. 10 of 5 acres and 138
poles to Patience Patterson. Lot No. 11 of 5 acres and 138 poles to Rebeccah Scott. Lot
No. 12 of 5 acre and 138 poles to Robert Exum. Lot No. 13 of 5 acres and 138 poles to
Joseph Exum. Land on Turneys Creek of Harpeth River, total of about 82 acres and 146
poles. This 17 Oct 1825. Signed by John Davis, Francis Newsom, William E. Newsom,
William Wrenn, and John Demoss, Commissioners. Oct Term 1825.

Page 506   Division of estate of Absalom Page, deceased.
Dec 9, 1825   We, being appointed Commissioners to divide said estate among the
heirs. We find that Martha Page, widow of Absalom Page, deceased, is entitled to $601.30½
and each heir being eleven in number is entitled to $672.46¼. This 3 Sept 1825. Signed by
William James, Joseph Love and David B. Love. Oct Term 1825.

Page 506   Account of estate of John Deaderage, deceased.
Dec 9, 1825   Made with Thomas Deaderick, admr. Persons listed, to wit,
Hewlett, David McGavock, J.B. Houston, Elliston for double tombstone and inclosing tomb,
N. Craddock, Henry Crabb for shroud, Doctor Shelby and McNairy, _____ Boyd for printing
tombstone, Doctor Newman, J.P. Erwin, Mr. Ewing, J. Bell agent for W.H. Love, Philip
Deatherage, Robert Dearing, James B. Houston, Judge Trimble, Craven Jackson, Joseph
Wood, J. Garner, P. Thompson, R. Garrett, J. & R. Woods, B.F. West, Doctor Ford, and
Doctor Bell. Oct Term 1825.

Page 507   Account of sale of estate of William Wallace, deceased.
Dec 9, 1825   Sold on 12 May 1825. Purchasers, to wit, R. Wallace, G. Saunders,
William Anderson, David Read one Bible, R.B. Wallace, Zachariah Gent, Reuben Wallace, J.B.
Demumbrum, William Read, Abitha Wallace, Henry M(illegible), Wilson Crockett, William
Shelton, Jacob Cagle, James Maxey, Jas. Smith, R. & B. Hall, Andrew M(illegible), James
Simmons, Jos. Lenox, Alfred G. Page, Isham W. Felts, John W. Page, Timothy Duratt, John
C. Glasgow, Lunsford Read, Jesse Simmons, Mathew Harris, Lewis G. Gower, B. Wallace,
James Rea, Eaton Wallace, Thomas Hunter, Blethel Wallace, Silas Equals, Theophilus Horn,
Elizabeth Wallace, and Eaton Wallace. David Read, admr. Oct Term 1825.

Page 508   Settlement of estate of Reuben Westmoreland, deceased.
Dec 10, 1825   Made with Tilman R. Daniel, admr. Persons listed, to wit, James
Perry, Lewis H. Brown, and Nathan Ewing. State of Tennessee, Giles County pursuant to an
order of the Davidson County Court. Charles C. Abernathy, D. Leatherman, Nathan Bass
and Joseph McDonald. Oct Term 1825.

Page 509   Division of estate of Reuben Westmoreland, deceased.
Dec 10, 1825   We have divided and set apart the personal estate among his heirs
and divisees accouding to his Last Will and Testament. To Elizabeth Westmoreland, widow
of the deceased, her third part of said estate containing a colt, mare, cow and calf, heifer,
bed, bedstead, bed cloths, dining table, riding gig and several other items including two
negroes and $151.30¼ money in the hands of Tilman R. Daniel. To William G. Westmoreland,
eldest son, a horse, china press and furniture, bed and bedstead and several other items. To
Jesse Westmoreland, mare, bed and bedstead and bed cloths and several other items. To
Laban Westmoreland, a horse, steers, and several other items. To Martha L. Westmoreland,
the last of the heirs, a horse, wagon and several other items. This 13 Aug 1825. Charles C.
Abernathy, D. Leatherman, Nathan Bass, and Joseph McDonald, Commissioners. Oct Term
1825.

Page 510   Account of notes of estate of Reuben Westmoreland, deceased.
Dec 12, 1825   Returned by Tilman R. Daniel, admr. Persons listed, to wit, Aron
Brown and Andrew Fay. The sum being equally divided between the four children of said
Reuben Westmoreland, deceased, William G., Jesse, Laban, and Martha L. Westmoreland. 7
Oct 1825. Signed by the above Commissioners. Oct Term 1825.

Page 511   Settlement of estate of Frederick Stump, deceased.
Dec 13, 1825   Made with Philip Shute, executor. Persons listed, to wit, N. Ewing,
_____ Norvell, E.H. Foster, M. Barrow, R.T. Walker for Jas. Hood, _____ Wilson, R.H. Barry,
John M. Hills, George W. Campbell's note for Bank Stock to let Rachel Stump have as much
of hers and her children's part of said estate, Mrs. Parker, J.W. Horton, Sheriff, and Robert
Walker. Paid to Doctor Sappington. Also Thomas Stagner, Duncan Robertson, _____
Bedwell, Daniel Brims, Balser Huffman, and Lewis Earthman rent of Race Place. Stephen
Cantrell and Daniel A. Dunham. Oct Term 1825.

Page 512   Inventory of estate of Thomas James, deceased.
Mar 6, 1826   Fourteen negroes and several other items listed. Elizabeth James
and Thomas G. James, executors. Jan Term 1826.

163

Page 512   Inventory of estate of Benjamin Casselman, deceased.
Mar 6, 1826   Taken Jan 26, 1826 by Andrew Casselman, executor. Several items
listed including 110 acres of land on Richland Creek also a bond on Jacob Casselman and
Benjamin Casselman of Wilson County, Tennessee for 267 acres of land in Wilson County.
Jan Term 1826.

Page 512   Will of Benjamin Casselman, deceased, of Davidson County.
Mar 6, 1826   27 Sept 1824. To my wife Amelia Casselman the home place where
I now live during her widowhood or lifetime if she lives a widow, with the stock, tools and
household furniture, then to decend to my three sons, Abraham, Benjamin and James
Casselman. To my son Abraham blacksmith tools. To my other two sons Lewis and David
Casselman a bond I have on Benjamin Casselman and Jacob Casselman of Wilson County,
Tennessee for 276 acres of land lying in Wilson County. Also John Bon is to have 30 acres
of land where he now lives and is marked out for him provided he pays $300.00, $50.00 to be
paid yearly. This money is to go to the use of my family to support and school them, if the
said Bon does not pay, the land is to be sold and money to go to the use of the family. The
reason why I do not mention anything to be given to my daughters, I have portioned them
off, viz, Sally Bond, Rhoda Bond, and Betsy Casselman. Betsy Casselman is to have a
saddle. Susan Casselman is to have a horse, saddle and bridle when she comes of age. I
appoint Andrew Casselman, executor. This Aug 27, 1825. Wit: James Casper and David
Cartwright. Jan Term 1±826.

Page 513   Hire of negroes of estate of William P. Bowers, deceased.
Mar 6, 1826   Isaac to John Bowers. Willis to Thomas Bowers. Readin to Lemuel
Bowers. Lewis, his wife and six children to William P. Bowers. Minerva to Lemuel Bowers.
Lewis to Presley M. Randall. E.P. Connell and George Campbell, admrs. Jan Term 1826.

Page 513   Inventory of estate of Abner Cowgill, deceased.
Mar 7, 1826   Several items listed. Edmond Melvin, admr. Jan Term 1826.

Page 514   Division of estate of Reuben Westmoreland, deceased.
Mar 7, 1826   Made with Tilman R. Daniel, admr. Persons listed, to wit, William
G. Westmoreland, William Owens, Robert Oliver, John McCarmack, Nathan Ewing, Charles
Adkinson, Laban Westmoreland, John Tilman, Elizabeth Westmoreland, and Reuben
Westmoreland, and Henry T. Butler.
Giles County, Tennessee. Charles C. Abernathy, Joseph McDonald and Nathan Bass,
Commissioners. Jan term 1826.

Page 515   Account of sale of estate of Isham Felts, deceased.
Mar 7, 1826   Several items listed. Hardy D. Felts, admr. Jan Term 1826.

Page 515   Inventory of estate of Josiah Mullen, deceased.
Mar 7, 1826   Several items listed. Notes on the following, to wit, Jason
Thompson, George Crockett, R. Higginbotham, John B. Lyon, S. Sutton, William Rutherford,
Shelby & McCall, William Hinton, Benjamin Joslin, E. Hall, (money to be collected and paid
to Jesse Mullins, deceased, in his lifetime), T. Morefield, and Maj. Hughs. Elizabeth Mullins,
executrix. Jan term 1826.

Page 516   Inventory of estate of John Graves, deceased.
Mar 7, 1826   Accounts against the following, to wit, Charles Herd, Edward
Keeling, John Roberts, William Hall, Thomas May, Mr. Abercrombe, John Puckett, Felix
Grundy, Martha Wilkinson, Doctor James Priestley, Thomas Hudson, Thomas Connell, Charles
Ballentine, James Priestley, Joseph McVey, Abel Nanny, Nanny & Finch, Isaac Hudson,
Robert Moseley, Gilliland's heirs, Nathaniel Childress, Wyatt Wilkinson, and Josiah Warner.
Also inventory of the property devised to the widow which are in her possession, five negroes
and other items. William Seat, executor. Jan Term 1826.

Page 516   Settlement of estate of Elisha Brewer, deceased, of Davidson
Mar 7, 1826   County. Dec 7, 1825. Commissioners found the administrators
charged with $550.21½ also an account on Jos. Kimbro for $4.00.00, also on Mason Philips
for $16.00 not collected. We found vouchers on the following, to wit, William Murphy, Dr.
Watson & Irons, Benajah Gray, David Irvins & Sons, James Roberts, William Nolin, Jeremiah

Ezell. Hugh Lockhart, John C(illegible), receipt of Jesse Barns, Nathan Ewing, Joseph White's account, William Harris, Samuel R. Cutchen, Samuel D. P(illegible), Adam Carper, John C. McLemore, John Warmouth, John G. Tate, James Collinsworth, to beef for family, Eli Brewer's account, W.W. B(illegible), and William Brewer. This 17 Dec 1825. Benajah Gray, J.P. and William H. Nance, Commissioners. Jan Term 1826.

Page 517   Settlement of estate of Williamson Adams, deceased.
Mar 8, 1826   Made with James Carter, admr. Vouchers, to wit, on Hugh Roland, David L. Thompson, E.H. Foster, L. Noell (Constable), James Grizzard, Philip Campbell, A. Porter & Son, William Brooks, George W. Gibbs, Solomon Clark, Jacob McGavock, Robert Elam, George Shall, James Ridley, Ed. H. East, John O. Ewing, Nathan Ewing, J.B. Houston, Robert Smiley, Beal Bosley, George Wilson, John Harding, Richard Drury, Isaac L. Crow, and William M. Hunter. John Buchanan and William Murphy, Commissioners. Jan Term 1826.

Page 518   Settlement of estate of Robert Thompson, deceased.
Mar 9, 1826   Accounts and notes against the estate paid by John Thompson, admr, to wit, Mrs. Brents, L. & J. Thompson, Nichols & Vaulx, Thomas Deaderick, Austin M. Wards, William McCann, Robertson & Waters, J.B. Houston, and Robert Thompson by Edward Smith. Half of a note given to John Overton by Robert Thompson as counselor and lawyer. Several other items listed. This Jan 17, 1826. Jonas Menifee and William Windle, Commissioners. Jan term 1826.

Oage 519   Rachel Boyd, widow support laid off.
Mar 10, 1826   The widow Boyd and family are allowed 5500 lbs pork, 12 bushels of salt, 85 barrels of corn, 60 lbs of coffee, 3 lbs tea, 175 lbs brown sugar, 25 lbs of loaf sugar, 2 lbs pepper, one lb of spice, 3 barrels of flour and 12 gallons of whiskey, 20 gallons of vinegar, 2 milch cows and calves. The widow is at liberty to purchase the above mentioned cows and calves if she chooses. Rachel Boyd is the widow of Richard Boyd, deceased. This 25 Nov 1825. Lewis Joslin, Shelton Hardgrave and Aaron Franklin, Commissioners.

Page 520   Settlement of estate of Benjamin Philips, deceased.
Mar 10, 1826   Made with William Williams, admr and executor of Joseph Philips, deceased, who was admr &c and guardian to Rebecca and Eliza, devisees &c of Benjamin Philips, deceased. Several vouchers on the following, to wit, McGavock, Armstrong, Cheatham, McNairy & Roan, Maxey, E.S. Hall, J. Nichol, Shelby & McCall, R. Hill guardian (Henton), R. Hydes, Mr. Williams, R. & Elliott (Rebeccah & Eliza), J. Sigler, G. Wilson, Robertson & Waters, Ewing, T. Washington, and T. Wells. 21 Jan 1826. E.S. Hall and M. Barrow, Commissioners. Jan term 1826.

Page 520   Negroes hired belonging to the estate of Zachariah Betts, dec'd.
Mar 10, 1826   Allen to John Betts, Henry to Charles L. Burn (Byrn), Daniel to Catherine Betts, Spurlet to John Betts, and Jesse, a child, to lowest bidder C.L. Byrn. Jan Term 1826.

Page 521   Account of sale of estate of Josiah Mullen, deceased.
Mar 10, 1826   Sold 4 Sept 1825. Purchasers, to wit, John Overton, John Bradford, Gilbert Washington, A.H. Brent, James Dobbs, James Ruff, H. Petway & Clark, J. Maxwell, William Pope, Jno. B. Manifee, William Williams, John Nichol, Edwin Smith, Jesse Wharton, Solomon Clark, B. Ridley, J. Lawrence, J. Cattles, M.H. Quinn, and Jo. T. Elliston. Elizabeth Mullens, executrix. Jan term 1826.

Page 521   Division of negroes of Bedford Brown, deceased.
Mar 10, 1826   Made on 30 Dec 1825, set apart and allotted to William Brown, one of the heirs of Bedford Brown, deceased, and it being represented to us that the other two heirs have heretofore had their allotments in view of the 26 negroes. William Brown drew Lot No. 2 consisting of 9 negroes. Signed by Will Williams, Thomas Martin, Jno. Hobson, and Paul Vaughn, Commissioners. Jan term 1826.

Page 522   Division of estate of Frederick Stump, deceased.
Mar 10, 1826   John F. and Thomas J. Stump, Complainants VS Frederick Stump's executors and legatees, Defendants. Commissioners to allot and make partition between the petitioners and the widow and children of Christopher Stump, deceased, legatees of Frederick

Stump, deceased, of all the negroes and money belonging to the estate of Frederick, deceased, remaining in the hands and control of said executors. They met at the court house in Nashville on 30 Dec 1825 and proved to the discharge of said duties Philip Shute and John Criddle, two of the executors of Frederick Stump and the petitioners John F. and Thomas J. Stump being present. Fifteen negroes valued at $4085.00. To John F. Stump assigned two negroes. To Thomas J. Stump three negroes, to Rachel Stump three negroes, to Tennessee M. Stump three negroes, and to Philip S. Stump two negroes. Jno. B. Craighead, William B. Lewis and D.A. Dunham, Commissioners. Jan Term 1826.

Page 523   Jeremiah Grizzard of William M. Harwood.
Mar 10, 1826   This day received of Jeremiah Grizzard 136 acres of land valued by said Grizzard to me one of his heirs at $1500.00. I hereby bind myself, my heirs &c in the division of the balance of the estate of said Jeremiah Grizzard among his lawful heirs. This 23 Jan 1822. Test: Caleb McGraw. Jan Term 1826.

Page 524   Settlement of estate of Benjamin Philip, deceased.
Mar 10, 1826   The estate of Joseph Philips in account with the estate of Benjamin Philips, deceased. Several vouchers listed. Signed by E.S. Hall and M. Barrow, Commissioners. Jan Term 1826.

Page 524   Additional inventory of estate of Absalom Page, deceased.
Mar 10, 1826   Returned by Samuel Shannon, executor. Received of Matthew Barrow, agent for Alexander Evan's heir of Stephen Brooks, $406.25. This Jan 24, 1826. Jan Term 1826.

Page 525   Settlement of estate of John Elliston, deceased.
Mar 11, 1826   Made by Joseph T. Elliston, executor. Vouchers on the following, to wit, Martin, Hobson, Link, Harris, McGavock, Haget, Brown, Merrell, Crenshaw, Hays, Newman, Thompson, Williams, Harman, Armstrong, Clark, Quinn, Ridley, Seay, Manchester, Goodlett, Hinton, Falwell, Wharton, Moseley, Faulkner, Ewing, Pilcher, Walker, Porter, Stephens, Cannon, Md. Williams, Shoeman, Shackleford, Sumner, McNairy, Bd. E. Clark, Wilbourn, Grizzard, Watson, Goodwin, Thompson, Bedford, Campbell, Norvell, Parish, Litton, McIntosh, Mullen, Methodist C(Church), Stuart, and Boyd. Cash of, to wit, John Hays, Newman, P. Moore, S. Clark, Demumbro, Ridley, Seay, Bateman, Brooks, Sumner, Goodlett, Falwell, Jesse Wharton, Ewing, Herrin, Gibson, Kingsley, Hynes, Knox, Sneed, Read, Porter, Gibbs, Erwin, McNairy, Bedford, J.M. Elliston, Smith, J. McNairy, N. NcNairy, Lockhart, Grizzard, Donelson, Grant, Price, Spence, Young, Watson, Vanleer, Thompson, Earthman, Sandalin, Phipps, Morrison, Trimble, Shelby, Brooks, Foster, Dunham, Bedford, Campbell, Litton, Fly, Crenshaw, Town Tax, Irwin, Hoover, J.B. Bank, Overton, McCombs, Hinton, Young, G. Boyd, Doctor Ewing, Gleaves, Doctor Overton, Doctor Newman, M(illegible), Crabb, Houston, Cartmell, Craddock, Waters, Ridley, G(illegible) by agent, Priestley, Yeatman, and Sommerville. 12 Jan 1826. J. Wharton and D.A. Dunham, Commissioners. Jan Term 1826.

Page 526   Division of estate of Robert Thompson, deceased, of Davidson
Mar 11, 1826   County. To divide the personal estate of Robert Thompson, deceased, among his heirs have done it as follows: To Philip Campbell a negro woman Harriet and her youngest child. To John Chadwell a negro girl Anne. To Nancy Thompson negro boy Dennis and girl Winna. To John Thompson a negro girl and house girl Rachel. Philip Campbell has to pay to John Chadwell $700.00 and to John Thompson $46.00. Nancy Thompson has to pay to John Thompson $33.00. This 19 Jan 1826. Signed by Jonas Manifee, Thomas Edmiston and William Windle, Commissioners.

Page 527   Settlement of estate of Foster Sayre, deceased.
Mar 13, 1826   Made by Samuel Seay, admr. Persons listed, to wit, J.W. McCombs, R. & W. Armstrong, William Arthur, E. Cooper, Mrs. Snow, Addison East, R.A. Higginbotham, Roane & Hays, R. Garrett, R. Stothart, N. Ewing, W. Parker, W. Kenner, P.S. Sayres, David Sayres, G. Wilson, David Irwin, Thomas G. Bradford, J. Norvell, E.S. Hall, ?.D. McLean, John L. Allen, ____ Elliot, H. Sayres, Jno. Sayres, Jacob McGavock, A. & G. McNeill, John Young, S. Bradford, D. Richardson, M. Campbell, J. Metcalf, B.S. Harrison, Jos. W. Horton, J. & R. Woods, and Francis McCoy. This Jan 21, 1826. Signed by Daniel A. Dunham and John Nichol, Commissioners.

Page 528   Settlement of estate of Henry Feribee, deceased.
Mar 13, 1826   Made with Thomas Feribee, admr and found estate to be worth $286.29 3/4 and from vouchers of $69.22. Balance $217.07¼. Thomas Buchanan and Henry White, Jr., Commissioners.

Page 529   Division of estate of John Elliston, deceased.
Mar 13, 1826   According to his Last Will, to wit, a house and lot on Market Street valued at $6500.00. A house with 71½ feet of ground part of Lot No. 12 at $1300.00. 10 feet of ground on Public Square at $1500.00. A negro boy named Henry at $200.00, and negro firl at $100.00. Total value to $9600.00 is three fourths which is the children's undivided share of the estate. A house with about 60 feet of ground fronting on Market Street part of Lot No. 14 at $2000.00. 90 feet of ground on Spruce Street at $1000.00. A negro girl named Charity has palsy, a negro woman Rachel with consumption, a negro woman Philis very old valued at $200.00. Total $3200.00. Is one fourth of the estate which is the widow's share according to the will. This 26 Jan 1826. Signed by Duncan Robertson, Samuel Seay, Addison East and Robert Woods, Commissioners.

Page 530   Division of Lot of L.P. Cheatham and Jno. Elliston, deceased.
Mar 14, 1826   Commissioners proceeded to lay off and divide between the heirs of John Elliston, deceased and Leonard P. Cheatham, Esquire, a certain half of Lot No. 14 in the town of Nashville conveyed to John and L.P. by James Ball by Deed of Conveyance dated 11 Apr 1822. And upon division have set apart and allotted to the heirs of said John Elliston, deceased, the northwestern half of said part of lot so conveyed and L.P. Cheatham the southeastern half of said lot. This 21 Dec 1825. Signed by Robert Woods, Henry Ewing and Duncan Robertson.

Page 530   Division of Lot of Micajah H. Lewis, deceased.
Mar 14, 1826   Plat on page 530. 20 feet for alley. Lot No. 1 to W.B. Lewis with 52 feet fronting on street. Lot No. 2 to Mary Ann Lewis with 57 feet on street. Lot No. 3 to Mary Ann Lewis one half of this lot and the other one half as Lot No. 4 is allotted to the children of Dr. Thomas A. Claiborne and wife Sarah, 30 feet. Lot No. 4 to the children of Dr. Thomas A. Claiborne. To William A. Lewis they allotted 52 feet fronting _____ Street and adjoining a 20 feet alley. 26 Oct 1825. Signed by John H. Eaton, Ephraim H. Foster, W. Tannehill and John Bell.

Page 531   Elizabeth Hooper, her dower laid off.
Mar 14, 1826   Plat on page 531. Elizabeth Hooper, widow and relict of Joseph Hooper, deceased. A tract of 662½ acres of land found and set apart to said widow 222½ acres of land including the mansion house and all the necessary out buildings. Land borders David Parker's tract and on Eastern Dry Fork of Whites Creek near the lower gate of said Hooper. This 11 Nov 1825. Signed by Samuel Weakley, Jr., surveyor, Paul Vaughn, Thomas Taylor, D.B. Love, William B. Ewing, John J. Hinton, N.H. Robertson, William Faulkner, Jno. Criddle, David Parker, Robert Taylor, and John Hobson, Commissioners.

Page 532   Davided real estate of Joseph Hooper, deceased.
Mar 14, 1826   Plat on page 531. No. 1 to James H. Hooper of 160½ acres, No. 2 to Elizabeth Hyde 136 3/4 acres, and No. 3 to Mary Ann Hooper of 147 3/4 acres. This 24 Jan 1826. Signed by Samuel Weakley, Duke W. Sumners and Will White.

Page 534   Divided real estate of Daniel Young, deceased.
Mar 15, 1826   Plat on page 534. No. 1 to Mary Young of 7 acres 58/100. No. 2 to Lucy Young of 8 acres and 107 poles. No. 3 to Hardy B. Herning of 13 acres. No. 4 to Senia Bagswell of 16 acres. No. 5 to William Young of 16 acres. No. 6 to Sarah Strother of 21 acres. No. 7 to Claiborne Y. Hooper of 17 acres. And No. 8 to Catherine Bryant of 17 acres. This 26 Jan 1826. Signed by Samuel Weakley, William B. Ewing, R.M. Ewing, Taswell Hyde, and Jordan Hyde, Commissioners.

Page 535   Settlement of estate of Elinor Young, deceased.
Mar 15, 1826   Persons listed, to wit, Zenas Tait, John Clinard, Daniel Buie, Morris Reighley, Jonathan Reader, Sarah F. Tait, Franklin Tait, John S. Cox, B.H. Lanier, Pharoah Hudgins, George Cagle, Jr., N. Perkins, Morgan McDaniel, Alexander Merriman, and William Taylor. B.H. Lanier, admr. Jan 24, 1826.

Page 536   Settlement of estate of Robert Searcy, deceased.
Mar 16, 1826   Made with Stephen Cantrell, executor. Persons listed, to wit, B.
Bedford, Mr. Cobb, Frances McGavock, James P. Clark, Andrew Hays, E.D. Jones, P.R.
Booker, William L. Bryles, Elijah Masingham, Andrew Erwin, Mr. Lareys, Mr. Robston, Jesse
Benton, Gen. Robertson, M. Stephens, A.W. Johnston, A. Erwin, Jr., Thomas B. Tunstall,
Duncan Robertson, J.C. McLemore, G.W. Gibbs, _____ Williams, C. Johnston, Esquire, A.
Balch, A.V. Brown, N.A. McNairy, John Catron, Thomas Crutcher, and E.S. Hall. This 28 Jan
1826. Signed by E.S. Hall and D.A. Dunham.

Page 539   Settlement of estate of James Priestly, deceased.
Mar 17, 1826   Made with Mrs. Sarah Priestly, admrx. Persons listed, to wit, A.W.
Johnston, Newman & Ewing, N. Talley, _____ Gleaves, John Newman, George Shall, Robert
C. Foster, E.H. Foster, Robert B. Curry, Jacob McGavock, George & Jacob Shall, Saunders &
Chandler, B.W. & W.H. Bedford, Henry Willis, Richard Smith, William Wray, James T. Love,
James Condon, Thomas Conly, R.P. Beauchamp, J.K. Kain, John Shelby, Robertson & Curry,
Ingram & Loyd, Robert Samples, Moses Drew, Joseph Litton, Leven Watson, William Harding,
E.H. Foster, John Graves, James B. Houston, A.G. Goodlett, Thomas Claiborne, W.A. Cook,
W. Campbell, A. Kingsley, Keeling, James Smith, John T. Priestley, James Priestley, P.M.B.
Priestley, Joseph L. Priestley, and Sarah Ann Priestley, Mrs. S. Priestley, Joseph Underwood,
Gen. Allen, Thomas Monroe, Anthony Foster, Blount Robertson, William L. Brown, John
Donelson, Ralph Crabb, Elizabeth Moore of Kentucky, and James Smith. This 26 Jan 1826.
Signed by R. Farquharson, R. McGavock and N.B. Pryor.

Page 541   Settlement of estate of William Wharton, deceased.
Mar 17, 1826   Made with Jesse Wharton, admr. Persons listed, to wit, Benjamin
Porter, J. Porter, D. Robertson, N.T. Walker, J.C. Hicks for coffin for deceased and wife,
William Maxey, S. Cantrell, J. Whitsett for timber at same mill, M. Porter for attending on
deceased's family, T.B. Craighead for tuition for William H. Wharton, McChesney for making
saw mill crank, J. Murry, William McCann, Mrs. Cobler for two granny fees for negroes, Mr.
Blackburn, Joseph T(illegible), B. Smith, Thomas Williams, G.M. Deaderick, Dr. Roan, Parson
Whitsett, Joseph T. Elliston, W. Carroll, S. Scales, R.C. Napier, Jo. Taylor, Thomas G.
Bradford, D. Irwin, Dr. Mays, R. Mosley, M. Bell, James M(illegible), Mrs. Childs, A. McFail
(McPhail) admr of D. McBean, J. Menifee schoolmaster, Mr. Howlett schoolmaster, M. Quinn,
Peter Bass, Dr. Hadley, H. Cromer, Thomas Edmiston, Thomas Yeatman, Mr. Craighead,
Joseph Scales, R. Gillespie for patent right for two log stills, Dr. Newman, John T. Dismukes
for Austin Wade, Samuel J. Ridley, jailor for keeping Edward A. Keeling in jail, David Snow,
S. Sanders, John Haywood, Dunham & Johns, Joseph Philips, Esquire, John Anderson, J.B.
Houston, Rev. T.B. Craighead, Christopher Stump, Herbert & Rice, J. Manley, George Bell,
E. Bennet, Charles Lewis, Joshua Porter, C. Talbot, Parson Moore, _____ Burrow, Thomas
Fletcher, and J. Wharton and Samuel J. Ridley for rent of plantation, mills, distillery &c.
This 23 Jan 1826. Signed by E.S. Hall and Stephen Cantrell, Commissioners.

Page 545   Division of negroes of Benjamin Philips, deceased.
Mar 17, 1826   By will of Benjamin Philips, deceased, and allotted to Eliza now
Eliza Wells, three negro slaves. William Philips drew Lot No. 1 consisting of three dollars.
Rebecca drew Lot No. 4 consisting of five negroes. Eliza drew Lot No. 2 consisting of four
negroes, and Hinton drew Lot No. 3 consisting of three slaves. Also named Rebeccah as
having to pay $160.40. This 3 Jan 1826. Signed by Richard Hyde, Beal Bosley, Jno. B.
Craighead and J. Wharton, Commissioners.

Page 546   Inventory of estate of Alexander McCombs, deceased.
Mar 18, 1826   Returned by Gabriel McCombs, admr, on 25 Jan 1826. Accounts
against Mrs. Judge Haywood, Mrs. Susan Haywood, Mr. Dugal, B.W. Bedford, Henry Burnett,
deceased, and Willis L. Shoemate's executors, Willis Barrow, E.H. Foster, Thomas Claiborne,
and John McNairy. Jan term 1826.

Page 546   Settlement of estate of John McCool, deceased.
Mar 20, 1826   Made by John H. Smith, admr. Persons listed, to wit, John Page,
William Caldwell, J.C. Philips, J. Page, Chester Shaw, James Hennon, A.H. Harris, J.
Sumner, Douglass & Criddle, Michael Santee, John H. Smith, and C. Stump. Jan Term 1826.

Page 547   Account of sale of estate of John Earthman, deceased.
Mar 20, 1826   Sold on 10 Dec 1825. Purchasers, to wit, R. McGavock, Thomas Dill, Polly Earthman, Jas. Faulkner, Gilbert Marshall, Thomas Woodard, Boyd McNairy, Ezekiel Cloyd, James H. Hooper, Lewis Earthman, and John Shelby. Signed by Polly Earthman, Lewis Earthman and Isaac Earthman. Jan Term 1826.

Page 547   Account of sale of perishable estate of George Wharton, deceased.
Mar 21, 1826   Purchasers, to wit, Samuel L. Wharton, John Morgan, Samuel Seay, Jos. Dickinson, David Ralston, Thomas Woodard, Jas. Faulkner, John Hinton, Edmond Goodrich, E. McCance, D. Robertson, Reuben Payne, C. Brooks, Beverly Coats, George Watkins, Thomas Stratton, Greenwood Payne, H. Harris, B. Williamson, N. Tally, S. Donelson, J. Wharton, Thomas Welch, D. Scruggs, and John T. Dismukes. Jan 7, 1826. Samuel Seay, executor. Jan term 1826.

Page 549   Settlement of estate of James Trimble, deceased.
Mar 22, 1826   Paid Gregory (grave digger), H. Petway, Jacob McGavock, J.W. McCombs for coffin, Nathan Ewing, A.B. Hawkins, Ilai Metcalf, D. Robertson, to Cumberland College, McClanton for taxes, N.A. McNairy, George Shall, Elezer for work on mill, Mrs. Smiley for work, James Carruthers, James Blackmore, Montgomery Bell, James Stuart, Woods & Knoles, Mrs. Garrett's account, A. Boyd, James McCampbell, Robert T. Walker, Jas. Walker, Miss Mary Poyzer, received rent to Presbyterian Church, Martin News for tombstone, E. Grant for brick, Thomas Crutcher for Female Academy Stock, Mr. Stephens a schoolmaster, William L. Brown, Esq., Philip Hurt, John Peck, subscription to build a church, Joseph Love for tobacco, Robertson & Sanderson, Joseph and Robert Woods, Robert B. Curry a Postmaster, R.P. Hays, A.W. Johnston, M.P. Walker, Abraham Maury for funeral expense, Doc. John O. Ewing, Nathan Ewing for copy of will, John Shute, Elliot, Andrew Hynes, A. Morrison's Bridge Toll, Pollock's account, John Nichols, Lewis Earthman for shingles for mansion house, Welch & Austin for roofing house, contribution to the Nashville Library, T. Washington, to Cumberland College for John Trimble, F.B. Fogg, Esq., and J.P. Clark. Other accounts of: John Graham and William Peebles, R. McGavock, Jacob McGavock, Nathan Ewing, J. Hardens, Jno. F. Stump, Sappington & Hickman, Higginbotham and as a Green's note, Josiah Horton, G. Buford, A. Kingsley, L. Temple, Bell & Higginbotham, Douglas' note, A. Wilkinson of J. Wheaton, R.W. Higginbotham, John Harding redeeming land of Thomas Shute, William E. Kennedy, Robert W. Green, F. Sanders, A. Walker, Jno. C. Sullivan, Thomas Aimes, A. Arnold, John Wilson, George Shall for rent of mansion house. 28 Jan 1826. Signed by Ephraim H. Foster, R. McGavock and John Nichols. Jan Term 1826.

Page 552   Will of James W. Sittler, deceased.
June 15, 1826   All my stock and profits I have in the firm of Isaac & James W. Sittler unto my brother Isaac Sittler, also all my interest in my father's estate. I am induced to make this my will in consequence of the manifold obligations I lay under, and benefits I have received from said Isaac Sittler. This 5 Jan 1813. Wit: Robert Searcy and E.S. Hall. Proven Apr term 1826.

Page 552   Will of Clement Whittimore, deceased.
June 15, 1826   To my wife Mary Whittimore the house and plantation whereon I now live together with the 260 acres of land including the same and all the rest of my property except what is herein after disposed of by this my will, all to remain her own during her life or widowhood. To my daughter Martha negroes Mary and her increase, Sally and her increase, also a negro boy named Isaac, one good bed and furniture, one mare and saddle and bridle. To my son Sterling during my wife's natural life and at her death or marries my negro Booker together with the house, plantation and 260 acres of land, my reason for this is that I have before given my other four sons, Lewis, Abram, Clement and William, a tract of land and a negro man each. I have 180 acres of land and upwards in Guilford County, North Carolina, whereon my daughter Elizabeth Dickey now lives. It is my will that my daughter Elizabeth Dicky have all the benefits of all proceeds for 15 years then it should be equally divided between my two daughters Nancy and Peggy. The rest of my estate to be divided among all my children, Lewis, Clement, Polly, Sterling to pay William and Abraham $100.00 each. This 13 Dec 1823. Wit: Jerm. Ezell, Robert Brown and Thomas Brown. Apr Term 1826.

Page 554   Will of Benjamin Prichard, deceased, of Davidson County.
June 15, 1826   To my two beloved sons Benjamin and William Prichard the plantation I now live on containing 497 acres to be equally divided between them. Benjamin is to have the mills and William is to have the home part of the plantation where I now live. To my daughter Sally Prichard 10 acres of land out of Benjamin's part of the land for a home for her during her natural life. To my beloved wife Joanna Prichard out of my son William Prichard's part of the land, the house I now live in and 12 acres of land during her life for support for her. To my wife during her life two negroes Simon and Genney all the property she brought with her, she may dispose with as she pleases. I also leave her one black mare. To my son Enoch Pritchard a negro Jesse. To my son Joseph Pritchard a negro Laban. To my son Enoch Pritchard two stills with all the tubs and utensils, also sorrel horse. To my son William one mare colt. The balance of my property to be equally divided between my four youngest daughters, Annis Prichard, Peggy Prichard, Nancy Prichard and Polly Prichard. The two negroes left my wife during her life named Simon and Ginney at her death to be equally divided between my four last named daughters. This 31 May 1822. Wit: Hugh Allison, Francis Cary and Thomas Wynn.
Additional to above will: To my son William Prichard one yoke of steers out of the property I left to my four daughters. Benjamin Prichard is to have the use of the negroes and steers to work on the mill for the space of six weeks. The corn and wheat to be equally divided between my wife and children, Joanna Prichard and Benjamin, Sally, Peggy, Annis, Nancy, Polly, and William. This 9 June 1822. Wit: Hugh Allison, Adam H. Berry and Benjamin Brittain. Apr Term 1826.

Page 556   Will of Thomas Hooper, deceased, of Davidson County.
June 16, 1826   To my beloved wife Jane T. Hooper one bed and furniture also her choice, also one negro woman and a negro boy, negro woman, one mare, also the land whereon I now live to be hers during her natural life or widowhood for the purpose of raising my two children Churchwell Hooper and Elizabeth Hooper. To my son Churchwell one tract of land on S(illegible) Creek, Davidson County containing 150 acres and one tract on Cumberland River lying below where George Hail now lives containing 100 acres, a negro man, a negro woman, and a negro boy, a negro girl named Juda the said Churchwell is to have part when he arrives at age of 21 years, except Juda which my wife Jane T. Hooper is to have until her death or marriage. To my daughter Elizabeth T. Hooper the tract of land whereon I now live after the death or marriage of her mother Jane T. Hooper Containing 150 acres and 40 acres on Cumberland River just below Hickmans Ferry and four small dowers of land part of Churchwell Hooper's widow after his death, also several negroes. Elizabeth is to be put into possession of all the estate I have given to her when she arrives at age of 21 years or her marriage. Remainder of my property to be equally divided between my wife and my children. This 15 Jan 1826. Wit: J.M. Lovell, Anne M. Hooper and Jesse Hooper. Apr Term 1826.

Page 557   Will of Pembroke Cartwright, deceased, of Davidson County.
June 16, 1826   To my son Jacob Cartwright my apple mill with two large troughs. To my son James Cartwright a negro boy and other property he has received. To my son Jesse Cartwright a negro girl and property he has already received of me also $100.00. To the heirs of my son David Cartwright, to wit, Jaconia Cartwright, Elbert Cartwright, Pembroke Cartwright, Emily Cartwright, Eliza Cartwright, and Sally Cartwright, the sum of $600.00 to be equally divided between them when they become of age or marries. To my grand daughter Pembroke Rutherford one bay mare. All the property that I may die possessed with except what is already bequeathed &c to be divided equally between Thomas Cartwright, Jacob Cartwright, James Cartwright, Betsy Rutherford, Robert Cartwright, Jesse Cartwright and the heirs of David Cartwright. I appoint Samuel L. Wharton and William Donelson, my executors. This 13 Aug 1818. Wit: Enoch Cunningham and John Cole.
Codicil: Made 16 Nov 1818. I give unto my son Thomas Cartwright the sum of $294.00 to be paid out of the proceeds of sale of my fattening hogs. To my grand daughter Polly Cartwright, daughter of my son James, a bed and furniture &c. To my grand daughter Pembroke Rutherford a bed and furniture &c. To my grand daughter Betsy Kittrell one cow and calf, set of knives and forks and other items. To my grand daughter Nancy Butterworth one sow and pigs. To my grand son John Hunter Cartwright one gray colt. To my grand daughter Pembroke Cartwright, daughter of Robert Cartwright, a bay horse. Wit: George Wharton and Samuel L. Wharton. Apr Term 1826.

170

Page 559   Settlement of estate of Robert Smiley, deceased.
June 17, 1826   Made with A.M. Smiley, admr. Several vouchers listed (no names).
R.C. Foster and J.P. Erwin. Apr Term 1826.

Page 560   Settlement of estate of George Hewlett, deceased.
June 17, 1826   Made with Ann M. Hewitt, admrx. Several vouchers listed and
accounts (no names). J.P. Erwin and Jo. Norvelle. Apr Term 1826.

Page 560   Settlement of estate of Joseph Coldwell, deceased.
June 17, 1826   Made with Sidney Coldwell and Stewart Pipkin, admrs. Persons
listed, to wit, David Campbell, S.M. Morris, B. Richmond, J.B. Williams, Richard Vaughn,
Benjamin Brown, Richard Joslin, Jury Tuhett and William McCrary. Apr Term 1826.

Page 561   Settlement of estate of William Carvin, deceased.
June 19, 1826   Made with Edward Carvin, admr. Persons listed, to wit, William
Neely, James Hennon, Felix Robertson, David Black, William Smith, John Dickinson, A.
Russell, Benjamin Rutherford, Thomas G. Watkins, Ezekiel Bass, James Winters, Andrew
Ewing, William Philips, William Sneed, Edward Carvin, John Farrow, Jeremiah Hinton, James
Swanson, and William Perkins. R. Weakley and Will Lytle, Commissioners. Apr Term 1826.

DAVIDSON COUNTY, TENNESSEE WILL BOOK # 9

1826 - 1832

Page 1   Inventory of estate of Pembroke Cartwright, deceased.
June 22, 1826   Taken by Samuel L. Wharton, executor, on 8 Feb 1826. Several
items listed, notes on James Cunningham, on Reuben Payne, on John Cunningham, on James
Cunningham, and one on George W(illegible). Apr Term 1826.

Page 1   Inventory of estate of Robert Vick, deceased.
June 22, 1826   Apr 15, 1826, taken by Wilson Crockett, admr. Several items listed.
Apr Term 1826.

Page 2   Settlement of estate of James Campbell, deceased.
June 22, 1826   Taken on Apr 21, 1826 by Sally Campbell, admrx and P.W.
Campbell, admr. Several negores sold also several vouchers listed (no names). Apr Term
1826.

Page 2   Sale of personal estate of Richard Boyd, deceased.
June 22, 1826   Made by Rachel Boyd, admrx, sold on 1 Dec 1825. Persons listed,
to wit, Josiah Horton, Robert Simpson, Alexander Richardson, Edward Raworth, Samuel B.
Davidson, Shelton Hargroves, Gilliam King, Henry Lile, John Johns, Sr., J.W. Harton, W.W.
Brown, C.W. Garrett, J. Woodward, J. Pinkerton, William Lofton, William Newsom, Wilkins
Whitfield, William Johns, John Little, Sr., Lewis Joslin, F.T. Blackwood, John McGavock,
Mathew Lee, W.H. Boyd, William E. Watkins, J. Harding, George P. Clark, and Jesse
Newland. Apr Term 1826.

Page 4   Additional inventory of estate of Richard Boyd, deceased.
June 23, 1826   A list of notes of hand due to Richard Boyd, deceased. Persons
listed, to wit, Samuel Elam, H.R. Cartmell, Edward & Orton, A. Stobaugh, Benjamin Joslin,
C.H. Jordon, Henry Cromer, James Page, John Buchanan, William Bebe, Terry Bradley, E.J.
Porter, C.H. Rooker, Jno. and Adam Barnhart, Jos. Benning, E. Talbot, William Rutherford,
Richard Joslin, Alexander McDowell, William Chandler, N. Peck, Jacob Sumner, Thomas
Coventon (Covington), William Sergant, J.P. Lymar, Frederick Horn, William Eilson, William
L. Barry, Samuel Hogg, C.V. Laramy, James Chavis, William Martin, Eli Harris, R. Barrate,
Rachel Legrand, David Allen, and Jesse Nowlin. Apr Term 1826.

Page 5   Settlement of estate of Zachariah Betts, deceased.
June 24, 1826   Persons listed, to wit, Jas. McDaniel, Lucy Watson, Richard
Harrison, John Maxey, George Hall, George Campbell, Watson & Connell, John Pavott, Levi
A. Baker, Frederick Lassiter, Shaw & Campbell, John S. Galbreath, Isaac L. Glasgow, John
R. Bevins, David Buie, James McDaniel, Allen Mathis, William P. Bowers, Beverly Harris,
George Perry, E.P. Connell, Seldon Bells, William L. Brown, and Foster & Hogg. John Segler
two notes. Signed by John Pirtle, J.P. and Charles L. Byrom. Apr Term 1826.

Page 6   Division of estate of Zachariah Betts, deceased.
June 24, 1826   Made 4 Feb 1826, between Caty Betts, John Betts, Seldon Betts,
Lovell Betts, Lemuel Bowers, Eliza Betts and Stockley Betts, the only legatees of Zachariah
Betts, deceased, and all being of lawful age do agree to divide the estate. Caty Betts,
widow, agrees to take one negro boy named Daniel for her full share. John Betts agrees to
take two negroes named Allen and Jesse for his share. Seldon Betts agree to take negro boy
Spirlet for his share. Lovell Betts agree to take $453.00 for his full share. Lemuel Betts
agree to take $453.00 for his share. Eliza Betts agree to take a negro man Henry at this
time. Stockley Betts agree to take the land and plantation whereon the said deceased lived
near the head of Manskers as his full share. Wit: E.P. Connell, William P. Byrn and Isaac
Walton. Apr Term 1826.

Page 7   Divided estate of William P. Bowers, deceased.
Hyne 24, 1826   Had $1767.54 3/4 in money given up by the administrators, as
follows, to wit, Hugh Tilford a negro girl Manervia and $716.50. To Lemuel Bowers $950.00
already received and $166.50 to receive. To Thomas Powell $423.00 in advance and negroes
Edward and Lewis. To John Bowers $449.00 in advance and negro Redin. To William Bowers
negroes Isaac and (?) his share. To Stephen C. Bowers negroes Lewis and Judy his wife
and two children named Jackson and Pomprey his share. To Lavina Bowers negroes Willie
and Mariah and Jack her share. 1st Feb 1826. Apr term 1826.

Page 8   Robert M. Burton and wife.
June 26, 1826   On 2nd day of Feb 1826 to set apart to Robert M. Burton and
Martha H., late Martha H. Donelson, his wife, a distributive share of the negro property of
the late William Donelson, deceased, agreeable to his will. Several negroes listed (38). To
the (illegible) oldest children and there is three younger and the widow their share. Signed
by Will Williams, E.P. Connell and Allen Mathis, Commissioners. Apr Term 1826.

Page 9   Sale of estate of John Goodwin, deceased.
June 26, 1826   Feb 10, 1826. Purchasers, to wit, Dempsey Jones, Walter Greer,
John Prichard, William Cannada, Nancy Goodwin, Andrew E. Speers, John Jones, John Arthur,
Jas. Cloyd, Houston Cooper, Henry Stuart, William Greer, Henry F. Clark, Jefferson Fowler,
John Exum, Isaac Greer, Jesse Reynolds, William Herrin, Mrs. Neal, William H. Shelton, John
K. Swenney, John E(illegible), Henry Stewart, John Berry, Silas Linton, Theoderick Hunt, Asa
Green, Archibald Connelly, William Jewell, Bayles Anderson, William Ellison, Lodwick B.
Beach, John Travilson, Thomas Hunt, Neal McNeal, Polly Goodwin, Elenor Goodwin, John
Carrington, William Greer, Samuel Spence, James Douglas, John Arthur, Elijah G(illegible),
and Philip Wills. John Jones, admr. Apr Term 1826.

Page 10   Additional inventory of Willis L. Shumate, deceased.
June 26, 1826   Taken by Cary Felts and Jeremiah Ezell, admrs. Persons listed,
to wit, J.K. Buchanan, Benjamin Wright, William Brooks, William (illegible), Nichol & Vaulx,
Luallen Campbell, George F. Hamilton, Sally Shumate, John Bell & Jeremiah Burnett, Arthur
Bland & N. Tomlin, William, alias Billy, Bibby, and J.W. Horton. Apr Term 1826.

Page 11   Division of land of John Pugh, deceased.
June 27, 1826   Plat on page 11. Widow's dower of 117½ acres. No. 1 to Sally
Pugh of 26 3/4 acres. No. 2 to Samuel Pugh of 25 3/4 acres. No. 3 to Polly Brown of 29
acres. No. 4 to Jonathan Pugh of 29 acres. No. 5 to Isaac G. Pugh of 29 acres. No. 6 to
Hampton Pugh of 25 acres and 33 poles. No. 7 to Hannah Davidson of 24 acres and 55 poles.
And No. 8 to John Pugh of 29½ acres. This 10 Feb 1826. Signed by Giles Harding, Giles H.
Page, John Johns, E. Raworth, and W.E. Watkins. John Davis, J.P. of Davidson County. Apr
Term 1826.

Page 14   Settlement of estate of Harris Ogilvie, deceased.
June 28, 1826   Made with W. Ogilvie, admr. Persons listed, to wit, Joel Elam, Henry Bailey, William Owen, James Butt, J.W. Horton, Newman & Lea, J.H. Haislett, James Stevenson, Nathan Ewing, John Nichol, J. & R. Woods, Nathaniel Bell, Lewis Ogilvie, Benjamin Bibb, Elizabeth Ogilvie, William Ogilvie guardian of A.S. Ogilvie, Thomas Sadler, John Bells, and T.S. Hall. Apr term 1826.

Page 15   Division of land of Joseph Coldwell, deceased.
June 28, 1826   Widow's dower of 45½ acres. No. 1 to Mary Coldwell of 5 acres and 46 poles. No. 2 to James Coldwell of 5 acres and 46 poles. No. 3 to Samuel Coldwell of 5 acres and 46 poles. No. 4 to Andrew Coldwell of 5 acres and 46 poles. No. 5 to Martha McCrary of 5 acres and 46 poles. No. 6 to Harriet Pipkin of 5 acres and 36 poles. No. 7 to Joseph Coldwell of 5 acres and 46 poles. Also No. 1 of 6acres and 51 poles, No. 2 of 3 3/4 acres and 25 poles, No. 3 of 7¼ acres, No. 4 of 7½ acres and 29 poles, No. 5 of 9 3/4 acres and 26 poles, No. 6 of 9 3/4 acres and 26 poles, and No. 7 of 9 3/4 acres and 26 poles allotted on 27 & 28 Mar 1826. Sworn 24 Apr 1826, Will Lytle, J.P. Signed by Samuel Weakley, Surveyor, and Henry Barnes, Henry Compton, James Cooper, and John Hodge. Apr Term 1826.

Page 18   Catherine Binkley, her dower.
June 29, 1826   Apr 5, 1826. The jurors met to lay off the dower ov Mrs. Catherine Binkley. Located on the bank of S. River at C. Ridles corner and Elam's corner. Signed by Joseph Burnett, John Hall, Jas. W. Wright, John Tate, David Casselman, Joseph Wilson, and Eleazer Hamilton. Apr Term 1826.

Page 18   Inventory of estate of Clemment Whittemore, deceased.
June 29, 1826   Several items including one large Bible and notes on Sterling Whittemore, William Whittemore, Robert Brown, Samuel V. Ensley, William Vaulx, J. Spruce, Benjamin Wright, and John Owens. Signed by Charles Hayes, admr &c. Apr Term 1826.

Page 19   Account of sale of estate of Abner Cowgill, deceased.
June 29, 1826   The amount of the sale was $196.42½. This 22 Apr 1826. Edmond Melvin, admr. Apr Term 1826.

Page 20   Settlement of estate of Corbin Noles, deceased.
Sept 4, 1826   Persons listed, to wit, N. Ewing, D. Higginbotham, E.H. Foster, C. Brooks, Jos. Norvill, Duncan Robertson, F. Sehumans, J.W. Sitler guardian of T(illegible) Noles, Lucy Noles, widow, and James Boyd, admr. This 26 July 1826. Will Lytle and Henry Ewing. July Term 1826.

Page 21   Inventory of estate of Corbin Noles, deceased.
Sept 4, 1826   Made by James Boyd, admr. The admr has charged himself with two hundred in bank paper which he never received at the time the inventory and that the said sum of money was in the pocket book of the descendent. 28 July 1826. July Term 1826.

Page 21   Settlement of estate of Ann Hay, deceased. Persons listed, to wit, James Campbell special legacy and guardian Sophronia W. Campbell, P.W. Campbell, William P. Seat a guardian of W.P. Campbell, William McDonald in right of Sophronia W. Campbell, and James G. Campbell and Albert G. Campbell and Eudalphus D. Campbell, Partick W. Campbell of lawful age, William P. Campbell of lawful age, James Lockhart guardians, Enoch Ensley guardian, Moses Eakin, Nathan Ewing, Henry Ewing, Joseph Norvill, and George Wilson. Apr Term 1826.

Page 22   Settlement of estate of George M. Deaderick, deceased.
Sept 4, 1826   Persons listed, to wit, Stephen Cantrell, J. Terry, Daniel B. and Susan D. Turner, Nathan Ewing, Jno. G. Deaderick a legacy, B.G. Murrell, Thomas J. Perkins, William Craig, Mrs. F(illegible), Samuel M. Perry, Charles D. McLean as admr of his wife, Mark Young, William Patterson, James Trimble, W.W. Gordon, Eliza R. D(illegible), Thomas Welch, D.A. Deaderick, David Nelson and wife, Jno. Sigler, Matthew Barrow, E. Hickman, John P. Hickman, Gideon Johnson, J.P. Clark, C. Johnson, Esq., Samuel Vance, deceased, George Shall, Mortimore Williams, Martin & Williams, A. Montgomery, Hardee D. Murrell,

Samuel Clay and wife, John Smith admr of D.S. Deaderick, G.W. Gibbs, Jno. Overton, Esq., William Windle admr of Robert Posey, deceased, J. McGavock, Joseph A. Deaderick, A.B. Hayes, Esq., M.L. Brown, Esq., Alfred M. Carter an legacy due himself and wife, C. Brooks, Outlaw's heirs, William Word executor of Jos. Cole, deceased, J. Master, F. Linch, J. & R. Woods, Jo. Litton, I. McNairy, and George Wilson. 24 July 1826. Wilkins Tannehill and Daniel A. Donelson, Commissioners. July Term 1826.

Page 24   Settlement of estate of John Bowle, deceased.
Sept 6, 1826   Made with Robert Hill, executor. Persons listed, to wit, Jno. Chambers, William Woodward, David Chambers, T.G. Bradford, Robert Armstrong, N. Ewing, Jno. Harding, Thomas Washington, Jno. Motherall, and William Hume. July 26, 1826. Will Lytle and A.W. Johnson. July Term 1826.

Page 24   Rebecca B. Spence, widow's dower.
Sept 6, 1826   July 26, 1826. Dower out of the estate of the late John Spence, deceased, located by lot of John Catron, Esqire, on Cherry Street, the dwelling house and building given to the children &c. Signed by Thomas Claiborne, Josiah Nichols, William Vaulx, Hays Blackman, Simon Bradford, D.S. Jamison, J. Philips, William King, Jordan Hyde, Samuel Seay, Addison East, and William H. Nance. July Term 1826.

Page 25   Mary Knox, widow years support.
Sept 6, 1826   Mrs. Mary Knox, widow of James Knox, deceased, is allowed $500.00 July 22, 1826. Signed by Duncan Robertson, Was. L. Hammons and R.C. Foster. July Term 1826.

Page 26   Lucy Noles, widow's support.
Sept 7, 1826   One years support for Lucy Noles and family of $300.00. Duncan Robertson and Colin S. Hobbs. July Term 1826.

Page 26   Polly Earthman, widow's support.
Sept 7, 1826   July 31, 1826. We, James Marshall, John Criddle and N.H. Robertson met to lay off to Polly Earthman, widow and relict of John Earthman, deceased, a support for her and her family the sum of $300.00. July Term 1826.

Page 26   Mady Dodson, widow's dower.
Sept 7, 1826   A jury met to lay off and set apart to Mary Dodson, widow of Allen Dodson, deceased, her dower of a tract of land. Signed by Joseph Burnett, Jos. Cook, John W. Murry, Frederick Binkley, Abraham Earhart, Robert Mann, Absalom Gleaves, Eli Cherry, Thomas Gleaves, William Stewart, A. Clopton, and Zachariah F. Robertson. July Term 1826.

Page 27   Division of land of William Cross' heirs.
Sept 7, 1826   Lot No. 1 to James Cross for 114 acres and 130 poles. Lot No. 2 to Powhatton Cross for 149 acres and 41 poles. Lot No. 3 to Nancy Black for 180 acres and 27 poles. Lot No. 4 to Eldridge Cross for 114 acres and 130 poles. Surveyed 1 Nov 1825, a tract of 559 acres and 8 sq. poles of land granted to Richard Cross by No. 1961 for 64 acres dated 20 May 1793 lying on the eastern waters of Mill Creek and bordered by lands of James McCristians and C. Hays. Joseph Burnett, D.S., Jeremiah Burnett, Benjamin Bell, Samuel Blair, and Charles Hays. July Term 1826.

Page 28   Martin Smith's children land divided.
Sept 8, 1826   The Commissioners met 25 July 1826 to lay off and set apart to the heirs of Martin Smith one fifth part of 200 acres of land belonging to the heirs of Thomas Smith, deceased, and to which the said children are entitled by a Deed of Conveyance from Stephen West and Elizabeth his wife one of the heirs. Bordered by David Adams and Robert B. Currey's line and containing 40 acres. Signed by Andrew Casselman, Jeremiah Terry, Philip Pipkin, David Adams, and William Windle. July Term 1826.

Page 28   Will of Newton E. Burnham, deceased, of Davidson County.
Sept 8, 1826   To my beloved wife Polly Burnham during her natural life all my lands, negroes and other estate whatever for her support and her children. To my children Sally and William Burnham and their heirs after the death of my wife all the lands and

negroes and other estate. I appoint my said wife sole executrix. This 14 July 1826. Wit: John Waters and William Crockett. July Term 1826.

Page 29   Will of James Mulherrin, deceased.
Sept 8, 1826   I wish as much of my plantation on which I live on sold to lift the mortgage on it which is about 300 acres will do. The land borders Mr. Murry's line, Capt. Sample, Cumberland River, and to where my son Charles lived. I owe debts to Mr. Ridley and Maj. John Buchanan which I wish to have (paid). I have 822 acres of land in Smith County, part of the Patsy Robertson tract which I wish to be sold to pay debts. I have or will have 500 acres of land warrants which I wish sold and have 1200 acres of land in Logan County, Kentucky to be sold to pay debts. If my wife should incline to buy the negro man peter and can do so with the proceeds of the crops or any balance may be left from the sale of the property before mentioned. I wish her to do so and keep him during her natural life or widowhood or set him free. I give to my wife the use of the house, outhouses, plantation &c and to provide for the use of my grandchildren that is left. My only child Charles Mulherrin who is incapable of taking care of himself and he would squander it without benefit to his children and much to his own injury considering these things that he has four children yet to be provided for without the fostering of a mother and therefore may be said to be without father or mother and believing it to be my duty to provide for them as it is my in my power. I wish the remaining part of the land I now live on to be divided into two equal parts, my grandson James to have that half which incoudes my present residence and the orchard and that half of the tract my grandson George is to have which extends near the mouth of the creek and as there is a tract of land between Judge Overton and myself in the Forked Deer Country upwards of 300 acres of which will belong to me, I wish same to be equally divided between my two grandsons Charles and Henry. My wife to have remaining property. I appoint John Overton formerly Judge and my wife Margaret Mulherrin, executor and executrix. This 3 June 1822. Wit: Philip L. Lovely and Elizabeth Broughton.
Codicil: I wish to sell what may be necessary towards the mouth of the creek the part including the house, plantation and orchard for the accommodation of my wife even if my Forked Deer land should be sold which I perfer to sell all the place which I am allotted. Wit: Philip L. Lovely and Elizabeth Broughton. July Term 1826.

Page 31   Will of John Tate, Sr., deceased, of Davidson County.
Sept 9, 1826   To my beloved wife Rebecca Tate during her natural lifetime, all my estate both real and personal to her only benefit and she may sell any of the estate that she sees proper and the proceeds to be equally divided among my heirs, also give to her $240.00 to do with as she pleases. At my wife's death the estate is to be sold and proceeds to be divided among my heirs having respect however to what each of them has received from me and deduct unto be made accordingly. Susanna Done(?) a horse, bed and saddle, to John Tate 66 acres of land lying on Suggs Creek whereon he now lives and a cow. To Zachariah Tate one mare and cow. To Sally Jamison a bed and a cow. To William H. Tate a cow. To Zedekiah Tate a cow. To Jane Fuqua a cow and bed and $20.00. Rebecca Tate a cow, bed and $20.00. To Nancy Brooks a cow, bed and #25.00. I appoint Zedekiah Tate, executor. This 21 Dec 1822. Wit: William Creel and Z.T. Robertson. July Term 1826.

Page 31   Will of Elizabeth Coots, deceased, of Davidson County.
Sept 11, 1826   To my beloved sister Lavinia Boyd 75 acres left to me by my father John Coots, deceased, and the same wherein he lived at the time of his death and the said parcel of land to remain as it now does in the possession of my mother Mary Coots and my sister Letitia Coots during their natural lives then to descend to my sister Lavinia Boyd and her lives. Also to Lavinia Boyd my mare valued at $200.00 to be paid at the death of my mother Mary Coots out of the personal property of said Lavinia Boyd $100.00 to be paid to my sister Polly Harris and the remaining $100.00 to my sister Esther Dickinson. My negro man Frank to my mother Mary Coots and at her death to my sister Lavinia Boyd. The undivided amount of the negroes in possession of my mother Mary Coots as left to me by my father John Coots, deceased, to my sisters Polly Harris and Esther Dickinson. Remainder of the estate to be equally divided among my sisters Polly Harris, Esther Dickinson and Rebecca Houser and Lavinia Boyd. I appoint Jason Thompson and my brother John Boyd, sole executors. This 13 July 1825. Ait: Andrew Wilson, Jason Thomas and Jason H. Thompson.
Codicil: 5 Dec 1825 - The 75 acres that I bequeathed to Levinia Boyd, I revoke, and I now will and bequeath that my brother and sister John Boyd and Lavinia Boyd be put into full

175

possession of said land at the death of my mother Mary or Molly Coots. Wit: A. Wilson and John Thompson. July Term 1826.

Page 33   Sale of estate of Benjamin Pritchard, Sr., deceased.
Sept 11, 1826   Made by Benjamin Pritchard, Jr., executor. Several items listed. Two negroes to the widow of the deceased. To Joseph Prichard a negro man. To Enoch Prichard a negro man. To William Prichard yoke of oxen. To John Berry a negro man. To S(illegible) a negro man. To John Prichard one negro girl. To Polly Prichard a negro girl. To Sally Prichard 36 bushels of corn and one lot of wheat. July Tern 1826.

Page 34   Inventory of estate of Nicholas Crossway, deceased.
Sept 12, 1826   Several items listed. This 28 July 1826. July Term 1826.

Page 34   Inventory of estate of John Tate, deceased.
Sept 12, 1826   A receipt from William Tate for $100.00 received as part of his legacy. Several items including a Bible. Signed by Zedekiah Tate, executor. July Term 1826.

Page 35   Inventory of estate of Thomas Hooper, deceased.
Sept 12, 1826   Several items listed. This 8 Apr 1826. Signed by William Lovell, executor. Also one note on Willoughby Douge and an account on William Rasberry. 17 July 1826. July Term 1826.

Page 35   Sale of estate of James Knox, deceased, of Nashville.
Sept 13, 1826   May 25, 1826. Persons listed, to wit, Nathaniel A. McNairy, Mrs. Knox, Mr. McGehee, and Mr. Martin. Joseph Anderson, admr. July Term 1826.

Page 36   Inventory of estate of Thomas H. Perkins, deceased, of Davidson
Sept 14, 1826   County. Persons listed, to wit, Nicholas Perkins, Jr., Sheriff of Williamson County, Thomas H. and Daniel Perkins, executors of Nicholas Perkins, Nicholas Seals and Nicholas Perkins, executors of Peter Perkins, Thomas L. Trotter. July 26, 1826. July Term 1826.

Page 36   Inventory of estate of John E. Linn, deceased.
Sept 14, 1826   July 8, 1826. Several items listed. Signed by Elmore Walker, admr. July Term 1826.

Page 36   Inventory of estate of Henry W. Sturdevant, deceased.
Sept 14, 1826   26 July 1826. Several items listed including a note on William Payne. Lucy Sturdevant, admrx. July Term 1826.

Page 37   Sale of estate of Pembroke Cartwright, deceased.
Sept 14, 1826   Made by Samuel L. Wharton, executor. Persons listed, to wit, James Hit (Hitt), David McGuire, Solomon McGuire, Douglas Puckett, Isham Butterworth, John Porter, Martin Pierce, Thomas Cartwright, Elizabeth Cartwright, James Cartwright, Mrs. Martin, William Porter, Isaac Newland, B. Thomas, Thomas Davis, William Boothe, John Wray, James Faulkner, Lewis Basye, Isaac McCaslin, Benjamin Bell, Robert Bates, William Williams, A. Cartwright, William Shaw, William Payne, L. Baker, A. Grizzard, Jas. Hunt, Isaac Walton, George Watkins, William Watkins, James Newland, John Beazley, John Cunningham, Henry Davis, John Orr, A. Cunningham, R.J. Williams, Jas. Cunningham. This 22 July 1826. July Term 1826.

Page 37   Inventory of estate of Joshua Cutchen, deceased.
Sept 15, 1826   On 21 Apr 1826 by Joseph Kimbro, admr. Several items listed. Persons listed, to wit, Susan Cutchen and Joseph Kimbro. Sale on 2 May 1826 at the late dwelling of said Joshua, deceased. July Term 1826.

Page 38   Sale of estate of Robert Cartwright, deceased.
Sept 15, 1826   On 9 Mar 1826. Persons listed, to wit, James Cartwright, Jas. Cunningham, Jno. Cunningham, John Wray, David Roulston, J. Newland, Thomas Cartwright, Elizabeth Cartwright, Enoch Cunningham, Enoch P. Connell, John Adams, Ambrose Grizzard, John Pierce, David Ralston and William Shaw. Thomas Cartwright, executor. July Term

1826.

Page 38   Henry R. Cartmell of Richard Boyd.
Sept 15, 1826   I, Richard Boyd of Davidson County sold unto H.R. Cartmell of
Nashville, a certain piece or part of Lot No. 10 fronting on Market Street, adjoining Joseph
T. Elliston's brickhouse, on 1st July 1825. Test: R. Weakley. July Term 1826.

Page 38   Inventory of estate of Henry Graves, deceased.
Sept 15, 1826   Eighteen negroes and several items listed. Persons listed, to wit,
Edmond Townson of Alabama, Richard C(illegible), S.T. Allen, Thomas Waller, J. Howlett a
Constable, Thomas Conley, John Puckett, Moses Drew, Abel Nancy, Mrs. Rhoda Goodrich,
and Rovert Ward. Signed by Sally W. Graves, executrix. July Term 1826.

Page 39   Division of negroes of Dr. William Dickson, deceased, of Davidson
Sept 15, 1826   County. The slaves to be divided between this two daughters
Cornelia Ann Dickson now Cornelia Ann Slith(?) and Mary F. Dickson. This 2 May 1826.
Edward Ward and H. Petway and Benjamin J. Jones, Commissioners. July Term 1826.

Page 40   Inventory of estate of James Maxwell, deceased.
Sept 16, 1826   Several negroes and other items listed including notes on Solomon
Clark, Micajah Fly, Frederick Harwell, David Maxwell, Daniel A. Dunham, John Nichols,
William E. Anderson, Jno. B. Craighead, Mr. Paine, George Woodward, and Jesse Woodward.
David Maxwell, admr. July Term 1826.

Page 40   Sale of property of Henry Graves, deceased.
Sept 18, 1826   Persons listed, to wit, Sally Graves, Isaac Hudson, John Morgan,
David Graves, James Love, Isaac W. Brooks, John Puckett, John Broughton, Leonard Keeling,
Nelson P. Carter, George E. Harris, Henry Ray, William D. Williams, Moses B. Fraser, David
T. Hatch, Robert Wood, John Kernel, William Murphy, John G. Wilborn, and H. Hill. Sally W.
Graves, admrx. July Term 1826.

Page 41   Inventory of estate of Robert Vick, deceased.
Sept 18, 1826   Taken on 5 May 1826 by Wilson Crockett, admr. Persons listed,
to wit, John B. Demumbrom, M.L. Gower, Reuben Wallace, Joel Vick, Silas Equals, Wilson
Crockett, William Richardson, Milley Vick, Isaac Anderson, Elizabeth Biggs, Jacob Binkley,
Frederick Gulledge, Thomas C. Smith, William Fuqua, Nathan Bennett, and Timothy Durat,
Hardy D. Felts, R.S.B. Hollice, Jos. Vick, Josiah Vick, Simon Everett, and George Hail. July
Term 1826.

Page 42   Inventory of sale of estate of James Maxwell, deceased.
Sept 20, 1826   Persons listed, to wit, Richard Johnson, E. Raworth, Jesse
Woodward, Robert Smith, James R. Bosley, Charles Bosley, William Grubbs, Jesse Wharton,
John Gillespie, William W. Brown, John Shute, William D. Cobler, D.A. Dunham, W.
Woodruff, Hugh Swaney, Edwin Smith, Jos. Pinkerton, Lewis Joslin, William Thomas, F.
McGavock, David Maxwell, Henry Wade, John Corbit, George Woodward, George Ament, A.
Tucker, I. Erwin, Durant & Jackson, Samuel Davidson, Philip Campbell, Sol. Clark, N.
Stevenson, John Logan, J.W. Harton, David Whiteside, John Nichols, John P. Harrison,
Stephen Cantrell, Adam G. Goodlett, James Scott, John Harding, A. Whitson, J. Morris, L.
McGavock, H.F. Newell, A. Waits, David McGavock, George P. Clark, W. McCann, and Mr.
Fly. David Maxwell, admr. July Term 1826.

Page 45   Patsey Page, her dower laid off.
Sept 22, 1826   Jurors met to lay off and set apart to Patsey Page, widow of
Absalom Page, deceased, her dower in a tract of land on which said Absalom Page lived
immediately before his death, of 287 acres bordering the north bank of Cumberland River
sixty two poles below the mouth of Wells Creek, a lane, a spring, the public road leading
from Clarksville intersects with the first lane, Smith's corner, and Brooks corner, including
the mansion house or houses and all out houses, spring house and one half of the spring.
Next they layed off to Patsey Page her dower in the tract of 105 3/4 acres nearly adjoining
the other tract, borders Thomas Talbot's corner, David Earhart's tract, and David Parkers'
line. This 19 Feb 1824. Benjamin Hyde, Mark R. Cockrill, Philip Shute, Jonas Menifee,
James Clemmons, Edwin Smith, Paul Vaughn, Martin Smith, Jacob C. Smith, John Rains, Jr.,

George Stull, and Samuel Stull.   Plat on page 46.   Samuel Shannon, executor of Absalom Page's will.   Apr Term 1826.

Page 47   Division of land of Benjamin Pritchett, Sr., deceased.
Sept 23, 1826   To William Prichard the dwelling house and farm where the descend formerly lived.   The land bordering a 640 acre tract of land granted by the State of North Carolina to Oliver Smith and conveyed to John Demoss to the decedent by deed dated 21 Jan 1817 and recorded in Davidson County Book M, page 132 on 4 Mar 1818, crosses south Harpeth &c.   Also laid off out of William Prichard's part 12 acres of land to Joanna Prichard, widow of the deceased, including the dwelling house where he formerly lived, marked in the plat A. Benjamin Prichard's begins at William Prichard's beginning corner and crosses south harpeth, borders Smith's line above the mill being Adam Berry's corner, and Elias Dobson's line.   Containing 322 acres being part of the deed from Demoss to said Prichard. We have also agreeable to a provision in well land off out of Benjamin Prichard's ¼art 10 acres of land to Sally Prichard borders Elias Dobson and marked in the plat B.   This 5 June 1826. Signed by John Davis, William Henry, Hugh Allison, Elias Dobson, David Moss, and A.H.Berry.   July Term 1826.

Page 49   Inventory of estate of John O. Ewing, deceased, of Davidson
Sept 29, 1826   County.   Several items listed including two Bibles, and a list of notes, viz, Mr. Adams brother-in-law of Hobbs, Mr. Almond a bricklayer, Col. Robert Armstrong, Dr. Christian Allen, Capt. William Armstrong, Dr. Robert T. Allen, Isaac Allen, Jeremiah Allen, deceased, John Boyd a painter, Henry Brown of near McMinnville, William Brown, Moses Bennett, T(illegible) Bradley, Jacob Bondurant, Mrs. Armstead Boyd, Samuel Bell, John N. Blankenship, William Boyd (of John), Moses Brown (a mulatto), Blackman (near Grundys), Col. Robert Baylor, Richard Cornelius, Michael Campbell, Elizabeth Criddle, Mr. Cothran of Rev. Whitsell, Charles Canady of Gen. Winchester, Lewis Carlton, Abner Cowgill, deceased, Mr. William Carroll, John Cattler (Cutler), John Connell, Irwin Cutler, Andrew Caselman, Richard Cotham, John Campbell, Rev. Thomas Craighead, Richard Clinton, Widow Campbell, James Campbell, David (a black man of Phil Thomas), Enoch Douge, Peter Douge, William Docherty of Hawkins, Mr. Davis of Thomas Edmondson, Maj. David Dunn, Dr. William R. Davenport of Gallatin, Robert Davis at Hoovers, Mr. Duff (a painter), Addison East, George M. Esseleman, Drs. Eldridge and Topp, Ezekiel Fitzhugh, Francis Farmer, John Folwell, Dr. Charles G. Fisher, James Fay, Isaac Folwell, Richard Garrett, Mr. Grant of Hamilton, Mr. Garrett of Thompson, Umphrey Guinn, Mr. Greer (Harpeth), Mr. Gill (a son-in-law of Dobbs), John Gowen, Sr., Mr. Greer (of Benjamin Anthony), widow Rhoda Goodrich, James Gould (of Hoggatt), George Gross, Dr. A.G. Goodlett, Abner B. Hawkins, Thomas Hardiman, Churchill Hooper, Henry Hall, John C. Hall, Charles M. Hall, Mr. Harris (of Ament), Edward D. Hobbs, William Howlett, Dr. George B. Hopson, Richard Hanks, James Hooper, Ceasar Hooper, Mr. Hamlett (of Dobbs), Mrs. Hightower, William Hubble, Richard Hyde, William R. Harmer, Dr. Jos. Hodge, Ezra Holsted, Drs. Hickman and McKinney, Dr. Henry Holmes, Thomas Haywood, Hamblin, Andrew Hays, Oakley Jones, Sarah Jefferson, Joseph Johnson (Lebanon), Mrs. Jackson widow of Craven Jackson, Mr. John Natchez Duke Sumner, Josiah Johnson, Thomas James, Maj. Jeffrey, Isaac Erwin, Drs. L.M. and S.H. Jordon, Thomas A. Jones, Reuben Kempt (at Bosleys), Mr. Kirkwood, Mr. Kirkland, Dr. William P. King, Walter Keeble, Mr. Loving (old man), William Livingston, Levin Shoemaker, Joshua Laurence, Capt. Lockhart, Sam Malloy, Cornelius McGraw, Hany (Henry) Malloy, Maj. Shaw (of Washn. estate), Dr. John Maxey, Dr. Boyd McNairy, David McGavock, John McNairy, Esq., Jehu Meddows, Benjamin Manning, Dr. Manning (of Huntsville), H. Miles, Maj. Thomas Murray, Miss Mitchell (of Rogersville), William Norris (near Sq. Bryants), Mr. Nelson Marsh (of Louisville), Nashville Thespian Society, widow Norman, Martin C. Harrow, Miss Nancy Owen, Mr. Owen ((illegible) County), John Phyzer, Dr. Granville Pierce, Mrs. Sarah Priestley, Eldridge N. Phipps, Gideon Parker (of McManners), Matthew Patterson, Dr. Charles Perkins, Dr. James R. Putman, Capt. Perry, Peter (of J. Grundy), Moses Patterson, Richard Phipps, Mr. Quinton (of George Crockett), Jones Read, Alexander Richardson, John F. Rhyal, Miss Ridley (of widow Elliston), Jonathan Rucker, Wright Ramsey, Silas Rainey, Drs. Roberts , Caldwell and Call, Robert Reaves, Mr. Redding, Samuel Read, Rachel (of Caswell), Marmaduke Reddit, Jacob C. Smith, Martin Smith, Ewing Spear, Moses Spear, Drewry Stull, Benjamin Sherwood, Mrs. Smith (mother of Martin), John Sperry, John Sharp, Mr. Sullivan (butcher), William Smith (gambler), Molly Stratton (Water Street), Moses Stevens, John F. Stump, Arville Shelby, Dr. Thomas Sappington, Mrs. Scudder, Christopher Stump, Lewis Sturdevant, Mrs. H. Temple, Mr. Turner (of H(illegible) and Thomas), John Thurston (of Judge

Campbell), Maj. Robert Turner, William H. Turner, Dr. Thornton, Dr. Dee Thomas, Henry Terrace, Henry Vanpett, widow Vaulx, William Vaulx, John S. V(illegible), Mr. Vanute, David Vaughn, William Wordley, Jesse Wharton, Mr. White, Joshua White, George Wilson, James M. Wilson, David Windle, Mr. Willis (of Rev. Dobbs), Thomas Waller, E. Whitney, Mr. Watson (of Stout), Mr. Wilson a carpenter, William Washington, William Whitsell, William Willis (of Sneed), Dr. Samuel Watkins, Dr. John M. Waters, Mr. Wilson a blacksmith, Capt. John Young, Mr. Yarbrough (of D. McGavock), Norvill & Pitcher & Jamison, Francis Morris, John Demoss, William Trippard, Nelson Thornton, William Garner, Jonas Menifee, Brown & Goodlett, Richard Joslin, John Criddle, Levin Watson, Samuel Shannon, William Bosworth, David R. Cole, William W. Goodwin, John Harrison, Mr. Reynolds (of Mrs. Boyd), Sophia Myers, Mr. Beaver (near Reads), Abraham H. Smith, Robertson & Elliott, Randal McGavock, Jr., Mr. Burnham, George Foster, S. Jefferson, William Kent, and Cox & Waggoner. Nathan Ewing, admr. July Term 1826.

Page 53   Ann Brannon and Eleanor Brannon of John Brannon.
Oct 3, 1826   We, John Brannon of Davidson County, am bound unto Ann Brannon and Eleanor Brannon of Davidson County for $60.00. This 5 May 1825. Condition is that Ann and Eleanor Brannon, executorx, admrs are deeded 10 acres of land lying on Beech Creek joining Martha Brannon. Signed by John Brannon, executor. Apr Term 1826.

Page 54   Inventory of estate of James Mulherrin, deceased.
Dec 11, 1826   Taken 16 June 1826. Twelve negroes and several items listed including a large Bible. Margaret Mulherrin, executrix. Oct Term 1826.

Page 55   Settlement of estate of David Cartwright, deceased.
Dec 12, 1826   Made with Samuel Seay, executor &c of George Wharton, deceased. Notes on Elizabeth Cartwright and Dempsey Powell, Pembroke Cartwright, Samuel L. Wharton, R. Farquharson, Robert Cartwright, Sr., and David Cartwright. Oct Term 1826.

Page 56   Inventory of estate of John Kellum, deceased.
Dec 12, 1826   Made on Oct 16, 1826. Several items listed including a bond on William Russell. Signed by Martha Kellum, admrx. Oct Term 1826.

Page 56   Account of sale of Reuben S. Thornton, deceased.
Dec 12, 1826   Made on 15 Sept 1826. Persons listed, to wit, H. Cummins, Mrs. Thornton, William Thompson, Everett Owen, John Fitzhugh, James Owen, William Ramsey, J.W. Ramsey, Demsey Corbett, William McAlpin, John Swain, William Ballew, Robert Black, James Corbitt, Jno. Scruggs, Jno. Brockman, Jabez Owen, Dr. Patterson, George Chadwell, J.W. Howlett, John Watson, Edmond Hyde, George Foster, Charles Branch, Thomas Boles, Jere Burnett, Benj. Turberville, Albert Rives, William Corbitt, P.C. Rives, Nathan Owen, Joseph H. McEwing, and Nelson Fields. J.H. Howlett, admr. Oct Term 1826.

Page 57   Inventory of estate of Benjamin Bibb, deceased.
Dec 13, 1826   Made on Oct 26, 1826. Several items listed including a Family Bible. Signed by Susannah Bibb, admrx and William Ramsey, Jr., Admr. Oct Term 1826.

Page 58   Will of Sally Hays, deceased, of Davidson County.
Dec 13, 1826   To my daughter Nancy Camel the bed and furniture that my mother left me, also give to my two sons Robert Hays and John Hays the whole of the land I own. The balance of my estate and all I possess to be equally divided among all my children after all my just debts are paid. It is my will that Nanna shall be free at my death and live on my land her lifetime and my son Robert to take care of her. Wit: Samuel Steele and Andrew Melvin. Oct Term 1826.

Page 58   Polly Thornton, her support laid off.
Dec 13, 1826   An order to lay off and set apart to Polly Thornton, widow and relict of Reuben S. Thornton, deceased, one years support for her family. Several items listed. This 15 Sept 1826. test: William Ramsey, J.P., William Ewing, James Condon, and Robert Scales. Oct Term 1826.

Page 59   Will of Samuel Chapman, deceased, of Nashville.
Dec 14, 1826   To Harrison Harper and Polly Harper, children of William Harper,
deceased, a part of Lot No. 180 in town of Nashville with the houses and improvements
thereon which was conveyed to me by their father by deed dated 12 Dec 1821 reserving to
Mrs. Elizabeth Harper, their mother, the use and occupation of one half of said ground and
the house she now occupies during her natural life. To Hiram White, son of Lewis White, a
part of said Lot No. 180 in Nashville which was conveyed to me by Elizabeth Harper,
executrix of William Harper, deceased, by deed dated 21 July 1823. To Nelson Raymon, son
of Nicholas Raymon, deceased, two Lots No. 11 and 12 in the town of Haysborough with the
improvements. To Samuel Chapman, Jr., son of Thomas Chapman formerly residing in the
State of New York, if living at the time of my death, and Lot No. 34 in the college land
adjoining Nashville and one half of Lot No. 42 in college lands, and the rest and residue of
my estate after my debts are paid and the above legatees I give and bequeath all the
property hereby given to him to his brothers or if they be dead to his and their heirs to be
equally divided between them. I appoint my friends Robert B. Curry, Martin New and Henry
Ewing of Nashville my executors. This 14 May 1825. Wit: Nathan Ewing and W.W. Goodwin.
Oct Term 1826.

Page 60   Inventory of estate of Elizabeth Coots, deceased.
Dec 14, 1826   75 acres of land, one negro man, one mare, eight head of cattle,
note on Robert Reaves, and other items. John Boyd, executor. Oct Term 1826.

Page 60   Inventory of estate of Edmond Owen, deceased.
Dec 14, 1826   Several items listed. Adam Hope, admr and Mary Owen, admrx.
Oct Term 1826.

Page 61   Will of Charles M. Wright, deceased.
Dec 14, 1826   To my beloved wife Polly Wright two beds and furniture and
several other household items. Several items to his beloved wife and James Hollis Hager
Wright equally divided and at her death to go to James Hollis Hager Wright for his use. To
my wife my bay mare and at her death to James Hollis Hager Wright. To my beloved wife
Polly Wright the east end of my plantation where I now live, the old improved part and
lastly at her death the land above named is to go to James Hollis Hager Wright. To my
beloved wife Polly Wright $100.00 in silver for her use during her life and at her death to
James H.H. Wright, at my death the money that is faound owning my estate and the
proceeds of $105.00 due me from Capt. Wilcher Bandy to be applied to paying all my just
debts and remainder to be divided between my beloved wife and James H.H. Wright.
Remainder to be divided among my children, Polly Hope, James Wright, Charles Wright,
Rebecca Cook, Jane Hager Hollis Wright, Elizabeth Umphries. This 24 Dec 1826. I
appointed Abe Gleaves and Samuel Steel, executors and Josiah D. Green. Oct Term 1826.

Page 62   Will of Peter Booth, deceased.
Dec 18, 1826   This 1 Sept 1826. Thomas Poole, Harrison Whitfield and Robert
Simpson came before me, John Davis, an acting Justice of the Peace, for the purpose of
proving the noncupative will of said Peter Booth who departed this life yesterday August the
thirty first and said that peter Booth at the time he made his noncupative will was of sound
mind, it being on Monday last the 28th August. To his cousin William Hobbs three negroes.
To his cousin Polly Hobbs $1000.00 in cash. To his sister Martha Porch the plantation and
tract of land on which he then lived with the crops growing and the balance of his negroes
and all and every other part of property not disposed of. He also named that henry
Whitefield was to take possession of his farm and negroes and to finish and house the crops
for which he was to receive $100.00 out of the crops. Also there was a tract of land taken
up in partnership between him and John Davis which he wanted a right made to. Signed by
Harrison Whitfield, Robert Simpson and Thomas Poole. Oct Term 1826.

Page 63   Settlement of estate of Willis L. Shumate, deceased.
Dec 19, 1826   Made by Jeremiah Ezell and Cary Felts, admrs. Several vouchers
listed. Notes and payments on the following persons, to wit, P. Scott and T.G. Bradford. 20
May 1826. George W. Charlton, M. Murphy and Henry White, Jr., Commissioners. Oct Term
1826.

Page 64   Inventory and sale of estate of Edward Sanderson, deceased.
Dec 22, 1826   Made on 22 Feb 1826 on Whites Creek, Davidson County. Persons listed, to wit, J.J. Hinton, B. Thomas, C. Brooks, R. Taylor, M.M. Hinton, E. Sanderson, T. Taylor, M.L. Findley, E. Smith, J. Maxey, A. Ray, J.W. Brooks, M. Fordham, J. Earhart, M. Gleaves, L. Scruggs, William Gill, ?. Nicholas, H. Seat, S. Elam, S. Wharton, J. McGavock, T. Morris, Thomas Dill, W. Wright, P. Clinard, P. Bashaw, J.W. Brooks, Jno. Brooks, Jno. Faulks, William Jones, Jas. Smith, J. Alexander, J. Scruggs, J. Yarborough, E. Anderson, H. Combs, W. Walker, Ed. Smith, R. Bates, Eli Smith, Jno. Turner, D.B. Love, R. Williams, Jno. Beauchan, A. Birdwell, J.E. Turner, and N.H. Robertson. William Faulkner, admr. Oct Term 1826.

Page 65   Sally Shumate, dower.
Dec 26, 1826   A dower to be layed off for Sally Shumate, widow and relict of Willis L. Shumate, deceased, land bordering land conveyed to James Glasgow, Floods boundary. This 22 Sept 1826. Signed by Joseph Burnett, James Pigg, William Vaulx, Godfrey Shelton, William P. Campbell, Samuel Blair, John Johnson, Owen D. W(illegible), Ralph S. McFaddin, George Peay, William Burnett, and Thomas Johnson, jurors. Oct Term 1826.

Page 65   Inventory of estate of Neal McDaniel, deceased.
Dec 26, 1826   Several items listed. William Faulkner, admr. Oct Term 1826.

Page 66   Inventory of estate of Newton E. Burnham, deceased.
Dec 26, 1826   Made Oct 26, 1826. Several items listed including one gold watch. Polly Burnham, admrx. Oct Term 1826.

Page 66   Inventory of estate of Philip Walker, deceased.
Dec 26, 1826   Made on 18 Oct 1826 by William H. Hamblin, admr. Several items listed including a bond on Enios Walker and a due bill on Samuel Hope. Oct Term 1826.

Page 66   Settlement of estate of Francis Wright, deceased.
Dec 26, 1826   Made by J.H. Hewlett, admr. Persons listed, to wit, Jno. A. Ewing, William Parkman, Wyatt Parkman, Nathan Ewing, Thomas Conley, and William Ramsey. Oct Term 1826.

Page 67   Negroes divided of estate of Frederick Stump, deceased.
Dec 27, 1826   In 1822 the executors proceeded to divide the estate between the families of John Stump and Christopher Stump, sons of Frederick Stump, after paying over to Barbara Cox, a daughter of said Frederick, a legacy left her two negroes. Left to John Stump 30 negroes, also left to Christopher Stump 30 negroes. John Stump bid off several items sold. The balance was set apart to Christopher Stump. This 27 June 1826. Signed by Philip Shute, Jno. Criddle and Thomas Shute. Oct Term 1826.

Page 67   Settlement of estate of Robert Williams, deceased.
Dec 27, 1826   Made by Nathan Williams, admr's report, viz, attendance on his father during his sickness, say eight weeks @$3.00 per wk $24.00. Clerk's fee for administration bond $1.00. To coffin and burial $6.00 - $7.00. Credit $31.00. By amount of sale pr account $6.50. By cash on hand at his death $22.00. $28.50. Balance due admr $2.50. Robert Hewitt and G.G. Washington, J.P. Oct Term 1826.

Page 68   Inventory of estate of Charles Wright, Sr., deceased.
Dev 27, 1826   To wit, 58 acres of land devised to James H. Hollis Wright also two notes on James H. Hollis Wright. $40.00 in hands of Absalom Gleaves to James H.H. Wright. Also several other items devised to James H.H. Wright. Absalom Gleaves, executor. This 25 Oct 1826. Oct Term 1826.

Page 68   Account of estate of Andrew Davis, deceased.
Dec 27, 1826   Made by Jacob D. Donelson, executor. Persons listed, to wit, McDaniel & Scruggs, J. Trimble, Light Nowlin, Nathan Ewing, John Bell, Nancy Davis, Thomas Gleaves, John T. Dismukes, B. Butterworth, William Donelson, B. Davis, Greenwood Payne, Alexander Dunham, J.W. Crunk, Henry Boothe, S. Donelson, and Thomas Cartright. Each legatee $723.83. Oct 18, 1826. "We have received fourteen hundred and forty seven dollars and 66/100 as guardian for Hardin Davis and Minton Davis having been appointed such

in the County of Bedford, Tennessee, 18 Oct 1826". Signed by Light Nowlin and S. Bigham. Oct Term 1826.

Page 69   Sale of estate of Joseph Philips, deceased.
Dec 27, 1826   Persons listed, to wit, M.R. Cockrill, William Williams, D.M. Sumner, Thomas Cartwright, P. Bashaw, R. Patterson, William Hinton, H. Seat, M. Pearce, G. Wharton, R. Wilson, Jabez White, William D. Philips, Jno. Lanier, John Pearce, John E. Turner, Thomas Stratton, Jos. F. Williams, J. Scruggs, F. Ford, John G. Porter, D. McGavock, J. Marshall, William Temple, Jos. McGavock, Severn Donelson, Jonas SH(illegible), S. Donelson, A. Ray, D. Robertson, John Patterson, B. Bashaw, D. Ralston, M. Gleaves, John McGavock, E.P. Sumner, M.P. Walker, M. Redding, F. McKay, and S. Hope. Signed by William and J.F. Williams. Several notes, viz, M. Bell, F. McKay, M. Horn, Jno. Earhart, J. Hooper, J. Marshall, W.D. Philips, V. Winfrey, J. Dickinson, N.H. Robertson, H. Harmon, E.P. Sumner, J. Hinton, E. Benoit, Jos. F. Williams, and William Williams. Oct Term 1826.

Page 70   Settlement of estate of Thomas H. Perkins, deceased.
Dec 28, 1826   Made by Robert Scales. Persons listed, to wit, Nathan Ewing & Brown, Peter Pinkston, Mary N. Perkins, Jonathan Hill, Robert B. Curry, Gordon & Walker, Murray & Ewing, Dr. Goodlett, Jno. C. Pryor, Dickinson & Cooper, A.M. Harwood, Capt. Jas. Walker, Const. Scales, Nicholas Perkins, William Smith, Martin Adams, William G. Childress, Thomas Edmiston, Dr. Smith, E.H. Foster, P. Craddock, J.B. Houston, Joel Waller; Thomas Hardeman, Richard Hanks, Edmond Reaves, Sheriff for D.M. Gee, Clerk of Williamson County, Jonathan Cooper, N.P. Perkins, H.R. Hill, T.J. Hord, Thomas G. Bradford, R.A. Higginbotham, Jno. P. Perkins, Jas. H. Maury, Gibbs & Fogg, F.B. Fogg, John Overton, N.L. Hardeman, W. Tannehill, M. Barrow, Thomas H. Perkins executor of Nicholas Perkins, Daniel Perkins, John D. Edney, and John Boyles. D.A. Dunham and Watthew Barrow, Commissioners. 24 Oct 1826. Oct Term 1826.

Page 72   Division of land to Albert and Orville Shelby.
Dec 28, 1826   Land plotted on page 72. No. 1 to Albert Shelby for 150 acres bordering Cumberland River on the south. No. 2 to Orville Shelby for 195 acres bordering on west by Albert Shelby and on the south by Cumberland River. The division of one half of 640 acres of land bequeathed by David Shelby, deceased, in his Last Will and Testament to his sons Orville Shelby and Albert Shelby. This 15 Aug 1826. E.S. Hall, J.P. Signed by Samuel Weakley, Thomas Crutcher, M.B. Lewis, D. McGavock, and R. Weakley. Oct Term 1826.

Page 73   Rachel Boyd, widow dower.
Dec 28, 1826   Plat on page 73. 176 acres was laid off for Rachel Boyd, widow of Richard Boyd, deceased, out of a tract of 528 acres, including the mansion house. The dower borders on the bluff of Cumberland River and the mouth of Overalls Creek. This 5 Oct 1826. Signed by Samuel Weakley, Surveyor, S.B. Davidson, John Hobson, Luke Hill, John F. Oneal, Robert Hill, Johnson Vaughn, Beal Bossley, Robert Goodlet, Henry Lytle, Andrew Word, and John Bosley. Oct Term 1826.

Page 73   Division of land of Daniel Binkley, deceased.
Dec 28, 1826   Made on 31 July 1826, the Commissioners met at the house of Mrs. Binkley and surveyed and set apart to each of the heirs of Daniel Binkley, deceased, consisting of 150 acres of land. Lot No. 1 to Ann Strong being on west banks of Stones River containing 20 acres and 125 poles. Lot No. 2 to Anthony Binkley on the bank of Stones River containing 17 acres and 80 poles. Lot No. 3 to Franklin Binkley of 11 acres and 25 poles on bank of Stones River. Lot No. 4 to Almeada Binkley of 13 acres and 35 poles on bank of Stones River. Lot No. 5 to Isaac Binkley containing 15 acres and 15 poles on bank of Stones River. Lot No. 6 to Mary Earhart of 15 acres and 15 poles on bank of Stones River. Lot No. 7 to John Binkley of 12 acres and 110 poles on bank of Stones River. Lot No. 8 to William Binkley of 12 acres and 110 poles on bank of Stones River. Lot No. 9 to Mahala Binkley of 10 acres on banks of Stones River. Lot No. 10 to Nelly Binkley of 10 acres on banks of Stones River. Lot No. 11 to Martha Binkley of 12 acres on banks of Stones River. This 31 July 1826. Joseph Burnett, George W. Charlton, James Baker, Hollis Wright, and John Hall. Oct Term 1826.

182

Page 75   Division of Lots in Nashville of estate of Richard C. Cross,
Dec 26, 1826   deceased. Plat on page 75. Lots on Broad Street and College
Street and Market Street. Lot No. 1 to Louisa Gordon of 45 feet on Market Street, Lot No.
2 to R. White of 80 feet on Market Street, Lot No. 3 to John Gordon of (not given) feet on
Market Street, one Lot unnumbered on Market Street, Lot No. 4 to Dolly Gordon for (not
given) feet on Market Street, Lot No. 5 to William Gordon of (not given) feet on Market
Street, Lot No. 6 to Richard Gordon for 58 feet on Market Street, 20 feet undivided on
Market Street and M(blank) line, 20 feet undivided on M(blank) line and College Street, Lot
No. 6 to Richard Gordon, part of Lot No. 6, on College Street, Lot No. 7 to T.J. Gordon of
(not given) feet on College Street, Lot No. 8 to M. Holmes of (not given) feet, Lot No. 9 to
P. Gordon of (not given) feet on College Street, Lot No. 10 to T.L. Gordon of (not given)
feet, Hoover Lot on College Street, and Black george on College Street and Broad Street. A
12 ft alley separates Lot No. 1 thru 6 and No. 6 to 10 and Hoover and Black George's lots.
Oct 27, 1826. Signed by Eli Talbot, Anthony M. Johnson, George Shall, Joseph T. Elliston,
and Richard Woods, Commissioners. Oct Term 1826.

Page 76   Settlement of estate of Joseph Philips, deceased.
Dec 29, 1826   Made by Josiah F. Williams, guardian. Persons listed, to wit, S.M.
Perry, R. & Sanderson, R. & Curry, M. Bibb, E. McCance, J. Lucas, E. Pritchett, P.
Tesh(illegible), McNairy & Shelby, _____ Pearce, W.D. Philips, Vanleer, Harper, Att. Foster,
Hooper, Cowden & Sanderson, S. Williams, Att.. Bell, Cantrell, Morrison, Wharton, and
William Williams, executor, Mr. Fuqua, Mr. Horn, D. McGavock, Mr. Wilkinson, Josiah Cook,
deficiency of estate of Benjamin Philips, Abernathy, Ray, Cartwright, Redding, Tyre, M.
Walker, McNairy & Roan, and Ewing. Commissioner William D. Philips. Will Williams,
executor. Oct Term 1826.

Page 78   Settlement of estate of Robert P. McFarland, deceased.
Mar 7, 1827   Made by Winney McFarland, admr. Persons listed, to wit, Thomas
Read's rent, Robert Smiley, John Runkle for house rent, Mrs. Webb for house rent, Ephraim
H. Foster, J.W. Horton, James Grizzard, Robert Farquharson, Samuel C. Martin, Thomas
Bradley, Robertson & Waters, Christopher Brooks, Jno. Topp, and Abner Field treasurer,
Illinois. Nelson Patterson and Nicholas B. Pryor, Esqrs. Jan Term 1827.

Page 79   Settlement of estate of Ezekiel Fitzhugh, deceased.
Mar 7, 1827   Made by Polly Fitzhugh, admrx and John Fitzhugh, admr. Persons
listed, to wit, William Ogilvie, D.L.F. Ezell, Nathan Ewing, John Cooper, Enoch Ensley, J.H.
Howlett, Jno. Rains, Jr., William Hamilton, W.W. Brown, J.W. Horton (Sheriff), Jas. Pickle,
Jos. Norvell, Robertson & Waters, Jas. Bell, B. Bibb admr of C. Bibb, deceased. Signed by
Thomas Edmiston, John Currin, Alexander Buchanan, Commissioners. 5 Jan 1827. Jan Term
1827.

Page 79   Inventory of estate of Willis L. Shumate, deceased.
Mar 7, 1827   Made by Cary Felts and Jeremiah Ezell, admrs. One judgement
on Joseph Williams, note on Caleb Goodrich, George F. Hamilton, and R.B. Turner. Others
listed, viz, Isaac Hewlett, Thomas Rutherford, Daniel (illegible), and Thomas Chitwell. Jan
Term 1827.

Page 80   Inventory of estate of William C. Marrs, deceased.
Mar 7, 1827   Taken 18 Nov 1826 by Samuel D. Power, admr. Several items
listed including one watch and notes on John C. McLemore, on Philip Alston. Note due by
said McLemore to said Marrs in bank notes on the Banks of the Mississippi. Jan Term 1827.

Page 80   Sale of estate of William C. Marrs, deceased.
Mar 8, 1827   Sold on 18 Nov 1826. Persons listed, to wit, Samuel D. Powers
one Bible for 25¢, George Keeling, Richard Crouch, Thomas Paine, and James H. Green.
Samuel D. Powers, admr. Jan term 1827.

Page 80   Settlement of estate of John Brice, deceased.
Mar 8, 1827   Made with Isaac Hudson, admr. Vouchers and amount found on his
books $230.54 3/4. A balance of $3.65¼. This 25 Jan 1827. Signed by Edmond Goodrich and
Alexander Walker, Esq., Commissioners. Jan Term 1827.

Page 81   John Fitzhugh of Polly, Mary and John W. Fitzhugh.
Mar 8, 1827   Received of Maj. John Fitzhugh, admr of the estate of Ezekiel Fitzhugh, deceased, $302.08 being so much of my distributive share of said estate. Jan 20, 1827. Signed by Polly Fitzhugh. Received of Maj. John Fitzhugh, admr of the estate of Ezekiel Fitzhugh, deceased, $171.62 being my share of estate. Jan 20, 1827. Signed by Mary L. Fitzhugh. Received of Maj. John Fitzhugh, admr of said Ezekiel Fitzhugh, deceased, $86.62 being my share. Jan 20, 1827. John W. Fitzhugh.

Page 81   Lucy Sturdevant, widow support.
Mar 8, 1827   The following was set apart for a years support for Lucy Sturdevant, widow of Henry Sturdevant, deceased, viz, 1000 lbs pork, all the corn after paying rent on the place, one cow and calf, 25 lbs sugar, and 12 lbs coffee. Dec 22, 1826. Edmond Goodrich, William Hope and William H. Hamblin, Commissioners. Jan Term 1827.

Page 81   Abigail Walker, widow support.
Mar 8, 1827   1000 lbs pork, 9 bushels wheat, 35 barels corn, 50 lbs sugar and coffee, salt, milch cow, ginned cotton, leather for shoes. Philip Walker the husband of Abigail Walker departed this life about the 25 day of June 1826. Dec 15, 1826. Signed by Edmond Goodrich, Martin Pierce and Simon Williams, Commissioners. Jan Term 1827.

Page 81   Mary Owen, widow support.
Mar 8, 1827   We, on 4 Dec 1826, laid off and set apart one years provisions for the support of Mrs. Polly Owen, widow of Edmond Owen, deceased. Several items listed. William Murphy and John Gowen, Commissioners. Jan Term 1827.

Page 82   Effey McNeal, widow support.
Mar 10, 1827   Effey McNeal, widow of Call McNeal, deceased. One lot of hogs 1500 <u>wright</u>, 35 barrels of corn laid off for the widow and children. B.H. Lanier, J.P. Jan Term 1827.

Page 82   Susanna Bibb, widow support.
Mar 10, 1827   We set apart for Mrs. Susanna Bibb, widow of Benjamin Bibb, deceased, one years support for her and her family. Several items listed. 10 Nov 1826. Michael D. Dunn, William Ewing and James Condon, Commissioners. Jan Term 1827.

Page 82   Will of John Haywood, deceased.
Mar 10, 1827   To Egbert Haywood in trust for my son George Haywood two negroes, Samuel and Austin. In case the Lynches should not recover the land from Howlet which I have bought from them and declared myself a trustee for the benefit of Thomas Haywood and his wife and children, then I give and devise the land in the Forked Deer Country bought from Col. John D. Love and had to be conveyed to the Lynches in case of their recovery. To my son Thomas the money deposited in the red case in my house $802.00 in Tennessee Bank notes for the purpose of enabling him to complete the purchase of the Lynches land which I desire to Egbert Haywood in trust for my daughter-in-law Susan Haywood and her children. Negroes to Egbert Haywood in trust for the benefit of the said Susan and her children. 19 Dec 1826. Wit: (illegible), Humphrey George and Samuel Edmondson. Jan Term 1827.

Page 83   Will of John Johns, Sr., deceased.
Mar 10, 1827   To my beloved son Joel Johns the tract of land whereon I now live containing 135 acres, also my negro man Andrew with all my stock, all my household and kitchen furniture also my farming utensils. The reason for giving Joel all my property is because I think him entitled to it for services he has rendered me since he was 21 years of age with the exception of $60.00 which my will is that Joel pay to John Little, Jr. My other children had the portion therefore. I appoint my son Joel Johns my sole executor. This 22 Feb 1826. Wit: Elizabeth Hopkins and Eveline B. Hopkins. Jan Term 1827.

Page 83   Settlement of estate of Ezekiel Fitzhugh, deceased.
Mar 15, 1827   We have this 20 Jan 1827 divided the personal estate of Ezekiel Fitzhugh, deceased, among the respective legatees, viz, Polly Fitzhugh, widow and relict of the deceased, Mary Fitzhugh his daughter and John Fitzhugh his son, the following, viz, Polly Fitzhugh amount of property bought at sale $302.08. She is entitled to $217.62 ($519.70 her

184

proportion), Mary received $571.02 and entitled to $519.70, and John Received $686.02 and entitled to $619.70. John Watson, John Currin, Alexander Buchanan and Isaac H. Howlett, Commissioners. Jan Term 1826(1827).

Page 84   Inventory of estate of William T. Norment, deceased.
Mar 15, 1827   Made 26 Jan 1827 by James Norment, admr. Two horses and one saddle and bridle. Jan Term 1826(1827).

Page 84   Division of negroes of Sarah Hays, deceased.
Mar 15, 1827   Andrew S. Hays was called upon to divide the negroes of Sarah Hays, deceased, on Jan 16, 1827. Four negroes listed, viz, Fanny, Ann, Isabel and Jack. Signed by Eli Cherry, Thomas Gleaves, William Wilson, and William Creel. Jan Term 1827.

Page 84   Sale of estate of Newton E. Burnham, deceased.
Mar 15, 1827   Persons listed, to wit, John Gambrel, William Thomas, L. Cato, John H. White, Jas. Mosley, Jos. Haley, and William Wood. Polly Burnham, executorx. Jan Term 1827.

Page 84   Sale of estate of John Tait, deceased.
Mar 15, 1827   Several items listed. By the consent of Rebecca Tait, widow of John Tait, deceased, and agreeable to the will of Zedekiah Tait, executor, also sold at the sale two grist mills and one saw mill and two acres of land where the mill stands. Jan Term 1827.

Page 85   Estate settled of Henry Hyde, deceased.
Mar 15, 1827   Made by Mrs. Mary Hyde, admrx. Oct 28, 1826. Persons listed, to wit, Jas. B. Craighead in Alabama, Jno. W. Bell in Nashville, Richard Hyde guardian for Mary D. Hyde, Jordan Hyde, Mosley Hyde, John J. Hyde, and Elizabeth Hyde, and A.D. Carden, Henry C. Cummins, Edmond Hyde, William Ewing, and John Caulfield. This 20 Jan 1827. William Ewing and John Caulfield, Commissioners. Jan Term 1827.

Page 85   Penelope Overton, dower.
Mar 15, 1827   Penelope Overton, widow and relict of Thomas Overton, deceased, was set apart for her dower 1510 acres of land. Land borders the bluff of the Cumberland River a little above the lower parcel of the island, and James Robertson's corner. This 24 Jan 1827. Signed by John Donelson, William Donelson, Thomas Gleaves, Joseph Cook, Absalom Gleaves, Matthew Gleaves, William Watson, Thomas Gleaves, Jr., William H. Tate, Jacob M. Bonderant, William Creeland, Andrew J. Donelson, jurors. Jan Term 1827.

Page 86   Sale of estate of Charles Wright, Sr., deceased.
Mar 16, 1827 $223.60. This 15 Jan 1827. Absalom Gleaves, executor.   Jan Term 1827.

Page 86   Division of negroes of George Wharton, deceased.
Mar 16, 1827   Twenty two negroes. Persons listed, to wit, Samuel Seay, George R. Wharton, Charles J.F. Wharton, Susan Wharton, and Alexander S. Wharton. This Dec 27, 1826. Josiah F. Williams, William Hope and William Williams, Commissioners. Jan Term 1827.

Page 86   Clay, Moorefield and Sledge, Division.
Mar 16, 1827   Commissioners appointed to divide a certain lot adjoining the town of Nashville deeded by John McNairy to Polly Williams Clay now wife of Thomas Moorefield, Elizabeth M. Clay now wife of John P. Sledge, and Joseph Coleman Clay a minor. They met on said lot on Jan 26, 1827. In presence of the above John P. Sledge, N.B. Pryor guardian of Joseph Coleman Clay, and agreed to divide into three equal parts as possible so as only to include a log house therein. Part No. 1 to begin at the north west corner of Lot No. 58(38?) running with said line towards Cherry Street about 60 feet to Thomas Moorefield. Lot No. 2 borders Lot No. 1 and Cherry Street, and Lot No. 3 borders Lot No. 2, Town Lot No. 58 (or 38?), John McNairy. Lot No. 1 was drawn to Joseph Coleman Clay, Lot No. 2 to Polly Moorefield, and Lot No. 3 to Elizabeth Sledge. Signed by Duncan Robertson, Joseph Gingry and Enoch Wilburn. Jan term 1827.

Page 87   Settlement of estate of George Wharton, deceased.
Mar 16, 1827   Persons listed, to wit, N. Ewing, William T. Dickinson, Francis
McKay, Enoch Cunningham, Jas. W. McCombs, Thomas Stratton, Samuel Shannon, R.
Farquharson, J.? and A.G. Ewing, McNairy & Roane & Ewing, Duncan Robertson, James
Dickinson, Thomas Wells, James E(illegible), Ira Bradford, D.W. Sumner, Paul Dismukes,
James Overton, R. Payne, William Hope, M.P. Walker, Jas. M. Walker, Wilson White, H.
Ewing, E.S. Hall, Jessy White, E. McCance, and B. Coats, Armstrong & Seay, and William
Shaw. 27 Dec 1826. Samuel Seay, executor. Stephen Cantrell and Will Lytle. Jan Term
1827.

Page 88   Sale of estate of Henry W. Sturdevant, deceased.
Mar 16, 1827   Persons listed, to wit, Lucy Sturdevant, William Sturdevant,
Carter Allen, John Hinton, Thomas Watkins, Edward Finch, Isaac Clements, John Orr, and
Jno. Fowlkes. Lucy Sturdevant, admrx. Jan Term 1827.

Page 88   Sale of estate of Edmond Owen, deceased.
Mar 16, 1827   Several items listed. Adam Hope and Mary Owens, admrs. Jan
Term 1827.

Page 89   Inventory of estate of Thomas H. Perkins, deceased.
Mar 16, 1827   To amount in the Nashville Bank of $350.00, when $150.00 was
paid by William Perkins, deceased, in his lifetime on the 24 Jan 1821 which is an over credit.
Robert Scales, executor. Jan Term 1827.

Page 89   Division of negroes of estate of William Donelson, deceased.
Mar 16, 1827   We, the Commissioners, has laid off and set apart to John
McGregor and Milberry his wife, late Milberry Donelson, their proportion of the negroes, six
in number. This 13 Jan 1827. Enoch P. Connell, Allen Mathis and Edmond Goodrich, Esqrs.
Jan Term 1827.

Page 90   Sale of estate of Philip Walker, deceased.
Mar 16, 1827   Sale on 15 Dec 1826. Mrs. Abigail Walker purchased several
items, also Henry Seat, John E. Turner, Ebenezer W. McCance, Benjamin J. Love,
Christopher Brooks, James D. Matthews, James Elezier, Daniel M. Frazer, John E. Minus,
William A. Williams, Samuel Watkins, William Sturdevant, Samuel B. Neely, Samuel Wood,
William Wiseman, widow White, William T. Norment, Robert Jenkins, Robert Bates, William
Hope, Henry Strange, Peter Bashaw, William Hurt, Adam Hope, and John Frazer. William H.
Hamblin, admr. Jan Term 1827.

Page 90   Sale of estate of Thomas Taylor, deceased.
Mar 17, 1827   A list of notes on, viz, William Grubbs, William Hathway, Richard
Bandy, John Scruggs, John (illegible), Henry Ray, James Scruggs, Elizabeth Earhart, Edward
Scruggs, James H. Hooper, Peter Bradford, Joseph Rolan, William M. Hinton, Edward Smith,
John B. Williams, Daniel Brown, E. Tracy, Henry Faulkes, Robert Taylor, Samuel Wharton,
James McGavock, Edward Scruggs, Sr., Martin Pearson, Bailey Taylor, Wallace Branch,
Martha Clay, C.M. Brooks, Thomas Taylor, Isaac Clemmons, and John Earhart, executor. Jan
Term 1827.

Page 91   Inventory of estate of Benjamin Pritchard, deceased.
Mar 17, 1827   Jan 15, 1827. Persons listed, to wit, William Henry, Hugh Allison,
John Ivey, Thomas Crofton, James Pritchard, Henry Clayton, Frederick Ivey, William
Kennedy, Lazarus Inman, Thomas Winn, Samuel Powers, Samuel Tennison, Turner Davis, John
Buck, William Shelton, Branch Anderson, George Koonce, John H. Davis, James Brown, John
Walker, Andrew Boyd, Abraham Weeks, Robert A.B. Buck, Thomas Craig, Thomas Walton,
Green B. Greer, John Winn, Benjamin Thompson, Samuel Smith, David Montgomery, William
Montgomery, John Whitley, Samuel Jonathan Stepleton, and George Wade.   Benjamin
Prichard, executor. Jan term 1827.

Page 91   Settlement of estate of Robert Sanderson, deceased.
Mar 17, 1827   Made with Zebulon P. Cantrell, admr. Persons listed, to wit, J.E.
Buck's estate, A. Hyns, J. & R. Woods, Armstrong & Seay, Dickson & Dyer, Dr. Thomas
Wells, J.P. Minnick, Samuel Edmondson, Isaac Sitler, J. Dwyer, E. Grizzard, A. & Knox,

186

Smith Johnson, William Brooks, M. Porter, B. Poyzer, Jas. & L. McGavock, Dr. R.B. Sappington, Dr. John A. Ewing, John Franklin, McNairy & Roane, Samuel V.D. Stout, J. Norvell, John M. Hill, _____ Houston, D. Perkins, Jas. Stevenson, D. Robertson, N. Ewing, Armstrong & Seay, D. & Dyers, G.W. Campbell, James Erwin, F. Fisher, Dr. Wells, J.P. Minich, M. & Grizzard, J. & J.W. Sitler, W. & C. Brooks, A. & Seay, Isaac Sitler, Brown & Knox, Cutler & Wilborn, Wright & Gordon, Campbell & Cantrell, R.K. Anderson, Duncan Robertson, _____ McNairy, _____ Harrison, S.V.D. Stout, E. Long, and John M. Hill. 10 Jan 1827. Samuel Seay and S.V.D. Stout. Jan term 1827.

Page 93   Sale of estate of Benjamin Bibb, deceased.
Mar 17, 1827   Sale on Nov 23, 1826. Persons listed, to wit, Susan Bibb, Jacob W. Rainey, Jos. H.W. Erwin, Dempsey Corbet, William Ramsey, John Fitzhugh, Thomas Spear, Frederick Owen, John B. Menifee, Henry Critchlow, Martin Davis, John Dobbs, E.N. Paterson, Michael Finney, David L. Thompson, W. Ramsey, Jr., James Condon, William Ramsey, Sr., John Scruggs, Langhorn Scruggs, Richard Wright, John Topp, Williamson Foster, and John Pope. Jan term 1827.

Page 94   Sale of estate of Call McNeill, deceased.
Mar 17, 1827   Sale on 25 Nov 1826. Several items listed. Hire of one negro boy to E.D. Hobbs. Daniel Buie, admr. Jan Term 1827.

Page 94   Will of Timothy Demonbrun, deceased.
Mar 19, 1827   I appoint my friend Joseph T. Elliston, Esquire, my executor and if he refuses to qualify or dies, then an administrator be appointed. As soon as convenient after my death, I will and desire that my executor proceed to sell the part of the Lot No. 45 in the town of Nashville on which I now live, also I wish him to dispose of all my personal estate. To my daughter Agnes Doza and such child or children as she may have living at the time of my death by Mr. Doza, in equal shares (the mother and the children) the sum of $500.00 and directing my executor to pay the legacy into the hands of the mother Mrs. Doza. To my daughter Julia Johnson $1000.00 in cash and hereby declare that the receipt of Mrs. Johnson single or married for the legacy, also to my daughter Mrs. Julia Johnson 290 acres of land part of the tract on which my son Timothy Demonbrun now lives in Davidson County to be laid off and allotted to her by my executor having regard to quality lot in such way as not to interfere with the plantation of my son Timothy in any way. To the three oldest sons of my daughter Julia Johnson now living to each of them the sum of $100.00 to be paid into the hands of the mother or any guardian until they come of age. To my son Timothy Demonbrun $1000.00 in cash, also 293 acres of land in Davisdon County including the farm and plantation on which he now lives. To my illegitimate son John Batteaste Demumbrun $500.00, also one third part of a tract of 440 acres of land for which I have a deed from Capt. Joshua Hadley. To my illegitimate daughter late Polly Demumbrun now married to (blank) $500.00 and also the one third part of said tract of 440 acres of land conveyed to me by Capt. Joshua Hadley. To my illegitimate son William Demumbrun $500.00 and the remaining third of said 440 acres. To my two sisters Catherine Demumbrun and Polly Demumbrun $500.00 each, these two sister, if alive, reside in the city or neighborhood of Montreal in Canada which my executor is to notify them of their interest in my estate and if they fail to acknowledge same within three years then it is to be equally divided among my legitimate heirs. All the rest and residue of my estate I wish to divide equally among all my legatees. This Sept 24, 1820. Wit: M. Fly, Nelson Thornton and Rphraim H. Foster. (Signed by Thimoti DemomBrun). Jan Term 1827.

Page 96   Inventory and sale of estate of Timothy Demonbrun, deceased.
Mar 19, 1827   An inventory of Capt. Timothy Demonbrun, deceased, inventory included one old negro woman Jane, one receipt and an acknowledgement of E.H. Foster for $1425.00 of which he, Foster, had paid Capt. Demombrun $50.00, sundry pieces of old household and kitchen furniture, one half of Lot No. 45, one account with Sally Parrish for $600.00 payable in Oct 1831 with a further sum of $50.00 pr year until the above date bearing date July 1826. J.T. Elliston, executor. The amount of sales of the estate of Capt. Timothy Demombrun Nov 1826 on credit of 12 months, household and kitchen furniture of $125.37½. A total in all $5712.25. Jan Term 1827.

Page 97   Inventory of estate of Peter Boothe, deceased.
Mar 19, 1827   Several negroes and several other items listed. Notes on the

187

following, to wit, William Knight, Wilkins Whitfield, John Bosley, Thomas W. Hobbs, William Roach, John Davis, Jervis Cutler, Henry Demoss, Francis Newsom, James C. Roach, Harrison Whitfield, Williamson B. Lofton, Thomas Lofton, Abraham Demoss, and Shelton Hardgraves. Martha Porch, admr. Jan Term 1827.

Page 97   Sale of estate of Sarah Hays, deceased.
Mar 19, 1827   Several items listed. Sold on Nov 24 & 25, 1826. Anderson S. Hays, executor. Jan Term 1827.

Page 98   Inventory of estate of Charles M. Hall, deceased.
Mar 19, 1827   Dec 22, 1826, Nancy B. Hall, admrx. Several items listed. Jan Term 1827.

Page 99   Sale of estate of John C. Ewing, deceased.
Mar 19, 1827   Persons listed, to wit, Dr. William P. Laurence, Henry Ewing, Alpha Kingsley, Mrs. Rhoda Boyd, Duncan Robertson, Lemira S. Ewing bought one silver watch, Nathan Ewing, Albert G. Ewing purchased all the medicine and apparatus belonging to the shop except the bathing tub, bed pan and (illegible) machine, and James Dobbs. Nathan Ewing, executor. Jan term 1827.

Page 100   Sale of estate of Nicholas Crossway, deceased.
Mar 20, 1827   Purchasers, viz, James Crossway, Edmond S. Moore, Landon Farrer, Pilmon Cole, John Rea, William Shaw, Isaac Moore, William Williams, Enoch Cunningham, William Strange, Charles B. Perry, George Campbell, Martin Pearce, James Hite, William P. Connel, Pilmore Crossway, John Kerby, George Perry, Thomas P. Yeats, Thomas Cartwright, Spencer Pearce, Ira Bradford, Edmond Smith, Isaac L. Glasgow, William Kennedy, William Watson, Allen Mathis, Anna Crossway, Henry Crossway, Eleazer Dorris, Severn Donelson, John Butterworth, John Newlin, David Ralston, James Hill, Thomas Powell, John Cole, Robert Dorris, John Betts, Lemuel Bowers, Jonas Sheviers, Philip Kiser, Reuben Noel, Pleasant Walker, David McGuire, William Cole, Lemington Crossway, Stephen Bowers, Mrs. Kiser, and Lowe Harrison. Jan Term 1827.

Page 102   Heirs division of estate of William Rains, deceased.
Mar 20, 1827   No. 1 to Hance H. Rains 24 acres. No. 2 to Charlotte Rains 24 acres, and No. 3 to Ursula Gowen of 24 acres. We find 194 acres being the remainder after 27½ acres being laid off to Wilford H. Rains, one of the devisees of said William Rains, out of the 194 acres have set apart to Hance H. Rains 24¼ acres of land. Ursula Gowen wife of Wilford B. Gowen. Several negroes to be divided. This 13 Jan 1827. Will Lytle, J.P. Samuel Weakley, Sr., and Commissioners Samuel J. Ridley and John Thompson. Jan term 1827.

Page 103   Sale of estate of Charles M. Hall, deceased.
Mar 20, 1827   Purchasers, to wit, Mary B. Hall, A. Hall, Sherwood Bryant, William Goode, A. Gleaves, Thomas Harding, C. Brooks, John G. Neely, James Ridley, Severn Donelson, Nelson P. Carter, John Broughton, Samuel Frossythe (Forsythe), Robert Goodlett, Robert Wood, Samuel Hite, William Perkins, Thomas Fuqua, E. Wilson, J.W. Royston, James Shane, David Stewart, James Blair, William Carpenter, J. Grant, Samuel Stull, Robert Hill, N. Williams, Peter Fuqua, Dempsey Corbit, Elisha Wilson, Robert Buchanan, Ed. Matthews, P. Northern, W.?. Carter, John McBride, Ealan Cason, Alexander Nailor, Archibald Hall, Thomas Ray, James Hoggatt, James Ridley, Robert Wood, Parks & Gibson, Thomas Terry, Thomas Wray, B. Richmond, William H. Horn, Jonas Shivers, Betsey Shropshire. Farm rented by Joel W. Royster. Nancy B. Hall, admrx. Jan term 1827.

Page 105   Settlement of estate of Ermine Johnson, deceased.
June 12, 1827   Made with Susan Lester, executrix. In the hands of the admrx $21.49 remaining unpaid. Apr 21, 1827. Isaac Hunter and William Wilkinson, Commissioners. Apr Term 1827.

Page 105   Settlement of estate of Daniel Binkley, deceased.
June 12, 1827   Absalom Gleaves and Herbert Towns appointed to settle with George W, Charlton, Esq., admr. Several notes and vouchers listed. This 18 Apr 1827. Apr Term 1827.

Page 106   Settlement of estate of Christopher C. Carter, deceased.
June 13, 1827   Made with W.O. Carter, admr. Several vouchers listed. Harbert
Towns, Absalom Gleaves and George W. Charlton, Commissioners. Apr Term 1827.

Page 106   Settlement of estate of William Gulledge, deceased.
June 13, 1827   Persons listed, to wit, Nathan Ewing, Norvell H. Robertson, Hardy
S. Bryan, St(illegible) Hunter, Wilson L. Gowers, William Holmes, Frederick Gulledge, Wilson
& Birdsong, Isaac Earthman, and Binkley & Morris.   Wilson L. Gower and Braxton Lee,
Esquires, Commissioners. Apr Term 1827.

Page 106   Settlement of estate of Reuben P. Biggs, deceased.
June 13, 1827   Made on Apr 14, 1827. Persons listed, to wit, Wilson Crockett,
Nathan Ewing, William Shelton, Dennis Dozier, John Lewis, and I.J. Everett. Apr Term 1827.

Page 107   Settlement of estate of Thomas Lane, deceased.
June 13, 1827   Made with Ralph S. McFaddin and Rebecca Lane, admrs. Several
vouchers listed, a balance due the minor heirs $150.00. This 28 Feb 1827. William H.
Nance, Guy McFaddin and James Hamilton, Commissioners. Apr Term 1827.

Page 107   Settlement of estate of Gabriel Fuqua, deceased.
June 13, 1827   Persons listed, to wit, Braxton Lee, Mr. Anderson, Nathan Ewing,
J. Horton, W. Crockett, and Dennis Dozier, and Wilson L. Gower. Apr Term 1827.

Page 107   Sale of estate of William T. Norment, deceased.
June 13, 1827   Sale on 17 Feb 1827, amounted to $160.56. Total amount of
money due the deceased at his death was $147.50 in notes. This 16 Apr 1827. James
Norment, admr. Apr Term 1827.

Page 108   Settlement of estate of John Baird, deceased.
June 13, 1827   Made by M.C. Dunn, executor. persons listed, to wit, John Nichol,
W.E. Owen, Thomas Crutcher, Jno. Harding, James Irwin, M. Hoover, McNairy & Roane,
George Shall, Jno. H. Smith, D. Robertson, A. Whiting, Dr. R.P. Hays, A.W. Johnson, Jas. P.
Clark, R.P. Garrett, Jas. McGavock, G. Wilson, Kirkman & Erwin, Nathan Ewing, Thomas
Wells, Jos. Marshall, S. Barnet, Nichol & Barry, George Ament, Pleasant Maynn,   Jas.
Stephens, W.M. Goodwin, W.H. Mason, George S. Yerger, Francis H. Baird and D. Craighead,
James Collins, and John R. Grundy, Thomas Welch, Robertson & Elliot, R.H. Barry, Jas.
Rucks an attorney, M. Portis for Dr. Shelby, Hynes & Knowles, James Ridley, William H.
Horn, Lewis Hope, William L. Brown, This 27 Apr 1827. Elihu S. Hall and Matthew Barrow,
Esquire, Commissioners. Apr Term 1827.

Page 109   Settlement of estate of John Graves, deceased.
June 13, 1827   Made with William Seat, executor. Persons listed, to wit, Jno. &
Douglas Puckett, Mr. Abercrombie, Jos. Priestley, Alexander Stewart, William & Samuel
Neely, John Barnhart, Stump & Cox, John Nichol, Jo. Norvell, J.W. Ferguson, Abel Manny, N.
Ewing, Graves Pennington, Alexander Martin, Thomas Joy(?), Harris Williams, John Maneys,
J.W. Horton, James Woodruff, Elizabeth Braten, Thomas Harding, Bernard Varden, Moses
Drew, Samuel May, Elizabeth C. Cole, Kinchen T. Wilkinson, E. Finch, A. Nanny, David
Hays, Jo. M. Cane, Russell Sullivan, James Brown, Isaac David, John Brown, Lemuel
Ballentine, Charles Herd, Edward A. Keeling, John Roberts, William Hall, Thomas May, John
Buckett, Felix Grundy, Martha Wilkinson, Thomas Hudson, Thomas Cannell, Charles
Ballentine, Joseph McVey, Nanny & Linch, Isaac Hudson, Robert Moseley, Gilliland heirs, J.W.
McComb, Alexander Stewart, Thomas Hanney, Samuel Mays, David Hays, Jno. McCanes,
Russell Sullivan, James Brown, John Brown, Charles Herds, Dr. Jos. Priestley, Nathaniel
Childress, Wyat Wilkinson, Josiah Warner, Leonard P. Cheatham, R.A. Higginbotham, and M.
Autry rent on old Meeting House. This 23 Apr 1827. William B. Lewis and Benjamin F.
Curry, Esquires, Commissioners. Apr Term 1827.

Page 111   Sale of estate of George Hathaway, deceased.
June 14, 1827   Sale on 27 Jan 1827. Purchasers, to wit, Langhorn Scruggs, John
Corbit, James Corbit, W.B. Brent, B. F(illegible), Barnett Davenport, William Hathaway.
William Hathaway, admr. Apr Term 1827.

Page 111   Inventory of estate of Charles M. Hall, deceased.
June 14, 1827   This 24 Feb 1827. Three negroes that John G. Neely hires Dec
23, 1826 and again hired out again, Sam hired to Peter Fuqua for $56.00 his wife Louisa and
three children, Joel Fuqua for clothing, Daniel Cairy two children, and little George to
Whitfield Moore $50.00. Signed by Nancy B. Hall, admrx. Apr Term 1827.

Page 111   Inventory of estate of Richard Stringfellow, deceased.
June 15, 1827   Made on Apr 11, 1827. Several items listed. William
Stringfellow, admr. Apr Term 1827.

Page 112   Additional inventory of estate of John Baird, deceased.
June 15, 1827   Made by Michael C. Dunn, executor, on Apr 30, 1825. Persons
listed, to wit, A. Whiting for rent of store, Thomas A. Duncan's note for an old house, office
rent from J. Rucks, office rent from J. Collinsworth, R.H. Barry rent of store, cash received
from Chapman & Neditel of Philadelphia by Gill & Porter, office rent from Foster & Fogg,
house rent from George S. Yerger, house rent from George Shall, notes for office rent from
James Collinsworth, William T. Crenshaw, John R. Grundy, and Nathan Ewing. Apr Term
1827.

Page 112   Inventory of estate of Martin W.B. Armstrong, deceased.
June 16, 1827   Made by Martin McCall, admr. Several items listed including
notes on the following, to wit, Edward Ward and A(illegible) Catron. Others listed, Spencer
Thomison whereabouts unknown, Mr. Foster, Maj. Sterling C. Robertson, Mr. White, Mr.
Fisher, a bond on William W. Williams, T.T. Armstrong, Andrew Roane, deceased, W.T.
Crenshaw, a plat of location on the Brassor (?) River marked "G", and Mark H. Smith of
Franklin. Apr Term 1827.

Page 113   Division of estate of John N. Crossway, deceased.
June 16, 1827   Total of $1016.43 minus $78.3¼ for expenses. $120.00 willed to
Lennington and Elias Crossway out of the above amount which leaves $818.11 3/4. Negroes
valued at $2753.11 3/4. To wit, Mrs. Kiser her share, and to James Crosway his share, to
Pilmon Crossway his share which he is to pay to the guardian of the minor heirs, and to
Henry Crossway his share, and to Lennington Crossway his share, and to Elias Crossway his
share. This 23 Feb 1827. Enoch P. Connell, John Pirtle, Esquires, and Charles L. Byrn,
Commissioners. Apr Term 1827.

Page 113   Inventory of estate of Samuel Chapman, deceased.
June 16, 1872   Sold on 18 Nov 1826. Purchasers, to wit, Graves Pennington,
Joseph W. Horton, H. Ewing, Christopher Brooks, J. Grizzard, William Murdough, George S.
Yerger, Edward Butler, Jas. W. McCombs, Richard Manly, Jacob Greenhalph(?), George W.
Boyd, and James Scruggs. Notes on the following, to wit, H.M. Pitman, Graves Pennington,
David Graves, Lemuel Dean, Pleasant Mayner, Jno. Maney (or Massey), M. Autry, James T.
Love, Christopher Brooks, William Brooks, Isaac G. Sandsberry, James A. Cannon, William
L. Ward, James C. Patton, James Grizzard, John Wright, and John E. Finn. Henry Ewing,
executor. Apr Term 1827.

Page 113   Inventory of estate of John Haywood, deceased.
June 16, 1827   Persons listed, to wit, Alexander Allen, _____ Anderson, James
Austin, _____ Benland, Charles Brun(?), And. Buchanan, R.D. Berry, _____ Betts, Matthew
Brooks, Montgomery Bell, Samuel Bell, Samuel Buchanan, Bennet Blackman, _____ Baham,
Richard Blanton, Abram Beavers, Benjamin Bibbs, David Cummins, William Chrisman, Edward
Clifton, James C(illegible), David Clinton, James Clinton, James Cochram, _____ Callender
(?), _____ Cannon, Moses Christerberry, Jno. Clinard, James Cor(illegible), _____ Connally,
Absalom Davis, Isaac Douglas, John D(illegible), William Edmondson, Robert Edmondson, John
L. Ewing, Samuel Edmondson, Jno. Fitzhugh, J. Fort, James Glasgow, Jno. Goodloe, Jno.
Gordon, James Grant, G.M. Gibbs, Humphrey George, Jno. Haynes, Jno. Huckaby, Charles
Hays, Jno. Hanks, Henderson heirs, Edward Harris, William Hewlitt, Constant H(illegible),
Rivhard Hightower, John Haywood, Jr., John Hicks, Alfred Harris, _____ Haskell, Adam
Hope, James K. Hope, William Kelton, W.T. Lewis, Richard Long, Alexander Loury (or
Lorrie), _____ McCann, William McClemmons, Samuel McCullock, _____ Mackie, _____
Montgomery, Jno. Mayfield, _____ Moore, _____ McKissick, _____ Napier, Elias Napier,
_____Noblett, John Newman, John Oliver, Archibald Overton, William Polk, T.H. Perkins,

Absalom Page, William Philips, Benjamon Pryor, William Pea, Hugh Pugh, Jos. Philips, Wright Ramsey, Jas. Reynolds, John Rains, Sr., _____ Rather, Clayton Rollins, Benjamin Sewell, Basset Stilth, Andrew Stobaugh, Hugh Stephenson, William Stark, S.H. Smith, James Turner, R(illegible) Turner, _____ Taylor, _____ Terrell, Thomas Tobb, Jno. Townsend, Willie Turbeville, James Watson, Peter Wright, Jenkin Whiteside, and Hartwell Wallace. Notes on, to wit, Ephraim Philips, James Parker, Jno. Davis, George Flinn, Thomas Archer, Joel Love, Henry Giles, Henry Fuller, James Gee, _____ Clea(illegible), J.H. Blass, Cosmo Madice, Benjamin Farmer, Joshua Barker, John Rolls, Abram Lundsly, John Vickus, Holman Southhall, Elijah Wilkins, Philip Sike, Thomas Cotton, Daniel Wilkes, William Kelly, William Tenpen, Mary Carter, Rob Bell, Jesse Pitman, Richard Sears, John Trimble, Hugh Greenwood, Stephen Stuart, Jesse Hamer, William Jackson, Henry Philips, Jacob Williamson, Thomas B. Whitmill, H. Speer, James Dalton, Richard Smith, Jos. Moore, James Taylor, David Taylor, George Taylor, William Armstrong. Egbert Haywood, admr. Apr Term 1827.

Page 115   Settlement of estate of James David, deceased.
Aug 31, 1827   Made with John Davis and George David, admrs. The amount of sale is $465.37½ and also received a note from William B. Robertson a citizen of Louisiana. A balance in the hands of the admrs of $465.12½. This July 16, 1827. Lewis Joslin, William E. Watkins and John McNairy Robertson, Commissioners. July Term 1827.

Page 116   Settlement of estate of Robert Parry, deceased.
Sept 3, 1827   Made with William Windle, admr. Persons listed, to wit, J.G. Deaderick, Orville Parry and David Parry. This 24 July 1827. Hinckey Petway, Gilbert G. Washington and Zebulon P. Cantrell, Commissioners. July Term 1827.

Page 116   Settlement of estate of Henry Burnett, deceased.
Sept 3, 1827   Made on 25 May 1827 by Elizabeth Seat, admrx. Persons listed, to wit, B.W. and W.H. Bedford, Dr. Robertson, _____ Newman, C. Felts, Dr. Richmond, F. Saunders, Elizabeth Seat, Henry Burnett, Joseph Burnett, and Richard Burnett. George W. Charlton, Nathan Williams, Jesse Bell, Joshua Ellis, Benjamin Bell, Commissioners. July Term 1827.

Page 117   Rebecca Lane, widow's dower.
Sept 3, 1827   Allotted to Rebecca Lane 52 1/3 acres. This 6 July 1827. Patrick W. Campbell, Godfrey Shelton, Joseph Burnett, James Pigg, Edwin Austin, Samuel Blair, Isaac Johnson, John M. Wright, Arvin D. Weaver, George Peay, George Hartman, William H. Nance, Jurors. Rebecca Lane, widow and relict of Thomas Lane, deceased. July Term 1827.

Page 117   Will of Rebecca K. Hardy, deceased.
Sept 3, 1827   I will that my just debts be paid out of my dower of my father Henson Hardy's estate. To my beloved sisters, Mary Ann and Elizabeth Hardy $100.00 each. The balance of my estate to be equally divided between my two sisters and two brothers, Mary Ann and Elizabeth, William and George W. Hardy. I appoint my friends Henry Ewing and Micajah Fly my executors. This 25 May 1827. Wit: William M. Harwood and Micajah Fly. July Term 1827.

Page 118   Sale of estate of Thomas Overton, deceased.
Sept 3, 1827   Purchasers, to wit, Mrs. Overton, Samuel Scott, Zachariah B. Pryor, Z. Payne and Robert Boothe. Note on P.H. Overton. Others listed, to wit, Benjamin Castleman, Thomas Gleaves, Thomas J. Winston, William Watson, Isaac Hudson, and William Ward. Patrick H. Overton, admr and Penelope Overton, Admrx. July Term 1827.

Page 118   Will of Thurston Head, deceased.
Sept 3, 1827   To Marth (Martha) Page all my whole estate of every kind except my silver watch which I give to William P. Brooks and Martha Page is to call all my debts and to pay all my debts. I appoint Marth Page my executrix. This 1 June 1827. John M. Chandain, Thomas Barlow and John C. Dittamore. July Term 1827.

Page 119   Will of Jane Neely, deceased.
Sept 3, 1827   I leave my body to be entered to the disposal of my children. To my daughter Polly Cook one half of my lan(land) and to my daughter Polly my grey mare and

two cows and my bed and furniture. To my son Samuel B. Neely the other half of my lan(land) whereon he now lives. This __ day of May ____. Wit: John Minus, John E. Minus and Benjamin Minus. July Term 1827.

Page 119   Nicholas Hail of Abraham Hail, receipt.
Sept 3, 1827   Received from Nicholas Hail sundry and miney and authority to collect certain money and estate in East Tennessee which in addition to a receipt given to the said Nicholas Hail dated 9 Apr 1825 which is written on the back of a note executed by said N. Hail to Sally Hail and Abraham Hail dated 5 Apr 1825 for certain property and money which is received by me in full satisfaction not only for any claim said Sally Hail might or could have either in law or equity to any other part or portion of the estate of said Nicholas Hail as her husband from whom she is now separated and also in full satisfaction to any and every part and portion of Nicholas Hail's estate to which I as one of the sons of the said Nicholas Hail might be entitled in law or equity. Signed by Abraham Hale. Test: Thomas Claiborn. July Term 1827.

Page 119   Nicholas Hail of Abraham and Sarah Hail.
Sept 4, 1827   I, Sally Hail of Davidson County and wife of Nicholas Hail, and I, Abraham Hail son of Nicholas Hail, are held and firmly bound unto said Nicholas Hail of Davidson County for $3000.00. This 5 Apr 1825. Wit: Thomas J. Hale and J.M. Lovell. July Term 1827.

Page 120   Settlement of estate of William Williams, deceased.
Sept 4, 1827   Made by Samuel Shannon, admr. Persons listed, to wit, Daniel Adams, C. Beaman, and paid to Matthew Patterson for coffin, Drs. Newman and Ewing, N. Ewing, and Dr. Maxey. This 26 July 1827. Buchanan H. Lanier, J.P. and David Ralston, Esqrs., Commissioners. July Term 1827.

Page 120   Will of David Harris, deceased.
Sept 4, 1827   To my dearly beloved wife Anny two beds and furniture, a grey horse and bay mare, three cows and calves, two sows and pigs, six head of sheep, table and cupboard and other items, also a negro man Ben which she is to fold during her lifetime and at her death the remains of her property willed to her her lifetime to be sold and equally divided among the heirs, my sons, to wit, John Harris, Thomas Harris, Peter Harris, George Harris, and Martin Harris. I appoint John Harris my executor. This 4 May 1827. Wit: Matthew Gleaves, Thomas Gleaves, Jr., and Silas H. McKay. July Term 1827.

Page 121   Sale of estate of John Haywood, deceased.
Sept 4, 1827   Made on 26 June 1827. Persons listed, to wit, Egbert Haywood, Alfred Balch, Dr. Patterson, Jno. B. Menifee, Silas Morton, H. Gwynn, Nicholas Tomlin, Alexander Buchanan, E.M. Patterson, James Condon, Kincaid Hope. E. Haywood, admr. July Term 1827.

Page 122   Will of Lewis King, deceased.
Sept 4, 1827   This 16 July 1827, I was requested to visit Lewis King on his sick bed, on my approaching him, said Major Shaw, I am glad to see you. I have been for some days very sick but am now a little better. I want you to write my will and if I should die I wish you to attend to my business. I told him that anything I could do for him I would. He then said I will tell what I want done. I have no heirs and Dicey has done her part in getting the property that we have. I want my debts paid and for my wife to have the balance to dispose of as she might think proper but I feel a good deal better and I don't wish to trouble my friends. I will not do anything about it now but if I get worse I will send for you. One the next day he appeared worse, his wife sent for me and when I went discovered he was much worse. I named to him my business was to arrange his business. He said Major you know my will as well as I do. I am very weak. I asked him several questions and he appeared in his senses but rather flity or (illegible) and irregular in his ideas and getting worse so fast that I did not think it proper to commit anything to writing. This 18 July 1827. Signed by Basil Shaw. July Term 1827.

Page 122   Will of John Bradford, deceased.
Sept 4, 1827   To my dear wife Elizabeth Bradford the tract of land whereon I now live also all the negroes I own, stock and including household and kitchen furniture and

everything on the plantation at my death during her life except the legacy left especially to my daughter Elizabeth who is hereafter mentioned, I wish she should have the benefit of at once. To my daughter Elizabeth Bradford my negro woman Susan and her children to have possession of at my death but she is to account for them in the proportion she may receive of my estate in the division with her brothers and sisters. To my daughter Elizabeth Bradford the choice of any negro girl I own not exceeding the age of 12 years for which she is not to account in the distribution of my property. At the death of my dear wife Elizabeth Bradford, that land whereon I now live should valued and that my son Frederick Bradford shall have the option of taking the land and to pay the legatees their proportion after deducting his first, in two, three and four years and if he refuses to take the land on these terms I wish any of my sons have the same liberty and if they refuse then the land is to be sold and proceeds be divided among all my children and my grandson John J. Cowden. A negro girl Jane and her increase be given to my son-in-law James Cowden. I appoint Armstead Bradford, John Cowden, Robert Bradford, Edward Bradford, and Frederick Bradford, my executors. This 15 Jan 1827. Wit: William Temple, William Blackwell and Robert Johnson. July Term 1827.

Page 123   Sale of estate of Richard Stringfellow, deceased.
Sept 4, 1827   Purchasers, to wit, Mrs. Nancy Stringfellow, M.K. Anderson, Miles Ashley, James Dawson, Thomas Park, William Stringfellow, Jesse Felps, Jacob Ross, B. Woodward, S. Sowell, J. Baxter, William Champ, B.D. Pack, H. Stringfellow, E. Harris, M. Usrey, William Harris, James Lovell, W. Strong, E. Harris, Clark Reel, and Eli Grimes. William Stringfellow, admr. July Term 1827.

Page 124   Settlement of estate of Thomas Overton, deceased.
Sept 4, 1827   Made with P.H. Overton, admr. Persons listed, to wit, P.H. Overton, Z. Payne, W. Ward, Thomas Gleaves, Jr., Benjamin Casselman, Z.B. Pryor, Thomas J. Winston, Samuel Scott, William Watson, Isaac Hudson, M. Gleaves, R. Payne, W.S. Norment, J.W. Horton, George Hall, William Chandler, Jubal Grant, M. Perkins, L.H. Brown, A Porter & Son, N. Ewing, J.W. Overton, J.O. & A.G. Ewing, A. Morrison, Will Hill, Dr. Maxey, J.E. Davis, J.M. Smith, W.H. Henderson, B. Coleman, W. Stobaugh, Richardson & Read, J. McGavock, D.B. Love, E. Young, and T. Dodson. Sheriff to lay off widow's dower. Cash paid E.S. Hall. Balance due the admr $182.75. This 28 July 1827. E.S. Hall and N.B. Pryor, Commissioners. July Term 1827.

Page 125   Division of landof Henry Burnett, deceased.
Sept 5, 1827   Made on 25 May 1827. A division of 384 acres into three equal tracts. Lot No. 1 of 127 acres and 128 poles bordering Robert Whytes' corner and Buchanan's line. Lot No. 2 of 122 acres and 45 poles bordering Whytes' corner and William Seat's corner and Buchanan's line. Lot No. 3 of 133 acres and 147 poles bordering William Seat, William Bibby, C. Felts, and to Flood's line. George W. Charlton, Joshua Ellis, Nathan Williams, Benjamin Bell, and Isaac Bell, Commissioners. Lot No. 1 drew by Richard Burnett, Lot No. 2 by Joseph Burnett, and Lot No. 3 by Henry Burnett. July Term 1827.

Page 127   Will of Thomas Kirkman, deceased, of Nashville.
Sept 5, 1827   To be buried in any decent Episcopalian or Methodist burying ground. My wife Eleanor Kirkman and with my good friend Washington Jackson and my trusty honest friend Bolton Jackson of Baltimore, be my executrix and executors. All my businesses be brought to a close as speedily as possible. One half of my property be placed in some good security and the other half to be at the disposal of my wife Eleanor so long as she remains unmarried if not then one third of all my worth to my wife Eleanor for her use and the remaining two thirds to be equally divided among my children, to wit, Tom, Mary, James, Jane, Hugh, John, and Alexander, the boys when they arrive at the age of twenty one years and the girls when at twenty years or married. This 27 July 1820. Wit: Jas. Jackson, Sr., and James Erwin.
Washington Jackson, Esq. and Bolton Jackson, executors and Ellen Kirkman, executrix VS Richard K. Call and Mary his wife, that a certain paper writing here exhibited in Court as the Last Will and Testament and codicil of Thomas Kirkman, deceased. It is considered that the paper writing be admitted to record &c.

Page 128   Inventory of estate of Thomas Kirkman, deceased.
Sept 5, 1827   Made by Eleanor Kirkman, admrx. Persons listed, to wit, Thomas

and James Kirkman (Florence), John Spina (Nashville), John Brahan (Huntsville), William Lytle, George Wilson, George Bell (Louisiana), William and Jas. Brown account Liverpool, George Coulter (Florence), William Kenner, Joseph Vaulx, John Lytle for rent of plantation (Rutherford County), Robert Weakley, Bowers & Wilkes (of Kentucky), Brenham & Marshall, J. & J. Samuel, Catherwood & Rankin, James C. Hayes' estate, Robert L. Harrison, F. Adams, J. & N. Hunt (of Indiana), R. Hooper, Samuel Lowry (of Ohio), David Miller, Jr. (of Alabama), J. & G. Robertson (of Kentucky), J. Fitzsimmons (of Alabama), John Pugh (of Indiana), John & S. Hodgen. Kirkman & Jackson are sued in Philadelphia for debts due, Little & Tilford, Richard Cochran, Hamilton & Donoho, William Stanton, Henry Cook, and estate of James Hanna. Several items listed. This 23 July 1827. Ellen Kirkman, admrx. July Term 1827.

Page 130 & 131   William Hobson's devisee.
Sept 6, 1827   Willie Barrow, devisee. George M. Deaderick, deceased, executors and Robert Weakley division of Upper Ferry Property. Plat on pages 130 and 131. Commissioners are to lay off and divide into two equal parts two certain tracts of land in the town of Nashville and known and called the Upper Ferry Property and set apart to Nathaniel A. McNairy and Catherine his wife, Ann M. Hewlett, Mary Knox, Anthony M. Johnson and Elizabeth his wife, and Joseph Vaulx and Susan his wife, devisees of William Hobson, deceased, one moiety thereof, and to Ann E. Barrow, executrix and devisee of Willie Barrow, deceased. Jesse Wharton and Stephen Cantrell, executors of george M. Deaderick, deceased, and Robert Weakley the other moiety thereof, this 20 July 1827 after surveying the premises have divided and laid the same off into ten lots &c with suitable made, streets and alleys running through (illegible). Lot No. 1 to Barrow and others of 100 feet on Broad Street and Water Street and Cross Alley and Bason Alley. Lot No. 2 to William Hobson heirs of 100 feet on Broad Street, Market Street and Cross Alley and Bason Alley. Lot No. 3 to Barrow and others of 260 feet on Market Street and Wharf Street and Cross Alley and Bason Alley. Lot No. 4 to William Hobson's heirs of 260 feet on Wharf Street and Water Street and Cross Alley and Bason Alley. Lot No. 5 to Barrow and others of 348 feet borders Stone Bridge, Branch Creek, Wharf Street and Bason Alley. Lot No. 6 to William Hobson's heirs of 348 feet borders Bason Alley, Branch Creek and Water Street. Lot No. 7 to Barrow heirs of 100 feet by 50 feet borders Water Street, Road and Wharf of Cumberland River and Corporation line. Lot No. 8 to William Hobson heirs of 75 feet borders Road, Water Street and Lot No. 9. Lot No. 9 to Barrow and others 250 feet borders Water Street, Lot No. 8 and Road and Lot No. 10. Lot No. 10 to William Hobson's heirs of 442 feet borders Water Street, Lot No. 9, Road, and the Cumberland River. 24 July 1827. John H. Smith, Anthony W. Vanleer, Simon Bradford, John Shelby, Bernard Vanleer, Samuel Seay, S.B. Marshall, And. Hynes, George Shall, and Hugh Roland. July Term 1827.

Page 133   Will of John Marlin, deceased.
Nov 29, 1827   To my son James Marlin 110 acres out of the tract I now live on. To my five daughters, Rachel, Polly, Peggy, Betsey, and Anne 30 acres of land to be sold and the money equally divided between them also two beds and furniture to my said daughters and other items. I appoint William Roach and Newton Edney, executors. This 15 Aug 1827. Wit: William B. Rutland and John Little. Oct term 1827.

Page 133   Will of Josiah E. Giles, deceased.
Nov 29, 1827   I wish 68 acres of land that I own in Sumner County, lying on Cumberland River and deeded from William Lytle Bledsoe to Mr. Sandford and myself sold, also my negro Isaac to be sold to some person living in the neighborhood of his wife in Sumner County. To Edward Stanhope Giles, my son, $2.00. To William Hodge Giles, my son, $5.00. To Thomas Newton Giles, my son, $5.00. To Louis Leroy Giles, my son, $5.00. To Nathaniel Calvin Giles, my son, $5.00. To Eliza Caroline Sh(illegible), my daughter, $5.00. To Peggy Blackwood Giles, my daughter, $100.00. To my wife Polly M. Giles and Patrick Gibson Giles, my son, my three servants, James, Phillis and Austin and all my household and kitchen furniture with all my stock of cattle and horses and other items also to my wife and son Patrick jointly all that part of my wife's father's estate which I have not received including the bond on Sally Gibson. Betsey Gibson since married to Dr. Sappington and Kate Gibson since married to Mr. Parrish. I appoint my nephew Milton Giles, my executor. This 30 Aug 1827. Wit: Robert Paine and Jno. B. Craighead. Oct Term 1827.

Page 134   Will of Frances Curtis, deceased, widow.

Nov 30, 1827   To my grandchildren Fanny and Patsey, daughters of my son William Curtis, subject to the use of their father. To Thomas Crutcher my negro girl Hagar in trust for the use of my daughter Molly Dunnivant during her natural life and at her death to go to my son William Curtis and his heirs, also to Thomas Crutcher my negro slave Pealus in trust for the use and benefit of my grand daughter Patsey Osborn wife of Alfred Osborn and at her death shall go to her children. To my son William Curtis a bed and furniture. To Patsey Osborn a bed and furniture. To my grand daughter Betsey Earhart a bed and furniture. To Franky, a free man of color who was once my slave and under whose kind attention I am breathing out the remnant of my years, $100.00. To my son William Curtis my mare. I appoint my friend Thomas Crutcher my executor. This 16 Feb 1827. Wit: Ephraim H. Foster and Simon Bradford. Oct Term 1827.

Page 135   Will of Hartwell Seat, deceased.

Nov 30, 1827   To my beloved wife one third part of my land during her natural life to be laid off as she may choose and at her death to be equally divided among all my children. Also to my beloved wife one equal child's part of all my other property to do with as she may think proper and a pentiful allowance out of my estate. I lend to my daughter Sally Campbell during her natural life one equal child's part of all my property and at her death to be equally divided among all her lawful heirs of her body. To my son William P. Seat one equal child's part of all my property. To my son Greer Seat one equal child's part of all my property. To my son Littleton Seat one equal child's part of all my property. I lend to my daughter Jinny Watkins during her natural life one equal child's part of all my property and at her death to be equally divided among her heirs. To my son John B. Seat one equal child's part of all my property. I lend to my daughter Peggy Humphries during her natural life one equal child's part of all my property and at her death to be divided equally among her heirs. I have herein set my hand and affixed my seal at my house in the County of Davidson, State of Tennessee. This 27 May 1824. I appoint Jeremiah Ezell and my beloved wife Rebecca Seat my executor and executrix. Wit: John Gowen and John J. Gowen. Oct Term 1827.

Page 136   A nuncupative will of mary Fowlkes, deceased.

Dec 3, 1827   This 23 July 1827. I, being in the presents of Mary Fowlkes, was requested give publicity to the following facts, viz, It was her wish that her son Thomas Henry Fowlkes shall have all monies due her by bond account also a few days previous to the above stated 23rd July she stated that it was her wish that Thomas H. Fowlkes should take choice of her negroes. She also wish for Nancy Payne to have a cow and calf and one bed. Signed by Martin Pierce and Rebecca Frazor. This was put in writing by me the day after her death which was on the 1st of Aug 1827. Test: William H. Hamblin. Martin Pierce and Rebecca Frazor.

Oct Term 1827. Court ordered that said paper writing be admitted to record. William H. Hamblin, admr and he having given bond with Moses B. Frazor and martin Pierce, his securities.

Page 137   Inventory of estate of John Moore, deceased.

Dec 4, 1827   Taken 16 Oct 1827. Several items listed including a note on John Webber, one on D.W. Davis, William P. Edds, H. Cromer, B. Scurlock, Samuel Hayney, Jas. Tindal, and John Woodcock. Fleming P. Wood, admr. This 17 Oct 1827. Oct Term 1827.

Page 137   Sarah Claiborne's heirs division.

Dec 4m 1827   Nashville, Oct 25, 1827. Division of Lot No. 87 in the plan of the town of Nashville among the heirs of Micajah G. Lewis was apportioned to the heirs of Mrs. Sarah Claiborne containing 111 feet and 9 inches front have subdivided it among the heirs of said Sarah as follows: To Abram P. Maury and his wife Mary E. _____ and to said Abram P. as assignee of William F.L. Claiborne two thirds of said 111 feet and 9 inches adjoining Lot No. 86 on the north east corner of which Wilkins Tannehill resides, said two thirds being 74 feet, 6 inches commencing at the south east corner of Lot No. 86, running south eastwardly with Summer Street 74 feet 6 inches then to the back line of Lot No. 87 &c.To Micajah G.L. Claiborne the residue of 11 feet and 9 inches being 37 feet and 3 inches lying between the parcel of ground of Abram P. and mary E.T. and that part of said Lot No. 87. Signed by William B. Lewis, Duncan Robertson and Stephen Cantrell, Commissioners. Oct Term 1827.

Page 138   William Hobson's heirs land divided.
Dec 5, 1827   Lot No. 1 to Nicholas Hobson of 15 acres, Lot No. 2 to Elizabeth
Johnson of 15 cres, Lot No. 3 to Ann Hewlett of 15 acres, Lot No. 4 to Susan Vaulx of 15
acres, Lot No. 5 to Samuel Hobson of 27 acres, Lot No. 6 to Catherine B. McNairy of 26
acres, Lot No. 7 to Mary Knox of 26 acres, Lot No. 8 to John Hobson of 27 acres, and Lot
No. 9 to Jane Lytle's heirs of 40 acres. This 15 Oct 1827. Signed by Stephen Cantrell on 17
Oct 1827. John McGavock, Samuel Weakley, Thomas Martin, Jos. F. Williams, and Paul
Vaughn, Commissioners. Oct Term 1827.

Page 140   Division of estate of Elizabeth Coots, deceased.
Dec 7, 1827   Agreeable to the Last Will and Testament of Elizabeth Coots,
deceased, I, John Boyd, executor, made the following division of the following property
between Polly Harris, Esther Dickinson, Rebecca Hoover, and Lavina Boyd, heirs of the
deceased. To Polly Harris four coverlids, one blanket, one bed, one stand of certains. To
Esther Dickinson one blanket, two coverlids, two counterpanes, one paliece(?), three pair of
hanes, one bed and bedstead, and one oven. To Rebecca Hoover one blanket, two coverlids,
one umbrella, three counterpanes, one bedstead and one chest. To Lavina Boyd three
counterpanes, two coverlids, one blanket, one spinning wheel, one stand of certains, and one
trunk. John Boyd, executor. Oct Term 1827.

Page 141   Estate divided of John Baird, deceased, late of Nashville.
Dec 8, 1827   One fourth of his estate. To Mrs. Baird, widow of said John
Baird, one half of the house and premises at present occupied by her as a dwelling, including
the store room and all the front on the Public Square and running back to Cherry Street
including the stable and an equal front on Cherry Street with that on the Square, also the
bond of Mrs. Baird with D. Craighead security given for furniture, also negroes (3), 110 feet
of ground on High Street being the part next to that owned by McGavock Grundy &c. To
John Baird, only son of said John Baird, deceased, one half of the house and premises above
named and next to estate of W. Eichbaum, also five and three fourths acres of land adjacent
to the Female Academy. To Mary Jane Baird the house and lot on College Street occupied
by Thomas H. Fletcher, also negro Harry also the notes of G.S. Yerger, J. Collinsworth and
Richard H. Barry, also a debt of A. Sneed. To Eliza Ann Baird the ground lying on Cherry
and Cedar Streets including a frame building being the residue of ground belonging to said
estate in that vincinity not above assigned, also the two lots in Tuscumbia and a share of
stock in the Nashville Female Academy. Signed by John P. Erwin, R. Farquharson, John H.
Smith, Samuel Tilford, and George Shall, Commissioners. Oct Term 1827.

Page 142   Settlement of estate of William Donelson, deceased.
Dec 18, 1827   Made by Jacob D. Donelson, executor. Persons listed, to wit, G.
Blackburn, _____ Bingham, Andrew Davis estate for mill stones, Sheriff Williamson, Sheriff
Rutherford, Crockett & Adams, S. Donelson, Charity Donelson, McNeal Fish & Co., _____
McDaniel for coffin, Walton, Abram Echols, William Hill, William Smith, Drs. Hogg &
Brinough, Severn Donelson, _____ Cartwright's executors, _____ Puckett for ferriages,
Nathan Ewing, A. Mathis, Harrison Smith, J. Guilford, E.S. Hall, Hogatt & Overton, L.P.
Cheatham, John Jennings, John C. McLemore, _____ Cage a surveyor, Attorney Rucker,
Sheriff Gleaves, John McGregor, Grundy & Trimble, and R.M. Burton, J.D. Donelson, John
Donelson, ext., John and William Donelson, and John Peyton, Peter Edwards, A(illegible)
Herrin, William Owen, S.D. Hays, Thomas H. Fletcher, S. Jones, David Andrews, T.G.
Bradford, John Orr, M.B. Mumford, H. & W. Gibbs, W. Black, J.P. Wiggins, T. Ingram,
William Black, Robert Hays, J.M. Lewis, W.P. Anderson, Elizabeth Donaldson, and _____
Lofton for land. J.D. Donelson, acting executor. This 24 Oct 1827. William B. Lewis and
Enoch P. Connel, Commissioners. Oct Term 1827.

Page 145   Account of sale of estate of James Mulherrin, deceased.
Dec 21, 1827   Sold on 30 June 1826. Purchasers, to wit, Nelson P. Carter,
James Gordon, Charles J. Love, Robert Goodlett, Robert Woods, William Carpenter, William
M. Harwood, Margaret Mulherrin, James Corbit, William Askins, John Kemal, Elisha Phillips,
John Sneed, J.S. Gross, Robert Hill, William Bryant, A.G. Goodlett, E. Grizzard, Ab. Manuel,
David L. Thompson, Scott's family Bible to James Buchanan, Jas. Grizzard, W. McMaury,
Jno. Buchanan, Thomas Everett, Walter O. Carter, Graves Pennington, N.P. Carter, John
Frazier, Eli P. Ballow, W.L. Pullam, W.A. Parkman, J. Broughton, Mary Francis, Margaret
Mulherrin, Samuel J. Ridley, Thomas Cherry, Laban Estis, and James Wilson. Margaret

Mulherrin, executrix. Oct Term 1827.

Page 147   Inventory and sale of estate of David Harris, deceased.
Dec 22, 1827   Persons listed, to wit, G.W. Harris and Thomas Gleaves.   John
Harris, executor. Oct Term 1827.

Page 147   Inventory and sale of estate of Lewis King, deceased.
Dec 22, 1827   Several items listed and persons listed, to wit, Harry Hudson,
Samuel C. Marlin, Lynch Hughs, Thomas B. Harman, Seth Curl, Daniel Brown, Stephen Lytle,
James Grizzard, John Runkle, James Tilford, James McGavock, John Webber, J.S. Ramsey,
Robert Bradford, Pleasant Staggs, George Jackson, Hugh Roland, Seack Dishon, R. Bucky,
Alexander M. Daniel, Stephen Sutton, and Thomas B. Coleman. James Grizzard, admr. Oct
Term 1827.

Page 148   Settlement of estate of Lemuel T. Turner, deceased.
Dec 26, 1827   Made with Stephen Cantrell, executor. Persons listed, to wit,
Mrs. Turner and J.W. Horton. 25 Oct 1827. William Lytle and M. Faulkner, Commissioners.
Oct Term 1827.

Page 149   Negroes divided of estate of Thomas Overton, deceased.
Dec 26, 1827   John Donelson, Edward Ward and W.W. Donelson (Edward Ward
being absent), Commissioners met to lay off and divide the personal estate of Thomas
Overton, deceased, among his heirs, to wit, John H. Overton negroes, Virgil, Alfred, Synder,
Nancy and Washington. Patrick H. Overton negroes, John Bundy, Shepard, a negro girl Alsey,
Charles, Jacob, and Rose. James G. Overton negroes, Ireland, Dolly, Eliza, Sampson, and
Clarissa. Harriet B. Hynson negroes, Louis, Caroline, Letitia, Juan, Claiborne, and Andrew.
Signed by Capt. John Donelson, Sr. and William Donelson, Commissioners. Also to Mrs.
Overton the following negroes, to wit, a negro woman Bibby, Milly, Jinney, Alce, Betsey,
Bill, Zilpha, Henry, William, John, and Milly. July 16, 1825. John Donelson, Sr., Edward
Ward and William Donelson. Oct Term 1827.

Page 150   Settlement of estate of William Wallace, deceased.
Dec 28, 1827   Made with David Read, admr. Persons listed, to wit, W. Crockett,
J. Earthman, C. Johnston, N. Ewing, D.B. Love, Sevier Drake, M. Gleaves, L.P. Cheatham,
J.W. Horton, Jno. Bell, C. Brooks, William Lytle, E. Daniel, D. Read, B.R. Wallace, R.W.
Gibson, J. Simmons, Jos. M(illegible), Binkley & Morris, Gabriel Saunders, John B.
Demumbron, E.H. Foster, R. Hyde, admr of Kagle's estate, R.B. Sappington, and Ambrose
Downs. Stephen Cantrell and Will Lytle, Commissioners. Oct Term 1827.

Page 151   Will of henry Crabb, deceased.
Jan 25, 1828   11 Mar 1826. Appointed John Bell, FrancisB. Fogg, David Barrow,
and his wife Jane Crabb, executors and executrix, and he insists upon Mr. Bell and Mr. Fogg
need no security. All books except such ones his wife may select be sold, let the proceeds
of the Louisiana plantation (crops) be appropriated some way. If needed to sell the
Tennessee property as executors thinks best to pay debts. After debts are paid the
plantation in Louisiana and negroes (except Edmund and family be brought back to
Tennessee) and take proceeds and invest in some good stock. My wife and each child to be
entitled to equal shares. My wife be paid annually but the stock never to be subject to sale
by her or any other person. To my wife her piano forte, all household and kitchen furniture
and stock she (illegible), may be left on the lot we live on, her choice of misc. works in my
library, negro Edmund his wife and children and Lucy Anne and the use of out house in the
southfield so long as she keeps my children together for their nurture and education and if
she married then to be equally divided between my wife and out children. So long as the
Louisiana plantation shall be kept up, Mr. Gillaspie and his family to have the priviledge of
living there and being supported out of its proceeds, he superintending it and he on its sale
to have the expense of returning his family to Tennessee paid out of my estate and $500.00
out of the proceeds. I wish my children well educated. Wit: James P. Clark. Jan Term
1828. Archibald W. Goodrich, George S. Yerger and Thomas A. Duncan said they were well
acquainted with the handwriting of said Henry Crabb. Court ordered said will to be
recorded.

Page 153   Will of Samuel J. Ridley, deceased.
Feb 23m 1828   I authorize my most affectionate wife Sally Ridley (whom I appoint my sold executrix with directions that she be not required to give security as such) to sell the lands I own in common with Jesse Wharton on Cumberland River, also the house and lot in the town of Nashville in copartnership with Braddock Richmond as she may wish. All my property that I may die possessed of or may be entitled to, I will to my wife Sally Ridley to do as she pleases except a negro boy Horace and a horse, saddle and bridle which I give to my nephew Charles Mulherrin out of the regards I have for him and for his living and remaining with my wife Sally Ridley until he arrives at the age of twenty one years. This 16 Nov 1827. Wit: R.C. Foster, Moses Ridley and Edmond Crutcher. Jan Term 1828.

Page 153   Will of William H. Brown, deceased.
Feb 23, 1828   One half of my property to be given to my sister Elizabeth McClain living in Somerset County, Pennsylvania and the other half to my sister Mary Ann Brown living in Washington County, Pennsylvania. I appoint William Lytle of Nashville my executor. This 3 Jan 1828. Wit: David Abernathy and John Beaty. Jan Term 1828.

Page 154   Will of Jordan Hyde, deceased.
Feb 26, 1828   To my brother Tazewell Hyde my plantation on Whites Creek where on my negroes now is living, also my horse mill which stands on said tract of land. To my brother Benjamin Hyde one negro boy Sam. To my brother Edmond Hyde a negro man Kinchen or $500.00 to be left in the trust of brother Tazewell Hyde. Balance of my negroes to brother Tazewell. To my brother Richard Hyde my ridong gray horse. Residue of my estate to my brother Tazewell Hyde whom I appoint as my executor. This 6 Dec 1827. Wit: Lewis Williams and Jonathan Drake. Jan Term 1828.

Page 155   Will of Janet Washington, deceased, widow of Thomas Washington,
Feb 28, 1828   late of Rutherford County, Tennessee. All the residue of my money (cash) be equally divided among all my children now living, my son Thomas only not to be included, with this only exception that my son William L. is to have over and above his equal share the sum of $200.00. To my son Gilbert G. my negro boy Randal. To my son Thomas J. $150.00. To my son James G. my negro Manuel and negro girl Julia Scott and my negro boy Simon. To my grandson John A. Read my negro girl Julia and negro man Solomon, in trust for the benefit of his mother and my daughter Mrs. Fanny S. Read wife of Thomas J. Read of Nashville. To my grandson Thomas son of my said daughter Mrs. Read, I give my negro Tom and when he comes of age he shall hold said negro for the sole use and benefit of his mother. To my son William L. my negro Henry. To Thomas the oldest son of my son Gilbert G. I give my negro Austin. To my grand daughter Margaret Adelaide Thompson I give my negro girl Mary, and to my grand daughter Mary Washington Thompson I give my negro girl Susan. To my grandsons William Masterson and Thomas Masterson, I give my negro Welen. To my daughter Mrs. Read my bureau and my wearing apparel and I wish her to divide all my beds and bedclothing among my children including herself and to my grandson John A. I give my saddle horse Jerry to hold in trust for his mother. All the residue of my estate to be sold and divided among all my children. I appoint my sons Thomas Washington and James G. Washington, executors. This 24 Sept 1827. Wit: Ephraim H. Foster and Robert Farquharson. Jan Term 1828.

Page 156   Sale of estate of Hartwell Seat, deceased.
Feb 28, 1828   Sold on 28, 29, and 31st Dec 1827. Purchasers, to wit, Rebecca Seat, William P. Campbell, P.W. Campbell, James Williams, Thomas Norward, John Stile, Samuel P. Ensley, Alex. Carper, Seth Neal, James G. Campbell, C.H. Walden, Joseph Derickson, Jno. Bell, John Kimbro, John Hays, Bernard Seat, Jno. M. Wright, Jos. P. Watkins, James Blackaby, William N. Hamilton, Thomas A. Taylor, Thomas Waller, W. Wilkins, Jno. Rice, George Peay, Sally Campbell, O.D. Wever, Edmond Austin, R.H. Wallace, John Sangster, Greenberry Osment, Reuben Burnett, Sterling Whitamore, J. Humphreys, E. Stafford, P. Cross, William Saunders, Turner Neil, T. Campbell, William Boaze, J.B. Seat, Littleton Seat, Jane Watkins, Margaret Humphrey, James Finney, and R.N. Wallace, David Cuff (Kuff), S. Campbell, Jesse Perkins, Thomas Collins, Sally Campbell, Candor McFaddin, Godfrey Shelton, Walter Keeble, Thomas Hill, Thomas K. Butler, Elisha Owens, Thomas Barnes, James Williams, Aaron Lewallen, James Hamilton, Jesse Bell, William Brewer, Adam Carper, Thomas Hatchet, and O. Lane. William P. Campbell, admr. Jan Term 1828.

Page 160   Inventory of estate of Hartwell Seat, deceased.
Mar 4, 1828   Taken 23 Oct 1827. Several items listed including one large Bible and notes on Godfrey Shelton, William Campbell, Elias S(illegible), John Waspool, Walter Keeble, Joel Davis, Spencer Zachry, James Campbell, and John Hill. William Campbell, admr. Jan Term 1828.

Page 161   Sale of estate of Battersby Ballow, deceased.
Mar 4, 1828   Sold on 9 Nov 1827. Purchasers, to wit, Mary Bellow, Martha Bellow, Miles Myers, James Lee, John Brown, John Vanderville, Edward H. East, William Ballow, Hollis Wright, William Hays, Eli Ballow, James Blair, John Charleton, Alexander Martin, Brittain Whitley, Nathan Williams, A.B. Clements, John Brinkley, William Strong, Thomas C.H. Ballow, and William Freeman. Notes on Thomas McNeil, John B. Buchanan and David Haynes. Mary G. Ballow, admrx. Jan Term 1828.

Page 162   Sale of estate of Nathaniel Ashley, deceased.
Mar 6, 1828   Sold on 30 Oct 1827. Purchasers, to wit, Joseph Meek, Lydia Ashley, David Arterbury, Greenbury Ashley, R.R. Brown, the widow, Frederick Harrell, Joel Swinney, Hugh Logan, (illegible) Ashley, John Bosley, Martin Ashley, and James R. Robertson. Lydia Ashley, admrx. Jan Term 1828.

Page 163   Sale of estate of Thomas Fowlkes, deceased.
Mar 6, 1828   The same being lent to Mary Fowlkes during her natural life and sold since her death, viz, on the 18 Sept 1827. Purchasers, to wit, Benjamin Butterworth, John Pierce, Thomas Cartwright, Martin Pierce, William Bower, Henry Fowlkes, William H. Hamblin, Jesse Butterworth, William Carter, Ans. Brown, M. Reading, John Frazor, Moses B. Frazor, Reuben Payne, Ira Bradford, James Cunningham, John Morgan, Eneas Walker, Thomas A. Bal(illegible), Adam Hope, James McCormac, William Porter, John Cunningham, Benjamin Bas(illegible), Benjamin H. Hill, Beverly E. Coots, Kitty Fisher, and John Gill. William H. Hamblin and William Hope, executors. 29 Jan 1828. Jan Term 1828.

Page 164   Sale of estate of Mary Fowlkes, deceased.
Mar 8, 1828   Sold on 27 Dec 1827. Purchasers, to wit, John Porter, Andrew E. Spear, Henry Graves, John M. and Jas. S. Dickson, Alexander Walker, William Strange, Martin Pierce, James McGavock, John Pierce, Enoch Cunningham, William Hope, John Morgan, Jonas Shivers, William Shaw, Robert J. Williams, James Cunningham, John Madey, Isham Butterworth, William Brewer, Thomas Stratton, Jonas Read, Thomas N. Cartwright, George Sanderson, James Eliza, Daniel M. Frazor, and John Adams. William H. Hamblin, admr. Jan term 1828.

Page 165   Valuation of personal estate of Josiah Mullen, deceased.
Mar 8, 1828   Called by Mrs. Elizabeth Mullen, widow and admrx of Josiah Mullen, deceased, on 4 Sept 1825. Several items listed including one watch. Signed by Hinchy Petway, Thomas Edmiston and John Thompson. Jan term 1828.

Page 165   Sale of estate of John Moore, deceased.
Mar 11, 1828   Sold on 30 Nov 1827 by F.P. Wood, admr. Purchasers, to wit, F.P. Wood, W. Scott, John Webber, Elizabeth Moore, H. Lankford, E. Moore, Collin Hobbs, A. Adams, J. Cloyd, Solomon Porter, and Thomas Harmon. Fleming P. Wood, admr. Jan term 1828.

Page 166   Inventory of estate of Charity Donelson, deceased.
Mar 10, 1828   Amount of several items $1532.00 of which sum $95.68 3/4 is due the minors of William Donelson, deceased, Andrew and Elizabeth Donelson it being for the undivided part of the horses sold at the sale. Also $4.81¼ property sold at the sale belonging to Mary E.O. Hamblin. Notes on Francis McKay, guardian of Thomas Dickinson, Daniel M. Frazor, Thomas N. Cartwright, Jacob D. Donelson guardian of Thomas Dickinson, Francis Rice, William Williams, and Reuben Payne. John Macgregor, admr. Jan term 1828.

Page 167   Sale of estate of Jacob W. Ramsay, deceased.
Mar 13, 1828   Nov 22, 1827. Purchasers, to wit, Elizabeth S. Ramsay, William Ramsay, Sr., William Ramsay, Jr., John Hogan, A.D. Carden, Elijah Gray, Samuel Ham, El. Ramsay, Edmond Hyde, Ed Hyde, Stephen Bradley, William Morris, Dr. C.M. Petterson, N.

Fields, Thomas Sidler, Dempsey Corbet, J.W. Campbell, J. Watson, Reb Sutton, B. Richmond, William Thompson, and A. Buchanan. William Ramsay, admr. Jan Term 1828.

Page 168   Inventory of estate of Josiah Horton, deceased.
Mar 13, 1828   Several negroes listed also several items listed. Notes on James Newell who lives in Arkansas about seven or eight years ago, George W. Gibbs, Stump & Cox, Stump & League(?), and Ephraim H. Foster. An Assignment of Jos. and Robert Woods against Ernest Benoit. This 1 Dec 1827. Joseph H. Horton, admr. Jan Term 1828.

Page 169   Inventory of estate of Robert C. Owen, deceased.
Mar 13, 1828   Taken 1 Nov 1827. Several items listed and notes on Samuel Tanner, M. Fly, Elias Dobson, William Hopkins, Elizabeth Key, Robert C. Rives, Miss Page, Robert Hughs, and J. Edmondson. Sandy Owen, admr. Jan Term 1828.

Page 170   Inventory and account of sale of William C. Ward, deceased, late
Mar 15, 1828   of Davidson County. Persons listed, to wit, John W. Jones, Lewis B. Allen, Ben. B. Jones, William Saunders, Edward Ward, John Wright, Meredith Wilkinson, William McNeill, Sarah Ward, Patrick H. Overton, Timothy Dodson, Jas. Shean, Thomas Gleaves, Jr., Jno. Vanderville, William Baldwin, Henry Hayes, William Brooks, William Donelson, Jno. W. Jones, A.G. Ward one horse omitted in the sale in Alabama, and Jno. Benford, Manson Rice, George Grimes, Jno. Coffee, P. Gresham, B. Kitchen. Total sales in Alabama $249.23. John Bell was indebted to intestate. 19 Jan 1828. Albert Ward, admr. Jan Term 1828.

Page 171   Sale of estate of Alice Collinsworth, deceased.
Mar 18, 1828   Made by James Collinsworth, admr. Purchasers, to wit, N. Kelly, William Hamilton, Alexander Carper, H. Wamoth, B.F. Collinsworth, S. Whitamore, Harriss S. Whitamore, Loyd Davis, W.P. Campbell, B. Kelly, H. Towns, James Walpole, Will Thompson, Thomas Wamoth, A. Mason, A. Collins, Jas. G. Campbell, Thomas Waller, E.B. Mason, James Collinsworth, Jane Walpole, Thomas Chilcut, and E. Ensley. Jan Term 1828.

Page 172   Sale of estate of Josiah Horton, deceased.
Mar 18, 1828   Made on Dec 10, 1827. Purchasers, to wit, Jesse Woodard, John Davis, William Porch, Matthew Lee, Jasper Aydelotte, Thomas K. Porter, Elijah Robertson, Elisha Nicholson, John C. Hous, Benjamin Bond, Lewis H. (illegible), Whitmel H. Boyd, Nancy Horton, William Grubbs, Samuel B. Davidson, Micajah Fly, John Wilkinson, Henderson Horton, William Gower, Jas. Lovell, S.B. Davidson, W.D. Horton, J.P. Harrison, Lewis Horn, and J.?. Harrison. Nancy Horton widow of the intestate. Joseph W. Horton, admr. Jan term 1828.

Page 173   Lucretia Morris, her dower.
Mar 19, 1828   Commissioners laid off and set apart to Lucretia Morris, widow and relict of Thomas Morris, deceased, her dower in the lands of which her husband died possessed. On 1 Feb 1828 laid off to her land borders Absalom Hooper. Containing 33 acres and 22 sq. poles of land being one equal third. Signed by William Weakley, John Butterworth, William Neely, William Ray, Henry Strange, Maxm. Reding, Timothy Demumbrum, William D. Philips, John Beazley, William Nicolson, Nelson Talley, and Eneas Walker. Jan term 1828.

Page 174   Inventory of estate of Thomas Morris, deceased.
Mar 19, 1828   Notes on John B. Jefferson, Sarah Jefferson and Robert Lanier, also on G.W. Waggoner, N.P. Jackson and G. Gill, John Beazley, John T. Hunter, J.H. Morris and Sally Morris, N.H. Robertson, James Yarborough, John Pane(illegible), James Binkley, David House, John Newland, J. Earthman, Jr.'s judgement on Jolly Parrish and T.N. Loving and Jesse Parrish, William Hopkins, N. Eddington and James Cantrell, C. Phelan, Isaac Newland, judgement against Lucy (illegible), and William Shaw. David Ralston, admr.   Jan Term 1828.

Page 174   Sale of estate of Thomas Morris, deceased.
Mar 19, 1828   Made by David Ralston, admr on 2 Nov 1827. Purchasers, to wit, Mrs. Morris, _____ Butterworth, Jno. Wingo, Jacob Reasoner, D. Ralston, B.J. Love, William Newland, Jno. Newland, _____ Philips, _.H. Robertson, Thomas Robertson, J. Faulkner, E. McCance, _____ Gill, Thomas Woodard, J.G. Porter, B.J. Love, Rolin Wingo, J.H. Morris,

Wallis Swann, William Bonner, J. Marshall, P(illegible) Tinsly, E. Cloyd, William Roach, N. Young, and J.F. Earthman. David Ralston, admr. Jan term 1828.

Page 176   Additional inventory of John O. Ewing, deceased.
Mar 20, 1828   It being inpart of his share of the firm of McNairy, Roane & Ewing which was received by me as admr of said decedent's estate of McNairy & Roane the surviving partners as follows, in notes, to wit, Jn. Avery, Miss Nancy Owen, John Bell, Philip Pipkin, A.B. Hawkins, Henry Bateman, William W. Goodwin, Samuel R. Anderson, Thomas Patterson, John Chapman, George Foster, Collin M. Cowandin, Welch & Austin, John Harrison, William Temple, Robert Purdy, John Broughton, Hugh F. Newell, William Garner, William B. Ewing, Edwin Smith, William Trippard, Nancy R. Owen, and Dr. Putman. Amount of books sold by A.G. Ewing after deducting the amount of his account $215.50. Frame for an electrical machine &c sold to Philip S. Fall $12.00. A note on Jeremiah Hinton received. Nathan Ewing, admr. Jan Term 1827(1828).

Page 177   Division of estate of Edward Sanderson, deceased, late of
Mar 22, 1828   Davidson County, made by William Faulkner, Esq., admr. He after throwing all advancements made to his heirs into hotchpotch together with the assets in the hands of the admr, we find that John Saunderson, the oldest child of said Edward, when last heard from resided in the State of Virginia and have no evidence before us of what he has received by way of advancement and therefore leave the full dividend of $800.07 in the hands of the admr for his use. We find adter deducting for advancements that Frances Patten is entitled to $277.07, also find that Edward Saunderson is entitled to $712.07, and also Polly Warren is entitled to $320.07, and also George E. Saunderson is entitled to $689.07, and also Elizabeth Wright is entitled to $174.25. There is also a judgement in the County Court of Sumner against John Brown and George Roberts for $194.32½ in favor of said intestate Edward Sanderson. Signed by William White and Robert Bradford, Commissioners. Jan term 1828.

Page 177   Inventory and sale of estate of Francis McKay, deceased.
Mar 22, 1828   Made by Polly McKay. Several items listed including notes, to wit, Samuel Weakley, William Wisenor, Wilson White, Nelson T. Raymond, William Shaw, Matthew Allen, Thomas J. Gill, Greenwood Payne, and C.M. Brooks. Purchasers of property sold on 8 Nov 1827, to wit, Polly McKay, David B. Love, Asa Hodges, James Woodard, John T. Hunter, M. Gleaves, J.F. Williams, Rolin Wingo, David Ralston, M.B. Frazer, Matthew Allen, N.H. Robertson, William Wisenor, Peter Reasoner, James S. Porter, A.H. Farley, James Dean, John Beauchamp, Dickinson McKay, Thomas J. Gill, Daniel Young, James Marshall, William Newland, William Gill, J.F. Merryman, and J.F. Earthman. Polly McKay, admrx. Jan term 1828.

Page 179   Inventory and sale of estate of Joseph Rowland, deceased.
Mar 26, 1828   Several items listed sold on 24 Nov 1827. Robert Lanier, admr.
Jan Term 1828.

Page 180   Mary G. Ballow, widow support.
Mar 26, 1828   We, Anthony Clopton, George W. Charlton, Esq., and E.H. East, layed off and set apart to Mary G. Ballow one years support for herself and family. Several items listed. 9 Nov 1827. Jan term 1828.

Page 180   Sale of estate of Robert C. Owen, deceased.
Mar 26, 1828   Total of sale $1036.54¼. This 3 Nov 1827. Sandy Owen, admr.
Jan term 1828.

Page 180   Additional inventory of estate of Philip Walker, deceased.
Mar 26, 1828   Persons named, to wit, Henry Seat, William Farmborough, Abigail Walker, and Ebenezer McCance. William H. Hamblin, admr. Jan term 1828.

Page 180   Polly McKay, widow's support.
Mar 28, 1828   We, the Commissioners, laid off one years support for Polly McKay and family, widow and relict of Francis McKay, deceased. Several items listed. 7 Nov 1827. David B. Love, David Hunter, and William Wisenor, Commissioners. Jan term 1828.

Page 181   Settlement of estate of Edward Sanderson, deceased.
Mar 28, 1828   Made with William Faulkner, admr. Several vouchers of $2972.60.
31 Dec 1827. Also account for negroes. Signed by Joseph Love and Benjamin Wilkinson,
Commissioners. Jan term 1828.

Page 181   Settlement of estate of Josiah Mullin, deceased.
Mar 28, 1828   Made by Elizabeth Mullin, admrx. Persons listed, to wit, J.
Newman, _____ Spear, _____ Ewing, _____ Sutton, E.H. Foster, Isaac Mullin, Jas. Roan, Jas.
Grizzard, J.W. McCombs, _____ Mount, Jason Thompson, George Crockett's house rent, John
Elliston's estate, _____ Bryant, Shelby McCall, _____ Hinton, _____ McMuns, _____ Bedford,
George Wilson, and Martin New. Jan 26, 1828. Jesse Wharton, Thomas Edmiston and N.B.
Pryor, Commissioners. Jan term 1828.

Page 182   Robert Weakley, Bond of Identity.
Mar 30, 1828   We, James Jackson, Sarah Hannah, James Kirkman, and James
Erwin are bound unto Robert Weakley for three hundred thousand dollars for the payment of
which we bind ourselves, our heirs, executors and assignees, jointly. Condition of the
obligation is such that Robert Weakley has become one of the sureties of Ellen Kirkman, who
is appointed executrix of the late Will and Testament of Thomas Kirkman, deceased, if said
Ellen Kirkman should be guilty of an maladministration &c of the assets coming to her
hands, Robert Weakley should be rendered liable as surety. This 16 July 1827. Test: Richard
H. Barry and Hugh Erwin. James Jackson, James Kirkman, James Erwin and Sarah Hannah.
Jan term 1828.

Page 182   Land divided of Isaac Battle, deceased.
Mar 30, 1828   Plat on page 183. Four divisions. One lot of 339.5 acres as
Allen's part. One lot of 200 acres as Susan's part. One lot of 374.5 as William's part, and a
lot of 150 acres as the dower lot. This 27 Oct 1827. William H. Nance, John Kimbro,
William Waldron, Charles Johnson, and William Scruggs, Commissioners. Jan term 1828.

Page 183   Negroes divided of James Turner, deceased.
Mar 30, 1828   Lot of four valued at $1347.50. Lot 4 of five valued at $1370.00.
Lot 2 to pay lot 1 $22.50. D. McGavock. We, Cary Felts and Charles Hays met 1st Jan
1828 and Medicus Turner drew Lot No. 1 and lot of horse head valued to $225.00 and 75
barrels of corn, 22 head of hogs and 15 head of sheep. Jan Term 1828.

Page 184   Land divided of Joseph Philips, deceased.
Mar 31, 1828   Plat on page 184. No. 1 of 117½ acres to Josiah ?. Williams and
Margaret T. Williams and Lot No. 2 of 117½ acres to William Williams and Sarah Williams.
Land lying in McLane's Bend of Cumberland River devised by Joseph Philips, deceased, to his
daughters Sammy Williams and Margaret T. Williams. Margaret's land borders a corner of
John Evan's preemption right, William Williams' corner. Sarah's land borners Lot No. 1 and
William Williams' line. Also at the request of the parties have made a division of a
distillery which they owned severalty the one half which was owned by Margaret T. Williams
we have gave to Sally Williams. This 24 Nov 1827. James McGavock, Sam Weakley, Duke
W. Sumner, Micajah Autry, and William Neely. Stephen Cantrell, J.P. Jan Term 1828.

Page 185   Lucretia Morris, widow's support.
Mar 31, 1828   We have allotted Lucretia Morris, widow, 2000 lbs of pork and
other items. This 31 Oct 1827. Nelson Tally, Pitt Woodard, Matthew Allen and David
Hunter, Commissioners. Jan term 1828.

Page 185   Nancy Horton, widow's support.
Mar 31, 1828   We give to Nancy Horton, a widow of Josiah Hunter, deceased,
her years support, several items listed. This 26 Nov 1827. Lewis Joslin, William Gaver and
Edward Raworth, Commissioners. Jan term 1828.

Page 186   Negroes divided of Richard Boyd, deceased.
Mar 31, 1828   To Joseph W. Horton who is the owner of John A.M. Boyd's share,
a negro boy Daniel. To Rachel Boyd, widow of said Richard Boyd, deceased, we give Fanny
and her child also Luke, Ann and Amanda, all children of Fanny and she is to pay to
Clementina Boyd $50.00. To Whitmel Boyd negro man Jim, a boy Alfred commonly called

Big Alfred, and a girl Harriet. To Clementina Boyd a negro man Isaac, girl Maria and a boy Lewis and $50.00 to be paid to her by Rachel Boyd. To Robert B. Turner and Sophronia L. his wife we give negro woman Nitty and her child boy Alfred commonly called Little Alfred, and boy Jacob. To Laodocia Boyd a negro woman Milly and child boy Miol and girl Charity. To Rachel Tennessee Boyd a negro man Sanchs, boy Stephen and a boy Ned. This 28 Dec 1827. Lewis Joslin, Giles Harding and Edward Raworth, Commissioners. Jan Term 1828.

Page 186   Land divided of Richard Boyd, deceased.
Apr 3, 1828   Plat on page 186. Land borders Cumberland River. Surveyed by John Davis and a plot of the town property made by one of the Commissioners. To Rachel T. Boyd Lot No. 1 of 47 3/4 acres. Lot No. 2 of 38¼ acres to Sophronia S. Turner. Lot No. 3 of 37 3/4 acres to Clementina H. Boyd and also lot in Nashville. Lot No. 4 of 72½ acres to Laodicia J. Boyd and also a lot in Nashville. Lot No. 5 of 72½ acres to Whitmel H. Boyd also lot in Nashville. Lot No. 6 of 68 acres to John A.M. Boyd also lot in Nashville. Widow's dower, Rachel T. Boyd, of 176 acres, also part of Lot No. 11 in original plan of Nashville. Market Street and Clark Street. School house and one acre lot goes with Lot No. 6. This 1 Feb 1828. Duncan Robertson, J.T. Elliston, Addison East, and Simon Bradford and Jacob McGavock, Commissioners. Jan term 1828.
John A.M. Boyd VS Whitmel H. Boyd and others, heirs of Richard Boyd, deceased. About the equal shares of the estate. Court ruled the division was a true one.

Page 189   Negroes divided of William R. Bell, deceased.
Apr 10, 1828   To James R. Skyles and his wife Eliza four negroes. To Robert Bell three negroes. To Clement L. Bell two negroes. To George Bell four negroes. To Henry C. Bell two negroes. To Hugh F. Bell two negroes. To Robert Bell pay Clement L. Bell $150.00, Hugh F. Bell is to pay Clement L. Bell $50.00. Hugh F. Bell to pay George Bell $50.00 which makes the above division equal between the several heirs. Wit: Henry C. Bell one of the heirs and of full age, and Thomas A. Duncan guardian for Clement L. Bell, Hugh F. Bell and George Bell and Robert Bell, minors. Dec 6, 1827. John Shute, George Shall and John Harding. Jan term 1828.

Page 189   Sale of estate of John Kellum, deceased.
Apr 10, 1828   Sale on 18 Nov 1826. Purchasers, to wit, Martha Kellum, Elijah Lake, Henry Richardson, John C. Glasgow, Gustavus Rape, Sinclair Scott, Thomas Allen, P.N. Thompson, Willie Carrington, William Scot, D.G. Thompson, William Russell, John McIlewain, (illegible), Benjamin Smith, Isaac Smith, Jacob Rape, and William Anderson. 18 Nov 1826. Alexander McIlwain and Martha Kellum, admrs. Jan term 1828.

Page 190   Martha Kellum, widow's support.
Apr 11, 1828   Martha Kellum, widow of John Kellum, deceased, several items listed. 14 Nov 1826. Thomas Scott, Elijah Lake and St. Clair Scott, Commissioners. Jan Term 1828.

Page 190   Inventory of estate of John Deatherage, deceased.
Apr 11, 1828   Made by William Compton, admr. Judgement recoovered against Thomas Deatherage in Davidson County Court $1983.75. The balance of the estate consisting of money and notes remains in the hands of Missers Foster and Fogg. This Jan 24, 1828. Jan term 1828.

Page 190   Negroes divided of Josiah Mullen, deceased.
Apr 11, 1828   Between Elizabeth Mullen and Joseph T. Elliston guardian for John Mullen which are as follows, three negroes to Elizabeth Mullen, four negroes to John Mullen upon which division Joseph T. Elliston guardian allows Elizabeth Mullen $150.00. This __ ___, 1828. Jan term 1828.

Page 191   Elizabeth S. Ramsay, widow's support.
Apr 11, 1828   Elizabeth S. Ramsay, widow and relict of Jacob W. Ramsay, deceased, given one years support of several items. This 21 Nov 1827. Michael C. Dunn, William Ewing and James Condon, Commissioners. Jan term 1828.

Page 191   Settlement of estate of John Earthman, deceased.
Apr 11, 1828   Persons listed, to wit, William Homes, E. Cunningham, E.S. Hall,

Jack E. Turner, James Grizzard, D.P. Davis, Solomon Clark, R. Chick, William Hope, N. Ewing, V. Casney, Lewis Earthman, B.H. Lanier, Hinley Moses, _____ Higginbotham, Polly Earthman her allowance, Jno. Hunter, Gerner Lanier, Jno. Huffman, William B. Cox, James H. Chick, Henry Holt, Dr. A.G. Goodlet, Sevier Drake, N.P. Jackson, R. Sister, M. Kellor, George Wilson, E.H. Foster, D.B. Love, William Ramsay, John Beazley, S. Shannon, Hynes Knowles and Woods, J. Earthman, _____ Earthman, Jr., _____ Criddle, _____ Ralston, _____ Tait, J.M. Cook, and _____ Brown. Jno. Stump and David Ralston, Commissioners. Jan term 1828.

Page 192   Inventory of estate of James Walker Sitler, deceased.
Aor 15, 1828   600 acres of land in Dickson County, a negro woman and one gray mare. Also notes on William and Robert Daniel, Robert and William Hamilton, one half lot on Public Square, one half lot No. 173, blacksmith shop 78 feet Water Street, 126½ acres of land purchased of Jabez White, house and lot in Columbia, 250 acres in Dickson County, one half of two houses and lots in Russellville, Kentucky, and several other items including one gold watch and one lot in Winchester, Franklin County. Notes on John C. McLemore, Brier M(illegible), Ralph Crabb, Josiah Nichol, Francis Sink, S. Crosthwait, Nicholas Gordon, Jas. S. Haynes, David Park, William Hamilton, Felix Grundy, Edward Ward, R.C. Napier, Crockett & Adams, George Shall, Daniel Saffrans, Decker & Dyer, N.E. Phipps, M. Fly, John Nichol, Jas. P. Peters, George Crockett, Jas. Stewart, Jacob Shall, Anderson & Knox, John Hodg(Hodge), W.F. Long, W.W. Lea, Joseph Minnich, R. & A. Lockhart, McCullough & Neal, Avery & Ward, Jas. H. Wilson, John K. Yerger, Jas. H. Perry, Reuben Searcy, Hynes, Knowles & Wood, Jesse Lincoln, S. Cantrell, Robert Bradford, J. & J.W. Sitler, Thomas Phillips, Moyers & McEwing, Jacob Moyers, Lem Crosby, Andrew Smith, Loyons & Lothers, George Pigg, Jas. Erwin, Isaac Robbins, Frederick Lapitee, Solomon Simmons, Samuel Seay (steamboad Robinson), Gleen & Lincoln, Thomas Fletcher, Jesse Brinson, George W. Campbell, Jas. Bright, D. Herbert for Gillespie & Russell, J.P. Peters, John Wilson, Thomas Whitmell, John Lewis, Benjamin Golson, George McDowel, Jordan C. Holt, James Sandford, Bates & Hightower, N. Patterson, John Davis, Jonathan Betts, Thomas Eastin, George Poyzer, Jenkin Whiteside, Joseph Coleman, John Basford, Thomas Patton & H. Curd, David & William Perkins, Edmond Hewlett, E.H. Marr, Thomas G. Bradford, John Stone, John G. Sims, Davis Cobler, Aron Gambrill, G.F. Maney, John M. Tilford, Martin & Scruggs, Stump & Cox, E.S. Hall, Jas. Tilford, Joseph H(illegible), Edwin Alexander, William McMinn, Peter Moyer, John P. Erwin, W. Barrow, Randolf Ross, William L. Brown, A.V. Brown, R. Battson, Jesse Russell, William Wilson & Sons, Barbara Sittler, Caroline Peck, Jesse Durdan, Peter Braushaw, Henry Dickinson, William Alderson, William Lytle, William Black, Keepon & Shaffer, Goldsmith Chandley, James Woods, Peter Bradshaw, Benjamin Talbot, Charles Bosley, H.W. Rutledge, John L. Hadley, Tennessee Knowles, William Keen, Jr., Joseph Smith, S.B.Marshall, Yeatman & Woods, Abernathy & Brothers, John R. Burke, R.H. Barry, Frederick Schen(illegible), William Hamilton, Jesse Park, James Dickinson, William Trippard, William Wilkinson, Jr., Samuel Star(illegible), H. Falkes, Exum Sumner, William Hope guardian, M.H. Quinn, John Harding, William Phillips, Jos. Horton, David Barrow & Co., B.S. Webber, Jas. Woods, William Gibson, David S. Jameson, John Overton, and Mack. Hichcock. For note given him to collect one suit for house and lot in Columbia. Isaac Sittler, admr. Jan Term 1828. (a very long inventory)

Page 194   Philip Shute receipt from Micajah Fly.
May 12, 1828   Philip Shute, executor of John Low, deceased, $1100.00 in full for part or portion of property that fell to Laurety Lowe daughter of said deceased agreeable to the last will of the deceased and agreeable to a settlement this day between Philip as executor. This 28 Sept 1825. Test: Edwin Smith and William Salisbury. Apr term 1828

Page 195   Will of Francis Hodge, deceased.
May 28, 1828   I lend to my well beloved wife Biddey Hodge one negro man Chain and a negro boy Jack during her natural life also a mare and her colt and other items. It is my desire that my son John Hodge shall let my wife Biddey have a sufficiency of ground to till &c and to occupy the building where I now live during her natural life. To my daughter Betsey Armstrong and her heirs a negro girl named Malina. To my son John Hodge a negro boy Jack (after the death of my wife). All the personal estate not lent nor given shall be sold and the money be equally divided between my son John Hodge and Betsey Armstrong, all the property I have loaned to my wife (except negro woman Chain) at my death. To my son James Hodge's legal heirs $1.00 full part of my estate. To my daughter Sarah Slaughter's

204

heirs $1.00 their share. To my son Robert Hodge $1.00. To my son George Hodge $1.00. To my daughter Prusilah Carrithers $1.00. After the death of my wife the negro woman Chain to be free and in care of my son John Hodge. This 2?, Feb 1822. Wit: Moses E. Carter, Robert McFaddin and William McFaddin. Apr Term 1828.

Page 196   Will of Christopher Christian, deceased.
May 28, 1828   To my son Christopher Christian and his heirs part of a lot on Water Street in the town of Nashville, 25 feet running back 60 feet, part of a lot on Market Street, my negro man George and all the rest of my estate of every kind. It is my desire that my wife Patty should have the house and occupation of all the above named property during her natural life or widowhood for the support of my son and her daughter Jinny (so long as she remains single) and the death or marriage of my wife. I wish the lots rented out. Negro George hired out and remains of my property sold. I appoint Robert B. Curry, Duncan Robertson and Henry Ewing my executors and guardian of my son until he attains the age 21 years. This __ day Oct 1827. Test: Nathan Ewing and Peyton Robertson. Additional to the will, thie 14 Jan 1828, incase my son Christopher should die before his mother leaving no issue in that event the property bequeathed to him shall go to his mother. Wit: Austin Gresham and Daniel McIntosh. Apr Term 1828.

Page 197   Inventory and account of sale of estate of Neal McDaniel,
May 28, 1828   deceased. Purchasers, to wit, William Faulkner, Jos. Sadler, _____ Cagle, Jr., _____ Hyde, _____ Jenkins, _____ Vaughn, _____ Perkins, Thomas Smith, F. Abernathy, Susan Jones, Thomas J. Stump, William B(illegible), _____ Knight, _____ C. Feelin, William West, Al. Merryman, Benjamin Smith, Joel Butler, Jesse E(illegible), J. Cagle, William Westmoreland, Mrs. Faulkner, and Peterson Vaden. (Most of the given names above were in the margin of the book and was not readable). William Faulkner, admr. Apr Term 1828.

Page 197   Settlement of estate of Thomas Kirkman, deceased.
May 28, 1828   Made with Ellen Kirkman, exrx. Persons listed, to wit, McNairy & Roane, Jas. W. McCombs, E.S. Hall, H.S. Bryan, Jas. Kirkman, Jno. Lytle, R. Weakley, A. Balch, Jno. Gill, Jr. & Co., William Lytle, Henry Crabb, Felix Grundy, Thomas and James Kirkman, Kirkman & Erwin, P. Maynor, A.V. Ward, James Jackson, Washington Jackson, Riddle & Forsythe, N. Ewing, John Jackson, Thomas Kirkman, Jr., A.B. Hubberd & Co., Mrs. B. Kirkman, John Goddard, James Erwin, W.W. Lanerd, Jno. S. Simpson, William E. Anderson, Jno. Estill, Hall & Fitzgerald, Henry Ewing, Duncan Robertson, Thomas Washington, Jno. W. Birn, George Wilson, George Bell, _____ Spence, W. & J. Brown, Jos. Brahan, _____ Wells, _____ Lytle, Lytle & McCullough, _____ Pope to Huntsville, _____ Coulter, P.F. Pearson, Ellen Kirkman, Jacob Reese, and William Livingston. Rent from three three story houses on the Square, from one two story house on the Square, from one two story house on Cedar Street, from half lot on Market Street, and proceeds of sales (of) lands in Alabama, house and lot in Huntsville, sales at auction of two houses and lots in Florence also part of lot in Florence, ten shares Florence Stock and Bank Stock, two lots in Smithland, Kentucky, and also negroes sold. Apr Term 1828.

Page 200   Inventory of estate of Josiah E. Giles, deceased.
May 28, 1828   Obligation of Sarah Elizabeth and Cath Gibson for $11.00 per acre for the fourth part of the tract owned by Patrick Gibson, deceased. Notes on, viz, William H. Giles, S.R. Roberts & Co., Chas. Goodall, James H. Giles, G. Ledsniger, John Townson, Elias Duncan, Nelson Cardwell, Henry E. Jones, Hen. Head, Ship Jackson, Eli Harris, James E. Jackson, T. Head, F. Childress, Chas. Carter, and Jacob Anglia. J.T. Elliston, admr. 12 Feb 1828. Sales to Lewis L. Giles and Josiah E. Giles.

Page 201   Inventory of estate of Martin Armstrong, deceased.
May 28, 1828   One claim against George W. Campbell in litigation in Chancery Court in Franklin. G.W. Gibbs, admr. Apr Term 1828.

Page 201   Settlement of estate of John O. Ewing, deceased.
June 9, 1828   Made with Nathan Ewing, admr. Persons listed, to wit, J. Hinton, McNairy, Roane & Ewing, William P. Lawrence, and Jno. R. Burk. Vouchers on, to wit, George W. Alford, Moses Stevens, Bakewell, Page & Bakewell, William W. Goodrum, William Garner, Hooser & Thomas, J.S. Simpson, Jacob C. Smith, William H. Barker, Robertson &

Elliott, Thomas N. Clark, Martin New, Henry Bateman, A.P. Maury, T.D. Lawrence, Gordon Norvell & Co., Samuel W. Carmack, William L. Ward & D. Avery, Isaac Allen, Z.P. Cantrell, R.P. Graham, Joseph Norvell, B(R). McMinn, C. Brooks, George Foster, Richard Tait, Elam Bless, and Lemira S. Ewing. Money due the minor orphan. This 14 Apr 1828. Elihu S. Hall and Robert C. Foster, Commissioners. Apr Term 1828.

Page 202   Inventory of estate of David Cartwright, deceased.
June 9, 1828   Made by Reuben Payne, admr. Note due on Samuel S. Wharton, a bond on Elizabeth Cartwright widow of David Cartwright, deceased, dated 9 Dec 1819, payable when the youngest child becomes of age. Also from Thomas and Jacob Cartwright, executors of the estate of Robert Cartwright, deceased, principal. Also interest paid to William Glasgow and his wife Jemima legatee of Elizabeth Cartwright. $151.00 paid Ans. Brown and Emily Brown, legatee $151.00, paid Thomas (illegible) and his wife $100.00, to Mrs. Elizabeth Cartwright $30.00 __ Dec 1826, and to Thomas and Jacob Cartwright for her note $56.62. Apr Term 1828.

Page 203   Hiring of negroes of Charles M. Hall, deceased.
June 9, 1828   Persons listed, to wit, Nancy B. Hall, William Brooks, Sr., Alphus Lyon, D. Avery, William Brooks, Jr., Samuel Watkins, Williamson H. Horn, Robert Goodlet, and Ellinor Cason. Farm rented to Thomas Harding. Nancy B. Hall, admrx. Apr Term 1828.

Page 203   Division of negroes of Thomas Garret, deceased.
June 9, 1828   Divided among his four children and Winney Richmond formerly Winney Garret, late widow of Thomas Garret, four negroes. Sally Mullen drew three negroes. Polly Garret drew four negroes. Lewis Ridley Garret drew three negroes. George Thomas Garret drew four negroes. For Mrs. Richmond formerly widow of Thomas Garret and each of her children, $930.00. Braddock Richmond whose wife's lot amounts to $930.00 is to pay Joseph T. Elliston guardian of Sarah Mullen and Polly Garret $22.00 the excess of his dividend. And George Thomas Garret is to pay to Jos. T. Elliston $17.00 the excess of his dividend. 14 Feb 1828. J. Wharton, Philip Pipkin, Andrew Casselman and Robert Johnston. Apr Term 1828.

Page 204   Settlement of estate of Ermine Johnson, deceased.
June 9, 1828   Division of the estate among her heirs and find that Isaac Johnson is indebted Edward C. Johnson 30¢ and that Atkinson Fairley is indebted Edward C. Johnson $29.32 and there is a receipt on W. Bedford for two notes to collect and return to the hands of William Faulkner. Also a receipt on Pain for collection for $230.80. William Wilkinson, Sr. and Jonathan Wilkinson, Commissioners. Apr Term 1828.

Page 204   Additional inventory of estate of Shelton Hardgraves, deceased.
June 9, 1828   Made by Susanna Hardgraves, admrx. Found notes on the following, viz, W.B. Loftin in favor of Thomas Loftin. The following debtors live in Louisiana (one note on Frederick Hobbs, and one on Elizabeth Miller. Apr Term 1828.

Page 204   Divided estate of Henry Graves, deceased.
June 9, 1828   Made between his legal representatives report as follows: Lot No. 1 of three negroes to Henry Graves. Lot No. 2 of two negroes to Samuel Graves. Lot No. 3 of two negroes to Sally W. Graves, widow. Lot No. 4 of two to Elizabeth Graves. Lot No. 5 of two negroes to Sutton Graves. Lot No. 6 of three negroes to John Graves. Lot No. 7 of four negroes to Martha Graves now Martha Jefferson. Each legatees part $542.85 3/7. Edmond Goodrich, Joseph W. Clay and Micajah Autry, Commissioners. Apr Term 1828.

Page 205   Land divided of John Earthman, deceased.
June 9, 1828   Plat on page 205. No. 1 to John H. Earthman of 33 acres and 60 poles. No. 2 to Samuel H. Earthman of 21½ acres. No. 3 to Mary C. Earthman of 27 acres. No. 4 to Huldah R. Earthman of 20 acres and 12½ acres. No. 4 to Isaac F. Earthman 63½ acres and 12 poles. Polly Earthman drew 88 3/4 acres. Polly Earthman, widow and relict of John Earthman, deceased, her land borders lands of James Marshall where he now lives near Duke W. Sumner and Isaac Hunter's tanyard. James Marshall, Isaac Hunter, Cornelius Waggoner, Martin Garret, and Jonathan Garret, Commissioners. D.B. Love, Special Deputy Sheriff. Apr term 1828.

Page 207   Settlement of estate of Howel Tatum, deceased.
June 10, 1828   Made by Stephen Cantrell, admr. Persons listed, to wit, N. Ewing, F.B. Fogg, J.P. Clark, and J.P. Wiggin and T.D. Wiggin. This 3 May 1828. Wilkins Tannehill and Robert Farquharson, Commissioners. Apr Term 1828.

Page 207   Settlement of estate of Robert E. Searcy, deceased.
June 11, 1828   Made with Stephen Cantrell, executor. Persons listed, to wit, George Ament, N. Ewing, Mrs. Isabella Searcy, Houston & Pilcher for rent of the house that now live in, B. & Jo. Shaw for rent of the house on Market Street, Houston & Anderson, C. Brooks, Thomas Welch, J. Horton a Sheriff, Jno. H. Eaton an Attorney for Mrs. Searcy, and Aldridge & Walker for repair on their house. This 2 May 1828. Wilkins Tannehill and William Lytle, Executors, Commissioners. Apr Term 1828.

Page 208   Settlement of estate of Pembroke Cartwright, deceased.
June 14, 1828   Made with Samuel L. Wharton, executor. Persons listed, to wit, A. Mathis, J. Newland, T. Cartwright, William P. Byrn, A. Cartwright, A. Brown, William Glasgow, and J. Beazley and N. Ewing. William Lytle, Esquire and Jno. H. Smith, Commissioners. Apr Term 1828.

Page 209   Nancy Philips, her dower.
June 14, 1828   We met to lay off to Nancy Philips, widow and relict of Samuel Philips, deceased, her dower in the real estate of which her said husband died seized and possessed in D. County, met at the residence of Nancy Philips and laid off and set apart to her land which consists of 163 acres and 136 Sq. poles. Land begins at a stake in the middle of the road leading from Nashville to Huntsville, including the mansion house in which Samuel Philips lived immediately before his death with all the out houses. This 21 Feb 1828. Alexander Buchanan, Abraham Whittemore, Thomas Bell, George Chadwell, and Samuel Edmondson, Commissioners. Apr Term 1828.

Page 210   Inventory of estate of David M. Richardson, deceased.
June 14, 1828   Made on Apr 21, 1828 by William Hope, admr. Several items listed including one silver watch. Apr term 1828.

Page 210   Inventory of estate of Shelton Hardgraves, deceased.
June 16, 1828   Several items listed including credits on James Cloud now in the hands of Foster & Smith which suit is commenced in the County of Williamson and one on John Davis, and one on Reuben League. Apr Term 1828.

Page 211   Account of sale of estate of Shelton Hardgraves, deceased, of
June 16, 1828   County. The hire of four negroes. Susanna Hardgraves, admrx.
Apr Term 1828.

Page 211   Inventory of estate of Mrs. Frances Curtis, deceased.
June 16, 1828   Notes, to wit, R.A. Higginbotham and J. Crockett, Charles G. Fisher and William L. Washington, J.R. Jefferson and S.S. Jefferson, Jonathan Wilkinson, and John Harrison. Four negroes, Henry and Montaville willed her grand daughter and delivered. Hagar willed to her daughter Mrs. Dunnivant and delivered. Peakes willed to Patsey Osborn and delivered. Nashville Apr 29, 1828. Thomas Crutcher, executor. Apr Term 1828.

Page 211   Additional inventory of estate of David M. Richardson, deceased.
June 16, 1828   Several items listed including $6.00 on John L. Bugg, $45.00 due him from myself May 1, 1828. William Hope, admr. Apr Term 1828.

Page 211   Sarah Graves, her dower.
June 16, 1828   Edmond Goodrich, John Maxey, Micajah Autry, Josiah F. Williams and Thomas Sample laid off and set apart to Sarah Graves her dower, land bordering McMurry's tract, and the bank of the Cumberland River. Containing 159½ acres being equal third. This 15 Mar 1828. Apr Term 1828.

Page 212   Settlement of estate of Abner Cowgill, deceased.
June 17, 1828   Made with Edmond Melvin, admr. Persons listed, to wit, William Wilson, William Hays, Mary Craves, William Sanders, Joseph Cook, James P. Thompson,

Morris Brewer, Timothy Dodson admr of Allen Dodson, deceased, Edmond Melvin and wife. Absalom Gleaves and George W. Charlton, Commissioners. Apr Term 1828.

Page 213   Settlement of estate of Robert Cartwright, deceased.
June 17, 1828   In account with Thomas and Jacob Cartwright, executors, on final setttlement of said estate. Persons listed, to wit, E.P. Connel, John T. Dismukes, J.D. Donelson, and N. Ewing. 7 Mar 1828. E.P. Connell, J.P. and E. Goodrich, Esqrs., Commissioners. Apr Term 1828.

Page 213   Susan Hardgraves, her support.
June 17, 1828   Widow and relict of Shelton Hardgraves, deceased. Several items listed for one year's provisions for her and her family. Jno. Davis, Moses Knight and Lewis Joslin, Commissioners. Apr Term 1828.

Page 214   Settlement of estate of William P. Bowers, deceased.
June 19, 1828   Several notes listed. Collection paid to the deceased, to wit, by John Harrison, William Campbell, Joshua Drake, Thomas Ragan, Joseph Dorris, John Jordan, James Bowers, Will Crawford, John Tomlinson, Samuel S(illegible), James B. Congers, and John Parrott. This 21 Apr 1828. Charles L. Byrn and John Pirtle, Commissioners. Apr Term 1828.

Page 214   Division of property of William Wallace, deceased.
June 19, 1828   Division of negroes. To David Reed and wife Lot No. 3 of Major and Charles. To Guilford Reed and wife Lot No. 4 of Henry and Isreal. To Benjamin Wallace Lot No. 5 of Chaney and Jeffrey. To John Wallace Lot No. 2 of Kinchen and $235.00. To William Wallace Lot No. 1 of Jane and child and $210.00. Mar 25, 1828. John Stump, William Faulkner, Stephen Cantrell, and Richard Hyde, Esquires, Commissioners. Apr Term 1828.

Page 215   Settlement of estate of Daniel Binkley, deceased.
June 19, 1828   Made with George W. Charlton, admr of estate. Note on Ephraim T. (illegible), Jacob Binkley and H. Gray, Marvel Lowe, and John Hall. This 15 Feb 1828. Herbert Towns and Absalom Gleaves, Commissioners. Apr Term 1828.

Page 215   Will of James Boyd, deceased, a butcher of Nashville.
Aug 11, 1828   My late wife Patsey who returned to my bed and board and has born to me a son named William it is my will that they share my property in the same manner as if no divorce had separated us and that said Patsey shall enjoy all the rights that my lawful wedded would be entitled to. This 22 July 1828. Wit: Adam G. Goodlett and George S. Grass and Duncan Robertson. July Term 1828.

Page 215   Will of Alexander Campbell, deceased.
Auf 11, 1828   To (son) James 139 acres of land it being 39 acres on the east part of my 60 acres survey on which he now lives and the 100 acres being my 100 acre survey adjoining the above. To my son Thomas all the rest of my land on Otter Creek including the houses and plantation on which I now live and one bed and furniture and one half of my household furniture. To my son Francis one bed and furniture having heretofore given him all I intended except the bed and furniture. To my daughter Sarah my negro girl Clary and the bed that is now called hers and its furniture and one half of my household furniture and I do not include beds and their furniture, also the gray horse. The rest of my property to be sold and the money be divided among all my children. I appoint my two sons Francis and Philip, my executors. This 25 Oct 1819. Wit: Thomas Edmiston and Allen Cotton. July Term 1828.

Page 216   Will of Sevier Drake, deceased.
Aug 11, 1828   To my beloved wife Mary P. Drake all the negroes which came by her (3), and also other items. To my only child, son Nathaniel S. Drake, after my debts first being paid, all the money and profits that arises from the sale of my land which I have sold my negro fellow Isaac and other items. To my sister Sally Criddle, for her attention to me now on my sick bed and past favors, my bureau. To my beloved old father John Drake my saddle and bridle. To my brothers my wearing cloths. if my son Nathaniel S. Drake not live to the age of twenty one, that his part of my estate go to his mother Mary P. Drake and the

balance of my estate be equally divided between my brothers and sisters. I appoint my brother Jonathan Drake my sole executor. This 1st May 1828. Wit: Thomas Heaton, Benjamin Hyde and Lewis Williams. July Term 1828.

Page 217   Will of William Gibson, deceased.
Aug 11, 1828   To his son Joseph Thompson Gibson all his property both real and personal, viz, two negro women, house, cows and household furniture &c, also my lot of graound in Nashville known by part of Lot No. 79. Nevertheless be it understood that his mother, my wife Rebecca Gibson, shall hold all the above mentioned property for her support and the support and education and love of Joseph Thomas Gibson until he arrives to the age of 21 years then she will deliver over the personal property to him except the lot which she, the said Rebecca, shall hold during her natural life. After my decease it will be optional with my wife Rebecca continue the business in conjunction with her brother Nathan Adams (which I recommend) but before such copartnership shall be entered into, all my debts shall be first paid. I appoint George Crockett, Thomas P. Adams and Robert Gibson to act as guardians to my son advise from my wife. This 9 Aug 1827. Wit: Robert Gibson, Thomas P. Adams and George Crockett. July Term 1828.

Page 218   Will of Diana Hoggatt, deceased.
Aug 12, 1828   To Mrs. Rhoda Clopton a featherbed &c. To Amanda F. Hoggatt a featherbed and bed furniture she has already selected. To my grandson Sandifer Hoggatt my bay horse. All the rest of my residue and remainder of my estate &c to my son James W. Hoggatt whom I also appoint my sole executor. This 9 July 1828. Wit: George Keeling and O. Gordon. July Term 1828.

Page 218   Will of Susan Gilliam, deceased.
Aug 12, 1828   To my sister Sally all my right title and interest in and to the tract or parcel of land whereon I now live lying and being on the waters of Trace Creek in Davidson County, containing 100 acres. Also to Sally all my right and title to a number of slaves bequeathed by legacy to me by my Aunt Molly Tucker of Dinwiddie County, Virginia, slaves being now in the possession of Cecila Champion of Sussex County, Virginia. Also to Sally all my goods and chattels and all property whatsoever I have or may die possessed of, also appoint my dear sister Sally to be sole executrix. This 24 Jan 1821. Wit: Leven Edney, John W. Allen, B. Russell Howland and Nathaniel Gilliam. July Term 1828.

Page 219   Will of William Goode, deceased.
Aug 12, 1828   I desire the executors take possession of the plantation I am now in possession of and carry on the farm &c. All the personal property except my negroes be sold and the negroes be hired out until my children becomes of age or marries. Each of them to have their part of the negroes. The executors to sell a tract of land I own in Barren County, Kentucky. I appoint my executors, David Vaughn and Reuben Payne. This 9 June 1828. Test: John E. Minus and R.A. Higginbotham. July Term 1828.

Page 220   Inventory of estate of Thomas Campbell, deceased.
Aug 12, 1828   Persons listed, to wit, James D. Smith, William Cook, Hornbach & Walker, McCann & Pettigrew, James M. Pettigrew, W.M. Winbum, James Gould, James Barrett, James A. Gibson, Peter Moseley, Arnold & Norvell, John McClelland, McClelland & Hall, John Young, John M. Tilford, Joseph H. Marshall, A. R(illegible), Murphy & Holland, John C. McLemore, Richard McConnell, Jas. Herron, Samuel Peters, John Fowler, John M. Pollock, J.C. Beckham, Dougherty & Foreman, Francis Mercer, Francis Wheatley, A.A. Kincannon, Moore & Croxwell, Jesse Lincoln, James Scott, William Chamberland, Robert Crockett, Charles Guiger, Jas. T. Eccles, Green & Mitchell, Jos. Finley, Chester's notes, Thompson's note, Moore's note, William L. Cobbs, Hodge's note, Fisher A. Han(illegible), Maj. Hockley, Silas Lock, Matthew Clanton, Robert Murry, W. King, A.B. Hawkins, Dr. A.G. Goodlet, W.B. Ament, E. Dibrell, in the hands of Gilchrist, W.O. Whitney, Giles Burditt, William Gann, W.P. Sar(illegible), _____ Carroll, Shirley & Snoddy, Robert Orrel, Phil Thomas, S.V.D. Stout, Dr. Overton, Andrew Woods, Tilford & King, Smith & Johnson, Philip Morris, J.R. Grundy, J.K. Chester, David Hughes, Champ Hughes, H. Crabb, Falls & Christy, Lafayette G(illegible), David Culp, William Bosworth, J.S. Moore, J.C. Muscrilla, James Moore, Thomas Norman, William Cook, Charles Rhea, Jos. H. Marshall, Thomas Walton, P.R. Rison, Jas. Putnam, Thomas A. Duncan, Thomas G. Billow, H. Harroldson, J.H. Freeman, Wyman Leftwick, Stephen T. Logan, Pleasant Staggs, J.S. Hamilton, John Lawrence, Joseph

Hyse, Mason & Banks, J.H. Martin, W.C. Anderson, J.G. Anderson, Paul Shirley, Patsey (blank), Jos. Park, William Scudder, A. Bynew & Co., A. Massey, William Edmondson, J.B. Grizzard, Shirley & Montague, S.H. Boone & Co., Harton & Cloud, C. McConnell, Murphree & Holland, P.A. Mirabin, J. Thomas, Campbell & McConnell, H.N. Martin, S.C. Martin, F.M. Patterson, G.W. Coalman, John McCollough, W.H. Horn, H. Bryant, N. Cartwright, H. Norvell, Collin A. Hogs, James Monks, David T. Hatch, Samuel Carmell, John Graham, M. Alexander, John Austin, C. Grant, Robert Hawkins, James Tilford, Alexander McDaniel, Edmondson & Robertson, Thomas P. Adams, John Gill, Jr. for rent, G. Wilson, Thomas Campbell, Constant A. Wilson, and Robert Murray. Received for one bale cotton sold by P. Shirley. There is some claims in Kentucky, viz, A. Byrn & Co., Russellville. John Byrn & Co., Wadesborough and others. List of money received of, to wit, Thomas Campbell, deceased, William Bosworth, Richard McConnel, Andrew Woods, C. Guiger, William King, T.T. Eccles Kentucky money, Silas Lock, Tilford & King, J.A. Gibson, McCann & Pettigrew, James D. Smith, James Gould, James Barret, Matthew Clanton, A. Revier, William B. Ament, Peter Moseley, Robert Hawkins, James Putnam, James M. Pettigrew, Hornback & Walker, and F. Wheatley. 17 July 1828. Corry McConnel, Trustee. Richard McConnell, admr. July Term 1828.

Page 224   Settlement of estate of John Lowe, deceased.
Aug 12, 1828   Philip Shute, executor. Paid to the following, viz, Allen for Tennessee and John's schooling, Jos. L. Ewing for tuition of Tennessee and John, Jno. R. Shaw for Tennessee and John's schooling, E. Smith for school books for Tennessee, Joseph Scales for Loretta's past leaves, Ewing for recording will, Richard Lowe note for Loretta, N. Moore for John, Jno. Brant for collecting money in Louisiana, _____ Dorris, N.A. Spear, R.H. Barry for John a book, E. Smith, M. Fly, Smith & Quinn, Jas. Nichols, Whitford & Williams, William Allen, Fountain P. Jones, Robertson & Elliot, Jno. L. Bugg, Mr. Carrington, A. Hume, S. Tilford, and Edwin Smith. Note on Jos. Colwell, one on Francis M(illegible), one on Thomas Brown, and two drafts of C. Stump. This 15 May 1828. Stephen Cantrell and Will Lytle, Commissioners. July Term 1828.

Page 226   Inventory and account of sales of estate of Francis Hodge, dec'd.
Aug 13, 1828   Sale on May 15, 1828. Purchasers, to wit, Abraham Castleman, John Hodge, George Hodge, Levin Cator, John Armstrong, Lewis C. Allen, William H. Allen, Joseph Bartlett, Legate McCrory, George Harding, James Ezell, William M. Bateman, Abraham Smith, William Hodge, Lewis Wallet, Allen Cotton, David Johnson, Rany Allen, Elisha Walker, Samuel Allen, Greenberry Cartwright, William Chestham, James Crow, Elisha Biggs, John Aust, Giles & Page, William Betts, Thompson Osbourn, Joshua Perry, and William Hamilton. John Hodge, executor. July Term 1828.

Page 228   Additional account of estate of Thomas Taylor, deceased.
Aug 13, 1828   Amount of sale was $40.00 too much. Robert Taylor, executor.
July Term 1828.

Page 228   Inventory of estate of William Johnson, deceased.
Aug 14, 1828   Several items listed. This 21 July 1828. Dursilla Johnson, admrx.
July Term 1828.

Page 228   Inventory of estate of Benjamin F. Lewis, deceased.
Aug 14, 1828   Taken 26 July 1828. Notes listed, to wit, J.M. Smith endorser William Lytle, C.M. Bradford by R.A. Higginbotham, William B. Lewis by William D. Griffing, J.W. Horton by G.W. Gibbs, W. King & W.F.L. Claiborne by W.W. Lea, Yeatman & Woods, William King, Solomon Clark, R. Armstrong, William Marshall by Samuel C. Martin, H. Roland, William Brooks, T.D. Lawrence, Alex. McCall, A. Kingsley by James Woods &Co., Philip Campbell by And. Hays & L.P. Cheatham, W.T. Crenshaw by Richard Barrett, G.W. Gibbs by John Boyd, T.D. Laurence by Floyd Hunt, James Clark, John McGavock handed D.B. Love. Accounts considered good, to wit, William Brooks, R.C. Napier, John Sigler, Alpha Kingsley, Ann Barrow, John Newman, William B. Lewis, William Lytle, Moses Norvell, John R. Burke, Watson & Burke, and Micajah Fly. Notes doubtful, to wit, A.B. Hawkins, R.W. Hart, John S. Davis, John B. Logan, B. (urp(illegible)), D. Brown, James Christian, W. Harper, Caleb Goodrich, Shadrack Bell, John Stump, Roger Dougal, John Stewart, James Long, Noel Watkins, H.N. Marlin, J.S. Hamilton, Pierce Floyd, Lewis Carlton, and John G. Anderson. Doubtful collection, to wit, John G. Anderson, Thomas Connally, Mr. McCombs Carpenter,

Mr. Gilman to E. Dobson, and B.W. Taylor's order on William Washington in favor of T.W. Gilman, Alfred Balch, Thomas Harper, Joseph H. (illegible), Robert Goodlet, Elijah Grant, Collin D. Hobbs, Mr. Chapman a fidler, Bernard McFaddin, Robert Hart, James W. Robertson, Stephen Saunders, John Wilcox, Wright Ramsey, Samuel Watkins, Robert Bradford, Russell B. Vannoy, John Gregory, Mrs. Galloway, Daniel Brinn, David Perkins, P. Craddock, H. Roland, and Dr. R.A. Higginbotham. James Woods, admr. July Term 1828.

Page 231   Account of sales of estate of David M. Richardson, deceased.
Aug 15, 1828   Sale on Mar 17, 1828. Purchasers, to wit, Hillory Lyle, Thomas Royster, James Elizar, William Hope, Severn Donelson, Thomas Watkins, Thomas Dill, William M.Winbourn, William Woodson, William M. Gwinn, Matthew P. Walker, Isaac Hooper, William W. Shaw, David Hunter, Max Redding, Adam Hope, Henry Strange, and Isham Butterworth. William Hope, admr. July Term 1828.

Page 232   Settlement of estate of Thomas Taylor, deceased.
Aug 14, 1828   Made with Robert Taylor, executor. Commissioners find that the executor chargeable with the sum of $5236.00, and vouchers and Commissioners allowed $272.36, leaving a balance of $5074.14. This 7 June 1828. Edmond Goodrich and Samuel S. Wharton. July Term 1828.

Page 232   Deborah Fowler, her support.
Aug 14, 1828   Deborah Fowler late widow of William Fowler, deceased, was laid off and apportion one years support for herself and family. Several items listed. This 10 May 1828. Elijah Lake, Herbert Tarpley and Thomas Scott. July Term 1828.

Page 233   Property returned of John L. Goodwin, deceased.
Aug 14, 1828   By John Jones. Rent of land and three negro children, Fanny, Benjamin and Jennings, also a bell. John Cooper one account $700.00. July Term 1828.

Page 233   Inventory and account of sale of estate of William Fowler, dec'd.
Aug 15, 1828   Purchasers, to wit, James Russell, Deborah Fowler one Bible, Martin Ussery, Sterling Fowler, G. Rape, Thomas Ferebee, Thomas Pack, E. Lake, P. Strange, Henderson Fowler, John Carrington, Jr., Jesse Reynolds, Frederick Martin, A.E. Speer, and C. Glasgow. This 28 July 1828. Deborah Fowler, admrx. July Term 1828.

Page 234   Paulina E. Richardson, her support.
Aug 15, 1828   Provisions for the support of Paulina E. Richardson and family for one year of several items were laid off. May 5, 1828. William H. Hamblin, William Wisenor and William Neely, Commissioners. July Term 1828.

Page 234   Inventory of estate of Alexander McCombs, deceased.
Aug 15, 1828   Made by Gabriel McCombs, admr. Cash received by B.W. Bedford, also of Mrs. Haywood, of Mrs. Susan Haywood, Mrs. Anderson, R. McGavock a Clerk in case of Cary Felts and Jeremiah Ezell, admrs of Willis L. Shumate VS Willie Barrow. Debts, to wit, Mrs. Dougal, Mrs. Woodcock and Henry Burnet, and Mrs. McMinn. This 24 July 1828. July Term 1828.

Page 235   Inventory of estate of Sevier Drake, deceased.
Aug 17, 1828   Several items listed including notes, viz, John Hutchinson, John Newnan, several on John Drake and Benjamin C. Drake, Jr. Jonathan Drake, executor. July Term 1828.

Page 236   Division of estate of William C. Ward, deceased.
Aug 17, 1828   Commissioners proceeded to divide the negroes of the estate of William C. Ward, deceased, and have allotted to the widow Sarah Ward, Albert G. Ward and Mary Indiana Ward their respective share, to wit, Lot No. 1 to Sarah Ward drew 30 negroes. Lot No. 2 to Albert G. Ward drew 32 negroes. Lot No. 3 to Mary Indiana Ward drew 32 negroes. This 29 Jan 1828. Edward Ward, Thomas Harding, William Watson, William Donelson, and Timothy Dotson. July Term 1828.

Page 236   Land divided of estate of Francis May, deceased.
Aug 17, 1828   Petition of Andrew J. May, as one of the devicees of Francis May,

deceased, that he together with Richard H. Barry and Mary L. his wife in right of his wife, James F. May and Margaret J. May are entitled to half of Lot No. 4 in town of Nashville fronting on Market Street, that they claim the same as devicees of their late father Francis May, also shows that James F. May and Margaret J. are minors under the age of 21 years and that Richard H. Barry is their guardian. This 6 July 1828. William Lytle, Thomas Critcher, Robert Farquharson, John Nichol, Stephen Cantrell, David McGavock, Elihu S. Hall, James Erwin, and John H. Smith, Commissioners appointed to divide land. Plat on page 238. July Term 1828.

Page 239   McGavock & Baird's heirs division of land.
Aug 17, 1828   The petition of Frances Baird, Mary Jane Baird by her guardian Thomas Crutcher, and Eliza Ann Baird and John Baird by their guardian Daniel Graham, heir devicees of John Baird, deceased, by his Last Will and Testament. John Baird in his lifetime jointly with Felix Grundy, Esq., a certain lot or parcel of land lying and being in the town of Nashville and known by Lot No. 135, containing about one acre. Felix Grundy conveyed all right, title, claim and interest which he had in said lot to John R. Grundy and he conveyed the same way to Jacob McGavock. This June 18, 1828. Stephen Cantrell, Hinchy Petway, Hugh Elliot, John Cheatham, and Charles J. Love appointed Commissioners to divide and partition Lot No. 135 in Nashville. Land on Vine Street between Francis Baird, Mary Jane Baird, Eliza Ann Baird, and John Baird, heirs &c of John Baird, deceased, late of Davidson County one part and Jacob McGavock of other part. This 23 July 1828.

Page 241   Land divided of William C. Ward, deceased.
Aug 20, 1828   Plat on page 241. Lot No. 1 of 221 2/3 acres and (blank) to Sarah Ward, wife and relict of William Ward, deceased, on Stones Lick. Lot No. 2 of 221 2/3 acres to Albert G. Ward on Stones Lick. Lot No. 3 of 221 2/3 acres to Mary Indiana Ward. Surveyed by Samuel Weakley Apr 26, 1828. Thomas Harding, James W. Hoggatt, William Watson, Edward Ward, and Timothy Dotson. July Term 1828.

Page 243   Estate divided of estate of John Baird, deceased.
Aug 20, 1828   The petition of Frances Baird, widow, Mary Jane Baird by her guardian James Crutcher, and John Baird and Eliza Ann Baird by their guardian Daniel Graham said that sometime in the year 1824 John Baird the husband of Frances, and the father of the rest of your petitioners died in Davidson County after making his Last Will and Testament in which he bequeathed all his real and personal estate to your petitioners to be equally divided amongst them and make Michael C. Dunn his executor. John died possessed of real estate of 160 feet of ground fronting Vine Street being part of Lot No. 135, and part of Lot No. 38 on College Street fronting on College Street, part of Lot No. 50 on College Street and Cedar Street, and a house and part of Lot No. 34 on College Street, and 5 3/4 acres of land adjoining the Female Academy. Court appointed John P. Erwin, Robert Farquharson, John H. Smith, Samuel Tilford, and George Shall, Commissioners, to set apart and allot to each their portion. To Mrs. Frances Baird, the widow of John Baird, we allot one half or an undivided equal moiety of the house and premises including the store house and all the front on the Public Square being part of Lot No. 38 and running back through Lot No. 50 to Cherry Street including the stable and part of said Lot No. 50 and to front equally the same distance on Cherry Street with the front on the Square, also 110 feet of Lot No. 135 on Vine Street said part of 110 feet to front on Vine Street and to adjoin and be next to Jacob McGavock's part of Lot No. 135, also to her own land with David Craighead security for furniture purchased at the executor's sale, three negroes. To John Baird, the only son, we allotted the other half &c of Lot No. 38 &c and one half of that part of Lot No. 50 assigned to Mrs. Baird, also fifty feet on the balance of Lot No. 135 on Vine Street adjoining to Mr. More and Mr. Eichbourn, also 5 3/4 acres of land adjoining the Female Academy purchased of George and Robert Bell all of which is in full of his portion of estate now divided. To Mary Jane Baird the house and lot on College Street being part of Lot No. 34 at present occupied by Thomas H. Fletcher also negro Harry, also the notes of George S. Yerger, J. Collinsworth and Richard H. Barry, ans also a debt of A. Sneed. To Eliza Ann Baird the ground lying on Cherry and Cedar Streets being part of Lot No. 50 including a frame house being the residue of the ground belinging to said estate and front 95 feet on Cherry Street and about 180 feet on Cedar Street, also the residue of the debt against Sneed, and also residue of the cash on hand. This 1 Aug 1828. July Term 1828.

Page 246   Will of Francis Hardgrave, deceased.
Nov 10, 1828   This 22 Feb 1827. To my beloved wife the whole right of my plantation on which I now live during her natural life, also my household furniture and also one third of my personal estate and at her death the land &c belonging, it containing of two different surveys which is 140 acres then to be the property of my son Shelton Hardgrave, also to him one corner cupboard, one desk and book case, also one bedstead and furniture, six table spoons and six tea spoons of silver. To my daughter Hannah Russel 47½ acres of land which she now lives on and at her death is to be James H. Russel, son of Andrew Russel and Hannah Russel. To my grandson Francis Hardgrave, son of John and Polly Hardgrave a negro boy John. It is my will that the quotas or dividends that shall come to Sally Moss, Nancy Mills and Hannah Russell natural lives and at their deaths to be equally divided between the heirs. I appoint my well beloved friends John Davis and Silas Dillahunt to be my sole executors. Wit: John Demoss, James Crowder, Silas Dillahunt, Daniel Dansbee and Johnson Vaughn. Oct Term 1828.

Page 247   Will of Jacob Cartwright, deceased.
Nov 10, 1828   To loan to my beloved wife Patience Cartwright during her widowhood all the use and benefits of my farm whereon I now live except about 15 acres of the cleared land on the west side of the farm for John Cartwright which I want him to have possession of when he comes of age. Also to my wife seven negroes, all the rents and profits of my lands on Whites Creek and in Sumner County for the purpose of raising and educating my three youngest children and in case of her death or marriage, my executors to take possession of the same for the purpose above. To my wife forever all my household and kitchen furniture not hereafter given away and also other items. To my daughter Harriet Mathis a yellow negro girl Kitty and a sorrel mare and colt and what I have heretofore given her. To my daughter Tabitha Cartwright a negro girl Harriet, one sorrel horse, bridle and saddle, a cow and calf, two beds and furniture and one bedstead &c. To my daughter Lizetta Hobdy the interest of $200.00 now which sum of $200.00 as well as what she may heretofore get from my estate, my will is that the principal be put into the hands of Enoch P. Connel as Trustee for her and at her death to be equally divided between her heirs. To my two sons, John and Marcus D. Lafayette Cartwright the plantation whereon I now live to be equally divided between them when the youngest comes of age reserving for my wife the use of the house and as much cleared land as will support her during her lifetime or widowhood. My son John shall have a gray horse now and at his arrival of age to have the use of part of my farm. To my two sons, Robert and Alexander Cartwright all my lands on Whites Creek also 69 acres in Sumner County to be equally divided between them when the youngest comes of age. Residue of my estate to be sold and equally divided among the seven. I appoint Enoch P. Connel and William P. Byrn, my executors. This 22 Sept 1828. Wit: William P. Connel and Martin Pierce. Jan Term 1828.

Page 248   Will of David Crockett, deceased.
Nov 10, 1828   To my mother Rebecca Crockett residing in Ireland the sum of $250.00 to be remitted to her by my executor as soon as convenient after my death. I wish all my estate of every description whatever converted into money and disposed of as follows, to my beloved wife Mary Crockett her heirs and assignees forever one half part of my estate to be paid by my executors whenever my estate is settled. To my son George Crockett and his heirs the remaining one half of my estate to be paid to him when he arrives at the age of 21 years and if he should die before age of 21 years, I give that part of my estate to my brother George Crockett and his heirs. I give to my wife the privilege of keeping any part of my paroperty she may think proper. I wish my copartner in trade to be permitted to settle the business in which we are concerned in such way as they think most advantage having full confidence in their honesty and integrity. I appoint my beloved wife Mary Crockett my executrix and my brother George Crockett and my brother-in-law Thomas P. Adams, as executors. This 13 Sept 1828. Wit: Samuel Hogg, Robert Gibson and David Park, Jr. Oct Term 1828.

Page 249   Inventory of estate of David Crockett, deceased, late a Merchant
Nov 14, 1828   of the town of Nashville and the late firm of George & David Crockett. Notes due the estate of Crockett, Park & Co. Several items sold 13 Oct 1828. Notes on, viz, Robert Gibson, George Crockett, John L. Brown, Joseph Sitton, Moses Stevens, George Childress, C.H. Dickinson, William Armstrong, Washington Barrow, A.W. Johnson, Thomas P. Adams, J.S. Smith, Rev. O. Jennings, William Anderson, Samuel Tilford, W.

Ament, Mrs. Martha Adams, Mrs. Mary Crockett and Dr. Hogg. Accounts due the late firm of George & David Crockett, viz, James McClure, John Moorhead, Bartholomew Walsh, William Bosworth, E. Traylor, Lovett Stevens, Steam Boat President, G. Webster, John Lee, Drewry Dance, William Rutherford, McKinney & Sumner, Bosworth & Swan, W. Bloodworth, Martha Adams, G. McKane, James Grizzard, W.W. White, George Davidson, Robert Campbell, Robert White, John Boyd, Isaac Sitler, John Owen, Dr. Rugsby, John Philips, John Gordon, Thomas P. Adams, John Bullock, William Campbell, William Murrel, Hewlett & Peterson, Luther Taylor, Mrs. Bradly, George Buford, Isaac Thomas, J.C. McLemore, William Keen, Jr., Jane Davis, Solomon Clark, Jesse Hunt, Richard Bradly, Arnold & Norvel, Thomas Bon(illegible), James Thomas, J. Bosley, G.W. Campbell, Jesse Wharton, Thomas Martin, J. Lockhart, J. Woodfin, Mrs. White, J.P. Brown, Braden & White, Col. Dickinson, Gill & Porter, J. Hughs, T. Washington, D. Walker, Mrs. Watson, B. Williamson, Mrs. Probart, S. Perkins (in Western District), Martha Adams, R. Johnson, L. Lay, John Fisher, Daniel Stewart, Fogg & Bullock, P. Anderson, Mrs. Simple, W.P. & L. Ewing, J. Boyd, Archibald Boyd, Michael Finney, William Neely, J. Barry, and William Duncan, and James Galbreath & C0. A list of accounts due the firm of G. & D. Crockett, Cain & Williams, Dr. Walker, J. Robinson, J. Hogan, McCarty & Davis, B. Reese, William Nichol, S. Keeling, R.C. Napier, Bass & Spence, S. & Z.P. Cantrell, and George Crockett, and Thomas P. Adam, executors. Oct Term 1828.

Page 251   Inventory of estate of William Gibson, deceased, late Merchant of
Nov 15, 1828   Nashville. Cash received from N. Adams, Brooks on account of
Mrs. Williamson, John P. Adams, D. Parkman, Col. Ridley, G. & D. Crockett, William Armstrong's note with E.H. Foster, and Edwin Sharp's note, Robert Johnson, Edward Lawrence, James D. Matthews, Samuel Wilson, Richard Sandifer, James Sharp, Robert Robertson, the estate of Abraham Cannon, deceased. Notes in the hands of Christopher Brooks for collection, Capt. Thomas Butler, Sharp & Bart(illegible), Sherwood Green, Mr. Lester, Mrs. Beck, Abraham Gleaves, W.W. Watson, Dr. Howlett, Judge Overton, William B. Holton (moved to Kentucky), John Wright, George Graham, William Allen, Miss McConnel (dead), estate of James Mulherrin, John Moss, Capt. Woodward, Capt. Whitsett, Miss Sally Watkins, Brittain Drake, Esq., Asa Shives, Miles Myers, Mrs. John, John Young, _____ Huffman, _____ Richardson, William H. White, William Downs, Capt. Benjamin Bibb, William Howlet, Joseph McErwin, Joseph Dougal, Freeman Abernathy, Mrs. Sarah Smith, Capt. S.W. Hope, Langhorn Scruggs, Benjamin N. Farrow, Alexander Fossett, Batier Ayry, William Brian, E. Dibrell, Joel D(illegible), T.E. Danson, Philip Thomas, A.C. Hall, Frederick Ivy, Jonas Meniote, Moses Lindsy, David Pinkerton, John Ray, Edward Scruggs, George Woodward, James Scruggs, Drewry Scruggs, Washington Jones, John Kelly, William Lovell, Daniel Mozell, Daniel Hoffman, John B. Logan, William Stewart, Joseph Hollinsworth, Josiah Corbitt, Thomas A. Duncan, Samuel Johnson, Thomas B. Howland, Greenby Lanier, William S. Henry, Mr. Ward, Mrs. Reese, William Rea, William Thomas, Robert Wood, Washington Pullum, Willis Ally, Hon. John Haywood, Philip Frynard, Mr. Frazer, Wily Ray, Nathan Williams, Mrs. Boyd, (illegible) McNairy, Mrs. Chapman, Jesse Wharton, (illegible) H. Robertson, _____ Drew, James Gray, Mrs. Barrow, Joseph Herron, John Sumner, John Boyd, Richard Sutton, James Norment, Capt. John Tapp, S.B. Marshall, Duncan Robertson, Gilbert Washington, William Keen, Jr., D. McIntosh, Mrs. Paine, S. McMannus, David Hughs, J.C. Wilson, Thomas Patterson, Mr. Pearl, Judge McNairy, Mrs. Caldwell, S.C. Genl. Green, Thomas Hamilton, Solomon Clark, Hugh Roland, Mr. Finly, Wilson Sanderlin, Thomas Barnett, E. Grant, Lewis G. Gown, Ethered Harris, Isaac Harvy, Joseph Campbell, Matthew Cayce, Moses Gee (name doubtful), Matthew Reese, David Ray, William Wood, Noel W. Watkins, William Greer, Daniel R(illegible), A. Long, William Burton, William Turner, Thomas (illegible), Thomas Taylor, Thomas Strong, William Sturdevant, Samuel Powers, James Nevins, William B. Drake, estate of Samuel Crockett, A. Simpson, Edwin Sharp to collect in Rutherford County, Jacob Binkley, Nathaniel Barksdale, John Perkins, Saniel Baker, Jacob Tilman, William Cox, Stephen Sanders, William Anderson, William H. Shelton, Miss Anderson, William Baker, Henry Ford, Mrs. Mayfield, Mrs. Fussell, Mrs. Sharp, Isaac Howlett received for C.C. Carter, William M. Bell, J.H. Fuquay, Isaac Earthman, Dr. J. Newman, ?. K. Dillon gone to Alabama, Robert E. Currey, James Porter, McCanly & Spence, Thomas C. Smith, Mrs. C. Cherry, Miss King, Absalom Hooper, Mrs. Perkins, Richard Ridgeway, James Scott, Thomas Patterson, M(illegible) Hannum formerly lived in Kentucky, Capt. Bracox, Thomas Cheatham, Mr. Menfield, Mrs. Cyne Sharp, Washington Jones, Sarah Scott, Spencer Payne, Alfred Arnold, Jeremiah Fisher, W.W. Leagood, Jno. L. Allen, William Pomroy, William Johnson, Esq., Greenwood Payne, Dr. J.W. Riley, Thompson & Wardlow, Samuel H. Handy in Ireland, Mrs. Allen (Stones River), J.A. Banton, S.V.D. Stout, Parson Lanier, John Simpson & Co., A.

214

A. McFaddin, Bass & Spence, L. Browning, J.P. Tyree, William Allen, G.W. Ferrell, William H. Maxwell note in Talbot hand for collection, David Park, Jr., Bignal Crook in Maxey hand for collection, N. Dotson, Jas. Grizzard, and G. & D. Crockett. Several items left by the late William Gibson in his will for the use of his widow and child. Robert Gibson and Thomas P. Adams, admrs. Claims proved and presented to the administrators, Dr. Samuel Hogg, Joseph & Robert Woods, Park & Gibson, Crockett Park & Co., Martha Adams, Watson & Burke, Jas. Stevenson, William & Jo. Woods, Field & Fobe, Thomas Elmes, Hanse & McClelland, A. Ross, McCombs & Robinson, William Nichol, Nathan Adams, Thomas P. Adams, Earp & Co., S. & Z.P. Cantrell, and H. Taland. (very long instrument)

Page 255   Inventory of estate of Lewis Earthman, deceased.
Nov 20, 1828   Several negroes listed also other items. Notes on the following, viz, Seawell, Boyd McNairy, Thomas A. Duncan, James Marshall, Exum P. Sumner, B.H. Lanier, James Felts, Harris Dolin, William & Jesse Etherly, William Trotter, Isaac Hunter, James Gilbert, John L. Young, Alexander Merryman, Enos Walker, David B. Love, A.H. Fairly, Abraham Dunnivant, Jonathan Garrett, George Rodgers, William Saylor, James Earthman, John Lamotte, James Sims, John Paradise, Frederick Carpenter, John R. Jefferson, Richard C. & Drury A. Phelan, Edward Vaughn, Samuel Leech, Peter Binkley, Douglas Pucket, Christopher Elmore, John Morgan, Henry Douglas, D.C. Atkinson & D.A. Phelan, Willis Cunningham, Buchanan Lanier, Esq., Wilson Crockett, A. Knight, David & Daniel Buie, Norvel H. Robertson, Henry Binkley, George J. Cagle, R.C. & T.C. Phelan, John Stump, James Staggs, Darby Izor, Edward Singleton, Nimrod Hooper, Dennis Duff, Jacob Stump, Joseph (illegible), ?. Merryman, Jesse Eatherly, Pleasant Easley, Wilson L. Gower, Elizabeth Nolin, Joel Philips, Pharaoh Hudgins, William G. Westmoreland, Joel Smith, Exum Plummer, James Vaughn, Obediah Jenkins, Eli Binkley, Peterson Vaden, Jeremiah Bell, Parker Paradise, Martin Garrett, Christopher Elmore, John Boyls, Michael Waggoner, estate of John Earthman to the estate of Lewis Earthman, Jacob House, James W. Johnson, John T. Hunter, Joel Man, John Newland, and Wilson Crocket's receipt for collection of a note on Allen Wright and Isaac Earthman, Jr. Judah Earthman, admrx and John S. Cox, admr. Oct Term 1828.

Page 257   Sale of estate of Lewis Earthman, deceased.
Nov 20, 1828   Sale on Sept 11, 1828, sold by Judah Earthman, admrx and John S. Cox, admr. Purchasers, to wit, William Barnes, Robert Bates, John S. Cox, ?.F. Drake, Judah Earthman ...(incomplete, pages 258 and 259 missing)

Page 260   Inventory of estate of James Boyd, deceased.
(no date)   (First page 259 missing) Sale by J.C. Benson, admr and Martha Boyd, admrx. Persons listed, to wit, Mr. McGavock, Mr. Avery, Mr. Tinsley, Collins Hobbs, J. Parrish, Jesse Smith, Mr. Sullivan, Mr. Gibbs, William Yates, William Watson, David Burgey, Mr. Murp(illegible), Mr. Moore, Sam Marlin, Charles McKerrihan (?), Mr. Madison, Sain Johnson, Oakley Jones, John Jobe, Ned (blank), Mr. Alfred, Davis Cobler, Mr. Champ, Isaac L. Crow, Mr. Cunningham, James Cook, Steamboat Courier, Mr. Cobbs, Mr. Craddock, Mr. Carpenter, Mr. Cutler, James Christian, Sam Tyree, John Touson, Philip Thomas, Mr. Osborne, E.D. Eddy, Robert Hughs, Andrew Hays, Mr. Howlett, Mr. Housley, William Hamilton, Thomas Hamilton, Maj. E.D. Hobbs, James B. Houston, Mr. Hawkins, Mr. Huntsinger, Mr. Hickins, Mr. Harding, Jon. Leak, A. Lockhart, J. Lockhart, Mr. Parks, John Page, Mr. Vaughn, Mrs. Smith, James Scott, P. Scudder, Seawell & Emmitt, Capt. Shaffer, Mr. Kent, Sam P. Greer, N. Gordon, Mr. Dibrell, Mr. Duger, E. Dobson, B. Yount, Mr. Forrest, Mr. Folwell, John Folwell, Andrew Woods, Mr. White, Mr. Wright, Mr. Watkins, C. Webb, Benjamin Weller, Mr. Whiteside, Thomas Weston, Mr. Womack, Mr. Williams, Richard Barrett, and Daniel H. Bigle. Notes drawn by Forrest in favor of James Boyd, notes drawn by H. Keyton in favor of Boyd, note drawn by James Hynes in favor of Boyd, note drawn by Oakley Jones in favor of Boyd, note drawn by James Fogg in favor of Boyd, note drawn by Thomas Norman in favor of Boyd, note drawn by S. Watson in favor of James Boyd, notes drawn by James Scott, James Sullivan, Thomas Massey, John Hurd, Jacob Cur(illegible) in favor of J. Boyd and paid by him, W. Howard's receipt Comstable, and William T. Brooks receipt Constable. Oct 24, 1828. Oct Term 1828.

Page 261   Land divided by Thomas Overton, deceased.
Nov 22, 1828   Plat on page 261. No. 1 to Harriet O. Henson of 398 acres, No. 2 goes to Patrick H. Overton of 398 acres that borders the Cumberland River, No. 3 goes to

James G. Overton of 601 acres, and No. 4 goes to John H. Overton of 477 3/4 acres. John Overton, Jacob D. Donelson, John L. Hadly, William Donelson and William Harris, Commissioners. Oct Term 1828.

Page 263   Settlement of estate of David Beaty, deceased.
Nov 24, 1828   Made with Robert Johnson, executor. Persons listed, to wit, Miss Ann Hope, Winiford Boyd, Andrew Boyd, Polly Boyd, Isaac Beaty, John Overton, David Adams, Stephen Sutton, Robert B. Currey, John Newman, Jacob McGavock, James Causon, Charles McLaughlin, Evan Brock, John Withrow, Thomas H. Clarke, Josiah Phelps, Nathan Ewing, Constant Perkins, Josiah Williams, R.B. Sappington, J.W. Horton, Ebenezer Alexander, James Campbell, Josiah Nick(illegible), and Lewis Sturdevant. Old notes on William German, Patrick Lyon, Jonathan Williams, and William Mark. Other names listed, viz, Thomas Hickman, Thomas Norris, Felix Grundy, Ephraim H. Foster, Oliver Keen, Hendly & Norwood, W. Prentiss, expense on Lewis from Lexington, Mr. Beck as council, T. Washington, McGavock & Ewing, S. Weakley for surveying, to removing negroes to the State of Indiana &c, R. Evans, purchased nine quarter section of land in Vige County, Indiana, Isaac Beaty, A. Clarke, to Lewis one of the heirs in 1824, items to Johnston at Evansville to remove to their land provisions &c April 1827, George Beaty for his legacy in 1825, expenses for several trips to Indiana and also trips to Kentucky and also trips to Alabama. This 30 Oct 1828. Hinchy Petway and Philip Campbell, Commissioners. Oct Term 1828.

Page 264   Alexander Stothart & Others, lot divided.
Nov 23, 1828   Commissioners appointed to partition Lot No. 100 in Nashville between Thomas ?. Duncan and Jane his wife formerly Jane M. Stothart, Alexander A. Stothart and William Stothart. Alexander A. Stothart drew 86 2/3 feet on High Street adjoining James Walker's house and lot. To William Stothart, second division or one equal third part adjoining the first and 86 2/3 feet on High Street. To Thomas A. Duncan and Jane his wife the remaining third part being also 86 2/3 feet on High Street. This 1 Sept 1828. Ephraim H. Foster, James A. Porter, William Carroll, George Shall, Jas. Walker, and George S. Yerger, Commissioners. Oct Term 1828.

Page 265   Settlement of estate of Samuel Chapman, deceased.
Nov 23, 1828   Made with Henry Ewing, executor. Persons listed, to wit, Graves Pennington, J.C. Petman, Maynor & Dean, John Maxey, James Grizzard constable, David Graves, C. Brooks, William Brooks, John Wright, John E. Finn, Maxey & Autry, Martin New, James W. McComb, John Maxey, Benjamin Barnes, N. Ewing, Foster & Fogg, and Samuel Chapman. Notes on Isaac G. Sandeberry, James C. Patton, Ward & Cannon, and Graves Pennington. This 31 Oct 1828. Robert Farquharson and Will Lytle. Oct Term 1828.

Page 266   Inventory of estate of Francis Hardgraves, deceased.
Nov 26, 1828   Several items listed including notes on Abram Demoss, Shelton Hardgraves, John Hardgraves, Johnson Vaughn, John Knight, Thomas Norman, Thomas Demoss, and John Wright. Oct 20, 1828. Jno. Davis and Silas Dillahunt, executors. Oct Term 1828.

Page 267   Land Divided of Severn Donelson, deceased.
Nov 26, 1828   Play on page 267. Lot No. 1 to Samuel Donelson of 106 acres, Lot No. 2 to Alexander Donelson of 106 acres, Lot No. 3 to Lucinda R. Donelson of 125 acres, Lot No. 4 to Thomas J. Donelson of 100 acres, Lot No. 5 to James R. Donelson of 125 acres, and Lot No. 6 to John Donelson, Jr. of 112 acres. Andrew Jackson, Andrew J. Donelson, William Watson, Timothy Dodson, and J.G. Martin, Commissioners. Oct Term 1828.

Page 268   Inventory of estate of Nancy Whittemore, deceased.
Nov 27, 1828   Made on Sept 6, 1828. Several items listed. Abraham Whittemore and John Hays, admrs. Oct Term 1828.

Page 269   Account of sale of estate of Sterling Davis, deceased.
Nov 27, 1828   Sold by Sm. Edmondson, admr. Several items listed. Nov 1, 1828.
Oct Term 1828.

Page 269   Inventory of estate of Thomas Watkins, deceased.
Nov 27, 1828   Made by Thomas Watkins, admr. Notes on William Hinton, John
McGavock, Jeremiah Mathis, Henry Strange, Severn Donelson, Ira Bradford, William
Sturdivant, Simon Williams, Duke W. Sumner, John L. Brown, William M. Hinton, Isham
Butterworth, Thomas J. Watkins, Pilmore Cole, Henry Crossway, B.J. Love, John J. Hinton,
William Gill, Jonathan W. Gill, James Wilkes, Wilson White, and Alexander Harrison. Oct
Term 1828.

Page 269   Will of Frederick Schuman, deceased, departed this life on 24th
Nov 27, 1828   instant. All his property and estate goes to Patsy Smith then
living with him. 26 Sept 1828. Nuncupative Will produced in Court by Betsy Smith on 28
Oct 1828 and thereupon Henry Gingry in right of his Catherine his wife who alleges himself
to be next of kin to said Frederick, deceased, and came into Court and questioned the will
being of Frederick. A jury was impaneled who gave oath to the above will. The jury
consisted of James Nichol, John Drennan, Charles L. Byrn, William Whittemore, William M.
Hinton, Robert Bates, James Gilman, Bailey W. Taylor, John Thompson, William A. Williams,
Thomas Vaughn, and Jeremiah Hinton, who claimed that the said paper is the nuncupative
will of Frederick Shuman, deceased.

Page 270   Drusilla Johnson, support laid off.
Nov 28, 1828   Absalom Gleaves, Thomas Gleaves and James R. Gleaves,
Commissioners, to set apart one years provisions for Drusilla Johnson and her family, several
items listed. Oct 21, 1828. Oct Term 1828.

Page 270   Settlement of estate of Neal McDaniel, deceased.
Nov 28, 1828   Made with William Faulkner, admr. All vouchers in hands of said
Faulkner. 28 Oct 1828. Jno. Stump and G.W. Boyd, Commissioners. Oct Term 1828.

Page 271   Inventory of estate of John Frazer, deceased.
Nov 28, 1828   Made on Nov 1, 1828 by Samuel D. Read, admr. Several items
listed. Oct Term 1828.

Page 271   Judith Earthman, widow's support.
Nov 28, 1828   Commissioners met to set apart and lay off to Judy Earthman
widow and relict of Lewis Earthman, deceased, several items. This Sept 10, 1828. Michael
Gleaves, James Marshall and Martin Garrett, Commissioners. Oct Term 1828.

Page 271   Sale of estate of William Johnson, deceased.
Nov 28, 1828   Made on 17 Oct 1828. Amounted to $281.45. This 21 Oct 1828.
Drusilla Johnson, admrx. Oct Term 1828.

Page 271   Henry Parker's indenture, Edgecomb County, North Carolina.
Nov 28, 1828   30 Aug 1814 by and between Geraldus Dorman, Susannah Dorman
and Zelpha Parker of one part and John H. Hall of other part. Witnesseth that the said
Geraldus Dorman, Susannah Dorman and Zelphia Parker took and placed Henry Parker, aged
seven years, an apprentice and servant to John H. Hall with him to (illegible) reside and
serve until he, the said apprentice, shall arrive at the age of twenty one years during with
which time the said apprentice his said master shall faithfully serve in all lawful business &c
in all things, behave himself towards his said master during the said time as an apprentice
and the said John H. Hall doth covenant, promise and agree to and will find and provide the
said apprentice sufficient meat, drink, apparel, washing and lodging and use his best
endeavors to instruct him in the art of a farmer. Oct Term 1828.

Page 272   Inventory of estate of William P. Anderson, deceased.
Nov 28, 1828   Made by William P. Anderson, Sr., admr. There being thirty
shares in the Nashville Bank in Nashville and one small rifle gun. 20 Oct 1828. Oct Term
1828.

Page 272   Settlement of estate of Sarah Hays, deceased.
Nov 28, 1828   Each legatee's part $131.88½. This 22 Oct 1828. William Creel,
Eli Cherry, William C. Wilson and Thomas Gleaves, Commissioners. Oct Term 1828.

Page 272   Inventory of estate of Elizabeth Donelson, deceased.
Nov 29, 1828   Several items listed. John Donelson, admr.

Page 273   Inventory of estate of Call McNeill, deceased.
Dec 1, 1828   Taken Oct 19, 1828. Note on Isaac Earthman, and several other
items, also note on James Hooper. Daniel Buie, admr. Oct Term 1828.

Page 273   Elizabeth Davis, widow's support.
Dec 1, 1828   We, James Condon, William Ewing, Silas M. Morton,
Commissioners, proceeded to lay off to Elizabeth Davis several items. This Oct 28, 1828.
Oct Term 1828.

Page 273   Inventory of estate of William Frazer, deceased.
Dec 1, 1828   On Oct 31, 1828 by M.B. Frazer. 60 acres of land in Davidson
County and one negro boy Mark. Oct Term 1828.

Page 273   Settlement of estate of Caleb Cherry, deceased.
Dec 2, 1828   Made with Thomas Cherry, admr. Several items listed. Oct 26,
1828. Micajah Autry and Graves Pennington, Commissioners. Oct Term 1828.

Page 274   Will of William Wilkinson, Sr., deceased.
Feb 23, 1829   To my dear wife Maumen Wilkinson one third part of my tract of
land on which I now live including the house and spring during her life or widowhood but she
is not at liberty to make use of no timber or firewood more than is for the use and benefit
of the place. I give the profits arising from the other two thirds of my land to my two sons
Hancel T. Wilkinson and Micajah H. Wilkinson, during the natural life of my wife Moumen
Wilkinson but not giving the said Hancel T. and Micajah H. Wilkinson the power of setting
people upon said land who are or may be disagreeable to my said wife. At the death of my
wife the above said tract of land to be sold and whatever it brings to be equally divided
between my four sons, Jonathan Wilkinson, William Wilkinson, Hancel T. Wilkinson, and
Micajah H. Wilkinson. To my son Jonathan Wilkinson a negro boy Dave, a horse, one cow
and calf, a bed and furniture, also a negro boy Ned. To my son William Wilkinson a negro
boy Mat, one horse, one cow and calf, one bed and furniture. To my daughter Milley Everett
$400.00 in cash, a cow and calf and bed and furniture also a $30.00 horse or $50.00 in
money which she chooses. To my son Hancel T. Wilkinson one negro boy Jo, one horse, one
cow and calf, one bed and furniture. To my son Micajah H. Wilkinson a negro boy Sam, one
horse, one cow and calf, one bed and furniture. To my wife Moumen Wilkinson one negro
man Tom, one horse, a cow and calf, one bed and furniture. All the remainder of my estate
to be equally divided into seven equal parts except one negro girl Marie and a horse and
after divided, the said girl and horse to be added to one of the seven parts and that part is
to be placed in the hands of my son William Wilkinson for the supporting of my daughter
Tresia Smiley and raising and educating her children during her lifetime then to be equally
divided amongsy the heirs of her body. This 27 Nov 1828. Wit: William Faulkner, Laban
Abernathy and Daniel Brim. My sons, Jonathan Wilkinson, William Wilkinson and Hansel T.
Wilkinson, my executors. Jan term 1829.

Page 275   Will of Pilmore Cole, deceased.
Feb 23m 1829   To my beloved wife Lydia Cole during her natural life or
widowhood all my land, stock and furniture, dues &c of every description for the purpose of
raising and educating my children and in case my wife should marry, my will is that my
estate should be divided between my wife and children. I appoint my wife above named my
executrix. This 3 Dec 1828. Wit: Enoch P. Connel and William P. Byrn. Jan Term 1829.

Page 276   Will of Henry McIlwain, deceased.
Feb 23, 1829   To my two sons namely John McIlwain and Alexander McIlwain the
tract of land I now live on to be equally divided between then and by their paying $200.00
apiece, viz, $100.00 to Isabella Boyd, also $100.00 to Polly Martin, also $100.00 to Anne
Joslin, and the other $100.00 to be equally divided between Peggy McIlwain and Betsey
McIlwain and Jane McIlwain only the price of a saddle a piece to be taken out of it for Polly
Martin and for Anne Joslin. I also reserve 15 acres of land where I now live for my three
daughters that are single yet during their life provided they remain single, namely, Peggy,
Betsey and Jane, also to my three daughters all the household and kitchen furniture together

218

with the stock of all kinds, also to my daughter Betsey $100.00 of the money now in the hands of William Bedford, also $100.00 to my daughter Jane now in the hands of William Bedford. I appoint my sons John McIlwain and Alexander McIlwain my executors. This 10 June 1824. Wit: Elijah Lake, Herbert Tarpley and Thomas Scott. Jan Term 1829.

Page 277   Inventory of estate of Elizabeth Donelson, deceased.
Feb 24, 1829   Exposed to sale on Nov 21 and 2nd 1828. Several items listed.
John Donelson, Jr., admr. Also a supplement of several items. Jan Term 1829.

Page 279   Inventory of estate of George T. Bowen, deceased.
Feb 24, 1829   Of books and other property also other items. This Jan 29, 1829.
Francis B. Fogg and Nathaniel Cross, admrs. Jan Term 1829.

Page 280   Settlement of estate of Thomas Overton, deceased.
Feb 24, 1829   Made with P.H. Overton, one of the admrs. Persons listed, to wit, for rent of Cox plantation, and Butler and McGregor. Balance due on J. Litton, J. Creel, John E. Davis, Hall and Fitzgerald, Isaac Sitler, J.D. Donelson, John Bell, and E.S. Hall. Allowance for admr travelling expenses going to Kentucky on business of the estate, Lexington, 200 miles. Amount paid over by John Overton, Jr., Trustee of the heirs of Thomas Overton, deceased, which monies arose from the sale of 345 acres of land in Jones Bend conveyed to said Thomas. John H. Camp sold by said John, trustee &c by direction of the heirs and devisees of said Thomas. Persons listed received, to wit, E.S. Hall, Thomas Deaderick, Richard Smith, J. Jameson, M.W.B. Armstrong, M. Adams, Alexander Porter, Henry Ewing, A.W. Vanleer, James Stewart, Greenwood Wood, Bass & Spence, Berryhill & McKee, Philip Hurt, William Black, P.H. Overton, Thomas Moore, Matthew Watson, J. McGavock, and Craighead. This 22 Jan 1829. Elihu S. Hall and Archibald W. Goodrich, Commissioners. Jan Term 1829.

Page 281   Account of sales of estate of David Buie, deceased.
Feb 24, 1829   Purchasers, to wit, Sally Buie, Josiah Cook, Daniel Buie, J. Buie, Jacob B. Binkley, Peter Knight, Samuel Crockett, William B. Cox, Anthony Hinkle, Buchanan Lanier, Thomas Smith, George Ramer, John Raimer, William Brumboland, William Pitt, Zenas Tait, Henry Binkley, Whitmel Harrington, James Jones, John Seat, Philip Riser, Humphrey Marshal, Thomas Culbertson, Niel McNiel, Seldon Betts, H.W. Ryburn, Jacob Reasoner, Willis Seat, Absalom Binkley, James Ennis, Thomas Hall, Samuel Railey, Isaac Brumboland, Thomas Warren, Laurg McDonald, Jonathan Reasoner, Robert Cranks, Lewis Smith, and Elijah McGraw. Notes found on William Crockett, Anthony Hinkle, Exum P. Sumners, Noah Smithwick note payable to York Freeman, Joseph Rush, Benjamin Bowles, Moses Odom, Peter Quin receipt for the collection of notes in State of Mississippi, John Loftin for the collection of notes in Mississippi, also Lewis Megn for collection in Mississippi, also William Millar's receipt for twelve rifle guns left with him to sell in the State of Mississippi, and to H.M. Oneal's receipt for the collection of an order on Levi Middleton. Henry Fry and Daniel Buie, admrs. Jan Term 1829.

Page 283   Account of sale of estate of Nancy Whittemore, deceased.
Feb 24, 1829   Purchasers, to wit, Sterling Whittemore, Abraham Whittemore, William Whittemore, Samuel V. Ensley, John Hays, Samuel W. Hope, James K. Hope, John Fitzhugh, John Whittemore, Hiram Gray, John W. Alexander, Thomas Lynch, Charles Hays, Turner Neal, John Kimbro, Jas. Blackman, Absalom Hamilton, and John Jenkins. Sale on 31 Oct 1828 by John Hays and Abraham Whittemore, admrs. Jan Term 1829.

Page 284   Estate divided of William Donelson, Jr., deceased.
Feb 24, 1829   We have met on this 20 Nov 1829 at the late residence of Mrs. Charity Donelson, deceased, in the presence of the heirs and the legal representatives to divide and allot the estate of William Donelson, Jr., deceased, and allotting to Andrew J. Donelson seven negroes worth $2350.00 it being $112.50 more than his distributive share, and likewise Elizabeth Donelson seven negroes worth $2100.00 it being $139.50 more than her share, and we the Commissioners have allotted amongst the distributees the estate of Mrs. Charity Donelson, deceased, and likewise the estate of her son William Donelson, deceased, a minor under the age of twenty one years which duty we have performed. Each share to be $816.66 2/3. To Severn Donelson, one of the distributees his share of the estate also to Jacob D. Donelson his share, both allotted also negroes, and also to John McGregor and

219

Milbury his wife their share also negroes, also to Robert M. Burton and Martha his wife their share also negroes, and also to Andrew J. Donelson his share also negores, and also to Elizabeth Donelson her share and negroes. We have also divided the stock of horses, cows, hogs, and sheep also the crop. Allen Mathis, Reuben Payne and John Pirtle, Commissioners. Confirmed by R.M. Burton, Severm Donelson, J.D. Donelson, John McGregor, Andrew Jackson guardian for A.J. Donelson son of William Donelson, deceased, Robert M. Burton guardian for Elizabeth Donelson minor heir of William Donelson, deceased, William McGwinn, and James D. Booth. 15 May 1828. Jan Term 1829.

Page 286   Estate divided of John Hoggatt, deceased.
Feb 25, 1829   Commissioners met to lay off and divide a balance of some negroes which was devised by John Hoggatt, deceased, to his wife Diana Hoggatt during her life and after her death to be divided to his children according to the will of John Hoggatt, deceased, have divided said negroes to the following persons, viz, James W. Hoggatt five negroes, to Agnes W. Hoggatt and her infant son Sandifer Hoggatt by his guardian for this purpose Albert W(illegible) being the heir and representative of John H. Hoggatt, deceased, seven negroes. We also allotted to the heirs and representatives of Abraham S. Hoggatt, deceased, seven negroes. Also allotted to Agnes W. Hoggatt and her son is valued at $1700.00, that allotted to James W. Hoggatt is valued at $1925.00, and that allotted to the representatives of Abram S. Hoggatt be valued at $1825.00. Also decided that two thirds of the share allotted to Abram S. Hoggatt representatives be divided and set apart to James W. Hoggatt, he having purchased the interest of Rhoda Clopton five negroes. This __ day of Nov 1828. Jno. W. Overton, Thomas Harding, Zachariah Noell and Thomas H. Everett, Commissioners. Jan Term 1829.

Page 287   Inventory of sale of estate of Frederick Schuman, deceased.
Feb 27, 1829   Bills of bills, purchasers, to wit, Cumberland College, James Bosley, James Cantrell, Dr. Overton, Dr. Roane, Hugh McGavock, Dr. Grigsby, Mr. Avery, Joseph Litton, Judge Catron, Benjamin Weller, Col. Rutledge, Gov. Houston, B. Walsh, C. McConnel, Thomas Wells, Mr. Yeatman, Judge Campbell, Dr. McNairy, Judge McNairy, E.H. Foster, Esq., Mr. Goodwin, James Walker, Maj. Hockley, William Murdough, James Edmondson, Thomas Irwin, Mr. Hoover, Col. Armstrong, Thomas Price, Jonathan Douglass, Solomon Clark, Isaac Sitler, R. Sutton, Stephen Cantrell, R.C. Napier, Dr. J. Shelby, William Temple, William Bosworth, Thomas Redd, Mr. Eichbaum, Mr. Welborn, Johnson & Moore, Presbyterian Church of Nashville, Mr. Shields, James Erwin, Allen Porter, James Stevens, Davidson County, Mr. Horton, Lawyer Craighead, Craighead's black man, Corporation of Nashville, Mark Young, Mr. Benson, and Mr. Lanning. Bills of bills and notes, to wit, Thomas C. Miller, J. Smith, Sam McMinn, Wilmott book account, Mr. Martin, Mr. Morris, (unknown) McGavock, _____ Sarington, _____ Abernathy, Mr. Taylor, Mr. Gibson, Lawyer Anthony, Mr. Kent, _____ Boyd, Mr. Gordon, Philip Thomas, Major Emmit, Judge Crabb, John Lyon, H. Long, Mr. Garner, McNairy & Sumner, R. Cartmel, Simon Glenn, and K. Webb. Jan Term 1829.

Page 287   Inventory of estate of Frederick Schuman, deceased.
Feb 27, 1829   Made by Frederick Schuman, Jr., admr on 19 Jan 1829. Several items listed including the Holy Bible in three Vols in German also one silver watch with a gold chain and two gold seals. This 1 Apr 1827. Jan Term 1829.

Page 288   Settlement of estate of Alexander McCombs, deceased.
Feb 27, 1829   made with Gabriel McCombs, admr. Persons listed, to wit, B.W. Bedford, Mrs. Haywood, William S. Haywood, Mrs. Anderson, R. McGavock, and Cary Felts and Jeremiah Ezell admrs of Willis L. Shumate. Others listed were N. Ewing, Jacob McGavock, L.P. Cheatham, David Wilmott, John K. Buchanan, and T.H. Fletcher. 28 Jan 1829. Benjamin W. Bedford and Will Lytle, Commissioners. Jan term 1829.

Page 289   Settlement of estate of Reuben S. Thornton, deceased.
Feb 28, 1829   This 29 Jan 1829, we find notes, receipts and lawful vouchers by T.H. Howlet one of the admrs. Persons listed, to wit, paid Edmondson, Patterson, Case, Wright, Wilson, Wells, Moseley, Hope, Scott, E. Owen, Goodrich, Bell, Frost, Garner, Baker, William Ramsey, Jr., William Ramsey, Sr., John Jenkins, Nathan Ewing, Zadock Forbs, John Hogan, Edmund Reeves, Dor. Waters, Doc. Robertson, Jabez Owen, Samuel Owen, and James Condon. The following vouchers, viz, William Ramsay constable, Nathan Ewing, Will

Williams, and J.O. & A.G. Ewing.   William Ewing, James Condon and Hays Blackman, Commissioners. Jan term 1829.

Page 290   Additional inventory of estate of Lewis Earthman, deceased.
Several items listed. Several notes due on Isaac Earthman, on Nicholas Nelson, Daniel Brim, Edward Daniel, Charles Cooper, Samuel Galloway, George W. Garrett, Logan Drake, Benj. J. Love, Judah Earthman, Eli Binkley, Joel and William Randolph, and Atkinson H. Fairley. Judah Earthman, admrx and Jno. S. Cox, admr. 19 Jan 1829. Jan Term 1829.

Page 290   Settlement of estate of William C. Man, deceased.
Feb 28, 1829   Made with Samuel D. Power, admr. Persons listed, to wit, J.C. McLemore, Philip Alston, McNairy & Roane, William Garner, John Wright, Nathan Ewing, and expense in sending for hearse and coffin and sending the corpse twenty miles $10.00. This 23 Jan 1829. Archibald W. Goodrich and Elihu S. Hall, Commissioners. Jan Term 1829.

Page 291   Settlement of estate of Call McNeil, deceased.
Mar 18, 1829   Made with Daniel Buie, admr. Persons listed, to wit, Lewis Earthman, Charles Bedwell, William B. Cox, Jonathan Wilkinson, Robertson Murphy, Reuben Chick, Isaac Earthman, Sr., Wilson Crockett, B.H. Lanier, Call McNeil's note to J. Earthman, Lewis Earthman, Benjamin Rawls, George C. Coonrod, Daniel Buie, William Carter, Lawrence Clinard, Douglass Puckett, F.M. McBride, Isaac Earthman, Jr., Exum P. Sumner, Archibald Thomas, and Mary Buie. Buchanan H. Lanier and David Ralston, Commissioners. Jan Term 1829.

Page 292   Inventory of estate of James Wetherald, deceased.
Mar 9, 1829   Several items listed including negroes and one Family Bible. Jan 2, 1829. Peggy Wetherald, admrx. Jan Term 1829.

Page 292   Account of John Spence, deceased.
Mar 9, 1829   Made by Joseph Spence, executor. Persons listed, to wit, J. Spence, Arthur Harris, Charles Stothern, Thomas Stothern, William C. Emmit, M.B. Murfree, Edw. H. Chaffin, George Shall, Mrs. R.B.S. Spence, H. Ewing, E.S. Hall, Jos. Spence guardian of Mary S. Crosthwait, Jos. Ward, David Patton, Samuel S. Jones, Mary Hamilton, B. Coleman's note of H. Hoover, D. Jameson, heirs of Milus & Sally S. Spence, and Jos. Spence guardian of Ann B. Spence. Jan term 1829.

Page 293   Inventory of estate of Janet Washington, deceased.
Mar 9, 1829   Made by Thomas and James G. Washington, executors of her will, Several negroes listed. Jan Term 1829.

Page 293   Sale of estate of Landon C. Farrar, deceased.
Mar 9, 1829   Made on 20 Nov 1828. Several items listed. Josiah Walton, admr.
Jan Term 1829.

Page 294   Land divided of estate of Williamson Adams, deceased.
Mar 9, 1829   Court directed us to divide the land belonging to the estate of Benjamin Adams, deceased. We have laid off and set apart to the minor heirs of Williamson Adams one lot, to wit, Lot No. 1 to Caroline Adams and Benjamin F. Adams a tract of land bordering Benjamin Bibb's north boundary line, William Ramsay's south boundary line. Lot No. 2 to John Drewry and Nancy his wife, land bordering south west corner of Lot No. 1 and borders on the east boundary line of the heirs of Benjamin Owen. Lot No. 3 to John Charlton and Susan his wife, land bordering on the north west corner of Lot No. 2 and borders Owen's north east corner and the north west corner of Lot No. 1. This 15 Nov 1828. Jeremiah Ezell, William Ramsay, William Black, William Ewing, and Isaac H. Howlett, Commissioners. Jan Term 1829.

Page 295   Division of personal property of Thomas Fowlkes, deceased.
Mar 9, 1829   Agreeable to his will between his two sons William P. Fowlkes and Thomas H. Fowlkes. Several negroes divided equally. 27 Dec 1828. Edmond Goodrich, Esq., Martin Pierce and William Neely, Commissioners. Jan Term 1829.

Page 295   Sale of estate of Lewis Earthman, deceased.
Mar 10, 1829   Made by Hudah Earthman, admrx and Jno. S. Cox, admr, on 22 Nov 1828. Several items listed. Jan Term 1829.

Page 296   Judith Earthman, her dower.
Mar 10, 1829   We, the Commissioners, met to lay off and set apart to Judith Earthman, widow and relict of Lewis Earthman, deceased, her dower of a tract of land in the middle of Earthman's Fork of Whites Creek and to a corner Lewis Earthman bought of Rachel Stump also to line of James Marshall's land, containing 197½ acres. Proceedings held on 18 and 19 Dec 1828. Samuel Weakley, James Faulkner, James Marshall, Matthew Porter, and Benjamin J. Love, Commissioners. Jan Term 1829.

Page 296   Inventory of estate of Carrel Jackson, deceased.
Mar 10, 1829   Stephen R. Roberts states that there is personal property now belonging to the estate of Carril Jackson, deceased. Not items listed. Stephen R. Roberts, admr. Jan Term 1829.

Page 297   Division of property of John Criddle, deceased. John H. Criddle drew Caleb and Aaron, Smith Criddle drew Ann and Anderson, Sally Criddle drew Siller and Alexander, E. Criddle drew Isaac and Minerva. This Dec 10, 1828. William Faulkner, Lewis Williams and Thomas Heaton. Jan Term 1829.

Page 297   Settlement of estate of John Graves, deceased.
Mar 10, 1829   Made with William Seat, executor. To rent of ferry at Haysboro for years 1825, 1826, 1827, and 1828. Persons listed, to wit, John Puckett and Foster & Fogg. This 30 Jan 1829. Leonard P. Cheatham, James P. Clark and George S. Yerger, Commissioners. Jan term 1829.

Page 297   Settlement of estate of Robert P. McFarland, deceased.
Mar 10, 1829   Made with Winney McFarland, admrx. Persons listed, to wit, J.H. Eaton, to board, tuition and clothing of Sally Jane. 19 Jan 1829. Jan Term 1829.

Page 298   Inventory of estate of Mary C. Knox, deceased.
Mar 10, 1829   Made on Jan 29, 1829. Several items listed including one negro man, two negro woman and three children. The above list belonging to the estate with the exception of the undivided interest in the business of Anderson and Knox. Joseph Vaulx, admr. Jan Term 1829.

Page 298   Inventory of estate of Archibald McLearin, deceased.
Mar 10, 1829   Persons listed, to wit, Kirkman & Livingston, Dr. Higginbotham, Mr. Garner for coffin, Jesse Collins, John Gregory, William Hindall, and Samuel Blair. Thomas A. Taylor, admr. Jan Term 1829.

Page 298   Additional inventory of estate of William Donelson, deceased. Several notes as property of John and William Donelson and joint property of John and William Donelson and John Peyton and the estate of said Donelson, deceased, is only entitled to one third part thereof, to wit, Rawley and Samuel Morgan's note, also John Fletcher, Cary Morgan, Travis C. Nash, and John P. Wiggin. This 6 Jan 1829. Jacob D. Donelson, Andrew Jackson and John Donelson, executors.

Page 299   Inventory of estate of Landon C. Farrar, deceased.
Mar 10, 1829   Taken 20 Nov 1828. Several items listed including one watch. John Beasley notes for collection, D.B. Love, A. Newlin, James Dickinson, William H. Hamblin, Samuel Wharton, J. Marshall, Jacob Donelson, William Stewart, Henry Raimer, Henry Ramor, and William Shaw. Josiah Walton, admr. Jan term 1829.

Page 299   Inventory of estate of Jacob Cartwright, deceased.
Mar 11, 1829   Made on 15 Nov 1828. Seven negroes and all the household furniture, kitchen furniture and all the farming utensils of every kind and other items to the widow, negroes and household items &c to Tabitha Cartwright, one colt to John Cartwright also negroes also other items. One note on James Crossway, one on Jesse Cartwright, account on William Goode, and on R. Payne, and John Betts. Enoch P. Connel and William

222

P. Byrn, executors. Jan Term 1829.

Page 300   Account of sale of estate of Jacob Cartwright, deceased.
Mar 11, 1829   Made on 15 Nov 1828. Purchasers, to wit, James McGavock, E.P. Connel, Thomas Powel, and James Scruggs. Enoch P. Connel and William P. Byrn, executor. Jan Term 1829.

Page 300   Ann Farrar, support.
Mar 11, 1829   We have set apart for the support of Ann Farrar and family for one year, several items listed. This 18 Nov 1828. Samuel Shannon, David Hunter and William Neely, Commissioners. Ann Farrar is widow and relist of Landon C. Farrar, deceased. Jan Term 1829.

Page 301   Settlement of estate of Philip Walker, deceased.
Mar 11, 1829   Made with William H. Hamilton, admr. Vouchers and allowance for support of children for two years &c. This 9 Jan 1829. Edmond Goodrich and Reuben Payne, Esqrs., Commissioners. Jan term 1829.

Page 301   Settlement of estate of John Tait, deceased.
Mar 11, 1829   Made with Zedekiah Tait, executor. Sold land and left balance of $862.37½. This 26 Jan 1829. R.C. Foster and G.W. Charlton, Esqrs., Commissioners. Jan term 1829.

Page 301   David Buie's widow's support.
Mar 11, 1829   We, Allen Knight, Exum P. Sumner and J. Earthman, Jr., Commissioners met to lay off one year's support to David Buie's widow, several items listed. This 11 Nov 1828. Jan Term 1829.

Page 302   Negro sold of estate of John Gee, deceased.
Mar 11, 1829   Sold negro slave Feb on 20 Dec 1828 and Jane Gee became the purchaser and gave bond with Robert Gee and Matthew Waggoner, securities. Jan 19, 1829. David Abernathy, Commissioner. Jan Term 1829.

Page 302   Additional inventory of Robert C. Owen, deceased.
Mar 11, 1829   Admr bill on Andrew Hays and received of William Beaty. 9 Jan 1829. Sandy Owen, admr. Jan term 1829.

Page 302   Inventory of estate of Call McNeil, deceased.
Mar 11, 1829   Hire of negroes belonging to the estate of Call McNeil, deceased, for 1829. Daniel Buie, admr. Jan Term 1829.

Page 303   Additional inventory of estate of Mary C. Knox, deceased.
Mar 11, 1829   Notes on the following, N.A. McNairy, Joseph Vaulx, also some window curtains and a gold watch. Joseph Vaulx, admr. Jan term 1829.

Page 303   Sale of estate of James G. Overton, deceased.
Mar 11, 1829   The sale of seven negroes. The total amount of sales $2055.00. Jan 20, 1829. Patrick H. Overton, admr. Jan Term 1829.

Page 303   Will of Sarah Priestley, deceased.
May 14, 1829   To my daughter Sarah Ann Hoover all my wearing apparel and all my household and kitchen furniture and including my clock and a stove and except my library of books, philosophical apparatus and excepting two feather beds, a large looking glass. To my son-in-law Philip Hoover my negro girl Anachy and her increase forever in trust that Hoover shall hold for the use and benefit of my son Philander Priestley during his natural life and at same time said negro and her increase be kept in the possession of my said son if he desires. And at the death of my son Philander, it is my desire that said Hoover his heirs &c shall turn over said negro girl and her increase to the legal heirs of my son Philander. To my son-in-law Philip Hoover all the rest and residue of my estate including my money and all debts due and owing to me and he is to let my son Philander have the use of my featherbed &c and he shall let my son Joseph have the use of one featherbed &c. Mr. Hoover shall divide the residue of my estate into four equal parts, one part to my son-in-law

Mr. Hoover, another fourth part to the children of my late son Doctor Jno. Priestley, deceased, to be paid over to their guardian, and the two remaining shares or equal fourth parts to my son-in-law said Hoover to hold in trust for the use of my sons Joseph and James equally. I appoint my son-in-law Philip Hoover my executor. This 13 Feb 1829. Wit: Ephraim H. Foster and Jno. M. Hill. Apr Term 1829.

Page 304   Will of Silas Dillahunty, deceased.
May 14, 1829   To my beloved wife Sally Dillahunty the plantation and all the land whereon I now live and another being the place I bought of William Greer to be hers until my son John arrives at the age of twenty one years at which time a division made of the two places between my two sons John and Joseph and should either of the two die before they arrive at the age of twenty one years leaving no heirs then his part to fall to the surviving brother. My son Joseph to have the place where I now live and my beloved wife Sally to have her lifetime in it. To my beloved wife Sally all my household and kitchen furniture and other items. To my four daughters, Hannah, Zany, Martha and Delilah, four negroes. Also to my two daughters Sally and Clementine two negroes. The negroes of my four oldest daughters be hires out until they become of age or marry, and the two belonging to my two youngest daughters to stay with my wife until the oldest arrive at the age of fifteen years and then to be divided between them and the negro that falls to Sally to be hired out &c. To my two sons John and Joseph, two negroes to be divided between them when my son John arrives at age of twenty one years. I appoint my beloved wife Sally Dillahunty and my friend John Davis my exrx and exr. This 18 Nov 1828. Wit: John Davis and James Gilliam. Apr Term 1829.

Page 306   Will of William P. Byrn, deceased.
May 15, 1829   To my beloved wife Tabitha Byrn during her natural life or widowhood all my lands, negroes and property for the purpose of raising and educating my children. To my two sons Preston and Jackson Byrn, at the death of my wife, all my lands to be equally divided between them and their heirs and in case my wife should marry, they are to have possession of the two-thirds not allowed for her and at her death to have possession of the rest fourth, I give unto my four daughters Jane Bowen, Harriet Wormack, Elizabeth and Mary Byrn to be equally divided between them. I appoint my friends Enoch P. Connel and Charles L. Byrn my executors. This 18 Mar 1829. Wit: Enoch P. Connel and Charles L. Byrn.
Codicil: 20 Apr 1829. Apr Term 1829.

Page 307   Inventory and accounts of sale of William Wilkinson, deceased.
May 17, 1829   Made 12 Feb 1829 by Jonathan and William Wilkinson, executors. Purchasers, to wit, Mrs. Wilkinson, Hansel Wilkinson, M.H. Wilkinson, Jon Wilkinson, O. Jenkins, Mat Waggoner one Holt Bible, J.E. Morris, Jno. McGavock, W.T. Wheeler, William M. Hinton, C.M. Brooks, _____ Neal, J.J. Brown, ?.A. Lester, ?.H. Wells, Jo James, G.G. Wair, _____ Stubblefield, Gen. White, D. Brim, D. Young, W. Faulkner, _____ Abernathy, J.J. Stump, H. Fairley, R. Merryman, J.E. Turner, Jas. McGavock, S. Huffman, W. Patterson, R. Brooks, J. Drake, Jas. Fox, Jno. Vaughn, R. Chick, William Ray, M. Porter, Jo Butterworth, William Hudgins, J.T. Merryman, R.J. Williams, Jno. Lanier, G. Ashley, William Porter, Jo. Phillips, A. Booker, Mrs. Smiley, Porterfield, J.R. Faulkner, William Faulkner, W.W. Garrett, Charles Abernathy, Freeman Abernathy, and Elizabeth Earhart. Apr Term 1829.

Page 309   Inventory of estate of Silas Dillahunt, deceased.
May 18, 1829   Notes on the following, to wit, John Carrington, John B. Carrington, Archibald Carrington, William Campbell, Abner Driver, Joseph H. Little, John Little, Stephen Little, Bryant Boon, John Haley, Harrison Whitfield, Samuel Barcliff, Moses E. E(illegible), John Jones, Thomas Garrett, William B. Rutland, Walter Green, William Greer, W.T. Greer, Elisha Rhodes, _oston Sawyer, William Roach, Dempsey Sawyer, Martin Foreland, Abraham Weeks, Nathaniel Gilliam, Andrew Varden, David Guin, John Berry, Moses B(illegible), James Prichard, Edmond Edney, and William Roach, Daviel Richardson, John D. Stoner, John Davis, William Taylor, Eldridge N. Phipps, James Claud, Elisha Nicholson, Jesse Garland, James Robertson, William H. Shelton, Francis Newsom, John Mills, Burwell Butler, William E. Newsom, Joab Harden to Silas Dillahunt and John Davis executors of Francis Hardgraves, Lewis C. Allen and Nathaniel Gilliam, John Knight, Joseph H. Little and Fleming G(illegible), William L. Demoss, and Norvel & Walker. Open accounts on viz, John W. Whitfield, Theophilus Fulgum, Green B. Taylor, Thomas Cartwright, Samuel Tennison, John

Patrick, Robert W. Phipps, James Demoss, Joseph Orton, John Johnson, Newton Rhodes, Henry M. Hutton, Thomas Williams, Thomas Eva, John Bell, Henry Roach, James Roach, John Taylor, James Rhodes, Joel Jones, Harrison Whitfield, John Napier, Nancy Wilson, Turner J. Evans, Calten Pollard, Thomas E. Gilliam, Walter Porch, William B. Evans, Barnet Varden, Nathaniel Gilliam, William Greer, William R. Evans, John Manley, Nathan Greer, William Canada, Henry Demoss, Walter Greer, Joel Taylor, Susanna Williams, William Greer, Sr., Bryant Boon, James Gilliam, Elisha Spence, William W. Williamson, and Thomas Garrett. Sally Dillahunt, exrx and Jno. Davis, exr. Apr Term 1829.

Page 311   Inventory of sale of estate of Thomas J. Moore, deceased.
May 18, 1829   Made on 27 Feb 1829. Purchasers, to wit, M. Redding, D.T. Hatch, S. Shannon, T. Dill, C. Neal, William Boner, W. Strange, J. McGavock, M. Gleaves, W.M. Hinton, ?.H. Robertson, S. Scruggs, J. Davis, R. McGavock, Jr., R. McGavock, J. Price, B.J. Love, H. Boner, J. Clemmons, Ed. Scruggs, and J.J. Hinton. M. Gleaves, admr. Inventory listed by M. Gleaves, admr, viz, several items including gold watch and notes on, to wit, John T. Hunter, James McGennis, N.B. Pryor, James Faulkner, R. McGavock, M. Gleaves, John Davis, William D. Philips, David B. Love, C.Y. Hooper, William B. Ewing, Eneas Walker, Joel M(illegible), and Thomas Moore. 29 Oct 1818. James Moore. This man James Moore is unknown to me, account on Joseph Gingry drawn by John Davis in favor of Thomas J. Moore on John Porter, James Woods, William Sheppard, William Williams, and E. Dibrell. Michael Gleaves, admr. Apr Term 1829.

Page 313   Settlement of estate of Francis May, deceased.
May 19, 1829   Made with John P. Erwin, executors. Persons listed, to wit, McGavock, Norvell, Maury, Hays, Jennings and McEwen, Hockley, Bradford, Spence, Mrs. Mays, Kirkman, R. Searcy, McChesney, Dickson, Philips, J. Jackson, Houston, D. Cummins, P. Bass, cash received by Judge White of Higgins, Gibbs, Price, Mary May, R.H. Barry, A.J. May, cash sent to Knoxville, B.M. Garner receipt of Campbell, Jo. Norvell, R.P. Hays, McEwen, Presbyterian Church, Hockley, C. Metcalf, William Rutherford, Jacob Dickinson, and Thomas B. Smith. Payment made to William S. May on account of clain as heir of Revenhill. Cash and negroes by H.L. White and John P. Erwin. Received of John P. Erwin the note on Joseph Norvel, R.P. Hays, McEwen, Presbyterian Church, Hockley, Thomas B. Smith, Dickinson, C. Metcalf, William Rutherford, B.M. Garner, and Higgins. The note received belonging one fourth to Andrew J. May, one fourth to R.H. Barry and Mary his wife, and one fourth each to James May and Margaret May for whom said Barry is guardian. 2 Sept 1828. Ephraim S. Hall and Wilkins Tannehill and Nicholas B. Pryor, Esquires, Commissioners. Apr Term 1829.

Page 314   Inventory of estate of James Knox, deceased.
May 19, 1829   An inventory of goods, debts, property and everything belonging to the late firm of Anderson & Knox, taken 3 Apr 1829. Amount of goods on hand this $6894.31. Persons listed, to wit, Samuel Seay, Patrick Clifford, John Muirhead, Boyd McNairy, W. Nichol, Alexander Patton & Co., Thomas Martin, NIcholas Hobson, Martin & Ballentine, Matthew Porter, John C. McLemore, Joseph Dwyer, John Decker, Robert McMinn, Thompson & Wardlow, Andrew Fay, Dr. Overton, Robert Lockhart, S.V.D. Stout, William Bosworth, John Donelly, Robert W. Green, Robert Goodlet, John S. Green, William and Robert Gibson, Joel Parrish, Thomas H. P(illegible), William Porter, J. & R. Woods, JOhn Wilson, Bridge stock, John Wright, John Harding, Samuel St(illegible), William Shegog, Enon & Johnson & Moore, Lewis Earthman, Isaac Earthman, Opie Dunnaway, Opie Lea, David Park, A. Cunningham & Co., Robert Robertson, James Read, William Brooks, J.M. Bondurant, Phelps & Duff, William Garner, William White, Hugh Blackwood, Susan H(illegible), Horace Green, Moses (illegible), R.M. Anthony, William Little, George Young, R. Phipps, William Williams, Isaac L. Crow, John Nichol, (illegible), M. Munford, Alpha Kingsley, James Grizzard, John McGarvey, Tappan & (illegible), S.P. Bellamy & Co., Hornback & Shegog, James D. Alexander, A.W. Johnson & Co., Nashville Bank Stock, Pleasant M. Miller, Andrew Hays, McIntosh & Anderson, Harton & Ellred, Ewing & Brown, H(illegible) Petway, Sharp & Barttison, John Thompson, N.H. Robertson, Thompson Coventry (note), John Shelby, N.A. McNairy, Gordon & Norvell & Co., Samuel Young, Richard Boyd, Samuel W. Hanby, David Scott & Co., Henry White, Sterling Brewer, Thomas Lawson, William Brent, Thomas J. Athey, Jacob Donelson, Miss Hyde, A. Lock, Jno. L. Brown, Thomas Stratton, James Sharp, H. Norvel, Kyle & Orr, E. Welborn, W.W. Watson, R. Weakley, Armstrong & McAl(illegible), Major Hockley, Walter Lewis, Andrew Jackson, Franklin & Reece, C. Brooks, A.B. Hawkins,

Major Campbell, M. Watson, Mrs. Swann, O. Seawell, Dr. Roane, Thomas P. Minor, A. Balch, William Faulkner, Irwin & McMannus, William Nichol, S. Bradford, Harris & Polk, Peter Legrand, Adams & Jones, John Whitaker, James W. Walker, William Hewlett, John Easly, Thomas Jerard, Lewis Willhite, Jno. Mosby, Abner Dovall, John Windrow, (illegible) Webster, C. Hardeman, Andrew Rogers, John Fly, A. Arnold, Sneed & Forest, J.H. Banton, N. Barksdale, J.H. Lyle, K. Tucker, T. Saunders, W.N. Holt, Thomas Goff, John Frost, Hartsville property, R. & D. Knox, Samuel D. Wilson, Wilson & Stewart, A. Braden & McIver, Park & Gibson, B. Hardeman, Jno. Brown, James Knox, Joseph Anderson, E.H. Foster, James Perry, R. Smiley, L. Browning, D. Brimuller, Robertson & Elliott, Maj. Lockart, M. Bell, William Hewlett, Call McNeil, R.C. Foster, Thomas Weston, A. Porter & Son, Mrs. Perkins, George Guy, Capt. Lake, B. Williamson, _____ Morris, J. & J.W. Sitler, William Maxwell, Thomas Wells, R. Saunderson, Z.P. Cantrell, J.C. Benson, John Lea, Whitford & Williams, Robert Marlin, O.B. Hays, P. Kinney, D. Shields, Mana Price, J. Beaty, Kirkman & Erwin, Jas. Grose, Judy Campbell, Culter, Jno. B. West, Jno. R. Menifee, W. Payne, Pierce, A. Latapie, James Woods, Paysent & Co., William Shields, Welch & Austin, William Vaulx, Paul Shirley, William Stewart, Samuel Seay, Abraham Ward, and Charles McGrew. 30 Apr 1829. Joseph Anderson surviving partner of Anderson & Knox. Apr Term 1829.

Page 317   Sale of estate of Sevier Drake, deceased.
May 19, 1829   Sold on 6 Sept 1828. Purchasers, to wit, John Drake, Jonathan Drake, James McGavock, Randol McGavock, Henry Deal, Benjamin Drake, Eli Drake, Lorenzo D. Burges, David R. Coal, George Cagle, Daniel Young, Abram Smith, George W. Waters, George Hoofman, Tazewell Hyde, and Henry O'Denelly. Jonathan Drake, executor. Apr Term 1829.

Page 318   Sale of estate of Mary C. Knox, deceased.
May 20, 1829   Sold by Joseph Vaulx, admr, on 14 Feb 1829. Several items listed.
Apr Term 1829.

Page 319   Sale of estate of John Snary, deceased.
May 21, 1829   Bills due on Archy Panes, A. Tapps, Ben Athey, Mr. Finney, George Ellis, John Priest, W. Barry, John Thompson, Thomas Bine, Elisha West, John Henry, Mr. Dorris, T. Kingsley, Mr. S(illegible), William McClure, John Hilsman, A. Adair, J.B. Finney, George Barnby, Thomas Athey, Otter Woloc, Joseph Matthew, William Marshall, Samuel Watson, George R. Dillon, John Hickman, Alfred Spell, T. Loach, W. Sansbury, John Miller, Robert Smith, Hugh Drennen, W. Wallace, W. Elliston, Henry Sides, P. Clifford, Joseph Markes, Joel Madison, Thomas Melson, Warren Hale, and S.V.D. Stuart. S.V.D. Stout, admr. Apr Term 1829.

Page 320   Robert and Eliza Farquharson, dower.
May 22, 1829   On 18 Apr 1829, we, John Nichol, Stephen Cantrell, Joseph Vaulx, Benjamin W. Bedford, and Richard H. Barry, met to lay off and set apart to Robert Farquharson and Eliza his wife her legal dower out of one half of Lot No. 37 of which her deceased husband James Porter died seized and possessed and the said jurors have appeared on the premises and Henry Ewing special guardian of the minor heirs of said James Porter, deceased, being also present. Lot No. 37 fronts on College Street or Public Square, next to part of said lot owned by Adam Caldwell's heirs, including the mansion house. Apr Term 1829.

Page 321   Settlement of estate of Charles M. Hall, deceased.
May 22, 1829   Several items listed. 28 Apr 1827. Absalom Gleaves and Edward H. East, Commissioners. Apr Term 1829. They settled with Nancy B. Hall, relatively to her administration on the estate.

Page 321   Settlement of estate of henry Graves, deceased.
May 22, 1829   Commissioners met to settle the estate of Henry Graves, deceased, between the heirs and Sarah Graves, admrx of the same and found against admrx $214.00 and vouchers in her favor also her distributive share. Apr 20, 1829. Josiah F. Williams, Micajah Autry and S.W. Goodrich, Commissioners. Apr Term 1829.

Page 322   Settlement of estate of Lewis Demoss, deceased.
May 22, 1829   Made with Abraham Demoss and John Demoss, executors. Amount

chargeable to the executors $1852.74 3/4 and a balance due by said executors $388.42¼. The sale of stock of horses, cattle, sheep and hogs and the money equally divided between Delilah Taylor, Abraham Demoss, John Demoss and Sally Driver. The balance of the estate is yet to be divided and also discovered from the record of a suit Demoss, executors VS Charles Hartly that $60.60 only was recovered. John Davis and Bryant Boon, Commissioners. Apr Term 1829.

Page 322   Settlement of estate of George Hathaway, deceased.
May 23, 1829   Made with William Hathaway, admr.   Several vouchers listed.
Addison East, Simon Glenn and Samuel McMannus, Esqr., Commissioners.

Page 323   Inventory of estate of Pilmore Cole, deceased.
May 23, 1829   Several items listed including notes on David Watkins and William
Coltharp. Lydia Cole, admrx. Apr Term 1829.

Page 324   Settlement of estate of Richard Stringfellow, deceased.
May 23, 1829   Made with William Stringfellow, admr.   Several vouchers listed.
Thomas Scott and Thomas Ferebee, Esqrs., Commissioners. Apr Term 1829.

Page 324   Division of estate of William Wilkinson, deceased.
May 23, 1829   We proceeded to divide the negroes belonging to the estate of
William Wilkinson, deceased. Lot No. 1 of two negroes to Mrs. Moumen Wilkinson, Lot No. 2
of three negroes to Milly Everett, Lot No. 3 of three negroes to Hansel T. Wilkinson, Lot
No. 4 of two negroes to Micajah H. Wilkinson, Lot No. 5 of two negroes to William
Wilkinson, Lot No. 6 of two negroes to Jonathan Wilkinson, and Lot No. 7 of two negroes to
Tresea Smiley. This __ day of Feb 1829.   James McGavock, Jno. Criddle and William
Faulkner, Commissioners. Apr Term 1829.

Page 325   Sale of estate of John Hoggatt, deceased.
May 23, 1829   Sale of property left to be sold at the death of Diana Hoggatt.
Purchasers, to wit, Anthony Clopton, William McMurry, Mr. Thornton, Nelson Carter, O.
Gordon, Joseph Clay, Robert Hill and J.W. Hoggatt. J.W. Hoggatt, executor.   Apr Term
1829.

Page 325   Settlement of estate of John Kellum, deceased.
May 25, 1829   A list of notes against the estate of John Kellum, deceased.
Persons listed, to wit, Washington S. Shelton, John Carrington, Josiah H. Alston, Benjamin
Smith, William Tarpley, Nathan Smith, Nathan Ewing and widow's allowance for one year.
Amount in the widow's hands for division $122.34 3/4. Martha Kellum, admrx.   Abraham
Demoss and Silas Dillahunt, Esqrs., Commissioners. Apr Term 1829.

Page 326   Settlement of estate of Charles Wright, deceased.
May 25, 1829   Made with Absalom Gleaves, executor.   Several vouchers listed.
John Hall, Esq., and Samuel Steele and Thomas Harding, Commissioners. 20 Apr 1829. Apr
Term 1829.

Page 327   Inventory of estate of Lewis Earthman, deceased.
May 25, 1829   Money collected from execution in the name of M. Lowe VS Hugh
Roland also Peter Knight note in favor of the admrs. 27 Apr 1829. Jno. S. Cox, admr and
Judah Earthman, admrx. Apr Term 1829.

Page 327   Settlement of estate of William T. Norment, deceased.
May 23, 1829   Made with James Norment, admr.   Leaving a balance of $55.67¼.
Apr 11, 1829. Edmond Goodrich and Micajah Autry, Commissioners. Apr Term 1829.

Page 327   Settlement of estate of Thomas Fowlkes, deceased.
July 6, 1829   Made with William H. Hamblin, one of the executors, including
hire of negroes, vouchers &c.   6 Feb 1829.   Edmond Goodrich and Reuben Payne, Esqrs.,
Commissioners. Apr Term 1829.

Page 328   Sale of estate of William Frazor, deceased.
July 6, 1829   Made by Moses B. Frazor, admr.   One negro boy Mark sold for

$390.00. Apr 20, 1829. Apr Term 1829.

Page 328   Will of Thomas Shivers, deceased.
Aug 25, 1829   To my wife Abergale the tract of land on which I now live during
her natural lifetime, also all my stock of every description, my household and kitchen
furniture, all farming and carpenters tools. To my daughter Liddy Cowle $50.00 at the death
of my wife. To my grandson Henry Holt son of Ro. (Robert) Holt one horse and saddle and
bridle at the death of my wife. To my son Jonas Shivers one bed and furniture at the death
of my wife. To my son John Shivers one bed and furniture at the death of my wife. To my
wife Abergale my negro girl Emma during her natural life and at her death said negro Emma
and her increase to be sold and the money to be equally divided between my daughter Liddy
Cowle and my sons Jonas Shivers and John Shivers. To my son-in-law Robert Holt $1.00 at
death of my wife. I appoint my wife Abergale Shivers, executrix. This 20 May 1829. Wit:
Nicholas Hewlett and Thomas Cartwright. July Term 1829.

Page 329   Negroes divided of estate of John Earthman, deceased.
Aug 20, 1829   On May 15, 1829. Commissioners met at the house of Mrs. Polly
Earthman, widow of John Earthman, deceased. Mrs. Polly Earthman has drawn Zenas a
negro boy and Mariah a negro girl valued at $500.00 by I.F. Earthman paying her $66.66 2/3.
Isaac F. Earthman one of the legal heirs drew David and Fanny and paying others and John
H. Earthman $16.66. Garrison Lanier and his wife Huldah K. being legal heirs drew Andrew
and Garrett and paying Mary C. Earthman $8.33 1/3. Samuel H. Earthman being legal heir
drew Alford, Eliza and Washington and paying Mary C. Earthman $8.33 1/3. John H.
Earthman a legal heir has drawn Silver and her two children. Mary C. Earthman a legal heir
drew Allen and Matilda. James Marshall, Lysander McGavock and Michael Gleaves,
Commissioners. July Term 1829.

Page 330   Land divided of estate of Andrew J. and Elizabeth Donelson,
devised by William Donelson, deceased, to his two children Andrew J. and Elizabeth
Donelson. Land lying on the north side of Cumberland River in Davidson County devised by
William Donelson, deceased, to his two children Andrew J. and Elizabeth Donelson, minors
under the age of twenty one years. To Andrew J. Donelson allotted and set apart the tract
of land known by the name of the Bunkers Hill containing about 616 acres likewise a tract of
land commonly called the Clements tract containing about 320 acres. Allotted to Elizabeth
Donelson the following tracts of land, to wit, one tract of land conveyed by Jesse Hudson to
William Donelson for 400 acres, another tract conveyed by Thomas Kilgore, another tract for
320 acres, one other tract deeded by George Blackmore for 123 acres, one other tract
deeded by said Blackmore for 8½ acres, another small tract by said Blackmore for 18 acres,
one small tract conveyed by Thomas Cartwright for 12½ acres, one other tract deeded by
George W. Deaderick for 20 acres, in all 602 acres. This 18 July 1829. Allen Matthis, E.P.
Connell, William Neely and Reuben Payne, Commissioners. July Term 1829.

Page 331   Inventory of estate of William P. Byrn, deceased.
Aug 26, 1829   Taken 20 July 1829. Several items listed, with one half belonging
to C.L. Byrn. One note on Lemuel Bowers. E.P. Connell and C.L. Byrn, executors. July
Term 1829.

Page 331   Inventory of estate of Silas Dillahunty, deceased.
Aug 26, 1829   Items bequeathed in his Last Will and Testament to his wife Sally
Dillahunty who has since deceased. Several items listed. One proven account on Samuel and
David P. Biers. John Davis, executor. July Term 1829.

Page 332   Inventory of estate of Robert Buchanan, deceased.
Aug 27, 1829   Several items listed including one silver watch and several
negroes. Francis Porterfield, admr. July Term 1829.

Page 332   Settlement of estate of John L. Goodwin, deceased.
Aug 27, 1829   Taken on 17 May 1828. Voucher No. 1 to a lawyer fee, No. 2 to
Mobley shoemaking, No. 3 to Cooper's account for labor done, No. 4 to Anderson, No. 5 to
the balance of John O. Bennett for making a coffin 75¢, No. 6 to James Cloid for the season
of a man to his stud horse, No. 7 to the County Clerk, No. 8 to the deceased John J.
Goodwin's note to the admr., No. 9 to Henry's schooling, No. 10 to Dillahunt's note on said

Goodwin, No. 11 to the admr for whiskey made use of at the two sales, No. 12 to John Jones whiskey, No. 13 to Rutlands school account, No. 14 to the cryers account for crying one of the sales of the estate, No. 15 to Sheriff receipt, No. 16 to admr's charge, No. 17 the clerk's receipt, and No. 18 to Stroud's school account. William H. Shelton and Thomas Scott, Commissioners. July Term 1829.

Page 333   Winney McFarland, widow dower.
Aug 31, 1829   We, the Commissioners, met to lay off and set apart to Winney McFarland her legal dower out of Lot No. 36 in the town of Nashville, on College Street including the dwelling house in which Robert P. McFarland, deceased, last lived before his death. This 17 June 1829. Samuel Tilford, Enoch W. Brookshire, Richard H. Barry, James Erwin and Enoch Welborn, Commissioners. July Term 1829.

Page 334   Account of estate of Jacob Dickinson, deceased.
Aug 31, 1829   Mrs. Patsey Dickinson alias Allen, admrx. To the hire of sundry negroes from the settlement of the estate on 23 July 1829, to wit, negroes. Persons listed, Lucy Gough and David. To boarding, clothing and schooling five children. To boarding and clothing negro children. To going after Abram, a negro who ran away in 1826. To a note on Mrs. P. McCoy. July Term 1829.

Page 334   Settlement of estate of Abraham S. Hoggatt, deceased.
Sept 2, 1829   Made with James W. Hoggatt, admr. Sale of property filed in office $466.34. For his share of the net proceeds of the sale of his father's estate after the death of Diana Hoggatt. Paid to, to wit, W.H. Robertson, R.A. Higginbotham, Robertson & Waters, William Hall, R. & W. Armstrong, McComb & Ward, S. Ewing, A. Hynes, A.H. Clopton, H. Trott, M. Hurt, D. Craighead, Clerk of Rutherford County cost of suit, and by payment in full to James W. Hoggatt, John H. Hoggatt, A. Clopton, and Amanda F. Hoggatt, the distributees $331.09. This July 27, 1829. Robert Farquharson and Nicholas ?. Pryor, Commissioners. July Term 1829.

Page 335   Settlement of estate of William T. Dickinson, a lunatic.
Sept 2, 1829   Made with Jacob D. Donelson, guardian. Persons listed, to wit, JOhn H. Smith, John Nichol, Kirkman & Erwin, James Elizer, W.R. Gibson, Sumner & Hunter, Wallace & Dixon, William Neely, Will R. Gibson, L. Browning, L.H. Farrar, John Price, Joe. Payne, Benjamin J. Love, George W. Campbell for horse, F. McKay, John Blackman, R. Payne, Patsey Dickinson, D. Frazor, Thomas E. Harrison, N. Ewing, Jos. W. Horton, Durley I(illegible), B.F. Lewis, Duke W. Sumner, Alexander Walker, James Bishop, Mary H. Sampson, A. Cunningham, Doctor Mathis, Winburn & Gwinn, R.J. Love, S. McG(illegible), S. Williams, Carter Allen, W.P. Walker, Robert Bradford, J. Curry, Smith & Moore, William A. Bradford, Polly McKay, C. & V. Walker, James Dillard, Campbell & McConnell, Gill & Porter, Sam Seay, Alfred Lyons, Thomas Wells, W.D. Philips, Park & Gibson, M. Autry, W. Shaw, John M. Hill, Thomas P. Adams, John Harmond, Thomas P. F(illegible), Will W. Guinn, John L. Bugg, James Clements, Will M. Winbourn, John Beasley, W. Wilkes, W. Hope, R. Payne, M. Philips, J.D. Donelson, A.W. Vanleer, Julia Dickinson, Thomas Walker, Isaac Sitler, Thomas Watkins, and Mr. Love. This 20 July 1829. Edmond Goodrich, John Pirtle and Enoch P. Connell, Commissioners. July Term 1829.

Page 337   Settlement of estate of Diana Hoggatt, deceased.
Sept 3, 1829   Made with James W. Hoggatt, executor of the Last Will and Testament of Diana Hoggatt, deceased. She bequeathed to Mrs. Rhoda Clopton a featherbed and furniture, to Amanda F. Hoggatt a featherbed and furniture, to Sandifer Hoggatt a bay horse, and lastly that she gave the residue of all her estate both real and personal to James W. Hoggatt. This 26 July 1829. Robert Farquharson and Nicholas B. Pryor, Commissioners. July Term 1829.

Page 338   Inventory of estate of Thomas Shivers, deceased.
Sept 4, 1829   Made on July 24, 1829. Several items listed. Abigail Shivers, executrix. July Term 1829.

Page 338   Settlement of estate of John Hoggatt, deceased.
Sept 4, 1829   Made with James W. Hoggatt, executor. Persons listed, to wit, Attorney Foster, W. B(illegible), Attorney Craighead, P. Mosely, Moore's heirs, R. Smith, J.

229

Handly, Z. Powell, E. Ward, E. M(illegible), S. Strong, J.W. Drake, and nineteen days attendance in Lincoln County on business of the estate. By payment made in full to John Hoggatt, James W. Hoggatt, Diana Hoggatt, and the heirs of A.S. Hoggatt in full. Paid cost to Franklin and cash paid Fogg and Fletcher for legal services. July 27, 1829. Robert Farquharson and Nicholas B. Pryor, Commissioners. Disposition of two bonds on William P. Anderson delivered to A. Clopton. July Term 1829.

Page 340   Land divided of estate of John Patterson, deceased.
Sept 7, 1829   Plat on page 340. Lot No. 1 to Jackson Davis and Elizabeth his wife for 10 3/4 acres and 22 poles, Lot No. 2 to John Patterson for 10 3/4 acres and 22 poles, Lot No. 3 to Margaret Patterson for 10 3/4 acres and 22 poles, Lor No. 4 to William Patterson for 16 3/4 acres, Lot No. 5 to Patsey Patterson for 18 acres, and to Ellen Patterson for 33 1/3 acres. Ellen Patterson, widow and relict of John Patterson, deceased, the land where on she now lives on Whites Creek. This 22 June 1829. Sam Weakley, S.D. Michael Gleaves, John J. Hinton, William Faulkner, William Ray, James H. Hooper, William Nicholson, and William R. Ewing, Commissioners. July Term 1829.

Page 342   Settlement of estate of Mary C. Knox, deceased.
Nov 16, 1829   Made with Joseph Vaulx, admr. Notes on the following, to wit, Nathaniel A. McNairy, O. Scruggs, N. Hobson, J.K. Raybourn, John Davis, H. Roland, William W. Goodwin, Ch: M. Nichol, A.W. Johnson, D. Thompson, J. Drennen, and Joseph Vaulx. N. Hobson guardian of Catherine A. Knox. Others listed, viz, Allen A. Hall, M. S(illegible), Jno. P. Erwin, Simpson, Dr. Robert Henderson for medical attendance on Mrs. Knox in Virginia, Mrs. Dorris, Dr. John Waters, and money belonging to estate of William Hobson, Sr., deceased. Robert Farquharson and Stephen Cantrell.

Page 343   Inventory of estate of Thomas J. Athey, deceased.
Nov 16, 1829   Made by William Brook, admr. Several items listed including one gold watch. A note on Simon Bradford and one account on Charles Walker. Oct Term 1829.

Page 343   Settlement of estate of Francis McKay, deceased.
Nov 17, 1829   Made with Polly McKay, admr. Produced $1396.91½ also produced vouchers of $1405.12½. This 30 Oct 1829. Samuel Shannon, David Hunter and John J. Hinton. Oct term 1829.

Page 343   Inventory of estate of Thomas Shivers, deceased.
Nov 17, 1829   Purchasers, to wit, John Cunningham, John S. Gilbreath, Thomas Cartwright, Charles F. Massey, Jonas Shivers, Mrs. Cole, Mrs. Shivers, John Pucket, Thomas F. Shaw, David Batson, Isaac Walton, William Williams, John Cole, and Mary B. Walker. Abigail Shivers, executrix. Oct Term 1829.

Page 344   Will of James Wright, deceased.
Nov 17, 1829   I loan to my wife Sarah Wright during her natural life or widowhood three negroes and my land which still remains to me, also my stock, household and kitchen furniture, farming tools &c except as much as will pay my debts. To my son James Wright three negroes which he has received and other property which he has received, to him and his heirs. I loan to my son Thomas Wright a negro girl Harriet also I confirm to him all the money and other property I have heretofore given him, to him and his heirs. I loan to my daughter Elizabeth Brown one negro woman Betty and her three children, and 80 acres of land on Buchanans Creek and borders Silas Morton's corner and Thompson line, also other items listed. I loan to my daughter Mary Morton one negro woman Rose and her two children also two negro boys John and Sam, also $400.00 which Silas Morton owes me together with other property which I have given her, to her and her heirs. I loan to my son Moses Wright three negroes and one wagon in his possession at this time together with other things which he has received amounting to $330.00 which property loaned to him during his life time, to him and his children but if he should leave no lawful children then the property here given will return to be equally divided amongst my other children. I loan to my son Aaron Wright three negroes and one bay mare now in his possession together with other articles which he has received amounting to $330.00 which I loan to him during his lifetime and to descend to his children but should he die without lawful children then the property here given will return to be equally divided among my other children. I loan to my daughter Anny Pigg four negroes with other things already given her for her and her children but if

230

she leaves no children at her death then the property will return to be equally divided among my other children. It is also to be understood that what remains of the property which I have not disposed of to my children in this will is at the death or marriage of my wife, be sold and the remaining be equally divided among my children. I appoint my two sons James N. Wright and Moses Wright, my executors. This 1 Feb 1828. Wit: James Whitsell and Thomas Haywood. Oct Term 1829.

Page 345   Settlement of estate of Howel Tatum, deceased.
Nov 17, 1829   Made with Stephen Cantrell, admr. Persons listed, to wit, Edwin M. Tatum one of the heirs, Micajah Wade intermarried with Eliza Tatum, John P. Wiggin, Andrew Erwin, Jr., guardian. This 29 Oct 1829. John P. Erwin and Robert Farquharson, Esqrs., Commissioners. Oct Term 1829.

Page 346   Will of Jones Read, deceased.
Nov 21, 1829   I desire all my negroes, stock, my farm and household and kitchen furniture be kept together and to be used to the best advantage under the superintended and direction of my executors during my wife's natural life for her support and that of the family of Mahala Frazor and herself with the assistance of the negroes of said Mahala to be also worked on my farm &c. At the death of my wife all the household furniture, stock of all kind and other personal property, excepting the negroes, shall be sold and equally divided, along with the negroes, into several parts, one share to my son William Read, one share to my son John Read, one share to my son Samuel D. Read, one equal share to my daughter Polly Rucker, one share to my daughter Mahala Frazor, one share to my grandson James H. Turner in trust for the use and benefit of my grandchildren the children of my son Thomas J. Read living at the time of my death or that may be born after. To my daughter Elizabeth Bondurant $150.00 to my daughter Nancy Quinn. I appoint my son Samuel D. Read and my grandson James H. Turner, executors. This 15 May 1829. Wit: William B. Ewing and Joseph Rice. Oct Term 1829.

Page 347   Will of Rebecca Hyde, deceased.
Nov 23, 1829   To my beloved son Benjamin Hyde one good featherbed and furniture also negro man Isaac. To the heirs of said Benjamin Hyde and my yoke of steers and oxcart. To my beloved son Richard Hyde my negro woman Jinsey and her child Martha. To my beloved son Edmond Hyde my negro man Jim. To my beloved grandson Christopher Hyde Stump the youngest son of John Stump my negro girl Eliza and two heifers. To my grand daughter Pannellee Stump daughter of said John Stump my side saddle. To my beloved daughter-in-law Polly Hyde, relict of my son Henry Hyde, one bed and furniture. To my beloved grand son Felix Hyde, son of Taswell Hyde, my negro boy Isaac. To my beloved grandson Edmond Hyde son of Taswell Hyde, my negro boy George and a sorrel horse colt. To my beloved son John Hyde my two negro girls, Mary and Sins. To my beloved son Taswell Hyde $10.00 in money. I desire that my old negro woman Franky to be emancipated after my death. The residue of my estate to be sold and monies to be applied to the payment of a certain note of hand I gave for the purchase of property at my late husband Henry Hyde's sale after his death and to pay my funeral expenses. I appoint my sons Richard and Benjamin Hyde, my executors. This 13 Feb 1829. Wit: Thomas Hickman, Noah Underwood and Musander Walker. Oct Term 1829.

Page 348   Inventory of estate of Rebecca Hyde, deceased.
Nov 24, 1829   Several items listed. Notes on viz, Benjamin Hyde, Richard Hyde, David Abernathy, Freeman Abernathy, Edmond Hyde, and Daniel Dunnavan. Benjamin J. Hyde, executor. Oct Term 1829.

Page 348   Inventory of estate of Daniel Brown, deceased.
Nov 24, 1829   Several items listed. John McDaniel, admr. Oct Term 1829.

Page 349   Inventory of estate of John Glenn, deceased.
Nov 24, 1829   Made by Humphrey Dunnevant, admr. Cash of $48.00 and clothing sold for $4.37½. Oct Term 1829.

Page 350   Settlement of estate of Mary C. Knox, deceased.
Nov 25, 1829   Made with Joseph Vaulx, admr. Persons listed, to wit, Allen A. Hall, M. Spofford, John P. Erwin, _____ Simpson, Dr. Henderson for medical attendance on

Mrs. Knox in Virginia (illegible), Mrs. Dorris, Dr. Jno. Waters, Sam Hobson, A.W. Johnson, N.A. McNairy, Sam Hobson for money received by him belonging to estate of William Hobson, deceased, and being amount of Mrs. Knox proportion thereof, O. Scruggs, D. Thompson, John Drennen, N. Hobson, and J.K. Raybourn, John Davis, H. Roland, Joseph Vaulx, W.W. Goodwin, and Charles Nichol. $1290.99 out of the above amount the estate owes Nicholas Hobson guardian of Catherine A. Knox $170.46 and the guardian N. Hobson to pay Dr. Henderson's bill. John Nichol, Robert Farquharson and Stephen Cantrell, Commissioners. Oct Term 1829.

Page 351   Will of Sandy Owen, deceased.
Nov 28, 1829   All my property to be divided equally between my two brothers Samuel Owen and James C. Owen. This will was witnessed on 6 Oct 1829 reducted to writing at his request and read and approved by him and he signed on Oct 30, 1829. Thomas R. Jennings and James Roane. Will produced in Court by Henry A. Wise, Esq. Sandy Owen during his last illness and a short time previous to his death at the house of Jos. P. Minnich in this County and said Owen requested them to witness the said Last Will and Testament. Ordered that Samuel Owen have letters of administration granted him on the estate of Sandy Owen, deceased with the will annexed and gave bond with James C. Owen and Everett Owen, securities.

Page 351   Will of Elihu Marshall, deceased, of Nashville.
Nov 28, 1829   To my beloved wife Elizabeth Marshall during her natural life all my real and personal property including my brick house and lot on Market Street in Nashville where I now reside also one female slave Rachel. At the death of my wife all the property to be equally divided between our children should the youngest be at that time twenty one years of age. But if the youngest shall not have arrived at age of twenty one years at the death of my wife then the property is to remain undivided until the youngest arrives at age of twenty one years. I appoint my wife Elizabeth Marshall, executrix. This Mar 7, 1829. Wit: William H. Barker, Addison East and Eben H. Burnett. Oct Tern 1829.

Page 352   Will of Michael Steane, deceased.
Nov 30, 1829   (A letter) Dear Brother. "I am sorry to inform you that a necessity I am going away to settle some business and shall never return to see you again any more forever. I hope you will give Aunt Rose her freedom and the house where lee lives and three hundred dollars in cash and hope you will give my sister Betsey one thousand dollars and give the Missionary Society five hundred dollars and the Bible Society five hundred dollars and settle up my just debts and distribute the balance among the poor and do whatever you please with the balance except give Mrs. Boyd __ dollars toward a tombstone for Jos. Boyd. I hope you will put a tombstone in my garden in commemoration for me. Give my love to all my relations and respects to all inquiring friends, accept the same yourself. So I remain your affectionate brother until death." Signed Michael Steane. Oct 1, 1829. Oct Term 1829.
John Ritchie and John Lee said that they were acquainted with the said Michael Steane in his lifetime and believe it to be his handwriting also Henry Shuttle witnesses same handwriting.

Page 353   Inventory of estate of Isaac F. Earthman, deceased.
Nov 30, 1829   Several items listed including notes, viz, Joseph Elmore, James Earthman, Jonathan Coollidge, also one on James Earthman payable to William Patton. Oct 27, 1829. Garrison Lanear, admr. Oct Term 1829.

Page 353   Joseph McBride's heirs divided.
Nov 30, 1829   Settle with George Hodge guardian of Mary McBride who has intermarried with Wright Stanley, Joseph McBride and Priscilla McBride, heirs of Joseph McBride, deceased. We find him indebted to Mary Stanley for $902.19, and to Joseph McBride after allowing for schooling, boarding and clothing $676.06, and to Priscilla McBride after paying all charges $755.19. We then proceeded to value the negroes and divide them. They valued at $1740.00. We allotted to Mary Stanley, Thomas and Martha valued at $515.00 and $65.00. And to Joseph we allotted James and Joseph valued at $525.00 and $55.00 to make equal to Priscilla we allotted to Henry and Rachel and child Abraham valued at $700.00 she having to pay Mary $65.00, to Joseph $55.00. This 19 Oct 1829. Philip Campbell and John Johns, Commissioners. Mary McBride, one of the minor heirs of Joseph

McBride, deceased, has intermarried with Wright Stanley, and George Hodge guardian of Joseph McBride and Priscilla McBride the younger heirs of Joseph, deceased. Oct Term 1829.

Page 354   Inventory of estate of Patrick Clifford, deceased.
Dec 1, 1829   Taken 30 Sept 1838. Several items listed including notes, viz, John G. Moore, G.W. Campbell, Charles Newnan, William Job, James H. Chick, Henry Folkes, James Campbell, John L. Smith, and M.S. Gross. Brent Spence, admr. Oct Term 1829.

Page 354   Inventory of estate of David Buie, deceased.
Dec 1, 1829   Sale of estate in the State of Mississippi $100.00, which there was no account received of W. Edwards $20.00, received of Jn. Andling $24.00, received of Jamison Vixberry $34.00, received $22.00 all of which was received in the State of Mississippi. Daniel Buie, admr. Oct Term 1829.

Page 355   Inventory of estate of Robert Buchanan, deceased.
Dec 1, 1829   Several items listed. Francis Porterfield, admr. A list of notes due, to wit, B.W.D. Carty rent, William Temple for rent on Brown Creek, Allen Quentien, J.K. Kane, Thomas Turley, and Brent Spence. Other names on the books of R. Buchanan, to wit, Joseph A(illegible), E.W. Bell, Alexander Drake, Jos. Greer, Ingram & Loyd, J. Manier, James Reid, Thomas Williamson, Judy Young, James Boon, Jesse Cartwright, Thomas Everett, Jeremiah Hinton, Miles Myers, Charles McClean, Samuel Vandigrift, and Thomas Weston. Oct Term 1829.

Page 355   Inventory of estate of Richard Joslin, deceased.
Dec 2, 1829   Several items listed. Lewis Joslin, admr. Oct Term 1829.

Page 356   Inventory of estate of Phil Claiborne, deceased.
Dec 1, 1829   One stud horse called Carolinian, one black mare and colt, and one sorrel mare. Thomas Claiborne, admr. Personal property sold to the highest bidder. Purchasers, to wit, Doctor Devereux J. Claiborne, Augustine Claiborne, William King, and Thomas Claiborne. This 21 Oct 1829. Oct Term 1829.

Page 356   David M. Richardson's estate settled.
Dec 2, 1829   Commissioners examined the accounts of William Hope of David M. Richardson and reported amount due the estate of $301.14 3/4, and vouchers of $308.4, and a note on Samuel M. Osborne. This 20 Oct 1829. Edmond Goodrich and Reuben Payne, Commissioners. Oct Term 1829.

Page 356   Sale of estate of Silas Dillahunt, deceased.
Dec 2, 1829   To be sold in the lifetime of his widow Sally Dillahunt. Purchasers, to wit, Joshus ?. Cloud, Abraham Mitchell, William B. Porch, Neil Little, John Little, Sr., Zachariah Mitchell, Frederick Ezell, Silas Linton, Robert P. Boyd, John Carrington, John B. Carrington, Henry Knight, Abner Driver, Thompson & Ragan, Henry Ellison, and Charles H. Ratcliff. Sales of chattel estate bequeathed to his wife Sally Dillahunt who has since deceased. Purchasers, to wit, Thomas Demoss for Zeny Dillahunty, Zahy Dillahunty, Martha Dillahunty, Delilah Dillahunty, John Dillahunty, and James Greer, Rosa House, Thomas W. Hobs, Thomas C. Casey, Henry Demoss, John Knight, John Pritchard, John B. Carrington, Edward Raworth, William Whitfield, Jos. Demoss, Hardy Mitchell, William Spence, Nath. Gillam, Samuel Bryant, William B. Porch, William F. Demoss, Martin Forehand, John Patrick, (illegible) Whitfield, Henry Hutton, (illegible) Campbell, (illegible) Williams, Thomas Cartwright, John Dennagan, Greenberry G(illegible), Isaac Jones, William B. Brown, John Davis, Neal Little, Isaac G(illegible), John Harwood, Willie Carrington, Robert B. Turner, Demsey Sawyers, Isaac C. Pritchard, Benjamin Boon, and Joab Harding. John Davis, admr. Oct Term 1829.

Page 358   Settlement of estate of David T. Etheridge, deceased.
Dec 2, 1829   Made with Dennis Dozier, admr. Vouchers, to wit, A. Russell, Christopher Desson, Nathan Ewing, Jacob McGavock, Wilson Crockett, Timothy Dusall, John Lewis, Robert Vick, William Fuqua, Joseph Page, M. Gleaves, William Wallace, G. Fuqua, and John Reese. Penny Duncan charges for her services as admrx and waiting on a negro woman. James Lovell and George's certificate. Oct 17, 1829. Wilson L. Gower, J.P.,

Braxton Lee and Wilson Crockett, Esquires, Commissioners. Oct Term 1829.

Page 359   Will of Hannah Holmes, deceased.
Feb 24, 1830   To my daughter Eliza Holmes as long as she remains single all my
real and personal estate and to do with whatever she may think proper. If my daughter
Eliza should marry I give to her two thirds of my estate and the other one third to my son
William Holmes. I appoint my daughter Eliza sole executrix. This 29 Dec 1829. Wit: Henry
Ewing and Oliver Hart. Jan Term 1820.

Page 360   Sale of estate of James Walker, deceased.
Feb 24, 1830   Several items listed. Peter J. Walker, admr. Jan Term 1830.

Page 361   Sale of negroes of estate of Thomas J. Athey, deceased.
Feb 24, 1830   The sale of two negro slaves were sold at the Jackson Hotel in
Nashville on 30 Jan 1830 to Mrs. Lucy W. Athey. William Brooks, admr. Jan Term 1830.

Page 352   Sale of estate of Elizabeth Craighead, deceased.
Feb 24, 1830   A list of notes and accounts, viz, James Fleming, Thomas
Stratton, Henry Seat, Joseph Butterworth, Bailey Turner, M. Autry, Eliza Putney, Matthew P.
Walker, Benjamon Morgan, Carter Allen, Edward Scruggs, Langhorn Scruggs, Leven Watson,
Alexander Harmon, William White, R.J. Williams, John Faulkes, William H. Watkins, George
Lowry, John Orr, David Craighead, William Temple, John B. Craighead, Edmond Goodrich,
Jane Craighead, John G. Gorman, Josiah Williams, A. Pucket, H. Niles, Polly Orr, John
Turner, and Jos. Litton. John B. Craighead, admr. Jan Term 1830.

Page 363   Inventory of estate of Rebecca Hyde, deceased.
Feb 25, 1830   A list of notes belonging to the said estate, to wit, Benjamin
O"Donnelly, Henry O"Donnelly, Benjamin Litton, Joseph Litton, Taswell Hyde, Richard Hyde,
Edmund Hyde and Benjamin's, Gilbert Marshall, James Marshall, David Abernathy, James
Hooper, James Fox, Hiram Wells, M(illegible) Walker, Abraham Walker, Freeman Abernathy,
Laban Abernathy, Jr., Alexander Luster, A.H. Farley, Daniel Dunnaway, Thomas Perdie,
Henry Deal, George Waggoner, Matthew Waggoner, Thomas Vaughn, Thomas Abernathy,
William L. Frensly and Nancy C. Frensly, Noah Underwood, Hardy Floods, Elizabeth James
and Thomas G. James, Morgan Brown, G.M. Fogg, John Stump and Albert G. Stump,
Adkerson Fairly, Seth Curland, and James H. Hooper. 2 Feb 1830. Benjamin Hyde,
executor. Jan term 1830.

Page 364   Will of George Bell, deceased.
Feb 25, 1830   One bay colt I give to my brother Hugh Bell. To my brother
Clement L. Bell my negro woman Bella and her four children. To my brothers Henry C. Bell
and Clement L. Bell all my other estate, all my other dear brothers and sisters I believe to
be eligibly and provided for. I appoint Henry Bell and Clement L. Bell my executors. This
14 Sept 1829. Wit: Samuel Seay, Joseph Gingry and Davis Cobler. Addition: To my brother
H.F. Bell my chain and seal. Wit: Boyd NcNairy. Jan Term 1830.

Page 364   Settlement of estate of Frances Curtis, deceased.
Feb 25, 1830   Made with Thomas Crutcher, executor. Persons listed, to wit,
Robert Farquharson, John Gregor a grave digger, McCombs, and Hall and Fitzgerald for
printing. Jan Term 1830.

Page 365   Will of John Criddle, deceased.
Feb 25, 1830   The land on which I now live to be sold for the purpose of raising
money to pay my part of a debt of $2400.00 due the _____ Branch Bank at Nashville by
Robert Lanear and myself, my part being $1300.00. I will that my negroes be hires out and
enough of the money arising from the hire be reserved to board, school and cloth my three
youngest children, Harriet, Amanda and James until the girls marry or arrives at the age of
eighteen years and until James shall have acquired a good English education or some trade
he chooses. To my daughter Harriet Criddle a negro girl Priscilla and one good featherbed
and furniture. To my daughter Amanda Criddle a negro girl Nancy and a good featherbed
and furniture. To my son James Criddle a negro boy William. The remainder of my estate
to be equally divided among all my children and my two grand children John Lanier and
Susan Lanier the part which their mother Eliza Lanier should have had if she had lived, her

234

part is one fifth part. I wish Robert Lanier father of my grandchildren John and Susan to have the power of selling the said negro and other property which may go to the said children John and Susan. I wish the land, stock, furniture &c be sold. It was willed by my mother that Monroe Moss shall have $100.00 when he arrives at age of twenty one years. I appoint my friend John Hobson, my executor. This 13 Oct 1829. Wit: Smith Criddle, William Weakley, and John Finks.

Codicil: To my grandchild John Lanier 100 acres which I own in Sumner County which land I bought of Robert Eaton and which lies on Manskers Creek. Wit: Smith Criddle and John Finks. Jan term 1830.

Page 366   Will of Susannah Criddle, deceased.

Feb 25, 1830   To my nephew Monroe Moss $100.00 when he arrives at the age of twenty one years. To my son John Criddle, at my death, all my other property of every description and that he is to give it to his children. I appoint my son John Criddle my sole and only executor. This 3 Mar 1823. Wit: Smith Criddle, Robert Trotter and James Bonner. Jan Term 1830.

Page 366   Sale of estate of William Key, deceased.

Feb 26, 1830   Several items listed. John Alford, admr. Jan term 1830.

Page 367   Will of James Wilkes, deceased.

Feb 26, 1830   To my beloved wife Mary Wilkes all my estate real and personal during her natural life. At the death of my wife Mary it is my desire that my property shall be equally divided between my three children William C. and Albert P. Wilkes and my infant daughter not yet named. I appoint William Grizzard, executor. This 18 Jan 1830. Wit: Henry A. Grizzard and Thomas Cartwright. Jan Term 1830.

Page 368   Will of David Adams, deceased.

Mar 1, 1830   My property ov every description (my plantation and wardrobe excepted) be advertised and sold and that my debts be paid and enjoin on my executors to purchase a negro woman (illegible) girl as my sister Betsey Adams may choose and I will to my sister Betsey Adams during her natural life and after her death to her children, should she die without any heir, to my brother John Adams. My mother Martha Adams is to have a lifetime estate in the plantation I now live on and my executor to provide such stock, farming utensils, household and kitchen furniture, sufficient for a small farm. It is my wish that my sister Betsey Adams should live with my mother and enjoy a support from my farm above while she remains unmarried and no longer unless by consent of my mother. The remains to be equally divided between my brother John Adams and my sister Betsey Adams at the death of my mother Martha Adams. To my brother John Adams one half of the tract of land I now live on and one half of the property &c to my sister Betsey Adams. My brother John Adams, executor. This 30 Dec 1829. Wit: Robert Woods, Matthew B. Dyer and A. Foster. Jan Term 1830.

Page 368   Sale of estate of Elizabeth Key, deceased.

Mar 1, 1830   Several items listed. John Alford, admr. Jan Term 1830.

NAME INDEX

241

GORDON: 135, 140, 149, 152, 155, 173, 182, 183, 187, 190, 196, 204, 209, 214, 215, 220, 225, 227
GORHAM: 8
GORMAN: 234
GOUGH: 229
GOULD: 131, 178, 209, 210
GOWEN (GOWIN, GOWN): 5, 8, 14, 16, 57, 74, 85, 90, 91, 103, 141, 152, 178, 184, 188, 195, 214
GOWERS: 4, 21, 29, 32, 34, 42, 43, 70, 93, 98, 117, 118, 120, 121, 125, 126, 160, 163, 177, 189, 200, 215, 233
GRAHAM: 110, 118, 124, 131, 169, 206, 210, 212, 214
GRAINGER: 4
GRANT: 166, 169, 178, 188, 190, 193, 210, 211, 214
GRASS: 150, 208
GRAVES: 13, 27, 31, 51, 65, 125, 128, 132, 151, 153, 160, 161, 164, 168, 177, 189, 190, 199, 206, 207, 216, 222, 226
GRAY (GREY): 1, 2, 5, 7, 8, 10, 13, 15, 17, 23, 24, 35, 39, 40, 43, 45, 48, 52, 55, 57, 66, 75, 76, 79, 90, 91, 97, 103, 112, 115, 118, 127, 129, 135, 141, 144, 146, 154, 157, 158, 159, 164, 165, 199, 208, 214, 219
GRAYHAM: 138
GRAYSON: 156
GREAVES: 6
GREEN (GREENE): 8, 17, 20, 31, 32, 33, 52, 57, 59, 65, 66, 68, 70, 73, 74, 76, 83, 84, 89, 93, 95, 96, 102, 103, 104, 107, 108, 111, 117, 118, 120, 121, 122, 123, 128, 131, 134, 138, 139, 140, 150, 155, 169, 172, 180, 183, 209, 214, 224, 225
GREENHALPH: 190
GREENWOOD: 191
GREER: 4, 13, 41, 57, 59, 62, 66, 91, 92, 105, 106, 110, 117, 120, 141, 144, 145, 151, 155, 156, 172, 178, 186, 214, 215, 224, 225, 233
GREGG: 132
GREGORY (GREGOR): 16, 23, 45, 132, 155, 169, 211, 222, 234
GRESHAM: 200, 205
GRIFFIN (GRIFFING): 5, 8, 16, 25, 42, 62, 79, 93, 95, 134, 146, 210
GRIFFITH: 65
GRIGSBY: 220
GRIMES: 193, 200
GRIMMER: 129
GRIZZARD: 7, 74, 105, 107, 109, 112, 114, 122, 124, 131, 135, 139, 152, 153, 158, 165, 166, 176, 183, 186, 187, 190, 196, 197, 202, 204, 210, 214, 215, 216, 225, 235
GROSE (GROSS): 156, 178, 196, 226, 233
GRUBBS: 4, 53, 122, 130, 132, 143, 177, 186, 200

GRUBER: 123
GRUNDY: 15, 19, 20, 22, 30, 31, 50, 80, 120, 122, 123, 131, 134, 152, 164, 178, 189, 190, 196, 204, 205, 209, 212, 216
GUIGER: 209, 210
GUILFORD: 196
GUIN: 224
GUIRE: 146
GULLEDGE (GULLAGE, GULLIDGE): 120, 125, 154, 160, 177, 189
GULLET: 31
GUNNING: 122
GUNTER: 9
GUPTON: 152
GUTHRIE: 17
GUY: 89, 149, 156, 158, 226
GWATHNEY: 43
GWYNN (GWYN, GUINN): 57, 178, 192, 211, 229

HACKNEY: 159
HADDOCK: 17, 23
HADLEY: 42, 62, 93, 94, 102, 113, 168, 187, 204, 216
HAGEN: 105
HAGET: 166
HAGGARD: 1, 47
HAIL: 6, 17, 28, 44, 86, 109, 119, 121, 170, 177, 192
HAILEY: 18
HAINE: 15
HAINEY: 84
HAISLETT (HAISLOP): 32, 173
HALE (HALES): 26, 27, 62, 150, 192, 226
HALEY (HALLY): 74, 185, 224
HALFACRE: 23
HALLS: 1, 3, 4, 7, 8, 13, 14, 15, 17, 18, 19, 20, 21, 23, 25, 27, 28, 30, 32, 33, 34, 35, 37, 47, 48, 49, 51, 53, 54, 56, 57, 58, 59, 62, 64, 70, 74, 75, 76, 79, 80, 84, 91, 100, 101, 107, 110, 113, 116, 124, 126, 131, 133, 134, 135, 136, 139, 140, 145, 148, 150, 151, 152, 153, 156, 157, 160, 163, 164, 165, 166, 168, 169, 172, 173, 178, 182, 186, 188, 189, 190, 193, 196, 203, 204, 205, 206, 208, 209, 212, 214, 217, 219, 221, 225, 226, 227, 229, 230, 231, 234
HALLOWELL: 35
HALLUM: 46
HALSTED (HOLSTED): 178
HAMBLIN (HAMBLEN): 29, 39, 44, 47, 48, 51, 58, 66, 67, 68, 73, 97, 178, 181, 186, 195, 199, 201, 211, 222, 227
HAMBLETON: 102
HAMER: 191
HAMILTON: 7, 8, 17, 23, 32, 35, 43, 57, 58, 62, 70, 74, 75, 76, 86, 105, 117, 118, 122, 128, 130, 132, 134, 146, 152, 153, 154, 156, 157, 172, 173, 178, 183, 189, 194, 198, 200, 204, 209, 210, 214, 215, 219, 221, 223

HAMLETT: 178
HAMLIN: 104
HAMM (HAM): 23, 199
HAMMER (HAMER): 35, 47
HAMMONS: 25, 50, 174
HAMPTON (HAMTON): 47, 55, 75
HANBY: 225
HANCE: 215
HANCOCK: 34, 35, 42, 75, 81
HANDLY: 230
HANDSBERRY: 122
HANDY: 214
HANEY: 3
HANKINS: 11
HANKS: 8, 84, 93, 146, 157, 178, 182, 190
HANNAH (HANNA): 6, 7, 8, 9, 22, 29, 31, 32, 36, 45, 57, 59, 79, 81, 100, 127, 194, 202
HANNEY: 189
HANNUMS: 22, 74, 96, 214
HANSBOROUGH: 99
HARBERSON: 13
HARBINSON (HERBISON): 45, 149
HARDEMAN (HARDIMAN): 79, 83, 178, 182, 226
HARDGRAVES (HARDGROVES): 19, 26, 53, 83, 155, 165, 171, 188, 206, 207, 208, 213, 216, 224
HARDING (HARDIN, HARDEN): 10, 14, 16, 17, 19, 20, 21, 25, 27, 30, 31, 38, 40, 44, 45, 64, 66, 67, 72, 76, 81, 82, 96, 104, 115, 122, 124, 130, 132, 138, 145, 150, 151, 156, 158, 165, 168, 169, 172, 174, 177, 188, 189, 203, 204, 206, 210, 211, 215, 220, 224, 225, 227, 233
HARDY: 3, 4, 5, 6, 7, 9, 40, 41, 52, 71, 72, 74, 80, 97, 104, 120, 191
HARE; 122
HARFORT: 132
HARGISS: 20
HARLAN (HARLIN): 24, 57
HARMER: 178
HARMON (HARMAN): 52, 70, 166, 182, 197, 199, 229, 234
HARNETT: 104
HARNEY: 52, 161
HARP: 1
HARPATH: 34
HARPER: 31, 36, 42, 98, 122, 180, 183, 210, 211
HARRELL: 199
HARRINGTON: 71, 219
HARRIS: 1, 3, 11, 12, 14, 15, 16, 27, 35, 52, 55, 59, 61, 79, 80, 81, 84, 93, 94, 102, 103, 104, 108, 109, 112, 115, 121, 122, 132, 144, 146, 154, 157, 163, 165, 166, 168, 169, 171, 172, 175, 177, 178, 190, 192, 193, 197, 205, 214, 216, 221, 226
HARRISON: 7, 34, 61, 86, 88, 94, 95, 96, 98, 113, 115, 118, 125, 128, 137, 139, 158, 159, 166, 172, 177, 179, 187, 188, 194, 200, 201, 207, 208, 217, 229

251

255